AMERICA THROUGH BRITISH EYES &

AMERICA Through British Eyes &

Compiled and Edited by ALLAN NEVINS

GLOUCESTER, MASS.

PETER SMITH

1968

Preface ⚬❧

MANY of the best books of British travel in the United States were famous when first issued, and not a few have remained well known generation after generation. Dickens's *American Notes for General Circulation* are still circulated; Mrs. Trollope's acidulous *Domestic Manners of the Americans* still goes through new editions; when an American publishing house celebrated its 125th anniversary in 1938, it was with a reissue of Harriet Martineau's *Retrospect of Western Travel*. No student of our Civil War period would think himself properly equipped if he had not read at least parts of William H. Russell's graphic *Diary North and South* and Edward Dicey's *Six Months in the Federal States*. British travel books began when the United States had barely achieved its independence, and they still come from the press with undiminished vigor. The works of D. W. Brogan, Mary Hamilton, and Graham Hutton remind us that the republic is as much the favorite observation-ground of Britons today as it was in the days of Charles Lyell and James Bryce.

Yet, however well known certain conspicuous titles are, the great body of this travel literature is unexplored by ordinary American readers—and, indeed, is largely inaccessible. Relatively few of the books are kept in print, and not many are to be found outside the largest libraries. For these reasons a real place exists for a volume that furnishes characteristic and interesting passages from several scores of the most illuminating works, and which summarizes the contents of a good many more. What a panorama of social detail, what a long gallery of portraits, from George Washington to Franklin D. Roosevelt, and what a series of striking incidents this crowd of British sojourners affords us! The editor has attempted to arrange his selections (and nearly all the passages, he believes, will be new to the ordinary reader), in such wise as to furnish a summary of the development of American society from the time when independence was new to the period of the Second World War. He has divided the travelers into five groups; and each group he has introduced by an essay, which tries to give an account of the circumstances attending the visits of the different writers, the reception they met, the views they formed, and the changes in their attitudes.

All this material from British pens is entertaining; it is also, the editor believes, instructive. We may add that it is unique, just as the relation between Britain and America is unique. No effort has been made to suppress harsh criticism, and none to emphasize sensational bits; instead, a truly representative quality has been sought. The headings given to the different selections are those of the editor. Alterations in the original text have been avoided except where a modernization of orthography or punctuation seems desirable. It must be remembered, however, that the texts of different editions often vary, and in particular that the American editions of various books were generally superior to the British, errors having been corrected.

The editor wishes to thank the publishers of copyright material in this book, most of whom are cited on the pages on which the material from their publications occurs. In addition, he wishes to acknowledge the quotation from J. B. Priestley's *Midnight on the Desert,* published by Harper and Brothers, copyright 1937 by J. B. Priestley, and that from L. P. Jacks' *My American Friends,* published by The Macmillan Company and Constable and Company, Ltd.

ALLAN NEVINS

New York
25 *May* 1948

Contents ❧

Part I

Travelers of the First Period, 1789-1825

Travelers of the First Period, 1789-1825

Utilitarian Inquiry ᨶ

THE nervous interest of Americans in the impressions formed of them by visiting Europeans, and their sensitiveness to British criticism in especial, were long regarded as constituting a salient national trait. One friendly English traveler, James Silk Buckingham, pronounced this sensitiveness to be our principal fault; and if we view it as a product of our American boastfulness, as Tocqueville did in condemning our 'irritable patriotism,' a decided fault it was. But it may be regarded in a kinder light; not as a product of our conceit, but as a set-off against it, a defensive armor—an admission that we were not so sure of our national merits as we liked to appear. It was certainly a natural phenomenon, the principal underlying causes of which are clearly evident. In the first place, long after the American people declared their political independence of the 'unnatral parient,' they remained in distinct cultural dependence upon her. As Lowell said, we read English books and thought English thoughts; with English salt on her tail our wild eagle was caught. A sense of this anomalous position made us value the British estimates of our cultural and social attainments as the estimates of a final authority. Every author who imitated Scott or Byron, every lawyer trained in English jurisprudence, every painter who studied Turner or Constable, every editor who filled his sheet with English press clippings, was interested in English pronouncements upon our position. Again, all Americans regarded themselves as the guardians and exponents of a wholly new set of political institutions. They were demonstrating to the world, they believed, novel principles in democracy and representative government, and they were eager to know what the world thought of the demonstration.

A considerable degree of unity is discernible in the whole mass of British writings on America, and from these hundreds of volumes it is possible to obtain a composite portrait with certain strongly marked lineaments. It is upon the external features of American life, of course, that the agreement is most emphatic. Our climate, our racial heterogeneity, and the energy and ingenuity we developed in battling with shaggy nature early stamped upon us some lasting traits. All visitors have noted our wooden architecture; from Cobbett and Basil Hall, commenting upon its flimsiness as compared with the brick and stone of Europe, to Arnold Bennett, who quoted William Morris in approbation of wood as a building material, and declared that the fine old wooden houses of Cambridge and Indianapolis were among the most comfortable and characteristic of the truly American objects. As for cuisine, the universal use of ice, iced drinks, and ice cream has always arrested European sojourners. The first travelers after the Revolution, like Wansey, mentioned the icehouses so common in both city and country as interesting novelties; a little later Dickens was struck by the unloading of whole floes of ice along Broadway every summer morning, and he and Lord Acton developed a weakness for the iced cobblers and juleps; while Sir Philip Burne-Jones decided that the humidity of American air made ice water a necessity. The earliest and the latest travelers encountered with the same lively curiosity our huge oysters, like that which caused Thackeray to tell James T. Fields at the Parker House that he felt as if he had just swallowed a baby; and, even more than the oysters, our terrapin, little-neck clams, soft-shelled crabs, bleeding duck, and shad. The grapefruit, which Henry W. Nevinson celebrated as the one indispensable rite of our breakfast, and which Clemenceau hailed as the greatest discovery of his last visit to the United States, came in at about the same time that hot breads waned, and long before the free lunch went out.

The American rocking chair was encountered in all its glory by Miss Martineau, and Nevinson marveled at the long line of summer-hotel rockers in which men sat reading the Sunday papers; though it took a German, Hugo Munsterberg, to tell us that the rocker habit and the chewing-gum habit are an expression of our 'motor-restlessness.' Such an excuse could not be given for our tobacco-chewing habit. But that almost disappeared a generation ago; Sir George Campbell, here in the late 'seventies, seems to have been the last to find it positively perilous to wade over the reeking floors of city hotels. Our lack of privacy in steamboat accommodations shocked Basil Hall in the time of Jackson, and Englishmen used to railway compartments, like James F. Muirhead, the author of Baedeker's guide to the United States, still exclaim over the lack of privacy in our sleeping cars. Since the rise of James Gordon Bennett in the 'thirties, few Englishmen have failed to devote caustic attention to our yellow press—or few Frenchmen either, for Max O'Rell and Bourget, coming at an interval of several years, each profess to have seen a lynching story capped by the head-line, 'Jerked to Jesus.' And so one might go on through a list that was long at the beginning and has constantly become longer as we have added skyscrapers, universal automobiles, telephones, elevators, perfect heating systems, sybaritic plumbing, and cheap and easy divorce to our distinctive comforts of life.

Much more significant is the general British agreement upon our external social and cultural traits. It is the universal verdict that Americans are in a hurry, and the emphasis upon this attribute has increased rather than decreased; Lord Bryce found that the tension of our life, great when he first arrived, was greater still a quarter century later. Tocqueville was unfavorably affected by 'the strange unrest' of the people. Herbert Spencer warned us that our constant hurry, anxiety, and overwork required sharp correction if we wished to preserve our health, and the first impression of H. G. Wells upon landing in New York was one of 'headlong hurry.' This bustle, of course, has always been naturally connected with the American passion for getting on and for making money. James Flint in describing the American character in 1819 adverted to our 'passion for money'; Mrs. Trollope a decade later quoted an Englishman as saying that during his long residence he had never heard Americans converse without mentioning the word 'dollar'; a shrewd young British journalist, G. W. Steevens, entitled his impressions of us 'The Land of the Dollar'; and Burne-Jones states that 'in snatches of conversation caught in the streets, the restaurants, and the cars, the continual cry is always, "Dollars—dollars—dollars."' W. L. George playfully describes himself as being infected after a short stay by the prevailing spirit, yearning for luxuries like high-powered automobiles, and wondering if he could not make $500 out of some 'deal.' Various early travelers agreed with Captain Thomas Hamilton that in the pursuit of the dollar the Americans practiced and boasted of transactions so dishonest that they would promptly land an English-man in Botany Bay, but the criticism of us on this score has signally decreased. One aspect of our hurry, our habit of racing through meals, of which Dickens and many other visitors have left such vivid accounts, also persists only in a milder form, the 'quick lunch'—the very phrase, Burne-Jones said, gave him indigestion—being its chief manifestation.

All travelers in America, from 1780 to the present day, have been impressed by the manliness of carriage and address evident among social groups that in other lands would be obsequious. Thus Dalton in 1821 remarked that nothing riveted his attention 'more forcibly than a certain apparent independence which every American carries about with him'; Burne-Jones found the assumption of equality with him-self by Boston cabmen 'startling'; and Baedeker from the beginning

rightly cautioned the explorer of the United States 'to reconcile himself
to the absence of deference or servility, on the part of those he considers his social inferiors.' According to Burne-Jones, our manners
were affected for the worse by this equality, but Bryce more perspica-
ciously thought that they are improved by it, and even Matthew
Arnold declared that it gave a more genial tone to social intercourse.
A number of Britons, from the amiable Charles Augustus Murray
in the 'thirties to Sir A. Maurice Low in this century, have denied an
alleged boast of the Americans that we have no classes. They forget
that in reality we boast only of having no frozen classes, and no foreign
observer has ever dared to deny that Americans can and constantly do
rise from the lowest social positions to the highest.

Taking manners in the narrow sense of the word, it is interesting
to note how frequently British visitors have criticized us for precisely
the same traits that Continental observers find in the Britons: for
coldness and brusqueness of demeanor, for a selfish attitude toward
fellow-travelers, and for lack of animation and gaiety. Adlard Welby
found even a Fourth of July celebration in the Middle West in Monroe's time a melancholy affair, and almost every description of a hotel
or boarding-house table before the Civil War emphasized the surly
repression of conversation. Yet Miss Martineau, one of the closest and
surest of observers, thought that 'the manners of Americans (in
America) are the best I ever saw.'

American family life has been severely criticized at certain points,
for though its general purity and dignity are admitted, Englishmen
are prone to regard it as lacking in domesticity. Thus in the first half
of the nineteenth century the American household, especially in the
Middle States, was rebuked for its extensive patronage of the frigid
and depressing boarding house, while later writers have represented
the apartment house as an enemy of the true fireside spirit. Arnold
Bennett gives us an amusing vignette of a young housewife, her nerves
unstrung by a sleepless night amid the noises that assail a Manhattan
apartment, flinging a matutinal plateful of eggs at her husband. The
difficulty of obtaining servants was always noted, however, as extenuat-
ing our failure to maintain a home after the English pattern, and
W. L. George wondered to see the mother in even a family with an
income of $10,000 a year doing her own housework.

Yet it is the exceptional British traveler who does not bear witness
to the overflowing American hospitality: not merely overflowing, but
inescapable and pitiless, as Sir Philip Gibbs lamented when he returned
home in exhaustion from an American lecture tour. Miss Martineau
and Augustus Murray tell us that the wealthy and the poor alike
opened the door to them without a moment's hesitancy. And while

a number of travelers found the American to be unresponsive, glum, and preoccupied with worldly cares, they universally agree that his good nature under any imposition is marvelous. Miss Martineau, for example, could not understand why travelers would pay for uneatable tavern meals without a word of remonstrance. Herbert Spencer made this easy-going tolerance the theme for a well-justified homily to us, and the leading American critical organ of the time, the old *Nation,* echoed his words sharply. It was all very well, said Spencer in effect, for Americans to take good naturedly an unavoidable accident, as Alexander Mackay found they did the breakdown of a stagecoach. But it is a different matter to accept without complaint an avoidable and unjustifiable evil, like an ill-paved street, the noise of hawkers, or the drunkard on a crowded car. The reason why Europeans show less of this meekness under abuse escaped Spencer: the more distinct class lines in Europe make the upper ranks of society more insistent upon their privileges.

A high standard of morality has, with several important reservations, been consistently attributed to Americans by our English observers. One of the reservations affected business as it was formerly carried on, one affected politics, and a third, the most important, had reference to our well-known tendency towards reckless violence. The corruption in some branches of our government struck so early a visitor as Fearon, who was here just after the War of 1812, while Marryat was told by a frank politician that his place was worth $600 a year, 'besides *stealings.'* We know that Bryce thought our municipal corruption, from the Philadelphia Gas Ring in the East to Kearneyism in California, the worst stain on our governmental record. So, also, early visitors who, like Faux and Ashe, wished to blacken our national character, could give lurid pictures of the rough-and-tumble fighting of the Southwest, the universal practice of dueling, the constant shooting affrays in the South, and the flogging of slaves to death; for, lurid as their pages were, they had all too large a basis of fact. Later travelers have not failed to dwell upon our high percentage of homicides, and our failure to stamp out lynching. H. G. Wells, for example, relates with horror how at the time of his stay three Negroes were burned in Springfield, Missouri, and 'the edified Sunday-school children hurried from their gospel-teaching to search for souvenirs among the ashes, and competed with great spirit for a fragment of charred skull.' Yet the early travelers all speak of theft and burglary as conspicuously rare, and describe the careless exposure of valuable merchandise in public. Until the Civil War it was the consensus of our visitors' opinion that while tippling was all too common among Americans, outright drunkenness was commendably infrequent. After the Civil War the rapid strides of the prohibition movement pleased some observers, and appeared to others, such as Burne-Jones, 'irritating and silly.' The relation between the two sexes has at all times seemed to observers a sound one, save for their inevitable and emphatic condemnation of miscegenation in the South. It is true that Mrs. Trollope thought the general standards of morality laxer here than in Europe, but in this she stands almost alone; Bryce said in the first edition of his *American Commonwealth,* and again in a magazine article in 1905, that our moral estate was much superior to that of all Western Europe, including Great Britain.

Thus a catalogue of American characteristics and phenomena upon which sojourners from the British Isles have generally agreed might be continued at tiresome length. All writers except the most censorious have warmly praised the activity of the American people in establishing benevolent and charitable institutions. A majority have displayed a tendency to wag their heads gravely over the effects of hot breads, hasty meals, calomel, tobacco, cocktails, hurry, and other vices upon our health. It is a rare and unobservant Briton who has not had some amusing illustration to relate of our Yankee brag—a brag which long magnified all our Revolutionary victories into battles of world-wide importance, which insisted that the Erie Canal was the wonder of modern times, a work as remarkable as the Pyramids or the Chinese Wall, which required every foreigner to confess the Capitol at Washington superior to any European building, and which offended Matthew Arnold by declaring, through the mouth of George Bancroft, that our democracy was as irresistible in its progress 'as the laws of eternity.'

But a clear view of the standpoint, the personalities, and the writings of the principal British writers upon America cannot be obtained except chronologically. They fall naturally, as they are divided in this volume, into four groups, which correspond roughly with the four quarters of the century.

The first of these groups may be briefly characterized as representatives of a period of practical investigation of America, and the fact that they can be so described should in itself dispel some of the popular illusions as to the haughtiness and superciliousness of the typical English traveler in this country.

The common view among Americans that the republic was an object of condescension on the part of all British critics until it confounded them by its successful emergence from the Civil War, though quite absurd, rests upon several foundations. It is little realized how numerous were our English visitors, and how varied were their objects in crossing the ocean and publishing their books. Most Americans think first of the three travelers who bear names distinguished in the history of English literature, Dickens, Captain Marryat, and Mrs. Trollope; and they happen to have been a rather severe trio. Moreover, it is human nature to remember critics whose judgments were harsh and whose attacks upon us aroused bitter controversy, and to forget the sympathetic writers who said little except in praise. As a further factor, many American investigators of the subject, most notably John Bach McMaster, in a brilliantly written chapter of the fifth volume of his history, have fallen into the error of confounding the early British travel-writers with what the Tory quarterlies and monthlies said about their books. Just as it was the tendency of these partisan periodicals to heighten any caustic criticism of this country, and to tone down any commendation, so in turn it has been the tendency of historians who like high colors to exaggerate somewhat the importance of this magazine censure.

Thus it is that we find John Graham Brooks, in his study of the subject, remarking that the era of condescension in British travels closed 'when England began really to respect us because of the national strength displayed in the Civil War.' Thus Henry Cabot Lodge, in his *One Hundred Years of Peace,* declares that the English systematically libeled the American people for a prolonged period, and that to these critics 'everything in the United States was anathema.' Yet if anyone takes the trouble to examine the serried shelves of British travels, he will find a surprising amount of honesty, friendliness, and generosity in even the one brief period during which Tory hostility found unrestrained voice.

From the ratification of the Constitution until the full opening of steam navigation across the Atlantic—that is, from 1788 till about 1825 —the predominant motive of the British traveler in coming to this country was utilitarian inquiry. He visited the United States to ascertain its potentialities as a field for investment, for erecting factories, for settling down as a farmer, for opening a store or commencing a professional career. Most of the travelers came over hopefully and returned with their hopes confirmed. The books they wrote were intended primarily to assist men who had a similar curiosity regarding the New World, and, emphasizing information at the expense of literary quality, were in some instances little more than guidebooks and gazetteers with a little thin description of men and manners superadded. It was an unhappy period in Great Britain—the period of the Napoleonic Wars, of a national debt approaching a billion pounds, of the poverty accompanying the Industrial Revolution, of unwise poor laws and acts restricting the freedom of speech and the press; and by contrast until 1812 all looked sunny, quiet, and prosperous in the United States.

Henry Wansey, who came over in 1794 and had the honor of eating at Washington's table, was interested in woolen manufactures and their prospects in America. Isaac Weld, who was here at the time that Pitt was spending $200,000,000 a year in fighting the French Directory, was perturbed by the war-torn condition of Europe, and determined to learn whether 'any part of these territories might be looked forward to as an eligible and agreeable place of abode.' A shrewd and energetic Scot was John Melish, who reached America in 1806 hoping to open up a brisk market for cotton goods in the South through Savannah, later looked for mercantile employment in the Middle States, and accepted bravely the manifold difficulties arising from the noninter-course and embargo laws. His friendly volumes are a perfect treasury of facts regarding American economic life. A different kind of dis-appointment was encountered by Henry B. Fearon, who was sent hither just after the War of 1812 by two-score English families, of the most varied pursuits, to spy out the land, and who undeservedly lost their confidence before his mission was completed. Very significant indeed were the visits of Morris Birkbeck and Richard Flower, who decided immediately after the war that Illinois offered large oppor-tunities for the English farmer, and undertook to settle a tract of 16,000 acres in the southeastern part of the state. Their just and whole-some writings on the Middle West brought out many families from the old country, and when in the middle 'twenties the question of slavery arose like a thundercloud over the prairies in Illinois, the Eng-lish community did much to determine that the state should be free soil.

Such travelers were practical men of the middle class, who found in the crudity and hardship of American life nothing to surprise or repel them; not tender-skinned gentlemen or literary workers, who might be pained by the coarse if vigorous tone of democratic man-ners. A majority of them had a marked tendency toward political radicalism. Of the view of William Cobbett, that irrepressible agitator who had been heavily fined for his attacks on British administration in Ireland, and imprisoned two years for his bitter comment on the flogging of English militiamen, it is unnecessary to speak. He might have found the United States as congenial a permanent home as did those other radical journalists supplied by Great Britain at this time to help us fight our party battles—'Jack' Binns and William Duane. Morris Birkbeck, settling down upon the fat prairies, rejoiced that he would no longer be 'ruled and taxed by people who have no more right to rule and tax us than consisted in the power of doing it.' Melish also, who might have ended his days here had only his business ventures prospered a little, observed that 'a republican finds here a republic, and the only republic on the face of the earth that deserves the name, where all are under the protection of equal laws—of laws made by themselves.' This bluff north-countryman took pains to see both Jefferson and Madison in the White House, listened to them with profound respect, and bore the United States not the slightest malice for its course preceding the War of 1812. Godfrey T. Vigne declared, in words echoed by still other travelers: 'That the American form of government is admirably adapted to a new country, that that country has astonishing resources, and that the Americans lose no time in making the most of them, that it has thriven under its institutions, and is at present enjoying an exemption from many evils incident to older countries, it would be an absurdity to deny.' The contrast between the unburdened position of the United States and the tax-crushed state of Europe was bitterly pointed out by Lieutenant Francis Hall when he said that the American worker had not yet discovered the necessity of yielding nineteen parts of his earnings to the Government to repay it for taking care of the twentieth. America, Fearon summed up his verdict, is 'the poor man's country.'

Our somewhat idealized conception of the age of the fathers, when Washington was in his first term, when it alarmed the public to find rival parties angrily rallying behind Jefferson and Hamilton, when men wore tricolored cockades to show their sympathy with the French Revolution, when the South was just beginning to talk of the cotton gin, when Boston was dubiously allowing her first theater to be opened, when whole populations were drifting in flatboats down the Ohio to the new country opened up by Wayne's victory, when Barlow, Freneau, and Dwight were the great names of our literature—our conception of this heroic age suffers little from the pages of Henry Wansey and Thomas Cooper. The latter, delighted at the remarkable prosperity of the country, the flourishing state of religion, and the absence of 'those vices that arise usually from idleness,' left part of his family here and went back to England to bring out the remainder. His account of a respectable Pennsylvania farmer in 1795 is given in this volume; he also describes a richer agriculturist, the owner of 300 acres with a good house and barns, who had in addition a gristmill, a sawmill, a distillery, a fish pond, an icehouse, and a smokehouse for curing pork—'a tolerably fair though a favorable specimen' of a holding in the Middle States. The chief deficiency he discovered was in culture. Literature was an amusement only, and the opportunities of knowledge were few among the Americans; 'their libraries are scanty, their collections are almost entirely of *modern* books; they do not contain the means of tracing the history of questions; this is a want which the literary people feel very much, and which it will take some years to remedy.'

Wansey thoroughly enjoyed his travels, and was pleased by the high general level of health, happiness, and material well being—a level he thought had risen since the ratification of the Constitution. While he liked the plain blunt manners of the Americans everywhere, their industry and common sense, he was most impressed by Connecticut, the land of steady habits. The fine new bridge across the Charles River at Cambridge he pronounced 'a most prodigious work for so infant a country—worthy of the Roman Empire,' while he made a respectful note of the public buildings of New York: the Exchange, the Society Library, Columbia College, the Governor's Mansion, and so on. So, too, he observed with pleasure in New England that there was 'a schoolhouse by the roadside in almost every parish,' though he was disappointed by Yale College, where he found the library small and its books badly preserved. Of modes of travel he gives an interesting account. The stage journey from Boston to New York cost him fourpence a mile; at the Bunch of Grapes, the best inn of Boston, he paid 5 shillings a day for board and bed, including a pint of good Madeira, and at Oeller's Hotel in Philadelphia $7 a week; and both in Boston and Philadelphia he was greatly tormented by 'the bugs.' Cooper at the same time (1794) had declared good inns common from Boston to Maryland, but that farther south taverns were 'scarce and dear,' so that the traveler had to rely on the profuse hospitality of the planters. The number of public personages whom Wansey met helped him to form a favorable impression of America.

In Boston they included Jedidiah Morse, the geographer. In New York he saw Joseph Priestley and Citizen Genêt at the Tontine Coffee House, where he lodged; Chancellor Livingston called upon him; he went to see General Gates on Long Island; the brother of John Jay entertained him at the Belvidere tea-house and the Indian Queen Tavern; and at the wharf he glimpsed Vice-President Adams, 'a stout, hale, well-looking man, of grave deportment, and quite plain in dress and person'; while at Philadelphia, in 'awe and veneration,' he breakfasted with Washington. The infrequency of suicide, insanity, or disease attributable to dissipation he especially remarked. 'In these States,' he declared, 'you behold a certain plainness and simplicity of manners, equality of condition, and a sober use of the faculties of the mind.'

But it was Henry B. Fearon who may best be taken as the type of the early British traveler. His very first observations upon landing in this country in August 1817 convinced him that he was in a freer and more prosperous land. A boy at the Manhattan dock, procuring for him two hackney coaches at a distance of a quarter mile, refused an English shilling, saying, 'For as how I guess it is not of value; I have been *slick* in going to the stand right away'; and the Englishman, admiring his independence, paid him a half dollar. Fearon noticed that the laborers on the water front, though no better dressed than in England, were less careworn, and that there were no beggars. Looking about the city, after taking up his residence at Mrs. Bradish's boarding house on State Street, he was impressed by 'the absence of irremediable distress.' The very Negroes, who abounded, were well dressed. The shopkeepers manifested their confidence in the universal honesty, an honesty impossible in any land where the population was needy, by exhibiting their goods loosely upon sidewalk stands. These shopkeepers, in remarkable and not altogether pleasing contrast with the obsequious English retailers, lounged inside at their counters with their hats on, or lay stretched at full length along them, puffing at cigars and spitting in all directions. When the visitor went to the Park Theatre, he saw another of the advantages of the American wage earner. The pit was full of workingmen who, in England, would not be able to buy a pint of porter; they had paid three quarters of a dollar for places, and were watching the play with complete enjoyment.

However, it was the simplicity of all American life, and the lack of display or hauteur on the part of her greatest men, which Fearon most commended, exclaiming: 'What a lesson in this does America teach!' At his boarding house, where he had a bed and four profuse meals for $2 a day, he mingled familiarly with the leading naval officers of the city—with Decatur, Brackenridge, Biddle, and Commodore Rogers. Taking the steamer *Chancellor Livingston,* a vessel of surprising dimensions and comfort, up the Hudson, he 'marked the thoughtful face of Vice-President Tompkins,' standing unassumingly with the other passengers. When he went out from Boston to Quincy to visit ex-President John Adams, now a well-preserved old gentleman of eighty-six, he was charmed by the cordiality of his reception. The day being Sunday, everyone attended church twice, and the minister was asked to dine. As a first course the guests had hasty pudding with molasses and butter; then followed veal, bacon, neck of mutton, potatoes, cabbages, carrots, and beans, with a couple of glasses of Madeira apiece. The talk ranged over England, America, and France, over religion, science, literature, and politics, and such names as Dr. Priestley, Miss Edgeworth, Kean, Byron, Moore, and Cobbett were discussed. Fearon saw with pleasure that the former President had a plain wooden house of only eight rooms, and a limited staff of servants.

It must not be thought that Fearon, any more than other amiable

English travelers of the time, liked everything he saw. Some of his complaints deal with obvious defects, and were to become familiar to Americans through a hundred repetitions. He was surprised by the sallow and unhealthy-looking complexions of the people. Their manners he thought chilly and indifferent, though they often displayed an impertinent curiosity about a stranger's private affairs and they ate with lightning rapidity, resenting any effort to infuse a little sociability into their public meals. In a score of ways they were lamentably careless of appearance. In New York, for example, the side streets were narrow and dirty, nearly every corner had a woodpile, which the sawyers were preparing for the fireplaces, and the pigs wandered about in droves. The citizens, even well-to-do leaders of the bar like Thomas Addis Emmet, were slovenly in dress; the shops made a slipshod, unattractive display of their wares; and the farmsteads Fearon visited on Long Island were depressingly unkempt. The high charges for merchandise (largely imported from England, after paying a steep tariff) were a disagreeable shock to him. Thus a hat that in London could be purchased for about a guinea cost 45 shillings in New York, books were costly and ill-printed, and a frame house sold for as much as did a brick house in the old country. Worst of all, Fearon concluded, 'there is, on the surface of society, a carelessness, a laziness, which freezes the blood and disgusts the judgment.'

But beneath the surface, Fearon thought more serious faults were observable. Though outright intoxication was rare, dram-drinking was practiced to an excessive degree, and many laboring men and Negroes were a little fuddled half the time. In New York alone there were 1500 spirit shops, and rum, which cost six and a half pence in the taverns, could be had for as little as twopence a glass in the dirtier dens. Moreover, racial prejudices were painfully in evidence for a democratic republic, and Fearon was unpleasantly astonished when he saw a New York barber order a Negro roughly out of his shop. The man explained, in the queer tongue that passed for English among some uneducated Americans of the city: 'I reckon that you don't know that my boss wouldn't have a single ugly or clever gentleman come to his store if he cut colored men.' Slavery, too, was a constant affliction to a man of Fearon's temperament. Halting a day at Middletown, Kentucky, he saw a Negro boy of fourteen brutally flogged by two strapping fellows, one relieving the other whenever his arms grew tired. A third man interfered after a time, but only on the ground that the boy belonged to a friend, whose property he was unwilling to see permanently injured; while the talk at table was all favorable to the whipping, one witness saying that it would have been no matter if the slave had been beaten to death. Throughout the Southwest, indeed,

Fearon saw much to repel him. Now he turns in aversion from the cruelty of a 'gander-pulling'; now, at Louisville, he is disgusted by the spitting, smoking, toddy-drinking, and the bolting of food; and now, at Natchez, he finds gambling, drunkenness, and other forms of profligacy shamelessly unconcealed. In New Orleans also he discovered that 'gambling houses throng the city,' and that all coffee houses were crowded from morning to night with gamesters. He could hardly be expected to discern the fact that this was as uncharacteristic of the real and permanent America as were the frontier-camp excesses in the Far West a generation later.

Worst of all, from the standpoint of an observer keenly interested in the success of our republican experiment, were the flaws of our government. At his State Street boarding house Fearon pricked up his ears when the naval officers began talking of the corruption and party favoritism practiced in contract-letting during the War of 1812. In all parts of the land, he concluded, the people too frequently fell under the sway of unprincipled politicians, so that, in general, 'American theory is at least two centuries ahead of American practice.' Nevertheless, he admitted that 'the principle of at least liberty is acknowledged, and the fact of a free government exists,' which was not the case in Great Britain.

Among the score of noteworthy travelers in the generation after the Revolution there was certain to be at least one of jaundiced eye and malicious tongue. William Faux, who stepped forward at the close of the Napoleonic Wars to 'shew Men and Things as they are in America,' was an English farmer, so credulous, coarse, and ill-natured as to excite the ridicule of the very magazines whose prejudice against the republic equaled his own. *Blackwood's* called him 'a simpleton of the first water, a capital specimen of a village John Bull, for the first time roaming far away from his native valley—staring at everything and grumbling at most.' He was a querulous traveler, venting his ill-humor at every fresh inconvenience or obstacle, and failing to penetrate beneath the raw, turbulent ways of a new community to its primitive virtues. He laboriously collected the exceptional cases of violence and dishonesty, and the sensational, highly spiced mess he served up was as misleading as would be an American chronicle of Whitechapel murders and wife beatings if offered as a study of London life. He did not hesitate even to garble the facts, as the *North American Review* conclusively proved; and indeed, critical examination of the book shows that parts of it are plagiarized, and other parts are invented.

Nevertheless, because of his frank presentation of matter that more delicate-minded writers would conceal, Faux's volume has a certain historical interest. A large part of his picture of Charleston is un-

questionably veracious. Staying at the Planters' Hotel (1818), he found
the table groaning with food. 'Besides turtle soup and turtle steaks,
the number of our viands was to me countless, and at present indescribable; and to every plate stood two half-pint decanters of rum,
brandy, or Hollands, to drink at dinner, instead of ale.' The Negroes
of the city swarmed everywhere. They were required to be off the
streets at ten o'clock at night, when a patrol with a drum marched
through the town, and none of them—not even the rich free Negro
John Jones, who owned the best inn of the city, and kept carriages
for hire—was allowed to ride a horse; but they were fat, healthy, and
happy. He visited the superb new steamship *Savannah,* then about
to start for Liverpool on her first voyage. Another of the notable
sights he met during his stay was President James Monroe, who came
to South Carolina on a tour and shook hands with Faux at church
—'an amiable, mild-looking gentleman, of about sixty, dressed in a
common hat, plain blue coat with gilt buttons, yellow kerseymere
waistcoat, drab breeches and white silk stockings, and a little powder
in his hair,' states the traveler. 'His eyes beam with an expansive
kindness, gentleness, and liberality, not often seen in persons of his
elevated station, and his physiognomy, viewed as a whole, announces
a noble, well-judging, and generous mind.' Faux also heard Robert
Y. Hayne argue a case in court in a pleasantly conversational style of
eloquence.

But what particularly horrified Faux in Charleston and in the country districts of the South was the physical violence of which he heard
on every hand. A fellow-guest at the Planters' Hotel told him that
he had lately met there a party of thirteen gentlemen, eleven of whom
had each killed his man in a duel. Reports of assaults· constantly
reached the Englishman's ears; and before he had stayed a week in
the city he learned that a poor fellow had been found in the streets
one morning almost murdered by robbers the evening before, 'having
his legs both broken and otherwise terribly bruised about his head and
breast.' Faux makes the incredible statement that this unfortunate had
been left to roast in the blazing sun till some man gave three Negroes
a dollar to remove him as a public nuisance. Somewhat more probable
is his description of a fire-eating young colonel at the hotel, who
wanted to fight the proprietor when the latter refused him credit; and
there is no reason at all for disbelieving his statement that two men
were sentenced to death during his stay, one for murder and the other
for stealing a slave. Theft was still a capital crime in more than one
state. In the back country Faux seems to have observed at first hand
no instance of the maltreatment of Negroes, though he complains that
their huts were 'miserable,' and that their ration, which consisted of

only a peck of cornmeal for each adult weekly, was utterly inadequate. But he heard of terrible acts of cruelty, such as doubtless did occur from time to time. He was present, he avers, at the exhumation near Columbia of the body of a slave, who had been whipped by his master and two other men from midnight till sunrise, when he expired; but this tale was at least exaggerated. On one great plantation near Camden he was impressed by the easy lot of the slaves, whose work was over by one o'clock if they labored diligently. 'Their condition seems in some respects better than that of the paupers of my native land,' he remarked, little dreaming how such statements would be resented by successors of his like Miss Martineau.

Of the Western country Faux drew an equally repellent picture. The richness of the soil, the low cost of living, the genial atmosphere of democracy, he all admitted. But he found the people lazy, dirty, and uncouth, living for the most part in one-room cabins, which he thought scarcely fit for pigs. For example, in a forty-mile ride between Vincennes, Indiana, and Princeton, Illinois, he saw nothing 'but miserable log holes, and a mean ville of eight or ten huts or cabins, sad neglected farms, and indolent, dirty, sickly, wild-looking inhabitants. Soap is nowhere seen or found in any of the taverns, east or west. Hence dirty hands, heads, and faces everywhere. Here is nothing clean but wild beasts and birds, nothing industrious generally, except pigs, which are so of necessity.' Labor was hard to obtain in Indiana and Illinois; corn had to be carried ten miles or more to mill or market; and drunken desperadoes like the 'Illinois Rowdies' were troublesome. The tendency of life in the backwoods, he warned his English readers, was to cause the settlers to lose all self-respect, so that they never bathed or dressed properly. He delights to quote men like the Kentucky planter who told him: 'Kentucky is morally and physically ruined—Deception is a trade and all are rogues. The West has the scum of all the earth.' Faux's summary of American life is amusing:

Low ease; a little avoidable want, but no dread of any want; little or no industry; little or no real capital, nor any effort to create any; no struggling, no luxury, and perhaps, nothing like satisfaction or happiness; no real relish of life; living like store pigs in a wood, or fattening pigs in a stye. All their knowledge is confined to a newspaper, which they all love, and consists in knowing their natural, and some political rights, which rights in themselves they respect individually, but often violate towards others, being cold, selfish, gloomy, inert, and with little or no feeling. The government is too weak and too like-minded to support and make the laws respected. . .

In contrast with this book, no better evidence could be offered of the general adaptability and fairness of the early British travelers than the accounts a half dozen men in the second and third decades of the century have given us of the Middle West. Morris Birkbeck and George Flower laid out the neighboring towns of Wanborough and Albion in Illinois late in 1818, and within a year had drawn 400 English and 700 Americans to their settlement. Birkbeck in particular was a man of great ability. In England he had been a tenant farmer, with a leasehold of 1500 acres, so successful that he acquired £10,000; but he was filled with resentment by his exclusion from the ballot, and by the heavy taxes and tithes to which he was subject. In America he became the founder of a thriving settlement, a leader in the early Western movement toward scientific agriculture, and a powerful champion of the antislavery forces of Illinois. He and both Richard and George Flower wrote books extolling the West as a place of settlement, while an attack upon their enterprise came from the sharp pen of Cobbett, whom these leaders believed to have been enlisted for the purpose by certain large Eastern land dealers.

One of the Illinois settlers was John Woods, and his *English Prairie,* an account of his trip west and of two years' residence there, offers many just and kindly comments upon American life. He found Pittsburgh (1820) 'a large place with upwards 7000 inhabitants,' some handsome brick buildings, and more of logs. 'Owing to the quantity of iron-works,' he says, confirming a remark made by the traveler Thomas Hulme a year earlier, 'it has a black and dismal appearance.' Several steamboats were in course of construction, and he learned that in high water vessels came up from New Orleans to Pittsburgh in 70 or 80 days; but he himself pushed on overland. The stage on which he traveled west was hardly more than a light wagon, covered at the top, with inadequate leather side curtains to let down in case of rain; it was much crowded with luggage, and the passengers had to walk up steep hills. Woods also complained that the country taverns charged exorbitant prices for meals, a breakfast near the Monongahela, for example, costing two shillings sixpence. At Cincinnati, 'a noble-looking town, by far the best I have seen in the western country,' he found 12,000 people, with a number of large factories and mills, and well-stocked stores. The cost of living in the West was then marvelously low. While boating down the Ohio—he obtained passage for himself and his family on an ark, 600 miles from Wheeling to Louisville, for $50—he was able to buy a hind quarter of a deer, weighing 16 pounds, for 50 cents. Faux, indeed, tells us that a good buck could be had in Ohio for a dollar. Catfish of 30 to 40 pounds weight were offered to Woods for a quarter. When he went into the city markets at Cincinnati, he found flour selling at only $4 or $5 a barrel, and fine peaches were but 14 cents a peck.

In the description of pioneer Ohio given by these contemporaneous travelers, Woods, Faux, and Welby, there are many graphic touches. The first-named was surprised to see that the more fashionable inhabitants of Cincinnati were as well clothed as Londoners. 'But the females of the middle and lower orders, though gaily dressed, often go without shoes and stockings; indeed, most of the females in the western country go without them, at least in the summer.' Land near the city was selling very high, up to $100 an acre. Welby complained of the wretched condition of the roads, of the greed of the land speculators, who had seized on the best tracts, and of the poor inns. 'As to the general want of cleanliness in the taverns, of which so much has been said *and so justly,* though the keepers of them have no doubt a large share of the blame, yet much may be said in their defence; the fact is, their customers are of so filthy habits that to have a house clean is almost impossible. . .' Faux was stunned with amazement when he visited the circuit court at Zanesville and saw the presiding judge

in the midst of three rustic, dirty-looking associate judges, all robeless, and dressed in coarse drab, domestic, homespun coats, dark silk handkerchiefs round their necks, and otherwise not superior in outward appearance to our low fen-farmers in England. Thus they sat, presiding with ease and ability over a bar of plain talkative lawyers, all robeless, very funny and conversational in their speeches, manners, and conduct; dressed in plain box-coats, and sitting with their feet and knees higher than their noses, and pointing obliquely to the bench of judges; thus making their speeches, and examining and cross-examining evidence at a plain long table, with a brown earthen jug of cold water before them, for occasionally wetting their whistles, and washing their quid-stained lips; all, judges, jury, counsel, witnesses, and prisoners, seemed free, easy, and happy. The supreme judge is only distinguished from the rest by a shabby blue threadbare coat. . .

Woods settled down near Wanborough, Illinois, as a neighbor to Birkbeck, paying $940 for a quarter section of land with two cabins, a stable, a well, and some livestock, while later he bought another quarter section for $480. Of Birkbeck's settlement he gives us a delightful picture. Soon after his arrival he found the English people holding a gala day in memory of a fair in Surrey, and playing cricket. The settlers all lived in cabins, and while the English insisted upon ceilings, wooden floors, and windows, many Americans did without them. Yet a double cabin with a porch between, floored and ceiled, cost only about $150, or the price of a team of horses. Most of the American settlers grew tobacco for home consumption. Woods tells us that many of them had been lifelong wanderers, having lived in a number of localities of the South and West; that they were litigious, and would bring suit even over a piggin worth only a shilling; and that they were prone to drunkenness. Indians and 'negers' they regarded with equal contempt, and treated both as inferior races. They were frequently shiftless. Yet one good trait was always prominent. 'They are a most determined set of republicans,' writes Woods, 'well versed in politics, and thoroughly independent.'

The most famous of the travelers of this early period, a man gifted with remarkable powers of observation and a remarkable style, William Cobbett professed to have little use for the Illinois settlements that he visited. He expatiated upon their remoteness from markets, their social crudity, and the dirt, disorder, and hardship inseparable from frontier life. But of his ten months of farming on Long Island and his two months of travel in rural Pennsylvania he has given us an account as engaging as it is concrete and detailed. Had he not limited his written observations upon America to agricultural affairs, his book would be one of the most valuable of all English travels. Cobbett loved country pursuits, having been 'bred up at a ploughtail,' and he rejoiced in the independence and snug prosperity of the American farmer as an illustration of the benefits of political and religious freedom. The United States was a land of husbandmen, and the very presidents and governors boasted of the title. 'A farmer here is not the poor dependent wretch that a Yeomanry-Cavalryman is, or that a Treason-Juryman is. A farmer here depends on nobody but *himself* and on his own proper means; and, if he is not at his ease, and even rich, it must be his own fault.'

Cobbett in Pennsylvania was as much impressed by the plenty and cheapness of life as was Woods in the West. In a Harrisburg tavern, where he procured lodging and board for $1.25 a day, the array of meats, fowls, sausages, and other dishes oppressed him. At a Lancaster inn with warm fires and clean beds he found 'the eating still more overdone than at Harrisburgh. Never saw such profusion. I have made a bargain with the landlord; he is to give me a dish of chocolate a day, *instead of dinner.*' The sight in a New York street of a sow dining off a full quarter of a fine leg of mutton led him to reflect mournfully upon the eagerness with which many a family in England would snatch the meat from her, and upon the wickedness of the Government responsible for such misery. He perceived that in Pennsylvania the farmer usually had two houses, one large and the other small; the father had built the first and, as the family waxed wealthier, his son had put up the other. Everywhere, too, he admired the big stone barns, a hundred feet long, with a driveway taking wagons up to the wide mows and granaries on the second floor. 'And then, all about them looks so comfortable, and gives such manifest proofs of ease, plenty, and happiness!' In the Long Island farms he missed the beauty of the Kent or Sussex farmstead, but he recognized the natural reasons for this deficiency:

Instead of the neat and warm little cottage, the yard, cow-stable, pig-stye, hen-house, all in miniature, and the garden, nicely laid out, and the paths bordered with flowers, while the cottage door is crowned with a garland of roses or honey-suckle; instead of these, we here see the laborer content with a shell of boards, while all around him is as barren as the sea-beach; though the natural earth would send melons, the finest in the world, creeping round his door, and though there is no English shrub, or flower, which will not grow and flourish here. This want of attention in such cases is hereditary from the first settlers. They found land so plenty, that they treated small spots with contempt. Besides, the *example* of neatness was wanting. There were no gentlemen's gardens, kept as clean as drawing-rooms, with grass as even as a carpet. From endeavoring to imitate perfection men arrive at mediocrity; and, those who have never seen, or heard of perfection, in these matters, will naturally be slovens.

Cobbett, because of the superior intellectual atmosphere of his native land and for other reasons, preferred living in Great Britain. He discerned numerous faults in both this country and its people. Excessive drinking—'this is the *great misfortune* of America!'—he repeatedly mentions. American birds and flowers, he said, anticipating an unjust remark of many English travelers, which has since been transferred to Australia, were numerous, but they were birds without song and flowers without perfume. Continually, however, he came back to the indefeasible advantages of American life, inherent in our political, religious, and economic freedom. Salt and glass cost only half as much as in Great Britain, because they were untaxed. Every farmer made his own soap and candles, a practice forbidden in England, where it would impair the tax revenue; and Cobbett recalled with anger how a poor woman at Holly Hill, for dipping some rushes in grease to serve as a light, had been subjected to a search of her house, and all but dragged off to jail.

And then, think of the *tithes!* I have talked to several farmers here about the tithes in England, and they *laugh*. They sometimes almost make me angry; for they seem, at last, not to believe what I say, when I tell them, that the English farmer gives, and is compelled to give, the Parson a tenth part of his whole crop and of his fruit and milk and eggs and calves and lambs and pigs and wool and honey. They cannot believe this. They treat it as a sort of *romance*.

Two of the writers of this period who were unfavorable to America, though not abusively so, Thomas Ashe and Isaac Weld, were not wholly reliable. Ashe dealt in the sensational, like Faux; Weld gave a serious account of ferocious New Jersey mosquitoes that bit through the thickest shoes, and actually quoted Washington as an authority for this marvel. Yet the latter's *Travels,* covering the years 1795-7, really offer us much information of value. He thought our manners cold and suspicious, our taverns crowded and ill-managed, and the gambling and cockfighting in Maryland and Virginia disgraceful; while he correctly stated that Princeton and the other colleges he visited 'better deserve the title of a grammar-school.' C. W. Janson came to America to make his fortune, lost what money he had, and vented his ill-humor in a mendacious volume. All the other travelers, however, were cordial in their attitude. Kendall gave a sober and faithful picture of the Northern States, discussing the Government and the various public institutions respectfully. Fanny Wright's visit to America resulted in a book (1821) even more laudatory than Cobbett's. Like Cobbett, she rejoiced to see our statesmen and generals enrolled among the farmers. 'And how proudly does such a man tread his paternal fields, his ample domains improving under his hand; his garners full to overflowing; his table replenished with guests, and with a numerous offspring whose nerves are braced by exercise and their minds invigorated by liberty.' Bristed, who made an encyclopedic study of American resources, Candler, and Lambert, were undistinguished travelers who looked about with a tolerant and appreciative eye, and predicted a glorious future for the nation.

Particularly well balanced was the account of America given at the very close of this period by Adam Hodgson, a Liverpool gentleman who wrote his volumes because 'the present situation of England had rendered the subject of emigration so interesting.' He was vigorous in condemning slavery, of which he saw the brutal side clearly. In Charleston he read a newspaper account of a young Negro woman's being burned to death the week before for murdering her master; and an acquaintance who had been staying at an inn near the scene said that many of the guests had gone to see the spectacle. Hodgson adds,

At a dinner party of five or six gentlemen, I heard one of the guests, who is reputed a respectable planter, say, in the course of conversation, that he shot at one of his slaves last year with intent to kill him for running away; that on another occasion, finding that two runaway slaves had taken refuge on his plantation, he invited some of his friends out of town to dinner and a *frolic;* that after dinner they went out to hunt the slaves, and hearing a rustling in the reeds or canes in which they believed them to be concealed, they all fired at their *game,* but unfortunately missed.

Hodgson attended a slave sale in Charleston, and was too moved to remain after he had seen a young woman, with a baby at her breast and three other children at her skirts, put on the platform to be auctioned; 'the little boys looking up at their mother's face with an air of curiosity, as if they wondered what could make her look so sad.' Staying in a lodging-house in New Orleans, the traveler's room adjoined that of the stalwart landlady, and every morning he was awakened by the blows with which she cowhided the black servants who had displeased her the preceding day. But he did not fail to recognize that most slaves were treated kindly, nor did he overemphasize slavery.

Hodgson was especially interested in the morality of the republic, and reported that in New England moral standards were generally better than in the mother country, in the Middle States they were about the same, and in the South they were worse. Gaming was 'dreadfully prevalent' in New Orleans, where the steamboats lining the shores of the Mississippi for more than a mile were said on Sundays to be one row of gambling shops; while the lewd and profane language of the Southwest disgusted him. But in New England he was delighted with the people. 'There I see on every side, a hardy, robust, industrious, enterprising population; better fed, better clothed, better educated than I ever saw before, and more intelligent, and at least as moral as the corresponding classes of our own countrymen.' He contradicted vigorously the assertion that the Americans were cold, saying that this was but their outward appearance, and that in his 7000 miles of travel he had found them at least as obliging as the English. He, too, thought well of America's prospects. 'It is destined, I trust,' he wrote, 'to exhibit to the world at large a grand and successful experiment in legislation.'

The young republic, in all, had much for which to be grateful in its earliest guests.

The Father of His Country; Southern Life [1] &

JOHN BERNARD, *one of the brightest English comedians and one of the shrewdest American managers of his time, was born in Portsmouth, England, in 1756, the son of a naval officer. He was articled to a solicitor, but his inclination for the stage was irresistible, and before he was twenty he was a member of the Norwich circuit (1774). A few years later he and his wife, a versatile actress, joined the Bath*

[1] From *Retrospections of America*, 1797-1811, New York, 1887, chapters 5 and 7; by permission of Harper and Brothers.

*Theatre, then and long the most important in England outside Lon-
don. It was here that he played in the first non-metropolitan performance of* The School for Scandal, *rehearsed under the direction of Sheridan himself. In 1787 he made his first appearance in London, where
he was associated with such men of the town as Sheridan, Selwyn, and
Fox, and was elected secretary of the famous Beefsteak Club.*

*At the age of forty-one, and at the height of his powers, Bernard
came to America, being engaged by Wignell, the Philadelphia manager, at £1,000 a year, then a tremendous salary. His first American
appearance was in New York, at the Greenwich Street Theatre, on
25 August 1797. During the next six years he played with the Philadelphia company, not only in comedy parts but in various Shake-
spearean roles, as Shylock, Falconbridge, Hotspur, and so on. His
career as a manager, however, belongs to Boston's theatrical history.
He became joint manager of the Federal Street Theatre there in 1806,
and remained until 1810. He had the honor of opening the first regular
theater in Albany, in 1813. Three years later he went upon a tour of
the country, becoming one of the earliest of American traveling stars,
but returned to Boston. His farewell performance occurred in the
Yankee capital in February 1819, in* The Soldier's Daughter; *and he
went home to England, where he died in 1828.*

*Bernard left in manuscript an autobiography of considerable length.
Of this his son, two years after his death, published some condensed
portions, under the title of* Retrospections of the Stage. *A London
edition was followed by one bearing a Boston imprint, in 1832. This
work, however, carried Bernard's career down only to his departure
from England to America. Portions of the autobiography dealing with
America, unfortunately not complete, the original manuscript having
been lost, were long years afterwards edited for publication by Bernard's heirs, and issued under the title of* Retrospections of America,
1797-1811, *in 1887, by Harper and Brothers, with an introduction, notes,
and index by Laurence Hutton and Brander Matthews. The actor-
manager covered a great deal of the country, from Charleston on the
south to the wilds of Ohio on the west, and Canada on the north. He
was an observant man, quick to see all that was significant in men
and manners about him, and shrewd in his conclusions. Moreover, he
was keenly appreciative of all that was best in American life, and
studied it with a zest born of liking. As a London clubman, intimate
with the Whig leaders, he had acquired a Whiggish turn of mind. His
geniality, wit, and intelligence made him friends wherever he went,
and placed him in a position to record much that is permanently
valuable. His book is sown thick with delightful anecdotes, and its
style is admirable.*

WASHINGTON AS A HOST AT MOUNT VERNON

OUR season [in 1798] was so prosperous that Wignell delayed his visit to Baltimore till the summer was far advanced, and, as his leave extended but to the middle of June, we opened the house only to close it, and adjourn to the capital of Maryland—which might well be termed the Bath of America—Annapolis.

In this little spot all the best of Philadelphian and Virginian society was concentrated, and here, I am convinced, the most stubborn anti-republican could not but have perceived the absurdity of the common notion that all must be on a level socially because they are so politically. America really contained a true nobility, men of talent, probity and benevolence, who had been raised by the public voice to a station which the public feeling bowed down to—a station not hereditary, or due to one man's caprice or another's intrigue, but unassailably based on merit, and open to everyone who chose to emulate the conduct of its possessor. From my Philadelphian friends I obtained introductions to several occupiers of this position—Mr. Howard, the chancellor, Judge Kelly, Governor Stone, General Davidson, and last, not least, the excellent Mr. Carroll, one of the subscribers to the Declaration of Independence. Perhaps the latter, as much as any man, was an illustration of my remarks. From the refinement of his manners, a stranger would have surmised that he had passed all his days in the *salons* of Paris. He had all that suavity and softness, in combination with dignity, which bespeak the perfection of good taste. This attested the character of his society. Ease may be natural to a man, but elegance—the union of propriety with ease—must be acquired; the art of respecting one's company as well as one's self necessarily implies that one's company is worth respecting. But Mr. Carroll possessed higher qualities than mere external polish. He had a heart that colored all his thoughts and deeds with the truest hues of humanity. No man was fonder of doing a good action, and, certainly, none could do it with a better grace.

A few weeks after my location at Annapolis I met with a most pleasing adventure, no less than an encounter with General Washington, under circumstances which most fully confirmed the impression I had formed of him. I had been to pay a visit to an acquaintance on the banks of the Potomac, a few miles below Alexandria, and was returning on horseback, in the rear of an old-fashioned chaise, the driver of which was strenuously urging his steed to an accelerated pace. The beast showed singular indifference until a lash, directed with more skill than humanity, took the skin from an old wound. The sudden pang threw the poor animal on his hind legs, and the wheel swerving upon the bank, over went the chaise, flinging out upon the road a young woman who had been its occupant. The minute before I had perceived a horseman approaching at a gentle trot, who now broke into a gallop, and we reached the scene of the disaster together. The female was our first care. She was insensible, but had sustained no material injury. My companion supported her, while I brought some water in the crown of my hat, from a spring some way off. The driver of the chaise had landed on his legs, and, having ascertained that his spouse was not dead, seemed very well satisfied with the care she was in, and set about extricating his horse. A gush of tears announced the lady's return to sensibility, and then, as her eyes opened, her tongue gradually resumed its office, and assured us that she retained at least one faculty in perfection, as she poured forth a volley of invectives on her mate. The horse was now on his legs, but the vehicle still prostrate, heavy in its frame, and laden with at least half a ton of luggage. My fellow-helper set me an example of activity in relieving it of the external weight; and, when all was clear, we grasped the wheel between us and, to the peril of our spinal columns, righted the conveyance. The horse was then put in, and we lent a hand to help up the luggage. All this helping, hauling, and lifting occupied at least half an hour, under a meridian sun in the middle of July, which fairly boiled the perspiration out of our foreheads. Our unfortunate friend somewhat relieved the task with his narrative. He was a New Englander who had emigrated to the South when young, there picked up a wife and some money, and was now on his way home, having, he told us, been 'made very comfortable' by the death of his father; and when all was right, and we had assisted the lady to resume her seat, he begged us to proceed with him to Alexandria, and take a drop of 'something sociable.' Finding, however, that we were unsociable, he extended his hand (no distant likeness of a seal's fin), gripped ours as he had done the heavy boxes, and, when we had sufficiently *felt* that he was grateful, drove on. My companion, after an exclamation at the heat, offered very courteously to dust my coat, a favor the return of which enabled me to take a deliberate survey of his person. He was a tall, erect, well-made man, evidently advanced in years, but who appeared to have retained all the vigor and elasticity resulting from a life of temperance and exercise. His dress was a blue coat buttoned to the chin, and buckskin breeches. Though, the instant he took off his hat, I could not avoid the recognition of familiar lineaments—which, indeed, I was in the habit of seeing on every sign post and over every fireplace—still I failed to identify him, and, to my surprise, I found that I was an object of equal speculation in his eyes. A smile at length lighted them up, and he exclaimed, 'Mr. Bernard, I believe?' I bowed. 'I had the pleasure of seeing you perform last winter in Philadelphia.' I bowed again, and he added, 'I have heard of you since from several of my friends at Annapolis. You are acquainted with Mr. Carroll?' I replied that that gentleman's society had made amends for much that I had lost in quitting England. He then learned the cause of my presence in the neighborhood, and remarked, 'You must be fatigued. If you will ride up to my house, which is not a mile distant, you can prevent any ill effects from this exertion, by a couple of hours' rest.' I looked round for his dwelling, and he pointed to a building which, the day before, I had spent an hour in contemplating. 'Mount Vernon!' I exclaimed; and then, drawing back, with a stare of wonder, 'Have I the honor of addressing General Washington?' With a smile, whose expression of benevolence I have rarely seen equaled, he offered his hand, and replied, 'An odd sort of introduction, Mr. Bernard; but I am pleased to find you can play so active a part in private, and without a prompter,' and then pointed to our horses (which had stood like statues all this time, as though in sympathy with their fallen brother), and shrugged his shoulders at the inn. I needed no further stimulus to accept his friendly invitation. As we rode up to his house we entered freely into conversation, first in reference to his friends at Annapolis, then respecting my own success in America and the impressions I had received of the country.

Flattering as such inquiries were from such a source, I must confess my own reflections on what had just passed were more absorbing. Considering that nine ordinary country gentlemen out of ten, who had seen a chaise upset near their estate, would have thought it savored neither of pride nor ill-nature to ride home and send their servants to its assistance, I could not but think that I had witnessed one of the strongest evidences of a great man's claim to his reputation—the prompt, impulsive working of a heart which, having made the good of mankind—not conventional forms—its religion, was never so happy as in practically displaying it. On reaching the house (which, in its compact simplicity and commanding elevation, was no bad emblem of its owner's mind), we found that Mrs. Washington was indisposed; but the General ordered refreshments in a parlor whose windows took a noble range of the Potomac, and, after a few minutes' absence, rejoined me.

Though I have ventured to offer some remarks on his less-known contemporaries, I feel it would be impertinence to say a word on the public merits of a man whose character has been burning as a beacon to Europe till its qualities are as well known as the names and dates

of his triumphs. My retrospect of him is purely a social one, and
much do I regret, for the interest of these pages, that it is confined
to a single interview. The general impression I received from his appearance fully corresponded with the description of him by the Marquis
de Chastelleux, who visited America at the close of the war.

The great characteristic of Washington [says he], is the perfect union which
seems to subsist between his moral and physical qualities; so that the selection
of one would enable you to judge of all the rest. If you are presented with
medals of Trajan or Cæsar, the features will lead you to inquire the proportions
of their persons; but if you should discover in a heap of ruins the leg or arm of
an antique Apollo, you would not be curious about the other parts, but content
yourself with the assurance.that they were all conformable to those of a god.

Though fourteen years had elapsed since this was written, I could
perceive that it was far from being the language of mere enthusiasm.
Whether you surveyed his face, open yet well-defined, dignified but
not arrogant, thoughtful but benign; his frame, towering and muscular,
but alert from its good proportion—every feature suggested a resemblance to the spirit it encased, and showed simplicity in alliance
with the sublime. The impression, therefore, was that of a most perfect whole; and though the effect of proportion is said to be to reduce
the idea of magnitude, you could not but think you looked upon a
wonder, and something sacred as well as wonderful—a man fashioned
by the hand of Heaven, with every requisite to achieve a great work.
Thus a feeling of awe and veneration stole over you.

In conversation his face had not much variety of expression: a look
of thoughtfulness was given by the compression of the mouth and
the indentation of the brow (suggesting an habitual conflict with and
mastery over passion), which did not seem so much to disdain a sympathy with trivialities as to be incapable of denoting them. Nor had
his voice, so far as I could discover in our quiet talk, much change,
or richness of intonation, but he always spoke with earnestness, and
his eyes (glorious conductors of the light within) burned with a steady
fire which no one could mistake for mere affability; they were one
grand expression of the well-known line: 'I am a man, and interested
in all that concerns humanity.' In our hour and a half's conversation
he touched on every topic that I brought before him with an even
current of good sense, if he embellished it with little wit or verbal
elegance. He spoke like a man who had felt as much as he had reflected, and reflected more than he had spoken; like one who had
looked upon society rather in the mass than in detail; and who regarded the happiness of America but as the first link in a series of
universal victories; for his full faith in the power of these results of

civil liberty which he saw all around him led him to foresee that it would, ere long, prevail in other countries, and that the social millennium of Europe would usher in the political. When I mentioned to him the difference I perceived between the inhabitants of New England and of the Southern States he remarked, 'I esteem those people greatly; they are the stamina of the Union and its greatest benefactors. They are continually spreading themselves too, to settle and enlighten less favored quarters. Dr. Franklin is a New Englander.' When I remarked that his observations were flattering to my country, he replied, with great good humor, 'Yes, yes, Mr. Bernard, but I consider your country the cradle of free principles, not their arm chair. Liberty in England is a sort of idol; people are bred up in the belief and love of it, but see little of its doings. They walk about freely, but then it is between high walls; and the error of its government was in supposing that after a portion of their subjects had crossed the sea to live upon a common, they would permit their friends at home to build up those walls about them.' A black coming in at this moment, with a jug of spring water, I could not repress a smile, which the General at once interpreted. 'This may seem a contradiction,' he continued, 'but I think you must perceive that it is neither a crime nor an absurdity. When we profess, as our fundamental principle, that liberty is the inalienable right of every man, we do not include madmen or idiots; liberty in their hands would become a scourge. Till the mind of the slave has been educated to perceive what are the obligations of a state of freedom, and not confound a man's with a brute's, the gift would insure its abuse. We might as well be asked to pull down our old warehouses before trade had increased to demand enlarged new ones. Both houses and slaves were bequeathed to us by Europeans, and time alone can change them; an event, sir, which, you may believe me, no man desires more heartily than I do. Not only do I pray for it, on the score of human dignity, but I can clearly foresee that nothing but the rooting out of slavery can perpetuate the existence of our union, by consolidating it in a common bond of principle.'

I now referred to the pleasant hours I had passed in Philadelphia, and my agreeable surprise at finding there so many men of talent, at which his face lit up vividly. 'I am glad to hear you, sir, who are an Englishman, say so, because you must now perceive how ungenerous are the assertions people are always making on your side of the water. One gentleman, of high literary standing—I allude to the Abbé Raynal—has demanded whether America has yet produced one great poet, statesman, or philosopher. The question shows anything but observation, because it is easy to perceive the causes that have combined to render the genius of this country scientific rather than imaginative.

And, in this respect, America has surely furnished her quota. Franklin, Rittenhouse, and Rush are no mean names, to which, without shame, I may append those of Jefferson and Adams as politicians; while I am told that the works of President Edwards of Rhode Island [2] are a text book in polemics in many European colleges.'

Of the replies which I made to his enquiries respecting England, he listened to none with so much interest as to those which described the character of my royal patron, the Prince of Wales. 'He holds out every promise,' remarked the General, of a brilliant career. He has been well educated by *events,* and I doubt not that, in his time, England will receive the benefits of her child's emancipation. She is at present bent double, and has to walk with crutches; but her offspring may teach her the secret of regaining strength, erectness, and independence.' In reference to my own pursuits he repeated the sentiments of Franklin; he feared the country was too poor to be a patron of the drama, and that only arts of a practical nature would for some time be esteemed. The stage he considered to be an indispensable resource for settled society and a chief refiner; not merely interesting as a comment on the history of social happiness by its exhibition of manners, but an agent of good as a school for poetry, in holding up to honor the noblest principles. 'I am too old and too far removed,' he added, 'to seek for or require this pleasure myself, but the cause is not to droop on my account. There's my friend, Mr. Jefferson, has time and taste; he goes always to the play, and I'll introduce you to him,' a promise which he kept, and which proved to me the source of the greatest benefit and pleasure.

As I was engaged to dine at home, I at length rose to take my leave, not without receiving from the General a very flattering request to call on him whenever I rode by. I had the pleasure of meeting him once after this in Annapolis, and I dined with him on a public occasion at Alexandria, my impressions each time improving into a higher degree of respect and admiration.

I have never heard of but one jest of Washington's, which was related to me by his aide-de-camp, my good friend, Colonel Humphreys. The General, rather priding himself on his riding, the Colonel was induced, one day when they were out hunting together, to offer him a bet that he would not follow him over one particular hedge. The challenge was accepted, and Humphreys led the way and took the leap boldly, but, to his consternation, discovered that he had mistaken the spot, and was deposited, up to his horse's girths, in a quagmire. The General either knew the ground better, or had suspected

[2] Bernard means Jonathan Edwards of the College of New Jersey.

something, for, following at an easy pace, he reined up at the hedge, and, looking over at his engulfed aide, exclaimed, 'No, no, Colonel, you are too *deep* for me!'

LIFE IN THE OLD DOMINION, 1799

The summer of 1799 I passed in Virginia, my professional visits, alternating between Richmond and Norfolk, being relieved by excursions to various parts of the state, at the invitation of that truly hospitable race—the planters. Among these I met men of high intelligence and even refinement, whose conviviality not making its agent its end, could be, like their own summers, as radiant as it was warm. No class of persons that I know of has been so harshly judged as the planters, the sins of the fathers having been visited upon the tenth generation. Abroad and at home, worthy persons whose hearts throw a mist round their brains have confounded the necessity of the present with the evil of the past, have let the crimes of a few discolor the many, and the iniquity of a system vouch for that of individuals. Herein has lain the error and the wrong. Unless a man has been willing to break up this system at the cost of his own utter ruin, he has been pronounced a selfish barbarian, a loathsome maggot complacently fattening on corruption. In nine cases out of ten the supporters of the system have been its greatest victims. I do not hesitate to say they have been among its sincerest detesters. It certainly is no enviable lot when a man, happening to be born on a particular spot which is cursed with an indisposable legacy, can be put in a pillory by every enthusiast who makes feeling, not fact, his rule of reasoning. I do not remember a single instance of a planter defending the origin of his possessions, or one who defended the continuance of slavery by other than this single argument: that human agency is required in the cultivation of the Southern soil, while the extreme heat is not to be supported save by Africans or natives. The Negro, if manumitted and paid for his labor, can live upon so little that he would not do half that is required; and, till the country becomes so populated that work shall become scarce, the white will never take his place.

As to the planters . . . in their manners they have ever been austere to their inferiors, and, when abroad, reserved with their equals; but all frost vanished the moment you crossed their threshold. That was a minute but instantaneous division between the frigid and the torrid zone; a warmth—truly Irish—succeeded, and you were welcomed to a land of liberty. In all their domestic arrangements the taste was

evidently French, with some local modifications which were not dis-
pleasing. Though deficient in architectural beauty or stability, many
of their dwellings were internally palaces. Their furniture, pictures,
and musical instruments were all imported from Europe. But this did
not surprise me so much as the tone of their conversation. Their
favorite topics were European, and I found men leading secluded lives
in the woods of Virginia, perfectly *au fait* as to the literary, dramatic, and personal gossip of London and Paris. But the mystery was
soon explained: they had all been educated in France or England,
(a practice which ceased at the Revolution), had made a tour of
the Continent, and maintained a voluminous correspondence ever
since. At one house I met with a gentleman who had participated
in my revels at the London clubs. His memory was a storehouse of
anecdote, which he flavored by a peculiarly happy faculty of imitation,
the rapturous manner in which the company recognized the originals
often making me look round to see if I was not once more snugly
ensconced over the piazza at Covent Garden.

Of the planters' ladies I must speak in terms of unqualified praise;
they had an easy kindliness of manner, as far removed from rudeness
as from reserve, which being natural to them (for they mixed with no
society) was the more admirable. In a woman I would always have
the heart to be the chief source of her fascination. The one thing I
did not quite approve of was the juvenile period at which they bloomed
and decayed. A lady here was in the habit of marrying nearly ten
years earlier than a European, so that at twenty, if she had proved a
fruitful olive, her husband's table was surrounded with tall shoots
sufficient to supply him with shade for the remainder of his days. At
thirty—the glowing summer of an English dame—she had fallen into
'the sere leaf'; and at forty—the autumn fullness of a royal taste, the
bel age of St. James's—the faces of these matrons of the West are cut
up into as many lines as a map of Europe. Nevertheless, to the influence of their society I chiefly attribute their husbands' refinement,
and, in proof, I cannot, perhaps, more amuse the reader than by showing the contrast of a planter's life some twenty years previous, when,
marriage being made a mere mode of conveying property, every
woman was looked on as an animal, and every house was a harem.

During summer he used to rise about nine, when he exerted himself to walk as far as his stables to look at the stud he kept for the
races; at ten he breakfasted on coffee, eggs, and hoe-cake, concluding
it with the commencement of his diurnal potations—a stiff glass of
mint sling—a taking disorder peculiar to the South. He then sought
the coolest room and stretched himself on a pallet in his shirt and
trousers, with a Negress at his head and another at his feet to keep

off the flies and promote reflection. Between twelve and one his throat would require another emulsion, and he would sip half a pint of some mystery termed bumbo, apple toddy, or pumpkin flip. He then mounted a pony, and, with an umbrella over his head, rode gently round his estate to converse with his overseers. At three he dined, and drank everything—brandy, claret, cider, Madeira, punch, and sangaree, then resumed his pallet, with his Negresses, and meditated until tea-time—though he was not particular about tea, unless friends with womenkind dropped in. The inflammation in his throat returned about dusk, and he prescribed for himself cooling washes until bed-time.[3] From this detail the reader will surmise that a planter was a reptile only to be preserved in spirits; but I must guard against the error that he was by choice a solitary toper. On the contrary, he strained every nerve to pick up companions, and it was only when in utter despair of obtaining this pleasure that he gave himself up to bumbo, Dinah, a mattress, and meditation. Many humorous instances were related to me of the plans he adopted to draw guests to his convivial roof in the untracked woods of the interior. One of the most striking was the following:

On the morning of 'a clear day'—a decided scorcher—he would order a wagon to be packed with a tub containing bottles of every compound in his closets—sling, nog, flip, and toddy, together with their elements, spirits, lemons, sugar, et cetera; a pair of rifles, shot, and powder; a fishing rod and tackle; soap, towels, clean linen, and nankeens; and a canvas awning with poles and cords to support it. He then took his seat in the vehicle, and, attended by a train of blacks, was driven slowly to the nearest highway, along which he proceeded till he came to a clear, clay-bottomed pond. The wagon was then backed into the water where the depth was breast-high, the poles were firmly driven into the bottom, the awning stretched over them, and the horses being turned into the woods, the proprietor disarrayed himself and descended into this local bath. After amusing himself with a few minutes' splashing, a board was slid down from the wagon to support him in a recumbent position, and the tub, like a richly freighted West-Indiaman, was committed to the deep and moored beside him. Arrangements were now made for the busi-

---

[3] See Winterbotham's *Historical, Geographical, Commercial, and Philosophical View of the United States* (1796), III, 275, for a similar description of the day of a typical Georgia planter. The Georgian rose at six, drank a glass of bitters, rode forth to tour his estate, and returned at eight o'clock for breakfast. Afterwards he rode to the nearest village or public house, to talk of prices and horse-racing, make trades, and play cards, and came back at four o'clock with some friends for dinner, which was prolonged till sunset. After dinner the occupation varied with the weather. Sometimes it was hunting deer by torchlight, sometimes more cards and conversation. Like the Virginian, the Georgia planter left nearly all work to overseer and slaves—or so Winterbotham states.

ness of the day: while one ebony was placed in charge of the cattle, another carried out a line from his floating fishing rod, standing ready to give him notice of a bite; a third placed his rifles on the tub, that he might pop at the first bird that offered; and two others were despatched in opposite directions to watch if travelers were approaching. Thus combining the four staple enjoyments of bathing, drinking, shooting, and fishing, this Western Sardanapalus marked the furnace in the skies burn away, but not with a contented heart. He sighed for a victim; his toils were spread and he hungered for his prey. In the deep solitude that reigned around, his ear was triply alive to human sounds; the creak of a cartwheel had more music for him than the finest notes of a thrush, and the sight of any person, not a Negro, more beauty than the loveliest landscape. If at length the form of a stranger appeared, he sprang from his plank and shouted an invitation to alight and take a drop of something sociable. If the traveler refused, up went the rifle to his shoulder, and compliance was demanded in the tone of a European footpad. The stranger now saw that pleasure was policy, however urgent might be his business; but if he were so unguarded as to yield to his next request to 'strip and take a swim,' he speedily found himself irretrievably in the clutches of this human alligator. The planter fixed in him all the claws of nog, flip, sling, and toddy, until the brain of the victim became so confused that the grinning Negroes had no difficulty in stowing him into the wagon, whereupon the poles were struck, the horses buckled in, and the delighted planter returned home with his prize, whom he probably cooped up in a backroom with a *chevaux-de-frise* of bottles, until, by some desperate effort, the captive made his escape.

Another and more civilized plan was to send the Negroes round at nightfall to the nearest inn (here very properly termed 'ordinaries'), with a note to any lady or gentleman putting up there, stating that if they did not like their accommodation, Mr. —— would be happy to see them at his house close by, to which a black with a lantern would conduct them. This system was often successful; for, in the old times, all you could obtain at these places were eggs and bacon, hoe-cake, and peach brandy; a bed stuffed with shavings, on a frame that rocked like a cradle, and in a room so well ventilated that a traveler had some difficulty in keeping his umbrella erect, if endeavoring, under this convenience, to find shelter from the rain while in bed. But as the planter's hospitality proved such an antagonist to the landlord's interests, the latter always had it made up to him in presents, so that all parties were well content; and, probably, the only sufferer in the end was the cerebellum of the guest. Whether the decline of such a spirit may be deplored or not, it is not to be wondered at. As emigrants began to pour into the woods a planter had seldom occasion to lift his rifle to his shoulder in demanding their society, but, on the contrary, he probably soon obtained those who required some such gesticulation to be got rid of.

I was much amused by a story I once heard of a proprietor sending to an inn one evening, when he was in unusually good spirits, to desire the company of any stray gentleman who would so far favor him; and his sable Mercury returning with a New England preacher who was journeying on a crusade against slavery, and who immediately commenced tracing a comparison between the planter and Beelzebub, which lasted until daylight.

The Three Chief American Cities in 1794 [1] &

HENRY WANSEY, *who was born in 1752 or 1753 and died in 1827, was a clothier of Warminster, England, who retired in middle life, and devoted himself to travel, reading, and antiquarian research. In 1789 he was chosen a fellow of the Society of Antiquaries, and he gave many years to the coauthorship of a history of the hundred of Warminster. He also published pamphlets upon wool growing, in which he was interested not only as a clothier, but as vice-president of the Bath and West of England Agricultural Society. Curiosity and 'some occurrences in business' led him to make his voyage to the United States in 1794. He landed in Boston early in May, traveled as far south as Philadelphia, and, returning to New York, set sail for England in July, taking with him copious notes upon all that he had seen, two tortoises, a flying squirrel, and many shrubs and plants.*

Wansey explains that he was enabled to write a volume of 250 pages upon America after only two months' stay because he had made a thorough preliminary study of works upon the young republic, and had drafted in advance all the questions for which he desired answers. He believed that a plain, matter-of-fact narrative was needed, because most of the recent accounts of the United States were prejudiced and inaccurate. Imlay, he said, had too much flattered the Americans, while the author of Letters on Emigration *had viewed everything transatlantic with a hostile eye. Brissot's* Travels *he made his* vade mecum, *and*

[1] From *An Excursion to the United States of North America in the Summer of* 1794, Salisbury, 1796, pp. 18-35, 57-66, 96-119.

found to be tolerably accurate, though he criticizes it in certain details. His own judgment of American society was highly favorable. 'In these States,' he sums up, 'you behold a certain plainness and simplicity of manners, which bespeak temperance, equality of condition, and a sober use of the faculties of the mind—the mens sana in corpore sano.' He admitted that 'the arts and improvements proceed very slow in America,' and that in the interior, many of the comforts of life were still lacking; but he still believed that for anyone not a man of luxury, America would afford a happy asylum. Politically, he predicted a happy future for a nation 'not founded on conquest, but on the sober progress and dictates of reason, and totally disencumbered of the feudal system, which has cramped the genius of mankind for more than seven hundred years past.'

Wansey's small volume was published in Salisbury in 1796, and reached a second edition in 1798. It is given in diary form, the rough jottings of day-to-day travel.

AN ACCOUNT OF BOSTON

ON our arrival, we enquired for the best house of entertainment; and were directed to the Bunch of Grapes, in State Street, kept by Colonel Coleman. It is nothing unusual in America for army officers to keep taverns. A man with the title of Major sometimes holds your horse, and Captains are digging by the roadside; it is a vestige of the Revolution. During the American war, a man's promotion was not measured so much by his rank or fortune as by his zeal and assiduity in the service of his country, and it was a cheap way of rewarding him for his services.

In the year 1740, Boston was esteemed the largest town in America, now Philadelphia and New York rank before it; nevertheless, it is a very flourishing place, full of business and activity. The merchants and tradesmen meet every day, from twelve to two o'clock, in State Street, as on an exchange. We enquired for a porter to fetch our luggage from the ship to the tavern, and a free Negro offered himself, for which service he required half a dollar. The Negroes in this State are all free, and are a respectable body of people. They have a freemasons' club, into which they admit no white person. However, I believe they are not yet admitted to hold offices of state, though they vote for them. This town, or city, contains about eighteen thousand inhabitants. State Street is the principal one, about twenty yards wide, is near the centre of the town, and leads down to the long wharf. Cornhill is another comfortable street for trade, but it put me in mind of Basingstoke. Their foot ways are not yet paved with flat stones, the horse and foot way being alike pitched with pebbles, with posts and a gutter to divide them, like the old-fashioned towns in England. The buildings, likewise, are but indifferent; many of them, as well as their churches, are weather-boarded at the side, and all of them roofed with shingles. A very awkward-looking railed enclosure, on the top of the houses, for drying clothes, gives them a very odd appearance. The part of the town called New or West Boston, is an exception to this, for the houses there are all neat and elegant (of brick), with handsome entrances and door cases, and a flight of steps.

At Colonel Coleman's, which is more properly a lodging house than a tavern, we were but very indifferently accommodated as to beds; generally two in a room, and not very cleanly, for we were much pestered with bugs. At two o'clock dinner was announced, and we were shewn into a room where we found a long table covered with dishes, and plates for twenty persons. We were served with salmon, veal, beef, mutton, fowl, ham, roots, puddings, et cetera, et cetera, each man had his pint of Madeira before him, and for this and our breakfast, tea, supper, and bed, we paid five shillings currency, for they make no separate charges, nor do they abate of their charges were you to dine out every day. There is no shyness in conversation, as at an English table. People of different countries and languages mix together, and converse as familiarly as old acquaintances. Three or four of our company were French emigrants. On one side of me sat a Mr. Washington, from Virginia (no relation to the President, or very distant), and on the other side a young man from Philadelphia, next to him a person from Newbury Port, three hundred and fifty miles north of Philadelphia. I found myself well entertained with their conversation, on many subjects new to me. In half an hour after the cloth was removed every person had quitted table to go to their several occupations and employments, except the Frenchmen and ourselves; for the Americans know the value of time too well to waste it at the table. Here I met a Mr. Armstrong, once a clothier at Corsham, in Wilts, near my native place. When we meet a countryman in a remote part of the world, we speak to him as an intimate acquaintance, though perhaps we have never seen each other before. This was the case at present. I took a walk with him to Bunker Hill and Brede's Hill, the ground where the Americans (June 17, 1775) first resisted the attack of the British. A Captain Greatan accompanied us, who was an officer on the spot at the very time. He described the whole action, and shewed us the place where Dr. Warren fell, the point where the attack began, and the road by which the Americans retreated. The action was not fought on Bunker Hill, as is on record, but on Brede's

Hill. It was but a detachment of the main army which were in action. We followed the same route the armies went, for two miles; we then filed off to the left, and came to the town of Cambridge, where the principal university in the State is established. It is called Harvard College, is an excellent institution, was founded about the year 1650, is well endowed, and supports three hundred students; two large handsome brick buildings separate from each other; a third has been taken down lately, to be rebuilt. We returned to Boston over the new bridge, a most prodigious work for so infant a country; a work, as Mr. Hobe observed, worthy the Roman Empire. It is a bridge over an arm of the sea, above one thousand eight hundred feet long, and about thirty-four wide, well lighted all the way into Boston, about a mile in length. This bridge is built entirely of wood, and cost about twenty-four thousand pounds, and marks the genius and spirit of the town of Boston. It had been opened for about five months when we passed it. About halfway over the bridge, we observed two iron rings; Captain Greatan, by one of them, lifted up a trap door, and discovered a large room below, capable of holding two hundred men, to which we descended by stairs, and saw the machinery by which the draw-bridge is lifted up for large vessels to pass. In hot weather this must be a most delightful cool retreat, as well as an excellent place for bathing.[2]

There are two other long wooden bridges leading from Boston, Mystic and Dorchester. The latter is built on the site of an ancient Indian bridge, part of the causeway of which still remains perfect; but these are not to compare with the new bridge. A very elegant theatre was opened at Boston about three months ago, far superior in taste, elegance, and convenience to the Bath, or any other country theatre that I ever yet saw in England. Mr. Hobe and I were there with Mr. and Mrs. Vaughan. The play and farce were *Inkle and Yarico,* and *Bon Ton;* I paid a dollar for a ticket. It held about twelve hundred persons. One of the *dramatis personæ* was a Negro, and he filled his character with great propriety. The dress of the company being perfectly English, and some of the actors (Jones and his wife) being those I had seen perform the last winter at Salisbury, in Shatford's company, made me feel myself at home. Between the play and farce, the orchestra having played 'Ca Ira,' the gallery called aloud for 'Yankee-doodle,' which, after some short opposition, was complied with. A Mr. Powell is the manager of the playhouse.[3] Mr. Goldsmith,

[2] For the early Boston bridges, see the *Memorial History of Boston,* III, 555.

[3] This theater was built by a stock company, with a subscribed capital of £6000, during 1793. An effort to present plays in 1792, in defiance of the state laws, had resulted in the arrest of a comedian, and in great public excitement; but the performances had soon been resumed.

the ingenious architect of this theatre, has also lately built an elegant crescent, called the Tontine, about fourteen or sixteen elegant houses, which let for near two hundred pounds sterling a year.

In Boston, they have forty hackney coaches, and for a quarter dollar you are carried to any part of the town.

. . . I went twice with Mr. Vaughan's family to the Unitarian chapel, the only one yet opened in America, and is a proof of the increased liberality of sentiment of the Bostonians. They have in a great measure lost that rigidity of manners, and vigilant way of keeping the Sunday, as to put people in the stocks who were seen walking in the streets during service. They no longer hang old women for witchcraft, as they did in the last century; yet at the same time they maintain a general sobriety of manners, and the places of public worship, of which I think they have eighteen, are all well attended. Mr. Freeman [4] is the minister of the Unitarians, who meet in what was called the King's Chapel, before the Revolution. It is one of the handsomest buildings in the town. He has a salary of about one hundred and fifty pounds a year, and the society is increasing. The clergy, however, refused to give him ordination on account of his opinions; upon which, the principals of the congregation met and ordained him themselves. Their form of prayer is Dr. Clarke's reformed liturgy, with no addition whatever; some part was left out, and a few alterations made. No creed preserved but that called the Apostles' Creed; they have a baptismal confession for adult persons, and another for children.

There are many beautiful scenes around the town, and many views of the sea, and the green mountains in the distant horizon westward form a beautiful ground to the landscape.

On the southwest side of the town, there is a pleasant promenade, called the Mall, adjoining Boston Common, consisting of a long walk shaded by trees, about half the length of the Mall in St. James's park. At one end you have a fine view of the sea. The common itself is a pleasant green field, with a gradual ascent from the seashore, till it ends in Beacon Hill, a high point of land, commanding a very fine view of the country. . .

NEW YORK CITY

We moored our vessel at Burling slip at four in the morning, and after a little refreshment I landed and enquired out the Tontine coffee-house. New York is much more like a city than Boston, having

4 James Freeman, 1759-1835, became pastor of King's Chapel in 1783, and soon converted this ancient Episcopal church into the first Unitarian church in America.

broad footways paved, with a curb to separate them from the road. The streets are wider, and the houses in better style. Boston is the Bristol, New York the Liverpool, and Philadelphia the London of America. The Tontine tavern and coffee-house [5] is a handsome large brick building; you ascend six or eight steps under a portico, into a large public room, which is the Stock Exchange of New York, where all bargains are made. Here are two books kept, as at Lloyd's, of every ship's arrival and clearing out. This house was built for the accommodation of the merchants, by Tontine shares of two hundred pounds each. It is kept by Mr. Hyde, formerly a woolen-draper in London. You can lodge and board there at a common table, and you pay ten shillings currency a day, whether you dine out or not. No appearance of shop windows as in London; only stores, which make no show till you enter the houses. House rent is very dear; a hundred pounds sterling a year is a very usual price for a common storekeeper.

Dined the first day with Mr. Comfort Sands, a considerable merchant, to whom I brought a letter from his son in London. In the evening called on Mr. Jay, brother to the Embassador, and took a walk with him and Mr. Armstrong to the Belvidere, about two miles out of New York towards the Sound—an elegant tea-drinking house, encircled with a gallery, at one story high, where company can walk round the building and enjoy the fine prospect of New York harbour and shipping. You have a delightful sea view from thence, commanding Staten, Long Island, and Governor's Island, Paulus Hook, Brooklyn and the Sound, names very familiar to us during the American War. There were also formerly fine orchards on the land side, but these were entirely cut down by the troops for winter firing.

From hence we crossed the Boston road, to another tea-drinking house and garden, the Indian Queen. This place was filled by Frenchmen with their families. Here they all wear the tricoloured cockade, I observed, whether aristocrats or democrats.

May 19. Dined with Mr. Jay, and in the evening went to the theatre with Mrs. Sands and her two daughters. Mrs. Cowley's play, *A Bold Stroke for a Husband,* with the farce of *Hob in the Well;* the actors mostly from England; price of admittance to the boxes, one dollar. A very bad theatre; a new one is going to be built by subscription, under the direction of Hodgkinson, the present manager. Mrs. Wrighten, who used to sing at Vauxhall twenty years ago, and was afterwards an actress at Bristol, is one of their principal female per-

---

[5] The Tontine coffee-house, which served as a merchants' exchange, was erected in 1792 on the northwest corner of Wall and Water Streets, and was for two generations prominent in the city's commercial history.

formers; her voice is as clear and shrill as ever. I think them altogether far inferior to the Boston company.

In 1740 there was but one printing press in New York; now there
are near twenty, and some map engravers. The following newspapers
are published at New York: the *Daily Advertiser, American Minerva,
Daily Gazette, Diary, Evening Post, Greenleaf's New York Journal,*
published Wednesdays and Saturdays, price to subscribers three dollars,
or thirteen shillings and sixpence per annum; and one other that I
do not know the name of.

At first my lodgings were at the Tontine coffee-house, but afterwards I moved to more private lodgings, at Mrs. Loring's, near the
Battery. This is the pleasantest situation imaginable. Our common
sitting room was fifty feet by thirty, and twenty in height, with windows on two sides of it. As we sat at dinner, we could see the vessels,
on one side the room, sailing out of the harbour; and on the other,
the same turning up Hudson's River, apparently sailing round the
house, withing fifty yards of us. We could also see Long Island,
Governor's, and Staten Islands, as well as the Narrows beyond them
all, where every ship must first appear before it can make the harbour;
and with our glasses we could descry them, oftentimes a day before
they came in. It was so much of sea that we could see the porpoises
roll and tumble about at no great distance from us. At this house
lodged Mr. Genêt, the late French Embassador; Mr. Joseph Priestley,
waiting the arrival of his father; Mr. Henry, of Manchester; Captain
Lindsey, formerly of his majesty's ship, the *Pearl* frigate, and two
or three gentlemen from Connecticut.

.   .   .

May 23. Though the rain has ceased, it is still hot and close, and
the night insupportable. I went this morning, with Mr. Priestley and
Mr. Henry, to breakfast with General Gates, the hero of Saratoga.[6]
He has a very pleasant country situation, about three miles from New
York, on the borders of the Sound; from whence you have a good
view of Long Island, and of the shipping. He received us very hospitably. His wife is a pleasant, chatty, fat little woman, of sixty; and
described to us a visit paid to them by an Indian warrior, whose dignity of manners and serious behavior were both engaging and respectable.—Seeing a servant holding a silver waiter, and carrying the
cups thereon, he observed, 'the servant was putting it to a wrong use;
a hole should have been drilled in it, and it should have been hung
round the neck, for then it would have made an excellent breast plate.'
He also remarked on the want of good judgment among the white

[6] General Gates lived in New York from 1790 until his death in 1806.

people, in having their bedrooms piled on the top of the others; 'walking upwards is so unnatural, especially when there was so much room on the ground; besides, you were in that situation so easily surprised by the enemy, who could put a fire under you, and burn you, while you were asleep.' Many other observations, equally odd, he also made, all of which I make no doubt he was convinced were according to the true dictates of nature and common sense, and the fitness and reason of things.

The old General, upon finding I came from Wiltshire, called me countryman, and said he was born not far from me, near Totness, in Devonshire. He is quite the Uncle Toby; all his ideas and expressions are still military; at the same time so modest as not to mention anything relating to Saratoga, or any of his own military achievements. We were speaking of the advance of land, and he informed us of a large tract within his own knowledge, bought five years ago, for threepence an acre, and lately sold again at four shillings. Chancellor Livingston, who called on us at Mrs. Loring's today, says that, on an average, in the last twelve months, they have doubled in value; that eighteen months ago, he was offered one hundred and twenty thousand acres at two shillings an acre; that a week after, when inclined to accept it, he found it had been sold at two shillings and sixpence; but that lately it had been disposed of at sixteen shillings an acre.

May 24, 1794. As I was getting up in the morning, I heard drums beating and fifes playing. I ran to the window, and saw a large body of people on the other side of the Governor's House, with flags flying, and marching two and two towards the waterside. What, thought I, can the meaning of this be? The peaceful Americans with the ensigns of war? What! have the Americans a standing army too in time of peace? The sound of the drum is what I have not heard since I left England. I hastened down stairs, and the mystery was soon explained; it was a procession of young tradesmen going in boats to Governor's Island, to give the State a day's work. Fortifications are there erecting for strengthening the entrance to New York harbour; it is a patriotic and general resolution of the inhabitants of this city to work a day gratis, without any distinction of rank or condition, for the public advantage, on these fortifications. Today, the whole trade of carpenters and joiners; yesterday, the body of masons; before this, the grocers, schoolmasters, coopers, and barbers; next Monday all the attorneys and men concerned in the law handle the mattock and shovel, the whole day, and carry their provisions with them. How noble is this! How it cherishes unanimity and love for their country! How much does it tend to unite all ranks of people, and render the social compact firm and united!

PHILADELPHIA AND PRESIDENT WASHINGTON

We now came to a small township called Frankfort, five miles from Philadelphia; it is a place of small consequence, though one of the oldest in the state, being built by the Swedish and Dutch settlers before William Penn came to America; two miles further, we passed Harrowgate Gardens on our right, where there are mineral springs; it is a place of entertainment and relaxation for the tradesmen of Philadelphia to partake of upon a Sunday, like those in the vicinity of London. We had now a distant view of the spires and steeples of Philadelphia, and the country all around as flat and level as about London; the road nearly as good. We drove on at the rate of nine miles an hour, and entered Kensington, a small village; then crossing Cohocksinck and Choquensquock rivers, we arrived at Philadelphia, ninety-two miles from New York, a distance often run by mail stages in one day, although no turnpike any part of the way. We entered the city by Front Street, and arrived at the City Tavern, in South Second Street, about noon. I slept at this house two nights, and met with my old tormentors, the bugs: it was a very unpleasant house to be lodged at; yet it was a principal tavern, where the books are kept of what ships arrive and clear out; and to this coffee-house the principal merchants resort every day; a public ordinary every day at two o'clock; about twenty of us dined there, but we could get hardly any attendance from the waiters, though we rang the bell incessantly.

Finding the Congress were still sitting, and expected to adjourn every day, I lost no time in going to hear the debates; after calling on a gentleman to whom I had a letter of introduction, I was accompanied by him, and heard an interesting debate on the political situation of the country in respect to Great Britain.

On entering the House of Representatives, I was struck with the convenient arrangement of the seats for the members; the size of the chamber was about one hundred feet by sixty; the seats in three rows formed semicircles behind each other, facing the Speaker, who was in a kind of pulpit near the centre of the radii and the clerks below him; every member was accommodated for writing, by there being likewise a circular writing desk to each of the circular seats; over the entrance was a large gallery, into which were admitted every citizen, without distinction, who chose to attend; and under the gallery likewise were accommodations for those who were introduced; but no person either in the gallery or under it is suffered to express any marks of applause or discontent at what is debated; it being understood they are present in the person of their representative: this has been a great error in the new French Government; an attempt, however, was once made to introduce it here (in March last) by a clapping of hands, at a speech which fell from Mr. Parker; but the whole house instantly rose to resent it, and adjourned their business, being then in a committee, and the galleries were cleared.

．　　　．　　　．

June 6. I had the honor of an interview with the President of the United States, to whom I was introduced by Mr. Dandridge, his secretary. He received me very politely, and after reading my letters, I was asked to breakfast.

I confess, I was struck with awe and veneration when I recollected that I was now in the presence of one of the greatest men upon earth —the GREAT WASHINGTON—the noble and wise benefactor of the world! as Mirabeau styles him—the advocate of human nature—the friend of both worlds. Whether we view him as a general in the field, vested with unlimited authority and power; at the head of a victorious army; or in the Cabinet, as the President of the United States; or as a private gentleman, cultivating his own farm; he is still the same great man, anxious only to discharge with propriety the duties of his relative situation. His conduct has always been so uniformly manly, honourable, just, patriotic, and distinterested that his greatest enemies cannot fix on any one trait of his character that can deserve the least censure. His paternal regard for the army while he commanded it; his earnest and sincere desire to accomplish the glorious object for which they were contending; his endurance of the toils and hazards of war, without ever receiving the least emolument from his country; and his retirement to private life after the peace plainly evince that this motives were the most pure and patriotic that could proceed from a benevolent heart. His letters to Congress during the war, now lately published in England, as well as his circular letter and farewell orders to the armies of the United States, at the end of the war, shew him to have been justly ranked among the fine writers of the age. When we look down from this truly great and illustrious character upon other public servants, we find a glaring contrast; nor can we fix our attention on any other great man without discovering in them a vast and mortifying dissimilarity!

The President in his person is tall and thin, but erect; rather of an engaging than a dignified presence. He appears very thoughtful, is slow in delivering himself, which occasions some to conclude him reserved, but it is rather, I apprehend, the effect of much thinking and reflection, for there is great appearance to me of affability and accommodation. He was at this time in his sixty-third year, being born February 11, 1732, O.S., but he has very little the appearance of age, having been all his lifetime so exceeding temperate. There is a certain anxiety visible in his countenance, with marks of extreme sensibility.

Notwithstanding his great attention and employment in the affairs of his well-regulated government, and of his own agricultural concerns, he is in correspondence with many of the eminent geniuses in the different countries of Europe, not so much for the sake of learning and fame as to procure the knowledge of agriculture, and the arts useful to his country.

I informed his Excellency, in the course of conversation, that I was a manufacturer from England, who, out of curiosity as well as business, had made an excursion to America to see the state of society there; to inspect their various manufactories, and particularly the woolen, with which I was best acquainted. The General asked me what I thought of their wool? I informed him that I had seen some very good and fine, at Hartford, in Connecticut, which they told me came from Georgia; but that in general it was very indifferent; yet from the appearance of it, I was convinced it was capable of great improvement. That, to my surprise, in the course of travelling two hundred and fifty miles, from Boston hither, I had not seen any flock of more than twenty or thirty sheep, and but few of these; from whence I concluded there was no great quantity grown in the states so as to answer any great purposes for manufacture. His Excellency observed that from his own experience he believed it capable of great improvement, for he had been trying some experiments with his own flocks (at Mount Vernon); that by attending to breed and pasturage, he had so far improved his fleeces as to have encreased them from two to six pounds apiece; but that since, from a multiplicity of other objects to attend to, they were, by being neglected, gone back to half their weight, being now scarcely three pounds. I took this opportunity to offer him one of my publications on the *Encouragement of Wool,* which he seemed with pleasure to receive.

Mrs. Washington herself made tea and coffee for us. On the table were two small plates of sliced tongue, dry toast, bread and butter, et cetera, but no broiled fish, as is the general custom. Miss Custis, her granddaughter, a very pleasing young lady of about sixteen, sat next to her, and her brother George Washington Custis, about two years older than herself. There was but little appearance of form; one servant only attended, who had no livery; a silver urn for hot water was the only article of expense on the table. She appears something older than the President, though, I understand, they were both born in the same year; short in stature, rather robust; very plain in her dress, wearing a very plain cap, with her grey hair closely turned up under it. She has routs or levees (whichever the people chuses to call them) every Wednesday and Saturday at Philadelphia, during the sitting of Congress. But the Anti-federalists object even to these, as tending to give a super-eminency, and introductory to the paraphernalia of courts.

After some general conversation, we rose from table to view a model, which a gentleman from Virginia, who had breakfasted with us, had brought for the inspection of the President. It was a scheme to convey vessels on navigable canals from one lock to another, without the expense of having flood gates, by means of a lever weighted by a quantity of water pumped into a reservoir.

The President has continual applications from the ingenious, as the patron of every new invention, which, good or bad, he with great patience listens to, and receives them all in a manner to make them go away satisfied.

In the evening I went to the new theatre, to see Mrs. Inchbald's play, *Every One Has His Faults,* with the farce of *No Song No Supper.* Mrs. Whitlock, sister to Mrs. Siddons, is the chief actress; and, to my surprise, I recognized Darley, one of the actors last winter at Salisbury, in the character of Crop. It is an elegant and convenient theatre, as large as that of Covent Garden; and, to judge from the dress and appearance of the company around me, and the actors and scenery, I should have thought I had still been in England. The ladies wore the small bonnets of the same fashion as those I saw when I left England; some of chequered straw, et cetera, some with their hair full dressed, without caps, as with us, and very few in the French style; the younger ladies with their hair flowing in ringlets on their shoulders; the gentlemen with round hats, their coats with high collars, and cut quite in the English fashion, and many in silk striped coats. The scenery of the stage excellent, particularly a view on the Schuylkill, about two miles from the city. The greatest part of the scenes, however, belonged once to Lord Barrymore's Theatre, at Wargrave. The motto over the stage is novel: 'The Eagle Suffers Little Birds to Sing. . .' When it was in contemplation to build this theatre, it was strongly opposed by the Quakers, who used all their influence with Congress to prevent it, as tending to corrupt the manners of the people and encrease too much the love of pleasure. It was, however, at length carried, and this motto from Shakespeare was chosen. It is applicable in another sense; for the State House, where Congress sits, is directly opposite to it, both being in Chestnut Street, and both houses are often performing at the same time. Yet the eagle (the emblem adopted by the American Government) is no way interrupted by the chattering of these mock birds with their mimic songs.

Sundry Observations upon
American Manners [1] ঽৡ

JOHN MELISH, *born in 1771, was a textile manufacturer of Glasgow, who early in 1806 sailed for Savannah with a consignment of his own goods, planning to make arrangements throughout the United States for a considerable export business. After traversing the Coastal States from Savannah to New Hampshire and Boston, he returned home in the spring of 1807, greatly distressed by the commercial friction between Britain and America. Again having business in the United States, particularly in Georgia, where large sums were owed him by half-insolvent debtors, he sailed for this country in the autumn of 1809. He was in New York when the Nonintercourse Act of March 1811 effectually destroyed his commercial business, and he employed the remainder of that year in a tour that carried him down the Ohio as far as Louisville, over much of the states of Ohio and Kentucky, and across the frontier at Niagara into Upper Canada. His* Travels in the United States of America, in the Years 1806 and 1807, and 1809, 1810, and 1811, Including an Account of Passages betwixt America and Britain, and Travels through Various Parts of Great Britain, Ireland, and Upper Canada, *was published in two volumes in Philadelphia in 1812.*

Melish was a keen businessman, and a strait-laced Scotchman in his outlook upon morals and manners. His chief interest was in economic conditions, and particularly in the growth of manufactures in America, and the state of trade. For the most part the style and matter of his work are exceedingly dry, for it abounds in elementary information—physical descriptions of the country, statistics of population and commerce, and accounts of climate, soil, and government, noted down in the most humdrum fashion. His plan, he says, was to take Morse's

[1] From *Travels in the United States of America in the Years* 1806 *and* 1807, *and* 1809, 1810, *and* 1811, Philadelphia, 1812, volume I, p. 31ff.; volume II, pp. 69-74, 111-14, 247-8, 355-8, 368-9.

Gazetteer of the United States, *and Arrowsmith's map, to examine them carefully upon his arrival in a new locality, to confirm or correct the information they gave by personal observation or interviews with informed persons, and to commit the results to paper as notes for his journal. Among those with whom he reports conversations were President Jefferson, who told him that he believed Norfolk would soon become the greatest seaport in the United States save New Orleans, outstripping New York, stated that turnpike roads would be general throughout the country in less than twenty years, and offered some observations upon the 'putrid effluvia' of stagnant water as a cause of malaria. He also saw President Madison for an hour in 1811, and chatted with him upon trade, manufactures, and British relations, A long description is given of the Rappite community at Harmony, Pennsylvania, where he was greatly impressed by the order and prosperity of the German community on its 9000-acre tract. Throughout the two volumes Melish evinces the warmest admiration of the United States. Its political system, he says, conferred 'a degree of freedom to mankind unknown in Europe, and securing to industry the reward of its merit—peace and plenty.' He believed that 'The contemplation of the subject is animating to the mind; it inspires confidence in the future destinies of the world; and calls forth sentiments of gratitude to the supreme Disposer of all events.'*

A NEGRO BURNED

Leaving Hely's [inn, near Savannah], we traveled two miles, when my fellow-traveler stopped to point out the post where two Negroes were executed for killing an overseer. The one was hanged, and the other was burned to death. I was informed that this mode of punishment is sometimes inflicted on Negroes, when the crime is very flagrant, to deprive them of the mental consolation arising from a hope that they will after death return to their own country. This may be good policy as respects the blacks; but, in mercy to the white people, I wish it could be avoided. When I looked at the scorched tree where the man had been tied, and observed the fragments of his bones at the foot of it, I was horrorstruck; and I never yet can think of the scene without a pang. What feelings must have been excited in those who saw the execution! Thirteen miles beyond this we reached Berry's tavern, 28 miles from Savannah, and here we stopped for the night. . . Saturday, 28th June, we rose at three o'clock, and settled our bill, which amounted to one dollar and thirty-one cents each. . .

CELEBRATING THE FOURTH AT LOUISVILLE, GEORGIA

This being the anniversary of American independence, the day was ushered in by the firing of great guns; and military companies had collected in Louisville from the whole country round. On my return to the tavern, I found a considerable number of the military assembled there. I was waited on by a committee of the artillery company, and received a very polite invitation to dine with them, which I accepted with pleasure, being anxious to observe the mode of celebrating this day, so important in the annals of America.

About 3 o'clock we sat down to dinner. The captain took his place at the head of the table, the oldest lieutenant at the foot; the committee gave the different orders, and all were on an equal footing. Several of the State officers dined with them.

After dinner they drank Madeira wine to a series of toasts, one for each State, which had been previously prepared. Among the number were 'The Day We Celebrate,' 'The Land We Live In,' 'The President of the United States,' 'Memory of General Washington,' 'Memory of Benjamin Franklin,' 'Memory of John Peirce,' et cetera. Each toast was followed by a discharge of artillery, and the music played an appropriate air. A number of excellent songs were sung, and the afternoon was spent with great conviviality and good humour.

Having several calls to make in the town, I left the table early, but returned again in the evening, when I found that the 'cordial drop' had added greatly to the elevation of the animal spirits of the company. They had also received an addition to their number, by several military officers high in command, among whom was Major General Jackson. Having occasion to give a toast, I availed myself of that opportunity to impress them with favorable sentiments towards my native country. America had been long regarded with a jealous eye by the councils of Britain, and an almost total alienation of affection was the consequence. I knew that Mr. Fox's administration was favorably disposed towards America, and I was inclined, as far as I had opportunity, to impress the Americans with that belief. Accordingly, after thanking the company for the honor they had conferred upon me, and assuring them of my own friendly regard for the country, I proposed as a toast, 'Mr. Fox, and the Independent Whigs of Britain. May their joint endeavors with the Government of the United States be the means of reconciling the differences between the two countries; and to the latest prosperity may Americans and Britons hail one another as brothers and as friends.' This was cordially received, and drank accordingly; and immediately after I was introduced to and politely received by the visiting officers.

THE RAPPITES: INDUSTRY AND RELIGION [2]

At sunrise next morning we heard the bell ring, and in a quarter of an hour thereafter the people were at their respective employments; all was bustle and activity. The innkeeper accompanied us to see the Society's shepherds and sheep. We passed Conasquensing Creek, by a wooden bridge ornamented with flowers, and observed a low meadow on our left, which we were informed had been drained with a good deal of labor, and was now converted into excellent pasture ground; a pleasure garden called the Labyrinth, and a Botanic Garden, being in the east end of it, right opposite to the bridge. Beyond this, on the side of the creek, were various houses for dyeing, fulling, and dressing cloth. The ground rises to a considerable elevation on the north side of the creek, and on our way up we perceived about 100 sheep, which we were told had just arrived from Washington, Pennsylvania, and had not yet been distributed among the main flock. On arriving at the sheep pens, we found the flock to consist of about 1000, and they were separated into three divisions. The first were all of the merino breed, the most of them full-blooded; the second about half merinos and half common; and the third were all common, with some merino rams amongst them. They were under the charge of three shepherds, who sleep beside them all night in movable tents; and a watchman from the town attends them during the night. We were informed that the society intended to increase the flock, as fast as possible, to 3000; and to progress with the manufacture of woolen cloth, which they found very lucrative, as fast as circumstances would permit.

After breakfast we visited the different branches of manufacture. In the wool loft, eight or ten women were employed in teasing and sorting the wool for the carding machine, which is at a distance on the creek. From thence the roves are brought to the spinning house, in the town, where we found two roving billies and six spinning

---

[2] George Rapp, 1770-1847, came to the United States in 1803 from Germany to find a home for the peculiar religious community he had established. He at once bought a tract of land in Butler County, Pennsylvania, where the following year some 600 supporters, nearly all people of the working classes, joined him. In 1805 the Harmony Society was formally organized as a Christian brotherhood, holding all property in common, and devoting themselves to preparation for the second coming of Christ, which Rapp believed to be imminent. After 1807, when a wave of religious enthusiasm swept the society, celibacy was strictly observed. Unsympathetic neighbors and visitors in Pennsylvania greatly annoyed the Rappites, and in 1814 they removed to a tract of 30,000 acres in Indiana.

jennies at work. They were principally wrought by young girls, and they appeared perfectly happy, singing church music most melodiously. In the weaving house sixteen looms were at work, besides several warpers and binders.

In our way through the town we observed shoemakers, taylors, and saddlers at work and we passed on to view the smith work, which is very extensive. They have four or five forges for ordinary work, and one for nails, at which we were diverted by observing a dog turning a wheel for blowing the bellows. It brought to my recollection the remark on the English by Dr. Franklin's Negro boy: 'Dese people make ebery thing workee, only de hog.'

From the blacksmith's we passed to the barns, which, we were told, contained a stock of grain sufficient to last a year, and that it was the intention of the Society to keep up that stock; but they did not mean to raise any grain for sale, their object being to apply all the surplus labor of the society to manufactures. Contiguous to the barns is an orchard, containing about 25 acres of ground, well stocked with grafted fruit trees, though they have not yet come to maturity. A hemp brake, on a new construction, the model of which they got from Kentucky, was behind the barns. It is driven by two horses, and is found to answer remarkably well. In this neighborhood is the brew house; but it was not in operation when we saw it. It is a convenient building, and at the back of it is a hop garden, and part of the hops were growing in at the windows. We likewise observed them growing very luxuriantly in most of the gardens in the town; so that the materials for beer and porter must be very abundant. We had some of the porter at the tavern, of as good a quality as I have ever tasted in London.

After dinner we visited the soap and candle works; the dye works; shearing and dressing works; the turners, carpenters, and machine-makers; and, finally, we were conducted through the warehouses, which we found plentifully stored with commodities; among others, we saw 450 pieces of broad and narrow cloth, part of it merino wool, and of as good a fabric as any that was ever made in London. We were told that they could sell the best broad cloth, as fast as made, at 10 dollars per yard.

From the warehouses we went to the Labyrinth, which is a most elegant flower garden, with various hedge rows, disposed in such a manner as to puzzle people to get into the little temple, emblematical of Harmony, in the middle. Mr. Rapp abruptly left us as we entered, and we soon observed him over the hedge rows, taking his seat before the house. I found my way with difficulty; but the doctor, whom I left on purpose, could not find it, and Mr. Rapp had to point it out to him. The garden and temple are emblematical. The Labyrinth represents the difficulty of arriving at Harmony. The temple is rough in the exterior, showing that, at a distance, it has no allurements; but it is smooth and beautiful within, to show the beauty of harmony when once attained.

From the Labyrinth we went to the Botanic Garden, which is well stored with valuable plants and herbs; and the two doctors pored over them more than an hour. We afterwards went to the doctor's house, where he showed us an elegant collection of plants, all natives of Harmony, which he had carefully arranged agreeably to the Linnæan system.

In the evening the Society assembled to divine service, and we attended, accompanied by our innkeeper, who conducted us to a seat appropriated for strangers. The church was quite full, the number of persons being not less than 500. The women sat all in one end; the men in the other. They were singing a hymn, in which they all joined with one accord, and so simply, yet so sweetly, did they sing, that it brought to my recollection the passage in Burns' 'Cotter's Saturday Night':

> They chant their artless notes in simple guise;
> They tune their hearts, by far the noblest aim.

After singing, they all knelt down to prayer. We followed their example; and never did I pray more devoutly. . . After prayer, Mr. Rapp delivered a sermon with great animation, to which all the congregation paid the most devout attention; after which, with a short prayer and benediction, he dismissed the assembly.

Our guide told us to remain a little, as they had, on our account, requested the band of music to attend. They assembled before the pulpit with their various instruments, namely, three violins and a bass, a clarinet, a flute, and two French horns. On these they entertained us with a great variety of airs, the most of them of the solemn kind, and some of them accompanied by vocal music.

After our return to the inn, we heard the night watch calling, 'Again a day is past, and a step made nearer to our end; our time runs away, and the joys of Heaven are our reward.' They repeat the latter sentence at 11, 12, 1, and 2 o'clock, and at 3 they call, 'Again a night is past and the morning is come; our time runs away, and the joys of Heaven are our reward.'

A BACKWOODS BREAKFAST

As I proposed to ride to New Philadelphia, 36 miles from Coshocton, and the road was altogether new to me, and often crossed the river,

I was anxious to be gone as soon as possible, and urged the landlady
to make all the haste she could. She said she would have the breakfast ready in a minute; but the first indication I saw of dispatch was
a preparation to twist the necks of two chickens. I told her to stop, and
she gave me a look of astonishment. 'Have you any eggs?' said I.
'Yes, plenty,' replied she, still keeping in a stooping posture, with the
chicken in her hand. 'Well,' said I, 'just boil an egg, and let me have it,
with a little bread and tea, and that will save you and I a great deal
of trouble.' She seemed quite embarrassed, and said she never could
set down a breakfast to me like that. I assured her I would take nothing
else. 'Shall I fry some ham for you along with the eggs?' said she.
'No,' said I, 'not a bit.' 'Well, will you take a little stewed pork?' 'No.'
. . . 'Preserve me, what will you take then?' *'A little bread, and tea,
and an egg.'* 'Well, you're the most extraordinary man that I ever
saw; but I can't set down a table that way.' I saw that I was only to lose
time by contesting the matter farther; so I allowed her to follow her
own plan as to the cooking, assuring her that I would take mine as
to eating. She detained me about half an hour, and at last placed upon
the table a profusion of ham, eggs, fritters, bread, butter, and some
excellent tea. All the time I was at breakfast she kept pressing me
to eat; but I kept my own counsel, and touched none of the dishes,
except the bread, tea and an egg. She affected great surprise, and
when I paid her the ordinary fare, a quarter of a dollar, she said it
was hardly worth anything. I mention the circumstance to show the
kind of hospitality of the landlady, and the good living enjoyed by
the backwoods people.

New Settlers in America, 1817 [1] &

HENRY BRADSHAW FEARON, *born in* 1770, *was sent to America
in* 1817 *by thirty-nine English families who were considering removing to the New World, and wanted a fuller knowledge of conditions and prospects in America than they could obtain from books.
He tells us that they were all educated and intelligent people, and
that the flow of population from the British Isles to the United States
was assuming a new character. 'It was no longer merely the poor, the*

[1] From *A Narrative of a Journey of Five Thousand Miles through America*, London,
1818, pp. 148ff., 183-196.

idle, the profligate, or the worldly speculative who were proposing to quit their native country; but men also of capital, of industry, of sober habits and regular pursuits; men of reflection, who apprehended approaching evils; men of upright and conscientious minds, to whose happiness civil and religious liberty were essential; and men . . . who wished to provide for the future support and prosperity of their offspring.' He landed in New York in August 1817, and sailed for home again in May 1818. In the intervening period, Fearon had traveled through New England, the Middle States, and the Western country—Ohio, Kentucky, and Illinois. Though he made a trip down the Mississippi to Natchez and New Orleans, he says almost nothing of the South in his volume, evidently feeling that his friends would not wish to settle in a slave-holding region.

*Fearon was an unprejudiced, intelligent, and conscientious observer, the first part of whose volume, though often superficial, contains much of value. He told his friends that the United States was a far better place for the unskilled laborer and for most mechanics than England —that it was 'the poor man's country'; but that shopkeepers would do no better than in London, though as well, and that professional men, especially doctors and lawyers, would do worse. He spoke favorably of the Government. Before he completed his tour, he was recalled to England because the publications of Morris Birkbeck regarding the Illinois country—*Notes on a Journey in America, *and* Letters from Illinois—*induced many of the thirty-nine families to invest money in the Illinois colony. Fearon was piqued, and his later letters were devoted largely to attacks upon Birkbeck's writings, which were indeed somewhat injudiciously favorable to the Western prairies and abounded in rash promises. Contrary to Birkbeck's statements, Fearon declared that the American farmer was but 'scantily remunerated.' Upon returning to London he collected his letters in book form.*

POOR 'REDEMPTIONERS' AT PHILADELPHIA

A PRACTISE which has often been referred to in connection with this country naturally excited my attention. It is that of individuals emigrating from Europe without money, and paying their passage by binding themselves to the captain, who receives the produce of their labour for a certain number of years.

Seeing the following advertisement in the newspapers, put in by the captain and owners of the vessel referred to, I visited the ship, in company with a boot-maker of this city:

THE PASSENGERS

On board the brig Bubona, from Amsterdam, and who are willing to engage themselves for a limited time, to defray the expenses of their passage, consist of persons of the following occupations, besides women and children, viz.: 13 farmers, 2 bakers, 2 butchers, 8 weavers, 3 taylors, 1 gardener, 3 masons, 1 mill-sawyer, 1 white-smith, 2 shoe-makers, 3 cabinet-makers, 1 coal-burner, 1 barber, 1 carpenter, 1 stocking-weaver, 1 cooper, 1 wheelwright, 1 brewer, 1 locksmith.— Apply on board of the Bubona, opposite Callowhill Street, in the river Delaware, or to W. Odlin and Co. No. 38, South Wharves.

Oct. 2.

As we ascended the side of this hulk, a most revolting scene of want and misery presented itself. The eye involuntarily turned for some relief from the horrible picture of human suffering which this living sepulchre afforded. Mr. —— enquired if there were any shoe-makers on board. The captain advanced; his appearance bespoke his office; he is an American, tall, determined, and with an eye that flashes with Algerine cruelty. He called in the Dutch language for shoe-makers, and never can I forget the scene which followed. The poor fellows came running up with unspeakable delight, no doubt anticipating a relief from their loathsome dungeon. Their clothes, if rags deserve that denomination, actually perfumed the air. Some were without shirts, others had this article of dress, but of a quality as coarse as the worst packing cloth. I enquired of several if they could speak English. They smiled and gabbled, 'No Engly, no Engly,—one Engly talk ship.' The deck was filthy. The cooking, washing, and necessary departments were close together. Such is the mercenary barbarity of the Americans who are engaged in this trade that they crammed into one of those vessels 500 passengers, 80 of whom died on the passage. The price for women is about 70 dollars, men 80 dollars, boys 60 dollars. When they saw at our departure that we had not purchased, their countenances fell to that standard of stupid gloom which seemed to place them a link below rational beings. From my heart I execrated the *European cause* of their removal, which is thus daily compelling men to quit the land of their fathers to become voluntary exiles in a foreign clime; yet Americans can think and write such sentiments as the following: 'We rejoice with the patriotic Hollanders at the return of the illustrious House of Orange to their first magistracy, and do not wonder at *their enthusiastic joy* upon the occasion, when they remember that this ancient family have been always the gallant and zealous defenders of *the rights and liberties of the Dutch people.*'

An interesting occurrence is said to have taken place the other day, in connection with the German Redemptioners (as by a strange misnomer the Dutch are denominated). A gentleman of this city wanted an old couple to take care of his house; a man, his wife, and daughter were offered to him for sale; he purchased them. They proved to be his father, his mother, and sister!!!

EMIGRATION CROSSING THE ALLEGHANIES

The farmers in Pennsylvania are many of them rich; some reside in first-rate houses, and are possessed of most of the conveniences of life. Those remote from a market generally distil their grain, finding whiskey to be the most convenient and profitable form under which to carry and dispose of their stock. The great body of these men are Germans, or of German stock. They are excellent practical farmers, very industrious, very mercenary, and very ignorant. The condition of the labourer is similar to that in other parts of the United States. The towns of Lancaster, Harrisburgh, and Carlisle, through which I passed, are all of them considerable in extent and in population. They each contain a large proportion of excellent brick buildings, and the usual erections of market houses, gaols, and churches, all evincing an extent of national prosperity and an advancement towards European establishments truly extraordinary, when we recollect that this is a country which may be said to be but of yesterday. The German character is very prevalent throughout this State. The original language is still preserved, and there are even native Pennsylvanians who cannot speak the English language.

Arrived at Chambersburgh, 157 miles from Philadelphia, I went to the inn where the stages from Baltimore and Philadelphia to Pittsburgh usually stop. These stages are two days in arriving here from the latter, and one from the former city. I secured a place, for which I paid 14 dollars (3 guineas), distance 140 miles. This town contains about 240 houses, of all sorts, two or three churches, a gaol and courthouse.

October. The stage started at three o'clock in the morning. A Mr. Flower, connected with Mr. Birkbeck, left Chambersburgh a few days previous, on his return from Illinois to England. What his views of this country are I have not learned, though I should conclude, from the reported statements of an acquaintance, with whom he conversed at Chambersburgh, that his estimation of America is highly favourable.

Arrived at eight o'clock at Loudon, at the foot of the north mountain, one of the Allegany ridges. There are here 17 log and 20 frame or brick houses. We were not allowed to breakfast at the tavern in this town, as one of the proprietors of the coach had a house at

M'Connel's Ville. The tavern at Loudon is cheerless and dirty; a number of waggoners were breakfasting. The election was a topic of violent debate; bets and, as a usual accompaniment, choler, ran high. We brought the latest intelligence of the returns. All had their hopes and fears. The landlord, who is of Dutch descent, was, as a matter of course, a Heisterite, because he was descended from a countryman. The Irish party, for similar reasons, supported Findlay. We were saluted by each at our departure, 'Huzza for Heister!' 'Huzza for Findlay!' My fellow-travellers were citizens of the world: they huzzaed for each with true philanthropic liberality. The final return throughout the State elected Mr. Findlay with a majority of 7000. I counted 30 regular stage waggons engaged in the transportation of goods to and from Pittsburgh. They are drawn by four strong well-fed horses, are made upon the model of English waggons, but about one-third less in size. They are from 20 to 35 days in effecting their journey. The articles sent from Philadelphia are hardware, and what are denominated 'dry goods.' This term includes all articles of woolen, linen, cotton, and silk. Those returned from Pittsburgh are farming produce, chiefly flour. It is necessary to understand that the road I am travelling is the only trading waggon route to the whole western country. This circumstance being taken into consideration, in addition to the fact that there is no water carriage, the number of conveyances, though great, is by no means extraordinary.

Proceeded up the north mountain, over a most excellent piece of road, which is part of the new national turnpike, proposed to extend from the head of the Potowmac to Wheeling, and when completed will be of immense importance to the western country, and indeed the whole Union, the connection of the old and new sections being at present materially impeded by excessively bad roads. At eleven o'clock, when near the summit of the mountains, we enjoyed a most extensive view of a large and beautiful valley, which must contain tens of thousands of acres that have not yet known the hand of the cultivator. The prospect, combining some grand mountain scenery, was the most magnificent I had ever beheld. The interest of the scene was also not a little heightened by the prospect of M'Connel's Ville, which we were approaching. This apparently delightful little town appeared secluded from the rest of the world, and one might have imagined it another Eden, cut off by means of woods and trackless wilds, and mountain snows, from the vices and the corruptions which, in every other quarter, visit and torment mankind. . .

M'Connel's Ville contains 40 houses, chiefly log.—Beef is now 10 cents a pound (5¼ d.); sometimes it is only 7 (3¾ d.); mutton is not consumed; fowls are 6s. 9d. per dozen; charge for breakfast, 2s. 3d.—

Passed several travellers on foot from Massachusetts, going with an intention of viewing the western country, and, if satisfied, of selecting a settlement previous to the emigration of their families; they fairly excelled our stage in expedition. Came up with 20 small family waggons; two of these were broken down, and the horses of all in a very bad condition; they were chiefly from Massachusetts, Jersey, and Connecticut. One of these was the joint property of a Dutch and an American family. My companions seemed to know at first sight from what state the emigrants travelled. The New Englanders were evidently better fitted for the great and unavoidable fatigues of removal than the natives of Jersey and Maryland. I thought I could even discover in the white inhabitants the effects of residing in free and in slave States. The genuine Yankies (New Englanders) are ignorant of slavery; they have been necessitated to labour with their own hands; they have not been demoralized by familiarity with a system that establishes a barrier between fellow-beings on account of their colour; they have not been taught that because their neighbour's face was (to use their own phrase) a *grade* darker than their own, he was therefore of an *inferior species* (as I am sorry to see contended for even by Mr. Jefferson); they have relied on their own resources, and the consequence is that they are more enterprising, more healthy, more enlightened, and altogether better suited to cultivate the wilderness with success, than their slave-holding neighbours. Even the women from New England were walking before their waggons, while the others were either riding or lagging behind.

These emigrants preferred travelling in companies, forming a oneness of interest, and securing an interchange of assistance when necessary. In difficult parts of this tract their progress was so slow as to be hardly perceivable. Ropes were attached to each side of the waggons, at which, while some were pulling, others were most unmercifully, though necessarily, whipping the horses, which dragged the waggons five yards at an effort. The getting these waggons and families over the mountains appeared little less than a continuance of miracles. I was prepared to expect much, but the reality has increased my ideas of the difficulty of this emigration a thousandfold.

Crossed the Juniatta—arrived at Dickenson's Tavern—proceeded to Bloody Run, where we arrived at half-past eleven, excessively fatigued —charged for supper and bed, 4s. 6d. In the latter part of this stage nothing could exceed the badness of the roads; yet the understanding between the driver and horses was so perfect that we proceeded, though with almost broken bones, with the exactness of mechanism. A London coachman would in half an hour have dashed the strongest

English stage to pieces, and probably broken the necks of his passengers.

Second day. Started at three o'clock in the morning: thermometer 10° above zero; at nine arrived at Bedford, where we were not allowed to breakfast, as a stage proprietor lived farther on. We all crossed over to the orchard of a farmhouse and stole some frozen apples, which our keen appetites caused us to enjoy.—Passed over the Dry Ridge, upon which were great numbers of family and stage waggons; some of the former were from the district of Maine, and had been out 80 days. The progress of our stage was so slow and painful that I preferred walking; this afforded me an opportunity of entering into the views and little histories of fellow-travellers. No person here need feel backward in asking questions, and all answer without hesitation or reserve. The women I found the most communicative; their husbands being chiefly engaged in dragging along their wretched nags. The first I conversed with was from Jersey, out 32 days; she was sitting upon a log, which served for the double purpose of a seat and a fire; their waggon had broken down the day before; her husband was with it at a distant blacksmith's; she had been seated there all night; her last words went to my heart: "Ah! Sir, I wish to God we had never left home.'

The view from the summit of Dry Ridge even exceeds the one before described. The scenery is bolder, and marked with a character of increased magnificence. The eye takes in at one glance the various ridges called the South, the Blue, the Cove, and the more extended chain, peculiarly denominated the Allegany. The calm serenity of the numerous valleys formed a pleasing contrast with the more stupendous works of nature with which we were so profusely surrounded. Although there is here much barren country, there is a good deal of fine fertile land. The most prevalent trees are the beech, black, red, and white oaks. Clay slate appears, thus far, to characterize these mountains.—We continued to overtake emigrants' waggons from Maryland, Jersey, Pennsylvania, Connecticut, Massachusetts, and district of Maine. One of the families was that of the brother-in-law and sister of Captain Riley, whose work, detailing his shipwreck and consequent captivity in Africa, has been reprinted in England, and attracted such general and well-deserved attention. This family were in great distress.

At five o'clock in the evening we reached the top of the Alleganies. Our stage was far behind. This day I had walked about 16 miles; and, as was the case the day before, we were not allowed to stop for dinner, there being no *coach proprietor* upon the road. The Fountain Inn is a miserable log house, or what you would call a dog hole; it

was crowded with emigrants. I asked for something to eat, but could
only obtain for answer, 'I guess whiskey is all the feed we have on
sale.' I have met with several similar instances, when I have asked,
'Have you any meat?' 'No'—'Either cold or hot will make no difference to me.' 'I guess I don't know.'—'Have you any fowls?' 'No.'—
'Fish?' 'No.'—'Ham?' 'No.'—'Bread?' 'No.'—'Cheese?' 'No.'—'Crackers
(biscuits)?' 'No.'—'I will pay you any price you please.' 'I guess we
have only rum and whiskey feed.'

The character of the mountain inhabitants appears cold, friendless,
unfeeling, callous, and selfish. All the emigrants with whom I conversed complained of the enormous charges at taverns. Log houses
are the only habitations for many miles. They are formed of the
trunks of trees, about twenty feet in length, and six inches in diameter,
cut at the ends, and placed upon each other. The roof is framed in
a similar manner. In some houses there are windows; in others the
door performs a double office. The chimney is erected outside, and
in a similar manner to the body of the house. Some have clay in their
chimneys, which is a precaution very necessary in these western palaces.
In some the space between the logs remains open; in others it is filled
with clay. The hinges are generally wood. Locks are not used. In some
there are two apartments; in others but one, for all the various operations of cooking, eating, sleeping, and, upon great occasions, washing.
The pigs also come in for their due share of the log residence.—By
eleven o'clock at night we safely arrived at Somerset, 237 miles from
Philadelphia.

Started at three o'clock on our third day's journey: thermometer
6° above zero.—Crossed Laurel Hill. A family from Massachusetts
had 'camped out' during the night. At five o'clock we found them
cooking potatoes for breakfast; they very freely offered us a portion
of their homely fare. Perhaps in Essex I should have thought this no
treat—on Laurel Hill it was a most acceptable one; so naturally does
our inclination adapt itself to our circumstances. This family consisted
of ten persons: an old lady, her son and his wife, with seven children,
of both sexes, from two to sixteen years of age; all in excellent health,
and full of life and spirits; despising difficulties, and anticipating a
rich reward when they arrived in the 'land of Canaan.'

The vegetation on this ridge appears superior to that of the Allegany; it is considered to take its name from the *calmia latifolia,*
which grows here profusely. The mountain called Little Chestnut
Ridge succeeds that of Laurel Hill, the difficulties of the road increasing; though those which we experienced were 'light as air,' compared
with those which the poor families were exposed to. The inconveniences of traveling principally arise, not from the mere height of these

mountains, but from the abundance of enormous stones and of mud holes. The road is not turnpike after the small space described previous to arriving at M'Connel's Ville. The trees on Chestnut Ridge are chiefly oak and chestnut; the soil appears chalky. This morning, after a walk of four hours, we halted for the coach to come up; though the pain of riding exceeded the fatigue of walking, yet the having it as a place of final resort was desirable; it refreshed us by *varying* the weariness of our bodies. At half-past ten at night we arrived at Greensburgh, a town only 36 miles from Pittsburgh. I was delighted with the near prospect of a few days' cessation from fatigue.

Started, the fourth day, at four o'clock in the morning, with the high treat of a turnpike road; but the advantages arising from this were but of short continuance. We had to descend Turtle Creek Hill, which, in consequence of recent rains, had become, if possible, even worse than Laurel Hill. We all got out, and, up to our knees in mud, took our turns in holding up the stage. This tract bore decided evidence of being imbedded with coal. At the foot of the hill I came up with a woman and girl, with two infants in their arms, who came, to use their own language, 'vrom Zomerzetzhire in Hingland.' Collecting from my remarks that I had been in their country, they spoke of it with heartfelt attachment; were sorry that they had ever been persuaded to leave it; they had been told that this was the first place in the world, but they had experienced nothing but difficulties since they had set their foot upon it. The husband was behind, dragging on their little all. I assisted them over a brook, and endeavoured to comfort them with the hopes that when they once got settled they would be well repaid for all their toil.

Passed through M'Nair's Town, a new log settlement; also Eastern Liberty Town, containing some brick houses, an hotel, and a large steam grist mill. At two o'clock we arrived at Hunter's hotel in Pittsburgh. The town was enveloped in smoke. The condition of the people from Chambersburgh to Greensburgh is that of an absence of wealth and of the conveniences of life, with, however, the means of obtaining a sufficient quantity of food. Their habitations, in our ideas, are extremely wretched; but in theirs, the contrary. The blacksmith and the tavern-keeper are almost the only occupations; the former earns from 20s. 6d. to 27s. per week; the profits of the latter must be great, judging from the high charges and bad quality. From Greensburgh to Pittsburgh, the improvement in size and *quality* of the houses is evident; and the cultivation and condition of the land are much superior. Many places bear the evident marks of wealth; the criterion for ascertaining which is, in this country, very tangible. Recurring to my old plan of estimation, I passed on the road from Chambersburgh to Pittsburgh, being 153 miles, 103 stage waggons, drawn by four and six horses, proceeding from Philadelphia and Baltimore to Pittsburgh, 79 from Pittsburgh to Baltimore and Philadelphia, 63 waggons, with families, from the several places following: 20 from Massachusetts, 10 from the district of Maine, 14 from Jersey, 13 from Connecticut, 2 from Maryland, 1 from Pennsylvania, 1 from England, 1 from Holland, and 1 from Ireland; about 200 persons on horseback, 20 on foot, 1 beggar, 1 family, with their waggon, returning from Cincinnati, entirely disappointed—a circumstance which, though rare, is by no means, as one might suppose, miraculous.

Energy and Prosperity of
American Farmers [1] &

WILLIAM COBBETT, *who won distinction as an author, politician, and farmer, was born in Surrey in 1766, the son of a small farmer. In his boyhood he worked in the fields, and as a gardener in the grounds of the Bishop of Winchester, but found means to educate himself. Enlisting as a soldier at the age of eighteen, he used his leisure, both in England and in New Brunswick, where he was stationed 1785-91, in mastering all the books upon which he could lay hands. His energy and his taste for writing raised him to the rank of sergeant major and won him the esteem of his superiors. Leaving the army, and marrying in New Brunswick, after a hurried visit to France he emigrated in the autumn of 1792 to the United States. Here his true career immediately began.*

Cobbett's first sojourn in America endured eight years and left him a figure of national importance. At the outset he made a slender living at Wilmington, Delaware, by teaching English to the French refugees there. But when Joseph Priestley reached America in 1794, driven from his home in Birmingham by a mob, and was received with enthusiasm by the Republicans, who seized the opportunity to abuse England and eulogize France, Cobbett turned to his pen to defend his native land. His first pamphlet, signed 'Peter Porcupine,' and called Observations on the Emigration of a Martyr to the Cause of Liberty, *at-*

[1] From *A Year's Residence in the United States of America*, London, 1818, chapters 9 and 11.

tracted wide attention by the vigor of its style and the virulence with which it abused Priestley and his admirers. Cobbett was at once drawn into the profession of journalism and pamphleteering.

He wrote many more essays over the same signature, and his attacks on the Republican party and its doctrines were highly effective. He defended Jay's Treaty, assailed Edmund Randolph over the Fauchet Affair, and abused the French leaders; his satire on the Jeffersonian doctrine of the equality of all men has been compared with Swift. In his excess of zeal he castigated some of the best American institutions, and did not spare even the Federal Constitution. At the same time, he praised Great Britain and British policy. Such a course was certain to raise up powerful enemies against him. In Porcupine's Gazette, *as he called the newspaper he had started, Cobbett angrily reviled the Spanish Minister De Yrujo—'Don Yarico'—and various American statesmen. Libel suits followed. Three times, moreover, he was called into court to answer to a suit for libel grounded on his famous charge that Dr. Benjamin Rush had killed most of his patients by excessive bloodletting. On the third trial, at the close of 1799, Cobbett was fined $5000, and the following year he returned to England.*

Here his career was quite as turbulent as in America. Regarded at first as the champion of monarchy and the existing Tory Ministry, he was honored by some of the party leaders, and introduced to Pitt. But he stubbornly opposed the Peace of Amiens in 1802, he soon began using his bludgeon in every direction, and his attacks on the Government of Ireland again brought him into the courts. He was fined £1000, and in 1803 began taking the radical side in politics, remaining for many years one of the ablest journalists of that party. In 1809, for his denunciation of the harsh punishment of some mutinous militiamen, he was again fined £1000, and imprisoned two years. But from jail he managed still to edit his Weekly Political Register, *and to superintend the affairs of his Hampshire farm. In 1817, having accumulated immense debts, said to exceed £34,000, he fled to America, where he at once acquired a small farm at Hyde Park, near North Hempstead, on Long Island. Here for two years he farmed and wrote, and* A Year's Residence in the United States *was one of the fruits of his stay.*

In this book, which was intended chiefly as a guide for emigrant farmers, Cobbett describes American farms, weather, and farming; recounts his experiments in introducing rutabaga culture; and offers his general observations on the character of the American people, whom he found to be industrious, prosperous, independent-spirited, hospitable, remarkably free from crime or beggary, materialistic, and a little given to tippling. The volume is in Cobbett's characteristic style, clear, direct, forcible, but without delicate lights or shades. In May 1819 *his house burned down, and he returned to England, bearing the bones of Thomas Paine with him. In subsequent years he entered Parliament, but had little influence there. He died in* 1835, *on his much-loved farm.*

LAND, LABOUR, AND IMPLEMENTS

Land is of various prices, of course. But as I am, in this chapter, addressing myself to *English farmers,* I am not speaking of the price of land either in the *wildernesses,* or of land in the immediate vicinage of great cities. The wilderness price is two or three dollars an acre; the city price is four or five hundred. The land at the same distance from New York that Chelsea is from London is of higher price than the land at Chelsea. The surprising growth of these cities and the brilliant prospect before them give value to everything that is situated in or near them.

It is my intention, however, to speak only of *farming land.* This, too, is of course affected in its value by the circumstance of distance from market; but the reader will make his own calculations as to this matter. A farm, then, on this Island, anywhere not nearer than thirty miles off, and not more distant than sixty miles from, New York, with a good farmhouse, barn, stables, sheds, and styes; the land fenced into fields with posts and rails, the woodland being in the proportion of one to ten of the arable land, and there being on the farm a pretty good orchard; such a farm, if the land be in a good state, and of an average quality, is worth *sixty dollars an acre,* or *thirteen pounds sterling;* of course, a farm of a hundred acres would cost one thousand three hundred pounds. The rich lands on the *necks* and *bays,* where there are *meadows* and surprisingly productive orchards, and where there is *water carriage,* are worth, in some cases, three times this price. But, what I have said will be sufficient to enable the reader to form a pretty correct judgement on the subject. In New Jersey, in Pennsylvania, everywhere the price differs with the circumstances of water carriage, quality of land, and distance from market.

When I say a good farmhouse, I mean a house a *great deal better* than the *general run* of farmhouses in England. More neatly finished on the inside. More in a *parlour* sort of style, though *round about* the house things do not look so neat and tight as in England. Even in Pennsylvania, and amongst the Quakers too, there is a sort of out-of-doors slovenliness, which is never hardly seen in England. You see bits of wood, timber, boards, chips, lying about, here and there, and pigs and cattle tramping about in a sort of confusion, which would make an English farmer fret himself to death; but which is here seen with great placidness. The outbuildings, except the barns, and except in the finest counties of Pennsylvania, are not so numerous or so capacious as in England, in proportion to the size of the farms. The reason is that the weather is so *dry*. Cattle need not covering a twentieth part so much as in England, except hogs, who must be warm as well as dry. However, these share with the rest, and very little covering they get.

Labour is the great article of expense upon a farm; yet it is not nearly so great as in England, in proportion to the amount of the produce of a farm, especially if the poor rates be, in both cases, included. However, speaking of the positive wages, a *good* farm labourer has *twenty-five pounds sterling a year* and his board and lodging; and a *good* day labourer has, upon an average, *a dollar a day*. A woman servant, in a farmhouse, has from forty to fifty dollars a year, or eleven pounds sterling. These are the average of the wages throughout the country. But then, mind, the farmer has nothing (for really, it is not worth mentioning) to pay in *poor rates;* which in England must always be added to the wages that a farmer pays; and, sometimes, they far exceed the wages.

It is, too, of importance to know, *what sort* of labourers these Americans are; for, though a labourer is a labourer, still there is some difference in them; and, these Americans are *the best I ever saw*. They mow *four acres* of *oats, wheat, rye, or barley* in a day, and, with a cradle, lay it so smooth in the swaths that it is tied up in sheaves with the greatest neatness and ease. They mow *two acres and a half of grass* in a day, and they do the work well. And the crops, upon an average, are all, except the wheat, *as heavy* as in England. The English farmer will want nothing more than these facts to convince him that the labour, after all, is not so *very dear*.

The cause of these performances, so far beyond those in England, is first, the men are *tall* and well-built; they are *bony* rather than *fleshy;* and they live, as to food, as well as man can live. And secondly, they have been *educated* to do much in a day. The farmer here generally is at the *head* of his *'boys,'* as they, in the kind language of the country, are called. Here is the best of examples. My old and beloved friend, Mr. James Paul, used, at the age of nearly *sixty,* to go at *the head of his mowers,* though his fine farm was his own, and though he might, in other respects, be called a rich man; and I have heard that Mr. Elias Hicks, the famous Quaker Preacher, who lives about nine miles from this spot, has this year, at *seventy* years of age, cradled down four acres of rye in a day. I wish some of the *preachers* of other descriptions, especially our fat parsons in England, would think a little of this, and would betake themselves to 'work with their hands the things which be good, that they may have to give to him who needeth,' and not go on any longer gourmandizing and swilling upon the labour of those who need.

Besides the great quantity of work performed by the American labourer, his *skill,* the *versatility* of his talent, is a great thing. Every man can use an *axe,* a *saw,* and a *hammer.* Scarcely one who cannot do any job at rough carpentering, and mend a plough or a waggon. Very few indeed, who cannot kill and dress pigs and sheep, and many of them oxen and calves. Every farmer is a *neat* butcher; a butcher for *market;* and, of course, 'the boys' must learn. This is a great convenience. It makes you so independent as to a main part of the means of housekeeping. All are *ploughmen.* In short, a good labourer here can do *anything* that is to be done upon a farm.

The operations necessary in miniature cultivation they are very awkward at. The *gardens are ploughed* in general. An American labourer uses a *spade* in a very awkward manner. They *poke the earth about* as if they had no eyes; and toil and muck themselves half to death to dig as much ground in a day as a Surrey man would dig in about an hour of hard work. *Banking, hedging,* they know nothing about. They have no idea of the use of a *billhook,* which is so adroitly used in the coppices of Hampshire and Sussex. An *axe* is their tool, and with that tool, at *cutting down* trees or *cutting them up,* they will do *ten times* as much in a day as any other men that I ever saw. Set one of these men upon a wood of timber trees, and his slaughter will astonish you. A neighbour of mine tells me a story of an Irishman, who promised he could *do anything,* and whom, therefore, the employer sent into the wood to cut down a load of wood to burn. He stayed a long while away with the team, and the farmer went to him, fearing some accident had happened. The man was hacking away at a hickory tree, but had not got it half down; and that was all he had done. An American, black or white, would have had half a dozen trees cut down, cut up into lengths, put upon the carriage, and brought home in the time.

So that our men who come from England must not expect that, in these *common labours* of the country, they are to surpass or even equal these 'Yankees,' who, of all men that I ever saw, are the most *active,* and the most *hardy.* They skip over a fence like a greyhound. They will catch you a pig in an open field by *racing* him down; and they are afraid of nothing. This was the sort of stuff that filled the *frigates* of Decatur, Hull, and Bainbridge. No wonder that they triumphed when opposed to poor pressed creatures, worn out by length of service and ill-usage, and encouraged by no hope of fair play. My Lord Cochrane said, in his place in Parliament, that it would be so; and so it was. Poor Cashman, that brave Irishman, with his dying breath, accused the Government and the merchants of England of withholding from him his pittance of prize money! Ought not such a vile, robbing, murderous system to be destroyed?

Of the same active, hardy, and brave stuff, too, was composed the army of Jackson, who drove the invaders into the Gulph of Mexico, and who would have driven into the same Gulph the army of Waterloo, and the heroic gentleman, too, who lent his hand to the murder of Marshal Ney. This is the stuff that stands between the rascals, called the Holy Alliance, and the slavery of the whole civilized world. This is the stuff that gives us Englishmen an asylum; that gives us time to breathe; that enables us to deal our tyrants blows, which, without the existence of this stuff, they never would receive. This America, this scene of happiness under a free government, is the beam in the eye, the thorn in the side, the worm i' the vitals of every despot upon the face of the earth.

An American labourer is not regulated, as to time, by *clocks* and *watches*. The *sun,* who seldom hides his face, tells him when to begin in the morning and when to leave off at night. He has a dollar, *a whole dollar,* for his work; but then it is the work of a *whole day.* Here is no dispute about *hours.* 'Hours were made for *slaves,*' is an old saying; and, really, they seem here to act upon it as a practical maxim. This is a *great thing* in agricultural affairs. It prevents so many disputes. It removes so great a cause of disagreement. The American labourers, like the tavern-keepers, are never *servile,* but always *civil.* Neither *boobishness* nor *meanness* mark their character. They never *creep* and *fawn,* and are never *rude.* Employed about your house as day labourers, they never come to interlope for victuals or drink. They have no idea of such a thing. Their pride would restrain them if their plenty did not; and thus would it be with all labourers, in all countries, were they left to enjoy the fair produce of their labour. Full pocket or empty pocket, these American labourers are always the *same men;* no saucy cunning in the one case, and no base crawling in the other. This, too, arises from the free institutions of government. A man has a voice *because he is a man,* and not because he is the *possessor of money.* And, shall I *never* see our English labourers in this happy state?

Let those English farmers, who love to see a poor wretched labourer stand trembling before them with his hat off, and who think no more of him than of a dog, remain where they are; or go off, on the cavalry horses, to the devil at once, if they wish to avoid the tax-gatherer; for they would here meet with so many mortifications that they would, to a certainty, hang themselves in a month.

There are some, and even many farmers who *do not work themselves in the fields*. But they all *attend* to the thing, and are all equally civil to their working people. They manage their affairs very judiciously. Little talking. Orders plainly given in a few words, and in a decided tone. This is their only secret.

The *cattle* and *implements* used in husbandry are cheaper than in England; that is to say, *lower-priced*. The wear and tear not nearly half so much as upon a farm in England of the same size. The climate, the soil, the gentleness and docility of the horses and oxen, the lightness of the waggons and carts, the lightness and toughness of the *wood* of which husbandry implements are made, the simplicity of the harness, and, above all, the ingenuity and handiness of the workmen in *repairing,* and in *making shift:* all these make the implements a matter of very little note. Where horses are kept, the shoeing of them is the most serious kind of expense.

AMERICAN PLENTY

The first business of a farmer is, here, and ought to be everywhere, to *live well:* to live in ease and plenty; to 'keep hospitality,' as the old English saying was. To *save money* is a secondary consideration; but any English farmer who is a good farmer there may, if he will bring his industry and care with him, and be *sure* to leave his pride and insolence (if he have any), along with his anxiety, behind him, live in ease and plenty here, and keep hospitality, and save a great parcel of money too. . .

That *anxious eagerness to get on,* which is seldom unaccompanied with some degree of envy of more successful neighbours, and which has its foundation first in *a dread of future want,* and next in a *desire to obtain distinction by means of wealth;* this anxious eagerness, so unamiable in itself, and so unpleasant an inmate of the breast, so great a sourer of the temper, is a stranger to America, where accidents and losses, which would drive an Englishman half mad, produce but very little agitation.

From the absence of so many causes of uneasiness, of envy, of jealousy, of rivalship, and of mutual dislike, *society,* that is to say, the intercourse between man and man, and family and family, becomes easy and pleasant; while the universal plenty is the cause of universal hospitality. I know, and have ever known, but little of the people in the cities and towns of America; but the difference between them and the people in the country can only be such as is found in all other countries. As to the manner of living in the country, I was the other day at a gentleman's house, and I asked the lady for *her bill of fare for the year.* I saw *fourteen* fat hogs, weighing about *twenty score apiece,* which were to come *into the house* the next Monday; for here they slaughter them all in one day. This led me to ask, 'Why, in God's name, what do you eat in a year?' The bill of fare was this, for this present year: about *this same quantity of hog meat, four beeves;* and *forty-six fat sheep!* Besides the *sucking pigs* (of which we had then one on the table), besides *lambs,* and besides the produce of *seventy hen fowls,* not to mention good parcels of *geese, ducks,* and *turkeys,* but not to forget a garden of three quarters of an acre, and *the butter of ten cows,* not one ounce of which is ever *sold!* What do you think of that? Why, you will say, this must be some *great overgrown farmer* that has swallowed up half the country; or some nabob sort of merchant. Not at all. He has only 154 *acres of land* (all he consumes is the produce of this land), and he lives in the same house that his English-born grandfather lived in.

Jefferson: Northern and Southern Travel, 1816-17 [1] &

FRANCIS HALL, *a lieutenant of the 14th Light Dragoons, landed in New York City at the beginning of March 1816, traveled north up the Hudson and made a tour of Canada, returned through western New York and Pennsylvania to Philadelphia, and went on through Baltimore, Washington, and Richmond to Charleston, whence he sailed for England in February 1817. Except for his denunciation of 'the spirit of speculation, in all professions of life,' and his warm condemnation of slavery, his views of the American nation were highly favorable. He had lofty hopes for the future of 'this transatlantick republic, great in extent of territory, in an active and well-informed population; but above all, in a free government, which not only leaves individual talent unfettered, but calls it into life by all the incitements of ambition most*

[1] From *Travels in Canada and the United States in 1816 and 1817,* Boston, 1818, chapters 3, 35, 37, and 38.

grateful to the human mind.' Though he considered the manners of Americans to be stiff and ungracious, he saw that beneath the surface the people had a rough friendliness. 'With this feeling,' he writes, 'I have often been tempted to consider the farmers of the backwoods the politest class of people in the States, because their manners spring from the true source, their feelings.' In Washington he met Commodore Decatur, and attended one of Dolly Madison's levees, where he wondered at the extraordinary stature of the western members—'the room seemed filled with giants'—but apparently did not see President Madison. The crowning event of his tour was his visit to Jefferson at Monticello, where he stayed overnight.

For a work by a military man a few years after the War of 1812, Hall's book was remarkably friendly. He thought that the United States was trying to act amicably toward Great Britain, and that the British should respond in kind. He was greatly pleased when an Elmira storekeeper offered to advance him money to go to New York without any other security than a British officer's word. His travels ended, Hall recorded his conviction that the political institutions of the United States generated 'intelligence, or a quick perception of utility, both general and individual . . . energy, and perseverance in carrying their plans into effect . . . gravity of manner and deportment, because they are habitually occupied upon matters of deep interest; taciturnity, which is the offspring of thought.' He published his Travels in London in 1818, and the volume was immediately reprinted in Boston.

A DAY AT MONTICELLO

Having an introduction to Mr. Jefferson, I ascended his little mountain on a fine morning, which gave the situation its due effect. The whole of the sides and base are covered with forest, through which roads have been cut circularly, so that the winding may be shortened or prolonged at pleasure. The summit is an open lawn, near to the south side of which the house is built, with its garden just descending the brow: the saloon, or central hall, is ornamented with several pieces of antique sculpture, Indian arms, mammoth bones, and other curiosities collected from various parts of the Union. I found Mr. Jefferson tall in person, but stooping and lean with old age; thus exhibiting that fortunate mode of bodily decay, which strips the frame of its most cumbersome parts, leaving it still strength of muscle and activity of limb. His deportment was exactly such as the Marquis de Chastellux describes it, above thirty years ago: 'At first serious, nay even cold,' but in a very short time relaxing into a most agreeable amenity; with an unabated flow of conversation on the most interesting topics, discussed in the most gentlemanly and philosophical manner. I walked with him round his grounds, to visit his pet trees, and improvements of various kinds; during the walk, he pointed out to my observation a conical mountain, rising singly at the edge of the southern horizon of the landscape: its distance, he said, was forty miles, and its dimensions those of the greater Egyptian pyramid; so that it accurately represents the appearance of the pyramid at the same distance; there is a small cleft visible on its summit, through which the true meridian of Monticello exactly passes; its most singular property, however, is that on different occasions it *looms* or alters its appearance, sometimes becoming cylindrical, sometimes square, and sometimes assuming the form of an inverted cone. Mr. Jefferson had not been able to connect this phenomenon with any particular season, or state of the atmosphere, except that it most commonly occurred in the forenoon; he observed that it was not only unaccounted for by the laws of vision but that it had not yet engaged the attention of philosophers so far as to acquire a name; that of *looming* being in fact a term applied by sailors to appearances of a similar kind at sea. The Blue Mountains are also observed to loom, though not in so remarkable a degree.

It must be interesting to recall and preserve the political sentiments of a man who has held so distinguished a station in public life as Mr. Jefferson. He seemed to consider much of the freedom and happiness of America to rise from local circumstances: 'Our population,' he observed, 'has an elasticity, by which it would fly off from oppressive taxation.' He instanced the beneficial effect of a free government in the case of New Orleans, where many proprietors who were in a state of indigence under the dominion of Spain have risen to sudden wealth solely by the rise in the value of the land, which followed a change of government. Their ingenuity in mechanical inventions, agricultural improvements, and that mass of general information to be found among Americans of all ranks and conditions he ascribed to that ease of circumstances which afforded them leisure to cultivate their minds, after the cultivation of their lands was completed.—In fact, I have frequently been surprised to find mathematical and other useful works in houses which seemed to have little pretension to the luxury of learning. Another cause, Mr. Jefferson observed, might be discovered in the many court and county meetings, which brought men frequently together on public business, and thus gave them habits, both of thinking and of expressing their thoughts on subjects, which in other countries are confined to the consideration of the privileged few. Mr. Jefferson has not the reputation of being very friendly to England. We should, however, be aware that a partiality in this aspect is not absolutely the duty of an American citizen; neither is it to be expected that the policy of our Government should be regarded in foreign countries with the same complacency with which it is looked upon by ourselves. But whatever may be his sentiments in this respect, politeness naturally repressed any offensive expression of them; he talked of our affairs with candor and apparent good will, though leaning, perhaps, to the gloomier side of the picture. He did not perceive by what means we could be extricated from our present financial embarrassments, without some kind of revolution in our Government. On my replying that our habits were remarkably steady, and that great sacrifices would be made to prevent a violent catastrophe, he acceded to the observation, but demanded if those who made the sacrifices would not require some political reform in return. His repugnance was strongly marked to the despotic principles of Bonaparte, and he seemed to consider France under Louis XVI as scarcely capable of a republican form of government; but added that the present generation of Frenchmen had grown up with sounder notions, which would probably lead to their emancipation. . .

The conversation turning on American history, Mr. Jefferson related an anecdote of the Abbé Raynal, which serves to show how history, even when it calls itself philosophical, is written. The Abbé was in company with Dr. Franklin and several Americans at Paris, when mention chanced to be made of his anecdote of Polly Baker, related in his sixth volume, upon which one of the company observed that no such law as that alluded to in the story existed in New England. The Abbé stoutly maintained the authenticity of his tale, when Dr. Franklin, who had hitherto remained silent, said, 'I can account for all this; you took the anecdote from a newspaper of which I was at that time editor, and, happening to be very short of news, I composed and inserted the whole story.' 'Ah! Doctor,' said the Abbé, making a true French retreat, 'I had rather have your stories than other men's truths.'

Mr. Jefferson preferred Botta's *Italian History of the American Revolution* to any that had yet appeared, remarking, however, the inaccuracy of the speeches. Indeed, the true history of that period seems to be generally considered as lost. A remarkable letter on this point lately appeared in print, from the venerable Mr. John Adams to a Mr. Niles, who had solicited his aid to collect and publish a body of revolutionary speeches. He says: 'Of all the speeches made in Congress, from 1774 to 1776 inclusive of both years, not one sentence remains, except a few periods of Dr. Witherspoon, printed in his works.' His concluding sentence is very strong: 'In plain English, and in a few words, Mr. Niles, I consider the true history of the

American Revolution, and the establishment of our present Constitution as lost forever; and nothing but misrepresentations, or partial accounts of it will ever be recovered.'

EARLY STEAMBOATING ON THE HUDSON

I embarked on the 9th of March, in the *Paragon* steam-packet, from New York to Albany. The winter had been less severe than usual, which induced the captain to attempt making his way up the Hudson earlier than is customary. These steam-boats are capable of accommodating from 2 to 300 passengers; they are about 120 feet in length, and as elegant in their construction as the awkward-looking machinery in the center will permit. There are two cabins, one for the ladies, into which no gentleman is admitted without the concurrence of the whole company. The interior arrangements, on the whole, resemble those of our best packets. I was not without apprehension that a dinner in such a situation, for above 150 persons, would very much resemble the scramble of a mob; I was, however, agreeably surprised by a dinner handsomely served, very good attendance, and a general attention to quiet and decorum. 'Truly,' thought I, 'these republicans are not so barbarous.' Indeed when the cabin was lighted up for tea and sandwiches in the evening, it more resembled a ballroom supper than, as might have been expected, a stagecoach meal. The charge, including board, from New York to Albany, 160 miles, is seven dollars.

We started under the auspices of a bright frosty morning. The first few minutes were naturally spent by me in examining the machinery, by means of which our huge leviathan, with such evident ease, won her way against the opposing current. But more interesting objects are breaking fast on the view; on our right are the sloping sides of New York Island, studded with villas, over a soil from which the hand of cultivation has long since rooted its woodland glories, substituting the more varied decorations of park and shrubbery, intersected with brown stubble and meadows; while on our left, the bold features of nature rise, as in days of yore, unimpaired, unchangeable; gray cliffs, like aged battlements, tower perpendicularly from the water's edge to the height of several hundred feet. Hickory, dwarf oak, and stunted cedars twist fantastically within their crevices, and deepen the shadows of each glen into which they occasionally recede; huge masses of disjointed rocks are scattered at intervals below; here the sand has collected sufficiently to afford space for the woodman's hut, but the 'narrow waterfall, which in summer turns his sawmill, is now a mighty icicle glittering to the morning sun; here and there a scarcely perceptible track conducts to the rude wharf, from which the weather-worn lugger receives her load of timber for the consumption of the city. A low white monument near one of these narrow strands marks the spot on which the good and gallant Hamilton offered the sacrifice of his life to those prejudices, which noble minds have so seldom dared to despise. He crossed from the state of New York to evade the laws of his country, and bow to those of false shame and mistaken honor. His less fortunate adversary still survives in New York, as obscure and unnoticed as he was once conspicuous.

Evening began to close in as we approached the highlands. The banks on either side towered up more boldly, and a wild tract of mountain scenery rose beyond them. The river, which had been gradually widening, now expanded into a capacious lake, to which the eye could distinguish no outlets; flights of wild fowl were skimming over its smooth surface to their evening shelter, and the last light of day rested faintly on a few white farmhouses, glimmering at intervals from the darkening thickets. Verplank's Point shuts the northern extremity of this first basin. The river continues its course within a cliff-bound channel, until, after a few miles, it again opens out amid the frowning precipices of West Point. Here are the same features of scenery as at Verplank's Point, but loftier mountains skirt the lake; and cliffs of a more gigantic stature almost impend above the gliding sail.[2] The moon was riding in a cloudless sky, and as her silver coloring fell on the gray cliffs of the left banks the mountains on the other side projected their deepened shadows, with increased solemnity, on the unruffled waters.

This was the land of romance to the early settlers; Indian tradition had named the highlands the prison within which Manetho confined the spirits rebellious to his power, until the mighty Hudson, rolling through the stupendous defiles of West Point, burst asunder their prison house; but they long lingered near the place of their captivity, and, as the blasts howled through the valleys, echo repeated their groans to the startled ear of the solitary hunter, who watched by his pine-tree fire for the approach of morning. The lights, which occasionally twinkled from the sequestered bay or wooded promontory, sufficiently told that these fancies, like the Indians who had invented or transmitted them, must by this time have given way to the unpoetic realities of civilized life.

Masses of floating ice, which had, at intervals through the evening, split upon the bow of our ark, became so frequent immediately on

[2] The average of these heights is probably 800 feet; the highest is reckoned at 1100—[Hall's note].

our passing West Point as to oblige us to come to anchor for the night; a pretty sure prognostick that there was nearly an end to our feather-bed traveling. The next morning we found ourselves lying close to the flourishing little settlement of Newburgh, on the right bank of the river. Our captain, having concluded to terminate his voyage here, moved over to Fishkill, on the opposite shore, to give us means of accommodating ourselves with conveyances in the best way we could.

FROM RICHMOND SOUTH TO CHARLESTON

A glance at the foregoing table [a list of stopping places, with such names as Percival's Tavern, Gholson's Tavern, and Adcock's Tavern] indicates the state of the country. The stages are no longer marked by towns and villages, but by solitary taverns and stage-houses. The best part of the country lies betwixt Petersburg and Fayetteville, being within the limits of the granite ledge. The soil is a mixture of sand and clay, tolerably fertile; the woods are generally of oak, hickory, and walnut, with here and there pine barrens and swamps—but I can say little of the state or appearance of the Carolinas, for at Richmond I exchanged my convenient Dearborn for a seat in the mail, to be conveyed at its discretion to Charleston.

In New England they have adopted the fashion of our stagecoaches; but the primitive 'democratical machine' is still used in the Southern States; to embark in one of which is no light service, for they break down on an average twice a week, so that the wrecks and the maimed are always to be found on the road. Betwixt Richmond and Petersburg all was well: the weather was fine, and our horses ran away but twice, killed but one pig, and lamed but one passenger. But on the morning of the 18th the wind came from south to northwest, and brought down the thermometer to 14°, with a heavy fall of snow, in which we set off in the dark, packed in every posture of purgatory, with trunks, packages, and elbows, squeezing and distorting our shivering limbs, while we were, at the same time, cheered with the anticipation of being upset among the holes and swamps, which, now concealed by snow, were to be guessed at in the dark by our Negro coachman, who, to do him justice, managed the matter with what seemed to me miraculous dexterity. I was not sorry to halt at Warrenton, and await the next day's mail; but in one night the Roanoke was frozen over, and the ferry stopped, so I went on to Fox's Tavern, near Louisburg, in a private conveyance with a gentleman I fell in with at the tavern.

I had occasion, during this part of my journey, to feel the truth of a common remark, that one suffers more through cold in a temperate or even warm climate than in a cold one. The cold in Canada is so completely subdued by stoves within and furs without doors, that it seldom causes inconvenience; whereas in Carolina, where I expected to have escaped its dominion, it made traveling highly disagreeable. The houses are all built of scantling, and are worse than anything in the form of dwellings, but the Negro huts; for they are penetrable at every crevice; while, from the usual mildness of the weather, doors have become altogether released from the duty of being shut. Indeed they have seldom a latch, and Mr. Fox, to whom I was deploring this neglect, observed that they generally considered a door's being shut as a sign nobody was at home. It must, however, be noticed that they had not for many years experienced such a severe cold as the present. The crew of a schooner, on Lake Pontchartrain, was frozen to death on the 18th. On the same day the mercury descended, at Baltimore, to 6° below zero, a more intense cold than was ever remembered to have been felt there.

Part II

Travelers of the Second Period, 1825-45

Travelers of the Second Period, 1825-45

Tory Condescension 〰

THAT the tone of British criticism changed sharply just before the third decade of the century was in part attributable to a change in the type of British traveler. Instead of men from the middle and working classes, there now came men from the upper and professional classes; instead of seekers after a living, there came seekers after new sights and experiences. The first steamship made her initial voyage across the Atlantic in 1819. Theretofore the passage had often been an interminable journey, as long as or longer than that of Faux, who left London on Christmas Day, 1818, and did not reach Boston until 4 April 1819; a journey on short rations of moldy food, in quarters cramped, comfortless, dirty, and verminous, with little or no heat, and foul water. Within two decades of that experience, the traveler could count on a comparatively quick and comfortable crossing. He need fear nothing worse than the stormy headwinds, which Dickens so vividly described—to many an added zest rather than a hardship. Thanks to the increasing ease of travel, and to the increasing value of America as a source of literary material, the professional authors and commentators, like Miss Martineau, Captain Marryat, Dickens, and Lyell, began to supplant the men who came to farm, like Birkbeck, to run newspapers, like Cobbett, to act, like Bernard, or to trade, like Melish.

Another pronounced influence was the activity of the great Tory reviews. The *Quarterly,* edited by the deformed and savage Gifford, was reinforced in 1817 by the establishment of *Blackwood's,* edited by Wilson and John G. Lockhart. The former magazine had been dealing blows both foul and fair in behalf of all Toryism—political, literary, economic, and religious; the latter now began squirting vitriol in an even more brutal way. Their attacks in 1818 and the subsequent years upon Keats, Shelley, Hazlitt, Leigh Hunt, and Byron are famous in literary history for their grossness and dastardliness. It was well said by Hazlitt that the *Quarterly* was 'a receptacle for the scum and sediment of all the prejudice, bigotry, ill-will, ignorance, and rancor afloat in the kingdom.' Naturally, they could not neglect America, the world's great object lesson in democracy and liberalism, the refuge of Cobbett and Priestley from English persecution, and the spot where Coleridge and Southey had dreamed of founding their ideal Pantisocracy. The *Quarterly* as early as 1814 had indulged in an angry assault upon America. In its first issue for 1819 it reviewed Fearon and Bristed in two articles that grossly exaggerated the unfavorable portions of both, suppressed what was favorable, and added new charges of astonishing recklessness. Immoral, irreligious, illiterate, brutal, dirty—this was the character of Americans, and it was 'the natural consequence of that spirit of republicanism on which she prides herself.' *Blackwood's* also began the year 1819 with articles that rejected America's claims to any degree of education, asserted that all the books she had produced might be burned without loss, and added that 'there is nothing to awaken fancy in that land of dull realities.' In 1820 the *Edinburgh* made room for Sydney Smith's famous article asking to know who read an American book or looked at an American picture. This hue and cry, in which lesser periodicals joined, was likely insensibly to affect the judgment of even the fairest and most liberal of the travelers in America.

The eagerness of conservative or reactionary men to rush to the defense of old English institutions by an attack on American democracy was intensified by the crisis that gave birth to the Reform Bill of 1832. To the old-school Briton of the Canning stamp it seemed by 1830 that his countrymen were following false political lights into a bottomless bog. Captain Marryat, although willing to admit that democracy was the best form of government for America as it existed at the time, bitterly opposed any imitation of it by Great Britain, and avowed that 'my great object has been to do serious injury to the cause' of that democracy in the Old World. His definition of our brand of republicanism was mob rule, and he tried to convince his readers that the American public selected second-rate men to occupy office, and insisted that they should act not independently, but as the agents of the majority, 'who are as often wrong as right.' Similar convictions were held by Captain Thomas Hamilton, whose pen had been trained by fiction writing, and whose *Men and Manners in America* was a very entertaining bit of portraiture. 'When I found the institutions and experiences of the United States deliberately quoted in the reformed Parliament as affording safe precedents for British legislation,' wrote this confirmed Tory, 'and learned that the drivellers who uttered such nonsense . . . were listened to with patience and approbation by men as ignorant as themselves, I certainly did feel that another work on America was wanted, and at once determined to undertake a task which inferior considerations would probably have induced me to decline.' His book is not an attack upon America, however, and does not illustrate its avowed thesis. The same may be said of the volume by that well-meaning, stolid London barrister, Godfrey T. Vigne, called *Six Months in America*. He liked the American people, admired their material progress, and admitted that their government 'is admirably adapted to a new country.' When, therefore, he predicted that the nation would fall to pieces 'probably within a half century by its own weight,' he was plainly contradicting his own evidence. But he was alarmed by the radical movement in England, and he also wished to raise a warning voice against democracy.

In short, it became easy and profitable for gentlemen of conservative minds to visit America at the very period in which the clamor of the Tory press, the storm that swept away the rotten boroughs, the rising Chartist agitation, and other phenomena were inflaming these gentlemen against both the American republic and the English democratic movement. When a Chartist leader of England declared that 'every workingman in the land has a right to a good coat, a good hat, a good dinner, no more work than will keep him in health, and as much wages as will keep him in plenty,' he was referring to a condition very like that which Cobbett, Melish, and Birkbeck had pictured as actually existing under our free government. A 'refutation' of these writers became desirable. Moreover, we must bear in mind that the new travelers came to a country whose manners had changed for the worse, upon the whole, since the time of Wansey and Cooper. It was the era of Jacksonian democracy, and the frontier had given a relaxed tone to the habits and speech of a large part of our population. Earlier travelers had found the careful gentility of Federalist days still in existence, and had confined their peregrinations largely to the Eastern seaboard, where social refinement was most in evidence. Now the newcomers were expected to go as far west as did Dickens, who penetrated to St. Louis, and outside the old settled communities they saw a society with many unmannerly traits—the tobacco-chewing steamboat passengers, the quick-feeding hotel guests, the tavern keepers who thought that a man must be an invalid if he objected to sleeping two in a bed, the illiterate, drawling, impertinent loafers at every new stop. They had a careful look at these 'men with the bark on,' and formed a dislike for their uncouth ways, which many an American of today, could he be taken back to that environment, would heartily share. And whereas the inexpert pen of an Ashe had made little im-

pression, Americans writhed under the sure descriptive vividness of
Dickens and Marryat.

One of these books of travel surpassed all others in violence. Of
Mrs. Trollope it can only be said that she was a censorious harridan,
determined at all costs to vent an unreasonable prejudice against us.
Unreasonable, but not inexplicable. It was the misfortune of this lady
that she went first to the yet uncouth, undisciplined town of Cincinnati, and there formed impressions that a subsequent acquaintance
with the best parts of the East should have caused her to revise. Cincinnati she found a place of about the size of Salisbury, with just
enough bustle to make it noisy and uncomfortable, a terrific odor
from the pork-packing plants, and a complete absence of attractive
architecture or of cultural institutions. Here she had to stay while her
business, meant to be the mainstay of her impractical husband as
well as herself, excited general ridicule and sank into decay. When
she departed it was first to visit Maryland and Virginia, where the
indolent ways of the people and the existence of slavery offended her.
It is not strange that she regarded us with hostility.

Mrs. Trollope defined the chief distinction between England and
the United States as the latter country's total want of refinement. The
best literary conversation she enjoyed in Cincinnati was with a strait-
laced ignoramus who attacked Byron for his immorality, thought
that Pope's 'Rape of the Lock' was inadmissible to any family circle
because of the very title, had never heard of Massinger or Ford, and
declared of Shakespeare: 'Shakespeare, madam, is obscene, and thank
God, we are sufficiently advanced to have found it out!' The Cincin-
natians, like all their countrymen, then delighted in the Barnum
type of museum. The chief of the two institutions of this kind in
the town boasted of waxworks and a representation of hell with lakes
of fire, mountains of ice, and imps of ebony, with other weird exhibits;
but to really scientific collections the people were indifferent. They
were woefully restricted as to amusements. Billiards and cards were
forbidden by law, public balls were unknown except at Christmas,
and there were no concerts or dinner parties. The chief public diversion, beyond any doubt, was the frequent revivals, and Mrs. Trollope
was justly shocked—like other British travelers before and afterwards
—at the hysteria, coarseness, and irreverence these religious orgies
exhibited. She gives many instances, some of them overdrawn, of
the boorishness of the citizens. The most striking was a colloquy she
heard between a rough greasy fellow and President Jackson, when the
latter, filled with grief over the recent loss of his wife, passed down
the Ohio on a steamboat:

'General Jackson, I guess?'

The General bowed assent.

'Why, they told me you was dead.'

'No! Providence has hitherto preserved my life!'

'And is your wife alive too?'

The General, apparently much hurt, signified the contrary, upon which the courtier concluded his harangue by saying, 'Aye, I thought it was the one or t'other of ye.'

Much that was exceedingly offensive in Mrs. Trollope's book had at the time a large degree of truth in it, and Americans, as the poet-editor Bryant said, would have done well to take it to heart. In her pages we find our best account of that affected delicacy to which so many visitors of the period allude. At Cincinnati a young German gentleman of good manners came to her in great anxiety because he had offended one of the leading families by pronouncing the word 'corset' in the presence of ladies, and did not know how to apologize. At a public garden there, a signboard representing a Swiss peasant girl holding a scroll evoked the anger of the ladies because the ankles of the figure were exposed, and a painter was hastily summoned to add a flounce. When Mrs. Trollope visited the Pennsylvania Academy in Philadelphia, she found that the gallery of antique statues was ordinarily entered by alternate groups of males and females, never by the two sexes together, and that the attendant would have been horrified if she had gone in when men were present. What she says of the emotional excess of camp meetings; of the vapidity, unsociability, and comfortlessness of boarding-house life; of the premature aging of laborers' wives under the burden of housework and child-bearing; of the frequency of sharp dealing in business; of the lack of interest in literary subjects—'I am much mistaken if a hundred untravelled Americans could be found who have read Boileau or La Fontaine'; of American boastfulness and lawlessness—all this was founded on just and precise observation. Not long after the appearance of her volume, the cry of 'A Trollope! A Trollope!' was sufficient to reduce any ill-mannered person in a theater or other public place to order.

It is the unfounded and thoroughly malevolent generalizations of Mrs. Trollope's volume that most condemn her judgment. She said of Americans that 'I do not like their principles, I do not like their manners, I do not like their opinions,' and she justified herself by making the most egregiously sweeping misstatements. 'I never,' she declared, 'saw an American man stand or walk well.' 'In England the laws are acted upon, in America they are not.' 'Long, disabling, and expensive fits of sickness are incontestably more frequent in every part of America than in England.' 'Persecution [religious] exists to a degree

unknown, I believe, in our well-ordered land since the days of Crom-
well.' 'The want of warmth, of interest, of feeling, upon all subjects
that do not immediately touch their concerns, is universal.' 'I very
seldom, during my whole stay in the country, heard a sentence elegantly turned and correctly pronounced.' 'In no rank of life do you
meet with young women in that delightful period of existence between childhood and marriage.' These are typical utterances, and the
few compliments she paid to the United States weigh as nothing in the
balance. She thought New York one of the finest cities in the world.
She admitted that one element of our boasted equality was undeniable
—that the son of poverty could rise to a position as high as that of
the son of wealth. She acknowledged that in material well-being
the average American was well in advance of the average European.
The neatness, cleanliness, and attractiveness of Philadelphia she genuinely admired. But even her compliments were paid in a tone that
grates upon the ear. How conspicuous was the chip she everywhere
carried on her shoulder is evident from an incident she relates of
travel in New York:

> The coach stopped to take in 'a lady' at Vernon; she entered, and completely
> filled the last vacant inch of our vehicle; for 'we were eight' before.
> But no sooner was she seated, than *her beau* came forward with a most
> enormous best-bonnet box. He paused for a while to meditate the possibilities—
> raised it, as if to place it in our laps—sunk it, as if to put it beneath our feet. Both
> alike appeared impossible; when, in true Yankee style, he addressed one of our
> party with, 'If you'll just step out a minute, I guess I'll find room for it.'
> 'Perhaps so. But how shall I find room for myself afterwards?'
> This was uttered in European accents, and in an instant half a dozen whiskey
> drinkers stepped from before the whiskey store, and took the part of *the beau*.
> 'That's because you'll be English travellers, I expect, but we have travelled in
> better countries than Europe—we have travelled in America—and the box will
> go, I calculate.'
> We remonstrated on the evident injustice of the proceeding, and I ventured to
> say that, as we had none of us any luggage in the carriage, because the space
> was so very small, I thought a chance passenger could have no right so greatly
> to incommode us.
> 'Right!—there they go—that's just their way—that will do in Europe, maybe;
> it sounds just like English tyranny, now—don't it? but it won't do here.' And
> thereupon he began thrusting in the wooden box against our legs, with all
> his strength.
> 'No law, sir, can permit such conduct as this.'
> 'Law!' exclaimed a gentleman very particularly drunk, 'we makes our own
> laws, and governs our own selves.'
> 'Law!' echoed another gentleman of Vernon, 'this is a free country, *we have
> no laws here,* and we don't want no foreign power to tyrannize over us.'
> I give the words exactly. It is, however, but fair to state that the party had

evidently been drinking more than a usual portion of whiskey, but, perhaps, in whiskey, as in wine, truth may come to light. At any rate the people of the Western Paradise follow the Gentiles in this, that they are a law unto themselves.

During this contest, the coachman sat upon the box without saying a word, but seemed greatly to enjoy the joke; the question of the box, however, was finally decided in our favor by the nature of the human material, which cannot be compressed beyond a certain degree.

After reading such a passage—and there are a dozen such—we can understand the unholy joy many Americans must have taken in treading upon this lady's toes.

Although she found America in arms against Basil Hall's book, and vehemently denying that it contained a single word of truth, it is actually a mild and flattering treatise compared with her own. Hall assured his readers that he had crossed the Atlantic with preconceptions wholly favorable to the United States; and so they were, except in one regard. His political convictions led him to believe that the American system was radically imperfect as a model for Great Britain. Our type of democracy placed no sufficient check upon the blind will of the majority, which made the men it elected to office mere tools, not leaders—so he said, with what seems to us an amazing disregard of the salient political fact of the Jacksonian period, the hero-worshipping implicitness with which the majority trusted its destinies to 'Old Hickory.' All his prejudices were aristocratic, and with remarkable fatuity he deplored our abolition of primogeniture as vulgarizing our society, and argued that our separation of the Church from the State was the destruction of 'the fly-wheel in a great engine.'

The political chapters are thus the poorest part of Hall's work, and he undoubtedly let his prejudices color his observations in this field. With keen curiosity, he attended a session of the New York Legislature, having been told that the members were chiefly farmers, shopkeepers, and country lawyers. A debate upon the revision of the State code confirmed his belief that such men had no statesmanship. 'The whole discussion, indeed, struck me as being rather juvenile. The matter was in the highest degree commonplace, and the manner of treating it still more so.' Yet he thought he saw the inveterate Yankee spirit of brag seize upon even this weak exhibition, for he reports one assemblyman as saying, 'with a chuckling air of confident superiority, but in perfect good humor—"Well, sir, what do you think of us? Don't we tread close on the heels of the mother country?"' It is likely that the traveler mistook the tone of this query. To Captain Hall, Washington was simply another Albany upon a larger scale. Though he differed from Mrs. Trollope as to the decorum of Congress, thinking it excellent, he was bored by the looseness of the discussion, and 'the long-winded, rambling style of the speeches.' Certain real faults of our political system he saw clearly enough. He justly condemned the constant injection of national politics into our local elections, noting that for the most insignificant offices men would stand, not upon their own qualifications, but as Adams men or Jackson men. The partial subserviency of our state judiciary to the popular caprice also offended him, and rightly, though much else that he said about the state governments was erroneous.

In perfect good humor, Captain Hall mentioned several amusing instances of that studied cultivation of hostility to Great Britain that English travelers have continued to regret down to recent times. He heard some boys spouting furious philippics against the mother country at a high school oratorical exhibition. 'Gratitude! Gratitude to England!' vociferated one. 'What does America owe to her? Such gratitude as the young lion owes to its dam, which brings it forth on the desert wilds, and leaves it to perish there. No! We owe her nothing! For eighteen hundred years the world had slumbered in ignorance of Liberty, and of the true rights of freemen. At length America arose in all her glory, to give the world the long-desired lesson!'—and so on. How, Hall reasonably inquired, could the two lands be on good terms while such instruction lasted?

The social observations of Captain Hall, as distinguished from the political, were on the whole honest, considerate, and, above all, sagacious. It is true that he liked to make English practice his touchstone; that the tendency of democracy seemed to him, as to Mrs. Trollope, to lower the level of intellectual attainment, and that he asserted, like Matthew Arnold later, that it was inimical to distinction of mind or art. But he was never contemptuous or lacking in good will. His picture of Charleston and the surrounding region needs only to be compared with that of Faux to be recognized as tolerant and kindly. He thought the American prison system in advance of the British, commenting upon the productive labor of the inmates, their better discipline, and their educational opportunities. His remarks upon the superficiality and lack of thoroughness met in Americans were quite fair. In that busy country, he explained, nobody has leisure to push any task to meticulous perfection. Instead, they always and naturally stop 'at that point, where the business in hand has reached that condition which is most certain of procuring for it a ready market—that is, when it has reached the degree of excellence suited to the average taste of the customers.' He greatly admired our enterprise in such fields as the distribution of ice. In Boston he was told that as much as 3000 tons annually were frequently sent to the South. In winter, with a brisk north wind, not a pound would be lost before the unloading at Charleston began, while in summer, if the ship ran into a hot wave, all her cargo had to be pumped overboard before she had passed the Virginia Capes. The captain went out of his way to praise 'the enthusiasm and the talents' enlisted in America in the cause of education.

One of his worst faults was that he was a bad traveler, unable to accept the hardships incident to a new country philosophically. Taking a steamboat down the Chesapeake to Baltimore, he was distressed when night fell to learn that only one passenger in three could have a berth, and that they would draw lots for sleeping places. Luckily, the lottery gave him a prize, and he did not have to stretch himself, like many others, on the lockers or deck. But, oh, he moaned:

Oh, the misery of a long night on board of a crowded steamboat! In the middle of the cabin blazed and smoked a red-hot stove, the ferruginous vapors of which were mixed with such a steaming and breathing of brandy, gin, and tobacco as, for my sins, I have seldom encountered before. These miseries were made worse by the half-whispered prosings of sundry berthless passengers—interminable personages, who would neither sleep themselves nor allow others to sleep. At last, when I had reached a most distracting pitch of restlessness, I got up and tried the open deck—but a nipping frost soon drove me below again. The tremor from the machinery, the puffing from the waste-pipe, the endless thumping from the billets of wood on their way to the furnace, the bawling of the engineers, the firemen, the pilots, the captains, stewards, and stewardesses, to say nothing of children crying, and the irritating pat-pat-pattering of the paddle-wheels, altogether formed an association of head-rending annoyances. . .

So, too, when he traveled by stage from Fredericksburg to Richmond, paying $5 for a trip of 66 miles, he first grumbled over the early hour for starting, and induced the stage driver to defer it from two a.m. to five. The party accompanying Hall crowded the vehicle, and he paid for an extra place to keep it vacant. It rained, causing more grumbling. 'Your feet get wet; your clothes become plastered with mud from the wheel; the trunks—generally placed with mischievous perversity on their edge—drink in half a gallon of water apiece; the gentlemen's coats and boots steam in the confined space; the horses are dragged and chafed by the traces; the driver gets his neckcloth saturated with moisture;—while everybody's temper is tried and found wanting!' The native Virginian passengers on this trip, two planters, fortified themselves at ten separate stops during the seventeen hours that the journey required with ten mint juleps apiece, but Hall had no taste for such decoctions. The roads, as this pace of four miles an hour testifies, were execrable. Still another grievance of the Englishman was the poor meals he sometimes had to devour. Thus after jolting all day over a corduroy road south of Winton, North Carolina, he was set down, as he relates, at a wretched inn table:

There was no bread, except some lumps of paste, resembling in color, weight, and flavor so many knobs of pipe clay, but got up expressly for us by those obliging people as wheaten cakes. Their own corn bread was probably very good of its kind, and, for those who like it, I dare say excellent. There was also fried eggs and bacon, and a dish which looked like apple fritters; but when the coatings of batter were removed, the joints of a small, half-starved hen made their appearance, the whole dish forming but one reasonable mouthful. We had brought tea with us, fortunately, and with some difficulty we got a little milk for the child; but, upon the whole, a worse meal we thought it impossible to find—till dinner time came round, and showed us the extent of our miscalculations.

Yet only rarely did Captain Hall evince that disposition to put the worst interpretation on everything he saw, which marked Mrs. Trollope's writings. He shook his head over the tippling that went on all about him, and states that it was customary in America to take a dram during breakfast, another after it, and so on at intervals of from half an hour to two hours a day. But he did us the justice to remark that we seldom went beyond tippling to drunkenness. A good deal of fault was found by American readers with his remarks upon the relations here between the two sexes. Like Mrs. Trollope and Francis Hall, he deplored the excessive strictness of the line drawn to separate men and women. It was the same at church, at a cattle fair in New England—though it is hard to see why he should expect women to attend a cattle fair—and in the drawing room. 'I seldom observed anything in America but the most respectful and icy propriety upon all occasions when young people of different sexes were brought together. Positively I never once, during the whole period I was in that country, saw anything approaching, within many degrees, to what we should call a flirtation.' The good captain cannot have been very observant; and he should have admitted that propriety, even if icy, is better than impropriety. But there is no reason to doubt his central assertion that the influence of women in American society was not so great as in the best English society. Again, while he condemned slavery, and declared that when slaves fell under the control of drunken or naturally cruel masters the results were horrible, he had the fairness to add that in all quarters of the globe, on ships of war, in English regiments, and in schools, he had witnessed scenes of as revolting tyranny as any Southern planter could well exercise. His most interesting passage upon slavery is his picture of a slave sale in Washington.

After various delays, the slave was put up to auction, at the end of the passage, near which four or five persons had by this time collected. There was a good deal of laughing and talking amongst the buyers, and several jests were sported on the occasion, of which their little victim took no more notice than if he had been a horse or a dog. In fact, he was not a chubby shining little Negro, with a flat nose, thick lips, and woolly hair, but a slender, delicate-looking youth, more yellow than black, with an expression every way suitable, I thought, with the forlorn situation in which he was placed—for both his parents, and all his brothers and sisters, he told me, had been long ago sold into slavery and sent to the Southern States, Florida or Alabama, he knew not where!

'Well, gentlemen,' cried the Deputy-Marshal, 'will you give us a bid? Look at him—as smart a fellow as ever you saw—works like a tiger!'

One of the spectators called out, 'Come, I'll say 25 dollars'; another said 35—another said 40—and at last 100 dollars were bid for him.

From the spot where I was standing, in the corner, behind the rest of the party, I could see all that was passing. I felt my pulse accelerating at each successive offer, and my cheek getting flushed—for the scene was so very new that I almost fancied I was dreaming.

The interest, after a time, took a different character, to which, however, I by no means wished to give utterance, or in any shape to betray; but at this moment the Deputy-Marshal, finding the price to hang at 100 dollars, looked over to me and said, 'Do give us a bid, sir—won't you?'

My indignation was just beginning to boil over at this juncture, and I cried out, in answer to this appeal, with more asperity than good sense or good breeding—'No! no! I thank God we don't do such things in my country!'

'And I wish, with all my heart,' said the auctioneer, in a tone that made me sorry for having spoken so hastily, 'I wish we did not do such things here.'

'Amen!' said several voices.

The sale went on.

Both this little incident and the manner in which it is related do credit to the heart of Captain Hall. Outside the political sphere, he made an honest and tactful effort to learn the truth concerning American conditions, bustling about at every stop, questioning everybody, taking notes, and making sketches with the aid of a Camera Lucida. Nor did he regard his own views as infallible. He frankly acknowledged in his book that 'I have often been so much out of humor with the people amongst whom I was wandering that I have most perversely derived pleasure from meeting things to find fault with'—a perversity that all travelers know, but few confess.

Beginning in 1835, a subtle change in the tone of British commentaries upon the United States can be discerned. That was the year in which Tocqueville published his *Democracy in America,* a work profoundly influential in all Europe. It was especially so in Great Britain, where liberal elements in politics took it up. After Tocqueville visited England and married an Englishwoman, his writings were widely quoted and his ideas echoed by many journals and reviews.

The best of all works of American travel, from a literary point of view, is to be found in most homes that possess even a modest collec-

tion of books, and should be familiar to most educated American
adults. It is a little difficult now to comprehend the mortification that
seized the continent upon the publication of Dickens's *American
Notes*. Undoubtedly a great deal of this pain arose from a sense on
the part of Americans that their hospitality had been ill-requited. Enthusiasm during Dickens's stay knew no bounds, and the young
author, whom the country loved as the creator of Pickwick, Oliver
Twist, Nicholas Nickleby, and Little Nell, was treated as if he had
been some great sovereign. In Boston his hotel was crowded with
deputations from city after city, state after state, begging him for the
honor of a visit. In New York the ceremonial Dickens dinner, at which
Irving presided and Bryant spoke, was the greatest event of its kind
since the Lafayette tour, while the Boz Ball caused more excitement
than any similar occasion until the visit of the Prince of Wales. Tickets
for the public receptions to Dickens sold at fabulous prices. The press
chronicled every movement he made. President Tyler entertained him
at a reception, and the President's daughter-in-law was in ecstasies later
to think that he and Irving had been speaking to her at the same time.
When it was known that the novelist was to write a book on his
experiences, expectation was on tiptoe. Nineteen hours after a copy
had reached New York it had been reprinted and was on sale. Within
two days the New York publishers had sold 50,000 copies, and the
3000 copies first consigned to Philadelphia were exhausted in half
an hour. After such lavish hospitality, such worship of his genius,
Dickens's criticisms seemed a woeful breach of good manners.

But part of the anger caused by the *American Notes* also arose
from its sure touch upon actual abuses. The three criticisms Dickens
chiefly emphasized, and by which he most hurt our feelings, were
upon the subjects of slavery, copyright, and our penal system; and
upon all three his censures have been justified by time. It took the
republic exactly half a century to accept his contention that it was
little better than highway robbery in us to allow Tom, Dick, or Harry
to steal the fruit of an Englishman's brain by publishing his books
without payment; but we finally did accept it by our copyright legislation of 1892. Many Philadelphians assailed Dickens rancorously because he denounced their system of solitary imprisonment as inhuman,
and declared that the men administering that system did not fully
realize what they were doing, but within a generation more liberal
ideas were sweeping the system away. Intelligent Southerners of today
must honor Dickens for the vigor of his reply to the current statement
that public opinion would always prevent any real cruelty to the
slaves:

Public opinion! Why, public opinion in the slave States *is* slavery, is it not? Public opinion, in the slave States, has delivered the slaves over to the gentle mercies of their masters. Public opinion has made the laws, and denied the slaves legislative protection. Public opinion has knotted the lash, heated the branding iron, loaded the rifle, and shielded the murderer. Public opinion threatens the abolitionist with death, if he ventures to the South; and drags him with a rope about his middle, in broad unblushing noon, through the first city in the East. Public opinion has, within a few years, burned a slave alive at a slow fire in the city of St. Louis; and public opinion has to this day maintained upon the bench that estimable Judge who charged the Jury, impanelled there to try his murderers, that their most horrid deed was an act of public opinion, and being so, must not be punished by the laws the public sentiment had made. Public opinion hailed this doctrine with a howl of wild applause, and set the prisoners free, to walk the city, men of mark, and influence, and station, as they had been before.

And what an enormous number of flattering, kindly, cheery compliments Charles Dickens, who himself had been a poor boy of the slightest formal education, who by hard work as well as genius had raised himself to be the idol of two nations, and who was a thorough democrat, paid the continent that lionized and feted him! In Boston, where he landed, he was all praise for the courtesy and attention of the Custom House officers, so different from the similar functionaries at home; for the Tremont House, a hostelry which he found hardly smaller than Bedford Square; for the hospitality of the many citizens who offered him their church pews and other kindnesses; for the brightness, cleanness, and general attractiveness of the city and its suburbs; and for the intellectual refinement of Boston and Cambridge alike. He declared that 'the public institutions and charities of this capital of Massachusetts are as nearly perfect as the most considerate wisdom, benevolence, and humanity can make them.' He had no words too high for Dr. S. G. Howe's work with the dumb and blind. When he visited the factories at Lowell, and compared them with the mills of Manchester, he admired the superior health, dress, and manners of the working girls, the pleasantness of the workrooms, the company hospitals, and the amusements of the employees, 'amusements that in Europe would be deemed 'above their class.' The contrast between their lot and that of the English factory girls, he said, was a contrast 'between the Good and the Evil, the living light and deepest shadow.'

Few visitors have spoken more admiringly of the neat rural scene of New England than Dickens. Coming to New York city, he found more to criticize. He had a severe word for the Tombs prison, where the inmates were without proper exercise or light, and another for the swine that still wandered the streets, gaunt, ugly brutes with blotched, diseased-looking hides, long legs, and such tremendous snouts that they hardly looked like hogs at all. But he had also many good words for the energy of the community, the gay dress of the people, and the deep leafy green squares. Philadelphia was 'a handsome city,' with a wonderful water system, and what he saw of Philadelphia society, he avowed, 'I greatly liked.' So much for the three leading municipalities of the country. He ventured to offer few generalizations upon the United States, his book being almost wholly descriptive, and very little analytic. Some of these are unflattering, to say the least; for he thought that the Americans had a dull and gloomy character, that they were too suspicious and jealous of one another, that they had a weakness for 'smart' business transactions, and that their devotion to trade stifled their interest in the refinements, both cultural and social, of life. Yet he also declared that 'they are, by nature, frank, brave, cordial, hospitable, and affectionate,' and asserted that he had never in England ben so won upon by new acquaintances as she had been here by the educated Americans. He throws out in passing many such agreeable comments as the following:

> By the way, whenever an Englishman would cry 'All right!' an American cries 'Go ahead!' which is somewhat expressive of the national character of the two countries.

It was the West that came off worst from Dickens's pen, and yet, if we keep only the *American Notes* in mind, without thinking of *Martin Chuzzlewit,* we cannot call it shockingly severe treatment. The spitting was no doubt just as bad as he describes it in his acount of the Pennsylvania canal boat—'a perfect storm and tempest of spitting.' There were no doubt many Westerners just as impertinently curious as the man who insisted on knowing where Dickens had bought his fur overcoat, and what he had paid for it, and what it weighed, and whether his watch was French, and where he had acquired it, and so on. The dirty loafers whom the novelist saw lounging at roadside inns along the stage route in Ohio could be duplicated now at the railway stations of Ohio villages. If Dickens misrepresented a typical log inn of northern Ohio by speaking of its 'bugs,' then scores of other British and American guests at like inns have lied. He thought the prairies monotonous, and so they were; he thought the Mississippi a frowzy, muddy stream, with low, unhealthy-looking banks, and so it was. But it ought also to be remembered that he spoke well of many of his fellow-travelers, and that his idyllic picture of one little mother who met her husband at St. Louis was thought by the critic Jeffrey to be the finest page he ever wrote. He testified that never once, during his American travels, did he see a woman 'exposed to the slightest act of rudeness, incivility, or even inattention.' Pittsburgh ('beautifully situated'), Cincinnati ('a beautiful city; cheerful, thriving, and animated'), and Columbus ('clean and pretty') have reason to treasure the kind statements Dickens made of them and the surrounding country.

After all, Dickens's chief mistake, as Andrew Lang said, was his failure to manifest that kind of tact that is simply a gentler word for cowardice. An older, shrewder, and less self-assertive man than he would have been as noncommittal as was Thackeray after his American tour; and we should be thankful that he was not so worldly-wise as to restrain his pen. The resentment of Americans was the greater from their knowledge that he was perfectly honest, and that he had the ear of the world and of posterity. President Felton of Harvard admitted that our prowess in tobacco spitting was quite as appalling as Dickens represented it to be, and a well-known passage in Thoreau's *Cape Cod* bears him out; but the America of 1840 did not want the fault advertised to the world. Our best newspapers said of Congress just what Dickens said, that although it contained statesmen as eminent as Clay and Webster, it also contained many profligate politicians who owed their seats to corrupt party machines. His comments upon the pigs of Broadway were decidedly less scorching than those in which editors had been indulging since the very beginning of the century. What he said of our rowdy press harmonized precisely with the comments that religious bodies and sober citizens were making upon the *Herald,* and with the bitterness against James Gordon Bennett, which made him an outcast from the best society during his whole life. He illustrated his remarks upon our too-frequent duels and assassinations with excerpts from the current newspapers, which spoke for themselves. But for Dickens to praise Niagara, or the Alleghanies, or Irving, or the decorum of a White House reception enthusiastically, as he did, could not earn him the forgiveness of men who writhed under his immortal indictment of our faults.

A feeble and impertinent reply to Dickens was made in 1843 in an anonymous pamphlet called *Change for American Notes,* which undertook to draw an acid picture of the evils flourishing in John Bull's Island. As a matter of fact, of course, no one had more sharply attacked English abuses—the workhouses, the wretched boarding schools, the slums, the election bribery, the debtors' prisons—than the novelist himself; 'What English institution has he spared from the highest to the lowest that contained abuses?' asked the *National Quarterly Review* a little later. The *Change for American Notes* deserves a place on the considerable shelf of American replies to British criticism published in these years, some of which displayed marked controversial ability. Prominent among these efforts were J. K. Paulding's *The United States and England* (1815), Robert Walsh's *Appeal from the Judgments of Great Britain* (1818), Paulding's *John Bull in America* (1824), Cooper's *Notions of the Americans* (1828), and Irving's tactful essay, 'English Writers on America,' in the *Sketch Book*. Basil Hall's book evoked an able anonymous essay, known to be written by Richard Biddle, in the *North American Review,* a magazine that consistently and effectively defended the United States from its English assailants.

The one writer of this period besides Mrs. Trollope who was grossly prejudiced was the Reverend Isaac Fidler, an Anglican divine of stiff, pompous, impracticable temper, who came to America in 1832 unwilling to abate a jot of his English accent, manners, or other anfractuosities, and with the ridiculous belief that he would instantly fall into a fat benefice. His disappointment soured his temper, already sufficiently crabbed. The chief interest of his book lies in its unconscious absurdity. When offered a situation in Ohio, he declined any such 'exile,' saying that the manners of the people were bad enough in the East, and that he knew they could not be improved by contiguity to forests, bears, and Indians. In Boston he called upon the well-known German-American scholar and liberal, Francis Lieber, and straightway fell into a heated quarrel with him about Basil Hall and the comparative state of the arts in England and America. Shaking his fist under Dr. Lieber's nose, vociferating that 'I am greatly mistaken if any first-rate professional man exists in all America,' and that 'there is hardly any village in England which does not possess residents of greater learning than in almost any large town in the United States,' Dr. Fidler bounced out of the house in a rage. A few days later we find him at the home of the affable lawyer and linguist, John Pickering. He distinguished himself there by telling a boy of sixteen, a friend of the Pickering family, that he ought to be caned for the laziness and negligence he had shown in his Sanscrit studies, quarreling with two other guests of the house, and dashing back to his lodgings to write the astonished Mr. Pickering a note in which he declared: 'England, as a nation, is among the nations what her aristocracy is among the aristocracies of the earth; she stands supreme, and will do so for generations. . . The native Americans sit wrapped up in self-complacency, and inhale the grateful fragrance of slavish adulation.'

Not much offense could be taken from the jeremiads of this priest who wrote himself down an ass in every paragraph in which he attacked us. Fidler loved such bits of Christian charity as the verdict, 'there is no dependence to be placed upon the promises or friendships of any person in this country.' He loved such veracious statements as that in Boston 'the soldiers were brutally insulted and stoned by the

American rabble, previous to any bloodshed in revolutionary battles.'
As a climax, he states that the Americans carry their principle of
every man for himself to such an extent that in the great cholera
epidemic of 1835 in New York, which he witnessed, the very doctors
abandoned their stricken patients to hasten from the city. In short,
Fidler makes up with Faux, Ashe, and Mrs. Trollope a quartette that
happily stood alone until Sir Lepel Griffin arrived.

A varying but always considerable degree of amiability was evinced
by Captain Marryat, Thomas Hamilton, and Charles Augustus Murray.
The first-named gave voice to a variety of wrongheaded Tory opinions,
such as that the absence of an established church conduced to irreligion; while he made the ludicrous mistake of predicting that in
twenty or thirty years, if let alone by the wretched Abolitionists, most
of the South would voluntarily become free soil. But he found some
surprising objects for commendation. Unlike the generality of British
travelers of that day, he pronounced Washington 'an agreeable city,
full of pleasant, clever people,' while his account of Philadelphia, with
its Sabbath-like quiet, shining cleanliness, and an array of libraries,
museums, and other institutions 'very superior to those of any other
city or town in America, Boston not excepted,' was equally generous.
While he gives some amusing instances of bad manners among the
Americans, he lays no extreme emphasis upon our spitting, our city
piggeries, and our other more deplorable faults. Probably the worst
of these illustrations is an incident that occurred while he was traveling from Louisville to Baltimore. He stopped at an inn, quite worn
out, and two hours later was aroused by a man who entered his room
without knocking, and demanded whether he was Captain Marryat.
The novelist assented:

'Well, now,' said he, giving a jump and coming down right upon the bed in
his great coat, 'I'll just tell you; I said to the chap at the bar, "Ain't the Captain
in your house?" "Yes," says he. "Then where is he?" says I. "Oh," says he,
"he's gone into his own room, and locked himself up; he's a d—d aristocrat, and
won't drink at the bar with other gentlemen." So thought I, I've read Marryat's
works, and I'll be swamped if he is an aristocrat, and by the 'tarnal I'll go up
and see; so here I am, and you're no aristocrat.'

'I should think not,' replied I, moving my feet away, which he was half
sitting on.

'O, don't move; never mind me, Captain, I'm quite comfortable. And how do
you find yourself by this time?'

'Very tired, indeed,' replied I.

'I suspicion as much. Now, d'ye see, I left four or five good fellows down
below who wish to see you; I said I'd go up first and come down to them. The
fact is, Captain, we don't like you should pass through our town without showing
you a little American hospitality.'

So saying he slid off the bed, and went out of the room. In a minute he re-turned, bringing with him four or five others, all of whom he introduced by name, and reseated himself on my bed, while the others took chairs.

'Now, gentlemen,' said he, 'as I was telling the Captain, we wish to show him a little American hospitality; what shall it be, gentlemen; what d'ye say— a bottle of Madeira?'

An immediate answer not being returned he continued,

'Yes, gentlemen, a bottle of Madeira; at my expense, gentlemen, recollect that; now ring the bell.'

'I shall be most happy to take a glass of wine with you,' observed I, 'but in my own room the wine must be at *my* expense.'

'At *your* expense, Captain; well, if it must be, I don't care; at *your* expense, then, Captain, if you say so; only you see, we must show you a little American hospitality, as I said to them all down below; didn't I, gentlemen?'

The wine was ordered, and it ended in my hospitable friends drinking three bottles; and then they all shook hands with me, declaring how happy they should be if I came to the town again, and allowed them to show me a little more American hospitality.

Few books of American travel in this period were more widely read and discussed than Thomas Hamilton's delightfully written *Men and Manners in America* (1833), by the author of a popular but long-since-forgotten novel of the day. He also had his conservative political prejudices, but he formed a very just idea of the American character.

The Americans were inferior to Englishmen in book education, Hamilton decided, and the tone of their conversation in even the best circles was pitched in a lower intellectual key; but they were inferior to no nation on earth in the knowledge acquired by actual observation, and possessing immediate practical utility. As for man-ners, he thought those of the New York merchants as good as those of similar groups in London or Liverpool, while the gentility of the best Southern circles was admirable. Like Dickens and others, he was shocked to hear the 'cuteness' of sharp or even fraudulent business transactions openly praised, a proof of our low standard of commer-cial morality. But he anticipated Dickens in his tribute to American hospitality, saying that it was equaled in no other country, and that nowhere else in the world would a man seeking acquaintances be so likely to find friends. He also took the occasional discourtesies that he met equably. Thus at a Worcester inn—perhaps the self-same inn where Dickens passed so pleasantly quiet a night—he found the fire surrounded by a crowd of stockmen and others, and had to elbow his way to get any warmth. They devoured a colossal supper of beef-steaks, broiled chicken, ham, cold turkey, toast, 'a kind of crumpet called waffles,' and so on, and settled down to a babel of commercial talk, all wearing 'the same keen and callous expression of worldly anxiety.' All this Hamilton described in a spirit of picturesque enjoyment rather than of censure. In England, he informs us, the man who wants to go to bed rings for the chambermaid; in American inns like that at Worcester, he goes to the bar and asks for a candle, receiving also a key to Room 63, which he hunts up unaided. Though it is the depth of winter, the uncurtained bed has only the scantiest coverlets and the poorest excuse for a pillow, but a tip to the servant girl soon makes everything right. Only rarely do we catch a captious accent in Hamilton's book, as in the last sentence of his description of a breakfast scene at Niblo's Hotel in New York:

The contrast of the whole scene with that of an English breakfast table was striking enough. Here was no loitering nor lounging; no dipping into newspapers; no apparent lassitude of appetite; no intervals of repose in mastication; but all was hurry, bustle, clamor, and voracity, and the business of repletion went forward, with a rapidity altogether unexampled. The strenuous efforts of the company were, of course, soon rewarded with success. Departures, which had begun even before I took my place at the table, became every instant more numerous, and in a few minutes the hall had become what Moore beautifully describes in one of his songs, 'a banquet hall deserted.' The appearance of the table under such circumstances was by no means gracious either to the eye or the fancy. It was strewed thickly with the *disjecta membra* of the entertainment. Here lay fragments of fish, somewhat unpleasantly odoriferous; there, the skeleton of a chicken; on the right, a mustard pot upset, and the cloth, *passim,* defiled with stains of eggs, coffee, gravy—but I will not go on with the picture. One nasty custom, however, I must notice. Eggs, instead of being eaten from the shell, are poured into a wine glass, and after being duly and disgustingly churned up with butter and condiment, the mixture, according to the degree of fluidity, is forthwith either spooned into the mouth, or drunk off like a liquid.

The echoes of indignation over Basil Hall's and Mrs. Trollope's books had not died down when an accomplished gentleman of the British court, Charles Augustus Murray, published a two-volume work (1839) that had a distinctly emollient effect. The fruit of three years of sightseeing, it was painstakingly polite. 'Let not sneers, nor petty interests, nor petty jealousies sever these ties of ancient kindred,' was his fervent wish in closing his book. Though he found some traits that displeased him, he almost always managed to attach saving reservations to his censure. He went out of his way to deny the charge made by certain fellow-Britons that the Yankee is suspicious, hard, and avaricious, instancing several occasions on which men had advanced him money on a draft without a pennyworth of security or a moment of hesitation. He denied that the taverns were bad, asserting that he had tried them in several states, and that he had 'never had reason to complain of want of cleanliness, good victals, or civility.' It was a general complaint of our visitors then, and for long afterwards, that meals could not be had except at stated hours. On the contrary, remarked Murray, he had often arrived at his inn at unseasonable moments, and within a few minutes had always been supplied with beefsteaks, potatoes, eggs, and other comestibles.

Of the kindliness of Americans also he says much. Near Leesburg, Virginia, one dark night, his wagon broke down in the midst of a terrific rainstorm. He made his way to the nearest house, which proved to be a tavern, and poured his tale of woe into the ear of the aged proprietor. The latter 'told me that I was welcome to his servant, horse, and cart to transport my luggage to the city, and that he should charge me nothing. I think it right to record this among the many refutations (which my experience affords) to the accusation of rudeness, so frequently and unjustly brought against the Americans.'

Later in his travels, Murray was engaged in some land business in the northern neck of Virginia, a backwoods country. Every night, after a day's ride, his little party sought out the nearest cabin. 'We were in every instance kindly and hospitably received,' he assures his readers; 'and though our hosts were in many instances very poor, we got generally a good supper of Indian corn cakes, buckwheat and wheat bread, coffee, milk, and broiled pork or venison, and slept comfortably, sometimes on beds, and sometimes in blankets, cloaks, or buffalo skins, on the floor.' Nothing that such a kindly man could say would grate on even the sensitive ear of the 'thirties. He denied the existence of a true social republicanism in the East, pointing to certain distinctions of wealth and family so strongly marked there. In the West he was shocked, like the Earl of Carlisle a little later, by a profanity that he believed unparalleled in the wide world—probably he heard some of the steamboat captains and mates whose powers in this direction have been celebrated by Mark Twain. He did not like Trumbull's paintings in the Capitol, nor the ruinous tomb at Mount Vernon, nor the ugly, uncomfortable character of the city of Washington. But in conclusion he insisted that no Briton should regard the land of the Yankees too smugly. 'Neither our own manners nor morals are so faultless as to justify our indulging in a tone of censure, sarcasm, or satire upon those of the Americans. I would remind you that many of the peculiar characteristics which we sometimes criticize so severely in them are the very same traits which French, German, and other European writers have observed as marking our own national character.'

A fairly good picture of life in certain Mississippi River towns in the 'thirties can be pieced together from Murray's pages. He went as far west as Fort Leavenworth, and roughed it well on the frontier, sleeping in the open and eating badger meat with gusto. He liked the frank democracy of the West. For example, he had seen the clerk of a steamboat and a grocer in a small Missouri River village sit down to grog and a hand at cards with a member of Congress and an army officer, the four laughing, swearing, and chatting together, and calling each other familiarly by their first names. But he did not like the gambling on the steamboats, where he saw $600 staked on a single card. Nor did he like the violence he met in some places:

The village of Keokuk is the lowest and most blackguard place that I have yet visited: its population is composed chiefly of the watermen who assist in loading and unloading the keelboats, and in towing them up when the rapids are too strong for the steam engines. They are a coarse and ferocious caricature of the London bargemen, and their chief occupation seems to consist in drinking, fighting, and gambling. One fellow, who was half drunk (or, in western language, 'corned'), was relating with great satisfaction how he had hid himself in a wood that skirted the road, and (in time of peace) had shot an unsuspecting and inoffensive Indian, who was passing with a wild turkey on his shoulder: he concluded by saying that he had thrown the body into a thicket, and had taken the bird home for his own dinner. He seemed quite proud of his exploit, and said that he would as soon shoot an Indian as a fox or an otter. I thought he was only making an idle boast; but some of the bystanders assured me that it was a well-known fact, and yet he had never been either tried or punished. This murderer is called a Christian, and his victim a heathen!

Galena was, according to the traveler, an equally vicious town, for alongside the honest immigrants from Cornwall, Ireland, and Germany, it had attracted many escaped criminals and army deserters to work in its mines. The wages were so high that they spent little more than half their time at work, and the remaining half in drinking, gambling, quarreling, dirking, and pistoling one another. Dubuque was still another town of the same type. All up and down the Mississippi lynchings were frequent. Five men had been strung up in Vicksburg alone during the summer of 1835 for alleged offences that, even if proved, did not justify capital punishment. Murder was actually a good deal more common than larceny or house-breaking, for 'so easily are money and food here obtained by labor, that it seemed scarcely worth a man's while to steal.' It must have been a decided relief to Murray to come to St. Louis and find it a dull little city. The manners of the people were actually prim. When the Englishman went to a ball, he was surprised by the mode of dancing. 'No imagination can conceive the rolling, the swinging, the strange undulations of the rotary pair,' he tells us; 'they frequently hold each other only by one hand, and the lady places her idle hand on her waist; while the gentleman flourishes his gracefully either above his own or his partner's head, or assigns to it some resting-place no less extraordinary than its movements. In some circles in the South, elbow-waltzing alone is permitted; the lady's waist is forbidden ground, and the gentleman is compelled to hold her by the points of the elbows.'

But the most comforting book to which Americans of this period could turn after Mrs. Trollope and Dickens was Miss Martineau's *Society in America,* for it was a thorough analysis, and yet emphatically favorable, and it came from a writer of authority. Her design was 'to compare the existing state of society in America with the principles on which it is professedly founded,' a severe basis of comparison, to say the least. It was written after a most searching examination of every section, for she resided months at a time in each, was entertained in every type of home from the White House to the log cabin, met nearly all the leaders of thought and affairs, and visited scores of public institutions. Obviously, we were far behind our professed principles, but she thought us, in general, well in advance of Europe.

Politically, Miss Martineau was especially warm in approbation. At first she had some doubt whether the will of the majority actually controlled the government, but she soon recognized that its ultimate ascendancy upon any issue was certain. She admired the division of authority between the states and the nation; she approved of the low cost with which we administered affairs; and she marked our intense patriotism. At first, too, she was alarmed to hear so much of the President's patronage and the evils connected therewith, but this talk she decided was exaggerated. The abolition riots of the time convinced her that allegiance to the law was weaker than it should be, while she was shocked to find that the word hatred was not too strong for our sectional prejudices; yet she affirmed that nullification was only a passing cloud, and seems to have feared little from domestic quarrels. The political disabilities under which women labored naturally struck her, as they did Fanny Wright, as indefensible in a democracy, though Europe exhibited the same evil. On the whole, she agreed with Washington that our government approached nearer to perfection than any other the world had yet seen. Catching the spirit of the Jacksonian era, she predicted an irresistible and peaceful advance towards 'an uncompromising democracy.' Her horror of the 'moral evils, the unspeakable vices and woes of slavery,' was qualified by the same hopefulness for the future. She was confident that universal emancipation

lay not far in the future, for once it was generally perceived that
the abolition of slavery must take place, the Americans would not long
let the great principle be obstructed by details. They 'have done more
difficult things than this,' she said, with unwise optimism, 'though
none assuredly greater.'

Miss Martineau laid it down as a fact that the manners of the Americans were the best she had ever seen. Some exceptions to the rule
she pointed out with considerable sharpness. The only vulgarity she
met was the vulgarity of an aristocracy of mere wealth. In Philadelphia, where she went much into society, she found that the Chestnut
Street ladies had nothing to do with the Arch Street ladies; the former
families traced their fortunes to their grandfathers, the latter only
to their fathers. In New York she observed that the merchants rose
early, snatched a hasty breakfast, and toiled in the heat and dust of
Pearl Street all day, while their wives bought $100 bonnets and other
extravagances. She could not understand why these households did
not live more economically, and thus permit their heads to work
less violently. Taking the country as a whole, the only circumstances
that impressed her unpleasantly were the apparent coldness and indifference of people in hotels and shops: the tobacco-chewing and
spitting, a 'nauseous subject,' which she dismissed in a paragraph;
the harsh tone of voice, especially in New England; and at first, but
not later, the prosy, droll style of conversation. She was able to look
with humor upon many of the idiosyncrasies of the time, as, for example, the practice of calling women either ladies or females. Thus
she quotes a rhetorical question from a religious lecturer: 'Who were
last at the cross? Ladies. Who were first at the sepulchre? Ladies.'
Naturally enough, she was not a little puzzled to reconcile the good
nature of all Americans with their habit of killing each other at the
drop of a hat—with the fact, for example, that in 1834 New Orleans
had more duels than days in the year, and fifteen in a single Sunday
morning. Indeed, our easy-going acceptance of minor hardships and
annoyances dismayed her. Once, traveling in Virginia, her party was
kept waiting interminably for a meal that, when served, proved
wretched:

> Everything on the table was sour; it seemed as if studiously so. The conflict
> between our appetites and the disgust of the food was ridiculous. We all presently
> gave up but the ravenous driver. He tried the bread, the coffee, the butter, and
> all were too sour for a second mouthful; so were the eggs, and the ham, and
> the steak. No one ate anything, and the charge was as preposterous as the delay;
> yet our paymaster made no objection to the way we were treated. When we were
> off again, I asked him why he had been so gracious as to appear satisfied.

'This is a newly opened road,' he replied; 'the people do not know yet how the world lives. They have probably no idea that there is better food than they set before us.'

'But do you not think it would be a kindness to inform them?'

'They did their best for us, and I should be sorry to hurt their feelings.'

'Then you would have them go through life on bad food, and inflicting it on other people, lest their feelings should be hurt at their being told how to provide better. Do you suppose that all the travellers who come this way will be as tender of the lady's feelings?'

'Yes, I do. You see the driver took it very quietly.'

In New England this keen-sighted woman was inclined to censure the excessive caution of the people, and especially their fear of brooking public opinion; when Dr. Channing's essay on slavery appeared, many people refused to read or discuss it. In the South, on the contrary, she condemned an excessive recklessness. Next to slavery, her harshest remarks were reserved for the position of women in America. She summed it up in a sentence—'woman's intellect is confined, her morals crushed, her health ruined, her weaknesses encouraged, and her strength punished.' The education of women was limited to a few ornamental pursuits, they incurred the horror of all about them if they evinced any freedom of mind in deciding what was their duty, instead of letting their parents or husbands decide it, and they lived an inactive domestic life, refusing all outdoor exercise. In all sections it was difficult, and in some impossible, for women to earn their own bread, only five occupations being open to them—teaching, needle work, mill work, work in printing offices, and the keeping of boarding-houses. However, we may gather from her own remarks upon children that she drew too dark a picture. American boys and girls, she said, 'have the advantage of the best possible discipline, that of activity and self-dependence.' The effects of this self-dependence often extended from girlhood to womanhood.

Miss Martineau's conclusion was stated with entire confidence. The American people, she said, had already realized many objects for which the rest of the world was still struggling; and they could not be discouraged by their faults, for they 'are in possession of the glorious certainty that time and exertion will infallibly secure all wisely desired objects.' Such was the verdict of the most thorough student of American life and institutions in the decade that we think of as a period of British abuse. It was not really a period of abuse at all, but simply a time of mixed criticism and praise, with the former a larger element than either before or afterward; but we insisted upon remembering the blame, and forgetting the praise.

A Naval Officer Sees All Sections, 1827-8 [1] ⤳

CAPTAIN BASIL HALL, *the son of a well-known Scotch geologist, was born in Edinburgh in 1788, and educated at the High School there. He entered the navy at the age of thirteen, saw active service during the Napoleonic Wars, and rose to the rank of post-captain in 1817. Amid his naval duties he preserved a marked taste for the scientific and literary, made ethnographical observations in the strange lands he visited, and wrote many valuable papers. In 1816, the year in which he accompanied Lord Amherst's embassy to China, he was made a fellow of the Royal Society. He interviewed Napoleon at St. Helena, an event to which he alludes in his American travels. During 1820-22 he was stationed on the Pacific Coast of South America and Mexico, and in 1824 he published two volumes of a journal kept while in this service. His retirement the same year was followed by his marriage to Margaret, daughter of Sir John Hunter, and he thenceforth devoted himself to travel, study, and writing. His first long tour, in company with his wife and their infant daughter, was to Canada and the United States in 1827-8. It is not by his account of it, however, that he is chiefly remembered in Great Britain, but by his interesting* Fragments of Voyages and Travels, *which were published in three series of three volumes each during the years 1831-40, and which have been frequently reprinted. He also wrote a romance,* Schloss Hainfeld (1836), *and a volume of sketches entitled* Patchwork (1841). *He died insane at Portsmouth three years later.*

In the year following his return from his American tour, Captain Hall published his Travels in North America *in three volumes (London, 1829). They had a remarkable popularity in Great Britain, reaching their third edition in 1830, and were reprinted in the United States and read with even greater avidity. Captain Hall landed at New York, and his first volume treats of his tour through that state to Niagara and in Canada; the second volume offers his observations upon New England and the Middle States as far south as Baltimore; while the third is devoted to the South and the Mississippi. The author was a bluff, honest, clear-headed, practical-minded mariner, whose High-Tory prejudices were all inimical to the crude demo-*

[1] From *Travels in North America in the Years* 1827 *and* 1828, Edinburgh, 1829, volume I, chapters 1, 4, 5; volume II, chapter 10; volume III, chapter 8.

cratic society he found in America, who had little tact with which to smooth his way, and who candidly sets down his displeasure with all that he disliked. His style is without elegance, but it speaks the man, and its dignity, which is evident particularly in the avoidance of all personal allusions, is a good trait. His is one of the first works of the kind to avoid the guidebook structure, and to aim at a truly analytical goal.

Hall's Travels exasperated the American public as had no earlier British work, and an astonishing chorus of rage went up from the press. Mrs. Trollope correctly says that 'the book was read in city, town, village, and hamlet, steamboat, and stage-coach, and a sort of war-whoop was sent forth unprecedented in my recollection upon any occasion whatever.' Men told her that the volume did not contain one word of truth from beginning to end; she was gravely assured that the British Government had commissioned Hall to write down the republic to check the growing admiration expressed for the United States in British circles; and an anonymous volume was published for the purpose not only of refuting the captain but of assailing his character and morals. In short, the work produced a 'moral earthquake' which had not entirely subsided when she left America in the summer of 1831. Mrs. Trollope warmly defended the book as a moderate though penetrating statement of American merits and defects.

METROPOLITAN HOTELS AND SHOPS

A THOUSAND years would not wipe out the recollection of our first breakfast at New York. At eight o'clock we hurried from the packet, and though certainly I most devoutly love the sea, which has been my home for more than half my life, I must honestly acknowledge having leaped on shore with a light heart, after four weeks of confinement. Few naval officers, I suspect, be they ever so fond of their business afloat, ever come to relish another ship, after commanding one of their own.

The *Florida,* our good packet, during the night had been drawn alongside of the wharf, so that we had nothing more to do than step on shore, stow ourselves into a hackney coach, and drive off. This carriage was of the nicest description, open both in front, and at the sides, and was drawn by small, sleek, high-bred horses, driven by a mulatto, whose broken lingo reminded me of the West Indies.

As we passed along, many things recalled the seaports of England to my thoughts, although abundant indications of another country lay on all hands. The signs over the shop doors were written in English; but the language we heard spoken was different in tone from what we had been accustomed to. Still it was English. Yet there was more or less of a foreign air in all we saw, especially about the dress and gait of the men. Negroes and Negresses also were seen in abundance on the wharfs. The form of most of the wheeled carriages was novel; and we encountered several covered vehicles, on which was written in large characters, ICE. I was amused by observing over one of the stores, as the shops are called, a great, staring, well-wigged figure painted on the sign, under which was written, Lord Eldon. A skinny row of white law books explained the mystery. The whole seemed at times more like a dream than a sober reality. For there was so much about it that looked like England that we half fancied ourselves back again; and yet there was quite enough to show in the next instant that it was a very different country. This indistinct, dreamy kind of feeling lasted for several days; after which it gradually faded away before a different set of impressions, which will be described in their turn.

But I am quite forgetting the glorious breakfast! We had asked merely for some fresh shad, a fish reported to be excellent, as indeed it proved. But a great steaming, juicy beefsteak also made its appearance, flanked by a dish of mutton cutlets. The shad is a native of American waters, I believe exclusively, and if so, it is almost worthy of a voyage across the Atlantic to make its acquaintance. To these viands were added a splendid arrangement of snow-white rolls, regiments of hot toast, with oceans of tea and coffee. I have not much title, they tell me, to the name of gourmand, or epicure; nevertheless, I do frankly plead guilty to having made upon this occasion a most enormous breakfast; as if resolved to make up at one unconscionable meal the eight-and-twenty preceding unsatisfactory diurnal operations of this nature, which had intervened since our leaving the good cheer of Liverpool. No ship, indeed, could be more bountifully supplied than our packet; but, alas for the sea! manage it as you will, the contrast between it and the shore, I am sorry to say, is very great. Nothing but shame, I suspect, prevented me from exhausting the patience of the panting waiters by further demands for toast, rolls, and fish; and I rose at last with the hungry edge of appetite taken off, not entirely blunted. The luxury of silver forks and spoons, Indian china teacups, a damask tablecloth, in rooms free from any close, tarry, pitchy, remainder-biscuit smell, space to turn about in, soft seats to loll upon, and firm ground on which to stand, with the addition of the aforesaid magnificent meal, formed altogether, whether from contrast or from intrinsic excellence, as lively a picture of Mahomet's sensual paradise as could be imagined.

In the course of the morning I walked to the Custom House with a very obliging person for whom I had brought letters; and it is due to the public functionaries of that establishment to say that I do not remember having been more civilly treated in the teasing matter of trunks and boxes in any one of the numerous countries in which I have had to undergo the tormenting ordeal of being overhauled. My friend merely stated that I came to America as a traveler, without any view to trade, and that the luggage specified in the list contained nothing but wearing apparel. A few magical words were then written by the collector to the examining officer, upon producing which everything was permitted to pass in the most agreeable style possible, so that not a fold of any part of our finery was disturbed. . .

We soon found there were different modes of living at the great hotels in New York. An immense table d'hôte was laid every day at three o'clock for guests who did not lodge in the house but merely took their meals there. I have seen from sixty to a hundred persons seated at one of those tables. There was also a smaller and less public dinner for the boarders in the house. If any of these persons, however, chose to incur the additional expense of a private parlour, which was about two dollars, or nine shillings a day extra, they might have their meals separately.

On the 17th of May, at eight o'clock, which is the breakfast hour at New York, we went down to the room where the other lodgers were already assembled to the number of twelve or fourteen. Our main object was to get acquainted with some of the natives, and this, we imagined, would be the easiest thing in the world. But our familiar designs were all frustrated by the imperturbable silence and gravity of the company. At dinner, which was at three o'clock, we were again baffled by the same cold and civil but very unsocial formality. All attempts to set conversation in motion proved abortive; for each person seemed intent exclusively on the professed business of the meeting, and having dispatched, in all haste, what sustenance was required, and in solemn silence, rose and departed. It might have been thought we had assembled rather for the purpose of inhuming the body of some departed friend than of merrily keeping alive the existing generation.

A young American naval officer, with whom I had formed a most agreeable and useful friendship, was good enough to accompany me after breakfast to a dock yard, or, as it is more correctly called, the navy yard—for there are no docks in America—at Brooklyn on Long Island. We had to cross two ferries in the course of the day, in double or twin boats, worked by steam, with the paddle wheel in the centre. The most curious thing I saw during this agreeable ramble was a floating wharf, made of wood, the inner end of which was attached to the edge of the quay by means of strong hinges, while the outer end, supported on a large air vessel, or float, rose and sunk with the tide. At high water the wharf stood on a level with the shore; but when it fell, the surface of the wharf had a considerable inclination, though not more than could be easily overcome by the carriages and carts, which drove in and out of the ferry boat at all times, with nearly equal facility.

The officers of the navy yard were most kind and attentive, and showed everything I wished to see without the slightest reserve, and with such entire frankness that I felt no scruple in examining the whole establishment. Amongst other things, I of course visited the great steam frigate, the *Fulton,* intended, I believe, as a floating battery for the defence of New York. This singular vessel is of the double construction, with a paddle wheel in the middle, placed beyond the reach of shot. The machinery is also secured in like manner, by a screen of oak, independently of the ship's bends or sides, which are five feet in thickness, formed of successive layers of thick planks, disposed alternately lengthwise and vertically. This wooden wall affords a defence, as I am told by engineers, not pervious even to a cannon-shot fired at point-blank distance. I afterwards went over several line-of-battle ships and frigates, most of them constructed of live oak, a timber which grows only in the Southern States, and is admirably suited to such purposes from its durability and strength.

I called in the course of the morning on Mr. De Witt Clinton, the Governor of the state of New York. I was no less surprised than pleased with the affability of his manners, and the obliging interest he took in my journey; for I had happened to hear him described only by persons opposed to him in politics, and I had not yet learnt to distrust such reports of men so distinguished in public life as the late Mr. Clinton. He offered me introductions to various parts of the country, and undertook to assist my researches; a promise which he fulfilled to the very hour of his death, about a year afterwards.

.   .   .

It is often useful in travelling to record at the instant those trivial but peculiar circumstances which first strike the eye of a stranger, since, in a short time, they become so familiar as entirely to escape attention. On this principle, I amused myself one morning by noting down a few of the signs over the shop doors. The following may, perhaps, interest some people:

Flour and Feed Store—Cheap Store—Clothing Store—Cake Store and Bakery—Wine and Tea Store, all explain themselves. *Leather and Finding Store* puzzled me at first. I learned, upon inquiry, that finding means the tape and other finishing of shoes and boots. *Uncurrent Notes Bought* required investigation. It means that of late years many towns and country banks had failed, or fallen into such bad repute that their notes were not held as good payment by the generality of people; while other persons, knowing exactly how the case stood, were enabled to turn their knowledge to account, and thus to make a profit by buying up the depreciated paper.

Liberty Street—Amos Street—Thirty-First Street—Avenue A are all more or less characteristic. The following is a literal copy of the sign before the inn door at Brooklyn, all the places named being on Long Island:

Coe S. Dowling's Stage & Livery Stable
Horses and Carriages to Be Let

Flatbush and Bath—Hempstead—Jerusalem—Hempstead Harbour —Cow Neck—Westbury—Mosquetoe Cove—Jericho—Oyster Bay— Huntington—Eastwoods—Dixhill—Babylon and Islip, Stage House.

FIRES IN NEW YORK

At two o'clock in the morning of the 20th of May, I was awakened by loud cries of 'Fire! fire!' and started out of bed, half dreaming that we were still at sea, and the packet in flames. In a few minutes the deep rumbling sound of the engines was heard, mingled in a most alarming way with the cheers of the firemen, the loud rapping of the watchmen at the doors and window-shutters of the sleeping citizens, and various other symptoms of momentous danger, and the necessity of hot haste.

So much had been said to me of the activity and skill of the New York firemen that I was anxious to see them in actual operation; and accordingly, having dressed myself quickly, I ran downstairs. Before I reached the outer door, however, the noise had well-nigh ceased; the engines were trundling slowly back again, and the people grumbling, not without reason, at having been dragged out of bed to no purpose. Of this number I certainly was one, but more from what I had lost seeing than from any other cause.

I was scarcely well asleep again before a second and far more furious alarm brought all the world to the windows. The church bells were clanging violently on all hands, and the ear could readily catch, every now and then, a fresh sound chiming in with the uproar with much musical discord, and all speaking in tones of such vehemence as satisfied me that now there would be no disappointment.

On opening the street door, I saw in the east a tall column of black smoke, curling and writhing across the cold morning sky, like a great snake attempting to catch the moon, which, in her last quarter, was moving quietly along, as if careless of the increasing tumult which was fast spreading over the city.

On the top of the City Hall, one of the finest of the numerous public buildings which adorn New York, a fire warden or watchman is constantly stationed, whose duty when the alarm is given is to hoist a lantern at the extremity of a long arm attached to the steeple, and to direct it towards the fire, as a sort of beacon, to instruct the engines what course to steer. There was something singularly striking in this contrivance, which looked as if a great giant, with a blood-red finger, had been posted in the midst of the city, to warn the citizens of their danger.

I succeeded by quick running in getting abreast of a fire engine; but although it was a very ponderous affair, it was dragged along so smartly by its crew of some six-and-twenty men, aided by a whole legion of boys, all bawling as loud as they could, that I found it difficult to keep up with them. On reaching the focus of attraction, the crowd of curious persons like myself began to thicken, while the engines came dashing in amongst us from every avenue, in the most gallant and business-like style.

Four houses, built entirely of wood, were on fire from top to bottom, and sending up a flame that would have defied a thousand engines. But nothing could exceed the dauntless spirit with which the attempt was made. In the midst of a prodigious noise and confusion, the engines were placed along the streets in a line, at the distance of about two hundred feet from one another, and reaching to the bank of the East River, as that inland sea is called, which lies between Long Island and the main. The suction hose of the last engine in the line, or that next the stream, being plunged into the river, the water was drawn up, and then forced along a leathern hose or pipe to the next engine, and so on, till at the tenth link in this curious chain it came within range of the fire. As more engines arrived, they were marshalled by the superintendent into a new string; and in about five minutes after the first stream of water had been brought to bear on the flames another was sucked along in like manner, and found its way, leap by leap, to the seat of the mischief.

I moved about amongst the blazing houses till driven back by the police, who laboured hard to clear the ground for the firemen alone. On retiring reluctantly from this interesting scene, I caught a glimpse of a third jet of water playing away from the back part of the fire, and on going round to that quarter, discovered that these energetic people had formed a third series, consisting of seven engines, reaching to a different bend of the river, down some alley, and not quite so far off.

The chief things to find fault with on this occasion were the needless shouts and other uproarious noises, which obviously helped to exhaust the men at the engines, and the needless forwardness, or it may be called foolhardiness, with which they entered houses on fire, or climbed upon them by means of ladders, when it must have been apparent to the least skilful person that their exertions were utterly hopeless. A small amount of discipline, of which, by the way, there was not a particle, might have corrected the noise; and the other evil, I think, might have been removed by a machine recently invented in Edinburgh and found to be efficacious on like occasions.

At the request of a committee of the Fire Department, I afterwards explained this simple and excellent device. It consists of a lofty triangle, as it is called, formed by three long poles joined at top, and carrying a socket, through which passes the nozzle or spout of a pipe connected with an engine below. By means of guys, or directing lines, this spout may be raised, lowered, or turned to the right or left. By means also of a proper adjustment of the legs, two of which may be brought close to the wall of the burning house, and the third pushed either backwards or forwards, a solid stream of water can be directed, in its unbroken state, full upon the timbers of a blazing roof, or it may be spouted into a room on fire, not only without danger to the firemen but with much greater precision and effect than by the ordinary methods, which generally have the effect of scattering the water in a shower over the flames, to no purpose.

The committee listened very attentively to my lecture, and inspected the drawings made to illustrate what was said. But I had the mortification, five months afterwards, to see three fine houses burned to the ground, two of which might have been saved, as an old fireman assured me on the spot, had this contrivance been introduced.

. . .

On the 21st of May I accompanied two gentlemen, about three o'clock, to a curious place called the Plate House, in the very centre of the business part of the busy town of New York.

We entered a long, narrow, and rather dark room, or gallery, fitted up like a coffee-house, with a row of boxes on each side made just large enough to hold four persons, and divided into that number by fixed arms limiting the seats. Along the passage, or avenue, between the rows of boxes, which was not above four feet wide, were stationed sundry little boys, and two waiters, with their jackets off—and a good need, too, as will be seen. At the time we entered, all the compartments were filled except one, of which we took possession. There was an amazing clatter of knives and forks; but not a word audible to us was spoken by any of the guests. This silence, however, on the part of the company, was amply made up for by the rapid vociferations of the attendants, especially of the boys, who were gliding up and down, and across the passage, inclining their heads first to one box, then to another, and receiving the whispered wishes of the company, which they straightway bawled out in a loud voice, to give notice of what fare was wanted. It quite baffled my comprehension to imagine how the people at the upper end of the room, by whom a communication was kept up in some magical way with the kitchen, could contrive to distinguish between one order and another. It was still more marvellous that within a few seconds after our wishes had been communicated to one of the aforesaid urchins, imps, gnomes, or whatever name they deserve, the things we asked for were placed piping hot before us. It was really quite an Arabian Nights' Entertainment, not a sober dinner at a chop-house.

The sole object of the company evidently was to get through a certain quantum of victuals with as much dispatch as possible; and as all the world knows that talking interferes with eating, every art was used in this said most excellent Plate House, to utter as few words as might be, and only those absolutely essential to the ceremony.

In giving the order to the sprites flitting about us, we had merely to name the dish wanted, which they conjured to the table, either in a single portion or plateful, or in any other quantity, according to the number of the party. If a farther supply was wanted, a half or a whole plateful was whispered for, and straightway it was laid before us. We had been told by old stagers of the excellence of the corned beef, and said to the boy we should all three take that dish. Off the gnome glanced from us like a shot, to attend to the beck of another set of guests, on the opposite side of the room; but, in flying across the passage, turned his face towards the upper end of the apartment and called out, 'Three beef, 8!' the last word of his sentence referring to the number of our box. In a trice we saw the waiters gliding down the avenue to us, with three sets of little covered dishes, each containing a plate, on which lay a large, piping hot slice of beef. Another plate was at the same time given, with a moderate proportion of mashed potatoes on it, together with a knife and a fork, on which was stuck a piece of bread. As the waiters passed along, they took occasion to incline their ears to the right and to the left, to receive fresh orders, and also to snatch up empty tumblers, plates, and knives and forks. The multiplicity and rapidity of these orders and movements made me giddy. Had there been one set to receive and forward the orders, and another to put them into execution, we might have seen better through the confusion; but all hands, little and big together, were screaming out with equal loudness and quickness—'Half plate beef, 4!'—'One potato, 5!'—'Two apple pie, one plum pudding, 8!' and so on.

There could not be, I should think, fewer than a dozen boxes, with four people in each; and as everyone seemed to be eating as fast as he could, the extraordinary bustle may be conceived. We were not in the house above twenty minutes, but we sat out two sets of company at each. The bill, reduced to English money, was nine shillings and sixpence in all, or three shillings and twopence each.

There may be, for aught I know, hundreds of such places in London, Liverpool, and elsewhere in England; but travelling, it is said, opens the eyes, and teaches people to see things which, in the ordinary jog-trot of life, they would either despise or be too busy for, or never hear about at all, or take no pains to visit if they did hear of them.

On the 22d of May I went to the Supreme Court of the state, in expectation of hearing a speech from Mr. Emmet, a distinguished counsellor. In this I was disappointed; but there was much to interest notwithstanding. Amongst other things, it was curious to hear one of the lawyers quote a recent English decision. The Chief Justice and two judges were on the bench; but I must say that the absence of the wigs and gowns took away much more from their dignity than I had previously supposed possible. Perhaps I was the more struck with this omission, as it was the first thing I saw which made me distrust the wisdom with which the Americans had stripped away so much of what had been held sacred so long. Apparent trifles such as these ought never, I think, to be measured by their individual importance, but in fairness to the subject should be taken in connection with myriads of associations, all combining to steady our habits, to let us know distinctly what we are about, and thus to give us confidence in one another, which after all is the real source of power and happiness in a state.

CONTRASTS OF FRONTIER NEW YORK

On the 19th of June we reached the village of Syracuse, through the very centre of which the Erie Canal passes. During the drive we had opportunities of seeing the land in various stages of its progress, from the dense, black, tangled, native forest up to the highest stages of cultivation, with wheat and barley waving over it; or from that melancholy and very helpless-looking state of things, when the trees are laid prostrate upon the earth, one upon top of another, and a miserable log hut is the only symptom of man's residence, to such a gay and thriving place as Syracuse, with fine broad streets, large and commodious houses, gay shops, and stagecoaches, waggons, and gigs flying past, all in a bustle. In the centre of the village, we could see from our windows the canal thickly covered with freight boats and packets, glancing silently past, and shooting like arrows through the bridges, some of which were of stone, and some of painted wood. The canal at this place has been made double its ordinary width, and being bent into an agreeable degree of curvature, to suit the turn of the streets, the formality is removed, as well as the ditch-like appearance which generally belongs to canals. The water, also, is made to rise almost level with the towing path, which improves the effect. I was amused by seeing, amongst the throng of loaded boats, a gaily painted vessel lying in state, with the words Cleopatra's Barge painted in large characters on her broadside.

In the course of 50-miles travelling we came repeatedly in sight of almost every successive period of agricultural advancement through which America has run, or is actually running. At one place we found ourselves amongst the Oneida tribe of Indians, living on a strip of land called a reservation, from being appropriated exclusively to these poor remains of the former absolute masters of the territory— the native burghers of the forest! They were dressed in blankets with leggings of skin laced not very tightly and reaching to the hide moccasins on their feet. Their painted faces, and lank, black, oily hair, made them look as like savages as any lion-hunting travellers could have desired.

In merely passing along the road it was of course difficult to form any conjecture as to how much of the country was cleared; especially as new settlers naturally cling to canals, roads, and lakes, and it was such settlers only that we saw. Sometimes our track lay through a thick forest for a mile or two; though, generally speaking, the country for some distance on both sides of the road was thickly strewed with houses. Every now and then we came to villages, consisting of several hundred houses; and in the middle I observed there were always several churches surmounted with spires, painted with some showy colour, and giving a certain degree of liveliness or finish to scenes in other respects rude enough. In general, however, it must be owned, there prevailed a most uncomfortable appearance of bleakness or rawness, and a total absence of picturesque beauty in these villages, whose dreary aspect was much heightened by the black sort of gigantic wall formed of the abrupt edge of the forest, choked up with underwood, now for the first time exposed to the light of the sun.

The cleared spaces, however, as they are called, looked to our eyes not less desolate, being studded over with innumerable great black stumps; or, which was more deplorable still, with all scorched, branchless stems of trees, which had undergone the barbarous operation known by the name of girdling. An American settler can hardly conceive the horror with which a foreigner beholds such numbers of magnificent trees, standing round him with their throats cut, the very Banquos of the murdered forest! The process of girdling is this: a circular cut or ring, two or three inches deep, is made with an axe quite round the tree at about five feet from the ground. This, of course, puts an end to vegetable life; and the destruction of the tree being accelerated by the action of fire, these wretched trunks in a year or two present the most miserable objects of decrepitude that can be conceived. The purpose, however, of the farmer is gained and that is all he can be expected to look to. His corn crop is no longer overshadowed by the leaves of these unhappy trees, which, in process of time, are cut down and split into railings, or sawed into billets of firewood—and their misery is at an end.

Even in the cultivated fields, the tops of the stumps were seen poking their black snouts above the young grain like a shoal of seals. Not a single hedge or wall was to be seen in those places, all the enclosures being made of solid logs, built one upon the top of another in a zigzag fashion, like what the ladies call a Vandyke border. These are named snake fences, and are certainly the most ungraceful-looking things I ever saw.

Most of the houses are built of rough unbarked logs, nicked at the ends so as to fit closely and firmly; and roofed with planks. The better sort of dwellings, however, are made of square timbers framed together neatly enough and boarded over at the sides and ends, and then roofed with shingles, which are a sort of oblong wooden slates. The houses are generally left unpainted, and being scattered about without order, look more like a collection of great packing boxes than the human residences which the eye is accustomed to see in old countries. In the more cleared and longer settled parts of the country we saw many detached houses, which might almost be called villas, very neatly got up, with rows of wooden columns in front, shaded by trees and tall shrubs running round and across the garden, which was prettily fenced in and embellished with a profusion of flowers.

Sometimes a whole village, such as that of Whitesborough, was composed entirely of these detached villas; and as most of the houses were half hid in the thick foliage of the elm trees round them, they looked cool and comfortable when compared with the new and half-burnt, and in many places burning country, only a few miles off.

The village of Utica stands a step higher in this progressive scale of civilization, for it has several church spires rising over it, and at no great distance an institution called Hamilton College, intended, I was told, for the higher branches of science. We also visited Syracuse, a village with extensive saltworks close to it, and had numerous opportunities of examining the Erie Canal, and the great high road to Buffalo;—so that what with towns and cities, Indians, forests, cleared and cultivated lands, girdled trees, log houses, painted churches, villas, canals, and manufactories, and hundreds of thousands of human beings, starting into life, all within the ken of one day's rapid journey, there was plenty of stuff for the imagination to work upon. . .

On the 20th of June we left Syracuse after a pleasant excursion to the saltworks at Salina in that neighborhood, and reached Auburn at nine o'clock at night, having passed through the villages of Elbridge and Brutus. Owing to the numerous and teasing stops, we did not average more than five miles an hour, though we often went over the ground at a greater rate.

The country during this day's journey, though not quite so recently settled as some we had seen before, presented nearly the same mixture of wide oceans of impervious-looking forests, dotted over, here and there, with patches of cleared land under every stage of the agricultural process. Some of the fields were sown with wheat, above which could be seen numerous ugly stumps of old trees; others allowed to lie in grass, guarded, as it were, by a set of gigantic black monsters, the girdled, scorched, and withered remnants of the ancient woods. Many farms were still covered with a most inextricable and confused mass of prostrate trunks, branches of trees, piles of split logs, and of squared timbers, planks, shingles, and great stacks of fuel; and often, in the midst of all this, could be detected a half-smothered log hut without windows or furniture, but well stocked with people. At other places we came upon ploughs, always drawn by oxen, making their sturdy way amongst the stumps, like a ship navigating through coral reefs, a difficult and tiresome operation. Often, too, without much warning, we came in sight of busy villages, ornamented with tall white spires topping above towers in which the taste of the villagers had placed green venetian blinds, and at the summit of all, handsome gilt weathercocks glittering and crowing, as it seemed, in triumph over the poor forest.

'Driver!' I called out upon one occasion, 'what is the name of this village?' 'Camillus, sir.' 'And what is that great building?' 'That is the seminary—the polytechnic.' 'And that great stone house?' 'Oh, that is the wool factory.'

In short, an Englishman might fancy himself in the vale of Stroud. But, mark the difference—at the next crack of the whip—hocus pocus! —all is changed. He looks out of the window—rubs his eyes, and discovers that he is again in the depths of the wood at the other extremity of civilized society, with the world just beginning to bud, in the shape of a smoky log hut, ten feet by twelve, filled with dirty-faced children, squatted round a hardy-looking female cooking victuals for a tired woodsman seated at his door, reading with suitable glee in the *Democratical Journal* of New York an account of Mr. Canning's campaign against the Ultra Tories of the old country.

SLAVERY ON A SOUTH CAROLINA PLANTATION

It appears that when the Negroes go to the field in the morning, it is the custom to leave such children behind as are too young to work. Accordingly, we found a sober old matron in charge of three dozen shining urchins, collected together in a house near the centre of the [slave] village. Over the fire hung a large pot of hominy, a preparation of Indian corn, making ready for the little folks' supper, and a very merry, happy-looking party they seemed. The parents and such children as are old enough to be useful go out to work at daybreak, taking their dinner with them to eat on the ground. They have another meal towards the close of day after coming home. Generally, also, they manage to cook up a breakfast; but this must be provided by themselves, out of their own earnings, during those hours which it is the custom, in all plantations, to allow the Negroes to work on their own account.

It was pleasant to hear that, in most parts of the country, the Negroes of America had the whole of Sunday allowed them, excepting, as I afterwards learnt, at certain seasons of the year and in certain sections of Louisiana; for example, where sugar is cultivated, it is occasionally of such consequence to use expedition that no cessation of labor is permitted. Generally speaking, the planters, who seem well aware of the advantage of not exacting too much service from their slaves, consider the intermission of one day, at the least, as a source rather of profit than of loss. A special task for each slave is accordingly pointed out daily by the overseer; and as soon as this is completed in a proper manner, the laborer may go home to work at his own piece of ground, or tend his pigs and poultry, or play with his children —in a word, to do as he pleases. The assigned task is sometimes got over by two o'clock in the day, though this is rare, as the work generally lasts till four or five o'clock. I often saw gangs of Negroes at work till sunset.

We went into several of the cottages, which were uncommonly neat and comfortable and might have shamed those of many countries I have seen. Each hut was divided into small rooms or compartments, fitted with regular bed places; besides which, they had all chimneys and doors, and some, though only a few of them, possessed the luxury of windows. I counted twenty-eight huts, occupied by one hundred and forty souls, or about five in each. This number included sixty children.

On returning to dinner, we found everything in perfect order. The goodness of the attendance in this house, together with the comfort, cleanliness, and cheerfulness of the whole establishment, satisfied me that by a proper course of discipline, slaves may be made good servants —a fact of which, I confess, I had begun to question the possibility. Regularity in arrangement—good sense and good temper—an exact knowledge of what ought to be done, with sufficient determination of character to enforce punctual obedience, are requisites, I suspect, more indispensably necessary in slave countries than in places where the service is voluntary.

It will easily be understood, indeed, that one of the greatest practical evils of slavery arises from persons who have no command over themselves, being placed, without any control, in command of others. Hence passion without system must very often take the place of patience and method; and the lash—that prompt but terrible instrument of power, and one so dangerous in irresponsible hands—cuts all the Gordian knots of this difficulty, and, right or wrong, forces obedience by the stern agony of fear, the lowest of all motives to action. The consequence, I believe, invariably is that where service is thus, as it were, beaten out of men, the very minimum of work, in the long run, is obtained. Judicious slave-holders, therefore, whether they be humane persons or not, generally discover, sooner or later, that the best policy by far is to treat these unfortunate dependents with as much kindness as the nature of the discipline will allow.

The gentlemen of the South sometimes assert that the slave population are rather happier than the labouring classes in the northern parts of their own Union, and much better off than the peasantry of England. There is no good purpose served by advancing such pretensions. They are apt to excite irritation, sometimes ridicule; and while they retard the cause of improvement, substantiate nothing in the argument, except the loss of temper. It signifies little to talk of the Poor Laws of England or the pauperism in the great cities on the American coast, for, after all, such allusions apply to a small portion only of the labouring classes; whereas, in a slave-holding country, the whole working population are included in this humiliating description. . . Have not ignorance, irreligion, falsehood, dishonesty in dealing, and laziness become nearly as characteristic of the slave as the colour of his skin? And when these caste marks, as they may almost be called, are common to the whole mass of the labouring population of the states in question, it is certainly not quite fair to place them on a level with the free New Englanders of America, or the bold peasantry of Great Britain.

THE GREAT AMERICAN LEXICOGRAPHER

In the evening I had the pleasure of being introduced to Mr. Noah Webster, of New Haven, a gentleman who has been occupied during the last forty years of his life in preparing a dictionary of the English language, which, I find, has since been published. He includes in it all the technical expressions connected with the arts and sciences, thus giving, he hopes, as complete a picture as possible of the English language, as it stands at this moment, on both sides of the Atlantic.

We had a pleasant discussion on the use of what are called Americanisms, during which he gave me some new views on this subject. He contended that his countrymen had not only a right to adopt new words, but were obliged to modify the language to suit the novelty of the circumstances, geographical and political, in which they were placed. He fully agreed with me, however, in saying that where there was an equally expressive English word, cut and dry, it ought to be used in preference to a new one. 'Nevertheless,' said he, 'it is quite impossible to stop the progress of language—it is like the course of the Mississippi, the motion of which, at times, is scarcely perceptible; yet even then it possesses a momentum quite irresistible. It is the same with the language we are speaking of. Words and expressions will be forced into use, in spite of all the exertions of all the writers in the world.'

'Yes,' I observed; 'but surely such innovations are to be deprecated?'

'I don't know that,' he replied. 'If a word becomes universally current in America, where English is spoken, why should it not take its station in the language?'

'Because,' I said, 'there are words enough already; and it only confuses matters and hurts the cause of letters to introduce such words.'

'But,' said he, reasonably enough, 'in England such things happen currently, and, in process of time, your new words find their way across the Atlantic, and are incorporated in the spoken language here.' 'In like manner,' he added, 'many of our words, heretofore not used in England, have gradually crept in there, and are now an acknowledged part of the language. The interchange, in short, is inevitable; and, whether desirable or not, cannot be stopped or even essentially modified.'

I asked him what he meant to do in this matter in his dictionary.

'I mean,' he said, 'to give every word at present in general use, and hope thereby to contribute in some degree to fix the language at its present station. This cannot be done completely; but it may be possible to do a great deal.'

I begged to know what he proposed to do with those words which were generally pronounced differently in the two countries. 'In that case,' said he, 'I would adopt that which was most consonant to the principles of the English language, as denoted by the analogy of similar words, without regarding which side of the water that analogy favoured. For example, you in England universally say *ch*ivalry—we as generally say *sh*ivalry; but I should certainly give it according to the first way, as more consistent with the principles of the language. On the other hand, your way of pronouncing the word deaf is def— ours, as if it were written deef; and as this is the correct mode, from which you have departed, I shall adhere to the American way.'

I was at first surprised when Mr. Webster assured me there were not fifty words in all which were used in America and not in England, but I have certainly not been able to collect nearly that number. He told me too, what I did not quite agree to at the time but which subsequent inquiry has confirmed as far as it has gone, that, with very few exceptions, all these apparent novelties are merely old English words, brought over to America by the early settlers, being current at home when they set out on their pilgrimage, and here they have remained in good use ever since.

Domestic Unmannerliness of the Americans [1] &

FRANCES TROLLOPE *is remembered as the author of the most prejudiced and most hotly discussed of all British books of travel in the United States, and as mother of two novelists, Anthony and Thomas Adolphus Trollope. Born in 1780 as Frances Milton, she married Thomas Anthony Trollope, a graduate of Oxford and a propertied barrister, in 1809. Lack of business capacity, a tendency towards speculation, and a series of unfortunate accidents plunged her husband deeper and deeper into poverty, until, having given up the law and betaken himself to farming, he was quite ruined. When his affairs were reaching the worst, in 1827, Mrs. Trollope went to the United States, taking with her two daughters and one son, and intending with the help of her friend Fanny Wright, the well-known woman lecturer, to find a profitable career for at least the boy. She soon determined to open a bazaar in Cincinnati for the sale of fancy goods and knick-knacks—of 'pincushions, pepper boxes, and pocket knives,' as Anthony Trollope later wrote. During 1828 her husband and another son, Thomas Adolphus, joined her in Cincinnati. They found the shop, 'an institution which was to combine the specialties of an athenæum, a lecture hall, and a bazaar,' still unbuilt. It was soon contracted for, and Mrs. Trollope's husband returned home, together with Thomas Adolphus, to send out a consignment of the goods required.*

This business venture soon proved a total failure. The bazaar was built, and has been described by another English traveler as the most 'absurd, ugly, and ridiculous' building in the town; but there was insufficient patronage. In 1831 Mrs. Trollope returned home in a frame of mind very unfriendly to the Americans. She had made some noteworthy friends in Cincinnati, including the clergyman-author Timothy Flint, the then well-known pioneer in viticulture, Nicholas Longworth, and the youth Hiram Powers, later famous as a sculptor. But in general the rather crude society of the fast-growing Western city had been repugnant to her, and her disposition was not softened by her money troubles. She immediately published her Domestic Manners of the Americans, *which was eagerly read in England. Soon afterwards the*

[1] From *Domestic Manners of the Americans*, London, 1832, chapters 5, 9, 14, 15, 26, 28, and 32.

family fled from Great Britain to escape its creditors, and Mrs. Trollope
thereafter supported it by literary work in Belgium.

The uproar produced in the United States by her ill-natured work
was tremendous. Lieutenant E. T. Coke, who traveled in America
the following year, found that the controversy it aroused had eclipsed
even the Tariff and the Bank War in popular interest. 'At every corner
of the street, at the door of every petty retailer of information for
the people, a large placard met the eye, with "For sale here, with
plates, Domestic Manners of the Americans, *by Mrs. Trollope." At*
every table d'hôte, on board of every steamboat, and in all societies,
the first question was, "Have you read Mrs. Trollope?" And one-half
the people would be seen with a red or blue half-bound volume in
their hand, which you might vouch for being the odious work, and
the more it was abused, the more rapidly did the printers issue new
editions.' Mrs. Trollope published other books of travel and many
novels, writing steadily until her death at Florence in 1863.

WANT OF ELEGANCE IN AMERICA

THE 'simple' manner of living in Western America was more distasteful
to me from its levelling effects on the manners of the people than from
the personal privations that it rendered necessary; and yet, till I was
without them, I was in no degree aware of the many pleasurable
sensations derived from the little elegances and refinements enjoyed
by the middle classes in Europe. There were many circumstances, too
trifling even for my gossiping pages, which pressed themselves daily
and hourly upon us, and which forced us to remember painfully
that we were not at home. It requires an abler pen than mine to trace
the connexion which I am persuaded exists between these deficiencies
and the minds and manners of the people. All animal wants are supplied profusely at Cincinnati, and at a very easy rate; but, alas! these go
but a little way in the history of a day's enjoyment. The total and
universal want of manners, both in males and females, is so remarkable that I was constantly endeavouring to account for it. It certainly
does not proceed from want of intellect. I have listened to much dull
and heavy conversation in America, but rarely to any that I could
strictly call silly (if I except the everywhere privileged class of very
young ladies). They appear to me to have clear heads and active in-
tellects; are more ignorant on subjects that are only of conventional
value than on such as are of intrinsic importance; but there is no
charm, no grace in their conversation. I very seldom, during my
whole stay in the country, heard a sentence elegantly turned and cor-

rectly pronounced from the lips of an American. There is always something either in the expression or the accent that jars the feelings and shocks the taste.

I will not pretend to decide whether man is better or worse off for requiring refinements in the manners and customs of the society that surrounds him, and for being incapable of enjoyment without them; but in America, that polish which removes the coarser and rougher parts of our nature is unknown and undreamed of. There is much substantial comfort, and some display in the larger cities; in many of the more obvious features they are as Paris or as London, being all large assemblies of active and intelligent human beings— but yet they are wonderfully unlike in nearly all their moral features. . . Captain Hall, when asked what appeared to him to constitute the greatest difference between England and America, replied, like a gallant sailor, 'the want of loyalty.' Were the same question put to me, I should answer, 'the want of refinement.'

LITERATURE AND PRUDERY

On one ocacsion . . . I passed an evening in company with a gentleman, said to be a scholar and a man of reading; he was also what is called a *serious* gentleman, and he appeared to have pleasure in feeling that his claim to distinction was acknowledged in both capacities. . . To me he spoke as Paul to the offending Jews; he did not, indeed, shake his raiment at me, but he used his pocket handkerchief so as to answer the purpose; and if every sentence did not end with 'I am clean,' pronounced by his lips, his tone, his look, his action fully supplied the deficiency.

Our poor Lord Byron, as may be supposed, was the bull's-eye against which every dart in his black little quiver was aimed. I had never heard any serious gentleman talk of Lord Byron at full length before, and I listened attentively. It was evident that the noble passages which are graven on the hearts of the genuine lovers of poetry had altogether escaped the serious gentleman's attention; and it was equally evident that he knew by rote all those that they wish the mighty master had never written. I told him so, and I shall not soon forget the look he gave me.

Of other authors his knowledge was very imperfect, but his criticisms very amusing. Of Pope, he said, 'He is so entirely gone by that in *our* country it is considered quite fustian to speak of him.'

But I persevered, and named 'The Rape of the Lock' as evincing some little talent, and being in a tone that might still hope for admittance in the drawing room; but, on the mention of this poem, the serious gentleman became almost as strongly agitated as when he talked of Don Juan; and I was unfeignedly at a loss to comprehend the nature of his feelings, till he muttered, with an indignant shake of the handkerchief, 'The very title!'

At the name of Dryden he smiled, and the smile spoke as plainly as a smile could speak, 'How the old woman twaddles!'

'We only know Dryden by quotations, Madam, and these, indeed, are found only in books that have long since had their day.'

'And Shakespeare?'

'Shakespeare, Madam, is obscene, and, thank God, *we* are sufficiently advanced to have found it out! If we must have the abomination of stage plays, let them at least be marked by the refinement of the age in which we live.'

This was certainly being *au courant de jour.*

Of Massinger he knew nothing. Of Ford he had never heard. Gray had had his day. Prior he had never read, but understood he was a very childish writer. Chaucer and Spenser he tied in a couple, and dismissed by saying that he thought it was neither more nor less than affectation to talk of authors who wrote in a tongue no longer intelligible.

This was the most literary conversation I was ever present at in Cincinnati.

YANKEE CURIOSITY

It is by no means rare to meet elsewhere, in this working-day world of ours, people who push acuteness to the verge of honesty, and sometimes, perhaps, a little bit beyond; but, I believe the Yankee is the only one who will be found to boast of doing so. It is by no means easy to give a clear and just idea of a Yankee; if you hear his character from a Virginian, you will believe him a devil; if you listen to it from himself, you might fancy him a god—though a tricky one; Mercury turned righteous and notable. . . In acuteness, cautiousness, industry, and perseverance he resembles the Scotch; in habits of frugal neatness he resembles the Dutch; in love of lucre he doth greatly resemble the sons of Abraham; but in frank admission, and superlative admiration of all his own peculiarities, he is like nothing on earth but himself.

The Quakers have been celebrated for the pertinacity with which

they avoid giving a direct answer, but what Quaker could ever vie
with a Yankee in this sort of fencing? Nothing, in fact, can equal
their skill in evading a question, excepting that with which they set
about asking one. I am afraid that in repeating a conversation which
I overheard on board the Erie Canal boat, I shall spoil it by forgetting
some of the little delicate doublings which delighted me—yet I wrote
it down immediately. Both parties were Yankees, but strangers to
each other; one of them having, by gentle degrees, made himself pretty
well acquainted with the point from which every one on board had
started, and that for which he was bound, at last attacked his brother
Reynard thus:—

'Well, now, which way may you be travelling?'

'I expect this canal runs pretty nearly west.'

'Are you going far with it?'

'Well, now, I don't rightly know how many miles it may be.'

'I expect you'll be from New York?'

'Sure enough I have been at New York often and often.'

'I calculate, then, 'tis not there as you stop?'

'Business must be minded, in stopping and in stirring.'

'You may say that. Well, I look then you'll be making for the Springs?'

'Folks say as all the world is making for the Springs, and I expect a good
sight of them is.'

'Do you calculate upon stopping long when you get to your journey's end?'

' 'Tis my business must settle that, I expect.'

'I guess that's true, too; but you'll be for making pleasure a business for once,
I calculate?'

'My business don't often lie in that line.'

'Then, may be, it is not the Springs as takes you this line?'

'The Springs is a right elegant place, I reckon.'

'It is your health, I calculate, as makes you break your good rules?'

'My health don't trouble me much, I guess.'

'No? Why, that's well. How is the markets, sir? Are bread stuffs up?'

'I an't just capable to say.'

'A deal of money's made by just looking after the article at the fountain's
head.'

'You may say that.'

'Do you look to be making great dealings in produce up the country?'

'Why, that, I expect, is difficult to know.'

'I calculate you'll find the markets changeable these times?'

'No markets ben't very often without changing.'

'Why, that's right down true. What may be your biggest article of produce?'

'I calculate, generally, that's the biggest as I makes the most by.'   .

'You may say that. But what do you chiefly call your most particular
branch?'

'Why, that's what I can't justly say.'

And so they went on, without advancing or giving an inch, till I was weary of listening; but I left them still at it when I stepped out to resume my station on a trunk at the bow of the boat, where I scribbled in my notebook this specimen of Yankee conversation.

A METHODIST CAMP-MEETING IN OHIO

We reached the ground about an hour before midnight, and the approach to it was highly picturesque. The spot chosen was the verge of an unbroken forest, where a space of about twenty acres appeared to have been partially cleared for the purpose. Tents of different sizes were pitched very near together in a circle round the cleared space; behind them were ranged an exterior circle of carriages of every description, and at the back of each were fastened the horses which had drawn them thither. Through this triple circle of defence we distinguished numerous fires burning brightly within it; and still more numerous lights flickering from the trees that were left in the enclosure. The moon was in meridian splendour above our heads.

We left the carriage to the care of a servant, who was to prepare a bed in it for Mrs. B. and me, and entered the inner circle. The first glance reminded me of Vauxhall, from the effect of the lights among the trees and the moving crowd below them; but the second showed a scene totally unlike anything I had ever witnessed. Four high frames, constructed in the form of altars, were placed at the four corners of the enclosure; on these were supported layers of earth and sod, on which burned immense fires of blazing pine wood. On one side a rude platform was erected to accommodate the preachers, fifteen of whom attended this meeting, and with very short intervals for necessary refreshment and private devotion, preached in rotation, day and night, from Tuesday to Saturday. . .

At midnight a horn sounded through the camp, which, we were told, was to call the people from private to public worship; and we presently saw them flocking from all sides to the front of the preachers' stand. Mrs. B. and I contrived to place ourselves with our backs supported against the lower part of this structure, and we were thus enabled to witness the scene which followed, without personal danger. There were about two thousand persons assembled.

One of the preachers began in a low nasal tone, and, like all other Methodist preachers, assured us of the enormous depravity of man as he comes from the hands of his Maker, and of his perfect sanctification after he had wrestled sufficiently with the Lord to get hold of

him, et cetera. The admiration of the crowd was evinced by almost
constant cries of 'Amen! Amen!' 'Jesus! Jesus!' 'Glory! Glory!' and the
like. But this comparative tranquillity did not last long; the preacher
told them that 'this night was the time fixed upon for anxious sinners
to wrestle with the Lord'; that he and his brethren 'were at hand to
help them,' and that such as needed their help were to come forward
into 'the pen.' . . . 'The pen' was the space immediately below the
preachers' stand; we were therefore placed on the edge of it, and
were enabled to see and hear all that took place in the very centre
of this extraordinary exhibition.

The crowd fell back at the mention of the *pen,* and for some minutes
there was a vacant space before us. The preachers came down from
their stand and placed themselves in the midst of it, beginning to
sing a hymn, calling upon the penitents to come forth. As they sang
they kept turning themselves round to every part of the crowd, and,
by degrees, the voices of the whole multitude joined in chorus. This
was the only moment at which I perceived anything like the solemn
and beautiful effect which I had heard ascribed to this woodland worship. It is certain that the combined voices of such a multitude, heard
at dead of night, from the depths of their eternal forests, the many
fair young faces turned upward, and looking paler and lovelier as
they met the moonbeams, the dark figures of the officials in the middle
of the circle, the lurid glare thrown by the altar fires on the woods
beyond, did altogether produce a fine and solemn effect that I shall
not easily forget; but ere I had well enjoyed it, the scene changed,
and sublimity gave place to horror and disgust.

The exhortation nearly resembled that which I had heard at 'the
revival,' but the result was very different; for, instead of the few
hysterical women who had distinguished themselves on that occasion,
above a hundred persons, nearly all females, came forward, uttering
howlings and groans so terrible that I shall never cease to shudder
when I recall them. They appeared to drag each other forward, and
on the word being given, 'let us pray,' they all fell on their knees;
but this posture was soon changed for others that permitted greater
scope for the convulsive movements of their limbs; and they were
soon all lying on the ground in an indescribable confusion of heads
and legs. They threw about their limbs with such incessant and violent
motion that I was every instant expecting some serious accident to
occur.

But how am I to describe the sounds that proceeded from this strange
mass of human beings? I know no words that can convey an idea of
it. Hysterical sobbings, convulsive groans, shrieks and screams the

most appalling burst forth on all sides. I felt sick with horror. As if their hoarse and overstrained voices failed to make noise enough, they soon began to clap their hands violently. . .

Many of these wretched creatures were beautiful young females. The preachers moved about among them, at once exciting and sooth-ing their agonies. I heard the muttered 'Sister! dear sister!' I saw the insidious lips approach the cheeks of the unhappy girls; I heard the murmured confessions of the poor victims, and I watched their tor-mentors, breathing into their ears consolations that tinged the pale cheek with red. Had I been a man, I am sure I should have been guilty of some rash act of interference; nor do I believe that such a scene could have been acted in the presence of Englishmen without instant punishment being inflicted; not to mention the salutary punish-ment of the treadmill, which, beyond all question, would, in England, have been applied to check so turbulent and so vicious a scene.

After the first wild burst that followed their prostration, the moan-ings, in many instances, became loudly articulate; and I then experi-enced a strange vibration between tragic and comic feeling.

A very pretty girl, who was kneeling in the attitude of Canova's Magdalene immediately before us, amongst an immense quantity of jargon, broke out thus: 'Woe! woe to the backsliders! I hear it, hear it, Jesus! when I was fifteen my mother died, and I backslided, oh Jesus, I backslided! take me home to my mother, Jesus! take me home to her, for I am weary! Oh John Mitchel! John Mitchel!' and after sobbing piteously behind her raised hands, she lifted her sweet face again, which was as pale as death, and said, 'Shall I sit on the sunny bank of salvation with my mother? my own dear mother? oh Jesus, take me home, take me home!'

Who would refuse a tear to this earnest wish for death in one so young and so lovely? But I saw her, ere I left the ground, with her hand fast locked, and her head supported by a man who looked very much as Don Juan might, when sent back to earth as too bad for the regions below.

One woman near us continued to 'call on the Lord,' as it is termed, in the loudest possible tone, and without a moment's interval, for the two hours that we kept our dreadful station. She became frightfully hoarse, and her face so red as to make me expect she would burst a blood vessel. Among the rest of her rant, she said, 'I will hold fast to Jesus, I will never let him go; if they take me to hell, I will still hold him fast, fast, fast!'

The stunning noise was sometimes varied by the preachers begin-ning to sing; but the convulsive movements of the poor maniacs only became more violent. At length the atrocious wickedness of the horrible scene increased to a degree of grossness that drove us from our station; we returned to the carriage at about three o'clock in the morning, and passed the remainder of the night in listening to the ever increasing tumult at the pen. To sleep was impossible. At daybreak the horn again sounded to send them to private devotion; and in about an hour afterwards I saw the whole camp as joyously and eagerly devouring their most substantial breakfasts as if the night had been passed in dancing; and I marked many a fair but pàle face that I recognized as a demoniac of the night, simpering beside a swain, to whom she carefully administered hot coffee and eggs.

VIOLENCE IN AMERICAN LIFE

During the summer that we passed most delightfully in Maryland, our rambles were often restrained in various directions by the advice of our kind friends, who knew the manners and morals of the country. When we asked the cause, we were told, 'There is a public house on that road, and it will not be safe to pass it.'

The line of the Chesapeake and Ohio Canal passed within a few miles of Mrs. S——'s residence. It twice happened during our stay with her, that dead bodies were found partially concealed near it. The circumstance was related as a sort of half-hour's wonder; and when I asked particulars of those who, on one occasion, brought the tale, the reply was, 'Oh, he was murdered, I expect; or maybe he died of the canal fever; but they say he had marks of being throttled.' No inquest was summoned; and certainly no more sensation was produced by the occurrence than if a sheep had been found in the same predicament.

The abundance of food and the scarcity of hanging were also favourite topics, as proving their superiority to England. They are both excellent things, but I do not admit the inference. A wide and most fertile territory, as yet but thinly inhabited, may easily be made to yield abundant food for its population: and where a desperate villain knows that he has made his town or village 'too hot to hold him,' he has nothing to do but to travel a few miles west, and be sure of finding plenty of beef and whiskey, with no danger that the law shall follow him, it is not extraordinary that executions should be rare.

Once during our residence at Cincinnati, a murderer of uncommon atrocity was taken, tried, convicted, and condemned to death. It had been shown on his trial that some years before he had murdered a wife and child at New Orleans, but little notice of it had been taken at the time. The crime which had now thrown him into the hands of justice was the recent murder of a second wife, and the chief evidence against him was his own son.

The day of his execution was fixed, and the sensation produced was so great from the strangeness of the occurrence (no white man having ever been executed at Cincinnati) that persons from sixty miles' distance came to be present at it.

Meanwhile some unco' guid people began to start doubts as to the righteousness of hanging a man, and made application to the Governor of the State of Ohio, to commute the sentence into imprisonment. The Governor for some time refused to interfere with the sentence of the tribunal before which he had been tried; but at length, frightened at the unusual situation in which he found himself, he yielded to the importunity of the Presbyterian party who had assailed him, and sent off an order to the sheriff accordingly. But this order was not to reprieve him but to ask him if he pleased to be reprieved, and sent to the penitentiary instead of being hanged.

The sheriff waited upon the criminal, and made his proposal, and was answered, 'If anything could make me agree to it, it would be the hope of living long enough to kill you and my dog of a son; however, I won't agree; you shall have the hanging of me.'

The worthy sheriff, to whom the ghastly office of executioner is assigned, said all in his power to persuade him to sign the offered document, but in vain; he obtained nothing but abuse for his efforts.

The day of execution arrived; the place appointed was the side of a hill, the only one cleared of trees near the town; and many hours before the time fixed, we saw it entirely covered by an immense multitude of men, women, and children. At length the hour arrived, the dismal cart was seen slowly mounting the hill, the noisy throng was hushed into solemn silence; the wretched criminal mounted the scaffold, when again the sheriff asked him to sign his acceptance of the commutation proposed; but he spurned the paper from him, and cried aloud, 'Hang me!'

Midday was the moment appointed for cutting the rope; the sheriff stood, his watch in one hand, and a knife in the other; the hand was lifted to strike, when the criminal stoutly exclaimed, 'I sign'; and he was conveyed back to prison, amidst the shouts, laughter, and ribaldry of the mob.

I am not fond of hanging, but there was something in all this that did not look like the decent dignity of wholesome justice.

HOME LIFE IN PHILADELPHIA

Let me be permitted to describe the day of a Philadelphia lady of the first class. . .

This lady shall be the wife of a senator and a lawyer in the highest repute and practise. She has a very handsome house, with white marble steps and door posts, and a delicate silver knocker and door handle; she has a very handsome drawing room (very handsomely furnished, there is a sideboard in one of them, but it is very handsome, and has handsome decanters and cut glass water jugs upon it); she has a very handsome carriage, and a very handsome free black coachman; she is always very handsomely dressed; and, moreover, she is very handsome herself.

She rises, and her first hour is spent in the scrupulously nice arrangement of her dress; she descends to her parlour neat, stiff, and silent; her breakfast is brought in by her free black footman; she eats her fried ham and her salt fish, and drinks her coffee in silence, while her husband reads one newspaper, and puts another under his elbow; and then, perhaps, she washes the cups and saucers. Her carriage is ordered at eleven; till that hour she is employed in the pastry room, her snow-white apron protecting her mouse-colored silk. Twenty minutes before her carriage should appear, she retires to her chamber, as she calls it, shakes, and folds up her still snow-white apron, smoothes her rich dress, and with nice care sets on her elegant bonnet, and all the handsome et cetera; then walks down stairs, just at the moment that her free black coachman announces to her free black footman that the carriage waits. She steps into it, and gives the word, 'Drive to the Dorcas Society.' Her footman stays at home to clean the knives, but her coachman can trust his horses while he opens the carriage door, and his lady not being accustomed to a hand or an arm, gets out very safely without, though one of her own is occupied by a work basket, and the other by a large roll of all those indescribable matters which ladies take as offerings to Dorcas Societies. She enters the parlour appropriated for the meeting, and finds seven other ladies, very like herself, and takes her place among them; she presents her contribution, which is accepted with a gentle circular smile, and her parings of broadcloth, her ends of ribbon, her gilt paper, and her minikin pins are added to the parings of broadcloth, the ends of ribbon, the gilt paper, and the minikin pins with which the table is already covered; she also produces from her basket three ready-made pincushions, four ink wipers, seven paper matches, and a pasteboard watch case; these are welcomed with acclamations, and the youngest lady present deposits them carefully on shelves, amid a prodigious quantity of similar articles. She then produces her thimble, and asks for work; it is presented to her, and the eight ladies all stitch together for some hours. Their talk is of priests and of missions; of the profits of their last sale, of their hopes from the next; of the doubt whether young Mr. This or young Mr. That should receive the fruits of it to fit him out for Liberia; of the very ugly bonnet seen at church on Sabbath morning, of the very handsome preacher who performed on Sabbath afternoon, and of the very large collection made on Sabbath evening. This lasts till three, when the carriage again appears, and the lady and her basket return home; she mounts to her chamber, carefully sets aside her bonnet and its appurtenances, puts on her scalloped black silk apron, walks into the kitchen to see that all is right, then into the parlour, where, having cast a careful glance over the table prepared for dinner, she sits down, work in hand, to await her spouse. He comes, shakes hands with her, spits, and dines. The conversation is not much, and ten minutes suffices for the dinner; fruit and toddy, the newspaper and the work bag succeed. In the evening the gentleman, being a savant, goes to the Wister Society, and afterwards plays a snug rubber at a neighbor's. The lady receives at tea a young missionary and three members of the Dorcas Society. And so ends her day.

For some reason or other, which English people are not very likely to understand, a great number of young married persons board by the year, instead of 'going to housekeeping,' as they call having an establishment of their own. Of course, this statement does not include persons of large fortune, but it does include very many whose rank in society would make such a mode of life quite impossible with us. I can hardly imagine a contrivance more effectual for ensuring the insignificance of a woman than marrying her at seventeen, and placing her in a boarding house. Nor can I easily imagine a life of more uniform dulness for the lady herself; but this certainly is a matter of taste. I have heard many ladies declare that it is 'just quite the perfection of comfort to have nothing to fix for oneself.' Yet despite these assurances, I always experienced a feeling which hovered between pity and contempt when I contemplated their mode of existence.

How would a newly married Englishwoman endure it, her head and her heart full of the one dear scheme—

'Well-ordered home, *his* dear delight to make'?

She must rise exactly in time to reach the boarding-table at the hour appointed for breakfast, or she will get a stiff bow from the lady president, cold coffee, and no egg. I have sometimes been greatly amused upon these occasions by watching a little scene in which the by-play had much more meaning than the words uttered. The fasting but tardy lady looks round the table, and having ascertained that there was no egg left, says distinctly, 'I will take an egg, if you please.' But as this is addressed to no one in particular, no one in particular answers it, unless it happens that her husband is at table before her, and then he says, 'There are no eggs, my dear.' Whereupon the lady president evidently cannot hear, and the greedy culprit who has swallowed two eggs (for there are always as many eggs as noses) looks pretty considerably afraid of being found out. The breakfast proceeds in sombre silence, save that sometimes a parrot, and sometimes a canary bird ventures to utter a timid note. When it is finished, the gentlemen hurry to their occupations, and the quiet ladies mount the stairs, some to the first, some to the second, and some to the third stories, in an inverse proportion to the number of dollars paid, and ensconce themselves in their respective chambers. As to what they do there it is not very easy to say; but I believe they clear starch a little, and iron a little, and sit in a rocking chair, and sew a great deal. I always observed that the ladies who boarded wore more elaborately worked collars and petticoats than anyone else. The plough is hardly a more blessed instrument in America than the needle. How could they live without it? But time and the needle wear through the longest morning, and happily the American morning is not very long, even though they breakfast at eight.

It is generally about two o'clock that the boarding gentlemen meet the boarding ladies at dinner. Little is spoken, except a whisper between the married pairs. Sometimes a sulky bottle of wine flanks the plate of one or two individuals, but it adds nothing to the mirth of the meeting, and seldom more than one glass to the good cheer of the owners. It is not then, and it is not there, that the gentlemen of the Union drink. Soon, very soon, the silent meal is done, and then, if you mount the stairs after them, you will find from the doors of the more affectionate and indulgent wives a smell of cigars steam forth, which plainly indicates the felicity of the couple within. If the gentleman be a very polite husband, he will, as soon as he has done smoking and drinking his toddy, offer his arm to his wife as far as the corner of the street, where his store or his office is situated, and there he will leave her to turn which way she likes. As this is the hour for being full dressed, of course she turns the way she can be most seen. Perhaps she pays a few visits; perhaps she goes to chapel; or, perhaps, she enters some store where her husband deals, and ventures to order a few notions; and then she goes home again—no, not home—I will not give that name to a boarding house, but she re-enters the cold heartless atmosphere in which she dwells, where hospitality can never enter, and where interest takes the management instead of affection. At tea they all meet again, and a little trickery is perceptible to the nice observer in the manner of partaking the pound cake, et cetera. After this, those who are happy enough to have engagements hasten to keep them; those who have not either mount again to the solitude of their chamber, or, what appeared to me much worse, remain in the common sitting room, in a society cemented by no tie, endeared by no connexion, which choice did not bring together, and which the slightest motive would break asunder. I remarked that the gentlemen were generally obliged to go out every evening on business, and, I confess, the arrangement did not surprise me.

It is not thus that the women can obtain that influence in society which is allowed to them in Europe, and to which both sages and men of the world have agreed in ascribing such salutary effects. It is in vain that 'collegiate institutes' are formed for young ladies, or that 'academic degrees' are conferred upon them. It is after marriage, and when these young attempts upon all the sciences are forgotten that the lamentable insignificance of the American woman appears; and till this be remedied, I venture to prophesy that the tone of their drawing rooms will not improve.

. . .

COOKING, AMUSEMENTS, AND MONEY-GETTING

In relating all I know of America, I surely must not omit so important a feature as the cooking. There are sundry anomalies in the mode of serving even a first-rate table; but as these are altogether matters of custom, they by no means indicate either indifference or neglect in this important business; and whether castors are placed on the table or on the sideboard; whether soup, fish, patties, and salad be eaten in orthodox order or not, signifies but little. I am hardly capable, I fear, of giving a very erudite critique on the subject; general observations, therefore, must suffice. The ordinary mode of living is abundant, but not delicate. They consume an extraordinary quantity of bacon. Ham and beef-steaks appear morning, noon, and night. In eating, they mix things together with the strangest incongruity imaginable. I have seen eggs and oysters eaten together; the sempiternal ham with applesauce; beef-steak with stewed peaches; and salt fish with onions. The bread is everywhere excellent, but they rarely enjoy it themselves, as they insist upon eating horrible half-baked hot rolls both morning and evening. The butter is tolerable, but they have seldom such cream as every little dairy produces in England; in fact, the cows are very roughly kept, compared with ours. Common vegetables are abundant and very fine. I never saw sea cale or cauliflowers, and either from the want of summer rain or the want of care, the harvest of green vegetables is much sooner over than with us. They eat the Indian corn in a great variety of forms; sometimes it is dressed green, and eaten like peas; sometimes it is broken to pieces when dry, boiled plain, and brought to table like rice; this dish is called hominy. The flour of it is made into at least a dozen different sorts of cakes; but in my opinion all bad. This flour, mixed in the proportion of one-third with fine wheat, makes by far the best bread I ever tasted.

I never saw turbot, salmon, or fresh cod; but the rock and shad are excellent. There is a great want of skill in the composition of sauces; not only with fish but with everything. They use very few made dishes, and I never saw any that would be approved by our savants. They have an excellent wild duck, called the Canvas Back, which, if delicately served, would surpass the black cock; but the game is very inferior to ours; they have no hares, and I never saw a pheasant. They seldom indulge in second courses, with all their ingenious temptations to the eating a second dinner; but almost every table has its dessert (invariably pronounced desart), which is placed on the table before the cloth is removed, and consists of pastry, preserved fruits, and creams. They are 'extravagantly fond,' to use their own phrase, of puddings, pies, and all kinds of 'sweets,' particularly the ladies; but are by no means such connoisseurs in soups and ragouts as the gastronomes of Europe. Almost every one drinks water at table, and by a strange contradiction, in the country where hard drinking is more prevalent than in any other, there is less wine taken at dinner; ladies rarely exceed one glass, and the majority of females never take any. In fact, the hard drinking, so universally acknowledged, does not take place at jovial dinners, but, to speak plain English, in solitary dram-drinking. Coffee is not served immediately after dinner, but makes part of the serious matter of tea-drinking, which comes some hours later. Mixed dinner parties to ladies and gentlemen are very rare, and unless several foreigners are present, little conversation passes at table. It certainly does not, in my opinion, add to the well-ordering a dinner table to set the gentlemen at one end of it, and the ladies at the other; but it is very rarely that you find it otherwise.

Their large evening parties are supremely dull; the men sometimes play cards by themselves, but if a lady plays, it must not be for money; no ecarté, no chess; very little music, and that little lamentably bad. Among the blacks I heard some good voices, singing in tune; but I scarcely ever heard a white American, male or female, go through an air without being out of tune before the end of it; nor did I ever meet any trace of science in the singing I heard in society. To eat inconceivable quantities of cake, ice, and pickled oysters—and to show half their revenue in silks and satins seem to be the chief objects they have in these parties.

The most agreeable meetings, I was assured by all the young people, were those to which no married women are admitted; of the truth of this statement I have not the least doubt. These exclusive meetings occur frequently, and often last to a late hour; on these occasions, I believe, they generally dance. At regular balls married ladies are admitted, but seldom take much part in the amusement. The refreshments are always profuse and costly, but taken in a most uncomfortable manner. I have known many private balls . . . where the gentlemen sat down to supper in one room, while the ladies took theirs, standing, in another.

What we call picnics are very rare, and when attempted, do not often succeed well. The two sexes can hardly mix for the greater part of a day without great restraint and ennui; it is quite contrary to their general habits; the favourite indulgence of the gentlemen (smoking cigars and drinking spirits) can neither be indulged in with decency nor resigned with complacency.

The ladies have strange ways of adding to their charms. They powder themselves immoderately, face, neck, and arms, with pulverized starch; the effect is indescribably disagreeable by daylight, and not very favourable at any time. They are also most unhappily partial to false hair, which they wear in surprising quantities; this is the more to be lamented, as they generally have very fine hair of their own. I suspect this fashion to arise from an indolent mode of making their toilet, and from accomplished ladies' maids not being very abundant; it is less trouble to append a bunch of waving curls here, there, and everywhere, than to keep their native tresses in perfect order.

Though the expense of the ladies' dress greatly exceeds, in proportion to their general style of living, that of the ladies of Europe, it is very far (excepting in Philadelphia) from being in good taste. They do not consult the seasons in the colours or in the style of their costume; I have often shivered at seeing a young beauty picking her way through the snow with a pale rose-coloured bonnet, set on the very top of her head; I knew one young lady whose pretty little ear was actually frost-bitten from being thus exposed. They never wear muffs or boots, and appear extremely shocked at the sight of comfortable walking shoes and cotton stockings, even when they have to step to their sleighs over ice and snow. They walk in the middle of winter with their poor little toes pinched into a miniature slipper, incapable of exploding as much moisture as might bedew a primrose. I must say in their excuse, however, that they have, almost universally, extremely pretty feet. They do not walk well, nor, in fact, do they ever appear to advantage when in movement. I know not why this should be, for they have abundance of French dancing-masters among them, but somehow or other it is the fact. I fancied I could often trace a mixture of affectation and of shyness in their little mincing unsteady step, and the ever-changing position of the hands. They do not dance well; perhaps I should rather say they do not look well when dancing; lovely as their faces are, they cannot, in a position that exhibits the whole person, atone for the want of tournure, and for the universal defect in the formation of the bust, which is rarely full or gracefully formed.

I never saw an American man walk or stand well; notwithstanding their frequent militia drilling, they are nearly all hollow chested and round shouldered; perhaps this is occasioned by no officer daring to say to a brother free-born 'hold up your head'; whatever the cause, the effect is very remarkable to a stranger. In stature and in physiognomy a great majority of the population, both male and female, are strikingly handsome, but they know not how to do their own honours; half as much comeliness elsewhere would produce ten times as much effect.

Nothing can exceed their activity and perseverance in all kinds of speculation, handicraft, and enterprise which promises a profitable pecuniary result. I heard an Englishman, who had been long resident in America, declare that in following, in meeting, or in overtaking, in the street, on the road, or in the field, at the theatre, the coffee-house, or the home, he had never overheard Americans conversing without the word DOLLAR being pronounced between them. Such unity of purpose, such sympathy of feeling, can, I believe, be found nowhere else, except, perhaps, in an ants' nest. The result is exactly what might be anticipated. This sordid object, forever before their eyes, must inevitably produce a sordid tone of mind, and, worse still, it produces a seared and blunted conscience on all questions of probity. I know not a more striking evidence of the low tone of morality which is generated by this universal pursuit of money than the manner in which the New England States are described by Americans. All agree in saying that they present a spectacle of industry and prosperity delightful to behold, and this is the district and the population most constantly quoted as the finest specimen of their admirable country; yet I never met a single individual in any part of the Union who did not paint these New Englanders as sly, grinding, selfish, and tricking. The Yankees (as the New Englanders are called) will avow these qualities themselves with a complacent smile, and boast that no people on the earth can

match them at over-reaching in a bargain. I have heard them unblush-
ingly relate stories of their cronies and friends, which, if believed
among us, would banish the heroes from the fellowship of honest men
forever; and all this is uttered with a simplicity which sometimes led
me to doubt if the speakers knew what honour and honesty meant.
Yet the Americans declare that 'they are the most moral people upon
earth.' Again and again I have heard this asserted, not only in conversation and by their writings, but even from the pulpit. Such broad
assumption of superior virtue demands examination, and after four
years of attentive and earnest observation and inquiry, my honest conviction is that the standard of moral character in the United States
is very greatly lower than in Europe. Of their religion, as it appears
outwardly, I have had occasion to speak frequently; I pretend not to
judge the heart, but, without any uncharitable presumption, I must
take permission to say that both Protestant England and Catholic
France show an infinitely superior religious and moral aspect to mortal
observation, both as to reverend decency of external observance, and
as to the inward fruit of honest dealing between man and man.

In other respects, I think no one will be disappointed who visits the
country expecting to find no more than common sense might teach him
to look for, namely, a vast continent, by far the greater part of which
is still in the state in which nature left it, and a busy, bustling, industrious population, hacking and hewing their way through it. What
greatly increases the interest of this spectacle is the wonderful facility
for internal commerce, furnished by the rivers, lakes, and canals, which
thread the country in every direction, producing a rapidity of progress
in all commercial and agricultural speculation altogether unequalled.

AMERICAN BOASTFULNESS

On the subject of national glory, I presume I got more than my
share of buffeting; for being a woman, there was no objection to their
speaking out. One lady, indeed, who was a great patriot, evinced much
delicacy towards me, for upon someone speaking of New Orleans, she
interrupted them, saying, 'I wish you would not talk of New Orleans;'
and turning to me, added with great gentleness, 'It must be so painful
to your feelings to hear that place mentioned!'

The immense superiority of the American to the British navy was a
constant theme, and to this I always listened, as nearly as possible, in
silence. I repeatedly heard it stated (so often, indeed, and from such
various quarters, that I think there must be some truth in it), that the
American sailors fire with a certainty of slaughter, whereas our shots

are sent very nearly at random. 'This,' said a naval officer of high reputation, 'is the blessed effect of your game laws; your sailors never fire
at a mark; whilst our free tars, from their practise in pursuit of game,
can any of them split a hair.' But the favourite, the constant, the universal sneer that met me everywhere was on our old-fashioned attachments to things obsolete. Had they a little wit among them, I am
certain they would have given us the cognomen of 'My Grandmother,
the British,' for that is the tone they take, and it is thus they reconcile
themselves to the crude newness of everything around them.

'I wonder you are not sick of kings, chancellors, and archbishops,
and all your fustian of wigs and gowns,' said a very clever gentleman
to me once, with an affected yawn; 'I protest the very sound almost
sets me to sleep.'

It is amusing to observe how soothing the idea seems that they are
more modern, more advanced than England. Our classic literature, our
princely dignities, our noble institutions, are all bygone relics of the
dark ages. . .

I was once sitting with a party of ladies, among whom were one
or two young girls whose curiosity was greater than their patriotism,
and they asked me many questions respecting the splendour and extent of London. I was endeavouring to satisfy them by the best description I could give, when we were interrupted by another lady,
who exclaimed, 'Do hold your tongues, girls, about London; if you
want to know what a beautiful city is, look at Philadelphia; when Mrs.
Trollope has been there, I think she will allow that it is better worth
talking about than that great overgrown collection of nasty, filthy,
dirty streets, that they call London.'

Once in Ohio, and once in the District of Columbia, I had an atlas
displayed before me, that I might be convinced by the evidence of my
own eyes what a very contemptible little country I came from. I shall
never forget the gravity with which, on the latter occasion, a gentleman . . . showed me, past contradiction, that the whole of the British
dominions did not equal in size one of their least important states; nor
the air with which, after the demonstration, he placed his feet upon
the chimney-piece, considerably higher than his head, and whistled
'Yankee Doodle.'

Washington in Jackson's Day;
Southern Slavery [1] 🦢

HARRIET MARTINEAU, *one of the most versatile and energetic of all women publicists, was born in 1802 in Norwich, England, the daughter of a cloth manufacturer. After a sickly childhood, she was thrown midway in her twenties upon her own resources. Her elder brother, father, and fiancé successively died, and she and her sisters lost all their money in the failure of the business in which it was invested. Her deafness was marked, and closed the profession of teaching to her; but she had already contributed to a Unitarian periodical. She at once commenced that career of authorship, which endured until her death in 1876, and which was truly amazing in its copiousness and industry. Though frail of body and frequently ill, she never seemed tired. After a hard day's work with the needle, for at first she made sure of her bread in that way, she would write until two or three o'clock in the morning, and yet be at the breakfast table at eight. Her first stories and essays were religious in character, and some of them were widely circulated in England and France. But she achieved a larger success when, after studying Adam Smith and other economists, she conceived the idea of a series of tales to illustrate the principles of political economy for the minds of the masses. The great London publishers rejected her proposal, but she finally found one who drove a hard bargain with her, and brought out the first tales. The demand at once ran high into the thousands. Lord Brougham said that it made him tear his hair to think that the Society for the Diffusion of Knowledge, which he had founded for this very purpose, had not a single man capable of doing what this little deaf girl from Norwich had done.*

Upon completing this work, and a supplemental series on taxation, which fully established her fame, Miss Martineau in 1834 visited America and made a tour lasting more than two years. Most educated Americans were acquainted with her writings. They took a keen interest in meeting her—a young woman of more than middle height, slender figure, and a face whose broad forehead and strong chin showed her vigor of mind and will. She was at first hospitably received wherever

[1] From *A Retrospect of Western Travel*, London, 1838, volume I, chapters 12 and 13; and *Society in America*, London, 1839, part II, chapter 5.

she went, her travels extending as far west as Mackinac and Chicago, and as far south as New Orleans. Among the enduring friendships she made at this time were those with Emerson and William Lloyd Garrison. But later, after she had made a public avowal of her antislavery sentiments at an Abolitionist mass meeting in Boston, she encountered much prejudice, and many slights and insults. The Southern press denounced her as a dangerous incendiary, and she was even constrained to abandon an intended trip down the Ohio River.

When she returned to England, Miss Martineau was besieged with offers from the London publishers for her impressions of America, and for her two works of three volumes each, Society in America, *and* A Retrospect of Western Travel, *she received a total of £1500. Her plan in the former was to present a systematic scrutiny of the American application of the principles laid down in the Constitution and the Declaration of Independence, and it is rather heavily philosophical and decidedly awkward in arrangement. The second records in much more interesting fashion the incidents of travel, impressions of distinguished persons, and descriptions of people and places. Both works, in spite of some glaring errors, were appreciatively received in America.*

LIFE AT THE CAPITAL IN 1835

WE arrived at Washington on the 13th of January 1835, the year of the short session of Congress, which closes on the 4th of March, so that we continued to see the proceedings of Congress at its busiest and most interesting time.

The approach to the city is striking to all strangers from its oddness. I saw the dome of the Capitol from a considerable distance at the end of a straight road; but, though I was prepared by the descriptions of preceding travellers, I was taken by surprise on finding myself beneath the splendid building, so sordid are the enclosure and houses on its very verge. We went round its base, and entered Pennsylvania Avenue, the only one of the grand avenues intended to centre in the Capitol which has been built up with any completeness. Our boarding house was admirably situated, being some little way down this avenue, a few minutes' walk only from the Capitol, and a mile in a straight line from the White House, the residences of the heads of departments, and the British Legation.

In Philadelphia I had found perpetual difficulty in remembering that I was in a foreign country. The pronounciation of a few words by our host and hostess, the dinner table, and the inquiries of visitors were almost all that occurred to remind me that I was not in a brother's house. At Washington it was very different. The city itself is unlike any other that ever was seen, straggling out hither and thither, with a small house or two a quarter of a mile from any other; so that in making calls 'in the city,' we had to cross ditches and stiles, and walk alternately on grass and pavements, and strike across a field to reach a street. Then the weather was so strange; sometimes so cold that the only way I could get any comfort was by stretching on the sofa drawn before the fire up to the very fender (on which days every person who went in and out of the house was sure to leave the front door wide open); then the next morning, perhaps, if we went out muffled in furs, we had to turn back and exchange our wraps for a light shawl. Then we were waited upon by a slave appointed for the exclusive service of our party during our stay. Then there were canvas-back ducks, and all manner of other ducks on the table, in greater profusion than any single article of food, except turkeys, that I ever saw. Then there was the society, singularly compounded from the largest variety of elements: foreign ambassadors, the American Government, members of Congress, from Clay and Webster down to Davy Crockett, Benton from Missouri, and Cuthbert, with the freshest Irish brogue, from Georgia; flippant young belles, 'pious' wives dutifully attending their husbands, and groaning over the frivolities of the place; grave judges, saucy travellers, pert newspaper reporters, melancholy Indian chiefs, and timid New England ladies, trembling on the verge of the vortex; all this was wholly unlike anything that is to be seen in any other city in the world; for all these are mixed up together in daily intercourse like the higher circle of a little village, and there is nothing else. You have this or nothing; you pass your days among these people, or you spend them alone. It is in Washington that varieties of manners are conspicuous. There the Southerners appear to the most advantage, and the New Englanders to the least; the ease and frank courtesy of the gentry of the South (with an occasional touch of arrogance, however), contrasting favourably with the cautious, somewhat *gauche,* and too deferential air of the members from the North. One fancies one can tell a New England member in the open air by his deprecatory walk. He seems to bear in mind perpetually that he cannot fight a duel, while other people can. The odd mortals that wander in from the western border cannot be described as a class, for no one is like anybody else. One has a neck like a crane, making an interval of inches between stock and chin. Another wears no cravat, apparently because there is no room for one. A third has his lank black hair parted accurately down the middle, and disposed in bands in front, so that he is taken for a woman when only the head is seen in a crowd. A fourth puts an arm round the neck of a neighbor on either side as he stands, seeming afraid of his tall wire-hung frame dropping to pieces if he tries to stand alone; a fifth makes something between a bow and a courtesy to everybody who comes near, and poses with a knowing air; all having shrewd faces, and being probably very fit for the business they came upon.

Our way of life was so diversified that it is difficult to give an account of our day; the only way in which one day resembled another being that none had any privacy. We breakfasted about nine, surrounded by the heaps of newspapers, documents, and letters, which the post and newsmen brought to the parliamentary members of our party. We amused ourselves with the different versions given by the *Globe* and the *Intelligencer*—the administration and opposition papers—to speeches and proceedings at which we had been present the day before; and were kindly made acquainted by our representative friend with the nature of much of his business, the petitions he had to present, the dilemmas in which he was placed by his constituents of different parties, and his hopes and fears about favourite measures in progress. The senator happened, from a peculiar set of circumstances, to be an idle man just now. He taught me many things, and rallied me on my asking him so few questions, while, in fact, my head was already so much too full with what was flowing in upon me from all sides that I longed for nothing so much as to go to sleep for a week. This gentleman's peculiar and not very agreeable position arose out of the troublesome question of Instructions to Representatives. Senators are chosen for a term of six years, one-third of the body going out every two years; the term being made thus long in order to ensure some stability of policy in the Senate. If the government of the state from which the senator is sent changes its politics during his term, he may be annoyed by instructions to vote contrary to his principles, and, if he refuses, by a call to resign, on the ground of his representing the opinions of the minority. This had been the predicament of our companion; and the question of resigning or not under such circumstances had become generally a very important and interesting one, but one which there was no means of settling. Each member in such a scrape must act as his own judgment and conscience dictate under the circumstances of the peculiar case. Our companion made a mistake. When the attempt to instruct him was made, he said he appealed from the new legislature of his state to the people who chose him. He did appeal by standing for the office of governor of the state, and was defeated. No course then remained but resigning, which he did immediately, when his senatorial term was within half a session of its close. He had withdrawn from the Senate Chamber, and was winding up his political affairs at the time when we joined his party.

At a little before eleven we usually set out for the Capitol, and passed the morning either in the Senate Chamber or the Supreme Court, unless it was necessary to make calls, or to sit to the artist who was painting my portrait, or to join a party on some excursion in the neighbourhood. We avoided spending the morning at home when we could, as it was sure to be entirely consumed with callers, and we became too much exhausted before the fatigues of the evening began. Much amusement was picked up in the artist's apartment in the Capitol; members and strangers dropped in, and the news of the hour circulated; but the Senate Chamber was our favourite resort. We returned home to dinner some time between four and six, and the cloth was seldom removed before visitors entered. The stream continued to flow in during the whole evening, unless we were all going out together. We disappeared, one by one, to dress for some ball, rout, levée, or masquerade, and went out, more or less willingly, according as we left behind us visitors more or less pleasant. The half hour round our drawing-room fire after our return was the pleasantest time of the day, weary as we were. Then our foreigners' perplexities were explained for us; we compared impressions, and made common property of what had amused us individually; and, in some sort, set our overcharged minds in order before we retired to rest.

Our pleasantest evenings were some spent at home in a society of the highest order. Ladies, literary, fashionable, or domestic, would spend an hour with us on their way from a dinner or to a ball. Members of Congress would repose themselves by our fireside. Mr. Clay, sitting upright on the sofa, with his snuffbox ever in his hand, would discourse for many an hour in his even, soft, deliberate tone on any one of the great subjects of American policy which we might happen to start, always amazing us with the moderation of estimate and speech which so impetuous a nature has been able to attain. Mr. Webster, leaning back at his ease, telling stories, cracking jokes, shaking the sofa with burst after burst of laughter, or smoothly discoursing to the perfect felicity of the logical part of one's constitution, would illuminate an evening now and then. Mr. Calhoun, the cast-iron man, who looks as if he had never been born and never could be extinguished, would come in sometimes to keep our understandings upon a painful stretch for a short while, and leave us to take to pieces his close, rapid, theoretical, illustrated talk, and see what we could make of it. We found it usually more worth retaining as a curiosity than as either very just or useful. His speech abounds in figures, truly illustrative, if that which they illustrate were but true also. But his theories of government (almost the only subject on which his thoughts are employed), the squarest and compactest that ever were made, are composed out of

limited elements, and are not, therefore, likely to stand service very
well. It is at first extremely interesting to hear Mr. Calhoun talk; and
there is a never-failing evidence of power in all he says and does which
commands intellectual reverence; but the admiration is too soon turned
into regret, into absolute melancholy. It is impossible to resist the conviction that all this force can be at best but useless, and is but too
likely to be very mischievous. His mind has long lost all power of
communicating with any other. I know of no man who lives in such
utter intellectual solitude. He meets men, and harangues them by the
fireside as in the Senate; he is wrought like a piece of machinery, set
agoing vehemently by a weight, and stops while you answer; he either
passes by what you say or twists it into a suitability with what is in
his head, and begins to lecture again. Of course, a mind like this can
have little influence in the Senate, except by virtue, perpetually wearing
out, of what it did in its less eccentric days; but its influence at home
is to be dreaded. There is no hope that an intellect so cast in narrow
theories will accommodate itself to varying circumstances; and there
is every danger that it will break up all that it can, in order to remould
the materials in its own way. Mr. Calhoun is as full as ever of his nullification doctrines; and those who know the force that is in him, and
his utter incapacity of modification by other minds (after having gone
through as remarkable a revolution of political opinions as perhaps any
man ever experienced), will no more expect repose and self-retention
from him than from a volcano in full force. Relaxation is no longer
in the power of his will. I never saw anyone who so completely gave
me the idea of possession. Half an hour's conversation with him is
enough to make a necessarian of anybody. Accordingly, he is more
complained of than blamed by his enemies. His moments of softness
in his family, and when recurring to old college days, are hailed by
all as a relief to the vehement working of the intellectual machine; a
relief equally to himself and others. Those moments are as touching
to the observer as tears on the face of a soldier.

One incident befell during my stay, which moved everybody. A
representative from South Carolina was ill, a friend of Mr. Calhoun's;
and Mr. Calhoun parted from us one day, on leaving the Capitol, to
visit this sick gentleman. The physician told Mr. Calhoun on his
entrance that his friend was dying, and could not live more than a very
few hours. A visitor, not knowing this, asked the sick man how he was.
'To judge by my own feelings,' said he, 'much better; but by the
countenances of my friends, not.' And he begged to be told the truth.
On hearing it, he instantly beckoned Mr. Calhoun to him, and said,
'I hear they are giving you rough treatment in the Senate. Let a dying
friend implore you to guard your looks and words so as that no undue

warmth may make you appear unworthy of your principles.' 'This was friendship, strong friendship,' said Mr. Calhoun to me and to many others; and it had its due effect upon him. A few days after, Colonel Benton, a fantastic senator from Missouri, interrupted Mr. Calhoun in a speech for the purpose of making an attack upon him, which would have been insufferable if it had not been too absurdly worded to be easily made anything of. He was called to order; this was objected to; the Senate divided upon the point of order, being dissatisfied with the decision of the chair; in short, Mr. Calhoun sat for two full hours hearing his veracity talked about before his speech could proceed. He sat in stern patience, scarcely moving a muscle the whole time; and, when it was all settled in his favour, merely observed that his friends need not fear his being disturbed by an attack of this nature from such a quarter, and resumed his speech at the precise point where his argument had been broken off. It was great, and would have satisfied the 'strong friendship' of his departed comrade if he could have been there to see it.

Our active-minded, genial friend, Judge Story,[2] found time to visit us frequently, though he is one of the busiest men in the world, writing half a dozen great law books every year; having his full share of the business of the Supreme Court upon his hands; his professorship to attend to; the District Courts at home in Massachusetts, and a correspondence which spreads half over the world. His talk would gush out for hours, and there was never too much of it for us; it is so heartfelt, so lively, so various; and his face all the while, notwithstanding his gray hair, showing all the mobility and ingenuousness of a child's. There is no tolerable portrait of Judge Story, and there never will be. I should like to bring him face to face with a person who entertains the common English idea of how an American looks and behaves. I should like to see what such a one would make of the quick smiles, the glistening eye, the gleeful tone, with passing touches of sentiment; the innocent self-complacency, the confiding, devoted affections of the great American lawyer. The preconception would be totally at fault.

With Judge Story sometimes came the man to whom he looked up with feelings little short of adoration—the aged Chief Justice Marshall. There was almost too much mutual respect in our first meeting; we knew something of his individual merits and services; and he maintained through life and carried to his grave a reverence for woman as rare in its kind as in its degree. It had all the theoretical fervour and magnificence of Uncle Toby's, with the advantage of being grounded upon an extensive knowledge of the sex. He was the father and the

---

[2] Judge Joseph Story, 1779-1845, was at this time a Justice of the Federal Supreme Court and Dane Professor in the Harvard Law School.

grandfather of women; and out of this experience he brought not only the love and pity which their offices and position command, and the awe of purity which they excite in the minds of the pure, but a steady conviction of their intellectual equality with men; and, with this, a deep sense of their social injuries. Throughout life he so invariably sustained their cause that no indulgent libertine dared to flatter and humour; no skeptic, secure in the possession of power, dared to scoff at the claims of woman in the presence of Marshall, who, made clear-sighted by his purity, knew the sex far better than either.

How delighted we were to see Judge Story bring in the tall, majestic, bright-eyed old man; old by chronology, by the lines on his composed face, and by his services to the republic; but so dignified, so fresh, so present to the time that no feeling of compassionate consideration for age dared to mix with the contemplation of him. The first evening he asked me much about English politics, and especially whether the people were not fast ripening for the abolition of our religious establishment; an institution which, after a long study of it, he considered so monstrous in principle and so injurious to true religion in practise that he could not imagine that it could be upheld for anything but political purposes. There was no prejudice here on account of American modes being different; for he observed that the clergy were there, as elsewhere, far from being in the van of society, and lamented the existence of much fanaticism in the United States; but he saw the evils of an establishment the more clearly, none the less, from being aware of the faults in the administration of religion at home. The most animated moment of our conversation was when I told him I was going to visit Mr. Madison on leaving Washington. He instantly sat upright in his chair, and with beaming eyes began to praise Mr. Madison. Madison received the mention of Marshall's name in just the same manner; yet these men were strongly opposed in politics, and their magnanimous appreciation of each other underwent no slight or brief trial.

Judge Porter [3] sometimes came, a hearty friend, and much like a fellow-countryman, though he was a senator of the United States, and had previously been, for fourteen years, Judge of the Supreme Court of Louisiana. He was Irish by birth. His father was vindictively executed, with cruel haste, under martial law, in the Irish rebellion; and the sons were sent by their noble-minded mother to America, where Alexander, the eldest, has thus raised himself into a station of high honour. Judge Porter's warmth, sincerity, knowledge, and wit are the pride of his

[3] Alexander J. Porter, born in Ireland in 1786, was admitted to the bar in Tennessee in 1807, and won political distinction in Louisiana. He was a judge of the State Supreme Court for some years following 1821, and United States Senator 1833-7.

constituents and very ornamental to the Senate. What their charm is by the fireside may be imagined.

Such are only a few among a multitude whose conversation filled up the few evenings we spent at home. Among the pleasantest visits we paid were dinners at the President's, at the houses of heads of departments, at the British Legation, and at the Southern members' Congressional mess. We highly enjoyed our dinings at the British Legation, where we felt ourselves at home among our countrymen. Once, indeed, we were invited to help to do the honours as English ladies to the seven Judges of the Supreme Court, and seven great lawyers besides, when we had the merriest day that could well be. Mr. Webster fell chiefly to my share, and there is no merrier man than he; and Judge Story would enliven a dinner table at Pekin. One laughable peculiarity at the British Legation was the confusion of tongues among the servants, who asked you to take fish, flesh, and fowl in Spanish, Italian, German, Dutch, Irish, or French. The foreign ambassadors are terribly plagued about servants. No American will wear livery, and there is no reason why any American should. But the British ambassador must have livery servants. He makes what compromise he can, allowing his people to appear without livery out of doors except on state occasions; but yet he is obliged to pick up his domestics from among foreigners who are in want of a subsistence for a short time, and are sure to go away as soon as they can find any employement in which the wearing a livery is not requisite. The woes of this state of things, however, were the portion of the host, not of his guests; and the hearty hospitality with which we were ever greeted by the minister and his attachés, combined with the attractions of the society they brought together, made our visits to them some of the pleasantest hours we passed in Washington.

Slight incidents were perpetually showing, in an amusing way, the village-like character of some of the arrangements at Washington. I remember that some of our party went one day to dine at Mr. Secretary Cass's, and the rest of us at Mr. Secretary Woodbury's.[4] The next morning a lady of the Cass party asked me whether we had candied oranges at the Woodburys'. 'No.' 'Then,' said she, 'they had candied oranges at the Attorney-General's.' 'How do you know?' 'Oh, as we were on the way, I saw a dish carried; and as we had none at the Cass's, I knew they must either be for the Woodburys or the Attorney-General.' There were candied oranges at the Attorney-General's.

When we became intimate some time afterward with some Southern

---

[4] Lewis Cass, of Michigan, 1782-1866, was Secretary of War from 1831 to 1836; Levi Woodbury, of New Hampshire, 1789-1851, was Secretary of the Navy from 1831 to 1834, and Secretary of the Treasury from 1834 to 1841.

friends, with whom we now dined at their Congressional mess, they gave us an amusing account of the preparations for our dinner. They boarded (from a really self-denying kindness) at a house where the arrangements were of a very inferior kind. Two sessions previous to our being there they had invited a large party of eminent persons to dinner, and had committed the ordering of the arrangements to a gentleman of their mess, advising him to engage a French cook in order to ensure a good dinner. The gentleman engaged a Frenchman, concluding he must be a cook, which, however, he was not; and the dinner turned out so unfortunately that the mess determined to ask no more dinner company while they remained in that house. When we arrived, however, it was thought necessary to ask us to dinner. There was little hope that all would go rightly, and the two senators of the mess were laughingly requested, in case of any blunder, to talk nullification as fast as possible to us ladies. This was done so efficaciously that, when dinner was over, I could not have told a single dish that was on the table, except that a ham stood before me, which we were too full of nullification to attack. Our hosts informed us, long afterward, that it was a bad dinner, badly served; but it was no matter.

At the President's I met a very large party, among whom there was more stiffness than I saw in any other society in America. It was not the fault of the President or his family, but of the way in which the company was unavoidably brought together. With the exception of my party, the name of everybody present began with J, K, or L; that is to say, it consisted of members of Congress, who are invited alphabetically, to ensure none being left out. This principle of selection is not, perhaps, the best for the promotion of ease and sociability; and well as I liked the day, I doubt whether many others could say they enjoyed it. When we went in the President was standing in the middle of the room to receive his guests. After speaking a few words with me, he gave me into the charge of Major Donelson, his secretary, who seated me, and brought up for introduction each guest as he passed from before the President. A Congressional friend of mine (whose name began with a J) stationed himself behind my chair and gave me an account of each gentleman who was introduced to me; where he came from, what his politics were, and how, if at all, he had distinguished himself. All this was highly amusing. At dinner the President was quite disposed for conversation. Indeed, he did nothing but talk. His health is poor, and his diet of the sparest. We both talked freely of the governments of England and France; I, novice in American politics as I was, entirely forgetting that the great French question was pending, and that the President and the King of the French were then bandying very hard words. I was most struck and surprised with the President's complaints of the American Senate, in which there was at that time a small majority against the administration. He told me that I must not judge of the body by what I saw it then, and that after the 4th of March I should behold a Senate more worthy of the country. After the 4th of March there was, if I remember rightly, a majority of two in favour of the government. The ground of his complaint was that the senators had sacrificed their dignity by disregarding the wishes of their constituents. The other side of the question is that the dignity of the Senate is best consulted by its members' following their own convictions, declining instructions for the term for which they are elected. It is a serious difficulty, originating in the very construction of the body, and not to be settled by dispute.

The President offered me bonbons for a child belonging to our party at home, and told me how many children (of his nephew's and his adopted son's) he had about him, with a mildness and kindliness which contrasted well with his tone upon some public occasions. He did the honours of his house with gentleness and politeness to myself, and, as far as I saw, to everyone else. About an hour after dinner he rose, and we led the way to the drawing room, where the whole company, gentlemen as well as ladies, followed to take coffee; after which everyone departed, some homeward, some to make evening calls, and others, among whom were ourselves, to a splendid ball at the other extremity of the city.

General Jackson is extremely tall and thin, with a slight stoop, betokening more weakness than naturally belongs to his years. He has a profusion of stiff gray hair, which gives to his appearance whatever there is of formidable in it. His countenance bears commonly an expression of melancholy gravity, though, when roused, the fire of passion flashes from his eyes, and his whole person looks then formidable enough. His mode of speech is slow and quiet, and his phraseology sufficiently betokens that his time has not been passed among books. When I was at Washington albums were the fashion and the plague of the day. I scarcely ever came home but I found an album on my table, or requests for autographs; but some ladies went much further than petitioning a foreigner who might be supposed to have leisure. I have actually seen them stand at the door of the Senate Chamber, and send the doorkeeper with an album, and a request to write in it, to Mr. Webster and other eminent members. I have seen them do worse; stand at the door of the Supreme Court, and send in their albums to Chief Justice Marshall while he was on the bench hearing pleadings. The poor President was terribly persecuted; and to him it was a real nuisance, as he had no poetical resource but Watts's hymns. I have seen verses and stanzas of the most ominous purport from Watts, in the President's very conspicuous handwriting, standing in the midst of the crowquill compliments and translucent charades which are the staples of albums. Nothing was done to repress this atrocious impertinence of the ladies. I always declined writing more than name and date; but senators, judges, and statesmen submitted to write gallant nonsense at the request of any woman who would stoop to desire it.

Colonel Johnson,[5] now Vice-President of the United States, sat opposite to me at the President's dinner table. This is the gentleman once believed to have killed Tecumseh, and to have written the *Report on Sunday Mails,* which has been the admiration of society ever since it appeared; but I believe Colonel Johnson is no longer supposed to be the author of either of these deeds. General Mason spoke of him to me at New York with much friendship, and with strong hope of his becoming President. I heard the idea so ridiculed by members of the federal party afterward that I concluded General Mason to be in the same case with hundreds more who believe their intimate friends sure of being President. But Colonel Johnson is actually Vice-President, and the hope seems reasonable; though the slavery question will probably be the point on which the next election will turn, which may again be to the disadvantage of the Colonel. If he should become President, he will be as strange-looking a potentate as ever ruled. His countenance is wild, though with much cleverness in it; his hair wanders all abroad, and he wears no cravat. But there is no telling how he might look if dressed like other people.

I was fortunate enough once to catch a glimpse of the invisible Amos Kendall,[6] one of the most remarkable men in America. He is supposed to be the moving spring of the whole administration: the thinker, planner, and doer; but it is all in the dark. Documents are issued of an excellence which prevents their being attributed to persons who take the responsibility of them; a correspondence is kept up all over the country for which no one seems to be answerable; work is done, of goblin extent and with goblin speed, which makes men look about them with a superstitious wonder; and the invisible Amos Kendall has the credit of it all. President Jackson's *Letters to His Cabinet* are said to be Kendall's; the *Report on Sunday Mails* is attributed to Kendall; the letters sent from Washington to appear in remote country newspapers, whence they are collected and published in the *Globe* as demonstrations of public opinion, are pronounced to be written by Kendall. Every mysterious paragraph in opposition newspapers relates

[5] Richard M. Johnson, of Kentucky, 1780-1850, was at this time in the House, and became Vice-President in 1837.
[6] Amos Kendall, of Kentucky, 1789-1869, was appointed Postmaster-General by Jackson in May 1835.

to Kendall; and it is some relief to the timid that his having now the office of postmaster-general affords opportunity for open attacks upon this twilight personage, who is proved, by the faults in the post-office administration, not to be able to do quite everything well. But he is undoubtedly a great genius. He unites with his 'great talent for silence' a splendid audacity. One proof of this I have given elsewhere, in the account of the bold stroke by which he obtained the sanction of the Senate to his appointment as postmaster-general.[7]

It is clear that he could not do the work he does (incredible in amount anyway) if he went into society like other men. He did, however, one evening; I think it was at the Attorney-General's. The moment I went in, intimations reached me from all quarters, and nods and winks, 'Kendall is here.' 'That is he.' I saw at once that his plea for seclusion (bad health) is no false one. The extreme sallowness of his complexion, and hair of such perfect whiteness as is rarely seen in a man of middle age, testified to disease. His countenance does not help the superstitious to throw off their dread of him. He probably does not desire this superstition to melt away; for there is no calculating how much influence was given to Jackson's administration by the universal belief that there was a concealed eye and hand behind the machinery of government, by which everything could be foreseen, and the hardest deeds done. A member of Congress told me this night that he had watched through four sessions for a sight of Kendall, and had never obtained it till now. Kendall was leaning on a chair, with head bent down, and eye glancing up at a member of Congress with whom he was in earnest conversation, and in a few minutes he was gone.

AN ATTEMPT ON JACKSON'S LIFE

There was a funeral of a member of Congress on the 30th of January; the interment of a representative from South Carolina, whose death I mentioned in connection with Mr. Calhoun. We were glad that we were in Washington at the time, as a Congressional funeral is a remarkable spectacle. We went to the Capitol at about half an hour before noon, and found many ladies already seated in the gallery of the Hall of Representatives. I chanced to be placed at the precise point of the gallery where the sounds from every part of the house are concentred; so that I heard the whole service, while I was at such a distance as to command a view of the entire scene. In the chair were the President of the Senate and the Speaker of the Representatives. Below

[7] *Society in America,* volume I, p. 60.

them sat the officiating clergymen; immediately opposite to them were the President and the heads of departments, one side the coffin, and the judges of the Supreme Court and members of the Senate on the other. the representatives sat in rows behind, each with crepe round the left arm; some in black; many in blue coats with bright buttons. Some of the fiercest political foes in the country; some who never met on any other occasion—the President and the South Carolina senators, for instance—now sat knee to knee, necessarily looking into each other's faces. With a coffin beside them and such an event awaiting their exit, how out of place was hatred there!

After prayers there was a sermon, in which warning of death was brought home to all, and particularly to the aged; and the vanity of all disturbances of human passion when in view of the grave was dwelt upon. There sat the gray-headed old President, at that time feeble, and looking scarcely able to go through this ceremonial. I saw him apparently listening to the discourse; I saw him rise when it was over and follow the coffin in his turn, somewhat feebly; I saw him disappear in the doorway, and immediately descended with my party to the Rotundo, in order to behold the departure of the procession for the grave. At the bottom of the stairs a member of Congress met us, pale and trembling, with the news that the President had been twice fired at with a pistol by an assassin who had waylaid him in the portico, but that both pistols had missed fire. At this moment the assassin rushed into the Rotundo where we were standing, pursued and instantly surrounded by a crowd. I saw his hands and half-bare arms struggling above the heads of the crowd in resistance to being handcuffed. He was presently overpowered, conveyed to a carriage, and taken before a magistrate. The attack threw the old soldier into a tremendous passion. He fears nothing, but his temper is not equal to his courage. Instead of his putting the event calmly aside, and proceeding with the business of the hour, it was found necessary to put him into his carriage and take him home.

We feared what the consequences would be. We had little doubt that the assassin Lawrence was mad; and as little that, before the day was out, we should hear the crime imputed to more than one political party or individual. And so it was. Before two hours were over, the name of almost every eminent politician was mixed up with that of the poor maniac who had caused the uproar. The President's misconduct on the occasion was the most virulent and protracted. A deadly enmity had long subsisted between General Jackson and Mr. Poindexter,[8] a senator of the United States, which had been much ag-

[8] George Poindexter, of Mississippi, 1779-1853, was United States Senator 1830-35.

gravated since General Jackson's accession by some unwarrantable language he had publicly used in relation to Mr. Poindexter's private affairs. There was a prevalent expectation of a duel as soon as the expiration of the President's term of office should enable his foe to send him a challenge. Under these circumstances the President thought proper to charge Mr. Poindexter with being the instigator of Lawrence's attempt. He did this in conversation so frequently and openly that Mr. Poindexter wrote a letter, brief and manly, stating that he understood this charge was made against him, but that he would not believe it until it was confirmed by the President himself; his not replying to this letter being understood to be such a confirmation. The President showed this letter to visitors at the White House, and did not answer it. He went further; obtaining affidavits (tending to implicate Poindexter) from weak and vile persons whose evidence utterly failed; having personal interviews with these creatures and openly showing a disposition to hunt his foe to destruction at all hazards. The issue was that Lawrence was proved to have acted from sheer insanity; Poindexter made a sort of triumphal progress through the states, and an irretrievable stain was left upon President Jackson's name.

Everyone was anxiously anticipating the fierce meeting of these foes on the President's retirement from office, when Mr. Poindexter last year, in a fit either of somnambulism or of delirium from illness, walked out of a chamber window in the middle of the night, and was so much injured that he soon died.

It so happened that we were engaged to a party at Mr. Poindexter's the very evening of this attack upon the President. There was so tremendous a thunderstorm that our host and hostess were disappointed of almost all of their guests except ourselves, and we had difficulty in merely crossing the street, being obliged to have planks laid across the flood which gushed between the carriage and the steps of the door. The conversation naturally turned on the event of the morning. I knew little of the quarrel which was now to be so dreadfully aggravated; but the more I afterward heard, the more I admired the moderation with which Mr. Poindexter spoke of his foe that night, and as often as I subsequently met him.

I had intended to visit the President the day after the funeral; but I heard so much of his determination to consider the attack a political affair, and I had so little wish to hear it thus treated, against the better knowledge of all the world, that I stayed away as long as I could. Before I went I was positively assured of Lawrence's insanity by one of the physicians who were appointed to visit him. One of the poor creature's complaints was that General Jackson deprived him of the British crown, to which he was heir. When I did go to the White

House, I took the briefest possible notice to the President of the 'insane attempt' of Lawrence; but the word roused his ire. He protested, in the presence of many strangers, that there was no insanity in the case. I was silent, of course. He protested that there was a plot, and that the man was a tool, and at length quoted the Attorney-General as his authority. It was painful to hear a chief ruler publicly trying to persuade a foreigner that any of his constituents hated him to the death; and I took the liberty of changing the subject as soon as I could. The next evening I was at the Attorney-General's, and I asked him how he could let himself be quoted as saying that Lawrence was not mad. He excused himself by saying that he meant general insanity. He believed Lawrence insane in one direction; that it was a sort of Ravaillac case. I besought him to impress the President with this view of the case as soon as might be.

It would be amusing if it were possible to furnish a complete set of the rumours, injurious (if they had not been too absurd) to all parties in turn, upon this single and very common act of a madman. One would have thought that no maniac had ever before attacked a chief magistrate. The act might so easily have remained fruitless! But it was made to bear a full and poisonous crop of folly, wickedness, and woe. I feared on the instant how it would be, and felt that though the President was safe, it was very bad news. When will it come to be thought possible for politicians to have faith in one another, though they may differ, and to be jealous for their rivals rather than for themselves?

SITTINGS OF THE SUPREME COURT

The places of resort for the stranger in the Capitol are the Library, the Supreme Court, the Senate Chamber, and the Hall of Representatives.

The former Library of Congress was burnt by the British in their atrocious attack upon Washington in 1814. Jefferson then offered his, and it was purchased by the nation. It is perpetually increased by annual appropriations. We did not go to the Library to read, but amused ourselves for many pleasant hours with the prints and with the fine medals we found there. I was never tired of the cabinet of Napoleon medals— the most beautifully composed piece of history that I ever studied. There is a cup carved by Benvenuto Cellini, preserved among the curiosities of the Capitol, which might be studied for a week before all the mysteries of its design are apprehended. How it found its way to so remote a resting place I do not remember.

Judge Story was kind enough to send us notice when any case was to be argued in the Supreme Court, which it was probable we might be able to understand, and we passed a few mornings there. The apartment is less fitted for its purposes than any other in the building, the court being badly lighted and ventilated. The windows are at the back of the judges, whose countenances are therefore indistinctly seen, and who sit in their own light. Visitors are usually placed behind the counsel and opposite the judges, or on seats on each side. I was kindly offered the reporter's chair, in a snug corner, under the judges and facing the counsel; and there I was able to hear much of the pleadings and to see the remarkable countenances of the Attorney-General, Clay, Webster, Porter, and others, in the fullest light that could be had in this dim chamber.

At some moments this court presents a singular spectacle. I have watched the assemblage while the Chief Justice was delivering a judgment; the three judges on either hand gazing at him more like learners than associates; Webster standing firm as a rock, his large, deep-set eyes wide awake, his lips compressed, and his whole countenance in that intent stillness which easily fixes the eye of the stranger; Clay leaning against the desk in an attitude whose grace contrasts strangely with the slovenly make of his dress, his snuffbox for the moment unopened in his hand, his small gray eye and placid half-smile conveying an expression of pleasure, which redeems his face from its usual unaccountable commonness; the Attorney-General, his fingers playing among his papers, his quick black eye and thin tremulous lips for once fixed, his small face, pale with thought, contrasting remarkably with the other two; these men, absorbed in what they are listening to, thinking neither of themselves nor of each other, while they are watched by the groups of idlers and listeners around them; the newspaper corps, the dark Cherokee chiefs, the stragglers from the Far West, the gay ladies in their waving plumes, and the members of either house that have stepped in to listen; all these I have seen at one moment constitute one silent assemblage, while the mild voice of the aged Chief Justice sounded through the court.

Everyone is aware that the wigs and gowns of counsel are not to be seen in the United States. There was no knowing, when Webster sauntered in, threw himself down, and leaned back against the table, his dreamy eyes seeming to see nothing about him, whether he would by and by take up his hat and go away, or whether he would rouse himself suddenly, and stand up to address the judges. For the generality there was no knowing; and to us, who were forewarned, it was amusing to see how the court would fill after the entrance of Webster, and empty when he had gone back to the Senate Chamber. The chief interest to me in Webster's pleading, and also in his speaking in the Senate, was from seeing one so dreamy and nonchalant roused into strong excitement. It seemed like having a curtain lifted up, through which it was impossible to pry; like hearing autobiographical secrets. Webster is a lover of ease and pleasure, and has an air of the most unaffected indolence and careless self-sufficiency. It is something to see him moved with anxiety and the toil of intellectual conflict; to see his lips tremble, his nostrils expand, the perspiration start upon his brow; to hear his voice vary with emotion, and to watch the expression of laborious thought while he pauses, for minutes together, to consider his notes and decide upon the arrangement of his argument. These are the moments when it becomes clear that this pleasure-loving man works for his honours and his gains.

WEBSTER AND CLAY CONTRASTED

Mr. Webster speaks seldom in the Senate. When he does, it is generally on some constitutional question, where his reasoning powers and knowledge are brought into play, and where his authority is considered so high that he has the glorious satisfaction of knowing that he is listened to as an oracle by an assemblage of the first men in the country. Previous to such an exercise he may be seen leaning back in his chair, not, as usual, biting the top of his pen, or twirling his thumbs, or bursting into sudden and transient laughter at Colonel Benton's oratorical absurdities, but absent and thoughtful, making notes, and seeing nothing that is before his eyes. When he rises, his voice is moderate and his manner quiet, with the slightest possible mixture of embarrassment; his right hand rests upon his desk, and the left hangs by his side. Before his first head is finished, however, his voice has risen so as to fill the chamber and ring again, and he has fallen into his favourite attitude, with his left hand under his coat tail, and the right in full action. At this moment the eye rests upon him as one under the true inspiration of seeing the invisible and grasping the impalpable. When the vision has passed away, the change is astonishing. He sits at his desk, writing letters or dreaming, so that he does not always discover when the Senate is going to a division. Some one of his party has not seldom to jog his elbow, and tell him that his vote is wanted.

There can scarcely be a stronger contrast than between the eloquence of Webster and that of Clay. Mr. Clay is now my personal friend; but I have a distinct recollection of my impression of his speaking while he was yet merely an acquaintance. His appearance is plain in the extreme, being that of a mere west-country farmer. He is tall and thin, with a weather-beaten complexion, small gray eyes, which convey the idea of something more than his well-known sagacity, even of slyness. It is only after much intercourse that Mr. Clay's personal appearance can be discovered to do him any justice at all. All attempts to take his likeness have been in vain, though upward of thirty portraits of him, by different artists, were in existence when I was in America. No one has succeeded in catching the subtle expression of placid kindness, mingled with astuteness, which becomes visible to the eyes of those who are in daily intercourse with him. His mode of talking, deliberate and somewhat formal, including sometimes a grave humour and sometimes a gentle sentiment, very touching from the lips of a sagacious man of ambition, has but one fault, its obvious adaptation to the supposed state of mind of the person to whom it is addressed. Mr. Clay is a man of an irritable and impetuous nature, over which he has obtained a truly noble mastery. His moderation is now his most striking characteristic; obtained, no doubt, at the cost of prodigious self-denial on his part, and on that of his friends of some of the ease, naturalness, and self-forgetfulness of his manners and discourse. But his conversation is rich in information, and full-charged with the spirit of justice and kindliness, rising, on occasion, to a moving magnanimity. By chances, of some of which he was totally unaware, I became acquainted with several acts of his life, political and private, which prove that his moderation is not the mere diffusion of oil upon the waves, but the true stilling of the storm of passion and selfishness. The time may come when these acts may be told; but it has not yet arrived.

. . .

His recollections of Europe are very vivid and pleasurable. We spent many an hour of my visit to him in Kentucky in talking over our mutual English friends, till we forgot the time and space we had both traversed since we parted from them, and looked up surprised to find ourselves, not at a London dinner table, but in the wild woods of the West. Mr. Clay has not kept up his knowledge of British life and politics so accurately as some of his brother-statesmen; but he is still full of the sayings of Castlereagh and Canning, of Lords Eldon and Stowell, of Mackintosh and Sydney Smith.

The finest speech I heard from Mr. Clay in the Senate was on the sad subject of the injuries of the Indians. He exposed the facts of the treatment of the Cherokees by Georgia. He told how the lands in Georgia, guaranteed by solemn treaties to the Creokees, had been surveyed and partitioned off to white citizens of the state; that, though there is a nominal right of appeal awarded to the complainants, this is a mere mockery, as an acknowledgment of the right of Georgia to divide the lands is made a necessary preliminary to the exercise of the right; in other words, the Indians must lay down their claims on the threshold of the courts which they enter for the purpose of enforcing these claims! The object of Mr. Clay's plea was to have the Supreme Court open to the Cherokees, their case being, he contended, contemplated by the Constitution. A minor proposition was that Congress should assist, with territory and appliances, a body of Cherokees who desired to emigrate beyond the Mississippi.

It was known that Mr. Clay would probably bring forward his great topic that day. Some of the foreign ambassadors might be seen leaning against the pillars behind the chair, and many members of the other house appeared behind and in the passages; and one sat on the steps of the platform, his hands clasped, and his eyes fixed on Mr. Clay as if life hung upon his words. As many as could crowd into the gallery leaned over the balustrade; and the lower circle was thronged with ladies and gentlemen, in the centre of whom stood a group of Cherokee chiefs, listening immovably. I never saw so deep a moral impression produced by a speech. The best testimony to this was the disgust excited by the empty and abusive reply of the Senator from Georgia, who, by the way, might be judged from his accent to have been about three months from the Green Island. This gentleman's speech, however, showed us one good thing—that Mr. Clay is as excellent in reply as in proposition; prompt, earnest, temperate, and graceful. The chief characteristic of his eloquence is its earnestness. Every tone of his voice, every fibre of his frame bears testimony to this. His attitudes are, from the beginning to the close, very graceful. His first sentences are homely and given with a little hesitation and repetition, and with an agitation shown by a frequent putting on and taking off of the spectacles, and a trembling of the hands among the documents on the desk. Then, as the speaker becomes possessed with his subject, the agitation changes its character, but does not subside. His utterance is still deliberate, but his voice becomes deliciously winning. Its higher tones disappointed me at first; but the lower ones, trembling with emotion, swelling and falling with the earnestness of the speaker are very moving, and his whole manner becomes irresistibly persuasive. I saw tears, of which I am sure he was wholly unconscious, falling on his papers as he vividly described the woes and injuries of the aborigines. I saw Webster draw his hand across his eyes; I saw everyone deeply moved except two persons, the Vice-President, who yawned somewhat ostentatiously, and the Georgian Senator, who was busy brewing his storm. I was amazed at the daring of this gentleman; at the

audacity which could break up such a moral impression as this Cherokee tale, so told, had produced, by accusing Mr. Clay of securing an
interest in opposition to Georgia 'by stage starts and theatric gesticula-
tions.' The audience were visibly displeased at having their feelings
thus treated, in the presence even of the Cherokee chiefs; but Mr. Clay's
replies both to argument and abuse were so happy, and the Georgian's
rejoinder was so outrageous that the business ended with a general
burst of laughter. The propositions were to lie over till the next day;
and, as I soon after left Washington, I never learned their ultimate fate.

The American Senate is a most imposing assemblage. When I first
entered it I thought I never saw a finer set of heads than the forty-six
before my eyes; two only being absent, and the Union then consisting
of twenty-four states. Mr. Calhoun's countenance first fixed my attention: the splendid eye, the straight forehead, surmounted by a load of
stiff, upright, dark hair, the stern brow, the inflexible mouth—it is one
of the most remarkable heads in the country. Next to him sat his
colleague, Mr. Preston, in singular contrast; stout in person, with a
round, ruddy, good-humoured face, large blue eyes, and a wig, orange
today, brown yesterday, and golden tomorrow. Near them sat Colonel
Benton, a temporary people's man, remarkable chiefly for his pom-
posity. He sat swelling amid his piles of papers and books, looking
like a being designed by nature to be a good-humoured barber or
innkeeper, but forced by fate to make himself into a mock-heroic
senator. Opposite sat the transcendent Webster, with his square forehead and cavernous eyes; and behind him the homely Clay, with the
face and figure of a farmer, but something of the air of a divine, from
his hair being combed straight back from his temples. Near them sat
Southard and Porter; the former astute and rapid in countenance and
gesture; the latter strangely mingling a boyish fun and lightness of
manner and glance with the sobriety suitable to the judge and the
senator. His keen eye takes in everything that passes; his extraordinary
mouth, with its overhanging upper lip, has but to unfold into a smile
to win laughter from the sourest official or demagogue. Then there
was the bright bonhomie of Ewing of Ohio, the most primitive-looking
of senators; and the benign, religious gravity of Frelinghuysen; the
gentlemanly air of Buchanan; the shrewdness of Poindexter; the somewhat melancholy simplicity of Silsbee; [9] all these and many others were
striking, and for nothing more than for their total unlikeness to each
other. No English person who has not travelled over half the world

[9] Thomas Ewing, of Ohio, 1789-1871, was United States Senator 1830-37; Theodore
Frelinghuysen, of New Jersey, 1787-1862, was Senator 1829-35; James Buchanan, of
Pennsylvania, 1791-1869, was Senator 1834-45; and Nathaniel Silsbee, of Massachusetts,
1773-1850, was Senator 1826-35.

can form an idea of such differences among men forming one assembly for the same purposes, and speaking the same language. Some
were descended from Dutch farmers, some from French Huguenots,
some from Scotch Puritans, some from English cavaliers, some from
Irish chieftans. They were brought together out of law courts, sugar
fields, merchants' stores, mountain farms, forests, and prairies. The
stamp of originality was impressed upon every one, and inspired a
deep, involutary respect. I have seen no assembly of chosen men, and
no company of the highborn, invested with the antique dignities of an
antique realm, half so imposing to the imagination as this collection
of stout-souled, full-grown, original men, brought together on the
ground of their supposed sufficiency, to work out the will of their
diverse constituencies.

In this splendid chamber, thus splendidly inhabited, we spent many
hours of many weeks. Here I was able to gain no little knowledge of
the state, political and other, of various parts of the country, from
my large acquaintance among the members of the Senate. When dull
official reports were read, and uninteresting local matters were discussed, or when the one interminable speaker, Benton, was on his
legs, one member or another of the body would come and talk with us.
I have heard certain of the members, stalking from their seats towards
those of the ladies, compared to cranes in search of fish; the comparison
is not a bad one.

I wished every day that the ladies would conduct themselves in a
more dignified manner than they did in the Senate. They came in
with waving plumes, and glittering in all the colours of the rainbow,
causing no little bustle in the place, no little annoyance to the gentlemen spectators, and rarely sat still for any length of time. I know
that these ladies are no fair specimens of the women who would
attend parliamentary proceedings in any other metropolis. I know
that they were the wives, daughters, and sisters of legislators, women
thronging to Washington for purposes of convenience or pleasure,
leaving their usual employments behind them, and seeking to pass
away the time. I knew this, and made allowance accordingly; but I
still wished that they could understand the gravity of such an assembly,
and show so much respect to it as to repay the privilege of admission
by striving to excite as little attention as possible, and by having the
patience to sit still when they happened not to be amused, till some
interruption gave them opportunity to depart quietly. If they had done
this, Judge Porter would not have moved that they should be appointed
seats in the gallery instead of below; and they would have been guiltless
of furnishing a plea for the exclusion of women, who would probably

make a better use of the privilege, from the galleries of other houses of parliament.

I was glad of an opportunity of hearing both the South Carolina Senators soon after my arrival in Washington. They are listened to with close attention, and every indication of their state of feeling is watched with the interest which has survived the nullification struggle. Mr. Calhoun on this occasion let us a little into his mind; Mr. Preston [10] kept more closely to the question before the body. The question was whether a vote of censure of the President, recorded in the minutes of the proceedings of the Senate the preceding session, should be expunged. The motion for the expunging was made by Colonel Benton, and rejected, as it had been before, and has been since; though it was finally carried, to the agony of the opposition, at the end of the last session (February 1837).

Mr. Preston was out of health, and unable to throw his accustomed force into his speaking; but his effort showed us how beautiful his eloquence is in its way. It is not solid. His speeches, if taken to pieces, will be found to consist of analogies and declamation; but his figures are sometimes very striking, and his manner is as graceful as anything so artificial can be. I never before understood the eloquence of action. The action of public speakers in England, so far as I have observed (and perhaps I may be allowed to hint that deaf persons are peculiarly qualified to judge of the nature of such action), is of two kinds; the involuntary gesture which is resorted to for the relief of the nerves, which may or may not be expressive of meaning, and the action which is wholly the result of study—arbitrary, and not the birth of the sentiment, and, therefore, though pleasing perhaps to the eye, perplexing to the mind of the listener. Mr. Preston's manner unites the advantages of these two methods, and avoids most of their evils. It is easy to see that he could not speak without an abundant use of action, and that he has therefore done wisely in making it a study. To an unaccustomed eye it appears somewhat exuberant; but it is exquisitely graceful, and far more than commonly appropriate. His voice is not good, but his person is tall, stout, and commanding, and his countenance animated.

Mr. Calhoun followed, and impressed me very strongly. While he kept to the question, what he said was close, good, and moderate, though delivered in rapid speech, and with a voice not sufficiently modulated. But when he began to reply to a taunt of Colonel Benton's that he wanted to be President, the force of his speaking became painful. He made protestations, which it seemed to strangers had better have been spared, that he would not turn on his heel to be President;

10 William C. Preston, of South Carolina, 1794-1860, was United States Senator 1832-42.

and that he had given up all for his own brave, magnanimous little state of South Carolina. While thus protesting, his eyes flashed, his brow seemed charged with thunder, his voice became almost a bark, and his sentences were abrupt, intense, producing in the auditory that sort of laugh which is squeezed out of people by the application of a very sudden mental force. I believe he knew little what a revelation he made in a few sentences. They were to us strangers the key, not only to all that was said and done by the South Carolina party during the remainder of the session, but to many things at Charleston and Columbia which would otherwise have passed unobserved or unexplained.

I was less struck than some strangers appear to have been with the length and prosy character of the speeches in Congress. I do not remember hearing any senator (always excepting Colonel Benton) speak for more than an hour. I was seldom present at the other house, where probably the most diffuse oratory is heard; but I was daily informed of the proceedings there by the representative who was of our party, and I did not find that there was much annoyance or delay from this cause. Perhaps the practise may be connected with the amount of business to be done. It is well known that the business of Congress is so moderate in quantity, from the functions of the general government being few and simple, that it would be considered a mere trifle by any parliament in the Old World; and long speeches, which would be a great annoyance elsewhere, may be an innocent pastime in an assembly which may have leisure upon its hands.

THE MORAL CONSEQUENCES OF SLAVERY

What social virtues are possible in a society of which injustice is the primary characteristic? in a society which is divided into two classes, the servile and the imperious?

The most obvious is Mercy. Nowhere, perhaps, can more touching exercises of mercy be seen than here. It must be remembered that the greater number of slave-holders have no other idea than of holding slaves. Their fathers did it; they themselves have never known the coloured race treated otherwise than as inferior beings, born to work for and tease the whites, helpless, improvident, open to no higher inducements than indulgence and praise, capable of nothing but entire dependence. The good affections of slave-holders like these show themselves in the form of mercy, which is as beautiful to witness as mercy, made a substitute for justice, can ever be. I saw endless manifestations of mercy, as well as of its opposite. The thoughtfulness of masters, mistresses, and their children about not only the comforts but the indulgences of their slaves was a frequent subject of admiration with me. Kind masters are liberal in the expenditure of money, and (what is better) of thought, in gratifying the whims and fancies of their Negroes. They make large sacrifices occasionally for the social or domestic advantage of their people, and use great forbearance in the exercise of the power conferred upon them by law and custom. . .

Little can be said of the purity of manners of the whites of the South; but there is purity. Some few examples of domestic fidelity may be found; few enough, by the confession of residents on the spot, but those individuals who have resisted the contagion of the vice amidst which they dwell are pure. Every man who resides on his plantation may have his harem, and has every inducement of custom and of pecuniary gain [11] to tempt him to the common practise. Those who, not withstanding, keep their homes undefiled may be considered as of incorruptible purity.

Here, alas, ends my catalogue of the virtues which are of possible exercise by slave-holders towards their labourers. The inherent injustice of the system extinguishes all others, and nourishes a whole harvest of false morals towards the rest of society.

The personal oppression of the Negroes is the grossest vice which strikes a stranger in the country. It can never be otherwise when human beings are wholly subjected to the will of other human beings, who are under no other external control than the law which forbids killing and maiming—a law which it is difficult to enforce in individual cases. A fine slave was walking about in Columbia, South Carolina, when I was there, nearly helpless and useless from the following causes. His master was fond of him, and the slave enjoyed the rare distinction of never having been flogged. One day, his master's child, supposed to be under his care at the time, fell down and hurt itself. The master flew into a passion, ordered the slave to be instantly flogged, and would not hear a single word the man had to say. As soon as the flogging was over, the slave went into the back-yard, where there was an axe and a block, and struck off the upper half of his right hand. He went and held up the bleeding hand before his master, saying, 'You have mortified me, so I have made myself useless. Now you must maintain me as long as I live.' It came out that the child had been under the charge of another person.

There are, as is well known throughout the country, houses in the free states which are open to fugitive slaves, and where they are concealed till the search for them is over. I know some of the secrets of such

---

[11] The law declares that the children of slaves are to follow the fortunes of the mother. Hence the practise of planters selling and bequeathing their own children [Miss Martineau's note].

places, and can mention two cases, among many, of runaways, which show how horrible is the tyranny which the slave system authorizes men to inflict on each other. A Negro had found his way to one of these friendly houses, and had been so skilfully concealed that repeated searches by his master (who had followed for the purpose of recovering him), and by constables had been in vain. After three weeks of this seclusion, the Negro became weary, and entreated of his host to be permitted to look out of the window. His host strongly advised him to keep quiet, as it was pretty certain that his master had not given him up. When the host had left him, however, the Negro came out of his hiding place and went to the window. He met the eye of his master, who was looking up from the street. The poor slave was obliged to return to his bondage.

A young Negress had escaped in like manner; was in like manner concealed; and was alarmed by constables, under the direction of her masters, entering the house in pursuit of her, when she had reason to believe that the search was over. She flew upstairs to her chamber in the third story, and drove a heavy article of furniture against the door. The constables pushed in, notwithstanding, and the girl leaped from the window into the paved street. Her master looked at her as she lay, declared she would never be good for anything again, and went back into the South. The poor creature, her body bruised and her limbs fractured, was taken up and kindly nursed; and she is now maintained in Boston, in her maimed condition, by the charity of some ladies there.

The following story has found its way into the Northern States (as few such stories do) from the circumstance that a New Hampshire family are concerned in it. It has excited due horror wherever it is known; and it is to be hoped that it will lead to an exposure of more facts of the same kind, since it is but too certain that they are common.

A New Hampshire gentleman went down into Louisiana, many years ago, to take a plantation. He pursued the usual method, borrowing money largely to begin with, paying high interest, and clearing off his debt, year by year, as his crops were sold. He followed another custom there, taking a Quadroon wife—a mistress, in the eye of the law, since there can be no legal marriage between whites and persons of any degree of colour, but, in nature and in reason, the woman he took home was his wife. She was a well-principled, amiable, well-educated woman; and they lived happily together for twenty years. She had only the slightest possible tinge of colour. Knowing the law that the children of slaves are to follow the fortunes of the mother, she warned her husband that she was not free, an ancestress having been a slave, and the legal act of manumission having never been performed. The husband promised to look to it; but neglected it. At the end of twenty years one died, and the other shortly followed, leaving daughters . . . I have reason to believe three, of the ages of fifteen, seventeen, and eighteen: beautiful girls, with no perceptible mulatto tinge. The brother of their father came down from New Hampshire to settle the affairs; and he supposed, as everyone else did, that the deceased had been wealthy. He was pleased with his nieces, and promised to carry them back with him into New Hampshire, and (as they were to all appearances perfectly white) to introduce them into the society which by education they were fitted for. It appeared, however, that their father had died insolvent. The deficiency was very small, but it was necessary to make an inventory of the effects to deliver to the creditors. This was done by the brother—the executor. Some of the creditors called on him and complained that he had not delivered in a faithful inventory. He declared he had. No: the number of slaves was not accurately set down; he had omitted the daughters. The executor was overwhelmed with horror, and asked time for thought. He went round among the creditors, appealing to their mercy, but they answered that these young ladies were 'a first-rate article,' too valuable to be relinquished. He next offered (though he had himself six children and very little money) all he had for the redemption of his nieces, alleging that it was more than they would bring in the market for house or field labour. This was refused with scorn. It was said that there were other purposes for which the girls would bring more than for field or house labour. The uncle was in despair, and felt strongly tempted to wish their death rather than their surrender to such a fate as was before them. He told them, abruptly, what was their prospect. He declares that he never before beheld human grief; never before heard the voice of anguish. They never ate, nor slept, nor separated from each other till the day when they were taken into the New Orleans slave market. There they were sold, separately, at high prices, for the vilest of purposes; and where each is gone no one knows. . .

It is well known that the most savage violences that are now heard of in the world take place in the Southern and Western States of America. Burning alive, cutting the heart out, and sticking it on the point of a knife, and other such diabolical deeds, the result of the deepest hatred of which the human heart is capable, are heard of only there. The frequency of such deeds is a matter of dispute, which time will settle. (I knew of the death of four men by summary burning alive, within thirteen months of my residence in the United States.) The existence of such deeds is a matter of no dispute. Whether two or twenty such deeds take place in a year, their perpetration testifies to the existence of such hatred as alone could prompt them. There is no doubt in my mind as to the immediate causes of such outrages. They arise out of the licentiousness of manners. The Negro is exasperated by being deprived of his wife—by being sent out of the way that his master may take possession of his home. He stabs his master; or if he cannot fulfill his desire of vengeance, he is a dangerous person, an object of vengeance in return, and destined to some cruel fate. If the Negro attempts to retaliate and defile the master's home, the faggots are set alight about him. Much that is dreadful ensues from the Negro being subject to toil and the lash; but I am confident that the licentiousness of the masters is the proximate cause of society in the South and Southwest being in such a state that nothing else is to be looked for than its being dissolved into its elements, if man does not soon cease to be called the property of man. This dissolution will never take place through the insurrection of the Negroes, but by the natural operation of vice. But the process of demoralization will be stopped, I have no doubt, before it reaches that point.

The Dark Side of Slavery, 1838-39 [1] &

FANNY KEMBLE'S *Journal of a Residence on a Georgian Planta-*
tion in 1838-39 first appeared in 1863— 'a sadder book the human hand
never wrote,' according to the Atlantic Monthly. *Fanny Kemble, a*
niece of Mrs. Siddons and a daughter of the famous actor Charles
Kemble, was born in 1809 and made her debut as Juliet at Covent
Garden at the age of nineteen, at once becoming a great favorite of the
public. Sheridan Knowles wrote The Hunchback *especially for her.*
In 1832 she accompanied her father to America, and the two achieved
an even more striking success there, being equally applauded. As she
says, in these years she 'literally coined money.' Meeting Pierce Butler,
a Southern planter, she married him in 1834 and went to reside on his
two large estates near Darien, Georgia, in total ignorance, she assures
us, of the fact that he was an extensive slave owner, or of what the
condition of the slaves was.

In her solitary situation on the Darien estates, living in a comfortless
frame house, without any of the amusements to which she had been
accustomed, she conceived the idea of writing a journal of her daily

[1] From *Journal of a Residence on a Georgian Plantation in* 1838-39, London, 1863, pp. 188-94.

*experiences on the model of the Journal kept by Monk Lewis during
his visit to his West India plantations. The Negroes on Pierce Butler's
estates esteemed themselves comparatively well off, as well they might
when they looked at the lot of those on neighboring tracts; while in
this part of the South they were very much better off indeed than on
some of the remote interior plantations. She was a clear-sighted, noble-
minded, warm-hearted woman, who at the outset believed that the
blacks about her were contented, and then for a time that they might
be made so. Her book relates in vivid and sincere style the story of her
tragic undeceiving. Its literary merits are considerable—she was later
the author of various poetical and dramatic works—but it is wholly
devoid of coloring for effect or of sensationalism. Her daily observations are stated in a matter-of-fact way, and such unconscious exaggeration as the book possesses arises from her excessive sensibility.*

*It was the slave woman, tasked with constant childbearing and field
work, with whom she sympathized most deeply, and of the terrible
physical ailments that resulted from the merciless combination of these
two burdens she writes with proper frankness. She tells us that on
Pierce Butler's well-managed plantations, as on others, the mothers
were driven afield to work under the lash within three weeks after
childbirth, and their infants, among whom the mortality was of course
excessive, were left to the care of youngsters still not quite old enough
for the field. She tells what she observed of the compulsion placed upon
some of these women to cohabit with their overseers or even white
masters. She tells of the floggings they received. One of her most striking passages relates at length the agony of a woman slave, Psyche, the
mother of two small children, when, supposing herself the property of
an overseer who had just purchased an Alabama plantation, she was in
daily fear of being separated from her husband and removed thither;
and the struggle that the writer, Fanny Kemble, had to wage with the
overseer and with Pierce Butler to keep the family united. She describes the wretched infirmaries on the estates, and the ghastly lack of
care given to the slaves on their deathbeds, in childbirth, and at other
seasons of illness—no fire, no medicines, no bandages, no bedclothing,
no lights. 'I groped my way out,' she states in describing one visit to
an infirmary, where sick slave women were lying on the bare earth in
nothing but filthy tattered clothing, 'and emerging on the piazza, all
the choking tears and sobs I had controlled broke forth, and I leaned
there crying over the lot of these unfortunates.'*

*Her description of the dirtiness and squalor of the slave huts is un-
doubtedly veracious. They had almost no furniture, their beds being
mere wooden frames with a bark covering; they abounded with fleas
and other vermin. The meals of the slaves were eaten without the aid*

of the most ordinary utensils, and consisted of nothing but meal or hominy. Work began at daybreak, the first food was eaten at noon— cooked over a fire kindled in the field—and the second meal was taken at night. She pictures a Negro dance and other merrymakings, but the tone of her book is one of almost unrelieved sadness. It can no more be neglected by the student of Southern society before the war than can Olmsted's volumes of Southern travels.

THE NEGROES AT HOME

THIS morning I have been to the hospital to see a poor woman who has just enriched Mr. Butler [2] by *borning* him another slave. The poor little pickaninny, as they called it, was not one bit uglier than white babies under similarly novel circumstances, except in one particular, that it had a head of hair like a trunk, in spite of which I had all the pains in the world in persuading its mother not to put a cap upon it. I bribed her finally, by the promise of a pair of socks instead, with which I undertook to endow her child, and, moreover, actually prevailed upon her to forego the usual swaddling and swathing process, and let her poor baby be dressed at its first entrance into life as I assured her both mine had been.

On leaving the hospital I visited the huts along the street, confiscating sundry refractory baby caps among shrieks and outcries, partly of laughter and partly of real ignorant alarm for the consequences. I think if this infatuation for hot head-dresses continues, I shall make shaving the children's heads the only condition upon which they shall be allowed to wear caps.

On Sunday morning I went over to Darien to church. Our people's church was closed, the minister having gone to officiate elsewhere. With laudable liberality I walked into the opposite church of a different, not to say opposite, sect: here I heard a sermon, the opening of which will, probably, edify you as it did me, viz., that if a man was *just in all his dealings* he was apt to think he did all that could be required of him—and no wide mistake either, one might suppose. But is it not wonderful how such words can be spoken here, with the most absolute unconsciousness of their tremendous bearing upon the existence of every slaveholder who hears them? Certainly the use that is second nature has made the awful injustice in the daily practise of which these people live a thing of which they are as little aware as you or I of the atmospheric air that we inhale each time we breathe. The bulk of the congregation in this church was white. The negroes

[2] In the original, Pierce Butler's name is represented by a dash.

are, of course, not allowed to mix with their masters in the house of God, and there is no special place set apart for them. Occasionally one or two are to be seen in the corners of the singing gallery, but any more open pollution by them of their owners' church could not be tolerated. Mr. Butler's people have petitioned very vigorously that he would build a church for them on the island. I doubt, however, his allowing them such a luxury as a place of worship all to themselves. Such a privilege might not be thought well of by the neighboring planters; indeed, it is almost what one might call a whity-brown idea, dangerous, demoralizing, inflammatory, incendiary. I should not wonder if I should be suspected of being the chief cornerstone of it, and yet I am not: it is an old hope and entreaty of these poor people, which I am afraid they are not destined to see fulfilled.

Dearest E——.[3] Passing the rice mill this morning in my walk, I went in to look at the machinery, the large steam mortars which shell the rice, and which work under the intelligent and reliable supervision of Engineer Ned. I was much surprised, in the course of conversation with him this morning, to find how much older a man he was than he appeared. Indeed his youthful appearance had hitherto puzzled me much in accounting for his very superior intelligence and the important duties confided to him. He is, however, a man upwards of forty years old, although he looks ten years younger. He attributed his own uncommonly youthful appearance to the fact of his having never done what he called field work, or been exposed, as the common gang negroes are, to the hardships of their all but brutish existence. He said his former master had brought him up very kindly, and he had learnt to tend the engines, and had never been put to any other work, but he said this was not the case with his poor wife. He wished she was as well off as he was, but she had to work in the rice-fields and was 'most broke in two' with labor and exposure and hard work while with child, and hard work just directly after child-bearing; he said she could hardly crawl, and he urged me very much to speak a kind word for her to massa. She was almost all the time in hospital, and he thought she could not live long.

Now, E——, here is another instance of the horrible injustice of this system of slavery. In my country or in yours, a man endowed with sufficient knowledge and capacity to be an engineer would, of course, be in the receipt of considerable wages; his wife would, together with himself, reap the advantages of his ability, and share the well-being his labor earned; he would be able to procure for her comfort in sickness or in health, and beyond the necessary household work, which the wives of most artisans are inured to, she would have no labor to

---

[3] The author's letters were addressed to Elizabeth Dwight Sedgwick in New England.

encounter; in case of sickness even these would be alleviated by the assistance of some stout girl of all work, or kindly neighbor, and the tidy parlor or snug bedroom would be her retreat if unequal to the daily duties of her own kitchen. Think of such a lot compared with that of the head engineer of Mr. Butler's plantation, whose sole wages are his coarse food and raiment and miserable hovel, and whose wife, covered with one filthy garment of ragged texture and dingy color, barefooted and bare-headed, is daily driven afield to labor with aching pain-racked joints, under the lash of a driver, or lies languishing on the earthen floor of the dismal plantation hospital in a condition of utter physical destitution and degradation such as the most miserable dwelling of the poorest inhabitant of your free Northern villages never beheld the like of. Think of the rows of tiny tidy houses in the long suburbs of Boston and Philadelphia, inhabited by artisans of just the same grade as this poor Ned, with their white doors and steps, their hydrants of inexhaustible fresh flowing water, the innumerable appliances for decent comfort of their cheerful rooms, the gay wardrobe of the wife, her cotton prints for daily use, her silk for Sunday church-going; the careful comfort of the children's clothing, the books and newspapers in the little parlor, the daily district school, the weekly parish church: imagine if you can—but you are happy that you cannot —the contrast between such an existence and that of the best mechanic on a Southern plantation. . .

On my return to the house I found a terrible disturbance in consequence of the disappearance from under cook John's safe keeping of a ham Mr. Butler had committed to his charge. There was no doubt whatever that the unfortunate culinary slave had made away in some inscrutable manner with the joint intended for our table: the very lies he told about it were so curiously shallow, childlike, and transparent, that while they confirmed the fact of his theft quite as much if not more than an absolute confession would have done, they provoked at once my pity and my irrepressible mirth to a most painful degree. Mr. Butler was in a state of towering anger and indignation, and, besides a flogging, sentenced the unhappy cook to degradation from his high and dignified position (and, alas! all the sweets of comparatively easy labor and good living from the remains of our table) to the hard toil, coarse scanty fare, and despised position of a common field hand. I suppose some punishment was inevitably necessary in such a plain case of deliberate theft as this, but, nevertheless, my whole soul revolts at the injustice of visiting upon these poor wretches a moral darkness which all possible means are taken to increase and perpetuate.

In speaking of this and the whole circumstance of John's trespass to Mr. Butler in the evening, I observed that the ignorance of these poor people ought to screen them from punishment. He replied that they knew well enough what was right and wrong. I asked how they could be expected to know it. He replied, by the means of Cooper London, and the religious instruction he gave them. So that, after all, the appeal is to be made against themselves to that moral and religious instruction which is withheld from them, and which, if they obtain it at all, is the result of their own unaided and unencouraged exertion. The more I hear, and see, and learn, and ponder the whole of this system of slavery, the more impossible I find it to conceive how its practisers and upholders are to justify their deeds before the tribunal of their own conscience or God's law. It is too dreadful to have those whom we love accomplices to this wickedness; it is too intolerable to find myself an involuntary accomplice to it.

I had a conversation the next morning with Abraham, cook John's brother, upon the subject of his brother's theft; and only think of the *slave* saying that 'this action had brought disgrace upon the family.' Does not that sound very like the best sort of free pride, the pride of character, the honorable pride of honesty, integrity, and fidelity?

A Writer of Sea Tales on America [1]

CAPTAIN FREDERICK MARRYAT, *the well-known novelist, was forty-five years old when he visited America in 1837, and as famous in the United States as in Great Britain. After an honorable naval career, in which during the Napoleonic Wars he had witnessed literally scores of engagements, and had attained the rank of commander, he had retired to civil life in 1830. His first book had appeared in 1829, and his labors as a writer of naval stories were thenceforth almost incessant.* Peter Simple *and* Jacob Faithful *were published in 1834, and* Mr. Midshipman Easy *and* Japhet in Search of a Father *in 1836.*

Marryat himself relates that when he had first landed in the United States, an errand boy who fetched him a package from a New York store gravely inquired whether Mr. Easy had left the King's service, and whether he had seen Mr. Japhet lately. The novelist was already a veteran traveler. Not only had he seen naval service in Burmese, North American, and West Indian waters as well as in Europe, but since retiring he had spent much time on the Continent. If we may

[1] From *A Diary in America, with Remarks on Its Institutions,* Philadelphia, 1839, volume I, chapter 2; volume II, chapters 31 and 32; and matter under 'Remarks.'

believe his own account, he had resolved during these wanderings to compare America with Europe. 'Do the faults of these people,' he wrote of the Swiss in his Diary on the Continent, *'arise from the peculiarity of their constitutions, or from the nature of their government? To ascertain this, one must compare them with those who live under similar institutions. I must go to America—that is decided.' He was, moreover, a little perplexed by the contradictory accounts of the republic brought home by different travelers, and wished to find out the facts for himself. He returned to England in* 1839, *and at once published in London* A Diary in America, with Remarks on Its Institutions, *in two series of three volumes each. The work was reprinted in Philadelphia by Carey and Hart, who were generous enough to pay Marryat* $2250 *for it and a novel.*

Marryat was everywhere well received in America. In Boston he was claimed as a kinsman through his mother, a native of that city, and in New York his visit coincided with the successful production of a nautical drama he had written, 'The Ocean Wolf, or the Channel Outlaw.' He felt, however, an undercurrent of sensitiveness, and bore it in mind in writing his volumes, which were meant to be studiously fair. He blames Miss Martineau severely for her many 'absurdities and fallacies,' though he notes that some of her errors originated in the desire of a few Americans to hoax the lady; and he ridicules Mrs. Trollope. His conclusions were generally favorable to the American character. He liked its energy and enterprise, saying that these were a natural development of English traits in an environment that demanded alertness and activity. He wrote that 'the mind can hardly calculate upon the degree of perfection and power to which, whether the states are eventually separated or not, it [the United States] may in the course of two centuries arrive.' But he had no liking for the government of the United States, though he recognized that it was the one best suited to existing circumstances. It was not a republican government at all, he asserted, but a democracy, by which he meant that it was a 'mob government'; the popular majority controlling it directly, instead of electing wise agents and permitting them to control it. He also formed the queer impression that the American climate resulted in a deterioration from the physique possessed by the original British settlers, and in several other ways he was unjust.

EFFECTS OF THE PANIC OF 1837

A VISIT, to make it agreeable to both parties, should be well timed. My appearance at New York was very much like bursting into a friend's house with a merry face when there is a death in it—with the sudden change from levity to condolence. 'Any other time most happy to see you. You find us in a very unfortunate situation.'

'Indeed I'm very, very sorry.'

Two hundred and sixty houses have already failed, and no one knows where it is to end. Suspicion, fear, and misfortune have taken possession of the city. Had I not been aware of the cause, I should have imagined that the plague was raging, and I had the description of Defoe before me.

Not a smile on one countenance among the crowd who pass and repass; hurried steps, careworn faces, rapid exchanges of salutation, or hasty communication of anticipated ruin before the sun goes down. Here two or three are gathered together on one side, whispering and watching that they are not overheard; there a solitary, with his arms folded and his hat slouched, brooding over departed affluence. Mechanics, thrown out of employment, are pacing up and down with the air of famished wolves. The violent shock has been communicated. like that of electricity, through the country to a distance of hundreds of miles. Canals, railroads, and all public works have been discontinued, and the Irish emigrant leans against his shanty, with his spade idle in his hand, and starves, as his thoughts wander back to his own Emerald Isle.

The Americans delight in hyperbole; in fact they hardly have a metaphor without it. During this crash, when every day fifteen or twenty merchants' names appeared in the newspapers as bankrupts, one party, not in a very good humor, was hastening down Broadway, when he was run against by another whose temper was equally unamiable. This collision roused the choler of both.

'What the devil do you mean, sir?' cried one; 'I've a great mind to knock you into *the middle of next week.*'

This occurring on a Saturday, the wrath of the other was checked by the recollection of how very favorable such a blow would be to his present circumstances.

'Will you! by heavens, then pray do; it's just the thing I want, for how else I am to get over next Monday and the acceptances I must take up, is more than I can tell.'

All the banks have stopped payment in specie, and there is not a dollar to be had. I walked down Wall Street, and had a convincing proof of the great demand for money, for somebody picked my pocket.

The militia are under arms, as riots are expected. The banks in the country and other towns have followed the example of New York, and thus has General Jackson's currency bill been repealed without the aid of Congress. Affairs are now at their worst, and now that such is the case, the New Yorkers appear to recover their spirits. One of the newspapers humorously observes—'All Broadway is like unto a new-made widow, and don't know whether to laugh or cry.' There certainly is a very remarkable energy in the American disposition; if they fall, they bound up again. Somebody has observed that the New York merchants are of that *elastic* nature that, when fit for nothing else, they might be converted into coach springs, and such really appears to be their character.

Nobody refuses to take the paper of the New York banks, although they virtually have stopped payment—they never refuse anything in New York—but nobody will give specie in change, and great distress is occasioned by this want of a circulating medium. Some of the shop-keepers told me that they had been obliged to turn away a hundred dollars a day, and many a Southerner, who has come up with a large supply of Southern notes, has found himself a pauper, and has been indebted to a friend for a few dollars in specie to get home again.

The radicals here, for there are radicals, it appears, in a democracy—

'In the lowest depths, a lower deep'—

are very loud in their complaints. I was watching the swarming multitude in Wall Street this morning, when one of these fellows was declaiming against the banks for stopping specie payments, and 'robbing a poor man in such a *w*illainous manner,' when one of the merchants, who appeared to know his customer, said to him—'Well, as you say, it is hard for a poor fellow like you not to be able to get dollars for his notes; hand them out, and I'll give you specie for them myself!' The blackguard had not a cent in his pocket, and walked away, looking very foolish. He reminded me of a little chimney-sweeper at the Tower Hamlets election, asking—'Vot vos my hopinions about primaginitur?' —a very important point to him certainly, he having no parents, and having been brought up by the parish.

I was in a store when a thoroughbred democrat walked in; he talked loud, and voluntarily gave it as his opinion that all this distress was the very best thing that could have happened to the country, as America would now keep all the specie and pay her English creditors with bankruptcies. There always appears to me to be a great want of moral principle in all radicals; indeed, the levelling principles of radicalism are adverse to the sacred rights of *meum et tuum*. At Philadelphia the ultra-democrats have held a large public meeting, at which one of the first resolutions brought forward and agreed to was—'That they did not owe one farthing to the English people.'

'They may say the times are bad,' said a young American to me, 'but I think that they are excellent. A twenty-dollar note used to last me but a week, but now it is as good as Fortunatus's purse, which was never empty. I eat my dinner at the hotel, and show them my twenty-dollar note. The landlord turns away from it, as if it were the head of Medusa, and begs that I will pay another time. I buy everything that I want, and I have only to offer my twenty-dollar note in payment, and my credit is unbounded—that is, for any sum under twenty dollars. If they ever do give change again in New York it will make a very unfortunate change in my affairs.'

A government circular, enforcing the act of Congress, which obliges all those who have to pay custom-house duties or postage to do so in specie, has created great dissatisfaction, and added much to the distress and difficulty. At the same time that they (the government) refuse to take from their debtors the notes of the banks, upon the ground that they are no longer legal tenders, they compel their creditors to take those very notes—having had a large quantity in their possession at the time that the banks suspended specie payments—an act of despotism the English government would not venture upon.

Miss Martineau's work is before me. How dangerous it is to prophesy. Speaking of the merchants of New York, and their recovering after the heavy losses they sustained by the calamitous fire of 1835, she says that although eighteen millions of property were destroyed, not one merchant failed; and she continues, 'It seems now as if the commercial credit of New York could stand any shock short of an earthquake like that of Lisbon.' That was the prophecy of 1836. Where is the commercial credit of New York now in 1837?!

The distress for change has produced a curious remedy. Every man is now his own banker. Go to the theatres and places of public amusement, and, instead of change, you receive an I.O.U. from the treasury. At the hotels and oyster cellars it is the same thing. Call for a glass of brandy and water, and the change is fifteen tickets, each 'good for one glass of brandy and water.' At an oyster shop, eat a plate of oysters, and you have in return seven tickets, good for one plate of oysters each. It is the same everywhere. The barbers give you tickets, good for so many shaves; and were there beggars in the streets, I presume they would give you tickets in change, good for so much philanthropy. Dealers, in general, give out their own bank notes, or as they are called here, *shin plasters,* which are good for one dollar, and from that down to two and a half cents, all of which are redeemable, and redeemable only upon a general return to cash payments.

Hence arises another variety of exchange in Wall Street.

'Tom, do you want any oysters for lunch today?' 'Yes!' 'Then here's a ticket, and give me two *shaves* in return.'

The most prominent causes of this convulsion have already been laid before the English public; but there is one—that of speculating in land—which has not been sufficiently dwelt upon, nor has the importance been given to it which it deserves; as, perhaps, next to the losses occasioned by the great fire, it led, more than any other species of overspeculation and overtrading, to the distress which has ensued.

THE WHITE SULPHUR SPRINGS OF VIRGINIA

We arrived first at the blue sulphur springs, and I remained there for one day to get rid of the dust of traveling. They have a very excellent hotel there, with a ballroom, which is open till eleven o'clock every night; the scenery is very pretty, and the company was good—as indeed is the company at all these springs, for they are too distant, and the traveling too expensive for everybody to get there. But the blue sulphur are not fashionable, and the consequence was we were not crowded, and were very comfortable. People who cannot get accommodated at the white sulphur remain here until they can, the distance between them being only twenty-two miles.

The only springs which are fashionable are the white sulphur, and as these springs are a feature in American society, I shall describe them more particularly.

They are situated in a small valley, many hundred feet above the level of the sea, and are about fifteen or twenty acres in area, surrounded by small hills covered with foliage to their summits; at one end of the valley is the hotel, with the large dining room for all the visitors. Close to the hotel, but in another building, is the ballroom, and a little below the hotel, on the other side, is the spring itself; but beautiful as is the whole scenery, the great charm of this watering place is the way in which those live who visit it. The rises of the hills which surround the valley are covered with little cottages, log houses, and other picturesque buildings, sometimes in rows, and ornamented with verandahs, without a second story above, or kitchen below. Some are very elegant and more commodious than the rest, having been built by gentlemen who have the right given to them by the company to whom the springs belong of occupying them themselves when there, but not of preventing others from taking possession of them in their absence. The dinners and other meals are, generally speaking, bad; not that there is not a plentiful supply, but that it is so difficult to supply seven hundred people sitting down in one room. In the morning, they all turn out from their little burrows, meet in the public walks, and go down to the spring before breakfast; during the forenoon, when it is too warm, they remain at home; after dinner they ride out or pay visits, and then end the day, either at the ballroom or in little societies among one another. There is no want of handsome equipages, many four-in-hand (Virginny long tails) and every accommodation for these equipages. The crowd is very great, and it is astonishing what inconvenience people will submit to rather than not be accommodated somehow or another. Every cabin is like a rabbit burrow. In the one next to where I was lodged, in a room about fourteen feet square, and partitioned off as well as it could be, there slept a gentleman and his wife, his sister and brother, and a female servant. I am not sure that the nigger was not under the bed—at all events, the young sister told me that it was not at all pleasant.

There is a sort of major-domo here, who regulates every department; his word is law, and his fiat immovable, and he presumes not a little upon his power—a circumstance not to be surprised at, as he is as much courted and is as despotic as all the lady patronesses of Almacks rolled into one. He is called the Metternich of the mountains. No one is allowed accommodation at these springs who is not known, and generally speaking, only those families who travel in their private carriages. It is at this place that you feel how excessively aristocratical and exclusive the Americans would be, and indeed will be, in spite of their institutions. Spa, in its palmiest days, when princes had to sleep in their carriages at the doors of the hotels, was not more in vogue than are these white sulphur springs with the élite of the United States. And it is here, and here only, in the States, that you do meet what may be fairly considered as select society, for at Washington there is a great mixture. Of course all the celebrated belles of the different states are to be met with here, as well as all the large fortunes, nor is there a scarcity of pretty and wealthy widows. The president, Mrs. Caton, the mother of Lady Wellesley, Lady Strafford, and Lady Caermarthen, the daughter of Carroll, of Carrollton, one of the real aristocracy of America, and a signer of the Declaration of Independence, and all the first old Virginian and Carolina families, many of them descendants of the old cavaliers, were at the springs when I arrived there; and I certainly must say that I never was at any watering place in England where the company was so good and so select as at the Virginia springs in America.

I passed many pleasant days at this beautiful spot, and was almost as unwilling to leave it as I was to part with the Sioux Indians at St. Peters. Refinement and simplicity are equally charming. I was introduced to a very beautiful girl here, whom I should not have mentioned particularly had it not been that she was the first and only lady in America that I observed to *whittle*. She was sitting one fine morning on a wooden bench, surrounded by admirers, and as she carved away her seat with her pen knife, so did she cut deep into the hearts of those who listened to her lively conversation.

There are, as may be supposed, a large number of Negro servants here attending their masters and mistresses. I have often been amused, not only here but during my residence in Kentucky, at the high-sounding Christian names which have been given to them. 'Byron, tell Ada to come here directly.' 'Now, Telemachus, if you don't leave Calypso alone, you'll get a taste of the *cow hide.*'

Among others attracted to the springs professionally was a very clever German painter, who, like all Germans, had a very correct ear for music. He had painted a kitchen dance in Old Virginia, and in the picture he had introduced all the well-known colored people in the place; amongst the rest were the band of musicians, but I observed that one man was missing. 'Why did you not put him in?' inquired I. 'Why, sir, I could not put him in; it was impossible; he never *plays in tune.* Why, if I put him in, sir, he would spoil the *harmony* of my whole picture!'

I asked this artist how he got on in America. He replied:

But so-so; the Americans in general do not estimate genius. They come to me and ask what I want for my pictures, and I tell them. Then they say, 'How long did it take you to paint it?' I answer 'So many days.' Well, then they calculate and say, 'If it took you only so many days, you ask so many dollars a day for your work; you ask a great deal too much; you ought to be content with so much per day, and I will give you that.' So that, thought I, invention and years of study go for nothing with these people. There is only one way to dispose of a picture in America, and that is to raffle it; the Americans will then run the chance of getting it. If you do not like to part with your pictures in that way, you must paint portraits; people will purchase their own faces all over the world: the worst of it is that in this country they will purchase nothing else.

During my stay here I was told one of the most remarkable instances that perhaps ever occurred of the discovery of a fact by the party from whom it was of the utmost importance to conceal it—a very pretty interesting young widow. She had married a promising young man, to whom she was tenderly attached, and who, a few months after the marriage, unfortunately fell in a duel. Aware that the knowledge of the cause of her husband's death would render the blow still more severe to her (the ball having passed through the eye into his brain, and there being no evident gun-shot wound), her relations informed her that he had been thrown from his horse, and killed by the fall. She believed them. She was living in the country, when, about nine months after her widowhood, her brother rode down to see her, and as soon as he arrived went into his room to shave and dress. The window of his room, which was on the ground floor, looked out upon the garden, and it being summer time, it was open. He tore off a portion of an old newspaper to wipe his razor. The breeze caught it, and carried it away into the garden until it stopped at the feet of his sister who happened to be walking. Mechanically she took up the fragment, and perceiving her husband's name upon it she read it. It contained a full account of the duel in which he lost his life! The shock she received was so great that it unsettled her mind for nearly two years. She had but just recovered, and for the first time reappeared in public, when she was pointed out to me.

Returning to Guyandotte, one of the travelers wished to see the view from the Hawk's Nest, or rather wished to be able to say that he had seen it. We passed the spot when it was quite dark, but he persisted in going there, and to help his vision borrowed one of the coach lamps from the driver. He returned and declared that with the assistance of the lamp he had had a very excellent view, down a precipice of several hundred feet. His bird's-eye view by candlelight must have been very extensive. After all, it is but to be able to say that they have been to such a place, or have seen such a thing that, more than any real taste for it, induces the majority of the world to incur the trouble and fatigue of traveling.

USE AND ABUSE OF LYNCH LAW

Englishmen express their surprise that in a moral community such a monstrosity as Lynch law should exist; but although the present system, which has been derived from the original Lynch law, cannot be too severely condemned, it must, in justice to the Americans, be considered that the original custom of Lynch law was forced upon them by circumstances. Why the term Lynch law has been made use of I do not know; but in its origin the practice was no more blameable than were the laws established by the Pilgrim Fathers on their first landing at Plymouth, or any law enacted amongst a community left to themselves, their own resources, and their own guidance and government. Lynch law, as at first constituted, was nothing more than punishment awarded to offenders by a community who had been injured, and who had no law to refer to, and could have no redress if they did not take the law into their own hands; the *present* system of Lynch law is, on the contrary, an illegal exercise of the power of the majority in opposition to and defiance of the laws of the country, and the measure of justice administered and awarded by those laws. . .

A circumstance occurred within these few years in which Lynch law was duly administered. At Dubuque, in the Ioway district, a murder was committed. The people of Dubuque first applied to the authorities of the state of Michigan, but they discovered that the district of Ioway was not within the jurisdiction of that state; and, in fact, although on the opposite side of the river there was law and justice, they had neither to appeal to. They would not allow the murderer to escape; they consequently met, selected among themselves a judge and jury, tried the man, and, upon their own responsibility, hanged him.

There was another instance, which occurred a short time since at Snakes' Hollow, on the western side of the Mississippi, not far from the town of Dubuque. A band of miscreants, with a view of obtaining possession of some valuable diggings (lead mines), which were in the possession of a grocer who lived in that place, murdered him in the open day. The parties were well known, but they held together and would none of them give evidence. As there were no hopes of their conviction, the people of Snakes' Hollow armed themselves, seized the parties engaged in the transaction, and ordered them to quit the territory on pain of having a rifle bullet through their heads immediately. The scoundrels crossed the river in a canoe, and were never after heard of.

I have collected these facts to show that Lynch law has been forced upon the American settlers in the Western States by *circumstances;* that it has been acted upon in support of morality and virtue, and that its awards have been regulated by strict justice. But I must now notice this practice with a view to show how dangerous it is that any law should be meted out by the majority, and that what was commenced from a sense of justice and necessity has now changed into a defiance of law, where law and justice can be readily obtained. The Lynch law of the present day, as practiced in the states of the West and South, may be divided into two different heads: the first is, the administration of it in cases in which the laws of the states are considered by the majority as not having awarded a punishment adequate, in their opinion, to the offence committed; and the other, when from excitement the majority will not wait for the law to act, but inflict the punishment with their own hands. . .

One or two instances in which Lynch law was called in to *assist* justice on the bench came to my knowledge. A Yankee had stolen a slave, but as the indictment was not properly worded, he knew that he would be acquitted, and he boasted so, previous to the trial coming on. He was correct in his supposition; the flaw in the indictment was fatal, and he was acquitted. 'I told you so,' he said, triumphantly smiling as he left the court, to the people who had been waiting the issue of the trial.

'Yes,' replied they, 'it is true that you have been acquitted by Judge Smith, but you have not yet been tried by *Judge Lynch*.' The latter judge was very summary. The Yankee was tied up, and cow-hided till he was nearly dead; they then put him into a *dugout* and sent him floating down the river. Another instance occurred, which is rather amusing, and, at the same time, throws some light upon the peculiar state of society in the West.

There was a barkeeper at some tavern in the state of Louisiana (if I recollect right) who was a great favorite; whether from his judicious mixture of the proportions in mint juleps and gin cocktails or from other causes, I do not know; but what may appear strange to the English, he was elected to an office in the law courts of the state, similar to our Attorney-General, and I believe was very successful, for an American can turn his hand or his head to almost anything. It so happened that a young man, who was in prison for stealing a Negro, applied to this Attorney-General to defend him in court. This he did so successfully that the man was acquitted; but Judge Lynch was as usual waiting outside, and when the attorney came out with his client, the latter was demanded to be given up. This the attorney refused, saying that the man was under his protection. A tumult ensued, but the attorney was firm; he drew his bowie knife, and addressing the crowd, said, 'My men, you all know me; no one takes this man, unless he passes over my body.' The populace were still dissatisfied, and the attorney, not wishing to lose his popularity, and at the same time wanting to defend a man who had paid him well, requested the people to be quiet a moment until he could arrange the affair. He took his client aside, and said to him, 'These men will have you, and will Lynch you, in spite of all my efforts; only one chance remains for you, and you must accept it: you know that it is but a mile to the confines of the next state, which if you gain you will be secure. You have been in prison for two months, you have lived on bread and water, and you must be in good wind; moreover, you are young and active. These men who wish to get hold of you are half drunk, and they never can run as you can. Now, I'll propose that you shall have one hundred and fifty yards law, and then if you exert yourself, you can easily escape.' The man consented, as he could not help himself; the populace also consented, as the attorney pointed out to them that any other arrangement would be injurious to his honor. The man, however, did not succeed; he was so frightened that he could not run, and in a short time he was taken, and had the usual allowance of cow hide awarded by Judge Lynch. Fortunately he regained his prison before he was quite exhausted, and was sent away during the night in a steamer.

At Natchez, a young man married a young lady of fortune, and, in his passion, actually flogged her to death. He was tried, but as there were no witnesses but Negroes, and their evidence was not admissible against a white man, he was acquitted; but he did not escape; he was seized, tarred and feathered, *scalped,* and turned adrift in a canoe without paddles.

Such are the instances of Lynch law being superadded, when it has been considered by the majority that the law has not been sufficiently severe. The other variety of Lynch law is when they will not wait for law, but, in a state of excitement, proceed to summary punishment.

The case more than once referred to by Miss Martineau, of the burning alive of a colored man at St. Louis, is one of the gravest under this head. I do not wish to defend it in any way, but I do, for the honor of humanity, wish to offer all that can be said in extenuation of this atrocity; and I think Miss Martineau, when she held up to public indignation the monstrous punishment, was bound to acquaint the public with the cause of an excitable people being led into such an error. This unfortunate victim of popular fury was a free colored man of a very quarrelsome and malignant disposition; he had already been engaged in a variety of disputes, and was a nuisance in the city. For an attempt to murder another colored man he had been seized, and was being conducted to prison in the custody of Mr. Hammond, the sheriff, and another white person who assisted him in the execution of his duty. As he arrived at the door of his prison, he watched his opportunity, stabbed the person who was assisting the sheriff, and then, passing his knife across the throat of Mr. Hammond, the carotid artery was divided, and the latter fell dead upon the spot. Now, here was a wretch who, in one day, had three times attempted murder, and had been successful in the instance of Mr. Hammond, the sheriff, a person universally esteemed. Moreover, when it is considered that the culprit was of a race who are looked upon as inferior; that this successful attempt on the part of a black man was considered most dangerous as a precedent to the Negro population; that, owing to the unwillingness to take life away in America, he might probably have escaped justice; and that this occurred just at the moment when the Abolitionists were creating such mischief and irritation—although it must be lamented that they should have so disgraced themselves, the summary and cruel punishment which was awarded by an incensed populace is not very surprising. Miss Martineau, however, has thought proper to pass over the peculiar atrocity of the individual who was thus sacrificed: to read her account of the transaction it would appear as if he were an unoffending party, sacrificed on account of his *color* alone.

THE AMERICAN LANGUAGE

The Americans boldly assert that they speak better English than we do, and I was rather surprised not to find a statistical table to that effect in Mr. Carey's publication. What I believe the Americans would imply by the above assertion is that you may travel through all the United States and find less difficulty in understanding, or in being understood, than in some of the counties of England, such as Cornwall, Devonshire, Lancashire, and Suffolk. So far they are correct; but it is remarkable how very debased the language has become in a short period in America. There are few provincial dialects in England much less intelligible than the following. A Yankee girl, who wished to hire herself out, was asked if she had any followers or sweethearts? After a little hesitation, she replied, 'Well, now, can't exactly say; I bees a sorter courted, and a sorter not; reckon more a sorter yes than a sorter no.' In many points the Americans have to a certain degree obtained that equality which they profess; and, as respects their language, it certainly is the case. If their lower classes are more intelligible than ours, it is equally true that the higher classes do not speak the language so purely or so classically as it is spoken among the well-educated English. The peculiar dialect of the English counties is kept up because we are a settled country; the people who are born in a county live in it and die in it, transmitting their sites of labor or of amusement to their descendants, generation after generation, without change; consequently, the provincialisms of the language become equally hereditary. Now, in America, they have a dictionary containing many thousands of words, which, with us, are either obsolete or are provincialisms, or are words necessarily invented by the Americans. When the people of England emigrated to the States, they came from every county in England, and each county brought its provincialisms with it. These were admitted into the general stock, and were since all collected and bound up by one Mr. Webster. With the exceptions of a few words coined for local uses (such as *snags* and *sawyers,* on the Mississippi) I do not recollect a word which I have not traced to be either a provincialism of some English county, or else to be obsolete English. There are a few from the Dutch, such as *stoup,* for the porch of a door, et cetera. I was once talking with an American about Webster's dictionary, and he observed, 'Well now, sir, I understand it's the only one used in the Court of St. James by the king, queen, and princesses, and that by royal order.'

The upper classes of the Americans do not, however, speak or pronounce English according to our standard; they appear to have no exact rule to guide them, probably from a want of any intimate knowledge of Greek or Latin. You seldom hear a derivation from the Greek pronounced correctly, the accent being generally laid upon the wrong syllable. In fact, everyone appears to be independent, and pronounces just as he pleases.

But it is not for me to decide the very momentous question as to which nation speaks the best English. The Americans generally improve upon the inventions of others; probably they may have improved upon our language.

I recollect someone observing how very superior the German language was to the English, from their possessing so many compound substantives and adjectives; whereupon his friend replied that it was just as easy for us to possess them in England if we pleased, and gave us as an example an observation made by his old dame at Eton, who declared that young Paulet was, without any exception, the most *good-for-nothingest,* the most *provoking-people-est,* and the most *poke-about-every-cornerest* boy she had ever had charge of in her life.

Assuming this principle of improvement to be correct, it must be acknowledged that the Americans have added considerably to our dictionary; but, as I have before observed, this being a point of too much delicacy for me to decide upon, I shall just submit to the reader the occasional variations, or improvements, as they may be, which met my ears during my residence in America, as also the idiomatic peculiarities, and having so done, I must leave him to decide for himself.

I recollect once talking with one of the first men in America, who was narrating to me the advantages which might have accrued to him if he had followed up a certain speculation, when he said, 'Sir, if I had done so, I should not only have *doubled* and *trebled,* but I should have *fourbled* and *fivebled* my money.'

One of the members of Congress once said, 'What the honorable gentleman has just asserted I consider as *catamount* to a denial'—(catamount is the term given to a panther or lynx).

'I presume,' replied his opponent, 'that the honorable gentleman means *tantamount.*'

'No, sir, I do not mean *tantamount;* I am not so ignorant of our language not to be aware that *cat*amount and *tan*tamount are *anon*ymous.'

The Americans dwell upon their words when they speak—a custom arising, I presume, from their cautious, calculating habits; and they have always more or less of a nasal twang. I once said to a lady, 'Why do you drawl out your words in that way?'

'Well,' replied she, 'I'd drawl all the way from Maine to Georgia, rather than *clip* my words as you English people do.'

Many English words are used in a very different sense from that which we attach to them; for instance, a *clever* person in America means an amiable good-tempered person, and the Americans make the distinction by saying, 'I mean English clever.'

Our *clever* is represented by the word *smart*.

The verb *to admire* is also used in the East, instead of the verb *to like*.

'Have you ever been at Paris?'

'No; but I should *admire* to go.'

A Yankee description of a clever woman:

'Well, now, she'll walk right into you and talk to you like a book'; or, as I have heard them say, 'she'll talk you out of sight.'

The word *ugly* is used for cross, ill-tempered. 'I did feel so *ugly* when he said that.'

Bad is used in an odd sense: it is employed for awkward, uncomfortable, sorry.

'I did feel so *bad* when I read that'—awkward.

'I have felt quite *bad* about it ever since'—uncomfortable.

'She was so *bad* I thought she would cry'—sorry.

And as *bad* is tantamount to *not good,* I have heard a lady say, 'I don't feel *at all good,* this morning.'

Mean is occasionally used for ashamed.

'I never felt so *mean* in my life.'

'We reckon this very handsome scenery, sir,' said an American to me, pointing to the landscape.

'I consider him very truthful,' is another expression.

'He stimulates too much.'

'He dissipates awfully.'

And they are very fond of using the noun as a verb, as—

'I *suspicion* that's a fact.'

'I *opinion* quite the contrary.'

The word *considerable* is in considerable demand in the United States. In a work in which the letters of the party had been given to the public as specimens of good style and polite literature, it is used as follows:

'My dear sister, I have taken up the pen early this morning, as I intend to write *considerable.'*

The word *great* is oddly used for fine, splendid.

'She's the *greatest* gal in the whole Union.'

But there is one word which we must surrender up to the Americans as their *very own,* as the children say. I will quote a passage from one of their papers:

'The editor of the Philadelphia *Gazette* is wrong in calling *absquatiated* a Kentucky *phrase* (he may well say phrase instead of *word*). It may prevail there, but its origin was in South Carolina, where it was a few years since regularly derived from the Latin, as we can prove from undoubted authority. By the way, there is a little *corruption* in the word as the *Gazette* uses it, *absquatalized* is the true reading.'

Certainly a word worth quarreling about!

'Are you cold, miss?' said I to a young lady, who pulled the shawl closer over shoulders.

'*Some*,' was the reply.

The English *what*, implying that you did not hear what was said to you, is changed in America to the word *how*.

'I reckon,' 'I calculate,' 'I guess,' are all used as the common English phrase, 'I suppose.' Each term is said to be peculiar to different states, but I found them used everywhere, one as often as the other. 'I *opine*' is not so common. . .

The verb '*to fix*' is universal. It means to do anything.

'Shall I *fix* your coat or your breakfast first?' That is—'Shall I brush your coat, or *get ready* your breakfast?'

Right away, for immediately or at once, is very general.

'Shall I fix it *right away?*'—i.e. 'Shall I do it immediately?'

In the West, when you stop at an inn, they say—

'What will you have? Brown meal and common doings, or white wheat and chicken *fixings?*'—that is, 'Will you have pork and brown bread, or white bread and fried chicken?'

Also, 'Will you have a *feed* or a *check?*'—A dinner, or a luncheon?

In full blast—something in the extreme.

'When she came to meeting, with her yellow hair and feathers, wasn't she *in full blast?*' . . .

There are two syllables—*um, hu*—which are very generally used by the Americans as a sort of reply, intimating that they are attentive, and that the party may proceed with his narrative; but, by inflection and intonation, these two syllables are made to express dissent or assent, surprise, disdain, and (like Lord Burleigh's nod in the play) a great deal more. The reason why these two syllables have been selected is that they can be pronounced without the trouble of opening your mouth, and you may be in a state of listlessness and repose while others talk. I myself found them very convenient at times, and gradually got into the habit of using them.

AFFECTED MODESTY

I cannot conclude this chapter without adverting to one or two points peculiar to the Americans. They wish, in everything, to improve upon the old country, as they call us, and affect to be excessively refined in their language and ideas; but they forget that very often in the covering, and the covering only, consists the indecency, and that, to use the old aphorism, 'Very nice people are people with very nasty ideas.'

They object to everything nude in statuary. When I was at the house of Governor Everett at Boston, I observed a fine cast of the Apollo Belvidere, but, in compliance with general opinion, it was hung with drapery, although Governor Everett himself is a gentleman of refined mind and high classical attainments, and quite above such ridiculous sensitiveness. In language it is the same thing: there are certain words which are never used in America, but an awkward substitute is employed. I cannot particularize them after this preface, lest I should be accused of indelicacy myself. I may, however, state one little circumstance, which will prove the correctness of what I say.

When at Niagara Falls, I was escorting a young lady with whom I was on friendly terms. She had been standing on a piece of rock, the better to view the scene, when she slipped down, and was evidently hurt by the fall; she had in fact grazed her shin. As she limped a little in walking home, I said, 'Did you hurt your leg much?' She turned from me evidently much shocked, or much offended; and not being aware that I had committed any very heinous offence, I begged to know what was the reason of her displeasure. After some hesitation, she said that as she knew me well, she would tell me that the word *leg* was never mentioned before ladies. I apologized for my want of refinement, which was attributable to my having been accustomed only to *English* society, and added that as such articles must occasionally be referred to, even in the most polite circles of America, perhaps she would inform me by what name I might mention them without shocking the company. Her reply was that the word *limb* was used. 'Nay,' continued she, 'I am not so particular as some people are, for I know those who always say limb of a table, or limb of a pianoforte.'

There the conversation dropped; but a few months afterwards I was obliged to acknowledge that the young lady was correct when she asserted that some people were more particular than even she was.

I was requested by a lady to escort her to a seminary for young ladies, and on being ushered into the reception room, conceive my astonishment at beholding a square pianoforte with four *limbs*. However, that the ladies who visited their daughters might feel in its full force the extreme delicacy of the mistress of the establishment, and her care to preserve in their utmost purity the ideas of the young ladies under her charge, she had dressed all these four limbs in modest little trousers, with frills at the bottom of them!

Journeys by Steamboat and Canal [1] &

CHARLES DICKENS. *Much less familiar than the* American Notes *are the letters of Dickens describing his travels in the United States, included in Forster's life of the novelist. Yet as Forster says, in a number of respects they are more interesting and important. The freshness of first impressions is in them; they are simple and direct, unweakened by some of the rhetorical additions of his printed book; and they are thoroughly* personal, *showing how his experiences arose, and hiding none of his views, favorable or unfavorable. Their vividness, buoyancy, and humor are unfailing, and show how vigorously Dickens met the difficulties of travel. 'Written amid such distraction, fatigue, and weariness as they describe,' says Forster, 'amid the jarring noises of hotels and streets, aboard steamers, on canal boats, and in log huts, there is not an erasure in them.' Dickens made them the groundwork of his* American Notes.

Dickens celebrated his thirtieth birthday (7 Feb., 1842) while in the United States. His half dozen first books, Sketches by Boz, Pickwick Papers, Oliver Twist, Nicholas Nickleby, The Old Curiosity Shop, *and* Barnaby Rudge, *had been devoured one after another as eagerly in America as in England, and he was given a reception of greater cordiality than that ever tendered any other foreign visitor save Lafayette. At dinners in Boston and New York he took the opportunity of bringing forward the subject of an international copyright agreement to protect the interests of authors of the two countries, and this aroused some hostile feeling. But in general his journey was one long ovation. He was welcomed in Boston by Longfellow, Bancroft, R. H. Dana, Channing, and others; in New York by Irving, Bryant, Fitzgreene Halleck, and all the principal gentlemen of the city; and in Washington by President Tyler.*

[1] From John Forster's *Life of Charles Dickens*, London, 1872-4, book III, chapters 5 and 6.

The novelist's original design was to make an extensive tour. He intended to go through Virginia to Charleston and Columbia, South Carolina; and, taking a carriage and saddle horse there, to push west 'through the wilds of Kentucky and Tennessee, across the Alleghany Mountains, and so on until we should strike the lakes and could get to Canada.' But being assured that such a journey would be quite too difficult for himself, and wholly out of the question for Mrs. Dickens, he gave it up. Fearing the heat of the South and the repugnant scenes of slavery, he went no further south than Richmond, returning thence to Baltimore. From Maryland he traveled through York, Harrisburg, Pittsburgh, Cincinnati, and Louisville to St. Louis; returning through Cincinnati, Columbus, and Cleveland to Buffalo, Niagara—which he viewed with something like ecstasy——and Montreal.

Dickens's second visit to the United States was made in 1867-8, *long after the first resentment over his scarification of American faults in* American Notes *and* Martin Chuzzlewit *had been forgotten; and again he was given a welcome of the warmest kind. At the public dinner offered him in New York he expressed his regret for any apparent unkindness in his writings, and his heartfelt friendship for the United States.*

ON BOARD THE CANAL BOAT. GOING TO PITTSBURGH, MONDAY, MARCH 28, 1842

WE left Baltimore last Tuesday the twenty-fourth at half-past eight in the morning, by railroad; and got to a place called York, about twelve. There we dined, and took a stagecoach for Harrisburgh, twenty-five miles further. This stagecoach was like nothing so much as the body of one of the swings you see at a fair set upon four wheels and roofed and covered at the sides with painted canvas. There were twelve *inside!* I, thank my stars, was on the box. The luggage was on the roof; among it, a good-sized dining-table and a big rocking-chair. We also took up an . . . intoxicated gentleman who got up behind, but in the course of a mile or two fell off without hurting himself, and was seen in the distant perspective reeling back to the grog-shop where we had found him. There were four horses to this land-ark, of course; but we did not perform the journey till half-past six o'clock that night. . . The first half of the journey was tame enough, but the second lay through the valley of the Susquehannah (I think I spell it right, but I haven't that American geography at hand), which is very beautiful. . .

I think I formerly made a casual remark to you touching the precocity of the youth of this country. When we changed horses on this journey

I got down to stretch my legs, refresh myself with a glass of whiskey and water, and shake the wet off my great coat—for it was raining very heavily, and continued to do so, all night. Mounting on my seat again, I observed something lying on the roof of the coach, which I took to be a rather large fiddle in a brown bag. In the course of ten miles or so, however, I discovered that it had a pair of dirty shoes at one end, and a glazed cap at the other; and further observation demonstrated it to be a small boy, in a snuff-coloured coat, with his arms quite pinioned to his sides by deep forcing into his pockets. He was, I presume, a relative or friend of the coachman's, as he lay atop of the luggage, with his face towards the rain; and, except when a change of position brought his shoes in contact with my hat, he appeared to be asleep. Sir, when we stopped to water the horses, about two miles from Harrisburgh, this thing slowly upreared itself to a height of three foot eight, and fixing its eyes on me with a mingled expression of complacency, patronage, national independence, and sympathy for all outer barbarians and foreigners, said, in shrill piping accents, 'Well, now, stranger, guess you find this a-most like an English a'ternoon—hey?' It is unnecessary to add that I thirsted for his blood. . .

We had all next morning in Harrisburgh, as the canal boat was not to start until three o'clock in the afternoon. The officials called upon me before I had finished breakfast; and as the town is the seat of the Pennsylvanian legislature, I went up to the capitol. I was very much interested in looking over a number of treaties made with the poor Indians, their signatures being rough drawings of the creatures or weapons they are called after; and the extraordinary drawing of these emblems, showing the queer, unused, shaky manner in which each man has held the pen, struck me very much.

You know my small respect for our House of Commons. These local legislatures are too insufferably apish of mighty legislation to be seen without bile; for which reason, and because a great crowd of senators and ladies had assembled in both houses to behold the inimitable and had already begun to pour in upon him even in the secretary's private room, I went back to the hotel with all speed. The members of both branches of the legislature followed me there, however, so we had to hold the usual levee before our half-past one o'clock dinner. We received a great number of them. Pretty nearly every man spat upon the carpet, as usual; and one blew his nose with his fingers—also on the carpet, which was a very neat one, the room given up to us being the private parlor of the landlord's wife. This has become so common since, however, that it scarcely seems worth mentioning. Please to observe that the gentleman in question was a member of the Senate, which answers (as they very often tell me) to our House of Lords.

The innkeeper was the most attentive, civil, and obliging person I ever saw in my life. On being asked for his bill, he said there was no bill: the honor and pleasure, et cetera, being more than sufficient. I did not permit this, of course; and begged Mr. Q.[2] to explain to him, that, travelling four strong, I could not hear of it on any account.

And now I come to the Canal Boat. Bless your heart and soul, my dear fellow—if you could only see us on board the canal boat! Let me think, for a moment, at what time of the day or night I should best like you to see us. In the morning? Between five and six in the morning, shall I say? Well! you *would* like to see me, standing on the deck, fishing the dirty water out of the canal with a tin ladle chained to the boat by a long chain; pouring the same into a tin basin (also chained up in like manner); and scrubbing my face with the jack towel. At night, shall I say? I don't know that you *would* like to look into the cabin at night, only to see me lying on a temporary shelf exactly the width of this sheet of paper when it's open (*I measured it this morning*) with one man above me, and another below; and, in all, eight and twenty in a low cabin, which you can't stand upright in with your hat on. I don't think you would like to look in at breakfast time, either, for then these shelves have only just been taken down and put away, and the atmosphere of the place is, as you may suppose, by no means fresh; though there *are* upon the table tea and coffee, and bread and butter, and salmon, and shad, and liver, and steak, and potatoes, and pickles, and ham, and pudding, and sausages; and three and thirty people sitting round it, eating and drinking; and savoury bottles of gin, and whiskey, and brandy, and rum, in the bar hard by; and seven and twenty out of the eight and twenty men, in foul linen, with yellow streams from half-chewed tobacco trickling down their chins. Perhaps the best time for you to take a peep would be the present: eleven o'clock in the forenoon: when the barber is at his shaving, and the gentlemen are lounging about the stove waiting for their turns, and not more than seventeen are spitting in concert, and two or three are walking overhead (lying down on the luggage every time the man at the helm calls 'Bridge!'), and I am writing this in the ladies' cabin, which is a part of the gentlemen's, and only screened off by a red curtain. Indeed it exactly resembles the dwarf's private apartment in a caravan at a fair; and the gentlemen, generally, represent the spectators at a penny a head. The place is just as clean and just as large as that caravan you and I were in at the Greenwich Fair last past. Outside, it is exactly like any canal boat you have seen near the Regent's Park, or elsewhere.

You never can conceive what the hawking and spitting is, the whole

---

[2] Dickens's secretary, hired in Boston.

night through. Last night was the worst. *Upon my honour and word* I was obliged, this morning, to lay my fur coat on the deck, and wipe the half-dried flakes of spittle from it with my handkerchief; and the only surprise seemed to be that I should consider it necessary to do so. When I turned in last night, I put it on a stool beside me, and there it lay, under a cross-fire from five men—three opposite; one above; and one below. I make no complaints, and shew no disgust. I am looked upon as highly facetious at night, for I crack jokes with everybody near me until we fall asleep. I am considered very hardy in the morning, for I run up, bare-necked, and plunge my head into the half-frozen water, by half-past five o'clock. I am respected for my activity, inasmuch as I jump from the boat to the towing path, and walk five or six miles before breakfast, keeping up with the horses all the time. In a word, they are quite astonished to find a sedentary Englishman roughing it so well, and taking so much exercise; and question me very much on that head. The greater part of the men will sit and shiver round the stove all day, rather than put one foot before the other. As to having a window open, that's not to be thought of.

We expect to reach Pittsburgh tonight, between eight and nine o'clock; and there we ardently hope to find your March letters awaiting us. We have had, with the exception of Friday afternoon, exquisite weather, but cold. Clear starlight and moonlight nights. The canal has run, for the most part, by the side of the Susquehannah and Iwanata [3] rivers; and has been carried through tremendous obstacles. Yesterday, we crossed the mountain. This is done *by railroad*. . . You dine at an inn upon the mountain; and, including the half hour allowed for the meal, are rather more than five hours performing this strange part of the journey. The people north and 'down east' have terrible legends of its dangers; but they appear to be exceedingly careful, and don't go to work at all wildly. There are some queer precipices close to the rails, certainly; but every precaution is taken, I am inclined to think, that such difficulties and such a vast work will admit of.

The scenery, before you reach the mountains, and when you are on them, and after you have left them, is very fine and grand; and the canal winds its way through some deep, sullen gorges, which, seen by moonlight, are very impressive, though immeasurably inferior to Glencoe, to whose terrors I have not seen the smallest *approach*. We have passed, both in the mountains and elsewhere, a great number of new settlements and detached log houses. Their utterly forlorn and miserable appearance baffles all description. I have not seen six cabins out of six hundred where the windows have been whole. Old hats, old

[3] So spelled in Forster; Dickens probably wrote Juniata.

clothes, old boards, old fragments of blanket and paper are stuffed into the broken glass; and their air is misery and desolation. It pains the eye to see the stumps of great trees thickly strewed in every field of wheat; and never to lose the eternal swamp and dull morass, with hundreds of rotten trunks, of elm and pine and sycamore and logwood, steeped in its unwholesome water; where the frogs so croak at night that after dark there is an incessant sound as if millions of phantom teams, with bells, were travelling through the upper air, at an enormous distance off. It is quite an oppressive circumstance, too, to *come* upon great tracts where settlers have been burning down the trees; and where their wounded bodies lie about, like those of murdered creatures; while here and there some charred and blackened giant rears two bare arms aloft, and seems to curse his enemies. The prettiest sight I have seen was yesterday, when we—on the heights of the mountain, and in a keen wind—looked down into a valley full of light and softness: catching glimpses of scattered cabins; children running to the doors; dogs bursting out to bark; pigs scampering home, like so many prodigal sons; families sitting out in their gardens; cows gazing upward, with a stupid indifference; men in their shirt sleeves, looking on at their unfinished houses, and planning work for tomorrow—and the train riding on, high above them, like a storm. But I know this is beautiful—very—very beautiful. . .

I told you of the many uses of the word 'fix.' I ask Mr. Q. on board a steamboat if breakfast be nearly ready, and he tells me yes, he should think so, for when he was last below the steward was 'fixing the tables'—in other words, laying the cloth. When we have been writing and I beg him (do you remember anything of my love of order, at this distance of time?) to collect our papers, he answers that he'll 'fix 'em presently.' So when a man's dressing he's 'fixing' himself, and when you put yourself under a doctor he 'fixes' you in no time. T'other night, before we came on board here, when I had ordered a bottle of mulled claret, and waited some time for it, it was put on table with an apology from the landlord (a lieutenant colonel) that 'he fear'd it wasn't fixed properly.' And here, on Saturday morning, a Western man, handing his potatoes to Mr. Q. at breakfast, enquired if he wouldn't take some of 'these fixings' with his meat. I remained as grave as a judge. I catch them looking at me sometimes, and feel that they think I don't take any notice. Politics are very high here; dreadfully strong; handbills, denunciations, invectives, threats, and quarrels. The question is, who shall be the next President. The election comes off in *three years and a half* from this time.

·   ·   ·

ON BOARD THE *MESSENGER* AGAIN. GOING FROM ST.
LOUIS BACK TO CINCINNATI. FRIDAY, FIFTEENTH
APRIL, 1842

Cincinnati is only fifty years old, but is a very beautiful city; I think
the prettiest place I have seen here, except Boston. It has risen out of
the forest like an Arabian-night city; is well laid out; ornamented in
the suburbs with pretty villas; and above all, for this is a very rare
feature in America, has smooth turf plots and well-kept gardens. There
happened to be a great temperance festival; and the procession mustered
under and passed our windows early in the morning. I suppose they
were twenty thousand strong, at least. Some of the banners were quaint
and odd enough. The ship carpenters, for instance, displayed on one
side of their flag the good ship *Temperance* in full sail; on the other,
the steamer *Alcohol* blowing up sky high. The Irishmen had a portrait
of Father Mathew, you may be sure. And Washington's broad lower
jaw (by the by, Washington had not a pleasant face) figured in all
parts of the ranks. In a kind of square at one outskirt of the city, they
divided into bodies, and were addressed by different speakers. Drier
speaking I never heard. I own that I felt quite uncomfortable to think
they could take the taste out of their mouths with nothing better than
water.

In the evening we went to a party at Judge Walker's, and were introduced to at least one hundred and fifty first-rate bores, separately and
singly. I was required to sit down by the greater part of them, and
talk! In the night we were serenaded (as we usually are in every
place we come to), and very well serenaded, I assure you. But we
were very much knocked up. I really think my face has acquired a
fixed expression of sadness from the constant and unmitigated boring
I endure. The L.L.'s have carried away all my cheerfulness. There is a
line in my chin (on the right side of the under lip), indelibly fixed
there by the New Englander I told you of in my last. I have the print
of my crow's foot on the outside of my left eye, which I attribute to
the literary characters of small towns. A dimple has vanished from
my cheek, which I felt myself robbed of at the time by a wise legislator.
But on the other hand I am really indebted for a good broad grin to
P. E., literary critic of Philadelphia, and sole proprietor of the English
language in its grammatical and idiomatical purity; to P. E., with
the shiny straight hair and turned-down shirt collar, who taketh all
of us English men of letters to task in print, roundly and uncompro-

misingly, but told me at the same time that I had 'awakened a new era' in his mind. . .

The last 200 miles of the voyage from Cincinnati to St. Louis are upon the Mississippi, for you come down the Ohio to its mouth. It is well for society that this Mississippi, the renowned father of waters, had no children who take after him. It is the beastliest river in the world. . .

Conceive the pleasure of rushing down this stream by night (as we did last night) at the rate of fifteen miles an hour; striking against floating blocks of timber at every instant; and dreading some infernal blow at every bump. The helmsman in these boats is in a little glass house upon the roof. In the Mississippi, another man stands in the very head of the vessel, listening and watching intently; listening, because they can tell in dark nights by the noise when any great obstruction is at hand. The man holds the rope of a large bell, which hangs close to the wheel house, and whenever he pulls it the engine is to stop directly, and not to stir until he rings again. Last night, this bell rang at least once in every five minutes; and at each alarm there was a concussion which nearly flung one out of bed. . . While I have been writing this account, we have shot out of that hideous river, thanks be to God; never to see it again, I hope, but in a nightmare. We are now on the smooth Ohio, and the change is like the transition from pain to perfect ease.

We had a very crowded levee in St. Louis. Of course the paper had an account of it. If I were to drop a letter in the street, it would be in the newspaper next day, and nobody would think its publication an outrage The editor objected to my hair, as not curling sufficiently. He admitted an eye; but objected again to dress, as being somewhat foppish, 'and indeed perhaps rather flash.—But such,' he benevolently adds, 'are the differences between American and English taste—rendered more apparent, perhaps, by all the other gentlemen present being dressed in black.' Oh, that you could have seen the other gentlemen! . . .

A St. Louis lady complimented Kate upon her voice and manner of speaking, assuring her that she should never have suspected her of being Scotch, or even English. She was so obliging as to add that she would have taken her for an American, anywhere: which she (Kate) was no doubt aware was a very great compliment, as the Americans were admitted on all hands to have greatly refined upon the English language! I need not tell you that out of Boston and New York a nasal drawl is universal, but I may as well hint that the prevailing grammar is also more than doubtful; that the oddest vulgarisms are received idioms; that all the women who have been bred in slave states speak more or less like Negroes, from having been constantly in their childhood with black nurses; and that the most fashionable and aristocratic (these are two words in great use), instead of asking you in what place you were born, enquire where you 'hail from!'

Lord Ashburton arrived at Annapolis t'other day, after a voyage of forty-odd days in heavy weather. Straightway the newspapers state, on the authority of a correspondent who 'rowed round the ship' (I leave you to fancy her condition), that America need fear no superiority from England in respect of her wooden walls. The same correspondent is 'quite pleased' with the frank manner of the English officers; and patronizes them as being, for John Bulls, quite refined. My face, like Haji Baba's, turns upside down, and my liver is changed to water when I come upon such things, and think who writes and who reads them. . .

They won't let me alone about slavery. A certain judge in St. Louis went so far yesterday that I fell upon him (to the indescribable horror of the man who brought him) and told him a piece of my mind. I said that I was very averse to speaking on the subject here, and always forebore, if possible; but when he pitied our national ignorance of the truths of slavery, I must remind him that we went upon indisputable records, obtained after many years of careful investigation, and at all sorts of self-sacrifice; and that I believed we were much more competent to judge of its atrocity and horror than he who had been brought up in the midst of it. I told him that I could sympathize with men who admitted it to be a dreadful evil, but frankly confessed their inability to devise a means of getting rid of it; but that men who spoke of it as a blessing, as a matter of course, as a state of things to be desired, were out of the pale of reason; and that for them to speak of ignorance or prejudice was an absurdity too ridiculous to be combated. . .

It is not six years ago since a slave in this very same St. Louis, being arrested (I forget for what), and knowing he had no chance of a fair trial, be his offence what it might, drew his bowie knife and ripped the constable across the body. A scuffle ensuing, the desperate Negro stabbed two others with the same weapon. The mob who gathered round (among whom were men of mark, wealth, and influence in the place) overpowered him by numbers; carried him away to a piece of open ground beyond the city; *and burned him alive*. This, I say, was done within six years in broad day; in a city with its courts, lawyers, tipstaffs, judges, jails, and hangman; and not a hair on the head of one of these men has been hurt to this day. And it is, believe me, it is the miserable, wretched independence in small things; the paltry republicanism which recoils from honest service to an honest man, but does not shrink from every trick, artifice, and knavery in business; that makes these slaves necessary, and will render them so, until the indignation of other countries sets them free.

They say the slaves are fond of their masters. Look at this pretty vignette (part of the stock-in-trade of a newspaper), and judge how you would feel, when men, looking in your face, told you such tales with the newspaper lying on the table. In all the slave districts, advertisements for runaways are as much matters of course as the announcement of the play for the evening with us. The poor creatures themselves fairly worship English people; they would do anything for them. They are perfectly acquainted with all that takes place in reference to emancipation; and *of course* their attachment to us grows out of a deep devotion to their owners. I cut this illustration out of a newspaper, which had a leader in reference to *the abominable and hellish doctrine of Abolition—repugnant alike to every law of God and Nature.* 'I know something,' said a Dr. Bartlett (a very accomplished man), late a fellow-passenger of ours, 'I know something of their fondness for their masters. I live in Kentucky; and I can assert upon my honour that, in my neighbourhood, it is as common for a runaway salve, retaken, to draw his bowie knife and rip his owner's bowels open as it is for you to see a drunken fight in London.'

SAME BOAT, SATURDAY, SIXTEENTH APRIL, 1842

Let me tell you, my dear Forster, before I forget it, a pretty little scene we had on board the boat between Louisville and St. Louis, as we were going to the latter place. It is not much to tell, but it was very pleasant and interesting to witness.

There was a little woman on board, with a little baby; and both little woman and little child were cheerful, good-looking, bright-eyed, and fair to see. The little woman had been passing a long time with a sick mother in New York, and had left her home in St. Louis in that condition in which ladies who truly love their lords desire to be. The baby had been born in her mother's house, and she had not seen her husband (to whom she was now returning) for twelve months, having left him a month or two after their marriage. Well, to be sure, there never was a little woman so full of hope, and tenderness, and love, and anxiety, as this little woman was: and there she was, all the livelong day, wondering whether 'he' would be at the wharf; and whether 'he' had got her letter; and whether, if she sent the baby on shore by somebody else, '*he' would know it, meeting it in the street*—which, seeing that he had never set eyes upon it in his life, was not very likely in the abstract, but was probable enough to the young mother. She was such an artless little creature; and was in such a sunny, beaming, hopeful state; and let out all this matter, clinging close about her heart, so freely; that all the other lady passengers entered into the spirit of it as much as she: and the captain (who heard all about it from his wife) was wondrous sly, I promise you, enquiring, every time we met at table, whether she expected anybody to meet her at St. Louis, and supposing she wouldn't want to go ashore the night we reached it, and cutting many other dry jokes which convulsed all his hearers, but especially the ladies. There was one little, weazen, dried-apple old woman among them, who took occasion to doubt the constancy of husbands under such circumstances of bereavement; and there was another lady (with a lapdog), old enough to moralize on the lightness of human affections, and yet not so old that she could help nursing the baby now and then, or laughing with the rest when the little woman called it by its father's name, and asked it all manner of fantastic questions concerning him, in the joy of her heart. It was something of a blow to the little woman that when we were within twenty miles of our destination, it became clearly necessary to put the baby to bed; but she got over that with the same good humour, tied a little handkerchief over her little head, and came out into the little gallery with the rest. Then, such an oracle as she became in reference to the localities; and such facetiousness as was displayed by the married ladies! and such sympathy as was shown by the single ones, and such peals of laughter as the little woman herself (who would just as soon have cried) greeted every jest with! At last, there were the lights of St. Louis—and here was the wharf—and those were the steps—and the little woman, covering her face with her hands, and laughing, or seeming to laugh, more than ever, ran into her own cabin, and shut herself up tight. I have no doubt that, in the charming inconsistency of such excitement, she stopped her ears lest she should hear 'him' asking for her; but I didn't see her do it. Then a great crowd of people rushed on board, though the boat was not yet made fast, and was staggering about among the other boats to find a landing place; and everybody looked for the husband, and nobody saw him; when all of a sudden, right in the midst of them—God knows how she ever got there—there was the little woman hugging with both arms round the neck of a fine, good-looking, sturdy fellow! And in a moment afterwards there she was again, dragging him through the small door of her small cabin, to look at the baby as he lay asleep!—What a good thing it is to know that so many of us would have been quite downhearted and sorry if that husband had failed to come.

But about the Prairie—it is not, I must confess, so good in its way as this; but I'll tell you about that, too, and leave you to judge for yourself. Tuesday the 12th was the day fixed; and we were to start at five in the morning—sharp. I turned out at four; shaved and dressed; got some bread and milk; and throwing up the window, looked down into the street. Deuce a coach was there, nor did anybody seem to be stirring in the house. I waited until half-past five; but no preparations being visible even then, I left Mr. Q. to look out, and lay down upon the bed again. There I slept until nearly seven, when I was called. . . Exclusive of Mr. Q. and myself, there were twelve of my committee in the party, all lawyers except one. He was an intelligent, mild, well-informed gentleman of my own age—the Unitarian minister of the place. With him and two other companions, I got into the first coach. . .

We halted at so good an inn at Lebanon that we resolved to return there at night, if possible. One would scarcely find a better village ale-house of a homely kind in England. During our halt I walked into the village, and met a *dwelling house* coming downhill at a good round trot, drawn by some twenty oxen! We resumed our journey as soon as possible, and got upon the looking-glass prairie at sunset. We halted near a solitary log house for the sake of its water; unpacked the baskets; formed an encampment with the carriages; and dined.

Now, a prairie is undoubtedly worth seeing—but more that one may say one has seen it than for any sublimity it possesses in itself. Like most things, great or small, in this country, you hear of it with considerable exaggerations. Basil Hall was really quite right in depreciating the general character of the scenery. The widely famed Far West is not to be compared with even the tamest portions of Scotland or Wales. You stand upon the prairie and see the unbroken horizon all round you. You are on a great plain, which is like a sea without water. I am exceedingly fond of wild and lonely scenery, and believe that I have the faculty of being as much impressed by it as any man living. But the prairie fell, by far, short of my preconceived idea. I felt no such emotions as I do in crossing Salisbury Plain. The excessive flatness of the scene makes it dreary, but tame. Grandeur is certainly not its characteristic. I retired from the rest of the party, to understand my own feelings the better; and looked all round, again and again. It was fine. It was worth the ride. The sun was going down, very red and bright; and the prospect looked like that ruddy sketch of Catlin's, which attracted our attention (you remember?); except that there was not so much ground as he represents, between the spectator and the horizon. But to say (as the fashion is, here) that the sight is a landmark in one's existence and awakens a new set of sensations is sheer gammon. I would say to every man who can't see a prairie—go to Salisbury Plain, Marlborough Downs, or any of the broad, high, open lands near the sea. Many of them are fully as impressive; and Salisbury Plain is *decidedly* more so.

We had brought roast fowls, buffalo's tongue, ham, bread, cheese, butter, biscuits, sherry, champagne, lemons, and sugar for punch, and abundance of ice. It was a delicious meal, and as they were most anxious that I should be pleased, I warmed myself into a state of surpassing jollity; proposed toasts from the coach box (which was the chair); ate and drank with the best; and made, I believe, an excellent companion to a very friendly companionable party. In an hour or so, we packed up, and drove back to the inn at Lebanon. While supper was preparing, I took a pleasant walk with my Unitarian friend; and when it was over (we drank nothing with it but tea and coffee) we went to bed. The clergyman and I had an exquisitely clean little chamber of our own: and the rest of the party were quartered overhead. . .

We got back to St. Louis soon after twelve at noon; and I rested during the remainder of the day. The soiree came off at night, in a very good ballroom at our inn—the Planter's House. The whole of the guests were introduced to us, singly. We were glad enough, you may believe, to come away at midnight; and were very tired. Yesterday, I wore a blouse. Today, a fur coat. Trying changes!

IN THE SAME BOAT. SUNDAY, SIXTEENTH [4] APRIL, 1842

The inns in these outlandish corners of the world would astonish you by their goodness. The Planter's House is as large as the Middlesex Hospital, and built very much on our hospital plan, with long wards abundantly ventilated, and plain whitewashed walls. They had a famous notion of sending up at breakfast time large glasses of new milk with blocks of ice in them as clear as crystal. Our table was abundantly supplied indeed at every meal. One day when Kate and I were dining alone together, in our own room, we counted sixteen dishes on the table at the same time.

The society is pretty rough and intolerably conceited. All the inhabitants are young. *I didn't see one gray head in St. Louis.* There is an island close by, called Bloody Island. It is the duelling ground of St. Louis; and is so called from the last fatal duel which was fought there. It was a pistol duel, breast to breast, and both parties fell dead at the same time. One of our prairie party (a young man) had acted there as

[4] Actually April seventeenth.

second in several encounters. The last occasion was a duel with rifles, at forty paces; and coming home he told us how he had bought his man a coat of green linen to fight in, woolen being usually fatal to rifle wounds. Prairie is variously called (on the refinement principle I suppose) para*a*rer; par*e*arer; and par*o*arer. . .

Part III

Travelers of the Third Period, 1840-70

Travelers of the Third Period, 1840-70

Unbiased Portraiture ॐ

AN era of detached appraisal, without much political philosophizing, followed the pamphleteering travels of the 'thirties. One reason for the change was the fact that, subsequent to the Reform Act of 1832, governmental issues aroused less and less alarm in England among the conservatives, particularly after Peel brought the Tories into power again in 1841. The attacks of the *Quarterly* and *Blackwood's* were more and more forgotten, and the motives behind them ceased to affect the judgment of the traveler. Moreover, it was now plain that the astonishing growth of the United States had passed beyond the rawness of youth, and the increasing wealth and power of the republic inspired a more respectful attitude in its visitors. A natural reaction followed upon the attacks of writers like Mrs. Trollope, Faux, and Fidler, which had all too evidently contributed to the American tendency, strong enough before, to regard England as an enemy.

One English traveler after another took occasion to denounce these libels. William E. Baxter, an Edinburgh merchant, in his *America and the Americans,* rejoiced that 'the incorrect and caricatured accounts of the United States,' offered by men who had catered to a temporary fashion for ridiculing and sneering at the republic, had yielded to the friendly pictures drawn by Sir Charles Lyell, Lord Carlisle, Colonel (later Sir) Arthur Cunynghame, and Lady Emmeline Stuart Wortley. Mrs. Houstoun, the author of a book of American travel called *Hesperos,* lifted her voice against the 'prejudice and fancied contempt' of earlier writers. Most important of all the new visitors, Alexander Mackay, a highly competent journalist as well as barrister, expressed in the preface to *The Western World* his regret that so many predecessors had evinced a predetermination to ridicule everything. It was time, he declared, for England to have 'a correct account of a great country, and a faithful portraiture of a great people.' Dedicating his work to Richard

Cobden, he treated all sides of the nation's life, from the party system and literature to canals and religious architecture.

Mackay was qualified to write what is the best book of the time upon America, three systematic and acute volumes, by his warm sympathy, for he was an ardent radical, and his long acquaintance with us, for he had lived in the United States some years before making the journey he describes. His work is pleasantly diversified—here a chapter on politics, there a descriptive account of a month of travel, here again a disquisition upon manners. Divesting himself wholly of condescension or reserve, he met all kinds of Americans as one of themselves, and was rewarded by an easy and frank intercourse with them. No observant man ought to say, he remarked, that the Americans are chilly and distant, for their fault was actually rather an excessive vivacity and openness:

During my preregrinations through the Union . . . I had frequent opportunity of seeing how English travellers demeaned themselves on passing through the country. I invariably found that those who met the Americans frankly and ingenuously were treated with the utmost kindness and warm-heartedness, and were consequently favourably impressed with the character of the people; whereas such as travelled through the country as if it were a compliment to the Republic that they touched its democratic soil, and as if the mere fact of their being Englishmen entitled them to treat all who came in their way with ill-dissembled hauteur and contumely, were left to find their way as they best could, the cold shoulder being turned to them wherever they went.

Almost the precise route of Dickens was covered by Mackay, with the addition of a circuit of the South; and it is interesting to contrast the equable and amiable pages of the barrister with the pungent vividness of the novelist. The hogs of Broadway and the squalor of the Five Points are barely mentioned in Mackay's full description of a city that he pronounced very fine. Instead, the emphasis falls upon the beauty of the bay and its islands, the attractiveness of the Battery, traversed in every direction by lines of 'magnificent trees,' the pleasant residential aspect of lower Broadway, with its terraces of houses 'both elegant and lofty, some being built of red brick, and others of gray granite from Massachusetts'; the bustle and crowded wealth of the wharves, with auctioneers here and there disposing of goods; the fine effect of the granite portico of the new Merchants' Exchange on Broadway; the forest of masts in the East River, and the crowd of steamship funnels in the lower Hudson—all concluding with an account of the wonderful new Croton aqueduct, which could bring 60 million gallons of water every day 33 miles to the city. Not a word is uttered against the fair fame of Philadelphia, with its symmetry of plan, flaring red brick houses, and shady streets; save that it was blazing hot when he arrived there, many horses dropping dead in the streets under a temperature of 104°. The decorous look of the soberly dressed people was as marked as the Quaker aspect of the town itself. Thus Mackay, seated on a hotel balcony, overheard a conversation between an army officer and his friend:

'Who, think you,' said the former, 'was the most flashily dressed man I met to-day?'

'Can't tell,' said his friend.

'Why, a corporal in my own company, to be sure,' added the officer. 'He looked like a blue jay among fantails.'

'Is he a Philadelphian?' inquired the other.

'No,' replied the officer. 'He's from "the land of steady habits." '

'Ah, from Connecticut,' said his friend; 'he must have passed through Broadway on his way here then.'

Baltimore pleased Mackay, though he did not agree with Lord Carlisle that it was the most beautifully situated of American towns, and though he thought its title of 'monumental city' affected in view of the fact that its only important monuments were the Washington pillar and a tasteless memorial to the dead of 1812. Upon Washington he made the stock remarks of the British traveler: that it was a thousand pities it had not grown symmetrically in both directions along the Potomac, as was intended, instead of wholly to the west, that its streets were too wide for the building façade, and its distance in every way too great, that the place looked like a collection of incipient country villages, that the plain brick government buildings, painted blue, were exceedingly ugly, and so on. But the Capitol itself he thought most imposing, and when viewed by moonlight, its milky white walls rising amid the fountains and shrubbery, a fairyland dream of magnificence. In the West he wrote of St. Louis with warm admiration for its rapid growth—it contained 34,000 people at the time!—and with a prediction that it would advance to the first place among inland cities and entrepots of trade. He had also the tact to speak well of the prairies, which Dickens had deemed rather depressing, saying that 'when the wind sweeps over them the effect is magnificent.' On his way home he halted at Rochester, the town Captain Basil Hall had described so slightingly, and he seemed not to know which to admire most—its rapid growth to a population of 30,000, the beauty of its situation on the Genesee, or the charm of its society, 'which is intellectual, highly cultivated, hospitable, frank, and warmhearted.'

It must not be thought that the clear-sighted Mackay had no criticisms. No traveler spoke with greater disgust of the filthy tobacco-chewing, which was a feature of American life everywhere south of the Hudson. He tells us that the floods of tobacco juice squirted all over the railway cars frequently forced him to take refuge on the platforms; that passengers would spit between his feet and over his shoulders; that he had seen a man take the quid from his mouth and draw ornamental figures on the window pane with it; and that at evening parties he saw young gentlemen in acute discomfort because they could not chew. He spoke with stern indignation of the racial prejudice so evident in the United States. Traveling from Philadelphia to Baltimore, he saw a white-skinned mulatto, neatly dressed, and of refined appearance, summarily ordered into the Jim Crow car by the conductor; the whites sneering at him as he departed, and the Negroes guffawing as he entered. 'He'll know his place better the next time, the b—y mongrel!' said one white man.

The excessive taste of Americans for speculation naturally struck him, and he describes several such evidences of it as the empty Baltimore suburb named Canton, which had paving and all other improvements save houses. Like Dickens, he gathered that while Washington had a few genuine statesmen, most of the Congressmen formed 'a crowd of brawling and obstreperous political adventurers who unfortunately play too conspicuous a part in the social drama of the capital.'

His picture of the manners of these men is repulsive. 'When neither house of Congress is sitting, groups of male idlers are constantly to be seen loitering in the streets, or smoking and chewing in crowds in front of the hotels, where they ogle with little delicacy the few women that pass; or noisily congregate in the barroom, treating themselves liberally to gin slings, sherry cobblers, and mint juleps.' In the rural districts, he thought, the voters were frequently misled by demagogy, but seldom corrupted, while in the large towns, especially those with a heavy Irish population, bribery was extensively practiced.

Mackay's analysis of slavery is at once more thoughtful and more moderate than that of Dickens, Mrs. Trollope, or even Miss Martineau. All Americans, he pointed out, acknowledged it to be a curse. 'It hangs about the social and political system like a great tumor upon the body, which cannot be suddenly cut away, without risking a hemorrhage that would endanger life, and which cannot be permitted to remain without incurring perils equally certain, though not so immediate.' He reminded English critics of a fact they continually ignored, that Congress had no power over slavery in the states. Unlike Miss Martineau, he believed that the Abolitionists were by their fanaticism delaying instead of forwarding emancipation, and that in any event early emancipation must be a chimera. Britons were wont to pride themselves upon the contrast between American slavery and the freedom they had effected in the West Indies, but Mackay showed that the boast had

little solid basis—that they were comparing a remote and petty difficulty
with a great evil existing in the very midst of a nation, and interwoven
with the social, political, and economic institutions of half of the republic. All this was a reasonable prelude to his scorching indictment of
slavery:

> It appears in its true light, in all its revolting atrocities, in the cotton-growing
> states. Whatever hideousness may be imparted to it by severity of toil and bru-
> tality of treatment, it there assumes without a mask. Badly housed, and not
> unfrequently scantily fed, the wretched slaves are driven, morning after morning,
> in hordes to the fields, where they labour till nightfall beneath a burning sun,
> and under the eyes and the lashes of superintendents, against whom they dare
> not, however well founded, prefer a complaint. To the unfeeling severity which
> characterizes the servitude of these states, there are, in the conduct of many
> planters, very honourable exceptions . . . ; but the candour of every American
> citizen who has travelled in the South will bear me out in the assertion that, in
> the practical working of slavery in the cotton-growing districts, humanity is the
> exception, and brutality the rule. It is unnecessary to dwell any longer upon
> this, or to specify the horrors which I myself have witnessed, and which would
> only be counterparts to the frightful catalogue, at the recital of which the better
> feelings of our nature have already so often revolted.

It is in his generalizations that Mackay's friendliness and fairness
are most evident. Americans were, he said, the cleanest people with
whom he had ever come in contact. They were far and away the most
prosperous. England paid four and a half times as much as the United
States to be governed, and was governed much worse, while English
inequality and privilege were the root of evils unknown in America.
'We present an imposing front to the world; but let us tear the picture
and look at the canvas. One out of every seven of us is a pauper. Every
six Englishmen have, in addition to their other enormous burdens, to
support a seventh between them, whose life is spent in consuming, but
in adding nothing to the source of their common subsistence.'

He praised the attitude of Americans toward education, which they
regarded 'in its true light—not merely as something that should not
be neglected, but as an indispensable coadjutor in the work of consolidating and promoting their schemes.' One of his many shrewd remarks explains why Americans had so little of that local attachment
which is strong in all Europe, and migrated so readily from state to
state, section to section. It was because they pinned their affections to
institutions rather than places, and cared only to have the same flag
over them and the same forms of government and society accompanying them. From this affection, reasoned Mackay, sprang the American
boastfulness, for every citizen believed himself implicated in the success of democracy, which was on test before the world, and was eager

to show himself the champion of democratic institutions. Hence, also, sprang the keen interest of most Americans in public affairs.

The one other English traveler writing between 1840 and 1860 whose work aimed at an encyclopedic goal, James Silk Buckingham, was an all-round reformer, interested in temperance, education, the betterment of the working classes, free trade, and universal peace, who came to speak as well as to observe, and whose lectures were heard or read by at least a million Americans. Nevertheless, his treatise is remarkably free from priggishness. The faults he found in us were precisely those which Miss Martineau, Mackay, the Earl of Carlisle, and other observers of the period noted—our unresting hurry; our tendency to live in hotels and boarding-houses; our excessive sensitiveness to English censure; and the failure of nearly everyone (particularly the young women, who kept late hours, ate hasty meals of pastry, cakes, and ice-cream, studied too hard, and took insufficient exercise) to look after bodily health. His pages on our yellow press are excellent, laying especial emphasis on a quality that in this modern day of the 'sob story' has become obsolete, their cynicism. Some faults that others overlooked he also treated, such as our extraordinary appetite for quack medicines. 'Fortunes are made in the shortest space of time by men who invent a new pill or potion; and there are at least twenty striking examples of this in the city of Philadelphia alone, though there are upwards of 400 regularly educated and practising physicians there.' He, like Dickens, unanswerably illustrated our violence by newspaper clippings of affrays and murders.

Yet Buckingham's total impression of America, as recorded in his eight detailed, fact-weighted, and rather dull volumes, was as complaisant as Mackay's. His tastes led him to examine our charitable and educational enterprises narrowly, and he was as much pleased by them as by our comparative liberalism in such fields as the penal code. If the republic were wisely governed, and preserved from luxury, intemperance, and war, he concluded, 'there are hardly any bounds to the expectations that may be formed of its future greatness.' He specially praised the educational facilities of the country, pronouncing the teachers of New York better than those of the national schools of England.

This same note of confidence in the splendid destiny of wealth and strength that awaited the United States runs through all the other books of travel of this period. Mackay, for example, warned Great Britain that America already offered, by her colossal industrial strides, a rivalry that might become disastrous to the mother land. Unless the latter hastened to meet the peril, the republic would absorb her capital and make her a comparatively weak nation. If the industry of 25 million

people, with limited means, had raised England to her existing pinnacle of greatness, what would the industry of 150 million accomplish
with the illimitable resources of North America? The United States
'is yet destined to rear up a fabric of commercial greatness, such as the
world has hitherto been a stranger to.' James Mursell Phillippo, whose
The United States and Cuba was published in 1857, predicted that at
the close of the century the young country would have a population
approaching 100 million, a remarkably accurate guess, and he elsewhere
asserted that in another half century 'she will be almost indubitably
the most powerful government on earth. There seems to be no limit to
her growth, and no possible hindrance to her taking the most prominent and leading position except that of internal dissensions.' Our
Mexican conquests and rapid expansion to the Pacific had much to do
with these prophecies. Yet as early as 1846, in his hastily written
Hochelaga, G. D. Warburton—brother of the author of a more famous
book of travels, *Crescent and Cross*—had asserted in the same terms:

> Most of the present generation among us have been brought up and lived in
> the idea that England is supreme in the Congress of Nations. I am one of that
> numerous class—long may it be a numerous one!—but I say with sorrow that a
> doubt crosses my mind, and something more than a doubt, that this giant son
> will soon tread on his parent's heels. The power of both increases rapidly in a
> geometric series, but with different multipliers. The merchant navy of the British
> islands has doubled since the war; that of America has trebled—the population
> of the former has increased by one half in the same period; the latter has
> doubled. . .

The dominant British opinion, to judge by volumes of travel, was
now emphatically convinced of the success of our republican form of
government. Phillippo took clear issue with Marryat and Hall, saying
that he hoped his readers would perceive that, so far as the system of
government went, in America 'little is left to be desired by the wise
and liberal of mankind.' He eulogized the humanity of our laws, the
efficiency of our justice, the freedom of our press, and our exemption
from crushing military burdens. All this he found to exert a salutary
effect on our manners; 'they exhibit a sort of republican plainness or
abruptness, but a simplicity withal that is quite in harmony with the
institutions of the country.' Baxter declared the American government
one of the most complicated, yet ingenious and practically perfect, that
had ever been devised, and burst into still stronger superlatives in his
admiration. 'I can conceive of no spectacle,' he said, 'displaying in a
greater degree the elements of grandeur, than 23 millions of men, educated, intelligent, and industrious, enjoying the freest political power,
and yet without the presence of a standing army.' Alexander Mackay

congratulated America upon starting from the point, in political and economic organization, 'to which society in Europe is only yet tending.'

A few hostile voices there still were. Edward Sullivan, later a baronet and a figure prominent in English politics, can hardly be listed among them, for he simply took the sober view that while many of our political practices were admirable, they were quite unsuited to Great Britain. But Hugh Seymour Tremenheere, a London barrister, went further; he wrote a comparison of the English and American Constitutions, in which the latter appeared in a very disadvantageous light. Nassau William Senior, one of the best-known economists of the time, long connected with Oxford and an indefatigable contributor to the *Edinburgh Review,* was the most vigorous in his attacks. He declared, in an essay evoked in 1856 by the cordial reception given to *Uncle Tom's Cabin* in England, that our government was wretched, for official posts were 'generally left to the inferior men whose ignorance, violence, or incapacity have led those who judge of America only through her public servants to look on her with merited contempt and disgust.' But the voices of friends like Alexander Mackay, whose volumes went through four British editions in 1850, Buckingham, and Baxter, bore down these unconvincing statements.

While in literary finish no book of travels between that of Dickens and that of Anthony Trollope just twenty years later stands conspicuously high, Alexander Mackay's bright pages are by no means alone in their readability. Charles Lyell, the eminent geologist, in 1845-9 published four pleasing volumes of description, in which natural scenery was usually emphasized over social and political interest. His account of the South in *A Second Visit to the United States* is especially valuable. In rural districts he found the manners exceedingly crude, but he seems to have endured impositions and impertinence with good-natured dignity. Thus in taking a molasses steamer, the *Andrew Jackson,* from Vicksburg to Cincinnati, he found that his fellow-passengers insisted upon knowing at once how old he was, how many children he had, how he liked the country, and many other particulars. 'As I was pacing the deck,' he continues, 'one passenger after another eyed my short-sight glass, suspended by a ribbon round my neck, with much curiosity. Some of them asked me to read for them the name inscribed on the stern of a steamer so far off that I doubted whether a good telescope would have enabled me to do more than discern the exact place where the name was written. Others, abruptly seizing the glass, without leave or apology, brought their heads into close contact with mine, and looking through it, exclaimed, in a disappointed and half reproachful tone, that they could see nothing.' A monocle would naturally excite attention, but there was no excuse for the similar treatment of Mrs. Lyell.

'Meanwhile the wives and daughters of passengers of the same class were sitting idle in the ladies' cabin, occasionally taking my wife's embroidery out of her hand, without asking leave, and examining it, with many comments, usually, however, in a complimentary strain.' Lyell was amused to find the train boy calling out, in the midst of the pine barren between Columbus, Georgia, and Chehaw, 'A novel, by Paul le Koch, the Bulwer of France, for twenty-five cents—all the go! more popular than the *Wandering Jew*.' He was equally diverted in going down to dinner the first night at his hotel in Jackson, Mississippi, to find that the landlord, a general of militia, called the large crowd of diners to order, proclaimed, in the loud voice of a herald, 'Gentlemen, we are a great people,' and then called out the names of all the viands on his long table and on the sideboard, beginning with 'beefsteak, with or without onions, roast turkey, pork, hominy, fish, eggs,' and other substantial dishes. But he was by no means so much pleased to find placards in various Southern towns demanding 'Forty-five or Fight,' and incessant talk of war with England over Oregon.

Lyell saw very little evidence of maltreatment of the Negroes in the South, and much evidence that they were treated well. At Tuscaloosa, for example, he stopped at a house where the domestic servants were allowed to give a supper to a large party of their friends, whom they feasted on roast turkeys (wild turkeys cost only twenty-five cents apiece), icecream, jelly, and cakes. The geologist's general observations upon the Negro were shrewd. He satisfied himself that they learned quickly, and that wherever they came into contact with advanced white people they reached a high level of culture. Everywhere they had acquired English, shaken off their African superstitions, taken to Christianity, accepted higher ideas of morality, and formed habits of neatness and cleanliness. By the end of the century, he predicted, there would be 12 million Negroes in America. Were it not for certain disturbing causes, 'I should cherish the most sanguine hopes of their future improvement and emancipation, and even their ultimate amalgamation and fusion with the whites, so highly has my estimate of their moral and intellectual capabilities been raised by what I have lately seen in Georgia and Alabama.' Of the general future of the South he also formed a favorable impression, noticing that in the old-settled communities the amenities of life were well developed. When he has a distinct piece of fault-finding, as in his declaration that 'drunkenness prevails' among the Georgia planters, he only mentions it casually.

Baxter's book abounds in truisms, or at least what a majority of English travelers of the time considered truisms. He maintained that we did not have enough home life, patronizing the boarding-house too much; that we overheated our homes; that we were excessively gallant to womenfolk, depriving them of independence and self-reliance; that we ate our meals too fast, and used an improper amount of fat in cooking; that our spitting and profanity were equally bad; that we had few beautiful women, but an unequaled number of pretty women; and that our charitable and reformatory institutions were marvelous. For his strictures he atoned by a consistent admiration of the American capacity for self-government, the educational system, and the material prosperity he saw everywhere. His book also contains a number of touches of human nature and humor. To illustrate our boastfulness, our we-can-whip-universal-natur'-spirit, he relates that while chatting with a gentleman in a Southern hotel he chanced to say that Providence had apparently designed the two nations to civilize the globe. 'Two nations!' broke in a little sharp-featured man. 'Guess there's only one, stranger; goin' to annex that island of yourn one of them fine days; don't know how little Vic will like that, but got to do it, and no mistake about that.' It was a Maine Yankee who, after insisting upon drawing from Baxter all his opinions regarding the United States, finally ejaculated: 'Well, now, I declare I know'd it; we air a great people, and bound to be tolerable troublesome to them kings.'

But a still more vivacious writer was Charles Mackay, a popular English lecturer, author of the well-known song, 'The Good Time Coming,' and at one time editor of the *London Illustrated News*. From him we had in 1859 one of our best antebellum pictures of New York City. He was vastly pleased by our Eastern metropolis, declaring Broadway, with its air of Parisian gaiety, finer than any English street. The St. Nicholas Hotel, a glittering white marble pile on Broadway, and the Metropolitan Hotel near by, had now eclipsed the Astor House in grandeur, and he impressively informed his readers that upon occasion the former made up 700 beds a night. London had no more imposing business houses than many that lined upper Broadway, like Stewart's and Haughwoot and Company's, some marble and some of brown stone. We were sadly behind London in possessing no cab service, and depending still on old-fashioned hackney coaches, the Irish drivers of which charged extortionate fees. But the streets swarmed with convenient white omnibuses, which pedestrians could halt and enter at any point, paying the driver through a hole in the roof; while on some of the avenues paralleling Broadway there were now horsecars. Mackay, like Trollope and R. H. Russell a few years later, was a little aghast at the enormous swaying crinolines worn by the ladies who made a fashionable parade of Broadway every afternoon. They were far larger than in London, and the Negresses ballooned about in them precisely like the white women. The streets, with their many Irish and German immigrants, their ragged, shouting newsboys, their firemen's parades, and their mass meetings to hear speeches by Fernando Wood and other candidates for office, were a perpetual show to the Englishman. He was glad to see that there was little overt vice, though he considered the police force inadequate, and learned from the press that crimes of violence were altogether too common. With special gusto he mentions the underground oyster saloons, which were scattered in every block along Broadway, and in which the bivalves were served under every conceivable form.

Good descriptions of Boston and Philadelphia also may be found in Charles Mackay. The former city, so intellectual in atmosphere, was something of a shock after New York. 'In walking along Washington Street,' the traveler states, 'and meeting a gentlemanly-looking person with a decent coat and a clean shirt, the traveller may safely put him down as either a lecturer, a Unitarian minister, or a poet; possibly the man may be, Cerberus-like, all three at once.' Mackay had his sarcastic moments, as when he suggested that the emblem of the United States should be, not an eagle, but a spittoon. But in general he was more than cordial to 'that great Republic, which is so rapidly rising to overshadow the world.'

For the first time, the Far West enters prominently into the writings of British travelers of this period. Alexander Mackay closed his three volumes by a chapter on California, its material secondhand but its tone glowing. William Chandless published in 1857 an entertaining but rather unreliable book called *A Visit to Salt Lake*. And a far more distinguished man, Richard F. Burton, already renowned for his Arabian travels, produced one of the classic volumes on the Old West in *The City of the Saints*. It details his journey from St. Joseph, Missouri, to San Francisco in 1860, and furnishes a graphic description of the Mormons as he saw them in the summer of that year. Introduced to Brigham Young, Governor Cumming, and other leaders, he was able to obtain much material on social and economic conditions which can be found nowhere else. His attitude is scientific, his temper is tolerant, and his conclusions are in the main favorable. In his four weeks in Salt Lake City, according to the historian H. H. Bancroft, he saw more than many a man did in four years.

Over all these travels the threat of a coming disaster to the nation now spread its black shadow—the disaster of sectional conflict. The English writers surveyed the rising storm with very different eyes. Miss Martineau had said in the 'thirties that secession would be impossible, since the slave states could not repress a servile revolt and fight back the Northern armies at the same time. Of the later observers, Baxter, writing on the very eve of the Civil War, thought that slavery was slowly giving ground, and that hopes might be entertained of its peaceful abolition. Charles Mackay, at the same time, did not believe that disruption was an immediate danger, though he thought it might occur when the United States had 100 million people. But two English travelers were more clear-sighted. Warburton predicted a civil war, ending in the abandonment of republican forms by the South: 'many of us will live to see an absolute monarch rule over the slave states,' he prophesied. Alexander Mackay believed that the nation had never struggled through a crisis like that which was approaching. The time was at hand, he wrote, 'when one of the two sections of the Union must obtain, in connection with this subject, a final and decisive victory over the other, or when the Union itself will be rent asunder.' Equally shrewd was his declaration that a great physical obstacle existed to the permanent separation of the North and South as two nations—the Mississippi. To the people of the West this artery was so essential that they would never relinquish control of its mouth to a foreign government.

The war came; and with the eyes of Europe upon us as never before in our national history, the reports of travelers were read with a new and keener interest in the Old World.

Of our numerous visitors from England during the Civil War, three only call for special mention—W. H. Russell, Anthony Trollope, and Edward Dicey. The first-named, one of the greatest of all war correspondents, a writer with an unusual faculty for observation and graphic description, came to our shores in March 1861, as a minister from a true Power, the London *Times*. By his very first letters to that organ he earned the hostility of the North. He was convinced at the outset, and remained so until his departure in April 1862, that the Union in its old integrity could never be restored, if only because the two sections were temperamentally and economically unfitted to live in harmony; and he also believed that the war would benefit them by chastening their temper. They would learn, he declared in the preface to *My Diary North and South* (1862), to work out their great experiment in government 'not in their old arrogance and insolence—mistaking material prosperity for good government—but in fear and trembling.' This resentment of our boastfulness and 'arrogance,' at which Englishmen had long merely laughed, had by now become marked in certain circles. The economist Senior had declared only half a dozen years earlier that 'we have long been smarting under the conceit of America—we are tired of hearing her boast that she is the freest and most enlightened country that the world has ever seen.' Russell was the more inclined to speak harshly because he was badly treated in this country, while he was unquestionably offended by the active anti-British feeling that he found.

His *Diary* is as rich in historical value as in interest, which is saying much. His energy and reputation at first carried him everywhere, and his courage made him signally outspoken. In New York, where Mayor Fernando Wood and half the press were opposed to the war, he was shocked by the apathy and want of patriotism. The historian Bancroft told him that we had the strongest, most beneficent government in the world, and that as a government it possessed no power of coercing the seceded states; to which view Samuel Tilden and Horatio Seymour assented. The pages of the *Herald* and several other journals were filled with the coarsest abuse of the Great Rail Splitter, but contained not a word to encourage the government in any decided policy. Horace Greeley, talking with Russell, was anxious for him to see the South. 'Be sure that you examine the slave pens,' he counseled. '*They* will be afraid to refuse you, and you can tell the truth.'

In Washington the correspondent found much bustle and nervousness, but complete uncertainty. He met Seward, Lincoln, whose natural sagacity impressed him favorably, and General Scott, whose conversation upon old battles entertained him; but he was more impressed by the universal office-hunting than by any preparations for war. When he saw the District of Columbia militia and volunteers drilling before the War Department Building, he set them down as a sorry crowd. 'Starved, washed-out creatures most of them, interpolated with Irish and flat-footed, stumpy Germans.' General Scott had only some 700 or 800 regulars to protect the capital. The President, unwilling to estrange the hesitating border states, seemed temporizing and timid. 'It is perfectly wonderful to hear people using the word Government at all, as applied to the President and his cabinet,' concluded Russell; 'a body which has no power "according to the Constitution" to save the country governed or itself from destruction.' Under the very shadow of the capitol he found people praying for the expulsion of Lincoln and the installment of Davis as President.

Crossing into the South, the correspondent found a far more belligerent spirit than among the Northerners. At Norfolk a crowd was yelling, 'Down with the Yankees! Hurrah for the Southern Confederacy!' and threatening the frigate *Cumberland*. On the Wilmington quay there were piles of shot and shell, which a resident identified as 'anti-abolitionist pills.' All along the railway in the Carolinas he found Confederate flags whipping in the breeze, troops waiting for the train, and an excited buzz about Fort Sumter, which had just been captured. At Charleston the fury, the animosity, and the eagerness for war astounded him. He went out to Morris Island, where there was a camp, full of life and excitement. Tents were pitched everywhere, the place was full of tall, well-grown young men in gray, and the opening of hostilities had plainly put everyone in high spirits:

In one long tent there was a party of roystering young men, opening claret and mixing 'cup' in large buckets; whilst others were helping the servants to set out a table for a banquet to one of their generals. Such heat, tobacco smoke, clamor, toasts, drinking, handshaking, vows of friendship! Many were the excuses made for the more demonstrative of the Edonian youths by their friends. 'Tom is a little cut, sir; but he is a splendid fellow—he's worth half a million of dollars.' This reference to a money standard of value was not unusual or perhaps unnatural, but it was made repeatedly; and I was told wonderful tales of the riches of men who were hanging round, dressed as privates, some of whom at that season, in years gone by, were looked for at the watering places as the great lions of American fashion. But Secession is the fashion here. Young ladies sing for it; old ladies pray for it; young men are dying to fight for it; old men are ready to demonstrate it. The founder of the school was St. Calhoun. Here his pupils carry out their teaching in thunder and fire. States' Rights are displayed after its legitimate teaching, and the Palmetto flag and the red bars of the Confederacy are its exposition. The utter contempt and loathing for the venerated Stars and Stripes, the abhorrence of the very words United States, the immense hatred of the Yankees on the part of these people cannot be conceived by anyone who has not seen them. I am more satisfied than ever that the Union can never be restored as it was, and that it has gone to pieces, never to be put together again, in the old shape, at all events, by any power on earth.

At Pensacola, Mobile, and New Orleans, he was struck by the same intense fighting spirit, reporting that 'as one looks at the resolute, quick, angry faces around him, and hears but the single theme, he must feel the South will never yield to the North, unless as a nation beaten beneath the feet of a victorious enemy.' When he saw the wretched camps of the Northern troops at Cairo, and looked at the still motley, undisciplined ranks of the volunteers gathered there, he was confirmed in his belief that the Federal could not meet the Confederates on equal terms. The South regarded itself as unbeatable. But from one other Southern belief, the belief that England would intervene, Russell strongly dissented. 'Why, I expect, sir,' one Charleston merchant told him, 'that if those miserable Yankees try to blockade us, and keep you from our cotton, you'll just send their ships to the bottom and acknowledge us.' Russell said no.

For in spite of his faith in the South's prowess, the journalist found much to dislike in its cause. In Montgomery, going to attend the Confederate Congress, he was disgusted to find a slave auction being held publicly in the near vicinity. A prime field hand was knocked down for $1000, and a bystander told Russell that 'niggers is cheap now—that's a fact.' He saw no force in the Southern argument that the slave was at least better off than the African savage. 'I doubt if the

aboriginal is not as civilized, in the true sense of the word, as any
Negro, after three degrees of descent in servitude.'

On several Louisiana plantations that Russell visited he failed to
find any abuse of the slaves. But the brutish labor of the women in the
canefields plainly disgusted him, as did the whole thought of slavery.
'Their clothing seemed heavy for the climate; their shoes, ponderous
and ill-made, had worn away the feet of their thick stockings, which
hung in fringes over the upper leathers. Coarse straw hats and bright
cotton handkerchiefs protected their heads from the sun. The silence
that I have already alluded to prevailed among these gangs also—not
a sound could be heard but the blows of the hoe on the heavy clods.
In the rear of each gang stood a black overseer, with a heavy-thonged
whip over his shoulder.' Throughout the lower South, moreover,
writer discovered 'a reckless and violent condition of society, unfavorable to civilization, and but little hopeful for the future.' He made up
his mind that he would rather be exposed to Turkish brigands than to
the bowie knives and derringers of the fiery Southerners. In short, he
was rather less inclined to sympathize with the Confederates than with
the North, and as he afterwards hinted, had he remained in America, he
might have contributed to a change of attitude on the part of the
London *Times.*

But it was Russell's too frank description of the rout at Bull Run
that, published by the London *Times,* gave him the distinction of
being the only English traveler who has been virtually forced to leave
America. His position was difficult before that battle, for his journal
was becoming detested in the North for its Southern sympathies. On
19 July 1861, he rode down from Washington with the Congressmen
and other light-hearted spectators who expected to see McDowell whip
the Confederates in a sort of gala spectacle. At first the reports from the
Federal troops were all favorable, and moving forward blithely after
a stop for lunch, Russell was amazed to find himself caught up and
whirled back like a straw on a floodtide of panic. One broken regiment after another came pouring northward in retreat, till the scene,
as he writes, assumed an aspect without any parallel of which he had
ever read. 'Infantry soldiers on mules and draft horses, with the harness
clinging to their heels, as much frightened as their riders; Negro servants on their masters' chargers; ambulances crowded with unwounded
soldiers; wagons swarming with men who threw out the contents in
the road to make room, grinding through a shouting, screaming mass
of men on foot, who were literally yelling with rage at every halt'—
thus he described the cowardly panic. Northern editors, even Greeley
and Bryant, did their best to conceal the shame and gravity of the
disaster, and when the English mails brought Russell's depiction of it

to America, the North raised a universal cry of anger. Anonymous letter writers threatened his life, the newspapers vied in denouncing him, he was menaced in the streets, and the attitude of the government toward his activities as a war correspondent became more chilly than ever.

When he was refused permission to join McClellan's forces at the front, late in 1861, he conceived that his usefulness was at an end, and before Delane could stop him, returned to England. It is not strange that, after seeing the makeshift Northern camps, the flight at Bull Run, and McClellan's interminable delays, he should have let stand in his book the judgment he formed in August 1861, that the republic was 'tumbling to pieces,' and that peace was possible in two years, 'but only by the concession to the South of a qualified independence.'

Dicey's book had a broader scope than Russell's and its friendliness to the North amply atoned for any injuries that the latter had inflicted upon American sensibilities. Appearing during 1863, it declared that 'the present war is working directly for the overthrow of slavery,' and presented a strong plea for the cause of the North. Ever since the attack on Fort Sumter, Dicey pointed out, the Union frontier had moved southwards, and the Confederate frontier had receded. The North already had won the border states, the Southwest, and the command of the sea, while a comparison of its resources with those of the Confederacy made the eventual result plain. But even when it had conquered, could it govern a sulky and rebellious people, a people so filled with hatred for the Yankees as Russell had pictured the Southerners? Yes. Once suppress the rebellion, was Dicey's wise answer, and the old loyalty would gradually return. The Confederate Army would surrender completely, the Secessionist leaders would be exiled, and the people would revert 'to the belief that they are better off under the Union than under any other form of government.' Dicey's book contains judicious chapters upon the border states and their sentiment, the Northern rally after the defeat of the Peninsular Campaign, public sentiment in the prairie states— 'the one point on which all Western men seemed agreed was that the insurrection must and should be suppressed'—and such significant social phenomena as a wartime commencement at Harvard.

Very little of the interest of Anthony Trollope's notable book, *North America,* is connected with the Civil War. He avowed a perfect neutrality between the North and South, and the ideas he presented upon the conflict showed a confusion that made this neutrality comprehensible. He went so far as to say that Southern secession was plainly unconstitutional, that Buchanan's conduct had been treasonable, and that it would have been criminal in Lincoln to approve the Crittenden

Compromise, offered to avert secession. Yet he also said that until the South used violence, he had hoped the North would let the erring sisters go in peace. He wrote that the war for the Union was a 'necessary' war, yet he held that there was no reason for according it English sympathy. The conclusion of the conflict that he thought most probable was a partial victory for the North. Like Russell, he did not believe the Union could be perfectly restored, but he hoped that the United States would bring Virginia and all the other border states under its free banner.

But much more interesting than Trollope's reserved comments on the war, which for his credit might have been more reserved still, were his utterances upon morals and manners. Characteristic in style, his entertaining book evinces the same realism and hearty good sense that appears in his novels. Good-natured, bluff, and manly, while also intensely British, he carries the reader along on the current of his steady-going observation. He had the disadvantage of seeing the United States in the winter, superficially, and in a time of intense confusion, but he had the advantage of being a man of the world, experienced in travel and society, with clear basic standards of appraisal. He stood squarely on his own feet, and it is evidence of the saliency of the faults previous travelers had mentioned that he emphasizes so many of them. The spoiled children who ordered beefsteak, cakes, and pickles for breakfast; the hurried meals, giving the poor novelist no opportunity to linger over his sherry or tea; the unhealthy look of the men, attributable to business worry and hot-air furnaces; the constant talk about money; the 'rowdy' character of religion; the Western swindlers, whose dishonesty arose from the keen, crude competition of the frontier; the corrupt politicians, now reinforced by corrupt contractors; and the mendacious newspapers, without editorial rectitude—all these faults Trollope espied. He wrote of these defects without passion, but with his native vigor.

Happily, some of his chapters were more original. Few men in the world were better equipped for a discussion of hotels, and his English prejudices were not overawed by the mere size and magnificence of ours. The clerks he found inattentive, the 'extras' cost too much, it was too difficult to take a bath or obtain a sitting room, and the meals were greasy and badly served. His criticism of our post office is also of course authoritative, for he was a postal official; and when he said that we made insufficient provision for the door-to-door delivery of mail, and was shocked by our use of all postal appointments as political rewards, he indicated defects that we have since remedied. Most high-spirited of all are the deliverances of the creator of Mrs. Proudie upon our women—their dress, fashions, and new social ideas. They horrified him. He had no sympathy with their demand for a larger place in the working and political worlds. Indeed, he was convinced that already we had carried our chivalry too far, and had encouraged women to think too confidently of their privileges. The ladies' doors and drawing rooms at the hotels, the ladies' cabins on the ferry boats, and the ladies' windows at the post office, seemed to him symptoms of an exaggerated deference. Like a true mid-Victorian, he attached importance to only one claim asserted by women. 'The best right a woman has is the right to a husband, and that is the right to which I would recommend every young woman . . . to turn her best attention.' In New York the manner in which women pushed themselves into public vehicles, accepting seats without a word of acknowledgment for the men who proffered them, seemed to him almost barbaric.

Naturally, the novelist took pains to pay an extended visit to Washington, and he visited the troops in Virginia, Kentucky, and Missouri, though he did not penetrate into the seceded states. The camp at Cairo, its ill-equipped soldiers weltering in a sea of mud, was as disagreeable to him as to Russell. Nor did he like the national capital. Its design was grand, he admitted, but there was no future prospect 'which can justify a hope that the design will be fulfilled.' As a whole, the Capitol was imposing; in detail, it was architecturally faulty. As for the White House, he was right in saying that its location on the low Potomac flats was unhealthy, but it is amusing to find him adding that 'we have private houses in London considerably greater.' Beyond doubt Washington during the winter of 1861-2, with the gloom and anxiety of the war heavy upon it, was a depressing place. When the weather was dry the dust was inches deep, and when it was wet the pedestrians waded in mud as thick as a ploughed field. A litter of war lay all about:

The streets of Washington were always full of soldiers. Mounted sentries stood at the corners of all the streets with drawn sabres—shivering with cold, besmeared with mud. A military law came out that civilians might not ride quickly through the streets. Military riders galloped over everyone at every turn, splashing about through the mud, and reminding one not unfrequently of John Gilpin. Why they always went so fast, destroying their horses' feet on the rough stones, I could never learn. But I, as a civilian, given, as the English are, to trotting, and furnished for the time with a nimble trotter, found myself harried from time to time by muddy men with sabres, who would dash after me, rattling their trappings, and bid me go at a slower pace. . . The streets of Washington, day and night, were thronged with army wagons. All through the city military huts and military tents were to be seen, pitched out among the men and in the desert places. Then there was the chosen locality of the teamsters and their mules and horses—a wonderful world in itself; and all within the city! Here horses and mules lived—or died—*sub dio,* with no slightest apology for a stable over them, eating their provender from off the wagons to which they were fastened. Here, there, and everywhere large houses were occupied as the headquarters of some officer, or the bureau of some military official. At Washington and round Washington the army was everything.

Elsewhere in the North Trollope, as he later wrote in his autobiography, was surprised by the persistence of the people in the ordinary pursuits of life. His chapter 'Ceres Americana' shows us how forcibly the teeming wealth of the Northwest was calculated to impress any alien from overseas. As he saw the endless fields of corn, he marveled to think that every ear bore a meal for a hungry man. At Buffalo and Chicago he began to appreciate 'what it was for a country to burst with its own fruits, and be smothered by its own riches.' In the former city the elevators poured 'rivers of wheat,' and in the latter one such structure held 500,000 bushels. With corn selling in the country at ten cents a bushel, the cost of living was of course remarkably low. At Dixon, Illinois, Trollope stayed at a hotel where he was told by a man and his wife that they received board, a small suite of rooms, and the maintenance of their horse for $2 a day. Nobody ever accused Trollope of being an unsocial man, and we cannot ascribe to his own defects of temper the unresponsiveness he found in the Westerners. 'I never held any conversation at a public table in the West,' he assures us. 'I have sat in the same room with men for hours, and have not had a word spoken to me. I have done my very best to break through the ice and I have always failed. A Western American man is not a talking man. He will sit for hours over a stove with his cigar in his mouth, and his hat over his eyes, chewing the cud of reflection.' This trait was hardly mentioned as a fault. But Trollope did find fault with the Western women, being 'generally hard, dry, and melancholy,' and prematurely aged at thirty; unquestionably many of them were cruelly overworked.

In this intelligent if confused and ill-constructed volume by Trollope Americans were able to find a son's emphatic contradiction of many of his mother's slanders. All question of the war apart, the novelist was genuinely our admirer. He did full justice, like most Britons, to American scenery, declaring that Niagara was of all the sights on earth the greatest, and enthusiastically commending the White Mountains, Alleghanies, and upper Mississippi. He sealed with his approval the patriotism that had already sent nearly 50,000 Illinoisans to the front; our invincible energy—'men in these regions do not mind failure, and when they have failed, instantly begin again'; and our optimism. He spoke well of a multitude of minor features, like the comfort of our homes, the residential attractiveness of Cleveland and Buffalo, and the convenience of the sleeping cars, even if they were dirty and noisy. What he said of American manners was often complimentary and always good-natured. For example, when he went to a tavern in Lexington, Kentucky, for a meal, he ate with seventy-five very dirty army teamsters. He tells us that they were orderly, well behaved, with more intelligence and better table manners than Englishmen of the same walk of life, and that he conceived an affection for them. 'It is always the same story,' he reflected. 'With us there is no level of society. Men stand on a long staircase, but the crowd congregates near the bottom, and the lower steps are very broad. In America men stand upon a common platform, but the platform is raised above the ground, and though it does not approach in height the top of our staircase, the average height is greater.'

Above all, Trollope admired our democracy, our equality of opportunity, and our insistence upon educating the masses. To these as causes he traced the fact that our wealth, intelligence, and general comfort and happiness were unrivaled. It is not you, he told his upper-class English readers, who would have been more happy in New York than in London; it is not myself. 'But it is this: if you and I can count up in a day all those on whom our eyes may rest, and learn the circumstances of their lives, we shall be driven to conclude that nine-tenths of that number would have had a better life as Americans than they can have in their spheres as Englishmen.' He never examined the rooms of an American without finding books in them; he learned that the readers of Tennyson, Thackeray, Dickens, Bulwer, Wilkie Collins, and—Martin Tupper, numbered ten thousand in America to every thousand in England; and he saw that the very coachmen and boot-blacks kept newspapers in their hands. In the West he was delighted by the manly dignity of poor cottagers who looked him in the eye and bade him sit down on their battered benches 'without dreaming of any such apology as an English cotter offers to a Lady Bountiful when she calls.' In leaving our shores he paid us a final tribute in feeling language:

When we speak of America and her institutions we should remember that she has given to her increasing population rights and privileges we could not give—which as an old country we probably can never give. That self-asserting, obtrusive independence which so often wounds us is, if viewed aright, but an outward sign of those good things which a new country has produced for its people. Men and women do not beg in the States; they do not offend you with tattered rags; they do not complain to heaven of starvation; they do not crouch to the ground for halfpence. If poor, they are not abject in their poverty. They read and write. They walk like human beings made in God's form. They know that they are men and women, owing it to themselves and to the world that they should earn their bread by their labour, and feeling that when earned it is their own. If this be so—if it be acknowledged that it is so—should not such knowledge in itself be sufficient testimony of the success of the country and of her institutions?

Words like these atoned for much that had seemed harsh in the judgments of the earlier British novelists, Dickens and Marryat; they must have heartened many an American reader and English sympathizer with us in the doubtful days of the war; and they struck a chord that was to be kept vibrating throughout the next two generations. The Tory and aristocratic class, which during the 'thirties and 'forties furnished the travelers who abused American institutions most roundly during the early 'sixties, furnished the writers and statesmen who took sides with the South against the Union. The plain democratic classes, which had furnished the travelers who had always seen much to admire and envy in American life, now furnished the sympathizers with the North. A good representative of those British laboring men who in Lancashire and elsewhere so unselfishly applauded the Federal Government in fighting the Civil War through to victory was residing in the North during the war—James D. Burn, author of a shrewd and well-written volume on *The Working Classes in the United States*. Burn found much to dislike in American ways. He condemned our sensational press, our cheap estimation of human life, the low character of our judiciary, the bounty-jumping and graft prominent during the conflict. He deplored the wartime restrictions upon personal liberty, and thought there was more demagogy in the United States than in England. But on the whole his book was most friendly; he was greatly pleased with the dignity and comfort enjoyed by workingmen, he admired our free school system, and he wholeheartedly sympathized with the Union. Declaring that the position of the humbler classes was much better in America than in Britain, he added: Without presuming to speculate on the future of America, I may be permitted to say that so long as the Constitution of the United States can be preserved, with honest statesmen to guard the rights and liberties of the people, so long will the country offer inducements to the laboring population of Europe to flock to her shores.

The war, terminating in Northern triumph, struck a deadly blow at that complacent ignorance of American history and institutions that had previously distinguished many Tory minds. T. C. Grattan states that Sir Charles Bagot, after he had been Minister to the United States and had become Governor-General of Canada, admitted in visiting Boston that he was totally ignorant of the significance of Bunker Hill. This, commented Grattan, afforded 'another proof of the insignificance attached by a certain idiosyncrasy of mind in England, regarding everything connected with America, beyond the fact that it was once an English colony, which waged a successful rebellion; and is an independent state, with rival interests, uncongenial feelings, and a cotton-growing, tobacco-chewing, sherry-cobbler-drinking, lynch-law practising, and slave-holding population.' Such contemptuous insularism could no longer exist. Nor was there any longer any desire in England to perpetuate it. After 1865 no one could withhold an acknowledgment of what Trollope called 'the success of the country and of her institutions.'

Metropolis and Summer Watering Place [1] &

JAMES SILK BUCKINGHAM *was one of the most intelligent, energetic, and liberal of British visitors to America before the Civil War. He was born in 1786 at Flushing, the son of a retired merchant, was early sent to the naval academy at Falmouth, and was appointed to a ship at the age of nine. During the naval wars with France he saw much active service, and was once captured by a French corvette and imprisoned at Corunna. He gave up his naval career in consequence of seeing a sailor 'flogged round the fleet' for desertion until he died under the lash. Buckingham's humanitarian instincts were at all times well developed. Marrying at nineteen, he was left penniless by the peculations of a trustee of the estate he had inherited, and commenced a remarkably varied and active career.*

For a time he was employed at the Clarendon Press at Oxford. Returning to the sea, he became captain of a West Indiaman at twentyone, and for some years made voyages with different vessels to many parts of the world. After wandering for some time in the East, in 1818 he established the Calcutta Journal; *but his attacks upon the government led five years later to the stoppage of his paper by the East India Company, and his expulsion from the country. Later, after he had appealed to Parliament for redress, the company awarded him a pension of £200 a year as damages. From 1832 to 1837 Buckingham sat as a member of Parliament for Sheffield, and distinguished himself as an untiring advocate of social reform. Meanwhile, he had made a perma-*

[1] From *America: Historical, Statistic, and Descriptive,* London, 1841, volume I, chapters 3, 4, and 9; volume II, chapter 23.

nent mark for himself in English journalism by founding the Athenæum (1828), *though it was not a success in his hands.*

Upon leaving Parliament Buckingham traveled in America, 1837-40, lecturing as he went upon temperance and other reforms he had espoused, and meeting with a warm reception from religious bodies and temperance societies. He was a voluminous writer, and his journeys in Syria and Palestine, on the Continent, and in the United States all led to useful books. When he died in 1855, he was engaged upon an interesting autobiography, which so far as completed not only tells the story of an adventurous life but reveals a manly, honest, kindly character. Only two volumes out of the intended four were published.

PEOPLE AND SCENES IN NEW YORK CITY

THE hotels are generally on a larger scale than in England. The great Astor House, which overlooks the Park from the west side of Broadway, is much larger in area than the largest hotels in London or Paris; it makes up 600 beds, and has a proportionate establishment to suit the scale of its general operations. It is built wholly of granite, is chaste in its style of architecture, and is called after the rich John Jacob Astor . . . who is now deemed not only the wealthiest man in the city, but, since the death of Stephen Girard of Philadelphia, is considered the richest individual in the United States; his income exceeding, it is said, a million of dollars annually, or nearly £250,000 sterling, from lands, houses, stocks, and permanent sources, unconnected with the risks of trade from which he has long since retired, having realized his immense wealth by a long life industriously and successfully devoted to the fur trade. The City Hotel is also very large. The Washington, the Waverley, the Mansion House, the American, the Carlton, the Clarendon, the Globe, and the Athenæum are all spacious establishments of the same nature; and others of a smaller size abound in every quarter.

Of places of public amusement there are a great number, including six theatres, which are well filled every night, though the majority of what would be called the more respectable classes of society, the most opulent, and the most religious members of the community do not generally patronize or approve of theatrical exhibitions under the present management. The large sums paid to English and other foreign actors and actresses who visit America are made up by the attendance of foreigners and persons not belonging to either of the classes before enumerated; and this will hardly be wondered at when it is stated that every one of these theatres was not only open but presented a combination of new and unusual attractions on the evenings of days kept by the classes named as days of religious observance; the one, the day set apart by the proclamation of the state government as a day of public thanksgiving; and the other, Christmas Day.

The private dwellings contain, as must be the case in all large cities, a great variety of kinds and descriptions. The older houses are small, and mostly built of wood, painted yellow or white. These are now confined to the residences of the poorer classes, and are fast disappearing in every quarter, their places being occupied by substantial buildings of brick, though here and there are a few with granite fronts. The style of decoration, in the steps of ascent, the area of railings, and the doors, is more florid and ornamental than in the best parts of London, and the interior of the principal houses may be described as spacious, handsome, and luxurious, with lofty passages, good staircases, large rooms, and costly and gorgeous furniture. There are many individual houses of much greater splendour in London than any to be seen in New York, especially in the mansions of the English nobility; but, on the whole, the number of large, commodius, and elegantly furnished private dwellings in New York is much greater in proportion to the whole population than those of London, and approaches nearer to the ratio of Edinburgh or Paris.

The streets are very unequal in their proportions and conditions. The great avenue of Broadway is striking from its continuous and unbroken length of three miles in a straight line; but its breadth, about eighty feet, is not sufficiently ample for the due proportion of its length. It is, moreover, wretchedly paved, both in the centre and on the sides. Large holes and deep pits are frequently seen in the former; and in the latter, while before some houses the slabs of stone are large, uniform, and level, there is often an immediate transition from these to broken masses of loose stones, that require the greatest caution to pass over, especially in wet or frosty weather. The lighting and cleansing of the streets are not nearly so good as in the large towns of England, the gas being scanty in quantity, the lamps too far removed from each other, and the body of scavengers both weak in numbers and deficient in organization. Some of the smaller streets are almost impassable in times of rain and snow; and, when not incommoded by a profusion of mud or water, they are prolific in their supply of dust. Many of the streets have trees planted along the edge of the foot pavement on each side, which in summer affords an agreeable shade, but in autumn it has the disagreeable effect of strewing the path with falling leaves, and in winter it makes the aspect more dreary.

A custom prevails, in the principal streets for shops, of having wooden pillars planted along the outer edge of the pavement, with horizontal beams reaching from pillar to pillar, not unlike the stanchions and crosspieces of a ropewalk. On these pillars, usually painted white, are pasted large printed placards, announcing the articles sold in the shop before which they stand; and from the under side of the horizontal beam are suspended, by hooks or rings, show boards with printed bills of every colour. This is especially the case opposite the bookstores. Another purpose which these pillars and beams serve is that of suspending awnings from the houses to the end of the pavement in summer, which must make the shade grateful to the foot passenger; but at all other times these wooden appendages, made as they are without regard to regularity or uniformity, are a great drawback to the otherwise good appearance of the streets. Broadway, which is greatly disfigured by these, is therefore much inferior to Regent Street in London in the general air of cleanliness, neatness, light, spaciousness, good pavement, and fine shops, by which the latter is characterized; and although the number of beautiful and gayly dressed ladies, who make Broadway their morning promenade, uniting shopping, visiting, and walking at the same time, gives it a very animated appearance on a fine day, between twelve and two o'clock, yet the absence of handsome equipages and fine horses, and the fewness of well-dressed gentlemen who have leisure to devote to morning promenades of pleasure occasions Broadway to be inferior in the general effect of brilliance and elegance to the throng of Regent Street on a fine day in May, between three and four o'clock. . .

The population of New York is estimated at present to be little short of 300,000. Of these perhaps there are 20,000 foreigners, including English and persons from Canada and the British possessions, and 30,000 strangers from other states of the Union, making therefore the fixed resident population 250,000 and the floating population about 50,000 more. The greatest number of these are engaged in commerce or trade, with a due admixture of professional men, as clergy, physicians, and lawyers. But among them all there are fewer than perhaps in any other community in the world who live without any ostensible·avocation. The richest capitalists still take a part in the business proceedings of the day; and men who have professedly retired and have no counting-house or mercantile establishment still retain so much of the relish for profitable occupation that they mingle freely with the merchants, and are constantly found to be the buyers and sellers of stock, in funds, or shares in companies, canals, railroads, banks, et cetera.

The result of all this is to produce the busiest community that any man could desire to live in. In the streets all is hurry and bustle; the very carts, instead of being drawn by horses at a walking pace, are often met at a gallop, and always in a brisk trot, with the carter standing in the front, and driving by reins. Omnibuses are as numerous as in London, many of them drawn by four horses, though the carriages are inferior to the English ones. Hackney coaches are also abundant, and superior in every respect to those of London. These, with private carriages, which, however, are few and plain, generally with a black coachman and footman, without display of livery or armorial bearings, added to gigs and other vehicles, make up a crowd of conveyances through the public streets, which, from their bad pavement, occasions as much rattling noise as in the most bustling parts of Piccadilly or Cheapside. The whole of the population seen in the streets seem to enjoy this bustle, and add to it by their own rapid pace, as if they were all going to some place of appointment, and were hurrying on under the apprehension of being too late.

Of the men thus seen in public, the greater part are well dressed, and the more fashionable among them more expensively than the same classes in England. Black cloth is the almost universal wear, and for the finest description of this the most extravagant prices are paid. Full cloth cloaks, with velvet or fur collars and linings, and rich tassels are much more numerous than with us; and the whole outer aspect of the moving crowd indicates greater gayety, and much more regard to personal appearance. The men are not generally as handsome, however, as they are well dressed. An almost universal paleness of countenance is seen, without the least tinge of ruddiness or colour; the marks of care and anxiety are also deeply furrowed on brows not yet bearing the impress of age; and a general gloom or sadness of countenance is the rule, and hilarity of aspect or cheerfulness of appearance the exception.

AMERICAN WOMEN

The women far exceed the men in the costliness of their dresses and in the gayety of their walking apparel. There is perhaps no city in the world in which so many expensively dressed ladies may be seen walking or shopping as on a fine morning may be met with in Broadway. Rich and bright-coloured silks, satins, and other similarly costly materials, with ermine-lined cloaks and the most expensive furs; white, pink, and blue satin bonnets, with ostrich feathers and flowers of the first quality are worn by all who assume to be genteel or rank in the class of ladies, and the whole force of the wardrobe seems to be exhausted in the walking costume. The women, moreover, are much handsomer than the men. They are almost uniformly good-looking; the greater number are what would be called in England 'pretty women,' which is something between good-looking and handsome, in the nice distinctions of beauty. This uniformity extends also to their figures, which are almost universally slender and of good symmetry. Very few large or stout women are seen, and none that we should call masculine. A more than usual degree of feminine delicacy, enhanced by the general paleness of complexion and slightness of figure, is particularly characteristic of American females; and the extreme respect and deference shown to them everywhere by men has a tendency to increase that delicacy by making them more dependent on the attention and assistance of others than English ladies of the same class usually are.

It is in private society, however, that one can best judge of both; and the result of my observation, after having seen much of them in domestic circles and in large and fashionable parties, was this: as wives and mothers, the American women appear to be exemplary in the extreme; and while the interior of their dwellings exhibits the greatest attention to everything that can give domestic comfort, an air of propriety and decorum reigns over all their establishments. In the private and social visits which we were permitted to pay to some of the families with whom we were on the most intimate footing, nothing could surpass the general good sense, amiability, intelligence, and benevolence which marked the conversation. The women were always equal to the men, and often superior to them, in the extent of their reading and the shrewdness of their observations; and though there is everywhere, on the part of American females, as far as we have seen them, a shrinking away from any share in political conversations (the notion studiously impressed on them by the men, and not unwillingly entertained by themselves, being that it is unbecoming the timid and retiring delicacy of the female character to meddle with political matters), yet, whenever they ventured to pass this barrier, and indirectly develop their views on public affairs, there seemed to me a clearness and a soundness in their remarks which sufficiently evinced their thorough understanding of the subject. The leading features of the female character here, however, in the best circles, are domestic fidelity, social cheerfulness, unostentatious hospitality, and moral and religious benevolence. There are perhaps ten times the number of women in good society in New York, who interest themselves in the support and direction of moral objects and benevolent institutions, than could be found in any city of the same population in Europe; and while the husbands are busily engaged in their mercantile or professional avocations, a good portion of the wealth they acquire is directed by the benevolent influence of their wives into useful and charitable channels.

In the gayer parties of fashionable soirees and balls the ladies do not appear to so much advantage as in the sunny promenade or in the private circle at home. Their fashionable parties are as injudiciously crowded with more persons than the rooms will accommodate as in London; three or four hundred is not an unusual number of guests; and though the rooms are spacious, yet the crowd is so uncomfortably great that the dancers have scarcely room to make a small circle in the middle of the dense mass; while those who do not dance must be content to remain wedged into one compact and solid phalanx, from which there is no moving, even for a change of position, till the dance is over; and even then it will sometimes take a quarter of an hour to elbow through the crowd from one room to another. I was asked at one of these fashionable parties, by a lady, what there was in the scene before us which characterized it as American, and wherein it differed from an English party of the same number and description. My answer was that the chief points of difference observable to me were these—that there were a greater number of pretty female forms and faces than were ever to be seen in an equal number of English persons, and especially among the younger portion; but there were no such examples of striking and surpassing beauty as one sometimes sees in one or two favoured individuals of a large party at home. There were no 'fine women' in the English sense of that term, comprehending the requisites of tall, full, and commanding figures, bold and striking as well as beautiful features, rosy colour, expressive eyes, and the noble air and carriage of a lofty and dignified rank. On the other hand, the American ladies were dressed more in the extreme of fashion, both as to form and materials; but there were no such splendid displays of jewels as one sees in an English party. The dancing was monotonous and indifferent; partly from languor, and partly, it is believed, from affectation of indifference, which is considered to be more genteel than vulgar vivacity—a weakness, no doubt, copied from the English.

The gentlemen in these fashionable parties appeared far less handsome in person and less polished in manners than the ladies; and many whom we saw were evidently very ill at ease, and had their thoughts occupied by other subjects than those immediately before them. The refreshments were all substantial as well as costly; if there was a fault in them, it was that they were generally too abundant; and the pressure of the supper rooms most frequently exceeded that of the apartments of the dance. Cards are rarely or never seen, the influence of the religious bodies on public opinion having banished these from general society; and the propriety of language among all classes of the men is remarkable, as not an oath or an imprecation, so often offending the ear in what are deemed the best circles in England, anywhere disturbs the general decorum of the scene. The same late hours as are followed in England unfortunately prevail here; and the most fashionable persons, though invited for eight, rarely come till ten or eleven, and parties of any extent in numbers are not often broken up till two or three in the morning.

Life in Old New Orleans, 1846 [1] &

CHARLES LYELL, *the famous geologist, visited the United States in 1841 and again in 1845-6, when he was already well known as the author of the* Principles of Geology, *which overthrew the catastrophic school in that science and gave the world the nomenclature for geological eras —Eocene, Miocene, and so on—which is now universally used. He was in his forties at the time, having been born in 1797 in Scotland, the son of a botanist. His journeys to America were primarily scientific in aim, and were exceedingly fruitful: he estimated the rate at which the falls of Niagara were receding, computed the annual average accumulation of alluvial soil in the delta of the Mississippi, studied the laying down of vegetable matter, as for future coal beds, in the Great Dismal Swamp of Virginia, and so on. But he was a man of great freshness of mind and intellectual curiosity, matured by an unusual education, for he had graduated at Oxford, been trained for the bar in London, and traveled very extensively in Europe. He was hence a keen observer of social and political life in the United States. His* Travels in North America, with Geological Observations, *was published in 1845, and his* A Second Visit to the United States of North America *in 1849.*

A FRANCO-AMERICAN CITY

February 23 (1846). The distance from Mobile to New Orleans is 175 miles by what is called the inland passage, or the channel between the islands and the mainland. We paid five dollars, or one guinea each, for berths in the *James L. Day* steamer, which made about nine miles an hour. Being on the low-pressure principle, she was so free from

[1] From *A Second Visit to the United States of North America,* New York, 1849, volume II, chapters 26, 27, and 28.

noise and vibration that we could scarcely believe we were not in a sailing vessel. The stunning sounds and tremulous motions of the boats on the southern rivers are at first so distracting that I often wondered we could sleep soundly in them. The *James L. Day* is 185 feet long, drawing now five and a half feet of water, and only seven feet when fully freighted. We sailed out of the beautiful bay of Mobile in the evening, in the coldest month of the year, yet the air was warm, and there was a haze like that of a summer's evening in England. Many gulls followed our ship, enticed by pieces of bread thrown out to them by the passengers, some of whom were displaying their skill in shooting the birds in mere wantonness. The stars were brilliant as the night came on, and we passed between the islands and mainland, where the sea was as smooth as a lake.

On board were many 'movers,' going to Texas with their slaves. One of them confessed to me that he had been eaten out of Alabama by his Negroes. He had no idea where he was going, but after settling his family at Houston, he said he should look out for a square league of good land to be had cheap. Another passenger had, a few weeks before, returned from Texas, much disappointed, and was holding forth in disparagement of the country for its want of wood and water, declaring that none could thrive there, unless they came from the prairies of Illinois and were inured to such privations. 'Cotton,' he said, 'could only be raised on a few narrow strips of alluvial land near the rivers, and as these were not navigable by steamers, the crop, when raised, could not be carried to a market.' He also comforted the mover with the assurance that there were swarms of buffalo flies to torment his horses, and sand flies to sting him and his family. To this the undismayed emigrant replied that when he first settled in Alabama, before the long grass and canes had been eaten down by his cattle, the insect pests were as great as they could be in Texas. He was, I found, one of those resolute pioneers of the wilderness, who, after building a log house, clearing the forest, and improving some hundred acres of wild ground by years of labor, sells the farm, and migrates again to another part of the uncleared forest, repeating this operation three or four times in the course of his life, and, though constantly growing richer, never disposed to take his ease. In pursuing this singular vocation, they who go southward from Virginia to North and South Carolina, and thence to Georgia and Alabama, follow, as if by instinct, the corresponding zones of country. The inhabitants of the red soil of the granitic region keep to their oak and hickory, the 'crackers' of the tertiary pine barrens to their light wood, and they of the newest geological formations in the sea islands to their fish and oysters. On reaching Texas, they are all of them at fault, which will surprise no geologist who has read

Ferdinand Roemer's account of the form which the cretaceous strata assume in that country, consisting of a hard, compact, siliceous limestone, which defies the decomposing action of the atmosphere, and forms table-lands of bare rock, so entirely unlike the marls, clay, and sands of the same age in Alabama.

On going down from the cabin to the lower deck, I found a slave dealer with sixteen Negroes to sell, most of them Virginians. I heard him decline an offer of 500 dollars for one of them, a price which he said he could have got for the man before he left his own state.

Next morning at daylight we found ourselves in Louisiana. We had already entered the large lagoon, called Lake Pontchartrain, by a narrow passage, and, having skirted its southern shore, had reached a point six miles north of New Orleans. Here we disembarked and entered the cars of a railway built on piles, which conveyed us in less than an hour to the great city, passing over swamps in which the tall cypress, hung with Spanish moss, was flourishing, and below it numerous shrubs just bursting into leaf. In many gardens of the suburbs, the almond and peach trees were in full blossom. In some places the blue-leaved palmetto and the leaves of a species of iris (*iris cuprea*) were very abundant. We saw a tavern called the Elysian Fields Coffee House, and some others with French inscriptions. There were also many houses with porte-cochères, high roofs, and volets, and many lamps suspended from ropes attached to tall posts on each side of the road, as in the French capital. We might indeed have fancied that we were approaching Paris, but for the Negroes and mulattoes, and the large verandahs reminding us that the windows required protection from the sun's heat.

It was a pleasure to hear the French language spoken and to have our thoughts recalled to the most civilized parts of Europe by the aspect of a city, forming so great a contrast to the innumerable new towns we had lately beheld. The foreign appearance, moreover, of the inhabitants made me feel thankful that it was possible to roam freely and without hindrance over so large a continent—no bureaus for examining and signing of passports, no fortifications, no drawbridges, no closing of gates at a fixed hour in the evening, no waiting till they are opened in the morning, no custom houses separating one state from another, no overhauling of baggage by *gens d'armes* for the octroi; and yet as perfect a feeling of personal security as I ever felt in Germany or France.

The largest of the hotels, the St. Charles, being full, we obtained agreeable apartments at the St. Louis, in a part of the town where we heard French constantly spoken. Our rooms were fitted up in the French style, with muslin curtains and scarlet draperies. There was a finely proportioned drawing room, furnished *à la Louis Quatorze,* opening into a large dining room with sliding doors, where the boarders and the 'transient visitors,' as they are called in the United States, met at meals. The mistress of the hotel, a widow, presided at dinner, and we talked French with her and some of the attendants; but most of the servants of the house were Irish or German. There was a beautiful ballroom, in which preparations were making for a grand masked ball to be given the night after our arrival.

It was the last day of the Carnival. From the time we landed in New England to this hour we seemed to have been in a country where all, whether rich or poor, were laboring from morning till night, without ever indulging in a holiday. I had sometimes thought that the national motto should be, 'All work and no play.' It was quite a novelty and a refreshing sight to see a whole population giving up their minds for a short season to amusement. There was a grand procession parading the streets, almost everyone dressed in the most grotesque attire, troops of them on horseback, some in open carriages, with bands of music, and in a variety of costumes—some as Indians, with feathers in their heads, and one, a jolly fat man, as Mardi Gras himself. All wore masks, and here and there in the crowd, or stationed in a balcony above, we saw persons armed with bags of flour, which they showered down copiously on anyone who seemed particularly proud of his attire. The strangeness of the scene was not a little heightened by the blending of Negroes, quadroons, and mulattoes in the crowd; and we were amused by observing the ludicrous surpise, mixed with contempt, of several unmasked, stiff, grave Anglo-Americans from the North, who were witnessing for the first time what seemed to them so much mummery and tom-foolery. One wagoner, coming out of a cross street, in his working dress, drove his team of horses and vehicle heavily laden with cotton bales right through the procession, causing a long interruption. The crowd seemed determined to allow nothing to disturb their good humor; but although many of the wealthy Protestant citizens take part in the ceremony, this rude intrusion struck me as a kind of foreshadowing of coming events, emblematic of the violent shock which the invasion of the Anglo-Americans is about to give to the old *régime* of Louisiana. A gentleman told me that, being last year in Rome, he had not seen so many masks at the Carnival there; and, in spite of the increase of Protestants, he thought there had been quite as much 'flour and fun' this year as usual. The proportion, however, of strict Romanists is not so great as formerly, and tomorrow, they say, when Lent begins, there will be an end of the trade in masks; yet the butchers will sell nearly as much meat as ever. During the Carnival, the greater part of the French population keep open house, especially in the country.

New Orleans, February 1846. Walking first over the most ancient part of the city, called the First Municipality, we entered the Place d'Armes and saw on one side of the square the old Spanish Government House, and opposite to it the Cathedral, or principal Catholic church, both in an antique style of architecture, and therefore strikingly unlike anything we had seen for many months. Entering the church, which is always open, we found persons on their knees, as in Catholic countries, although it was not Sunday, and an extremely handsome quadroon woman coming out.

In the evening we went to the French opera, and were much pleased with the performance, the orchestra being the best in America. The audience were very quiet and orderly, which is said not to be always the case in some theatres here. The French Creole ladies, many of them descended from Norman ancestors, and of pure unmixed blood, are very handsome. They were attired in Parisian fashion, not overdressed, usually not so thin as the generality of American women; their luxuriant hair tastefully arranged, fastened with ornamental pins, and adorned simply with a colored ribbon or a single flower. My wife learned from one of them afterward that they usually pay, by the month, a quadroon female hairdresser, a refinement in which the richest ladies of Boston would not think of indulging. The word Creole is used in Louisiana to express a native-born American, whether black or white, descended from old-world parents, for they would not call the aboriginal Indians Creoles. It never means persons of mixed breed; and the French or Spanish Creoles here would shrink as much as a New Englander from intermarriage with one *tainted,* in the slightest degree, with African blood. The frequent alliances of the Creoles, or Louisianians, of French extraction with lawyers and merchants from the Northern States help to cement the ties which are every day binding more firmly together the distant parts of the Union. Both races may be improved by such connection, for the manners of the Creole ladies are, for the most part, more refined; and many a Louisianian might justly have felt indignant if he could have overheard a conceited young bachelor from the North telling me 'how much they were preferred by the fair sex to the hard-drinking, gambling, horse-racing, cock-fighting, and tobacco-chewing Southerners.' If the Creoles have less depth of character and are less striving and ambitious than the New Englanders, it must be no slight source of happiness to the former to be so content with present advantages. They seem to feel, far more than the Anglo-Saxons, that if riches be worth the winning, they are also worth enjoying.

The quadroons, or the offspring of the whites and mulattoes, sat in an upper tier of boxes appropriated to them. When they are rich, they hold a peculiar and very equivocal position in society. As children, they have often been sent to Paris for their education, and, being as capable of improvement as any whites, return with refined manners, and not unfrequently with more cultivated minds than the majority of those from whose society they are shut out. By the tyranny of caste they are driven, therefore, to form among themselves a select and exclusive set. Among other stories illustrating their social relation to the whites, we were told that a young man of the dominant race fell in love with a beautiful quadroon girl, who was so light-colored as to be scarcely distinguishable from one of pure breed. He found that, in order to render the marriage legal, he was required to swear that he himself had Negro blood in his veins, and, that he might conscientiously take the oath, he let some of the blood of his betrothed into his veins with a lancet. The romance of this tale was, however, greatly diminished, although I fear that my inclination to believe in its truth was equally enhanced when the additional circumstance was related that the young lady was rich.

Some part of the feeling prevailing in New England, in regard to the immorality of New Orleans, may be set down to the fact of their theatres being open every Sunday evening, which is no indication whatever of a disregard of religion on the part of the Catholics. The latter might, with as much reason, reflect on the Protestants for not keeping the doors of their churches open on weekdays. But as a great number of the young mercantile men who sojourn here are from the North, and separated from their families, they are naturally tempted to frequent the theatres on Sundays; and if they do so with a sense that they are violating propriety, or acting against what in their consciences they think right, the effect must be unfavorable to their moral character.

During our stay here we passed a delightful evening in the St. Charles theatre, seeing Mr. and Mrs. Kean in the *Gamester* and in *The Follies of a Night*. Her acting of Mrs. Beverly was perfection; every tone and gesture full of feeling, and always lady-like, never overwrought, in the most passionate parts. Charles Kean's acting, especially in Richard, has been eminently successful during his present tour in the United States.

While at New Orleans, Mrs. Kean told my wife she had been complimented on speaking English so well; and some wonder had been expressed that she never omitted or misplaced her h's. In like manner, during our tour in New England, some of the natives, on learning that we habitually resided in London, exclaimed that they had never heard us confound our v's and w's. *The Pickwick Papers* have been so universally read in this country that it is natural the Americans should imagine Sam Weller's pronunciation to be a type of that usually spoken in the old country, at least in and about the metropolis. In their turn, the English retaliate amply on American travelers in the British Isles: 'You don't mean to say you are an American? Is it possible? I should never have discovered it, you speak English so well!'—'Did you suppose that we had adopted some one of the Indian languages?' —'I really never thought about it; but it is wonderful to hear you talk like us!'

Looking into the shop windows of New Orleans, we see much which reminds us of Paris, an abundance of articles manufactured in the Northern States, but very few things characteristic of Louisiana. Among the latter I remarked, at a jeweler's, many alligator's teeth polished and as white as ivory, and set in silver for infants to wear round their necks to rub against their gums when cutting their teeth, in the same way as they use a coral in England.

The tombs in the cemeteries on the outskirts of the town are raised from the ground, in order that they may be above the swamps, and the coffins are placed in bins like those of a cellar. The water is seen standing on the soil at a lower level in many places; there are often flowers and shrubs round the tombs, by the side of walks made of shells of the Gnathodon. Over the grave of one recently killed in a duel was a tablet, with the inscription—'Mort, victime de l'honneur!' Should anyone propose to set up a similar tribute to the memory of a duelist at Mount Auburn, near Boston, a sensation would be created, which would manifest how widely different is the state of public opinion in New England from that in the 'First Municipality.'

Among the signs of the tacit recognition of an artistocracy in the large cities is the manner in which persons of the richer and more refined classes associate together in the large hotels. There is one public table frequented by bachelors, commercial travelers, and gentlemen not accompanied by their wives and families, and a more expensive one, called the Ladies' Ordinary, at which ladies, their husbands, and gentlemen whom they invite have their meals. Some persons who occupy a marked position in society, such as our friend the ex-Senator, Mr. Wilde, often obtain leave by favor to frequent this ordinary; but the keepers of the hotels grant or decline the privilege as they may think proper.

A few days after the Carnival we had another opportunity of seeing a grand procession of the natives, without masks. The corps of all the different companies of firemen turned out in their uniform, drawing their engines dressed up with flowers, ribbons, and flags, and I never saw a finer set of young men. We could not help contrasting their healthy looks with the pale, sickly countenances of 'the crackers' in the pine woods of Georgia and Alabama, where we had been spending so many weeks. These men were almost all of them Creoles, and thoroughly acclimatized; and I soon found that if I wished to ingratiate myself with natives or permanent settlers in this city, the less surprise I expressed at the robust aspect of these young Creoles the better. The late Mr. Sydney Smith advised an English friend who was going to reside some years in Edinburgh to praise the climate:—'When you arrive there it may rain, snow, or blow for many days, and they will assure you they never knew such a season before. If you would be popular, declare you think it the most delightful climate in the world.' When I first heard New Orleans commended for its salubrity, I could scarcely believe that my companions were in earnest, till a physician put into my hands a statistical table, recently published in a medical magazine, proving that in the year 1845 the mortality in the metropolis of Louisiana was 1:850, whereas that of Boston was 2:250, or, in other words, while the capital of Massachusetts lost 1 out of 44 inhabitants, New Orleans lost only 1 in 54; 'yet the year 1845,' said he, 'was one of great heat, and when a wider area than usual was flooded by the river, and exposed to evaporation under a hot sun.'

It appears that when New Orleans is empty in the summer—in other words, when all the strangers, about 40,000 in number, go into the country, and many of them to the North, fearing the yellow fever, the city still contains between 80,000 and 100,000 inhabitants, who never suffer from the dreaded disease, whether they be of European or African origin. If, therefore, it be fair to measure the salubrity of a district by its adaptation to the constitution of natives rather than foreigners, the claim set up for superior healthiness may be less preposterous than at first it sounded to my ears. I asked an Irishman if the summer heat was intolerable. 'You would have something else to think of in the hot months,' said he, 'for there is one set of mosquitoes who sting you all day, and when they go in toward dusk, another kind comes out and bites you all night.'

The desertion of the city for five months by so many of the richer residents causes the hotels and the prices of almost every article in shops to be very dear during the remainder of the year. 'Goods selling at Northern prices' is a common form of advertisement, showing how high is the usual cost of all things in this city. The Irish servants in the hotel assure us that they cannot save, in spite of their high wages, for whatever money they put by soon goes to pay the doctor's bill, during attacks of chill and fever.

Hearing that a guidebook of New Orleans had been published, we wished to purchase a copy, although it was of somewhat ancient date for a city of rapid growth. The bookseller said that we must wait till he received some more copies from New York, for it appears that the printing even of books of local interest is done by presses 2000 miles distant. Their law reports are not printed here, and there is only one newspaper in the First Municipality, which I was told was very characteristic of the French race; for, in the Second Municipality, although so much newer, the Anglo-Americans have, during the last ten years, started ten newspapers.

We were very fortunate in finding our old friend, Mr. Richard Henry Wilde, residing in the same hotel, for he had lately established himself in New Orleans, and was practicing in the courts of civil law with success. The Roman law, originally introduced into the courts here by the first settlers, was afterwards modified by the French, and assimilated to the Code Napoleon, and finally, by modern innovations, brought more and more into accordance with the common law of England. Texas, in her new constitution, and even some of the older states, those of New England not excepted, have borrowed several improvements from the Roman law. Among these is the securing to married women rights in property, real and personal, so as to protect them from the debts of their husbands and enable them to dispose of their own property.

American Culture and American Prospects [1] ϟ

ALEXANDER MACKAY. *For almost forty years following its publication in 1849, Mackay's* Western World *was the most complete and penetrating account of American institutions written by an Englishman, being supplanted only by Bryce's* American Commonwealth. *The author based it upon no brief and hurried observation of the republic. He had spent some years in the United States before he commenced the tour he describes in his* Western World, *and which itself consumed a large part of the years 1846-7. As he said, 'to comprehend the social life of America, the working of its political institutions, and the bearing of its polity upon its moral development, it is absolutely essential that a man should step aside from the hotel, the railway and the steamer,*

[1] From *The Western World, or, Travels in the United States in* 1846-47, London, 1850, volume I, chapter 3; volume II, chapter 7; volume III, chapters 8 and 11.

and live with *the people, instead of living, as the mere traveller does,* beside *them.'*

   Mackay, who was born in 1808 and died in 1852, was admitted as a barrister to the Middle Temple in 1847. At the time he visited America in 1846-7 he was on the staff of the London Morning Chronicle, *and remained with it until 1849. In 1851 he was sent to India by the chambers of commerce of the large northern cities of England to inquire into the possibility of raising cotton extensively there. Mackay's point of view in looking at the United States was that of a convinced liberal. As the following selections show, he thoroughly realized the crudities of American character and life, but there was not a trace of ill-nature in his laugh over them. Of the superiority of the American political system to the British, and of a good many American ways and institutions, he was thoroughly convinced.*

MR. MACKAY MEETS A JEFFERSON BRICK

In addition to the roundabout journey by sea, the city of New York is approached from Boston by three different routes, each of which is a combination of railway and steamboat travelling. The Long Island Railway being blocked up by snow, I selected the route by Norwich in preference to that by Stonington, the former curtailing the sea voyage by about thirty miles, a serious consideration, as the navigation of the Sound was then rather perilous, owing to the masses of ice with which it was obstructed. . .

   It was a beautiful starlight night, the deep blue of the sky looking almost black in contrast with the snow which lay thick upon the ground. The train whisked over the face of the country like a huge overponderous rocket, the wood fire of the engine throwing up a shower of sparks, which spread into a broad golden wake behind us. On the platform of the adjoining car I found a fellow-traveller, who, like myself, had sought refuge from the heat. Our mutual sympathy for fresh air soon led us into conversation, during which I inquired of him as to the general character and social position of those who journeyed along with us.

   'Well,' said he, 'you see, as to position, they are much of a muchness; but some do one thing, and some another; some are farmers, who have been to Bosting to sell shoes—some are merchants from the West, who have also been to that ere city for winter stock—some do nothin' that nobody knows on, but manage to make a gentlemanly livin' on it; and some are spekelators, who have been to the East to do a stroke of business; I'm a spekelator myself, but none of your dubitatious sort;

I've lots for sale in Milwaukie, and Chicago—if you do anything in that line, stranger, I'm your man.'

Having assured him that I had no intention of becoming a landed proprietor on Lake Michigan, or elsewhere, I begged him to explain that portion of his harangue which connected farmers with dealings in shoes. I had heard much of the fertility of the American soil, but was not aware that such articles ranked among its products.

'Why, our people,' said he, 'can turn their hands to a'most anything, from whippin' the universe to stuffin' a mosquito. These 'ere New England farmers, you see, farm it in the summer time, but their poor sile givin' them nothin' to do in the winter, they take to it indoors, and work for months at the last. They sell their shoes in Bosting for home consumption, and to send to Europe, Chainy, and South America.'

I had scarcely received this piece of information as to the winter occupation of New England farmers, when we suddenly came to a halt under a sort of shed, which I was informed was the Norwich station. We were still eight miles from Alleyn's Point, where we were to take the steamer, and were soon informed by the conductor that we must stop at Norwich until news of her arrival should reach us. I could not exactly see the advantage of stopping for such a purpose— eight miles from the coast—but was obliged to swallow my disappointment. The truth was that the Sound was so obstructed with ice that, for the last two days, no steamer had ventured down from New York; and it was on the mere chance of finding one that might take us up to town that we were trundled off from Boston.

As we might be detained till morning, we all scrambled to the nearest hotels to secure sleeping quarters for the night. Alas! not only was every hotel full to overflowing, but there was not, in the whole town, a spare bed to be had for love or money. The passengers by the trains of the two previous days were still close prisoners in Norwich, as were also those who had arrived during the same period to proceed by the Long Island Railway. Here, then, were upwards of a thousand persons suddenly added to the population of a small town, creating a demand for pillows and mattresses, for which the supply was anything but adequate.

After a patient but unsuccessful search for a bed, I returned to the hotel nearest the station, where I found most of my fellow-unfortunates in noisy assemblage convened, venting their imprecations against the railway company, which they held responsible for all the annoyances of the journey. Everybody was sure that everybody had an action at law against the directors; and if everybody had been anybody else but himself, he would have had no hesitation in testing the point.

It was fortunate for us that the hotel was not unprovided with edibles. Whilst supper was being prepared, we were huddled into a small apartment, which did duty as an ante-chamber to a room behind it, fitted up as a bar-room, in which the more noisy of the company had congregated, discussing gin sling and politics, and the prospects more immediately before them. When supper was announced, the race for seats was appalling. Being near the door I was pushed in without any effort of my own, and was amongst the first to be accommodated with a seat. There was plenty, enough for the most craving appetites, and sufficient variety to meet any conceivable eccentricity of taste. The bacon and ham were good; but ludicrous in the extreme were the attempts at chops and the faint imitations of steak. There were several varieties of fish, including oysters, which latter were boiled into a sort of black broth; there were innumerable sweets and sweetmeats, fowl in every mode of preparation, very white bread and very black bread, Indian corn prepared in half a dozen different ways, with tea and coffee, beer, and every variety of spirituous liquor. We were all very hungry, and for some minutes forgot our annoyances in appeasing our appetites, the episode winding up by each man paying half a dollar to a sallow-looking sentry in yellow shirt sleeves, who stood at the door to receive it.

Such as were so inclined now disposed of themselves for sleep. The ponderous but very comfortable arm chairs, which invariably form the chief feature in the garniture of an American taproom, were immediately appropriated, as were also the chairs and tables in the adjoining rooms. Some laid themselves down upon the floor, with billets of wood for pillows. I had luckily been able to seize upon a chair, and sat for some time musing upon the strangeness of my position. On my left sat a large burly man, in the attire of a farmer, and who, like myself, seemed indisposed to slumber. He chewed with unusual vehemence; and my attention was first attracted to him by the unerring certainty with which he expectorated over one of them, into a spittoon, which lay between two sleepers on the floor. He occasionally varied his amusement by directing his filthy distillations against the stove, from the hot side of which they sometimes glanced with the report of a pistol. By and by we got into conversation, when I discovered that he was from the Granite State, as New Hampshire is called, and that he was on his way to Oregon, via New York and Cape Horn, a distance of 15,000 miles, but of which he seemed to make very light. His only trouble was that he would be too late for the ship, which was to sail on the following day. I observed that in that case his disappointment must be very great, inasmuch as many weeks must elapse ere a similar opportunity again presented itself to him. He assured me that it would be very trifling, for he had made up his mind, since he had supped, should he miss the ship, to 'go West' to 'Illinois state.' I was astonished at the facility and apparent indifference with which he abandoned the one purpose for the other. But it is this flexibility of character that is at the very foundation of American enterprise. Let your genuine Yankee find one path impracticable, and he turns directly into another, in pursuing which he never permits his energies to be crippled by futile lamentations over past disappointments.

About five in the morning we were once more put in motion by the welcome intelligence that a steamer had arrived, and was in waiting for us at Alleyn's Point. We embarked about seven o'clock some miles above the mouth of the Thames River. The morning was bright and cold, and we had a keen cutting breeze in our faces as we dropped down towards the Sound. We stopped for some minutes to take in passengers at New London, one of the seaport towns of Connecticut, very prettily situated on the right bank of the river, close to its junction with the Sound. On the opposite bank is a tall obelisk, raised to the memory of some Americans who are said to have been treacherously massacred, during the Revolutionary War, by a troop of British soldiers. Whilst looking at this, two men, who were on deck, advanced and stopped within a pace or two of me. The elder, and spokesman of the two, was about forty-five years of age and was dressed in a long overcoat, which was unbuttoned and hung very slovenly down to his heels. He stooped, not at the shoulders, but from the stomach, whilst his sallow face was furrowed like a newly ploughed field. His lips were thin to a degree, his mouth being marked but by a sharp short line; and when he looked at you, it was with nervous and uneasy glances, furtively shot from beneath a pair of shaggy half-gray eyebrows. His expression was malignant, his *tout ensemble* repulsive. I instinctively turned away from him, but it seems I was not to escape, for, having brought me, as he thought, within hearing distance, he muttered *to* his companion, but evidently *at* me—'Yes, there's a moniment raised to the eternal shame of the bloody Britishers; but we'll take the change out of them for that yet, or Colonel Polk's not my man, by G—d!' I looked at him, mechanically, as he uttered these words. He stood between me and his companion, as motionless as a statue, his eye, which turned neither to the right nor to the left, apparently fixed on the distant shore of Long Island, but with ears erect, in evident expectation of some rejoinder to this flattering harangue. Deeming it more prudent to make none, I turned away and paced the deck, which I had the satisfaction of perceiving caused him no little disappointment. He was one of the few in the seaboard and commercial states who had been seized with the Oregon mania; and so powerfully did the poison operate upon him that it was with difficulty that he could keep from biting.

On leaving New London, a few minutes sufficed to bring us to the Sound, the shore of Long Island being dimly visible to the southward. Its waters were then smooth and glassy; but, sheltered and landlocked though it be, the Sound is sometimes the scene of the most terrific and disastrous tempests. Our steamer was not one of the floating palaces which usually ply on these waters; and, being neither more nor less than the ferry boat connecting Long Island with the mainland, presented us with none of the accommodations generally found on this route. A more unshaven-looking crew, therefore, than sat down to breakfast can hardly be imagined. The majority of beards were of thirty-six-hours' growth, and it was amusing to watch the degree to which each had taken advantage of its accidental immunity. Some merely peered through the skin, others were wildly luxuriant. Some were light, some dark, some utterly black, some red, some sandy, and some had a smack of blue in them. The ladies, who had come aboard at New London, kept as shy from us as if we had escaped from Worcester.

After breakfast I seated myself by the stove and commenced reading, but had been thus engaged only a few minutes when I was accosted by a stout, short, elderly gentleman, dressed in snuff-coloured cloth from head to foot, who made me his confidant so far as to inform me that we had been very lucky in getting a boat. Having nothing to object to so obvious a proposition, I categorically assented, in the hope of being able to resume my book. But in this I was disappointed, for he was soon joined by a middle-aged man, with a very self-sufficient expression, who asked me—

'Didn't our Prez'dent's message put the old Lion's back up?'

The steamer by which I had arrived being the first that had left Liverpool after the receipt in England of the President's warlike message, the most intense interest was manifested on all hands to know the effect which it had produced in Europe. I, therefore, replied— 'Considerably.'

'We expected it would rile him a bit—rayther—we did,' added he.

'Didn't it frighten him a leetle?' asked the gentleman in snuff colour.

'As an Englishman, I would fain be spared the humiliating confession,' replied I, 'particularly as the whole will be published in the papers, in the course of a few hours.'

This, as I expected, only made them the more curious. The first speaker returned to the charge, urging me to let them know what had taken place, and advising me, at the same time, that I might consider myself among friends; and that the Americans were not a 'crowin' people.'

'Well, gentlemen,' said I, 'if you can sympathize with a fallen enemy, I have no objection to speak plainly with you.' They shook their heads affirmatively, and showed, by drawing closer to, that they really meant kindly towards me.

'The publication of the message,' I continued, 'was all that was necessary to shake to its foundation the European settlement of 1815. Prince Metternich immediately dismissed Reis Effendi across the Balkan. M. Guizot notified Abd-el-Kader that the Triple Alliance was at an end; whilst England, in alarm, threw herself into the hands of Russia, entering into an alliance offensive and defensive with that Power; and, as a guarantee of good faith, giving up the temporary possession of Tilbury Fort to the Autocrat, whose troops now garrison the key of the Thames.'

'Is that the way the British Lion took the lash of "Young Hickory"?' asked the first speaker; 'Well, I swan—'

'He needn't have been scared in such a hurry, neither,' said the gentleman in snuff colour; 'for maybe we didn't mean it, after all.'

'The Lion must have been considerably scared,' added I, 'thus to seek protection from the Bear.'

Both gentlemen hereupon looked at each other, pressed their lips, shook their heads, and unbuttoned their coats that they might breathe the more freely; and, after regarding me for some time with an air of evident compassion, turned suddenly round, and graciously left me to my own reflections. They were soon the centre of a group of eager listeners, to whom they detailed the important news which they had just heard.

'Well, I declare!' I overheard the snuff-coloured gentleman say, 'but we air a greater people than I thought for!'

'I knowd it,' said a long Yankee from Maine; 'we're born to whip universal nature. The Europeans can't hold a candle to us already, e'en a'most—'

'We have certainly,' continued the snuff-coloured gentleman, thoughtfully, 'done what Napoleon himself couldn't do. We have introduced foreign troops into England. The mere wag of our President's tongue has garrisoned her greatest fort with Cossacks and Rooshians.'

Such of my fellow-voyagers by the *Hibernia* as overheard the conversation enjoyed it greatly, as indeed did most of those who were within reach of our voice, who were amused at the gullibility of the two elderly gentlemen.

The truth is that the more belligerent of the American people imagined that the President's message was sure to set the Old World in a flame, and were mortified beyond measure on ascertaining the little impression which it had really produced.

As we approached the city, the Sound gradually narrowed, and when near Hell Gate, a straitened passage through which the water rushes at some periods of the tide with a velocity which renders its navigation rather hazardous, we became fairly embedded in ice, which, broken into masses of various sizes, completely covered the surface of the water, and through which it was with extreme difficulty that we made our way. Mass after mass grated along the sides of the boat, and then went—crunch-crunch—under the lusty paddle wheels, coming up, broken in piecemeal, in our wake. It was long dark ere we reached the city. Light after light first appeared upon our right, then on our left, then before, and finally all around us, as we became gradually environed by the city and its insular suburbs. It was with difficulty we groped our way alongside one of the crowded wharves. The long terraces of shops and warehouses, which skirted the harbour, presented one continuous blaze of light; and from the multitude of figures which flitted rapidly to and fro it would have been evident, had other tokens been wanting, that we were about to land in a great and bustling city. Eight o'clock was tolling from the nearest steeple as I stepped ashore; and immediately, from spire to spire, on all sides, the hour rang merrily through the keen night air. I jumped into a sleigh, and in less than an hour's time was oblivious to all my fatigues in a comfortable room in the second story of the Astor House.

SOUTHERN TRAVEL AND TRAVELLERS

Columbia, the seat of government in South Carolina, is situated on the banks of a river called the Congaree, a stream of petty dimensions in America, but one which would cut a very respectable figure in the geography of a European kingdom. The town contains a population scarcely so numerous as that of Horsham, and would be esteemed as a fair specimen of a parliamentary borough in England. One would think that in selecting a site for their capital, fertility in the circumjacent region would be a *sine qua non* with any people. But not so with the Carolinians, who, in order to have it in as central a position as possible, have placed it in the midst of one of the most barren districts of the state. Luckily, its limited population renders it easy of supply, for it is difficult to see how a large community could subsist on such a spot, unless they could accommodate themselves to pine cones as their chief edible. But Palmyra managed to subsist in the desert, and so may Columbia in the wilderness, which is the only appellation which can properly be bestowed upon the dreary and almost unbroken expanse of pine forest which surrounds it. Notwithstanding all its disadvantages in point of position, Columbia is, on the whole, rather an interesting little town. There is about it an air of neatness and elegance, which betokens it to be the residence of a superior class of people—many of the planters whose estates are in the neighbourhood making it the place of their abode; as well as the governor, the chief functionaries of state subordinate to him, and some of the judges. There is little or nothing connected with the government buildings worthy of attention, their dimensions being very limited, and their style of a simple and altogether unambitious description. The streets, as in the majority of the southern towns of more recent origin, are long, straight, and broad, and are lined, for the most part, with trees, prominent amongst which are to be found the gay and flaunting 'Pride of India.' Here, in this small, quiet, and unimposing-looking town, are conducted the affairs of a sovereign state at a cost of under £50,000, including not only the salaries of all its functionaries political, judicial, and municipal, but also the payment of the members of the legislature during their attendance at its annual sitting. South Carolina, however, is not so fortunate as to be free of debt like her northern namesake. Her absolute obligations exceed three millions of dollars, to which is to be added a contingent debt of about two millions, making her present total debt exceed five millions of dollars. On her absolute debt she now pays about 170,000 dollars a year by way of interest, or about £40,000, nearly as much as is required to defray the annual expense of the government of the state. She is not without something to show, however, as a set-off to the liabilities which she has incurred. Her public works are more numerous than extensive and are proportionate to her existing wants. By means of some of these, a communication by boats has been opened between the capital and the seaboard.

From Columbia I proceeded by railway towards Augusta. For the first half of the way the country was very uninteresting, being comparatively flat and sandy, and covered, for the most part, with the interminable pitch pine. Indeed the pine barrens extend, with but little interruption, almost the entire way between the two places, the distance between them being from eighty to ninety miles. Here and there are some long stretches of marshy ground, over which the railway is carried, not by embankments, but upon piles, which impart to it a dangerous and shaky appearance. I was not surprised at the anxiety which almost every passenger manifested to get over these portions of the line without accident, especially when I learnt that there was danger in being detained upon them after night-fall. It was not simply, therefore, by the dread of a break-neck accident that they were animated, their fears being divided between such a possibility and any contingency which might expose them to the nocturnal miasmas of the marshes.

Whilst passing over one of these flimsy and aerial-looking viaducts, I left the carriage in which I was seated for the platform outside. In doing so, I perceived that I was followed by a little wiry-looking man of about forty years of age, who had evidently, before my making the movement, been regarding me for some time with the most marked attention. He was dressed in a pair of coarse gray trousers, a yellow waistcoat, and a superfine blue swallow-tailed coat, profusely bespangled with large and well-burnished brass buttons. His face, which had a sickly pallor about it, was strongly lined, and marked with a mingled expression of shrewdness and cunning, which gave it some fascination, at the same time that it bordered on the repulsive. He was becoming prematurely gray, his hair sticking out from his head as strong and crispy as catgut. I instinctively shrunk from him as he approached me, for I saw a large capital note of interrogation in each of his little and restless light-blue eyes. Desirous of not being interrupted, I pulled out a notebook, with which I feigned to be engaged. Either the pretence was apparent to him, or, having made up his mind to address me, he was not going to be balked by a trifle. So approaching me still nearer, he put a finishing pressure upon the tobacco which was between his teeth, and the remaining juice of which he vehemently squirted over the platform of the succeeding carriage. Having done this he bent his head forward, opened his mouth wide, and the reeking quid fell at my feet. I turned half aside in disgust, and was meditating a retreat in to the carriage when—

'Good day, stranger,' broke upon my ear, and intimated that I was too late.

'Good day,' I replied, glancing at him at the same time; but he was not looking at me, for his eye was so vacantly intent upon the wilderness before us that, for the moment, I doubted his having addressed me at all.

'How d'ye do?' said he again, after a few seconds' pause, nodding his head, and looking me for a moment full in the face, after which his eye again riveted itself upon the forest.

'As well as a stranger could expect to be under such a sun in these stewing latitudes,' I rejoined, at the same time wiping the perspiration, which was flowing very freely, from my face.

'You don't chew, p'raps?' added he, offering me his tobacco box; on declining which he quietly replenished from its contents the void which the ejection of the last quid had left between his jaws.

'P'raps you snuff?' he continued.

I made a negative motion.

'Smoke?' he added.

'Occasionally,' I replied.

'I don't—it's a dirty habit,' said he, at the same time ejecting a quantity of poisoned saliva, a portion of which falling upon the iron railing which surrounded the platform, he rubbed off with his finger, which he afterwards wiped upon his trousers.

'In no way can the use of tobacco be regarded as a very cleanly habit,' I remarked, looking at the stain which the operation had left upon the garment in question. But if he heard, he affected not to hear me, for after a brief pause, changing the subject—

'Maybe you'll be no Scotchman, I'm thinkin',' said he.

'Maybe you're mistaken if you think so,' replied I.

'I opined as much from your tarting wrapper,' he added, alluding to a small shepherd's tartan plaid which I carried with me for night travelling.

'It has something of a Scottish look about it,' I remarked drily.

'Then,' said he, 'I was right in my position.'

'I did not say you were wrong,' rejoined I.

'Stranger,' added he, 'had I been wrong, you'd 'a' said so.'

I looked again at my notebook, in the hope that he would take the hint. But I was mistaken, for, after a brief silence, he continued—

'I'm fond of Scotchmen,' looking at the same time hard at me, to see what effect was produced by the announcement of so astounding a piece of patronage.

'Indeed,' I remarked, as unconcernedly as possible; at which he seemed somewhat annoyed, for he looked as if he expected me to grasp his hand.

'I'm a Scotchman myself,' he added, fixing his eye upon me again.

I was sorry to hear it, but looked unmoved, simply replying by the monosyllabic ejaculation, 'Ah.'

'Not exactly a Scotchman,' he continued, correcting himself, 'for I was born in this country, and so were my father and grandfather before me.'

'Then you have a longer line of American ancestors than most of your fellow-countrymen can boast of,' I observed.

'We don't vally these things in this country,' said he in reply. 'It's what's above ground, not what's under, that we think on. Been long in this country, stranger?'

'Some months.'

'How much longer be you going to stay?' he added.

'That's more than I can tell,' replied I, 'the length of my stay depending on a variety of circumstances.'

'You couldn't mention them?' he inquired coolly, expectorating over his right shoulder, to the imminent danger of another passenger who had just emerged from the carriage, and who, by a jerk of his body, missed the filthy projectile.

'If I were disposed to do so,' said I, rather amused at his impudence, 'we should be at Augusta long before I could detail them all.'

'I'm going further on,' added he, as if to intimate that he would give me an opportunity of finishing my story on quitting Augusta.

'But I am not; and we are now but a few miles from it,' I observed.

'Maybe you're on government business?' said he, endeavouring to extort by piecemeal that of which he was denied an ample narration.

'Maybe I'm not,' was all the satisfaction he had.

'I don't think you're in the commercial line,' he continued, unabashed; 'and you don't look as if you was travelling for pleasure neither.'

'It's very singular,' was my reply.

'How long d'ye think you'll stay in this free country?' he asked, baffled in his cross examination as to my objects and pursuits.

'Until I'm tired of it,' said I.

'When will that be?' he inquired.

'Perhaps not till I'm homesick,' said I.

'That'll be very soon,' said he; 'for most Europeans get homesick mightily soon after comin' here.'

'You give but a poor account of your country,' I observed.

'You're mistaken, stranger,' he remarked. 'I don't mean homesick.'

'You said homesick,' rejoined I.

'But I meant, sick of home,' he added, in a tone of great emphasis; 'for they can't be long in the midst of our free institootions without agettin' dead sick of their tyrannical governments.'

'It depends a great deal upon their turn of mind, and a little upon their strength of stomach,' I remarked; for at that moment the tobacco juice was oozing rapidly from either corner of his mouth. He did not comprehend the allusion, and I judged it as well to leave him in the dark.

.   .   .

AMERICAN EDUCATION AND LETTERS

The results of the general attention to popular education characteristic of American polity are as cheering as they are obvious. It divorces man from the dominion of his mere instincts, in a country the institutions of which rely for their maintenance upon the enlightened judgments of the public. Events may occur which may catch the multitude in an unthinking humour, and carry it away with them, or which may blind the judgment by flattering appeals to the passions of the populace; but on the great majority of questions of a social and political import which arise, every citizen is found to entertain an intelligent opinion. He may be wrong in his views, but he can always offer you reasons for them. In this, how favourably does he contrast with the unreasoning and ignorant multitudes in other lands! All Americans read and write. Such children and adults as are found incapable of doing either are emigrants from some of the less favoured regions of the older hemisphere, where popular ignorance is but too frequently regarded as the best guarantee for the stability of political systems.

In a country of whose people it may be said that all read, it is but natural that we should look for a national literature. For this we do not look in vain in America. Like its commerce, its literature is as yet comparatively young, but like it in its development it has been rapid and progressive. There is scarcely a department of literature in which the Americans do not now occupy a respectable and prominent position. The branch in which they have least excelled, perhaps, is the drama. In poetry they have been prolific, notwithstanding the practical nature of their pursuits as a people. A great deal of what they have produced in this form is valueless, to say nothing else; but some of their poets have deservedly a reputation extending far beyond their country's bounds. Of the novels of Cooper it is not necessary here to speak. There is an originality in the productions of Pierpont, and a vigour in those of Halleck, a truthfulness as well as force in the verses of Dana, and a soothing influence in the sweet strains of Bryant, which recommend them to all speaking or reading the glorious language in which they are written. In the bright galaxy of historical authors, no names stand higher than do those of some of the American historians. The fame of Prescott has already spread, even beyond the wide limits of Anglo-Saxondom. The name of Bancroft is as widely and as favourably known, his history of the United States, of which only a portion has as yet appeared, combining the interest of a romance with fidelity to sober realities. In biographical literature and in essays of a sketchy character, none can excel Washington Irving; whilst in descriptive writing and in detailing 'incidents of travel,' Stevens has certainly no superior. Many medical works of great eminence are from American pens; and there is not a good law library in this country but is indebted for some of its most valuable treasures to the jurisprudential literature of America. Prominent amongst the names which English as well as American lawyers revere is that of Mr. Justice Story. Nor have American theologians been idle, whilst jurists and physicians have been busy with their pens. Dwight, Edwards, and Barnes are known elsewhere as well as in America as eminent controversialists. Nor is the country behind in regard to science, for not only have many valuable scientific discoveries been made and problems solved in it, but many useful works of a scientific character have appeared, to say nothing of the periodicals which are conducted in the interests of science. The important science of economy has also been illustrated and promoted by the works of American economists, whilst Americans have likewise contributed their share to the political and philological literature of the world. The American brain is as active as American hands are busy. It has already produced a literature far above mediocrity, a literature which will be greatly extended, diversified, and enriched as by the greater spread of wealth the classes who can most conveniently devote themselves to its pursuit increase.

It is but natural that a government which does so much for the promotion of education should seek to make an ally of literature. Literary men in America, like literary men in France, have the avenue of political preferment much more accessible to them than literary men in England. There is in this respect, however, this difference between France and America, that whilst in the former the literary man is simply left to push his way to place, in the latter he is very often sought for and dragged into it. In France he must combine the violent partisan with the litterateur before he realizes a position in connection with his government. In America the litterateur is frequently converted into the politician, without ever having been the mere partisan. It was thus that Paulding was placed by President Van Buren at the head of the Navy Department, that Washington Irving was sent as minister to Spain, and Stevens dispatched on a political mission to Central America. It was chiefly on account of his literary qualities that Mr. Everett was sent as minister to London, and that Mr. Bancroft was also sent thither by the cabinet of Mr. Polk. Like Paulding, this last-mentioned gentleman was for some time at the head of a department in Washington, previously to his undertaking the embassy to London. The historian exhibited administrative capacity as soon as he was called upon to exercise it; whilst in this country he has earned for himself the character of an accomplished diplomatist, a finished scholar, and a perfect gentleman. But Mr. Bancroft's future fame will not depend upon his proved aptitude for administration or diplomacy. As in Mr. Macaulay's case, so with him, the historian will eclipse the politician.

As is the case in this country, the periodical and newspaper press occupies a very prominent position in the literature of America. Periodicals, that is to say, quarterlies, monthlies, and serials of all kinds, issue from it in abundance; the reviews and magazines being chiefly confined to Boston, Philadelphia, and New York.

In connexion with American newspapers, the first thing that strikes the stranger is their extraordinary number. They meet him at every turn, of all sizes, shapes, characters, prices, and appellations. On board the steamer and on the rail, in the counting-house and the hotel, in the street and in the private dwelling, in the crowded thoroughfare and in the remotest rural district he is ever sure of finding the newspaper. There are daily, triweekly, biweekly, and weekly papers, as with us; papers purely political, others of a literary cast, and others again simply professional; whilst there are many of no particular character, combining everything in their columns. The proportion of daily papers is enormous. Almost every town, down to communities of 2000 in number, has not only one but several daily papers. The city of Rochester, for instance, with a population a little exceeding 30,000, has five; to say nothing of the biweekly and weekly papers which are issued in it. I was at first, with nothing but my European experience to guide me, at a loss to understand how they were all supported. But I found that, in addition to the extent of their advertising patronage, which is very great, advertisements being free of duty in America, the number of their readers is almost coextensive with that of the population. There are few in America who do not both take in and read their newspapers. English newspapers are, in the first place, read but by a few; and in the next, the number of papers read is small in comparison with the number that read them. The chief circulation of English papers is in exchanges, newsrooms, reading rooms, hotels, taverns, coffee-houses, and pothouses, but a fraction of those who read them taking them in for themselves. Their high price may have much to do with this. In America the case is totally different. Not only are places of public resort well supplied with the journals of the day, but most families take in their paper, or papers. With us it is chiefly the inhabitants of towns that read the journals; in America the vast body of the rural population peruse them with the same avidity and universality as do their brethren in the towns. Were it otherwise, it would be impossible for the number which now appear to exist. But as newspapers are multiplied, so are readers, everyone reading and most subscribing to a newspaper. Many families, even in the rural districts, are not contented with one, but must have two or more, adding some metropolitan paper to the one or two local papers to which they subscribe.

The character of the American press is, in many points of view, not as elevated as it might be. But in this respect it is rapidly improving, and, as compared to what it was some years ago, there is now a marked change in it for the better. There may be as much violence, but there is less scurrility than heretofore in its columns; it is also rapidly improving in a literary point of view. There are several journals in some of the great metropolitan cities, which, whether we take into account the ability with which they are conducted or the dignity of attitude which they assume, as favourably contrast with the great bulk of the American press as do the best-conducted journals of this country.

The American papers, particularly in the larger commercial towns, are conducted with great spirit; but they spend far more money in the pursuit of news than they do in the employment of talent. Their great object is to anticipate each other in the publication of news. For this purpose they will either individually, or sometimes in combination, go to great trouble and expense. During the progress of the Oregon controversy a few of the papers in New York and Philadelphia clubbed together to express the European news from Halifax to New York, by horse express and steamer, a distance of 700 miles, and this too in winter. The most striking instance of competition between them that ever came under my observation was the following. For some time after the breaking out of the Mexican War, the anxiety to obtain news from the South was intense. There was then no electric telegraph south of Washington; the news had therefore to come to that city from New Orleans through the ordinary mail channels. The strife was between several Baltimore papers for the first use of the telegraph between Washington and Baltimore. The telegraph office was close to the post office, both being more than a mile from the wharf, at which the mail steamer, after having ascended the Potomac from the Acquia Creek, stopped, and from which the mail bags had to be carried in a wagon to the post office. The plan adopted by the papers to anticipate each other was this. Each had an agent on board the steamer, whose duty it was, as she was ascending the river, to obtain all the information that was new, and put it in a succinct form for transmission by telegraph the moment it reached Washington. Having done so, he tied the manuscript to a short heavy stick, which he threw ashore as the boat was making the wharf. On shore each paper had two other agents, one a boy mounted on horseback, and the other a man on foot, ready to catch the stick to which the manuscript was attached the moment it reached the ground. As soon as he got hold of it he handed it to the boy on horseback, who immediately set off with it at full gallop for the telegraph office. There were frequently five or six thus scrambling for precedence, and as they sometimes all got a good start, the race was a very exciting one. Crowds gathered every evening around the post office and telegraph office, both to learn the news and witness the result of the race. The first in secured the telegraph, and in a quarter of an hour afterwards the news was known at Baltimore, forty miles off, and frequently before the mail was delivered, and it was known even at Washington itself. On an important occasion one of the agents alluded to as being on board beat his competitors by an expert manœuvre. He managed, unperceived, to take a bow on board with him, with which, on the arrival of the boat, he shot his manuscript ashore, attached to an arrow, long before his rivals could throw the sticks ashore to which theirs was tied. Next evening, however, when still more important news was expected, and arrived, he was in turn outwitted. On her way up the boat touches at Alexandria, on the south side of the river, to leave the bags directed to that town, and take others from it. On this occasion one of the newspapers had a relay of horses between Washington and Alexandria, the rider receiving the news from the agent on board at the latter place, and galloping off with it to the capital. The bow was then of no use, for by the time the news-laden arrow was shot ashore, the intelligence designed for the rival paper was being telegraphed ahead to Baltimore. It will thus be seen that the American press partakes of that 'go-aheadism' which characterizes the pursuit of business in so many of its other departments in America.

THE CHARACTER OF AMERICAN SOCIETY

The Americans are almost universally known to be a sensitive people. They are more than this; they are oversensitive. This is a weakness which some travellers delight to play upon. But if they understood its source aright, they would deal more tenderly with it. As a nation, they feel themselves to be in the position of an individual whose permanent place in society has not yet been ascertained. They have struggled in little more than a century into the first rank among the powers of the earth; but, like all new members of a confined and very particular circle, they are not yet quite sure of the firmness of their footing. When they look to the future, they have no reason to doubt the prominency of the position, social, political, and economical, which they will assume. But they are in haste to be all of that they are yet destined to be; and although they do not exact from the stranger a positive recognition of all their pretensions, they are sensitive to a degree to any word or action on his part which purports a denial of them. It must be confessed that this weakness has of late very much increased. A sore that is being constantly irritated will soon exhibit all the symptoms of violent inflammation. The feelings of the American people have been wantonly and unnecessarily wounded by successive travellers who have undertaken to depict them, nationally and individually, and who, to pander to a prevailing taste in this country, have generally viewed them on the ludicrous side. It is a mistake to fancy that the Americans are impatient of criticism. They will submit to any amount of it that is fair, when they discover that it is tendered in an honest spirit. What they most wince at is the application to them and their affairs of epithet tending to turn them into ridicule. You may be as severe as you please with them, even in their own country as well as out of it, without irritating them, provided it appears that your intention is not simply to raise a laugh at their expense. When I first went to Washington, I was cautioned by one who knew the Americans well not to suppress my real sentiments concerning them, but to be guarded as to the terms and the manner in which I gave utterance to them. They have been so frequently unjustly dealt with by English writers that they now suspect every Englishman of a predetermination to treat them in a similar manner. I acted upon the advice which I received, and for the six months during which I resided in the capital I freely indulged in criticism of men and things, without, so far as I could ascertain, giving the slightest offence to anyone. But there are cases in which a look, a shrug of the shoulder, or a verbal expression may cause the greatest irritation. In this country it is difficult to understand this sensitiveness on the part of the American people. England has her fixed position in the great family of nations and at the head of civilization—a position which she has long occupied and from which it will be some time ere she is driven. We care not, therefore, what the foreigner says or thinks of us. He may look or express contempt as he walks our streets, or frequents our public places. His praise cannot exalt, nor can his contempt debase us, as a people. The desire of America is to be at least abreast of England in the career of nations; and every expression which falls from the Englishman, showing that in his opinion she is yet far behind his own country, grates harshly upon what is after all but a pardonable vanity, springing from a laudable ambition.

The Americans are much more sensitive at home than they are abroad. Their country is but yet young; and when they hear parties abroad, who have never seen it, expressing opinions in any degree derogatory to it, they console themselves with the reflection that the disparaging remark has its origin in an ignorance of the country, which is judged of, not from what it really is, but simply as a state of but seventy years' growth. Now in Europe it is but seldom that seventy years of national existence accomplishes much for a people. It is true that more has been done for mankind during the last seventy than perhaps during the previous 700; but the development of a nation in Europe is a slow process at the best, as compared with the course of things in this respect in America. The American, therefore, feels that if the European would suspend his judgment until he saw and heard for himself, it would be very different from what it is when begotten in prejudice and pronounced in ignorance. This takes the sting from such disparaging criticism abroad as he may chance to hear. But if it is offered at home, unless it is accompanied with all the candour and honesty in which such criticism should alone be indulged in, he has no such reflection to take refuge in, and it wounds him to the quick. If, notwithstanding all the evidences which the country affords of unexampled prosperity, universal contentment, social improvement, and material progress, the foreigner still speaks of it, not in terms of severity, but in those of contempt—in terms, in short, which the American feels and knows are not justifiable—he can only refer the criticism to a predetermination to turn everything into ridicule, and is consequently not unjustly offended. Such, unfortunately, is the predetermination with which a large proportion of English travellers in America enter the country, demeaning themselves, during their peregrinations through it, with an ill-disguised air of self-importance, unpalatable to a people who have become jealous from unmerited bad treatment. The consequence is that every Englishman in America is now on his good behaviour. He is not regarded as candid until he proves himself the reverse, but as prejudiced and unfriendly until he gives testimony of his fairness and honesty.

If the Americans are more sensitive at home than they are abroad, they are more boastful abroad than they are at home. The one is a mere weakness, the other frequently an offence. Many in Europe judge of the American people from the specimens of them who travel. There are, of course, many Americans that travel, who, if they partake largely of the national vanity attributed to them all, have the tact and the courtesy to conceal it. Indeed, some of the best specimens of Americans are, for obvious reasons, those who have travelled much from home. But the great mass of American travellers enter foreign countries with as thick a coat of prejudice about them as Englishmen generally wear in visiting America. The consequence is that they commit the fault abroad at which they are so irritated when committed in regard to themselves by the foreigner in America. With the American abroad, however, this fault assumes the reverse phase of that taken by it when committed by the foreigner in America. The Englishman, for instance, who is disposed to view everything in America through a jaundiced eye, and to draw invidious comparisons between the two countries, exalts his own by running down the other. The American, on the other hand, having the same object in view, approaches it from the opposite side, drawing comparisons favourable to his country, not by disparaging others, but by boasting of his own. This may be the weaker, but it is certainly the less offensive manifestation of a common fault. It would be erroneous to suppose that the national vanity, which so many Americans exhibit abroad, is prominently manifested at home. At all events it is not obtruded upon the stranger. The evidences of the country's greatness, both present and prospective, are before him when in the country; and to recapitulate them to him under these circumstances would be but to tell a tale twice over. . .

Intimately connected with the pride of country, which generally distinguishes the Americans, is the feeling which they cherish towards their institutions. Indeed, when the national feeling of an American is alluded to, something very different is implied from that which is generally understood by the term. In Europe, and particularly in mountainous countries, the aspect of which is such as to impress itself vividly upon the imagination, the love of country resolves itself into a reverence for locality irrespective of all other considerations. Thus the love which a Swiss bears to his country is attached to the soil constituting Switzerland, without referenec to the social or political institutions which may develop themselves in the cantons. And so with the Scottish mountaineer, whose national attachments centre upon the rugged features of his native land. It is seldom that the national feeling exhibits itself to the same extent in the breast of one born and bred in a country surpassingly rich, perhaps, in all the productions which minister to the comforts of life, but destitute of those rough and stern features which so endear his country to the hardy mountaineer. It is quite true that inspiriting historic associations may frequently produce feelings of national attachment similar to those inspired by a grand and imposing development of external nature; it is thus that some of the most patriotic tribes on earth are the inhabitants, not of the rugged mountain defile, but of the rich and monotonous plain. But the American exhibits little or none of the local attachments which distinguish the European. His feelings are more centred upon his institutions than his mere country. He looks upon himself more in the light of a republican than in that of a native of a particular territory. His affections have more to do with the social and political system with which he is connected than with the soil which he inhabits. The national feelings which he and a European cherishes, being thus different in their origin and their object, are also different in their results. The man whose attachments converge upon a particular spot of earth is miserable if removed from it, no matter how greatly his circumstances otherwise may have been improved by his removal; but give the American his institutions, and he cares but little where you place him. In some parts of the Union the local feeling may be comparatively strong, such as in New England; but it is astonishing how readily even there an American makes up his mind to try his fortunes elsewhere, particularly if he contemplates removal to another part of the Union, no matter how remote, or how different in climate and other circumstances from what he has been accustomed to, provided the flag of his country waves over it, and republican institutions accompany him in his wanderings.

Strange as it may seem, this peculiarity, which makes an American think less of his country than of the institutions which characterize it, contributes greatly to the pride which he takes in his country. He is proud of it, not so much for itself as because it is the scene in which an experiment is being tried which engages the anxious attention of the world. The American feels himself much more interested in the success of his scheme of government, if not more identified with it, than the European does in regard to his. The Englishman, for instance, does not feel himself particularly committed to the success of monarchy as a political scheme. He will support it as long as he is convinced that it conduces to the general welfare; and, judging it by this standard, it is likely that he will yet support it for a long time to come. He feels his honour to be involved in the independence of his country, but does not consider himself to be under any obligations to prove this or that political system an efficient one. The political scheme under which he lives he took as part and parcel of his inheritance in a national point of view, and his object is to make the best of it. It is very different, however, with the American. He feels himself to be implicated not only in the honour and independence of his country, but also in the success of democracy. He has asserted a great principle, and feels that, in attempting to prove it to be practicable, he has assumed an arduous responsibility. He feels himself, therefore, to be directly interested in the success of the political system under which he lives, and all the more so because he is conscious that in looking to its working mankind are divided into two great classes—those who are interested in its failure, and those who yearn for its success. Every American is thus, in his own estimation, the apostle of a particular political creed, in the final triumph and extension of which he finds both himself and his country deeply involved. . .

It is this feeling which renders the establishment of monarchy an impossibility in the United States. The American not only believes that his material interests are best subserved by a democratic form of government, but his pride is also mixed up with its maintenance and its permanency. It is a common thing for Europeans to speculate upon the disintegration of the Union, and the consequent establishment, in some part or parts of it, of the monarchical principle. These speculations are generally based upon precedents, but upon precedents which have in reality no application to America. The republics of old are pointed to as affording illustrations of the tendencies of republicanism. But the republics of old afford no criterion by which to judge of republicanism in America. The experiment which is being tried there is one *sui generis*. Not only are the political principles established different from those which have heretofore been practically recognized, but the people are also in a better state of preparation for the successful development of the experiment. The social condition of the ancient republics was as different from that of America as night is from day. The political superstructures which arose in them conformed themselves more or less to the nature of their bases. The result was not republicanism, but oligarchy.

President Lincoln and President Davis, 1861 [1] ❧

WILLIAM HOWARD RUSSELL *was born in 1821 near Dublin, was educated at Trinity College and Cambridge, and in the early 'forties became connected with the London* Times. *He at first thought of following a legal career, and was called to the bar in 1851, but his work for the press soon claimed all his attention. In 1843 he reported the O'Connell meetings in Ireland for the* Times, *in 1849-50 he was sent as correspondent to the scene of the Danish-Prussian War, and when the Crimean War broke out in 1853 he went to the front. His letters to the* Times *became the chief source of enlightenment for the English public, and were so popular that they were later reprinted in two volumes. By his exposure of the mismanagement of the war he did more than anyone else to cause the fall of the Aberdeen Ministry, and his name by 1856 was familiar throughout Europe and America. He was in India during the Sepoy Mutiny, being present at the siege and capture of Lucknow, and receiving the Indian war medal. In January 1860, he commenced the publication of the* Army and Navy Gazette, *of which he was editor and chief proprietor. But when the American Civil War threatened to break out, the* Times *engaged him and hurried off to the United States. He was regarded, at the time he landed in New York, as one of the foremost journalists of the time and an authority upon military affairs.*

Russell's career following the Civil War was as full of action as the years preceding it. He was at home in England until 1866, when he went to witness the Austro-Prussian War, and was at the battle of

[1] From *My Diary North and South*, New York, 1862, chapters 5, 6, and 23.

Koniggratz. He toured the Mediterranean with the Prince of Wales in 1868. When the Franco-Prussian War began, he hurried to the scene, and was in the thick of it from the battle of Wörth to the surrender of Paris; while later he gave a vivid description of the Communard outbreak. During the 'seventies he was with the Prince of Wales in India, and with Lord Wolseley during the Zulu War. He accompanied the Duke of Sutherland in touring the United States and Canada in 1881, and in the resulting book Hesperothen described some of the changes since his Civil War visit. Later he was with Wolseley in the Egyptian campaign. In 1895 he was knighted, and in 1907 he died.

SEWARD, LINCOLN, CHASE, AND OTHERS

March 27th. In a moderately sized and very comfortable apartment, surrounded with bookshelves and ornamented with a few engravings, we found the Secretary of State seated at his table, and enjoying a cigar; he received me with great courtesy and kindness, and after a time said he would take occasion to present me to the President, who was to give audience that day to the minister of the new kingdom of Italy, who had hitherto only represented the kingdom of Sardinia.

I have already described Mr. Seward's personal appearance; his son, to whom he introduced me, is the Assistant-Sectretary of State, and is editor or proprietor of a journal in the state of New York, which has a reputation for ability and fairness. Mr. Frederick Seward is a slight delicate-looking man, with a high forehead, thoughtful brow, dark eyes, and amiable expression; his manner is very placid and modest, and, if not reserved, he is by no means loquacious. As we were speaking, a carriage drove up to the door, and Mr. Seward exclaimed to his father, with something like dismay in his voice, 'Here comes the Chevalier in full uniform!'—and in a few seconds in effect the Chevalier Bertinatti made his appearance, in cocked hat, white gloves, diplomatic suit of blue and silver lace, sword, sash, and ribbon of the Cross of Savoy. I thought there was a quiet smile on Mr. Seward's face as he saw his brilliant companion, who contrasted so strongly with the more than republican simplicity of his own attire. 'Fred, do you take Mr. Russell round to the President's, whilst I go with the Chevalier. We will meet at the White House.' We accordingly set out through a private door leading to the grounds, and within a few seconds entered the hall of the moderate mansion, White House, which has very much the air of a portion of a bank or public office, being provided with glass doors and plain heavy chairs and forms. The domestic who was

in attendance was dressed like any ordinary citizen, and seemed perfectly indifferent to the high position of the great personage with whom
he conversed, when Mr. Seward asked him, 'Where is the President?'
Passing through one of the doors on the left, we entered a handsome
spacious room, richly and rather gorgeously furnished, and rejoicing
in a kind of *demi-jour,* which gave increased effect to the gilt chairs and
ormolu ornaments. Mr. Seward and the Chevalier stood in the center
of the room, whilst his son and I remained a little on one side. 'For,'
said Mr. Seward, 'you are not supposed to be here.'

Soon afterwards there entered, with a shambling, loose, irregular,
almost unsteady gait, a tall, lank, lean man, considerably over six feet
in height, with stooping shoulders, long pendulous arms, terminating
in hands of extraordinary dimensions, which, however, were far exceeded in proportion by his feet. He was dressed in an ill-fitting,
wrinkled suit of black, which put one in mind of an undertaker's
uniform at a funeral; round his neck a rope of black silk was knotted
in a large bulb, with flying ends projecting beyond the collar of his
coat; his turned-down shirt collar disclosed a sinewy muscular yellow
neck, and above that, nestling in a great black mass of hair, bristling
and compact like a ruff of mourning pins, rose the strange quaint face
and head, covered with its thatch of wild republican hair, of President
Lincoln. The impression produced by the size of his extremities, and
by his flapping and wide-projecting ears may be removed by the appearance of kindliness, sagacity, and the awkward bonhomie of his face;
the mouth is absolutely prodigious; the lips, straggling and extending
almost from one line of black beard to the other, are only kept in order
by two deep furrows from the nostril to the chin; the nose itself—a
prominent organ—stands out from the face, with an inquiring, anxious
air, as though it were sniffing for some good thing in the wind; the
eyes, dark, full, and deeply set, are penetrating, but full of an expression which almost amounts to tenderness; and above them projects the
shaggy brow, running into the small hard frontal space, the development of which can scarcely be estimated accurately, owing to the irregular flocks of thick hair carelessly brushed across it. One would say
that, although the mouth was made to enjoy a joke, it could also utter
the severest sentence which the head could dictate, but that Mr. Lincoln would be ever more willing to temper justice with mercy and to
enjoy what he considers the amenities of life than to take a harsh view
of men's nature and of the world, and to estimate things in an ascetic
or puritan spirit. A person who met Mr. Lincoln in the street would
not take him to be what—according to the usages of European society
—is called a 'gentleman'; and indeed, since I came to the United States,
I have heard more disparaging allusions made by Americans to him

on that account than I could have expected among simple republicans, where all should be equals; but at the same time, it would not be possible for the most indifferent observer to pass him in the street without notice.

As he advanced through the room, he evidently controlled a desire to shake hands all round with everybody, and smiled good-humoredly till he was suddenly brought up by the staid deportment of Mr. Seward, and by the profund diplomatic bows of the Chevalier Bertinatti. Then, indeed, he suddenly jerked himself back, and stood in front of the two ministers, with his body slightly drooped forward, and his hands behind his back, his knees touching, and his feet apart. Mr. Seward formally presented the minister, whereupon the President made a prodigiously violent demonstration of his body in a bow which had almost the effect of a smack in its rapidity and abruptness, and, recovering himself, proceeded to give his utmost attention, whilst the Chevalier, with another bow, read from a paper a long address in presenting the royal letter accrediting him as 'minister resident'; and when he said that 'the king desired to give, under your enlightened administration, all possible strength and extent to those sentiments of frank sympathy which do not cease to be exhibited every moment between the two peoples, and whose origin dates back as far as the exertions which have presided over their common destiny as self-governing and free nations,' the President gave another bow still more violent, as much as to accept the allusion.

The minister forthwith handed his letter to the President, who gave it into the custody of Mr. Seward, and then, dipping his hand into his coat pocket, Mr. Lincoln drew out a sheet of paper, from which he read his reply, the most remarkable part of which was his doctrine 'that the United States were bound by duty not to interfere with the differences of foreign governments and countries.' After some words of compliment, the President shook hands with the minister, who soon afterwards retired. Mr. Seward then took me by the hand and said, 'Mr. President, allow me to present to you Mr. Russell, of the London *Times*.' On which Mr. Lincoln put out his hand in a very friendly manner, and said, 'Mr. Russell, I am very glad to make your acquaintance, and to see you in this country. The London *Times* is one of the greatest powers in the world—in fact, I don't know anything which has much more power—except perhaps the Mississippi. I am glad to know you as its minister.' Conversation ensued for some minutes, which the President enlivened by two or three peculiar little sallies, and I left agreeably impressed with his shrewdness, humor, and natural sagacity.

In the evening I dined with Mr. Seward, in company with his son,

Mr. Seward, Jr., Mr. Sanford, and a quaint, natural specimen of an American rustic lawyer, who was going to Brussels as Secretary of Legation. . .

March 28th. I was honored today by visits from a great number of members of Congress, journalists, and others. Judging from the expressions of most of the Washington people, they would gladly see a Southern Cabinet installed in their city. The cold shoulder is given to Mr. Lincoln, and all kinds of jokes and stories are circulated at his expense. People take particular pleasure in telling how he came towards the seat of government disguised in a Scotch cap and cloak, whatever that may mean.

In the evening I repaired to the White House. The servant who took my hat and coat was particularly inquisitive as to my name and condition of life; and when he heard I was not a minister, he seemed inclined to question my right to be there at all; 'for,' said he, 'there are none but members of the Cabinet, and their wives and daughters, dining here today.' Eventually he relaxed, instructed me how to place my hat so that it would be exposed to no indignity, and informed me that I was about to participate in a prandial enjoyment of no ordinary character. There was no parade or display, no announcement, no gilded staircase, with its liveried heralds, transmitting and translating one's name from landing to landing. From the unpretending antechamber, a walk across the lofty hall led us to the reception room, which was the same as that in which the President held his interview yesterday.

Mrs. Lincoln was already seated to receive her guests. She is of the middle age and height, of a plumpness degenerating to the *embonpoint* natural to her years; her features are plain, her nose and mouth of an ordinary type, and her manners and appearance homely, stiffened, however, by the consciousness that her position requires her to be something more than plain Mrs. Lincoln, the wife of an Illinois lawyer; she is profuse in the introduction of the word 'sir' in every sentence, which is now almost an Americanism confined to certain classes, although it was once as common in England. Her dress I shall not attempt to describe, though it was very gorgeous and highly colored. She handled a fan with much energy, displaying a round, well-proportioned arm, and was adorned with some simple jewelry. Mrs. Lincoln struck me as being desirous of making herself agreeable; and I own I was agreeably disappointed, as the Secessionist ladies at Washington had been amusing themselves by anecdotes which could scarcely have been founded on fact.

Several of the ministers had already arrived; by and by all had come, and the party waited only for General Scott, who seemed to be the representative man in Washington of the monarchical idea, and to absorb some of the feeling which is lavished on the pictures and memory, if not on the monument, of Washington. Whilst we were waiting, Mr. Seward took me round and introduced me to the ministers and to their wives and daughters, among the latter, Miss Chase, who is very attractive, agreeable, and sprightly. Her father, the Finance Minister, struck me as one of the most intelligent and distinguished persons in the whole assemblage—tall, of a good presence, with a well-formed head, fine forehead, and a face indicating energy and power. There is a peculiar droop and motion of the lid of one eye, which seems to have suffered some injury, that detracts from the agreeable effect of his face; but, on the whole, he is one who would not pass quite unnoticed in a European crowd of the same description.

In the whole assemblage there was not a scrap of lace or a piece of ribbon, except the gorgeous epaulettes of an old naval officer who had served against us in the last war, and who represented some branch of the Naval Department. Nor were the ministers by any means remarkable for their personal appearance.

Mr. Cameron, the Secretary of War, a slight man, above the middle height, with gray hair, deep-set keen gray eyes, and a thin mouth, gave me the idea of a person of ability and adroitness. His colleague, the Secretary of the Navy, a small man, with a great long gray beard and spectacles, did not look like one of much originality or ability; but people who know Mr. Welles declare that he is possessed of administrative power, although they admit that he does not know the stem from the stern of a ship, and are in doubt whether he ever saw the sea in his life. Mr. Smith, the Minister of the Interior, is a bright-eyed, smart (I use the word in the English sense) gentleman, with the reputation of being one of the most conservative members of the Cabinet. Mr. Blair, the Postmaster-General, is a person of much greater influence than his position would indicate. He has the reputation of being one of the most determined Republicans in the Ministry; but he held peculiar notions with reference to the black and white races, which, if carried out, would not by any means conduce to the comfort of happiness of free Negroes in the United States. He is a tall, lean man, with a hard, Scotch, practical-looking head—an anvil for ideas to be hammered on. His eyes are small and deeply set, and have a rat-like expression; and he speaks with caution, as though he weighed every word before he uttered it. The last of the ministers is Mr. Bates, a stout, thick-set, common-looking man, with a large beard, who fills the office of Attorney-General. Some of the gentlemen were in evening dress; others wore black frock coats, which it seems, as in Turkey, are considered to be *en regle* at a Republican ministerial dinner.

In the conversation which occurred before dinner, I was amused to observe the manner in which Mr. Lincoln used the anecdotes for which he is famous. Where men bred in courts, accustomed to the world, or versed in diplomacy, would use some subterfuge, or would make a polite speech, or give a shrug of the shoulders as the means of getting out of an embarrassing position, Mr. Lincoln raises a laugh by some bold west-country anecdote, and moves off in the cloud of merriment produced by his joke. Thus, when Mr. Bates was remonstrating apparently against the appointment of some indifferent lawyer to a place of judicial importance, the President interposed with, 'Come, now, Bates, he's not half as bad as you think. Besides that, I must tell you, he did me a good turn long ago. When I took to the law, I was going to court one morning, with some ten or twelve miles of bad road before me, and I had no horse. The judge overtook me in his wagon. "Hollo, Lincoln! Are you not going to the courthouse? Come in, and I'll give you a seat." Well, I got in, and the judge went on reading his papers. Presently the wagon struck a stump on one side of the road; then it hopped off to the other. I looked out, and I saw the driver was jerking from side to side in his seat; so says I, "Judge, I think your coachman has been taking a little drop too much this morning." "Well, I declare, Lincoln," said he, "I should not wonder if you are right, for he has nearly upset me half a dozen of times since starting." So, putting his head out of the window, he shouted, "Why, you infernal scoundrel, you are drunk." Upon which, pulling up his horses and turning round with great gravity, the coachman said, "By gorra! that's the first rightful decision you have given for the last twelve-month."' Whilst the company were laughing, the President beat a quiet retreat from the neighborhood of the Attorney-General.

It was at last announced that General Scott was unable to be present, and that, although actually in the house, he had been compelled to retire from indisposition, and we moved in to the banqueting hall. The first 'state dinner,' as it is called, of the President was not remarkable for ostentation. No liveried servants, no Persic splendor of ancient plate, or *chefs d'œuvre* of art, glittered round the board. Vases of flowers decorated the table, combined with dishes in what may be called the 'Gallo-American' style, with wines which owed their parentage to France, and their rearing and education to the United States, which abounds in cunning nurses for such productions. The conversation was suited to the state dinner of a cabinet at which women and strangers were present. I was seated next Mr. Bates, and the very agreeable and lively secretary of the President, Mr. Hay, and except when there was an attentive silence caused by one of the President's stories, there was a Babel of small talk round the table, in which I was surprised to find a diversity of accent almost as great as if a number of foreigners had been speaking English. I omitted the name of Mr. Hamlin, the Vice-President, as well as those of less remarkable people who were present; but it would not be becoming to pass over a man distinguished for nothing so much as his persistent and unvarying adhesion to one political doctrine, which has made him, in combination with the belief in his honesty, the occupant of a post which leads to the Presidency, in event of any occurrence which may remove Mr. Lincoln.

After dinner the ladies and gentlemen retired to the drawing room, and the circle was increased by the addition of several politicians. I had an opportunity of conversing with some of the ministers, if not with all, from time to time, and I was struck by the uniform tendency of their remarks in reference to the policy of Great Britain. They seemed to think that England was bound by her antislavery antecedents to discourage to the utmost any attempts of the South to establish its independence on a basis of slavery, and to assume that they were the representatives of an active war of emancipation. As the veteran Commodore Stewart passed the chair of the young lady to whom I was speaking, she said, 'I suppose, Mr. Russell, you do not admire that officer?' 'On the contrary,' I said, 'I think he is a very fine-looking old man.' 'I don't mean that,' she replied; 'but you know he can't be very much liked by you, because he fought so gallantly against you in the last war, as you must know.' I had not the courage to confess ignorance of the captain's antecedents. There is a delusion among more than the fair American who spoke to me that we entertain in England the sort of feeling, morbid or wholesome as it may be, in reference to our reverses at New Orleans and elsewhere, that is attributed to Frenchmen respecting Waterloo.

On returning to Willard's Hotel, I was accosted by a gentleman who came out from the crowd in front of the office. 'Sir,' he said, 'you have been dining with our President tonight.' I bowed. 'Was it an agreeable party?' said he. 'What do you think of Mr. Lincoln?' 'May I ask to whom I have the pleasure of speaking?' 'My name is Mr. ——, and I am the correspondent of the New York ——.' 'Then, sir,' I replied, 'it gives me satisfaction to tell you that I think a great deal of Mr. Lincoln, and that I am equally pleased with my dinner. I have the honor to bid you good evening.' The same gentleman informed me afterwards that he had created the office of Washington correspondent to the New York papers. 'At first,' said he, 'I merely wrote news, and no one cared much; then I spiced it up, squibbed a little, and let off stories of my own. Congressmen contradicted me—issued cards—said they were not facts. The public attention was attracted, and I was told to go on; and so the Washington correspondence became a feature in all the New York papers by degrees.' The hum and bustle in the hotel tonight were wonderful. All the office-seekers were in the passages, hungering after senators and representatives, and the ladies in any way related to influential people had an *entourage* of courtiers sedulously paying their respects. Miss Chase, indeed, laughingly told me that she was pestered by applicants for her father's good offices and by persons seeking introduction to her as a means of making demands on 'Uncle Sam.'

DAVIS AND HIS CABINET IN MONTGOMERY

May 9th. Today the papers contain a proclamation by the President of the Confederate States of America, declaring a state of war between the Confederacy and the United States, and notifying the issue of letters of marque and reprisal. I went out with Mr. Wigfall in the forenoon to pay my respects to Mr. Jefferson Davis at the State Department. Mr. Seward told me that but for Jefferson Davis the Secession plot could never have been carried out. No other man of the party had the brain or the courage and dexterity to bring it to a successful issue. All the persons in the Southern States spoke of him with admiration, though their forms of speech and thought generally forbid them to be respectful to anyone.

There before me was 'Jeff Davis's State Department'—a large brick building, at the corner of a street, with a Confederate flag floating above it. The door stood open and 'gave' on a large hall, whitewashed, with doors plainly painted belonging to small rooms, in which was transacted most important business, judging by the names written on sheets of paper and applied outside denoting bureaus of the highest functions. A few clerks were passing in and out, and one or two gentlemen were on the stairs, but there was no appearance of any bustle in the building.

We walked straight upstairs to the first floor, which was surrounded by doors opening from a quadrangular platform. On one of these was written simply, 'The President.' Mr. Wigfall went in, and after a moment returned and said, 'The President will be glad to see you; walk in, sir.' When I entered, the President was engaged with four gentlemen, who were making some offer of aid to him. He was thanking them 'in the name of the Government.' Shaking hands with each, he saw them to the door, bowed them and Mr. Wigfall out, and turning to me, said, 'Mr. Russell, I am glad to welcome you here, though I fear your appearance is a symptom that our affairs are not quite prosperous,' or words to that effect. He then requested me to sit down close to his own chair at his office table, and proceeded to speak on general matters, adverting to the Crimean War and the Indian Mutiny, and asking questions about Sebastopol, the Redan, and the Siege of Lucknow.

I had an opportunity of observing the President very closely: he did not impress me as favorably as I had expected, though he is certainly a very different-looking man from Mr. Lincoln. He is like a gentleman—has a slight, light figure, little exceeding middle height, and holds himself erect and straight. He was dressed in a rustic suit of slate-colored stuff, with a black silk handkerchief round his neck; his manner is plain, and rather reserved and drastic; his head is well formed, with a fine full forehead, square and high, covered with innumerable fine lines and wrinkles, features regular, through the cheekbones are too high and the jaws too hollow to be handsome; the lips are thin, flexible, and curved, the chin square, well defined; the nose very regular, with wide nostrils; and the eyes deep-set, large, and full— one seems nearly blind, and is partly covered with a film, owing to excruciating attacks of neuralgia and tic. Wonderful to relate, he does not chew, and is neat and clean-looking, with hair trimmed and boots brushed. The expression of his face is anxious, he has a very haggard, careworn, and pain-drawn look, though no trace of anything but the utmost confidence and the greatest decision could be detected in his conversation. He asked me some general questions respecting the route I had taken in the states.

I mentioned that I had seen great military preparations through the South, and was astonished at the alacrity with which the people sprang to arms. 'Yes, sir,' he remarked, and his tone of voice and manner of speech are rather remarkable for what are considered Yankee peculiarities. 'In Eu-rope' (Mr. Seward also indulges in that pronunciation) 'they laugh at us because of our fondness for military titles and displays. All your travelers in this country have commented on the number of generals and colonels and majors all over the states. But the fact is, we are a military people, and these signs of the fact were ignored. We are not less military because we have had no great standing armies. But perhaps we are the only people in the world where gentlemen go to a military academy who do not intend to follow the profession of arms.'

In the course of our conversation, I asked him to have the goodness to direct that a sort of passport or protection should be given to me, as I might possibly fall in with some guerrilla leader on my way northwards, in whose eyes I might not be entitled to safe conduct. Mr. Davis said, 'I shall give such instructions to the Secretary of War as shall be necessary. But, sir, you are among civilized, intelligent people who understand your position and appreciate your character. We do not seek the sympathy of England by unworthy means, for we respect ourselves, and we are glad to invite the scrutiny of men into our acts; as for our motives, we meet the eye of Heaven.' I thought I could judge from his words that he had the highest idea of the French as soldiers but that his feelings and associations were more identified with England, although he was quite aware of the difficulty of conquering the repugnance which exists to slavery.

Mr. Davis made no allusion to the authorities at Washington, but he asked me if I thought it was supposed in England there would be war between the states? I answered that I was under the impression the public thought there would be no actual hostilities. 'And yet you see we are driven to take up arms for the defense of our rights and liberties.'

As I saw an immense mass of papers on his table, I rose and made my bow, and Mr. Davis, seeing me to the door, gave me his hand and said, 'As long as you may stay among us you shall receive every facility it is in our power to afford you, and I shall always be glad to see you.' Colonel Wigfall was outside, and took me to the room of the Secretary of War, Mr. Walker, whom we found closeted with General Beauregard and two other officers in a room full of maps and plans. He is the kind of a man generally represented in our types of the 'Yankees'—tall, lean, straight-haired, angular, with fiery, impulsive eyes and manner—a ruminator of tobacco and a profuse spitter—a lawyer, I believe, certainly not a soldier; ardent, devoted to the cause, and confident to the last degree of its speedy success.

The news that two more states had joined the Confederacy, making ten in all, was enough to put them in good humor. 'Is it not too bad these Yankees will not let us go our own way, and keep their cursed Union to themselves? If they force us to it, we may be obliged to drive them beyond the Susquehanna.' Beauregard was in excellent spirits, busy measuring off miles of country with his compasses, as if he were dividing empires.

From this room I proceeded to the office of Mr. Benjamin, the Attorney-General of the Confederate States, the most brilliant perhaps of the whole of the famous Southern orators. He is a short, stout man, with a full face, olive-colored, and most decidedly Jewish features, with the brightest large black eyes, one of which is somewhat diverse from the other, and a brisk, lively, agreeable manner, combined with much vivacity of speech and quickness of utterance. He is one of the first lawyers or advocates in the United States, and had a large practice at Washington, where his annual recipts from his profession were not less than £8000 to £10,000 a year. But his love of the card table rendered him a prey to older and cooler hands, who waited till the sponge was full at the end of the session, and then squeezed it to the last drop. . .

Being invited to attend a levee or reception held by Mrs. Davis, the President's wife, I returned to the hotel to prepare for the occasion. On my way I passed a company of volunteers, one hundred and twenty artillerymen, and three field pieces, on their way to the station for Virginia, followed by a crowd of 'citizens' and Negroes of both sexes, cheering vociferously. The band was playing that excellent quick-step 'Dixie.' The men were stout, fine fellows, dressed in coarse gray tunics with yellow facings and French caps. They were armed with smooth-bore muskets, and their knapsacks were unfit for marching, being waterproof bags slung from the shoulders. The guns had no caissons, and the shoeing of the troops was certainly deficient in soling. The Zouave mania is quite as rampant here as it is in New York, and the smallest children are thrust into baggy red breeches, which the learned Lipsius might have appreciated, and are sent out with flags and tin swords to impede the highways.

The Border in Wartime; Concord and Its Writers [1] &

EDWARD DICEY, *best known as the editor of the London* Daily News *in 1870 and of the London* Observer *from 1871 to 1889, was born in 1832 in Leicestershire, the son of an English country gentleman. He was graduated at Oxford, where he took honors, and became an active journalist and magazine writer. He spent six months in America for the* Spectator *during the first half of 1862. Later in life (1875) he became a member of the bar, and was treasurer of Gray's Inn 1903-4. His best books are those he wrote upon Egyptian affairs:* England and Egypt *(1884),* The Story of the Khedivate *(1902), and* The Egypt of the Future *(1907). But his work upon the United States has many merits. Its thoughtfulness and fairness, and especially its warm friendliness toward the North at a time when most English gentlemen and writers sympathized with the South, made a happy impression upon*

[1] From *Six Months in the Federal States*, London, 1863, volume II, chapters 1, 5, 6, and 15.

*American readers. Dicey sternly rebuked the Britons who sneered at
the United States, and told them that they were playing with fire among
powder barrels. 'Mr. Dicey has a manly, English way of accepting
the preponderant evidence concerning the crisis he came to study,'
remarked the* Atlantic. *'He seldom gets entangled in trivial events,
but knows how to use them as illustrations of great events.' It added
that there was 'scarcely an offense against good taste or good feeling
in Mr. Dicey's volumes,' and that they bore 'honorable testimony to
the accuracy of his observations, as well as to his powers of comparison
and judgment.' Dicey's brother, A. V. Dicey, after the Civil War
became even better known to Americans, being a constant contributor
to the New York* Nation *and other periodicals.*

WASHINGTON AND THE ARMY OF THE POTOMAC, 1862

FROM the windows of my lodgings, I looked out upon the mile-long
Pennsylvania Avenue, leading from the broad Potomac River, by the
marble palace of the President's, up to the snow-white Capitol, and
every hour of the day almost I was disturbed while writing by the
sound of some military band, as regiment after regiment passed, marching southwards. The Germans have brought with them into their new
fatherland the instinct of instrumental music, and the bands are fine
ones, above the average of those of a French or English line regiment.
The tunes were mostly those well known to us across the water—'Cheer,
Boys, Cheer,' the 'Red, White, and Blue,' and 'Dixie's Land' being the
favorites. For the war had brought out hitherto no war-inspired melody,
and the quaint, half-grotesque, half passion-stirring air of

'John Brown's body lies a-mould'ring in the grave,'

was still under McClellan's interdict. But yet, be the tunes what they
may, the drums and fifes and trumpets rouse the same heart beatings
as in the Old World, and teach the same lessons of glory and ambition
and martial pride. Can this teaching fail to work? is the question that
I asked myself daily, as yet without an answer.

Surely no nation in the world has gone through such a baptism of
war as the people of the United States underwent in one short year's
time. With the men of the Revolution the memories of the Revolutionary War had died out. Two generations had passed away to whom
war was little more than a name. The Mexican campaign was rather a
military demonstration than an actual war, and the sixteen years which
had elapsed since its termination form a long period in the life of a nation whose whole existence has not completed its first century. Twenty

months ago there were not more than 12,000 soldiers in a country of 31,000,000. A soldier was as rare an object throughout America as in one of our country hamlets. I recollect a Northern lady telling me that, till within a year before, she could not recall the name of a single person whom she had ever known in the army, and that now she had sixty friends and relatives who were serving in the war; and her case was by no means an uncommon one. Once in four years, on the fourth of March, two or three thousand troops were collected in Washington to add to the pomp of the Presidential Inauguration; and this was the one military pageant the country had to boast of. Almost in a day this state of things passed away. Our English critics were so fond of repeating what the North could not do—how it could not fight, nor raise money, nor conquer the South—that they omitted to mention what the North *had* done. There was no need to go farther than my windows at Washington to see the immensity of the war. It was curious to me to watch the troops as they came marching past. Whether they were regulars or volunteers it was hard for the unprofessional critic to discern; for all were clad alike, in the same dull, gray-blue overcoats, and most of the few regular regiments were filled with such raw recruits that the difference between volunteer and regular was not a marked one. Of course it was easy enough to pick faults in the aspect of such troops. As each regiment marched, or rather waded through the dense slush and mud which covered the roads, you could observe many inaccuracies of military attire. One man would have his trousers rolled up almost to his knees; another would wear them tucked inside his boots; and a third would appear with one leg of his trousers hanging down, and the other gathered tightly up. It was not unfrequent, too, to see an officer with his epaulettes sewed on to a common plain frock coat. Then there was a slouching gait about the men, not soldier-like to English eyes. They used to turn their heads round when on parade, with an indifference to rule which would drive an old drill sergeant out of his senses. There was an absence, also, of precision in the march. The men kept in step; but I always was at a loss to discover how they ever managed to do so. The system of march, it is true, was copied rather from the French than the English or Austrian fashion; but still it was something very different from the orderly disorder of a Zouave march. That all these and a score of similar irregularities are faults, no one—an American least of all—would deny. But there are two sides to the picture.

One thing is certain, that there is no physical degeneracy about a race which could produce such regiments as those which formed the army of the Potomac. Men of high stature and burly frames were rare, except in the Kentucky troops; but on the other hand, small, stunted men were almost unknown. I have seen the armies of most European countries; and I have no hesitation in saying that, as far as the average raw material of the rank and file is concerned, the American army is the finest. The officers are, undoubtedly, the weak point of the system. They have not the military air, the self-possession which long habit of command alone can give; while the footing of equality on which they inevitably stand with the volunteer privates deprives them of the *esprit du corps* belonging to a ruling class. Still they are active, energetic, and constantly with their troops. Wonderfully well equipped, too, at this period of the war, were both officers and men. Their clothing was substantial and fitted easily, their arms were good, and the military arrangements were as perfect as money alone could make them. It was remarkable to me how rapidly the new recruits fell into the habits of military service. I have seen a Pennsylvanian regiment, raised chiefly from the mechanics of Philadelphia, which, six weeks after its formation, was, in my eyes, equal to the average of our best-trained volunteer corps, as far as marching and drill exercise went. Indeed, I often asked myself what it was that made the Northern volunteer troops look, as a rule, so much more soldier-like than our own. I suppose the reason is that across the Atlantic there was actual war, and that at home there was at most only a parade. I have no doubt that, in the event of civil war or invasion, England would raise a million volunteers as rapidly as America has done—more rapidly she could not; and that, when fighting had once begun, there would only be too much of grim earnestness about our soldiering; but it is no want of patriotism to say that the American volunteers looked to me more business-like than our own. At the scene of war itself there was no playing at soldiering. No gaudy uniforms or crack companies, no distinction of classes. From every part of the North; from the ports of New York and Boston; from the homesteads of New England; from the mines of Pennsylvania and the factories of Pittsburgh; from the shores of the Great Lakes; from the Mississippi valley; and from the far-away Texan prairies these men had come to fight for the Union. It is idle to talk of their being attracted by the pay alone. Large as it is, the pay of thirteen dollars a month is only two dollars more than the ordinary pay of privates in the Federal army during peace times. Thirteen shillings a week is poor pay for a laboring man in America, even with board, especially during the war, when the wages of unskilled labour amounted to from twenty to thirty shillings a week. It is false, moreover, to assert, as the opponents of the North are fond of doing, that the Federal armies were composed exclusively, or even principally, of foreigners. In the North, the proportion of foreign immigrants to native-born Americans is about thirty per cent, and the same proportions were observed in the

Federal volunteer army. Judging from my own observation, I would say that the percentage of foreigners amongst the privates of the army of the Potomac was barely ten per cent. But in the West, which is almost peopled with Germans, foreigners are, probably, in the majority. The bulk of the native volunteers consisted of men who had given up good situations in order to enlist, and who had families to support at home; and for such men the additional pay was not an adequate inducement to incur the dangers and hardships of war. Of course, wherever there is an army, the scum of the population will always be gathered together; but the average *morale* and character of the couple of hundred thousand troops collected around Washington was extremely good. There was very little outward drunkenness, and less brawling about the streets than if half a dozen English militia regiments had been quartered there. The number of papers purchased daily by the common soldiers and the amount of letters which they sent through the military post was astonishing to a foreigner, though less strange when you considered that every man in that army, with the exception of a few recent immigrants, could both read and write. The ministers, also, of the different sects, who went out on Sundays to preach to the troops, found no difficulty in obtaining large and attentive audiences.

The general impression left upon me by my observations of the army of the Potomac was a very favourable one. All day, and every day while I resided at Washington, the scene before my eyes was one of war. An endless military panorama seemed to be unrolling itself ceaselessly. Sometimes it was a line of artillery struggling and floundering onwards through the mud—sometimes it was a company of wild Texan cavalry, rattling past, with the jingle of their belts and spurs. Sometimes it was a long train of sutlers' wagons, ambulance vans, or forage carts drawn by the shaggy Pennsylvanian mules. Orderlies innumerable galloped up and down, patrols without end passed along the pavements, and at every window and doorstep and street corner you saw soldiers standing. You had to go far away from Washington to leave the war behind you. If you went up to any high point in the city whence you could look over the surrounding country, every hillside seemed covered with camps. The white tents caught your eye on all sides; and across the river, where the dense brushwood obscured the prospect, the great army of the Potomac stretched miles away, right up to the advanced posts of the Confederates, south of the far-famed Manassas. The numbers were so vast that it was hard to realize them. During one week 50,000 men were embarked from Washington, and yet the town and neighbourhood still swarmed with troops and camps, as it seemed, undiminished in number. And here, remember, I saw only one portion of the gigantic army. Along a line of two thousand miles or so, from the Potomac down to New Mexico, there were at that time Federal armies fighting their way southwards. At Fortress Monroe, too, Ship Island, Mobile, and at every accessible point along the Atlantic seaboard expeditions numbered by tens of thousands were stationed, waiting for the signal to advance. At this time the muster roll of the Federal army numbered 672,000 men, or, at least, that number were drawing pay daily from the Treasury, though a large allowance must be made for absentees and non-effectives.

Try to realize all this, and then picture to yourself what its effect, seen in fact, and not portrayed by feeble description, must be upon a nation unused to war. The wonder to me is that the American people were not more intoxicated with the consciousness of their newborn strength.

AN EXCURSION TO THE FRONT

At the time of my visit to Blencker's camp, the army was hourly awaiting orders to march on Manassas. Within a week or so afterwards, the news came that the Confederates had evacuated the mud forts and quaker guns, which had kept McClellan so long at bay, and were retiring upon Richmond. Ten days had not passed before Yankee energy had reconstructed the railroad which led from Alexandria to Manassas Gap; and the offer having been made me to accompany the first trial trip after the completion of the line, I gladly availed myself of it. It was the loveliest of spring mornings when I left Washington early to join the expedition. A steamboat carried us off from the foot of the chain bridge to Alexandria. The wide river was covered with fleets of transports, dropping down with the tide to convey provisions to the army which had just begun to sail for the peninsula. The wharves of Alexandria were covered with troops waiting for embarkment. The great river steamers, which lay alongside, were crowded with troops singing and cheering lustily. The whole nation was overjoyed with the thought that at last the day of the 'masterly inaction' was over, and that the long-expected hour of victory had struck. The army shared in the general enthusiasm; and there were few, I think, who contemplated even the possibility of a temporary reverse. I own, laying claim as I do to no pretensions as a military authority, that I shared in that impression. It seems to me even now incredible at times, that that grand army, which I watched for days and weeks defiling through Washington, should not have swept all before it; and I confess that I still believe its failure was due to want of generalship. The nation, at any rate, at that time was confident, proud of its general, proud of its army, proud of its coming victory; and when the 'Young Napoleon'—with that partial affectation of the Napoleonic style he was so partial to—declared in the address he issued, almost on the day of which I write, that hereafter his troops 'would ask no higher honor than the proud consciousness that they belonged to the army of the Potomac,' he uttered a boast which found an echo in every Northern breast.

My companions on the excursion, among whom were Mr. Hawthorne and Mr. N. P. Willis, were all Northerners; and all of them, the ladies especially, showed a natural feeling of pride at the appearance of the troops about to start on that ill-fated expedition. It struck me, however, curiously at the time, how all the party talked about our excursion as if we were going to visit a strange country. The sacred soil of Virginia seemed as imperfectly known to them as Ireland is to myself; and they looked upon their excursion with much the same sort of interest as I should do on a trip across St. George's Channel.

Half an hour's sail brought us to Alexandria. Like most of the old Virginia and Maryland towns, it has a very English air about it; the red brick houses, the broad sleepy streets, the long straggling wharves might have been imported direct from Norfolk or Lincolnshire. The town itself was crammed with troops; but neither then nor on the other occasions when I visited it was there anything to be seen of the inhabitants. They had left the place for the most part, or lived in retirement. Closely connected as the little town is with Washington, it was bitterly 'secesh'; and the citizens of Alexandria showed their dislike of the Federal army of occupation by every means in their power. The women, as may be supposed, displayed their animosity most outspokenly. Unless they were foully belied, they used to take pleasure in insulting the private soldiers with epithets which will not bear repetition. The common Yankee soldiers seemed to feel these insults from women with a susceptibility I felt it hard to account for. English soldiers, under like circumstances, would have retorted with language still more unmentionable, or would have adopted the spirit of General Butler's famous order without compunction. But the Americans appeared to writhe under these insults. The bad language of the Alexandria women was constantly complained of in the papers as a bitter personal injury. I remember one stalwart Massachusetts soldier in the hospital, who complained seriously that when he was recovered, and went back to duty, he should be subjected again to the abuse of these Southern ladies; and said—'It was so hard to bear'. . .

At the wharf, a train was waiting to convey our party. It was the first which had started, and the resumption of the traffic was a sign of returning peace and order. But the event excited no comment in that gloomy, sullen town, and only a few boys and Negroes were collected together to witness our departure. Slowly we moved on through the dead streets till we reached the camps outside the town, and then, passing onwards at an increased speed, we were soon in the hilly Virginia country, which a few days before had been occupied by the Confederate forces.

The country through which our road lay impressed me strangely with a sense of desolation. If the reader knows the Surrey Downs, near Albury, and can fancy what they would be if the mansions and cottages were all removed, if the woods were replaced by pine forests, and if the place of roads was supplied by mud tracks, and if the whole district was intersected by steep gullies filled with clear sparkling torrent streams, he will have a pretty good notion of what northern Virginia is like. For miles and miles together you passed through long tracts of pine wood, broken by patches of deserted fields, where the brushwood was growing up again amidst the stumps of the forest trees, which had been cleared years ago. Every now and then you came to an open space, where you caught a glimpse of the distant Blue Ridge Mountains, and then you passed again into the gloomy pine-wood shade. Along the journey of twenty miles or so, you never saw a village; and the number of houses that you passed might be counted on your fingers. In the fields there was no one working; the snake fences were broken down; at the roadside stations there were no passengers; and the few people loitering about gazed sullenly at us as we passed. Actual traces of the war there were not many. We passed a few deserted camps, and a house or two which had been burnt down by one of the two armies which had occupied the soil in turn; but that was all. Indeed, the look of desolation could have proceeded but partially from the presence of the war. I never saw the same aspect elsewhere, even in states which had suffered as much from invasion. The state of the fields and fences, and roads and farmhouses betokened a decay of much longer standing than that of a year's time. The exhaustion of the soil, even more than the havoc of men, was the cause of the deserted air which hung over everything. With the wasteful system of tobacco-growing and slave labour, Virginia is rapidly sinking back into its primitive desolation.

At last we emerged from the pine woods, and began to ascend by a steep incline—an open table-land—at whose foot ran the now famous stream of Bull Run. Here we had to move slowly, and stop every few hundred yards to remove huge logs, which had been rolled across the rails to obstruct the passage. Then, reaching the tops of the incline, we found ourselves in the centre of Manassas camp. It had hardly yet been visited since the departure of the Confederates; everything which could be destroyed had been burnt before their retreat; and the whole ground for miles was covered with the debris of an army's stores. Smashed carriages, broken arms, empty coffins, charred planks, decaying skeletons of horses, pots, pans, and cartridges lay heaped together in a weird disorder. A detachment of Federal soldiers were on duty there, collecting any remnants of the stores which were worth preserving; but otherwise, there was not a soul visible. The few soldiers' huts which were left standing were knocked hastily together with the rudest planks, and swarmed inside with vermin of every description. A foul smell of charred animal matter hung about the place, and flights of crows were feeding upon the garbage strewn on every side. The whole ground was covered with stray leaves of tracts and Bibles, which some Southern religious society had obviously been distributing amongst the troops. Letters, too, were to be picked up by dozens; and, indeed, the collectors of curiosities amongst our party had their researches richly rewarded.

As to the value of the fortifications, I could form no opinion. To me they appeared of the rudest and poorest description of earthworks; and I fancy were intended rather to protect the retreat of the army in case of a sudden attack than to keep off the enemy. On the other hand, the position of Manassas in itself was obviously a strong one. The wide plateau on which it stood sloped down rapidly towards the north; so that an army advancing from Washington would have had to mount this slope, exposed to the full fire of the enemy's batteries. At this time, by the way, there was an embittered discussion going on in the American press as to whether the Confederates had manned their works with wooden cannon, in order to give a false impression of strength. The Antislavery party asserted positively that such was the case, and that McClellan had been frightened from attacking Manassas by a scarecrow. The Democratic party asserted as stoutly that the whole story was an invention. Curious to say, the fact of the existence of the 'quaker guns' was never either demonstrated nor disproved. I can only say that soldiers who were at Manassas assured me that they had seen the wooden cannon on their first arrival. On the other hand, persons who took more trouble to investigate the truth came to the conclusion that there was no evidence of the fact; but to me the definite result seemed to be that, from some cause or other, the Federal commanders failed invariably to obtain reliable information as to the position and movements of the Southern army.

Our visit was but a short one, for the train had to return early, in order to avoid the risk of travelling through that half-hostile country after dark. On our return to the cars, we came upon a strange living evidence of the results of this strange war. Huddled together upon a truck were a group of some dozen runaway slaves. There were three men, four women, and half a dozen children. Anything more helpless or wretched than their aspect I never saw. Miserably clothed, footsore, and weary, they crouched in the hot sunlight more like animals than men. They seemed to have no idea, no plan, and no distinct purpose. They were field hands, on a farm some score of miles off, and had walked all night; so at least they told us. Now they were going North as far as Washington, which appeared to them the end of the world. They had no fear of being recaptured, partly, I think, because they had reached Northern troops, still more because their home seemed to them so far away. With the exception of one woman, who was going to look for her husband, who was hired out somewhere in the District of Columbia, they talked as if they had no friends or acquaintances in the new land they were travelling to. For the present they were content that they could sit in the sun without being forced to work. Some of our party gave them money, and broken victuals, which they valued more. I overheard one of the men saying to a woman, as he munched some white bread he had picked up, 'Massa never gave us food like that.' Poor things, if their idea of freedom was white bread and rest, they must have been disappointed bitterly! As strangers and guests of official personages, it was impossible for us to do anything for them. We got them a lift upon the truck to Alexandria. But whenever I think of that incident, I wish that we could have done, that we had done, more. Before we reached the town they got down, and our roads parted. What became of them heaven knows.

Instead of returning by the river from Alexandria, the train carried us to the foot of the long chain bridge which crosses the Potomac in front of Washington. For hours we found it impossible to cross, as a division of 16,000 men were marching over on their way to Alexandria, to embark for the Peninsula. With colours flying, and bands playing, regiment after regiment defiled past us. In the gray evening light, the long endless files bore a phantom aspect. The men were singing, shouting, cheering; under cover of the darkness, they chanted 'John Brown's Hymn,' in defiance of McClellan's orders, and the heavy tramp of a thousand feet beat time to that strange weird melody. As the New England regiments passed our train, they shouted to us to tell the people at home that we had seen them in Dixie's Land, and on the way to Richmond. Ah, me! how many, I wonder, of those who flitted before us in the twilight, came home themselves to tell their own story?

FEELING ON THE BORDER

There can be no doubt that the common people of Tennessee, like the inhabitants of all the Southern States, believed sincerely that the 'Lincoln hordes' were coming down to destroy their property, burn their houses, and murder their wives and children. Extraordinary as such an illusion was, it could be accounted for partly by the comparative isolation of the South, partly by the extent to which the lower classes received all their intelligence and all their opinions from their leaders, and still more by the morbid nervousness which the existence of a slave population is sure to beget amongst the dominant race. By degrees the people of Tennessee were becoming convinced that the Northerners had no intention of interfering with their property, or of treating them as subjects of a conquered country; and that, in fact, life and property were far safer under a Federal government than they had been under the Confederate rule. Again, the war was too near at hand, and the danger too imminent for Tennessee to appreciate fully that the battle had been fought and lost. It was easy enough for an indifferent spectator in the North to see that the Confederates were fighting a losing fight in the border states, and that even a return of fortune to their arms would only prolong a hopeless struggle; but, to men living in Tennessee, it was not so easy to take a wide view of the case. If Beauregard had won the battle of Pittsburgh Landing, or had defeated the Federals at Corinth, it was quite possible, though not probable, that Nashville might have been reoccupied for the time by the Confederates; and their return would have been the sure signal for a reign of terror of which all who had given in their adhesion to the new government might reasonably have feared to be the victims. Moreover—and I believe this to have been the chief explanation—as long as the war lasts there can be no cordial restoration of Union feeling in any Southern state. Men may grow convinced of the folly of secession, may even wish for the triumph of the Union; but their hearts must be, after all, with the side for which their kinsmen and friends are fighting. I suppose there is hardly a family in Tennessee which has not some member in the ranks of the Confederate army. It is this conflict of affections which makes all civil war so hateful. How hateful it is, in truth, never came home to me till I saw it actually. I have known myself of a wife whose husband was fighting for the South, while her father and brother were in the Federal army. I knew, too, of a mother who had only two sons, one in the North, and the other in the South, both fighting in the armies that were ranged opposite to each other in front of Yorktown.

So I, or any one, could name a hundred instances of father fighting against son—brother against brother—of families divided—of homes where there was mourning whenever the news of battle came, no matter which side had won the victory. I have dwelt thus somewhat at length on the reasons why I think the sullen attitude of Tennessee might be accounted for, because I am anxious not to convey the impression that I believe in the Southern or rather the Confederate doctrine of an innate and unconquerable aversion between the North and South. If once the insurrection were suppressed, and order restored, I have little doubt the Southern States would acquiesce in what was inevitable. There is no difference in race, or language, or religion, or geographical position to keep the two divisions of the Union apart. Whether the difference in domestic institutions would prove an insuperable cause of disunion, I cannot say. If it should so prove, the North will suppress or remove this cause before it consents to the disruption of the Union. This is the only fact of which I feel positive.

In old English books about travel in Switzerland, it used to be a stock remark that you could tell whether a canton was Protestant or Catholic by the relative cleanliness or dirtiness of the towns. How far the fact was true, or how far, if true, it established the truth of the Protestant religion, I could never determine; but a similar conclusion may certainly be drawn with regard to the free and the slave states. You may lay it down as a rule throughout America that wherever you find slavery, there you have dirt also. Nashville . . . is one of the cleanest and brightest of towns at a distance; but when you come close the illusion vanishes. There is no excuse there for want of cleanliness. The position of the town makes drainage easy; the stone used so plentifully is clean of itself; and water is abundant. The only thing wanting seemed to be the energy to keep the place clean. The hotel where I was stopping was in itself an institution (in American phrase) of the country. It was the best in the city; and Nashville was always celebrated as one of the most thriving and prosperous cities in the South. Hotel-keeping was not suffering, like other trading concerns, from the depression of the moment. The hotel was crammed with guests, and had been crammed throughout the previous winter. Outside it was handsome enough, but internally, I say without hesitation, it was the dirtiest and worst managed hotel it had ever been my fortune to stop at. The dirt was dirt of old standing, and the mismanagement must have been the growth of years long preceding the days when secession was first heard of. The bar, as I mentioned, was closed by order; but the *habitués* still hung about the scene of their former pleasures. In the hall there were a number of broken shattered chairs, and here, with their legs stretched in every conceivable position, a number of well-dressed respectable-looking persons used to loaf all day long, smoking and chewing. They did not seem to have anything to do, or much to say to each other; but they sat there to kill time by looking at one another. The floor was as dirty as successive strata of tobacco juice could make it; and, at the slightest symptom of chill in the air, the stove was kindled to a red-hot heat, and the atmosphere was made as stifling as the cracks in the doors would permit it to become. The passages were as filthy as want of sweeping could make them; and dirty cloths, slop pails, and brooms were left lying about them, all day and every day; the narrow wooden staircases were such as you would hardly see in England leading to the poorest of attics; and the household arrangements were as primitive as was consistent with the dirtiness peculiar to civilized life. As to the meals, their profusion was only equalled by their greasiness, and by the utter nondescriptness of their component victuals. The chicken pie tasted uncommonly like the stewed mutton, and both were equally unlike any compound I ever ate before. I could understand why it was thought unnecessary for the Negroes to waste soap and water on washing; but the same reason could not apply to their jackets and shirts, which I presume once were white. The servants were all Negroes, and all, naturally enough, devoted their minds to doing as little work and taking as long about it as possible. What seemed more odd than all, none of the habitual residents—some of them persons of property— appeared to be aware that the establishment was dirty and uncomfortable. The heat of the house must have been fearful in summer and the smells pestilential; for, with a Southern climate, the style of building maintained was that of the small rooms and narrow passages of England. Nor was this a single instance. The other hotels in the city were worse; and some of my friends who have travelled through the Southern States have assured me that, except in the very large towns, the hotels are invariably of the same description. The truth is that where the whites think it beneath them to work, and where the Negroes will not work unless they are forced, you cannot expect domestic comfort.

. . .

THREE GREAT AUTHORS

Concord has nearer and dearer claims to the thoughts of all English-speaking people than the memory of an obscure battle. It is the home of Emerson and Hawthorne. An old-fashioned, sleepy, New England village; one broad, long, rambling street of wooden houses, standing for the most apart, and overshadowed by leafy trees; a quiet village green or two; shady, dreamy-looking graveyards, filled with old moss-covered tombstones of colonists who lived and died subjects of the Crown of England; a rich, marshy valley, hemmed in by low-wooded hills; and a dull, lazy stream, oozing on so slowly through many turnings that you fancy it is afraid of being carried out to the ocean that awaits it a few miles away—these are the outward *memorabilia* of Concord. Passing through the village, you come to a roomy country house, buried almost beneath trees, and looking the model of a quiet English parsonage; and then, entering it, it must be some fault of your own if you are not welcome at the kindly home of Emerson.

His is not a face or figure to which photographs can do justice. The tall spare form, the strongly marked features, and the thin scanty hair are all, to the English mind, typical, as it were, of that distinct American nationality of which Mr. Emerson has been the ablest, if not the first, exponent. In repose, I fancy, his prevailing expression would be somewhat grave, with a shade of sadness; but the true charm of his face can be learnt only if you hear him speaking. Then, when the 'slow wise smile,' as someone well called it, plays about that grim-set mouth, and the flow of those lucid sentences, so simple and yet so perfect, pours forth in calm, measured sequence, the large liquid eyes seem to kindle with a magnetic light, and you feel yourself in the presence of a living power. You may sit at his feet or not—that is a matter for your own judgment, but a Gamaliel is there. Hearing him thus speak, I understood, better than I had learnt from his writings, the influence which Mr. Emerson has wielded over the mind of America, and how Concord has become a kind of Mecca, of which the representative man of American thought is the Mahomet.

Some quarter of a mile further on, hidden almost by the overhanging hill at whose foot it stands, out of sight and hearing of the village world, you come to the home of Mr. Hawthorne—a quaint, rambling, pleasant house, which appears to have grown up no one knows how, as some houses do, and to have culminated mysteriously in an Italian campanile tower; so that it is rather a tower with a house attached, than a house surmounted by a tower. It is a fitting place for a romancer to have fixed his dwelling in. Right above the house there stretches a pine wood, so quiet and so lonely, so full of fading lights and shadows, and through whose trees the wind sighs so fitfully that it seems natural for all quaint fancies and strange memories to rise there unbidden. As to the tenant of the turret and the pine wood, I could not, if I wished, describe him better than by saying that he is just what, not knowing him, you fancy the author of *The Scarlet Letter* ought to look like. I suppose that most persons form an idea to themselves of the outward look and aspect of any author they have learnt to care for; and I know that, as far as my own experience goes, the idea is but seldom realized.

The author, when at last you meet with him in the flesh, may be better than your idea, but he is not the person you had pictured to yourself and dwelt on fondly. Now, if you were to place Mr. Hawthorne amongst a thousand persons, I think anyone that had read his writings would guess at once, amongst all that crowd, which the author was. The grand, broad forehead; the soft wavy hair, tangling itself so carelessly; the bright dreamy hazel eyes, flashing from beneath the deep massive eyebrows; and the sweet smile, so full at once of sad pathos and kindly humour, all formed for me the features one would have dreamed of for the author, who, more than any living writer, has understood the poetry of prose. It is a fancy of mine—a fancy, inspired, perhaps, by the atmosphere in which I formed it—that Nature, when she began to make Mr. Hawthorne, designed him for a man of action, and then, ere the work was done, she changed her mind, and sought to transform him into a poet, and that thus the combination of the two characters—of the worker and the dreamer—came out at last in the form of the writer of romance. Well, if Concord had been the scene of an English Waterloo, I am afraid I should still think of it with the kindliest of memories—should, indeed, remember it only as the dwelling place of men who have won fresh triumphs for English words, triumphs to me far dearer than those of English arms.

It was my fortune, too, to see—though but for a short period—the great poet of America. Of all pleasant summer houses, the houses round Boston seemed to me the pleasantest; and of such houses I know of none pleasanter than the one standing on the Mount Auburn Road, where General Washington used to dwell, and where Longfellow dwells now. The pleasant lawn, the graceful rooms, filled with books and pictures and works of art, formed the fit abode for the poet who has known so well how to use the sweet stately rhythm of the English hexameter; and of that abode the host, with his graceful manners, his refined and noble countenance, and his conversation, so full of learning and poetic diction, seems the rightful owner. But of this I would say nothing further, for I felt that, if I was in the presence of a great poet, I was in the presence also of a greater sorrow.[2]

[2] On 10 July 1861, Longfellow's second wife died from injuries received by fire.

The North and West in Wartime [1] ॐ

ANTHONY TROLLOPE, *who was born in London in* 1815, *and died
in* 1882, *was the son of the famous Mrs. Trollope who wrote* Domestic
Manners of the Americans. *He was forty-six years old when he visited
the United States in the fall of* 1861, *and had already published some of
his best novels, including* Barchester Towers, Doctor Thorne, *and*
Framley Parsonage. *He was at this time employed in the British post
office, and had recently made a trip on postal business to the West
Indies, which had given him the material for a volume of travels called*
The West Indies and the Spanish Main. *For many years he had
entertained an ambition to follow in his mother's footsteps in the United
States, and to write a book descriptive of the country. The outbreak
of the Civil War, an event in which he took a keen interest, led him
to think that such a volume might be popular and profitable. He therefore made a contract with Chapman and Hall, and obtained permission
from the postal authorities to have a leave of absence for nine months.
He set out for the United States in August, and returned home in May*
1862. *By this time he had perfected his indefatigable method of producing literary work according to an hourly schedule, and his book on
the United States was a mere interlude between* Framley Parsonage
and Orley Farm; *for a connection with the* Cornhill Magazine, *which
he established in* 1861, *marked the beginning of the high tide of his
success as a novelist.*

*As Trollope later asserted, he worked hard at the task he had set
himself in America, and saw much of the manners and institutions of
the people. Not only did he observe men and scenes diligently, but he
gave careful study to the operations of the government, and thrust into
his book much material that can be found, in more accurate form, in
any good manual of civics. He himself admits that his* North America,
*as he entitled it, for he visited Canada as well as the United States, was
not very well done. 'It was tedious and confused, and will hardly, I
think, be of future value to those who wish to make themselves acquainted with the United States.' The arrangement is indeed poor,
and there is an intolerable amount of padding, while as a prophet of
future tendencies he lacked perspicacity. In his autobiography he makes*

[1] From *North America*, London, 1862, volume I, chapters 3, 9, 10, 14, 17; volume II,
chapters 5 and 6.

the strange assertion, for which his book affords no real warrant, that
he had vigorously predicted the success of the North in the struggle.
He did incline to that opinion, but he asserted it without vigor, he be-
lieved the victory would be only partial, and he thought the Union could
hardly be restored in its old character. To Americans his remarks on
the war seemed cold and unsympathetic. In England the book was well
received by the public and critics, and his total receipts for it, £1250,
very considerably exceeded those he had obtained from Barchester
Towers. *Some other English travelers of subsequent years have tes-*
tified to its value as an introduction to the United States. While not
readable as a whole, some portions of it have an enduring value as a
picture of the North in wartime.

Trollope made four later trips to America on post-office business, but
did not write of them.

PROHIBITION IN PORTLAND

THE ways of the people seemed to be quiet, smooth, orderly, and
republican. There is nothing to drink in Portland of course, for, thanks
to Mr. Neal Dow, the Father Mathew of the state of Maine, the Maine
Liquor Law is still in force in that state. There is nothing to drink, I
should say, in such orderly houses as that I selected. 'People do drink
some in the town, they say,' said my hostess to me: 'and liquor is to be
got. But I never venture to sell any. An ill-natured person might turn
on me, and where should I be then?' I did not press her, and she was
good enough to put a bottle of porter at my right hand at dinner, for
which I observed she made no charge. 'But they advertise beer in the
shop windows,' I said to a man who was driving me—'Scotch ale and
bitter beer. A man can get drunk on them.' 'Wa'al, yes. If he goes to
work hard and drinks a bucketfull,' said the driver, 'perhaps he may.'
From which and other things I gathered that the men of Maine drank
pottle deep before Mr. Neal Dow brought his exertions to a successful
termination.

The Maine Liquor Law still stands in Maine, and is the law of the
land throughout New England; but it is not actually put in force in
the other states. By this law no man may retail wine, spirits, or, in truth,
beer, except with a special license, which is given only to those who
are presumed to sell them as medicines. A man may have what he likes
in his own cellar for his own use—such at least is the actual working
of the law—but may not obtain it at hotels and public houses. This
law, like all sumptuary laws, must fail. And it is fast failing even in
Maine. But it did appear to me from such information as I could col-

lect that the passing of it had done much to hinder and repress a habit of hard drinking, which was becoming terribly common, not only in the towns of Maine, but among the farmers and hired labourers in the country.

HARVARD UNIVERSITY

The University is not so large as I had expected to find it. It consists of Harvard College, as the undergraduates' department, and of professional schools of law, medicine, divinity, and science. In the few words that I will say about it I will confine myself to Harvard College proper. . . The average number of undergraduates does not exceed 450, and these are divided into four classes. The average number of degrees taken annually by bachelors of art is something under 100. Four years' residence is required for a degree, and at the end of that period a degree is given as a matter of course if the candidate's conduct has been satisfactory. When a young man had pursued his studies for that period, going through the required examinations and lectures, he is not subjected to any final examination as is the case with a candidate for a degree at Oxford and Cambridge. It is, perhaps, in this respect that the greatest difference exists between the English universities and Harvard College. With us a young man may, I take it, still go through his three or four years with a small amount of study. But his doing so does not insure him his degree. If he has utterly wasted his time he is plucked, and late but heavy punishment comes upon him. At Cambridge in Massachusetts the daily work of the men is made more obligatory; but if this be gone through with such diligence as to enable the student to hold his own during the four years, he has his degree as a matter of course. There are no degrees conferring special honour. A man cannot go out 'in honours' as he does with us. . . Nor are there prizes of fellowships and livings to be obtained. It is, I think, evident from this that the greatest incentives to high excellence are wanting at Harvard College . . . and consequently, the degree of excellence attained is no doubt lower than with us. But I conceive that the general level of the university education is higher there than with us; that a young man is more sure of getting his education, and that a smaller percentage of men leaves Harvard College utterly uneducated than goes in that condition out of Oxford or Cambridge. The education at Harvard College is more diversified in its nature, and study is more absolutely the business of the place than it is at our universities.

The expense of education at Harvard College is not much lower than at our colleges; with us there are, no doubt, more men who are absolutely extravagant than at Cambridge, Massachusetts. The actual authorized expenditure in accordance with the rules is only £50 per annum, i.e. $249; but this does not, by any means, include everything. Some of the richer young men may spend as much as £300 per annum, but the largest number vary their expenditure from £100 to £180 per annum; and I take it the same thing may be said of our universities. There are many young men at Harvard College of very small means. They will live on £70 per annum and will earn a great portion of that by teaching in the vacations. There are thirty-six scholarships . . . and there is also a beneficiary fund. Many are thus brought up to Cambridge who have no means of their own, and I think I may say that the consideration in which they are held among their brother students is in no degree affected by their position. I doubt whether we can say so much of the sizars and bible clerks at our universities. . .

It is required that every student shall attend some place of Christian worship on Sundays; but he, or his parents for him, may elect what denomination of church he shall attend. . . The young men for the most part live in College, having rooms in the College buildings; but they do not board in these rooms. There are establishments in the town under the patronage of the University, at which dinner, breakfast, and supper are provided. . . Every young man not belonging to a family resident within a hundred miles of Cambridge, and whose parents are desirous to obtain the protection thus provided, is placed, as regards his pecuniary management, under the care of a patron, and his patron acts by him as a father does in England by a boy at school. He pays out his money for him and keeps him out of debt. . . The rules with regard to the lodging and boarding-houses are very stringent. Any festive entertainment is to be reported to the President. No wine or spirituous liquors may be used, et cetera. It is not a picturesque system, this; but it has its advantages.

There is a handsome library attached to the College, which the young men can use; but it is not so extensive as I had expected. The University is not well off for funds by which to increase it. The new Museum in the College is also a handsome building. The edifices used for the undergraduates' chambers and for the lecture rooms are . . . very ugly red-brick houses standing here and there without order. There are seven such, and they are called Brattle House, College House, Divinity Hall, Hollis Hall, Holsworthy Hall, Massachusetts Hall, and Stoughton Hall. It is almost astonishing that buildings so ugly should have been erected for such a purpose.

LOWELL'S UTOPIAN FACTORY SYSTEM

That which most surprises an English visitor on going through the mills at Lowell is the personal appearance of the men and women who work at them. As there are twice as many women as there are men, it is to them that the attention is chiefly called. They are not only better dressed, cleaner, and better mounted in every respect than the girls employed at manufactories in England, but they are so infinitely superior as to make a stranger immediately perceive that some very strong cause must have created the difference. We all know the class of young women whom we generally see serving behind counters in the shops of our larger cities. They are neat, well dressed, careful, especially about their hair, composed in their manner, and sometimes a little supercilious in the propriety of their demeanour. It is exactly the same class of young women that one sees in the factories at Lowell. They are not sallow, nor dirty, nor ragged, nor rough. They have about them no signs of want, or of low culture. . .

One would of course be disposed to say that the superior condition of the workers must have been occasioned by superior wages; and this, to a certain extent, has been the cause. But the higher payment has not been the chief cause. Women's wages, including all that they receive at the Lowell factories, average about 14s. a week, which is, I take it, fully a third more than women can earn in Manchester, or did earn before the loss of the American cotton began to tell upon them. But if wages at Manchester were raised to the Lowell standard, the Manchester women would not be clothed, fed, cared for, and educated like the Lowell women. The fact is that the workmen and workwomen at Lowell are not exposed to the chances of an open labour market. They are taken in, as it were, to a philanthropical manufacturing college, and then looked after and regulated more as girls and lads at a great seminary than as hands by whose industry profit is to be made out of capital. This is all very nice and pretty at Lowell, but I am afraid it could not be done at Manchester. . .

The following extract is taken from the handbook to Lowell: 'Mr. F. C. Lowell had in his travels abroad observed the effect of large manufacturing establishments on the character of the people, and in the establishment at Waltham the founders looked for a remedy for these defects. They thought that education and good morals would even enhance the profit, and that they could compete with Great Britain by introducing a more cultivated class of operatives. For this purpose they built boarding-houses, which, under the direct supervision of the agent, were kept by discreet matrons'—I can answer for the discreet matrons at Lowell—'mostly widows, no boarders being allowed except operatives. Agents and overseers of high moral character were selected; regulations were adopted at the mills and boarding-houses, by which only respectable girls were employed. The mills were nicely painted and swept'—I can also answer for the painting and sweeping at Lowell—'trees set out in the yards and along the streets, habits of neatness and cleanliness encouraged; and the result justified the expenditure. At Lowell the same policy has been adopted and extended; more spacious mills and elegant boarding-houses have been erected'— as to the elegance, it may be a matter of taste, but as to the comfort there is no question—'the same care as to the classes employed; more capital has been expended for cleanliness and decoration; a hospital has been established for the sick, where, for a small price, they have an experienced physician and skilful nurses. An institute, with an extensive library, for the use of the mechanics, has been endowed. . .' Then the account goes on to tell how the health of the girls has been improved by their attendance at the mills, how they put money into the savings banks, and buy railway shares and farms; how there are thirty churches in Lowell, a library, banks, and insurance offices; how there is a cemetery, and a park, and how everything is beautiful, philanthropic, profitable, and magnificent.

Thus Lowell is the realization of a commercial Utopia. Of all the statements made in the little book which I have quoted I cannot point out one which is exaggerated, much less false.

MILWAUKEE COMPARED WITH ENGLISH TOWNS

Milwaukee is a pleasant town, a very pleasant town, containing 45,000 inhabitants. How many of my readers can boast that they know anything of Milwaukee, or even have heard of it? To me its name was unknown until I saw it on huge railway placards stuck up in the smoking rooms and lounging halls of all American hotels. It is the big town of Wisconsin, whereas Madison is the capital. It stands immediately on the western shore of Lake Michigan, and is very pleasant. Why it should be so, and why Detroit should be the contrary, I can hardly tell; only I think that the same verdict would be given by any English tourist. It must be always borne in mind that 10,000 or 40,000 inhabitants in an American town, and especially in any new Western town, is a number which means much more than would be implied by any similar number as to an old town in Europe. Such a population in America consumes double the amount of beef which it would in

England, wears double the amount of clothes, and demands double as much of the comforts of life. If a census could be taken of the watches it would be found, I take it, that the American population possessed among them nearly double as many as would the English; and I fear also that it would be found that many more of the Americans were readers and writers by habit. In any large town in England it is probable that a higher excellence of education would be found than in Milwaukee, and also a style of life into which more of refinement and more of luxury had found its way. But the general level of these things, of material and intellectual well-being—of beef, that is, and book learning—is no doubt infinitely higher in a new American than in an old European town. Such an animal as a beggar is as much unknown as a mastodon. Men out of work and in want are almost unknown. I do not say that there are none of the hardships of life . . . but want is not known as a hardship in these towns, nor is that dense ignorance in which so large a proportion of our town populations is still steeped.

TROOPS LEAVING LA CROSSE

I got out upon the quay and stood close by the plank, watching each man as he left the vessel and walked across towards the railway. Those whom I had previously seen in tents were not equipped, but these men were in uniform and each bore his musket. Taking them all together they were as fine a set of men as I ever saw collected. No man could doubt on seeing them that they bore on their countenances the signs of higher breeding and better education than would be seen in a thousand men enlisted in England. I do not mean to argue from this that Americans are better than English. I do not mean to argue here that they are even better educated. My assertion goes to show that the men generally were taken from a higher level in the community than that which fills our own ranks. It was a matter of regret to me, here and on many subsequent occasions, to see men bound for three years to serve as common soldiers, who were so manifestly fitted for a better and more useful life. . .

In the old countries population is thick, and food sometimes scarce. Men can be spared, and any employment may be serviceable, even though that employment be in itself so unproductive as that of fighting battles or preparing for them. But in the Western States of America every arm that can guide a plough is of incalculable value. Minnesota was admitted as a state about three years before this time, and its whole population is not much above 150,000. Of this number perhaps 40,000 may be working men. And now this infant state with its huge territory and scanty population is called upon to send its heart's blood out to the war.

And it has sent its heart's best blood. Forth they came—fine, stalwart, well-grown fellows, looking to my eye as though they had as yet but faintly recognized the necessary severity of military discipline. To them hitherto the war had seemed to be an arena on which each might do something for his country, which that country would recognize. . . Of these men whom I saw entering on their career upon the banks of the Mississippi, many were fathers of families, many were owners of land, many were educated men capable of high aspirations—all were serviceable members of their state. There were probably there not three or four of whom it would be well that the state should be rid. As soldiers fit, or capable of being made fit for the duties they had undertaken, I could find but one fault with them. Their average age was too high. There were men among them with grizzled beards, and many who had counted thirty, thirty-five, and forty years. . .

The first great misery to be endured by these regiments will be the military lesson of obedience, which they must learn before they can be of any service. It always seemed to me when I came near them that they had not as yet recognized the necessary austerity of an officer's duty. Their idea of a captain was the stage idea of a leader of dramatic banditti, a man to be followed and obeyed as a leader, but to be obeyed with that free and easy obedience which is accorded to the reigning chief of the forty thieves. 'Wa'll, Captain,' I have heard a private say to his officer, as he sat on one seat in a railway car with his feet upon the back of another. And the captain has looked as though he did not like it.

MUD, SOLDIERS, AND GUNBOATS AT CAIRO

The free state of Illinois runs down far south between the slave states of Kentucky to the east, and of Missouri to the west, and is the most southern point of the continuous free-soil territory of the Northern States. This point of it is a part of a district called Egypt. . . Fever and ague universally prevail. Men and women grow up with their lantern faces like spectres. The children are prematurely old; and the earth which is fruitful is hideous in its fertility. Cairo and its immediate neighbourhood must, I suppose, have been subject to yearly inundation before it was 'settled up.' At present it is guarded on the shores of each river by high mud banks, built so as to protect the point of land. These are called the levees, and do perform their duty by keeping out the body of the waters. The shore between the banks is, I believe, never above breast deep with the inundation; and from the circumstances of the place, and the soft, half-liquid nature of the soil, this inundation generally takes the shape of mud instead of water.

Here, at this very point, has been built a town. Whether the town existed during Mr. Tapley's time I have not been able to learn. At the period of my visit it was falling quickly into ruin; indeed I think I may pronounce it to have been on its last legs. At that moment a galvanic motion had been pumped into it by the war movements of General Halleck, but the true bearings of the town, as a town, were not less plainly to be read on that account. Every street was absolutely impassable from mud. I mean that in walking down the middle of any street in Cairo a moderately framed man would soon stick fast and not be able to move. The houses are generally built at considerable intervals and rarely face each other, and along one side of each street a plank boarding was laid, on which the mud had accumulated only up to one's ankles. I walked all over Cairo with big boots, and with my trousers tucked up to my knees; but at the crossings I found considerable danger, and occasionally had my doubts as to the possibility of progress. I was alone in my work, and saw no one else making any such attempt. A few only were moving about, and they moved in wretched carts, each drawn by two miserable, floundering horses. These carts were always empty, but were presumed to be engaged in some way on military service. No faces looked out at the windows of the houses, no forms stood in the doorways. A few shops were open, but only in the drinking shops did I see customers. In these silent, muddy men were sitting—not with drink before them, as men sit with us—but with the cud within their jaws, ruminating. Their drinking is always done on foot. They stand silent at a bar, with two small glasses before them. Out of one they swallow the whiskey, and from the other they take a gulp of water, as though to rinse their mouths. After that, they again sit down and ruminate. . .

But our visit to Cairo had been made rather with reference to its present warlike character than with any eye to the natural beauties of the place. A large force of men had been collected there, and also a fleet of gunboats. We had come there fortified with letters to generals and commodores, and were prepared to go through a large amount of military inspection. But the bird had flown before our arrival; or rather the body and wings of the bird, leaving behind only a draggled tail and a few of the feathers. There were only a thousand soldiers at Cairo when we were there—that is, a thousand stationed in the Cairo sheds. Two regiments passed through the place during the time, getting out of one steamer onto another, or passing from the railway into boats.

One of these regiments passed before me down the slope of the river bank, and the men as a body seemed to be healthy. Very many were drunk, and all were mud-clogged up to their shoulders and very caps. In other respects they appeared to be in good order. It must be understood that these soldiers, the volunteers, had never been made subject to any discipline as to cleanliness. They wore their hair long. Their hats or caps, though all made in some military form and with some military appendance, were various and ill-assorted. They were all covered with loose, thick, blue-gray greatcoats, which no doubt were warm and wholesome, but which from their looseness and colour seemed to be peculiarly susceptible of receiving and showing a very large amount of mud. Their boots were always good; but each man was shod as he liked. Many wore heavy overboots. . .

The generals and commodores were gone up the Ohio River and up the Tennessee in an expedition with gunboats, which turned out to be successful, and of which we have all read in the daily history of this war. They had departed the day before our arrival, and though we still found at Cairo a squadron of gunboats—if gunboats go in squadrons—the bulk of the army had been moved. There was left there one regiment and one colonel, who . . . gave us permission to see everything that was to be seen. Four of these gunboats were still lying in the Ohio, close under the terminus of the railway, with their flat, ugly noses against the muddy bank, and we were shown over two of them. They certainly seemed to be formidable weapons for river warfare, and to have been 'got up quite irrespective of expense.' So much, indeed, may be said for the Americans throughout the war. They cannot be accused of parsimony. The largest of these vessels, called the *Benton,* had cost £36,000. These boats are made with sides sloping inwards, at an angle of 45 degrees. The iron is two and a half inches thick, and it has not, I believe, been calculated that it will resist cannon shot of great weight, should it be struck in a direct line. But the angle of the sides of the boat makes it improbable that any such shot should strike them; and the iron, bedded as it is upon oak, is supposed to be sufficient to turn a shot that does not hit it in a direct line. The boats are also roofed in with iron, and the pilots who steer the vessel stand encased, as it were, under an iron cupola. I imagine that these boats are well calculated for the river service.

DISAGREEABLE TRAITS OF MISSOURIANS

As regards the people of the West, I must say that they were not such as I expected to find them. With the Northerns we are all more

or less intimately acquainted. . . They are talkative, intelligent, inclined
to be social, though frequently not sympathetically social with ourselves;
somewhat *soi-disant,* but almost invariably companionable. As the traveller goes southward into Maryland and Washington, the type is not
altered to any great extent. The hard intelligence of the Yankee gives
place gradually to the softer, and perhaps more polished manner of
the Southern. But the change thus experienced is not so great as is that
between the American of the Western and the American of the Atlantic
States. In the West I found the men gloomy and silent—I might almost
say sullen. A dozen of them will sit for hours round a stove, speechless.
They chew tobacco and ruminate. They are not offended if you speak
to them, but they are not pleased. They answer with monosyllables, or,
if it be practicable, with a gesture of the head. They care nothing for
the graces, or shall I say, for the decencies of life? They are essentially
a dirty people. Dirt, untidiness, and noise seem in nowise to afflict
them. . . Indifference to appearances is there a matter of pride. A foul
shirt is a flag of triumph. A craving for soap and water is as the wail
of the weak and the confession of cowardice. This indifference is carried into all their affairs, or rather this manifestation of indifference. A
few pages back, I spoke of a man whose furniture had been sold to
pay a heavy tax raised on him specially as a secessionist; the same man
had also been refused the payment of rent due him by the Government,
unless he would take a false oath. I may presume that he was ruined
in his circumstances by the strong hand of the Northern army. But
he seemed in nowise to be unhappy about his ruin. He spoke with
some scorn of the martial law in Missouri, but I felt that it was
esteemed a small matter by him that his furniture was seized and sold.
No men love money with more eager love than these Western men,
but they bear the loss of it as an Indian bears his torture at the stake.
They are energetic in trade, speculating deeply whenever speculation
is possible; but nevertheless they are slow in motion, loving to loaf
about. They are slow in speech, preferring to sit in silence, with the
tobacco between their teeth. They drink, but are seldom drunk to the
eye; they begin it early in the morning and take it in a solemn, sullen,
ugly manner, standing always at a bar; swallowing their spirits, and
saying nothing as they swallow it. They drink often and to great excess;
but they carry it off without noise, sitting down and ruminating over
it with the everlasting cud within their jaws. I believe that a stranger
might go into the West, and passing from hotel to hotel through a
dozen of them, might sit for hours at each in the large everlasting
public hall, and never have a word addressed to him. . .

I cannot part with the West without saying in its favour that there
is a certain manliness about its men, which gives them a dignity of

their own. It is shown in the very indifference of which I have spoken. Whatever turns up the man is still there—still unsophisticated and still unbroken. It has seemed to me that no race of men requires less outward assistance than these pioneers of civilization. They rarely amuse themselves. Food, newspapers, and brandy smashes suffice for life; and while these last, whatever may occur, the man is still there in his manhood.

NEW YORK'S OUTSTANDING DEFECTS

Speaking of New York as a traveller I have two faults to find with it. In the first place there is nothing to see; and in the second place there is no mode of getting about to see anything. Nevertheless New York is a most interesting city. It is the third biggest city in the known world—for those Chinese congregations of unwinged ants are not cities in the known world. In no other city is there a population so mixed and cosmopolitan in their modes of life. And yet in no other city that I have seen are there such strong and ever-visible characteristics of the social and political bearings of the nation to which it belongs. New York appears to me infinitely more American than Boston, Chicago, or Washington. . . Free institutions, general education, and the ascendancy of dollars are the words written on every paving stone along Fifth Avenue, down Broadway, and up Wall Street. Every man can vote, and values the privilege. Every man can read, and uses the privilege. Every man worships the dollar, and is down before his shrine from morning to night. . .

In saying that there is very little to be seen in New York, I have also said that there is no way of seeing that little. My assertion amounts to this—that there are no cabs. To the reading world at large this may not seem to be much, but let the reading world go to New York, and it will find out how much the deficiency means. In London, in Paris, in Florence, in Rome, in the Havana, or at Grand Cairo, the cab driver or attendant does not merely drive the cab or belabour the donkey, but he is the visitor's easiest and cheapest guide. In London, the Tower, Westminster Abbey, and Madame Tussaud are found by the stranger without difficulty, and almost without a thought, because the cab driver knows the whereabouts and the way. Space is moreover annihilated, and the huge distances of the English metropolis are brought within the scope of mortal power. But in New York there is no such institution.

In New York there are street omnibuses as we have—there are street cars such as last year we declined to have—and there are very excellent

public carriages; but none of these give you the accommodation of a
cab, nor can all of them combined do so. The omnibuses, though clean
and excellent, were to me very unintelligible. They have no conductor
to them. To know their different lines and usages a man should have
made a scientific study of the city. To those going up and down
Broadway I became accustomed, but in them I was never quite at my
ease. The money has to be paid through a little hole at the driver's
back, and should, as I learned at last, be paid immediately on entrance.
But in getting up to do this I always stumbled about, and it would
happen that when with considerable difficulty I had settled on my own
account, two or three ladies would enter, and would hand me, without a
word, some coins with which I had no lifelong familiarity in order that
I might go through the same ceremony on their account. The change
I would usually drop into the straw, and then there would arise trouble
and unhappiness. Before I became aware of that law as to instant payment, bells used to be rung at me, which made me uneasy. I knew I
was not behaving as a citizen should behave, but could not compass
the exact points of my delinquency. And then when I desired to escape,
the door being strapped up tight, I would halloo vainly at the driver
through the little hole; whereas, had I known my duty, I should have
rung a bell, or pulled a strap, according to the nature of the omnibus
in question. . . I heard it asserted by a lecturer in Boston, Mr. Wendell
Phillips, whose name is there a household word, that citizens of the
United States carried brains in their fingers as well as their heads,
whereas 'common people,' by which Mr. Phillips intended to designate
the remnant of mankind beyond the United States, were blessed with
no such extended cerebral development. Having once learned this fact
from Mr. Phillips, I understood why it was that a New York omnibus
should be so disagreeable to me, and at the same time so suitable to
the wants of the New Yorkers.

And then there are street cars—very long omnibuses—which run
on rails but are dragged by horses. They are capable of holding forty
passengers each, and as far as my experience goes carry an average
load of sixty. The fare of the omnibus is six cents or threepence. That
of the street car five cents or twopence halfpenny. They run along
the different avenues, taking the length of the city. In the upper or
new part of town their course is simple enough, but as they descend
to the Bowery, Peckslip, and Pearl Street, nothing can be conceived
more difficult or devious than their courses. . .

The street cars are manned with conductors, and therefore are free
from many of the perils of the omnibus, but they have perils of their
own. They are always quite full. By that I mean that every seat is
crowded, that there is a double row of men and women standing down

the centre, and that the driver's platform in front is full, and also the conductor's platform. . .

And now as to the other charge against New York, of their being nothing to see. How should there be anything there to see of general interest? In other large cities, cities as large in name as New York, there are works of art, fine buildings, ruins, ancient churches, picturesque costumes, and the tombs of celebrated men. But in New York there are none of these things. Art has not yet grown up there. One or two fine figures by Crawford are in the town—especially that of the sorrowing Indian at the rooms of the Historical Society; but art is a luxury in a city which follows but slowly on the heels of wealth and civilization. Of fine buildings—which indeed are comprised in art—there are none deserving special praise or remark. It might well have been that New York should ere this have graced herself with something grand in architecture; but she has not done so. Some good architectural effect there is, and much architectural comfort. Of ruins of course there can be none; none at least of such ruins as travellers admire, though perhaps some of that sort which disgraces rather than decorates. Churches there are plenty, but none that are ancient. The costume is the same as our own; and I need hardly say that it is not picturesque. And the time for the tombs of celebrated men has not come. A great man's ashes are hardly of value until they have all but ceased to exist.

The visitor to New York must seek his gratification and obtain his instruction from the habits and manners of men. The American, though he dresses like an Englishman and eats roast beef with a silver fork—or sometimes with a steel knife—as does an Englishman, is not like an Englishman in his mind, in his aspirations, in his tastes, or in his politics.

Part IV

Travelers of the Fourth Period, 1870-1922

Travelers of the Fourth Period, 1870-1922

Analysis ව

In the mere names of the principal British writers upon America after the Civil War we have an unmistakable evidence of the superior character these travels assumed. In all the century-long literature of the subject no descriptive passages show greater vividness and stylistic felicity than those of Kipling; no social and political analysis approaches that of James Bryce in thoroughness or discernment; no sociological generalizations are so forcible as H. G. Wells's; and we have among the other visitors Matthew Arnold, Herbert Spencer, E. A. Freeman, Frederic Harrison, Arnold Bennett, and Chesterton. But it is not only the eminence of the authors but the new character of the books that lifts the more recent treatment of the United States to a higher level: a change of character that may be summed up in the statement that for the first time analysis became the dominant note. It completely triumphed over mere narration and description.

The very vastness of the subject now exerted a compulsion in that direction, for no picture of a continental nation embracing nearly a hundred million people could be given except by resort to generalizations. English travelers could more readily synthesize their observations because they were now free from certain tasks and disabilities that had hampered the contemporaries of Miss Martineau and Alexander Mackay. They didn't have to waste time debating whether democracy was a success or a failure, for the nation of Lincoln had ended that debate; they didn't have to worry about the excessive American susceptibility to praise and blame; they could assume that if not all Englishmen admired America, nearly all of them respected her; and the most peculiar of all American institutions, slavery, had been swept away. The ground had been cleared of a deal of impedimenta. In some of these English writings, like Arnold's and Herbert Spencer's, the analysis is carried to a point where two or three salient theses only are discussed; in others, most notably Bryce's, it is unprecedentedly elaborate.

But the analytic character of nearly all these volumes is so plain that a parallel rather than a chronological survey of them is required.

First, however, it must be pointed out that between the close of the Civil War and the arrival of the earliest eminent Englishman, Freeman, in 1881, there appeared a series of strictly journalistic volumes upon the burning question of the day—the race question. The visit of that versatile and unresting newspaperman, G. A. Sala, in 1879-80, resulted in a flashily superficial treatment of it. A much more ambitious and bombastic, but equally worthless work was W. H. Dixon's *The White Conquest* (1876), which presented as the central fact of American life a vast struggle for supremacy between the Caucasian on one side, the Negroes, Indians, and Chinese on the other. His account of Louisiana groaning under the carpetbaggers, blacks, and Federal troops; of the black ascendancy in South Carolina; of the vicious half-breed element in southern California; of Mormon polygamy; of family feuds in lower Illinois; and of life among the tribes of Indian Territory, who had intermarried with the Negroes and still sold squaws—this account, luridly touched with rhetoric, made America look rather like a seething jungle than a nation. Though he predicted the end of Negro domination in the South, he believed that the race question had 'wrecked a third part of America'; and observing the Chinese, he declared that all along the Pacific Coast 'the rice-eater is pushing the beef-eater to the wall.'

David Macrae's *The Americans at Home* (1870) is a much fairer, more thorough, and more acute book. Of the half-ruined South he gives a graphic study, the fruit of diligent personal observation and inquiry. Everywhere he could, he talked with Confederate officers, walked with them over the battlefields, and collected their views of Lee and other commanders. On the Northern side he interviewed Grant, noting that his shrewd, gray, impenetrable eye and pleasant expression made him look 'as if he had something in him which he was amused at your trying to find out'; and he talked with President Johnson, finding 'a great deal of the bulldog in his broad, heavy, strongly marked face, with an expression of dogged obstinacy, especially about the lips, which are firmly pressed together as when a man is facing a cold blast.' Macrae had many illuminating chats with the freedmen of the South, whose immediate outlook seemed dark to him, and he saw the Virginia Constitutional Convention at work in Richmond, with Negroes participating in a debate that was 'rather showy than good.' But he never doubted that the Civil War would shortly be found beneficial to the South, where 'the lazy luxury that was enervating her people is no longer possible.' The owner of a tobacco factory in Richmond he found favorable to free labor:

I like it better than slavery. I would not go back to the slavery system if I could. Labour is cheaper now and more easily managed. Formerly you had to keep order with the cowhide. If a man was stubborn you had to whip him. You had paid $600 or $800 for him, and you could not afford to let him lie idle. But now, if a man is disorderly, or won't work, you tell him to take his jacket and go. . . Then, again, in slave times you had to keep the factory going whether you were making money or not, for the men were always on your hands.

The best treatise upon the race question, however, is Sir George Campbell's *White and Black* (1879), the work of a hard-headed Scotchman who had attained eminence in the Indian administration. He visited the rural districts as well as towns of Virginia, the Carolinas, and Georgia, and talked with the Negroes wherever he went. Politically, he concluded that the period of carpetbag rule had been rather a scandal than a permanent injury, and that there had been more pilfering than plundering. He sympathized with the upheaval of the whites, and their recapture of the state governments, but he did not think it right for them to insist upon the total exclusion of Negroes from office—upon an absolutely solid South. Any scheme of arbitrary disfranchisement he particularly opposed, though he had no objection to an educational qualification for the ballot. His social and economic views were equally liberal and wise. If there were any difference in intellectual capacity between the white and black races, he thought it neither very wide nor evident. 'I am told on all hands,' he remarked, 'that some pure Negroes show an educational capacity quite equal to that of good whites.' Both as hired laborers and as farmers, he saw that they were absolutely indispensable to the South, and remarked that if under the spur of long-continued ill-treatment the colored people of any particular locality began migrating *en masse* to the North, this fact would be brought home forcibly to the South—a prediction justified during World War I. The two peoples should realize their interdependence:

All that is now wanting to make the Negro a fixed and conservative element in American society is to give him encouragement to, and facilities for, making himself by his own exertions a small landowner; to do, in fact, for him what we have sought to do for the Irish farmer. Land in America is so much cheaper and more abundant that it would be infinitely easier to effect the same object there. I would by no means seek to withdraw the whole population from hired labor; on the contrary, the Negro in many respects is so much at his best in that function that I should look to a large class of laborers remaining; but I am at the same time confident that it would be a very great benefit and stability to the country if a large number should acquire by thrift an independent position as landowning American citizens. . . The whites certainly cannot do without them; already the great drawback to the Southern States is the want of that great influx of foreign population which causes the North and West to progress in a geometrical ratio. Evidently their true policy is to make the most of the excellent population which they have, and they quite see it. The blacks, again, certainly cannot do without the whites; their own race is not sufficiently advanced to fulfill the functions now in the hands of the whites.

A good deal of notice was given in these and other journalistic books to a second question, which took on prominence after the war, that of woman's rights. Anthony Trollope's portrait of the middle-class American woman as a pushing Jezebel, carrying her insistence on special privilege to a point that outraged all his ideas of feminine delicacy, was emphatically repudiated by Sir George Campbell. But the most detailed and sympathetic treatment of the woman's movement was that by the well-known English social worker and suffragist, Emily Faithfull, in *Three Visits to America* (1884). In both the political and economic spheres, it was now a remarkably vigorous movement. She was greeted in New York on her first visit, at a reception in Steinway Hall, by journalists like Mrs. Mary Booth, editor of *Harper's Bazaar,* and Mary E. Dodge, editor of *Hearth and Home;* by authors like Mrs. Stoddard; and by women physicians, artists, singers, business executives, and even clergywomen.

When Miss Martineau visited America in the 'thirties she discovered only five occupations open to women, but now Miss Faithfull found more than 400 in Massachusetts alone. In fact, merely between her first visit in 1872 and her second in 1882, the introduction of the typewriter and telephone threw open wide new fields of employment to women. She was impressed, too, by the increase in outdoor exercise for women in this decade. At Vassar, over which Professor Maria Mitchell, the eminent woman astronomer, showed her in 1883, she found the students constantly using the Hudson for boating or skating. Lawn tennis had become popular everywhere, and Central Park showed its daily bevies of young women on horseback. President Angell told her at Michigan University that the curriculum taxed the physical powers of the girls no more than those of the men, and she was assured there and at Cornell that women were welcomed because 'they give classroom conversation that delicate, chaste, and humane tone that the recognition of women among the readers of books has been giving to English literature during the last hundred years.' A new era for women had opened, in short, between the visits of Fanny Wright and Miss Faithfull, between 1820 and 1870.

The number of American women distinguished in the professions was clearly a gratifying surprise to Miss Faithfull, and she proudly mentions the wide following of Grace Greenwood as a journalist, the fact that Dr. Mary Putnam Jacobi and some other women physicians earned $10,000 to $20,000 a year, and the demands that drew Mrs. Livermore upon a lecture tour of 25,000 miles annually. She still found a good deal of which to complain in the economic inequality of men and women. In the teaching profession the latter were paid far less than the former, a circumstance that Colonel T. W. Higginson explained to her by saying: 'We have in the United States first half educated the women, and then, to restore the balance, only half paid them.' In the civil service at Washington there was as yet no approach to equality in promotion, and Kate Fields assured her that in the newspaper world women enjoyed no such opportunities as men. But all in all, Miss Faithfull found both the attitude of the nation toward women, and that of women toward life, excellent.

The publication of Herbert Spencer's, Matthew Arnold's and E. A. Freeman's impressions of the United States all occurred within a half dozen years in the 'eighties, a fitting prelude to the first edition of Bryce's monumental work. None of these men was a trained observer, and none spent much time in this country. It is hence but natural that we should find Spencer quite at variance with the facts in his statement of the position of the political boss, whom he grotesquely pictures as leading 20,000 voters to the polls. Actually our 'bosses' are not demagogues seeking the voters, but men secretly manipulating the political machinery. Spencer was equally wrong in his idea that the United States was given a ready-made paper constitution in 1787, which it would slowly have to adjust to actualities; for our Constitution represented a long, sure, and natural growth, as Bryce showed in tracing it from its colonial origins. It was natural for Arnold to make the error of saying that our landscape east of the Alleghenies 'in general is not interesting,' an opinion he changed when on his second visit to America he lived for a time in the Berkshires. Freeman's queer idea that politics is not so constant a subject of conversation here as in England would not have lasted long if he had stayed over till the great Mugwump campaign of 1884. But in general the three men are to be listened to with profound respect, and the two greatest will long provoke Americans to thought.

Matthew Arnold's primary objection to America was in a limited sense shared by Freeman, and in a still more limited sense endorsed by Bryce: American life, he thought, was culturally uninteresting. It did not have enough that was beautiful, he said—look at our monotonous landscapes, ugly place names, and shoddy architecture; it did not have enough that was distinguished—look how our passion for democracy glorifies the average man, how our yellow press vulgarizes everything it touches, and how we reconcile ourselves to our defects by a blind brag. The remedy Arnold prescribed was the creation of a spirit of true criticism, which would awaken in the American breast a sense of awe and reverence for whatever is truly distinguished. While Arnold's vision of America was defective, there was force in what he said, and Freeman, who had written earlier and somewhat less philosophically, would have approved of much of the indictment. He himself had condemned our newspapers as being for the most part ignorant, ill-written, and offensively personal, while he had objected vehemently to our place names as ill-assorted and artificial. But Freeman found America deficient in the highest interest primarily because he was a historian, and we lacked historical monuments. For that shortcoming the sole cure is time; and as Arnold acknowledged in his essay upon Grant, and Freeman in his remarks upon the old-world look of towns like Bristol, Pennsylvania, we do our best with the history we have. As for Spencer, in this connection he said simply that America was unformed, and would long remain so.

When Arnold accused the United States of being content with mediocre attainments and quoted with approval Lowell's remark that we were 'the most common-schooled and least cultured people in the world,' he touched a truth of which another facet was pointed out by Freeman. Arnold called us a nation of Philistines, a vast, stodgy, middle-class people; Freeman a nation of 'general readers.' 'It seemed to me,' said the historian, 'that in America the reading class, the class of those who read widely, who read, as far as they go, intelligently, but who do not read deeply—the class of those who, without being professed scholars, read enough and know enough to be worth talking to—form a larger proportion of mankind than they do in England. On the other hand, the class of those who read really deeply, the class of professed scholars, is certainly much smaller in proportion in America than it is in England.' Both men thought our culture lacked depth, though they defined culture very differently.

To turn from our defects to our merits, all three again emphatically agreed that the level of material well-being in America is worthy of the unqualified envy of Europe. Arnold told us that poor men, though not men of moderate wealth, were much better off here than anywhere else, society being so constituted as to favor those of small income; and that either we or our good fortune had solved 'the social problem.' Spencer was astonished at the immense development of our material civilization, its extent, wealth, and magnificence, which he attributed partly to our political institutions, and more largely to the factors Arnold had suggested by fortune—our unapproached natural resources, our inheritance of European science, and our native energy. Freeman, too, in commenting upon the munificence of the founders of American colleges, recognized the same happy fact, though for the most part he simply took it for granted.

However, in the exhortations they chiefly pressed upon America the three men differed sharply. Spencer was deeply alarmed by the growth of bossism and corruption in the republic, as he might well be, and feared that we were in danger of losing our liberties somewhat as the medieval Italian states had done. But Arnold felt no alarm whatever on this score. The corruption was exaggerated, he said—'it is not the wide and deep disease it is often represented; it is such that the good elements in the nation may, and I believe will, perfectly work it off.' Spencer wished us, in our headlong rush, to pause for the sake of our health and the greater enjoyment of life. Arnold wished us to pause to give more attention to the cultivation of the mind, and the pursuit of the things of the spirit. In *A Word More about America,* he made a tart remark concerning Spencer's crusade against state socialism, which he reprobated, while in his New York speech Spencer made a tart remark in criticism of Arnold's concentration upon culture as the one and sufficient goal of life. Freeman's criticisms were all good dogmatic British criticisms of detail, with much hard sense in them. We should not give our town names the French termination *ville,* but English terminations; we should pay more attention to research study in our colleges; we should have better paved streets and roads; we ought not to be so fond of titles; we were too much inclined to take the law into our own hands, an indication that we were undergoverned; our ignorance of England was most deplorable, and so on.

Arnold in particular, who committed the error of stating his opinion of America before he visited us, is decidedly misleading in some of his observations. In saying that our life lacked interest, he had in mind an excessively narrow definition of 'interest,' while his reasons for believing even that kind of interest nonexistent are by no means all valid. Our landscapes are not monotonous, our architecture Freeman thought promising, and Bryce has explained some of the countertendencies that prevent democracy from dragging everything down to a dead level. Arnold betrayed his distinct limitations of sympathy when he remarked that Benjamin Franklin was our greatest man, and that he could not understand why we insisted on placing Lincoln upon a lofty pedestal. His sweeping inclusion of nearly all Americans under the term 'Philistines' has been derided by no less a fellow-Briton than J. F. Muirhead, who thinks that we have too much imagination and too little smugness for that. But for all that, Arnold could not write a volume upon this country without hitting many truths squarely on the head. He admitted that America was quite as well off without a snobbish aristocracy like Britain's, just as Freeman admitted that we were quite as well off without any castles in our history. He admitted that it was worth while to penalize the wealthy a little to make the wage-earner more comfortable. Our atmosphere of buoyancy and geniality pleased him. Finally, his warnings to us that we do not sufficiently cultivate our sense of reverence, that we are prone to cynicism, materialism, and bragging, and that we must not rely too much on mere machinery or institutions were all to be taken to heart.

In one other writer of the decade, Sir Lepel Griffin, we have an amusing reversion to Mrs. Trollope. Nothing pleased him. 'America,' he declared with a sweeping gesture, 'is the country of disillusion and disappointment, in politics, literature, culture, and art; in its scenery, its cities, and its people. With some experience of every country in the civilized world, I can think of none except Russia in which I would not prefer to reside, in which life would not be more worth living, less sordid and mean and unlovely.' This Indian official, who might well be left to oblivion had not Arnold used his criticism as a text, was equally displeased by our scenery, our literature, our women, and our hotels. He thought the Mississippi 'a superb volume of pea soup,' and apropos of our passion for defacement, remarked that it would not be long till the walls of the Grand Canyon would invite travelers to purchase Conger's Chest Shields; he referred to 'the obscene ravings of Walt Whitman,' and 'the milk and water of Mr. W. D. Howells'; he was sure that 'more pretty faces are to be seen in a single day in London than in a month in the States'; and he found our hostelries a common lounge for the street loafers. Naturally, he expatiated upon our lynchings, our municipal bosses, our pension grabbing, and our wartime corruption; and as a crowning insult, he told us that the thing best worth seeing in the United States was the pork packing of Chicago. Sir Lepel came just fifty years after his due time, and we are not likely to look upon his kind again.

The supercilious egotism of Sir Lepel, the narrowness of scope and unsureness of tread, which mark even the volumes by Arnold, Freeman, and Spencer, throw into greater contrast the remarkable comprehensiveness and sagacity of the work that appeared as the decade was closing—Bryce's *American Commonwealth* (1888). It represents, as we now have it after its repeated revisions, the work of long decades. Bryce's first visit to America resulted, he states, in a swarm of bold generalizations, half of which he discarded after his second visit, in 1881; of the remaining half, still others went overboard when he returned from a third visit, in 1883-4; and before the first edition of his book appeared, two subsequent trips had dispelled further errors, and had given him an understanding of new truths. In addition to these repeated visits, Bryce had prepared himself by studying our history with care, and by making a host of American friends, with whom he assiduously corresponded. He contributed to our leading journals of opinion. It is impossible not to ascribe some of his ready sympathy with American manners and institutions to his Scotch-Irish blood, the blood of a strain that has contributed so much to American achievement. The philosophical insight of his two volumes, their expository persuasiveness, and their literary charm united to make their publication a landmark in the annals of political literature. Bryce and Tocqueville stand alone, and Bryce both corrects and amplifies Tocqueville.

With the political and constitutional chapters of Bryce's book hundreds of thousands of Americans have become familiar through its use as a school and college text. He heartily subscribed to the fundamental tenets of democracy, asserting the truth of the apparent paradox that in general the wisdom of the mass is greater than the wisdom of the select few, a truth that he believed history had proved. While he realized the baffling nature of many of America's unsolved problems, such as racial friction and our shameful municipal corruption, he was optimistic that the future would find answers for them. It is frequently an unreasoning optimism, but it represents an instinctive hopefulness that practically all Americans share. In theory, the Americans were still committed to the principle of *laissez faire,* but in practice Bryce perceived that the states—which could try new experiments with little danger—were going farther in governmental interference than most European countries; he instanced our severe restrictions upon the sale of liquor, our industrial legislation, and our establishment of state universities, agricultural experiment stations, and multiform inspecting authorities. These experiments he applauded, saying that 'no people is shrewder than the American in perceiving when a law works ill, nor prompter in repealing it.'

In his survey of our social life, Bryce was chiefly impressed by the effectiveness with which our boasted principle of equality continued to operate. The enormous gap between our multimillionaires and our poor was palpable, and he saw reasons for believing that it would more and more increase 'by the growth of a very rich class at one end of the line, and of a very poor class at the other end.' But he found no such worship of wealth as foreigners supposed to exist here, and hardly even an exaggerated respect for it; we made an amazing fuss over the doings of our richest folk, but this was rather because we had a simple feeling of wonder and curiosity about wealth. The very rich were admired as a famous runner or jockey is admired, 'but do not seem to receive either flattery or social deference'—unless, of course, they have amassed their fortunes by a display of remarkable talents. As for social precedence in general, Bryce thought it almost nonexistent. Even men in high official station do not give themselves airs, and are not encouraged by others to assume a superior mien. He instances a little scene he witnessed in the office of the Commander-in-Chief in Washington: some rather shabby Western tourists happened to push in, and, seeing the room occupied, began to retreat, when the famous General called them back, saying, 'Walk in, ladies; you can look around; you won't disturb me—make yourselves at home.' The gain in manners consequent upon our social equality Bryce esteemed to be far in excess of the loss. 'I do not think that the upper class loses in grace,' he wrote, 'I am sure that the humbler class gains in independence.' Matthew Arnold had taken much the same view, praising the spirit that discarded all those invidious social discriminations, which an Englishman wrapped up in the distinction between 'Mr.' and 'Esquire.'

However, like Arnold, Bryce deemed the effects of democracy upon our cultural life by no means uniformly good. Among the ten salient features of American intellectual activity and outlook that he listed, two only are praiseworthy, and eight are blameworthy. We wished to be abreast of the best thought and work of the world, he said, and to have every form of literature and art excellently represented. We also had a warm admiration for literary or scientific eminence, and an enthusiasm for the qualities of genius, with a keen desire to discover them. Unfortunately, these excellences were offset by an excessive fondness for bold and striking effects; an absence of refined taste, and a disposition to regard anything brilliant as obviously superior to first-rate work in a quiet style—a novel by Scott as superior to one by Jane Austen, for example; a lack of respect for canons or traditions; an inadequate appreciation of special knowledge or experience; a love of intellectual novelties whether good or bad; a desire for quick and showy results; and a tendency to identify bigness with greatness. There was nothing specifically democratic in our literature, Bryce concluded, and it differed no more from English literature than did the Scotch school of letters headed by Burns, Hume, and Scott. This is true if we except the writings and influence of a poet whom Bryce probably disregarded—Walt Whitman.

Bryce is a severer critic of America than most men who have not read him thoroughly realize; for his occasional severity is softened not only by his more frequent praise, but by his admirable habit of tracing every fault to its origins, which lie frequently in mere environment or circumstance. Like Arnold, he criticizes the American people for their want of the highest intellectual distinction; but unlike Arnold, he shows how natural—nay, inevitable—this want had been. Its causes he states as five: the many distractions of American life, our atmosphere of absorption in material progress, the absence of historical objects calculated to stimulate the imagination, the fact that Europe's generous cultural production so largely supplies the deficiency of our own, and the superficiality induced by our constant newspaper reading. Now of all these causes, only the first and last can really be rated as sins for which we are censurable, and even the first is so only in an uncertain degree. Moreover, Bryce took a more hopeful view of the future in this regard than did Arnold. He pointed to the development in fiction writing during the 'eighties, and to an improvement in many fields of exact scholarship, as evidences that our comparative cultural sterility might not last long; evidences that a quarter century later, writing of the wonderful development of our universities, he found strengthened. In the political field, he was at the same pains to define the causes of the faults of American democracy, faults four in number:

> First, a certain commonness of mind and tone, a want of dignity and elevation in and about the conduct of public affairs, an insensibility to the nobler aspects and finer responsibilities of national life.
>
> Secondly, a certain apathy among the luxurious classes and fastidious minds, who find themselves of no more account than the ordinary voter, and are disgusted by the superficial vulgarities of public life.
>
> Thirdly, a want of knowledge, tact, and judgment in the details of legislation, as well as in administration, with an inadequate recognition of the difficulty of these kinds of work, and of the worth of special experience and skill in dealing with them. Because it is incompetent, the multitude will not feel its incompetence, and will not seek or defer to the counsels of those who possess the requisite capacity.
>
> Fourthly, laxity in the management of public business. The persons entrusted with such business being only average men, thinking of themselves and thought of by others as average men, with a deficient sense of their high responsibilities, may succumb to the temptations which the control of legislation and the public funds present, in cases where persons of a more enlarged view and with more of a social reputation to support would remain incorruptible.

Other writers upon America had done us the service of defining our chief maladies, but Bryce was the first to offer a thorough diagnosis and prognosis of them; his object was not merely to describe, but to explain, and he enabled us to see ourselves as we had never done before.

Taking American life as a whole, our ablest critic pronounced it indubitably pleasanter than English life not merely for the poor, as most of his predecessors had admitted, but for people of all worldly conditions. This was because the naturalness of social intercourse was not checked by class lines, nor by the rancors between religious sects, which disturb so large a part of Europe; because of the kindliness and

consideration of Americans—traits no doubt partly referable to the
ease with which a comfortable subsistence is procured; and because of
the humorous turn that Americans love to give social intercourse. The
greatest drawback to this pleasantness he thought equally plain. It
was the gray monotony of American life. Her cities were too uniform,
too much of the nation was flat, her institutions had too few local variations, and there was less difference between a Mississippian and an
Oregonian than between a Yorkshireman and a Cornishman. Perhaps
Bryce exaggerated this uniformity. Other travelers, like Max O'Rell and
J. F. Muirhead, found the differences between a Southerner and a
Yankee very great and pleasantly picturesque. But Bryce's general conclusion is not likely to evoke much dissent from any quarter:

> Life in America is in most ways pleasanter, easier, simpler than in Europe;
> it floats in a sense of happiness like that of a radiant summer morning. But life
> in one of the great European centers is capable of an intensity, a richness blended
> of many elements, which has not yet been reached in America. There are more
> problems in Europe calling for a solution; there is more passion in the struggles
> that rage round them; the past more frequently kindles the present in a glow
> of imaginative light. In whichever country of Europe one dwells, one feels that
> the other countries are near, that the fortunes of their peoples are bound up
> with the fortunes of one's own, that ideas are shooting to and fro between them.

Not even Bryce could cover the whole ground; for want of space
he had to omit his chapters on natural scenery and its effect upon
American life, and some of the topics he had not fully discussed
were treated in detail, and with more personal impressions than he
cared to give, by later travelers. Several of these may be summarily dismissed. G. W. Steevens came here during the Presidential campaign
of 1896, and gives a vivacious narrative of the hectic summer during
which half the nation badged itself with silver and half with gold.
Nowhere is there available a better discription of the mass meetings,
rallies, the parades of businessmen in Chicago and New York, and the
wistful enthusiasm of workmen and farmers for Bryan. Steevens gives
characteristic sketches of both nominees:

> If you want to see a Presidential candidate you ring the bell and walk in and
> see him. That is what he is there for. I rang and walked in; Mr. McKinley was
> sitting on a rocking chair in a little office not ten feet from the door. His strong,
> clean-shaven face has a suggestion of Charles Bradlaugh; there is the same lofty
> and massive forehead, the same mastiff power of chin and jaw. Clear eyes, wide
> nose, full lips—all his features suggest dominant will and energy rather than
> subtlety of mind or emotion. He had on the frock coat in which he was pres-
> ently to address deputations, and loosely tied brown slippers in which he was
> not. He also was not unmindful of the spittoon. Yet . . . not to be tedious, his
> personality presents a rare combination of strength and charm.

For Bryan the English journalist caught some of the infectious silverite enthusiasm. He first saw him in a carriage in Washington, 'a compact, black-coated figure, a clean-shaven, clear-cut face, a large, sharp nose, and a square mouth and jaw. With the faint blue stubble on his face, and his long, grizzly hair, he suggests an actor to the English mind.' But when Steevens heard him speak in a Washington park the impression of an actor vanished:

A little girl in silver tripped along the platform rail, and presented a bunch of silver roses. The shrieks became delirium. For a moment the square, black figure stood absolutely still. Then slowly he reached forth the hand, like St. Paul in the Bible. The din went on unabated. Still very slowly, he raised an arm above his head and made passes—one, two, three—in each direction of the crowd. Gradually silence crept over the mass of heads, and then the orator opened his lips. In a voice low but plain, hoarse but very rich, he began. He was glad to see once more those among whom he had spent four years of official life. 'We'll give you four years more,' shrieked my friend over the station. A broad and winning smile broke over the candidate's mouth, and again the mob screamed. A most admirable demagogue!

Equally concerned with mere externals, though wider in range, is Philip Burne-Jones's *Dollars and Democracy* (1904). The one thing new that the celebrated painter discovered was New York society. We must smile over his statement that the Four Hundred occupy a position here somewhat analogous to that of the nobility in England, that 'the middle classes accept them cheerfully as the best available substitute for the dukes and duchesses whom, in their heart of hearts, the Americans love so well,' and that they 'are like little kings and queens in the small world they represent.' His comments upon the extreme frivolity of society, its lack of distinction or repose, and its pitiable snobbery possess more truth. For the rest, Burne-Jones's book is filled with rather shallow disquisition upon the rush of American life, ice water, crowded streetcars, the insolence of servants, the 'monstrosities' called skyscrapers, the yellow press, its front pages 'like a bad dream,' the constant talk of dollars, and the dirtiness of Chicago. He did like our enameled baths, our telephones, and our electric lights, yet when he visited Charles Eliot Norton at Shady Hill, and found all of these conveniences lacking, he breathed a sigh of homesick relief. His little account of the interview in which he failed to persuade Roosevelt to allow his picture to be painted is unconsciously amusing, for in some ways Burne-Jones was rather obtuse.

It is a much more thorough and penetrating analysis that we meet in James F. Muirhead's *America the Land of Contrasts* (1898) and in A. Maurice Low's *America at Home* (1907), the one the work of a traveler who studied America comprehensively in writing Baedeker's guide, the other of an able journalist long resident in America. It was Muirhead's book that Prince Henry of Prussia read in preparation for his visit. Mr. Muirhead could well dedicate it to 'the land that has given me what makes life most worth living,' for he had married an American girl. One of his chapters is 'An Appreciation of the American Woman,' in which he makes it clear that he liked our feminine population for a great variety of reasons—they are more individual and varied than English women, their minds are more agile and imaginative, and their fresh innocence is unmatchable. Mr. Muirhead used to astonish Americans by saying that the Daisy Miller of James's story struck him as a girl of whom, because of her essential sweetness, refinement, and freshness, we could not be too proud.

In its pleasantly smooth literary style Muirhead's volume reminds us of Captain Thomas Hamilton or Alexander Mackay, and in the quiet justice of its observations it sometimes approaches Bryce. The author gives us repeated witty touches, as when he compares New York city to a lady in ball costume, with diamonds in her ears and her toes out at the boots. In the large view the inconsistencies of American life—our energy and phlegm, our insistence on luxury and indifference to comfort, our matter-of-fact practicality and our love of spiritualists and faith cures— appeared to him more prominent than any set of consistent traits. He perhaps failed to remember how inconsistent all human nature, in every individual and every nation, is. But the prevailing tone of his volume, of course, is quite as cordial as Bryce's. Like Bryce, he inclined to the belief that the distinguishing feature of American society, as compared with European, lay in our closer approach to equality, and like Bryce again, he held that this equality made intercourse far freer and pleasanter. Even Matthew Arnold had mentioned the 'buoyancy, enjoyment, and freedom from restraint that are everywhere in America' as attributable to our exemption from any aristocratic incubus. Muirhead remarked that an American simply could not understand the uneasy sense of inferiority that a British author or scientist would show to a mere duke:

It is not easy for a European to the manner born to realize the sort of extravagant, nightmare effect that many of our social customs have in the eyes of our untutored American cousins. The inherent absurdities that are second nature to us exhale for them the full flavor of their grotesqueness. The idea of an insignificant boy peer taking precedence of Mr. John Morley! The idea of *having to* appear before royalty in a state of partial nudity on a cold winter day! The necessity of backing out of the royal presence! The idea of a freeborn Briton having to get out of an engagement long previously formed on the score that 'he has been *commanded* to dine with H.R.H.' The horrid capillary plaster necessary before a man can serve decently as an opener of carriage doors! The horsehair envelopes without which our legal brains cannot work! The unwritten law by which a man has to nurse his hat and stick throughout a call unless his hostess specially asks him to lay them aside!

Perhaps the chief fault of American society, if we may believe Mr. Muirhead, is our tendency to attach too much importance to materialistic effects. We do not see the folly of spending $100 where $10 would meet all the demands of good taste; we make too showy a display of American beauty roses and lilies of the valley at weddings and receptions; we fit up our hotels with oppressive tapestries, vases, and furniture; and our rich people show a tasteless magnificence in their private cars and their houses. The author condemned the social practice under which American girls allow their young men admirers to spend money so freely on them, as a practice that rubs some of the bloom off of romance. Like so many others, Mr. Muirhead also lamented the way in which people with any money spoil their children. He avers that he actually saw a little girl of five appear alone in a hotel dining room, order an indigestible breakfast, and silence the misgivings of the waiter with the rebuke, 'I guess I pay my way.'

A much fuller discussion of our humor is found in Muirhead than in any earlier writer. He was probably right in his conviction that the American and Scotch forms of humor are almost the same, and are both more subtle than the British form. He remembered hearing John Morley quote to an English audience Carlyle's statement about Sterling: 'We talked about this thing and that—except in opinion not disagreeing'; and he says there was a lapse of a half minute before the audience saw that the remark had a humorous turn, whereas in Scotland or America the perception would have been instant. But much of our humor was distasteful to him. He deplored its crudeness, as in the headline over the hanging of three Negroes—'Three Chocolate Drops'; its buffoonery, as in *Innocents Abroad;* and its irreverence, as in the advertisement of a patent filter being 'what it was in the beginning, is now, and ever shall be.' But he noted that our humor was not only a lubricant of society, as Bryce did, but a valuable safety valve, moderating partisan and other resentments; in the election of 1888 the Democrats enjoyed as much as the Republicans such squibs as one carried on a parade banner in Philadelphia—'No frigid North, no torrid South, no temperate East, no Sackville West.' As for the American press, his view of it coincided exactly with Arnold's and Freeman's: it was vulgar, trivial, and intrusive, though enterprising, and it represented a lower level of life than the English newspaper. Our sports, too, he considered more weakly developed than England's. Our love of outdoor play was not nearly so widespread or genuine as in the mother country, and the commercial spirit had more deeply pervaded our games.

A unique feature of Muirhead's volume was a chapter called 'Baedekeriana,' a web of conclusions drawn from his 35,000 miles of investigative travel in the United States. Our open railway cars he greatly preferred to the English compartments for long distances, saying that the sociability and free movement they offered were indispensable. His chief objection to our sleeping cars was our failure to place all the berths for women at one end, though their indiscriminate position among those of the men worries few Americans. Against our railways as a whole he alleged the frequency of accidents, and the slowness of the branch-line trains. Our river and lake steamboats were distinctly better than any he had seen elsewhere, and fully deserving the name of floating palaces. Our flat, clumsy-looking, but comfortable and spacious ferries were another source of admiration. A very different story he tells of the telegraph and postal service, both less prompt and accurate than in Great Britain; in fact, he strongly suspected on one occasion that a telegram had been sent by train, not wire. Muirhead's remarks upon our hotels supplement those made by Trollope forty years earlier. On the whole, he liked the American plan of charging an inclusive price for board and meals, despite its wastefulness; he defended our hotel clerks, boasting that several had actually seemed to regard him as an equal; and he thought our summer hotels, with their wide, shady balconies, and their pleasantly social atmosphere, quite incomparable. But he objected to the noisiness of the rooms in many city hotels, and thought they ought to provide smoking rooms for men; while he completely missed one European type of hostelry:

While we are on the question of defects in American hotels, it should be noticed that the comfortable little second-class inns of Great Britain are practically unknown in the United States. The second-class inns there are run on the same lines as the best ones; but in an inferior manner at every point. The food is usually as abundant, but it is of poorer quality and worse cooked; the beds are good enough, but not so clean; the table linen is soiled; the sugar bowls are left exposed to the flies from week-end to week-end; the service is poor and apt to be forward; and (last but not least) the manners of the other guests are apt to include a most superfluous proportion of tobacco-chewing, expectorating, an open and unashamed use of the toothpick, and other little amenities that probably inflict more torture on those who are not used to them than would decorous breaches of the Decalogue.

The best parts of Mr. Low's books are those political chapters that reflect his long experience of official life in Washington. His explanation of the political boss-ship illuminates a subject many Americans as well as Britons have failed to understand. His discrimination between the city boss and state boss, between Croker and Platt, is brief but pointed. Few will question his general characterization of the Americans, for his description of them as a moral people, resentful of social inferiority, gallant toward women, gregarious, hard-working, spontaneous and genuine in address, free spenders of money, usually hurried, and enterprising and ambitious is familiar. The chief fault of the book is a certain exaggeration of the materialistic inclination of the United States, which is assuredly great enough without overemphasis. 'The struggle for wealth in the United States is desperate and ceaseless,' he says. 'Money is what everyone wants, and money is what everyone is trying to obtain.' This is a statement that should be qualified, as should Mr. Low's view of the complete power of money over politics and the press. He discusses the American girl and her despotic position, such social traits as the horror of *décolleté* dress in inland towns, our pleasure resorts, and life at the national capital intelligently, but his handling of more difficult topics, such as the Negro problem, is inadequate. The constant overtone of the volume, half heard throughout, is his wonder over our wealth, our resources, and our future. He speaks of our boastfulness, but excuses it on the ground that we have done so much to justify it. Waiting in a public room of the White House during Roosevelt's administration, he heard one of two other men standing near ejaculate, 'By George, we *are* a great people!' and the rejoinder, 'Greatest in the world!' These exclamations he thinks only natural.

Two travelers who reflect clearly the same admiration of American power, prosperity, and progressiveness, and the general British desire for harmonious relations with America, which accompanied and followed the Spanish War, are William Archer, whose *America Today* was published in 1899, and W. T. Stead, whose *Americanization of the World* appeared in 1902. Enthusiasm is not too strong a word for the attitude of either. Stead, hailing the advent of America to a position as the greatest of world powers, declared that this emergence was 'the greatest political, social, and commercial phenomenon of our times.' He described the influence that the republic was exerting for the growth of democracy throughout the world, the improvement of the material condition of mankind, the diffusion of education, and the strengthening of international peace. Archer, dwelling upon the success of the United States in meeting one problem after another, and rejoicing in the final welding of North and South during the Spanish War, struck the same note:

The United States of America, let us say, is a rehearsal for the United States of Europe, nay, of the world. It is the very difficulties over which the croakers shake their heads that make the experiment interesting, momentous. The

United States is a veritable microcosm; it presents in little all the elements which go to make up a world, and which have hitherto kept the world, almost unintermittently, in a state of battle and bloodshed.

Both men made a plea for a close partnership between England and America, that of Stead being unprecedentedly hearty. Declaring that the right of the United States 'to claim the leading place among English-speaking nations cannot be disputed,' he recalled statements by Lord Derby and Cecil Rhodes that had looked toward a political connection between the two nations, and quoted Balfour's remark that the idea of a conflict between them 'carries with it something of the unnatural horror of civil war.' He suggested that Great Britain, in token of the new amity among the Anglo-Saxon peoples, celebrate the Fourth of July, and that we reciprocate by observing Magna Charta Day. Archer was similarly pleased to note that the old rancors were disappearing since England had shown her friendship during the war. 'Millions of people,' he observed, 'who had hitherto felt no touch of racial sympathy, and had been conscious only of a vague historical antipathy, learned with surprise that England was in no sense their natural enemy, but rather, among all the nations of Europe, their natural friend.'

G. W. Steevens, like Basil Hall long before him, had deplored the tone in which the instruction of our public schools had treated Great Britain. Our historical texts, as he showed by extracts, always spoke of British soldiers as 'insolent,' of the Tories as 'brutal,' of the English institutions as 'hateful,' and of the English government as 'tyrannical.' Matthew Arnold had also mildly expressed his opinion that the Revolution was not an uprising against despotism, but was rather simply the act of 'sensible young people getting rid of stupid and overweening guardians who misunderstood and mismanaged them,' a view the later American historians have endorsed. Now Mr. Archer looked forward to the day when our schools would teach a fairer view of Anglo-American relations, a day that has long since dawned. He and Stead both tried to impress upon Englishmen the superior character of many features of American civilization, and the advantages that would accrue to the mother country from a close relationship. Stead, for example, made amends for much English abuse of our journalism by saying that our illustrated magazines, our women's magazines, and our periodicals for juveniles were far better than similar publications in England. Archer spoke warmly of American literature, and pointed out the indebtedness of the English language to the United States for the addition of many useful new terms, and the preservation of many old ones. 'Let the purists who sneer at "Americanisms," ' he remarked, 'think for one moment how much poorer the English language would be today if North America had become a French or Spanish instead of an English continent.'

Fortunately, not all the mirrors held up to Uncle Sam at the close of the nineteenth and beginning of the twentieth centuries were so flattering. Rudyard Kipling in 1899 published his *From Sea to Sea*, letters of travel written to Indian newspapers in 1887-9, which for the first time gave general currency to his hasty and decidedly hypersarcastic impressions of a trip across the United States. His so-called *American Notes* had first appeared in book form in 1891, had evoked many protests, and had been almost completely suppressed. In the interim he had married an American girl, of an aristocratic New York and Vermont family, he had bought a home three miles north of Brattleboro, Vermont, on which he had erected a $50,000 house named 'The Naulahka,' and he had lived continuously in this country from 1892 till the summer of 1896. When his American impresssions reappeared in 1899, Kipling was the most individual and powerful figure in the literary world of the day, a man who had created a new movement in poetry and fiction. Compared with his books like *Plain Tales from the Hills, Barrack Room Ballads, The Light That Failed, Life's Handicap,* and *The Jungle Books,* all of which had now appeared, his two hundred pages of scattering and ill-tempered jottings on the United States were plainly mere journalism, and their disagreeable passages were not more taken to heart by Americans than they should have been.

Landing in San Francisco, the twenty-five-year-old Kipling did not like our ignorant and inquisitive reporters, our casual way of stabbing Chinamen on street corners, the spittoons 'of infinite capacity and generous gape,' which he saw being assiduously used at the Palace Hotel, or the nasal tones in which the Americans spoke an almost unknown tongue. 'The American has no language. He has dialect, slang, provincialism, accent, and so forth.' The novelist was justly indignant when, explaining to an interviewer that San Francisco was hallowed ground to him because it was Bret Harte's city, the interviewer informed him that California had long since repudiated Bret Harte because of his residence in England! An encounter with a bunco-steerer who took Kipling for a very green Englishman, and haled him off to a card game in a shady corner of the town, delighted the writer, who fooled the crook to the top of his very crooked bent. Even in writing of his delightful visits to a certain club, Kipling found opportunity to retell stories of the lawless days of the Vigilance Committee, imparted to him by the members. San Francisco, which had taken Kipling into its best circles, invited him to dinners and teas, and boasted of her matchless cable cars, felt that he had treated her scurvily. But the treatment she received was kindness itself compared with that he gave Chicago.

For Chicago, with its dirty tangle of interminable level streets, its smoke-filled air, its preoccupation with money, and its total lack of beauty in these ante-World's Fair days, gave Kipling an opportunity to draw some horrifying pictures for his Indian newspaper. At the Palmer House, which he deemed over-gilded and over-mirrored, but which an American described as 'the finest hotel in the finest city on God Almighty's earth,' he found 'a huge hall of tesselated marble crammed with people talking about money and spitting about everywhere.' It was a fit introduction to an uncouth, money-mad population. Invited by a cab driver to see the glories of the town, Kipling peered into canals black as ink, and rattled down oppressive streets of business houses screaming with loud advertisements. The cabman was amazed when the author, shown a famous saloon paved with silver dollars, declared that 'A Hottentot would not have been guilty of this sort of barbarism,' and was enraged when Kipling refused to believe 'that the snarling together of telegraph wires, the heaving up of houses, and the making of money is progress.' The Chicago newspapers were just then carrying on a fish-wife war with the New York press over the location of the Columbian Exposition, and this, with their inaccuracy, bad grammar, slang, and want of dignity, gave him a peculiarly unfavorable impression of that Midwestern journalism that had also displeased Arnold. Toward the stockyards he was respectful. But a church service was the final shock:

[1] It was a circus really, but that the worshippers did not know. There were flowers all about the building, which was fitted up with plush and stained oak and much luxury, including twisted brass candlesticks of severest Gothic design.

To these things and a congregation of savages entered suddenly a wonderful man, completely in the confidence of their God, whom he treated colloquially and exploited very much as a newspaper reporter would exploit a foreign potentate. But, unlike the newspaper reporter, he never allowed his listeners to forget that he, and not He, was the centre of attraction. With a voice of silver and with imagery borrowed from the auction room, he built up for his hearers a heaven on the lines of the Palmer House (but with all the gliding real gold, and all the plate glass diamond), and set in the centre of it a loud-voiced, argumentative, very shrewd creation that he called God. One sentence at this point caught my delighted ear. It was apropos of some question of the Judgment, and ran:

'No! I tell you God doesn't do business that way.'

He was giving them a deity whom they could comprehend, and a gold and jewelled heaven in which they could take a natural interest.

[1] From Rudyard Kipling's *From Sea to Sea,* copyright 1899, 1907, by Rudyard Kipling; reprinted by permission of Mrs. G. Bambridge, Macmillan and Company, Ltd., and Doubleday and Company, Inc.

But Kipling was by no means determinedly hostile to the Americans. As he put it, they were raw, lawless, 'almost more conceited than the English,' and cocksure, 'but I love them.' In one of his chapters he relates how he assured a scoffer, whom he met on a train between Salt Lake and Omaha, of his faith in the tremendous future of the Yankees. 'At present there is too much balcony and too little Romeo in the life plays of his fellow citizens. Later on, when the proportion is adjusted, and he sees the possibilities of his land, he will produce things that will make the effete East stare. He will also be a complex and highly composite administrator. There is nothing known to man that he will not be, and his country will sway the world with one foot as a man tilts a see-saw plank!' The scenic beauty of the West was given due tribute by the impressionable young man, who thought that neither pen nor brush could ever adequately portray the splendors of the Yellowstone Gorge; he felt that he had really lived after he had landed his salmon in the Clackamas; and as a climax, he went on a pilgrimage to Elmira to see Mark Twain, and laid his admiration at the humorist's feet. He and Mark Twain had a long talk about copyright, *Tom Sawyer*, the art of autobiography, and other literary topics. Young Kipling confesses that he would have given much to have had the courage to ask Clemens for the corn-cob pipe he was smoking, and when Mark Twain put his hand on the Englishman's shoulder, the latter felt that it was an investiture of the Star of India, blue silk, trumpets, and diamond all complete. It is on this note of humble admiration for a great American genius that he closes his sketches.

The four other novelists who wrote their impressions of the United States between 1906 and 1922, H. G. Wells, Arnold Bennett, W. L. George, and G. K. Chesterton, spent each only a limited time in this country. Wells and Chesterton were here for six or seven weeks, and Mr. George, whose stay was longest, for but ten months. Bennett devoted himself almost wholly to impressionistic description, which has never been written with more verve; Chesterton found in American life merely the themes for a dozen essays, some of which carried him into domains distant from the United States. None of the four attempted the formal study of manners and institutions that we find in Miss Martineau, Alexander Mackay, or Muirhead. Mr. Wells modestly compared himself with an ant crawling over the carcass of an elephant, though as a competent American critic said, he might better be compared to a hawk soaring over a landscape. Mr. George frankly admitted his 'presumption' in writing a book, for 'one tells oneself that one cannot condense within those few months the necessary evperience, and especially the necessary repose, which would make it possible to arrive at balanced judgments.' Yet we would lose something if any one of these volumes had not been written, and the first, that by H. G. Wells, really drove home certain criticisms that nobody had tried to drive home before.

For Wells brought one of the most highly individual points of view of all the British travelers in America. Whereas men like Bryce, Archer, and Low all looked at us from the same general standpoint, Wells came distinctly as a Socialist, and a Socialist with trenchant ideas about the direction human progress must take. Other travelers were interested in the America of the present, but Wells was interested in the America of the future. Symbolically, he refused at Boston to go visit the graves of Emerson and Hawthorne at Concord, and at Washington to make a pilgrimage to Mount Vernon, for his concern was with the America of 1976, not 1776. When he saw a roomful of university students more or less intent upon Greek, he lamented their waste of time over an obsolete study. In every way he was an unconventional critic, not afraid to blurt out unconventional opinions. Sir Lepel Griffin had recoiled in horror from the single paper mill first planted at Niagara, and Lord Bryce in the later editions of *The American Commonwealth* had deplored the way in which factories and hotels had spoiled that scenic wonder since his original visit, but Wells hoped that the time would soon come when the social and industrial processes of America would capture the falls entire; he delighted to foresee the moment when 'all the froth and hurry of Niagara at last, all of it, dying into the hungry canals of intake, should rise again in light and power, in ordered and equipped and proud and beautiful humanity, in cities and palaces and the emancipated souls and hearts of men.' At the time of his visit America had just thrown an English labor agitator, William MacQueen, into jail on the unfounded charge that he was an anarchist and had incited a Paterson mob to a riot; and some newspapers were engaged in hounding Maxim Gorky out of the country on the silly ground of his relations with Mme. Andreieva, who stood to him precisely as George Eliot had stood to George Lewes. These two instances of American injustice stirred Wells deeply, and he never tired of denouncing both.

Yet, like the other three novelists, he was a thoroughly friendly critic, without a trace of superciliousness. He and W. L. George were both drawn to the United States by their very trust in its greatness, their confidence in the ability of its people to achieve a still greater future. In a chapter called 'Growth Invincible' Wells relates how, as he watched the rich, busy country fly past on a trip from Chicago to Washington, 'I got still more clearly the enormous scale of this American destiny.' Gigantic vigor and growth, in fact, Wells saw as the fundamental attribute of the nation. Coming into New York harbor, he noted how the skyscrapers dwarfed the Goddess of Liberty. Emerging at Chatham Square suddenly upon the Cyclopean stone arches of Brooklyn Bridge, he was astonished by that monster. He stared at the torrent of Fifth Avenue, and found that certain clubs at which he dined far surpassed any in London. At Ellis Island he watched immigrants rolling in at the rate of nearly a million a year. In vast, smoky Chicago 'growth forced itself upon me again as the dominant American fact.' The universities impressed him, and he stated that in sociology, education, and psychology, studies close to his heart, 'America is producing an amount of work immense in comparison with our own British output.'

But against the background of all this wealth and might, Wells was troubled by a consciousness of the thrust of certain menacing evils, and of baffling problems. He was alarmed to see our enormous aggregations of private riches, and thought they needed checking. Arriving at the time when the Federal income tax law had been declared unconstitutional, he decided that the Statue of Liberty meant liberty for property, not man. The reckless, childish spending, which he saw on the part of the rich and their children, amused and disgusted him. He tells of one artless squanderer who, typifying the rest, was rebuffed by a London picture dealer. 'If you want a Boticelli that size, Mr. Record,' the dealer declared, 'I can't find it; you'll have to have it made for you.' The conglomeration of palaces and shops on Fifth Avenue was eloquent, to Wells's eye, of the fact that there was but one link between the residents. 'The link is just spending. You come to New York and spend; you go away again.' Equally on the surface lay the evil of lynching, while the evil of child labor was too prominent to be missed.

Indeed, child labor flaunted itself in the traveler's face. Returning home on the subway one night at two A.M. after a supper and talk with Abraham Cahan, he noted 'a childish-faced delicate little creature of eleven years old or so, wearing the uniform of a messenger boy,' who 'drooped with fatigue, roused himself with a start, edged off his seat with a sigh, and disappeared.' This was the year John Spargo published his *Bitter Cry of the Children*. Wells was told that 1,700,000 Americans under fifteen years of age were toiling in factories, mines, fields, and workshops—that in the South, children of five or six worked in the mills twelve hours a day. The abuse was clearly connected with a more inclusive evil, our commercial ruthlessness. Looking at the Standard Oil Company and its list of crushed competitors, he decided that, in practice, strictly honest trading could hardly exist. Commercial corruption and political corruption he treated in the same chapter, and the latter he regarded more indulgently than the former. In Chicago he entered 'Hinky Dink's' saloon, chatted with 'a pretty tough gathering' of loafers there, and formed a favorable impression of the boss himself. Wells saw the good as well as the bad side of the boss system. 'He is very kind to all his crowd. He helps them when they are in trouble, even if it is trouble with the police; he helps them find employment when they are down on their luck; he stands between them and the impacts of an unsympathetic and altogether too careless social structure in a sturdy and almost parental way.'

Below both kinds of corruption, he decided, not very profoundly, lay our huge exclusive preoccupation with money getting, and what the press called corruption was only an acute expression in individual cases of this general fault. His conception of the cure he stated with irritating vagueness—he believed we should face the task of 'creating imaginatively and bringing into being a new state.' But he was glad to see our *laissez faire* individualism submitting to an appreciation of the need for certain curbs. President Roosevelt was talking of the limitation of inheritance, revolts had formed against the trusts, the railways were being regulated, and so on—all of which Wells approved as signs of 'the birth strength of a splendid civilization.'

For everywhere and above all, Wells was outraged by the lawlessness, disorder, and chaos of American life. Throughout his volume he harps upon the need for discipline, constructiveness, and fixed purpose. New York's immense activity gave him a sense of 'soulless gigantic forces.' Chicago, with the reek and dirt of its stockyards, the endless smoking chimneys and blazing furnaces from Harvey to Pullman, the wilderness of grain elevators, factories, and warehouses along the river, the dust and clangor of State Street, seemed simply 'one hoarse cry for discipline.' The entire economic process struck him as equally untamed and savage, sprawling and wasteful—a process of letting lawless men find one new abuse after another for the government and public opinion to curb. Even our foundations and legacies, such as our gifts to universities and museums, he described as a litter of disorder, like the toys that too tired children leave on the nursery floor after a day of play. They were simply 'the impusive generosity of a mob of wealthy persons, with no broad common conceptions, with no collective dream.' Wells's visit coincided with the attack of Steffens on the shame of the cities, of Ida Tarbell on our oil corporations, of Robert Hunter on poverty, and of Lawson on Frenzied Finance. Upton Sinclair, Wells was glad to record, had achieved a popular success with *The Jungle* that had been denied his romance of *Manassas*. The Americans, so recently complacent, seemed to him now alert and questioning, aroused to a thorough consideration of the intricate issues of the day. It was high time:

¹ The essential question for America, as for Europe, is the rescue of her land, her public service, and the whole of her great economic process from the anarchic and irresponsible control of private owners—how dangerous and horrible that control may become the Railway and Beef Trust investigations have shown—and the organization of her social life upon the broad, clean, humane conceptions of modern science. In every country, however, this huge problem of reconstruction, which is the alternative to a plutocratic decadence, is enormously complicated by irrelevant and special difficulties. In Great Britain, for example, the ever-pressing problem of holding the empire, and the fact that one legislative body is composed almost entirely of private landowners hampers every step towards a better order. Upon every country in Europe weighs the armor of war. In America the complications are distinctive and peculiar. She is free, indeed, now to a large extent from the possibility of any grave military stresses, her one overseas investment in the Philippines she is evidently resolved to forget and be rid of at as early a date as possible. But, on the other hand, she is confronted by a system of legal entanglements of extraordinary difficulty and perplexity, she has the most powerful tradition of individualism in the world, and a degraded political system, and she has in the presence of a vast and increasing proportion of unassimilable aliens in her substance—Negroes, south European peasants, Russian Jews, and the like—an ever-intensifying complication.

What Wells says upon the problem of the Negro and the immigrant met sharp dissent at the time. Shocked by our indifference to the color problem—'hardly any Americans at all seem to be in possession of the elementary facts in relation to this question'—he was moved to deep admiration by the heroism with which thousands of Negroes were striving toward a higher station. As between Booker Washington, who inclined to accept the fact of racial separation, and W. E. B. DuBois, who rebelled against it, he agreed with the latter. Racial differences would always exasperate intercourse until people were trained to ignore them, he thought; the most miserable and disorderly countries in the world are those in which two races keep up a jarring, continuous discrimination against each other. 'You must repudiate separation,' he told Washington, who shook his head. As for immigration, he thought we were getting altogether too much of it, and about a decade later the United States decided he was right. It was not the difficulty of Americanizing the newcomers that troubled Wells, for he recognized that this process was fairly easy; it was the difficulty of giving attention to our proper national tasks while we were digesting a raw mass of humanity. The immigrants weakened the ranks of organized labor, they increased the amount of municipal corruption, they complicated

¹ Quotations in this introduction from H. G. Wells's *The Future in America*, copyright 1906, by Harper and Brothers; Arnold Bennett's *Your United States*, copyright 1912, by Harper and Brothers; and W. L. George's *Hail, Columbia*, copyright 1921, by Harper and Brothers, are by permission of the publishers.

the processes of economic and social development, and above all, they retarded the development of a true national consciousness and will. Whether we might not have a duty to help these questing peoples, whether the accession of strength and blood they brought might not repay us for the retarding of our institutional development Wells did not consider.

Compared with Wells, Bennett's *Your United States* is simply an excellent piece of literary photography of our surface aspects. There are vivid descriptive bits in Wells. When he speaks of 'the friendly peering snarl' of Roosevelt's face, 'like a man with the sun in his eyes'; when he says that certain closed Fifth Avenue palaces, with their blinds down, 'conveyed a curious effect of a sunlit child excursionist in a train who falls asleep and droops against his neighbor'; when he speaks of a school as 'a waving froth of flags and flushed faces'— we recognize a genuine literary artist. But as a descriptive volume, Bennett's is superior to any other of the period. He aims at expressing his impressions in broad, sweeping strokes. 'I think of American cities as enormous agglomerations in whose inmost dark recesses innumerable elevators are constantly ascending and descending,' runs a typical sentence. He disposed of the sleeper in a sentence: 'I confess I had not imagined anything so appalling as the confined, stifling, malodorous promiscuity of the American sleeping car, where men and women are herded together on shelves under the drastic control of an official aided by Negroes.' Bennett's travels were bounded, like Wells's, by New York, Boston, Chicago, and Washington. He 'did' the Capitol in thirty minutes, thus revenging himself upon Yankees who had treated Westminster Abbey with similar disrespect; and he saw nothing of the real workings of our universities, nothing of the social and economic processes into which Wells had peered, nothing of rural life. He did well, in ending his book, to say that he would not stand by any view propounded in it. The first tremendous impact of the United States upon a sensitive and discerning man—that was what he attempted to reproduce. With his quick observation, vivid phrase, knack of seeing the dynamic side of life, and intense modernity, he succeeded.

His modernity it was that made him think he had never been in a perfect home until he was entertained in the well-warmed, well-plumbed, well-lighted, well-planned, well-furnished domiciles of wealthy Americans. Modernity intensified his disgust when the world-renowned Limited, which bore him from New York to Chicago, met a series of accidents, and he reached the latter city seventy minutes late. Rapid transit in our great cities was naturally a keen disappointment to him, and he denounced our overcrowded subways and noisy elevated lines in almost the terms used by New Yorkers and Chicagoans. On the other hand, our modern city hotels made him lyrical with praise. Declaring that it had always been his secret ambition to be a hotel manager, he waxed dithyrambic in cataloguing 'the calm orderliness of the bedroom floors, the adequacy of wardrobes and lamps, the reckless profusion of clean linen, that charming notice one finds under one's door in the morning. "You were called at seven-thirty, *and answered,*" the fundamental principle that a bedroom without a bathroom is not a bedroom, the magic laundry, which returns your effects duly starched in eight hours, the bells which are answered immediately, the thickness of the walls, the radiator in the elevator shaft, the celestial invention of the floor clerk,' and other virtues of our hostelries. He found our theaters, unlike those of Europe, really built so that every person in the audience could see the stage. His modernity made him chant the romance of the skyscraper:

> The elevator ejects you. You are taken into dazzling daylight, into what is modestly called a business office; but it resembles in its grandeur no European business office, save such as may have been built by an American. You look forth from a window, and lo! New York and the Hudson are beneath you, and you are in the skies. And in the warmed stillness of the room you hear the wind raging and whistling, as you would have imagined it could only rage and whistle in the rigging of a three-master at sea. There are, however, a dozen more stories above this story. You walk from chamber to chamber, and in answer to inquiry learn that the rent of this one suite—among so many—is over thirty-six thousand dollars a year! And you reflect that, to the beholder in the street, all that is represented by one narrow row of windows, lost in a diminishing chessboard of windows. And you begin to realize what a skyscraper is, and the poetry of it.

Bennett, after a hasty glance at our universities, particularly Columbia and Harvard, suspected that they were too luxurious to be first-rate places for study. Yet on Morningside Heights the sight of a Chinese student tabulating from the world's press, in a modern history laboratory, a record of the globe day by day, gave him a thrill. His chief revolt against an expression of modernism related to the apartment house, which he pictures as an ogre devouring children, income, domesticity, and even initiative and self-reliance—a conception with altogether too much truth in it. He corrected its undue harshness, however, after visiting the Bronx, and seeing the comfortable four-room flat of a wage-earner who could pay only $26 a month, and the seven-room flat, at $45 a month, of a poor doctor who enjoyed 'no end of conveniences—certainly many more than in any flat that I had ever occupied myself!' And if he was dubious as to Harvard, where he saw a mere comic magazine housed in a spacious and costly building that some London newspapers would envy, he was all admiration for elementary education as he saw it exemplified at the Horace Mann School in New York. The palatial structure seemed to have no end, and in each of the scores of classrooms the children were fiercely dragging knowledge out of the communicative teachers with a zest he could not understand. One group was learning geography with the aid of a stereoscopic magic lantern, and when they had examined a view of a Russian village street, the teacher asked those with any questions to stand up. 'And the whole class leaped furiously to its feet, blotting out the entire picture with black shadows of craniums and starched pinafores.' If the dominant impression of America conveyed by Stead is power, and by H. G. Wells is gigantic disorder, that given by Bennett is vitality.

It was as natural for the delineator of the 'Five Towns' to like busy, prosperous, and progressive America as it was for Wells, who saw in it a vast and highly favorable sociological laboratory. There are not many generalizations in Bennett's book, and most of these are negative. He did not find the overwhelming hurry of which he had heard so much, even the New York Stock Exchange being much quieter than the Paris Bourse. He was not asked for his opinions of the United States until he had been here fully a fortnight. The national boasting under which he had expected to be drowned was nowhere in evidence. Neither was the insolence of train boys, policemen, and other public servants. But the few positive generalizations the novelist does advance are favorable, and the most important of these is his conviction that the United States, besides being rich and energetic, is culturally a land of some achievement and more promise. Winslow Homer's water colors were one of the pleasant surprises of his visit, and he longed to collect a trainload of New York, Boston, and Chicago dilettanti and lead them by the ears to the quiet museum in Indianapolis in which these creations were housed. He remarks that this allegedly Philistine nation may well hold up its head when it remembers that it has produced in Poe the one literary artist who has deeply influenced French imaginative writers since Byron; in Whitman one of the world's supreme poets; in Mark Twain the greatest pure humorist of modern times; and in addition, Stanford White, 'the incomparable McKim,' 'the miraculous Henry James,' and 'the only two Anglo-Saxon personalities who in graphic art have been able to impose themselves on modern Europe—Whistler and John Sargent.' Bennett gravely rebukes the superior Europeans who sneer at the ordinary American tourist:

The plausible argument is that the mass of such tourists are inferior in intellect and taste to the general level of Europeans who display curiosity about history or art. Which is probably true. But it ought to be remembered by us Europeans (and in sackcloth!) that the mass of us with money to spend on pleasure are utterly indifferent to history and art. The European dilettante goes to the Uffizi and sees a shopkeeper from Milwaukee gazing ignorantly at a masterpiece, and says: 'How inferior this shopkeeper from Milwaukee is to me! The American is an inartistic race!' But what about the shopkeeper from Huddersfield or Amiens? The shopkeeper from Huddersfield or Amiens will be flirting about on some entirely banal beach—Scarborough or Trouville—and for all he knows or cares Leonardo da Vinci might have been a cabman; and yet the loveliest things in the world are, relatively speaking, at his door! When the European shopkeeper gets as far as Lucerne in August, he thinks that a journey of twenty-four hours entitles him to rank a little lower than Columbus. It was an enormous feat for him to reach Lucerne, and he must have credit for it, though his interest in art is in no wise thereby demonstrated. One has to admit that he now goes to Lucerne in hordes. Praise be to him! But I imagine that the American horde 'hustling for culture' in no matter what historic center will compare pretty favorably with the European horde in such spots as Lucerne.

All general curiosity is, to my mind, righteousness, and I so count it to the American. Not that I think that American curiosity is always the highest form of curiosity, or that it is not limited. With its apparent omnivorousness it is often superficial and too easily satisfied—particularly by mere words. Very seldom is it profound. It is apt to browse agreeably on externals.

Freeman and Arnold, rebuking this vice of superficiality, had tried to believe it more marked in America than England; Arnold Bennett thought it the common fault of both nations, and refused to say in which it appeared the more prominent. The power of thinking things through, the determination to grasp a truth in its entirety, the refusal to blink unpleasant phenomena, 'demands intellectual honesty—a quality which has been denied by Heaven to all Anglo-Saxon races.' But after visiting the Homer room in Indianapolis and the Innes room in the Chicago Art Institute, he refused to believe that America could not foster a vital art.

Chesterton, unlike Bennett, is a writer of many generalizations, which are frequently paradoxical, sometimes unsound, and even when sound are sometimes pushed by his characteristic style into the limits of the fantastic. He brought his sense of humor with him, as he showed when, being asked by the interviewers in New York what he thought had caused the recent 'crime wave' there, he replied that it might be due to the number of British travelers who had recently landed. But above all, he brought his habit of looking for the oblique facets of truth, of standing facts on their heads to find what would drop out of their pockets. He begins his *What I Saw in America,* characteristically, by asserting that travel narrows the mind, a statement in behalf of which much can be said. New York, he pursues, is a cosmopolitan city, but it is not a city of cosmopolitans, another remark possessing much force, since the most alien people in New York are usually the least international in outlook. Replying to those who condemn the electric signs on Broadway as ugly though useful, he declares that they are beautiful but useless. An entire chapter is devoted to the development of the thesis that the Atlantic—the gulf between England and America—is widening, not narrowing. This, explains the ingenious Mr. Chesterton, is because all countries are growing apart from one another, as witness Ireland's separation from England, and Norway's from Sweden; while it is traceable in even greater degree to the deepening of national differences between England and the United States. When he was a boy he read *The Autocrat of the Breakfast Table,* written in an English as pure as Ruskin's, precisely as if it had been an English book; but now that he is a man, he cannot read O. Henry's short stories as if they were English, for the slang, the idiom, the dizzy and involved metaphors are radically different from any English style. So Chesterton pursues his way westward to Nebraska, throwing up a shower of paradoxical sparks all along the way. He had arrived expecting to find the United States a land of skyscrapers, he says, but as soon as he left New York he perceived that it was a land of the very opposite architecture. 'I saw forests upon forests of small houses stretching away to the horizon as literal forests do; villages and towns and cities. And they were, in another sense, literally like forests. They were all made of wood.'

Despite the extremes in generalization into which his passion for saying the unusual led him, Chesterton did light upon some conclusions that are more than half truths. America is really a paradoxical land, and so lent itself to his talent. Our very youth is paradoxical, as Chesterton pointed out when he said that we are youthful both in the sense of being progressive, of using the latest inventions, and in the sense of being primitive, raw, and unformed in certain respects. The perfection of our telephone system is marvelous. On the other hand, there are whole patches and sections of our manners that struck the essayist as quite Early Victorian. 'I cannot help having this sensation, for instance, about the arrangement for smoking in the railway carriages. There are no smoking carriages, as a rule; but a corner of each of the great cars is curtained off mysteriously, that a man may go behind the curtain and smoke. Nobody thinks of a woman doing so. It is regarded as a dark, bohemian, and almost brutally masculine indulgence; exactly as it was regarded by the dowagers in Thackeray's novels.' The illustration here is not quite happy, for we do have smoking cars, and much feminine smoking, but he does point to an undoubted social fact. Again, Chesterton demonstrated his shrewdness when he told English readers that they exaggerate the interest of Americans in European politics; that there are millions upon millions of people in the Middle West who have hardly more concern over Anglo-Irish relations than the Chinese do over the question whether their Ambassador in England shall dine at the Savoy or the Ritz. His explanation of certain differences in the national humor of Great Britain and the United States, while inadequate, does really cast some illumination upon the popular psychology of the two lands:

Suppose an American soldier said to an English soldier in the trenches, 'The Kaiser may want a place in the sun; I reckon he won't have a place in the solar system when we begin to hustle.' The English soldier will very probably form the impression that this is arrogance; an impression based on the extraordinary assumption that the American means what he says. The American has merely indulged in a little art for art's sake, an abstract adventure of the imagination; he has told an American short story. But the Englishman, not understanding this, will think the other man is boasting, and reflecting on the insufficiency of the English effort. The English soldier is very likely to say something like, 'Oh, you'll be wanting to get home to your old woman before that, and asking for a kipper with your tea.' And it is quite likely that the American will be offended in his turn at having his arabesque of abstract beauty answered in so personal a fashion. Being an American, he will probably have a fine and chivalrous respect for his wife; and may object to her being called an old woman. Possibly he in turn may be under the extraordinary delusion that talking of an old woman really means that the woman is old. Possibly he thinks the mysterious demand for a kipper carries with it some charge of ill-treating his wife; which his national sense of honor swiftly resents. But the real cross purposes come from the contrary direction of the two exaggerations, the American making life more wild and impossible than it is, and the Englishman making it more flat and farcical than it is; the one escaping the house of life by a skylight and the other by a trap door.

A score of British and French travelers found on the surface of American life a constant talk about dollars. Arnold Bennett pushed the fact aside with the remark that in all lands men talk of money, and no men more than authors, Balzac's correspondence being fuller of francs than any American stockbroker's is of dollars. Chesterton gets a little below the surface with the discovery that one reason why Americans mention dollars is that they have no false idea of their vulgarity, while another is that they are fond of talking of measurements. Whereas an Englishman will say that philanthropists have given the town a park, the Yankee will say they have given it a park of 300 acres worth $500,000.

The familiar Chestertonian dogmas—his belief in the superiority of medieval to modern life, of the provincial culture to metropolitan culture, of Catholicism to Calvinism, of jollity and good living to austerity—crop out somewhat eccentrically throughout the book. In the Middle West, quite rationally, Chesterton perceived the real strength of the American manhood and character. But this great agricultural section, to a determined medievalist, fell short of the glories of the twelfth century. The farmers grew their own physical food, but for mental and spiritual pabulum, instead of crowning their brows with laurel, devising morality plays, pageants, and fairs, and celebrating saints' days, they went to the movies and read the magazines. In short, they took their culture from the cities. They had no Catholic poetry or piety. An honest member of a Midwestern farm bureau would laugh over the essayist's invitation to return to the position of a medieval peasant, and Chesterton knew it. But for all that, he still preferred Main Street to the great industrial city. 'They have not heard the ancient noise either of arts or arms; the building of the cathedrals or the marching of the crusade. But at least they have not deliberately slandered the crusade and defaced the cathedral. And if they have not produced the peasant arts, they can still produce the peasant crafts.' It is impossible to take Chesterton in this vein seriously except by a total refusal to take him literally. If he means that a growth of distinctive local culture is desirable in every section, we can give him a qualified assent. Puritanism and feminism he treated to as caustic a denunciation as he did industrialism, asserting that a union of these two sinister isms had produced our lamentable addiction to fads and crankiness. As for democracy, he found no ray of hope for its future save 'in a dogma about the divine origin of man,' a statement that would have made Thomas Jefferson speechless with indignation. This leads Chesterton, in a wild *non sequitur,* to declare that 'so far as that democracy becomes or remains Catholic and Christian, that democracy will remain democratic.'

Several of the opinions emphasized by Chesterton were emphasized also by W. L. George, who in most ways—in his aggressive championship of feminism, for example—stood at an opposite pole in outlook. They seem to have thought alike about Prohibition. Chesterton had two reasons for invincible hostility to it. It was a blow at the gaiety of life, and it was also a product of industrialism. 'The real reason behind Prohibition,' he frowningly grumbles, 'is simply the plutocratic power of the pushing employers who wish to get the last inch of work out of their workmen.' Mr. George, though less outspoken, also regretted Prohibition because 'it has done immense damage to conviviality,' and because he felt an atmosphere of hypocrisy hanging about it, as about other manifestations of Puritanism. The first American he asked regarding it, a stranger, replied, 'O, I'm for Prohibition. Can you tell me where I can get a drink?' He chronicles the facts concerning our ineffectual enforcement of the Volstead Act, our wholesale bootlegging, and our consumption of substitutes worse than liquor itself. 'I have come across a number of men who supported Prohibition,' he writes, 'and their cellars were full of liquors.' Nevertheless, all question of his own disapproval apart, he prophesied that in the end Prohibition would triumph:

My own belief is that in the United States of America liquor will practically disappear. Liquor is to a certain extent sustained by the unpalatable nature of the Prohibition drinks; the beer is nothing but a ghost of the real beer; apple cider, loganberry juice, and such like are fit to make a school treat sick. The only good Prohibition drink is water. But the resources of industrial chemistry will by degrees produce the illusion we need. It is the only thing we need in life. Drink itself will go because it is not being given to the young generation. That is not only a question of shame, but a question of supply. As the stocks go down, as enforcement grows more rigid, drink will grow more and more difficult to obtain. The father will naturally keep it for himself, and a vague sort of shame will prevent him from introducing his son to liquor. So the young generation will grow up without it, not wanting what it does not know; by degrees, as the old drinking generation dies out, the only drunkards will be people afflicted by a new kind of depravity, who will drink whiskey as they now snuff cocaine.

Another point of agreement between the two novelists is their liking for the region that Meredith Nicholson has celebrated as the valley of democracy. Mr. George was deeply disappointed by New England. He could not understand the continuing reverence with which the rest of America regarded that ancient seat of culture. Though he did justice to the charming architecture, and though he liked the character of the Yankee farmer, which—showing 'an air of moderation and reserve, tinged with a little suspicion, and informed with a certain kindness'— suggested a Scotch type, he felt that, essentially, the old New England was dying, and a new England rising in industrial smoke. Boston, for example, except for an aloof and exhausted aristocracy, which he amusingly sketches, was now a polyglot city of immigrants. On the basis of the pages devoted to them in the telephone book, he estimated there must be at least 20,000 O'Briens in the city. Gazing in Copley Square at the Italian who retailed grapes from a pushcart, he envisaged him as a triumphant sentinel representing the army of occupation that had captured Boston. The signs of the Common did not say, 'Please Keep Off the Grass,' but 'Keep Off the Grass. If You Want to Roam, Join the Navy.' This, as he reflects, is not at all the way they would have expressed it in the days of Emerson. As a modernist, like Bennett, as one who shared Wells's confidence that industrial change will conquer beauty and ease for all men, whereas the old New England meant beauty and ease for only a few, he did not regret the change—

The spectacle of New England today, and even the spectacle of Boston, with its swarming tenements, its crowds of yelling children, its resounding trolley cars, all this is really sane and splendid and full of promise for a luminous future.

He was merely disappointed by it.

'But to me the Middle West is the true America,' wrote Mr. George. He was dazed by the clash of its trolley cars, blinded by the flame and smoke of its steel furnaces, and overwhelmed by the endless fields of wheat and corn. The Minnesota State Fair, with its palaces of grain, fruit, and livestock, persuaded him that he had found the land of Cockayne where pigs ran about roasted and asking to be eaten. From the cathedrals of America he turned in indifference to find satisfaction in the architectural beauty of the Minneapolis grain elevators, magnificent in their lofty towers, their rounded purity of line, and their spectral whiteness. 'I have seen nothing nobler than these factories of the moon,' he testifies. Crime itself comported with the scale of the land, and he learned with a sense of fitness that 3000 automobiles had been stolen in Chicago in eight months. The conviction that ambition was inevitable in America, for the nation contained food for ambition on every hand, grew upon him when he visited Tulsa. Twenty years earlier there had been no Tulsa; now it contained 72,000 people. Four years earlier the old frontier lawlessness had so persisted that it had been necessary to put an armed guard by the cash box of one of the big saloons. Now the head of the Exchange National Bank, located in a building of fifteen stories, lamented to Mr. George that though he had reserved a certain space for expansion, the bank had outgrown it in six months. A combination of natural wealth and hard work was making the Middle West:

They do work enormously hard. For instance, in Tulsa, Oklahoma, the trolley cars which make for the business district are almost empty at 8:30 A.M. By that time nearly everybody is at work. And, at Chicago, I was interested by a big business building opposite my hotel, when I noticed that at nine o'clock in the evening many of the offices were still tenanted. I began to watch that building. At nine o'clock work was going on in thirty-eight offices; at 10:15 P.M. there was energy still in ten; at 11:35 P.M. three offices were preparing to break into the next day. I don't know what happened next, for I went to bed; I am not from Chicago.

In Chicago work is dramatic; its spirit is impressive; I cannot ignore a picture postcard I bought there; it bears merely these words, 'Experience is a dead loss if you can't sell it for more than it cost you.' A variation of an immortal truth . . . which may shock some gentle souls. Well, it doesn't shock me. I like the extremism of it, just as I like the massive place where this sentiment circulates. I like Chicago, I like the colossal lines of its point of view, its religion of utility, its gospel of fitness, just as I like its streets, its attempt on South Michigan Boulevard to force even the lakeside into straight lines.

Vitality, modernity—these had emerged from Arnold Bennett's book as the salient traits of American life, and they emerged again from Mr. George's, but with a third added; for he insisted that our pioneer spirit counted powerfully. Our vitality made us take the arts so seriously. He commented on the solidity of the Western bookshops, displaying the works of Galsworthy, Conrad, Clemence Dane, Chesterton, and many books on democratic and sociological questions. Our vitality made us fill our press with screaming headlines like 'Ruth Up—Oh, Babe! She's a Ball Player!' It accounted for our lyricism over business, the romance and dignity of which we were always chanting. It helped explain the lavish magnificence of American hospitality.

We are not accustomed to being shown a house in detail—the labor-saving appliances at work; told the story of the pieces of furniture, of the pictures. The Americans are never weary of this, because their vitality is enormous. It is not only nerves which permit them to do so many things in a single day; it is not only their magnificent climate, which is bright and bracing like champagne; it is the rude strength of a race not yet sophisticated; it is the hunger for impressions of a race just entering into possession of its powers.

The same vitality stamps our amusements, like golf and dancing. It and the pioneer spirit together impel the American to develop his natural wealth with an extraordinary intensity, an intensity that Bryce decades before had deplored.

In Mr. George's book, however, alongside an enthusiasm like Arnold Bennett's, we return to a criticism almost as severe and searching as that of H. G. Wells. It is not concerned with such large problems as Wells confronted, and it does not propound any remedy so comprehensive as Wells asked in his demand for state-mindedness. But Mr. George finds fault with our national restlessness, our tendency to excess, and our self-consciousness. Americans were proud of their country, but he was glad to see that they made reservations. 'Many of them will criticize America in a temperate spirit, and, more and more, I suspect, the educated American is reacting against certain features of American civilization, such as haste and noise.' After our hectic rush, he was glad to return to the repose of England. Also, like almost all Englishmen since Washington's day, he disliked our children, forming an impression that they were hard, sophisticated, and spoiled. The hard child was a natural product of the hard home, which he thought characteristic of America. In his remarks upon our hearthstones, in fact, a very distinct British prejudices appears.

They felt bare, untenanted; they were too neat, too new; they indicated that the restaurant, the theatre, the cinema, were often visited; one missed the comfortable accumulation of broken screens, old fire irons, and seven-year-old volumes of the *London Illustrated News*, which make up the dusty, frowsy feeling of home. The American home is not a place where one lives, but a place where one merely sleeps, eats, sits, works. You will say that makes up home life, but it does not; there is something else, which can arise only out of a compound of dulness, boiled mutton, an ill-cut lawn, a dog, a cat, and some mice to keep the cat amused.

This is doing less—or more—than justice to the American middle-class habitation.

But the chief and most amazing accusation Mr. George brought against us, an accusation no other Briton had ever made, was that we mistreat our women! In the city, where the servant problem defied solution, he found the housewife terribly overworked. She was sur-rendering, so he imagined, intellectual interests that had been hers before the war. She was giving up children. But the position of the housewife he thought much worse on American farms, 'where she is sacrificed to the financial ambitions of her husband.' Mr. George cites a horrifying little play on the subject, and refers to a short story in a woman's magazine about a farmer's wife who had inherited $600, and meant, for the first time in her life, to buy the family some Christ-mas gifts, when her husband appropriated the money to purchase six tombstones. Such evidence is worth little, but Mr. George might have found an inexhaustible mass of perfectly valid testimony. Though the lot of the American woman—particularly the farm woman—has im-mensely improved in the last few years, there is yet room for more improvement, Mr. George's opinion that we must look to machinery to effect it is sound. After the long succession of British visitors who exclaimed over our gallantry to women and our habit of heaping lux-uries upon their heads, it is well to have one critic point to the ob-verse of the shield. Yet the novelist remains friendly even when he is criticizing. He praises our courts and prison systems more than they deserve, and he concludes his volume with the remark that 'America is a great country for a young man to get born in.'

Thus we come to the end of this list of travelers. Much might be said of still other books—of the volume by John Ayscough (Monsignor Drew), which is of special interest to Catholics; of Mrs. Asquith's and Clare Sheridan's bundles of hasty impressions, the latter teeming with personalities; of Stephen Graham's volume on the South, a happy descriptive chronicle of a tramp through a section that later travelers have too much neglected, and which both he and W. L. George found charming in its contentment, leisure, and quiet; of Dr. A. E. Shipley's survey of some American universities; and of Lord Birkenhead's rapid sketch of wartime America. Despite the forbidding bulk of America and the complexity of American civilization, the stream of English volumes appraising some aspect or aspects of both seems to grow larger, not smaller. It is seldom now that a Briton who is a complete stranger to us, as were so many travelers before the Civil War, essays a volume on American life; most of them are written by men and women whose names are sufficiently well known to command a ready hearing. Volumes of travel, too, are of late years more freqquently than of old the product of a lecture tour. A higher proportion than formerly are narrow in scope and superficial in content, but there remain a reassuring number that are neither.

Taken all in all, these British travels are an indispensable source of information upon American social, economic, and political history. The books that the Americans themselves have produced in the same field, such as Olmsted's invaluable records of travel in the South before the Civil War, are few and far between. An American can seldom view the culture of even another section than that in which he was reared with sufficient detachment to write a first-rate study of institutions and manners. Men, customs, and ways of thought and action have not the shock of novelty that will inspire a vivid description, or will suggest questions that lead to a penetrating analysis. An Englishman is just enough of a stranger to see us with a fresh and curious eye, eager for every new impression; he is not enough of an alien, as most Continental Europeans are, to confuse nonessentials with essentials, or to mistake the meaning of what he sees. Simply as works or travel, books like those of Basil Hall, Dickens, Mackay, Anthony Trollope, and Muirhead, and Arnold Bennett have a recognized literary position; but to us they are much more—they are among the most vital records of our national past.

The War-torn South [1] &

DAVID MACRAE, *who was born in 1837 and died in 1907, was a Scottish minister and missionary, a graduate of the University of Glasgow, and well known as a writer and scholar. He was a friend of George Gilfillan, the critic, of Professor John Stuart Blackie, and of other Scotchmen of letters. He toured the United States in 1867-8, describing his experiences in two volumes,* The Americans at Home; *and shortly before his death he returned, his* America Revisited *and* Men I Have Met, *which includes reminiscences of his more eminent*

[1] From *The Americans at Home,* Edinburgh, 1870, volume 1, chapters 20 and 30.

Scotch friends, being posthumously published. The second work is much slighter and less important than the first. In both the emphasis falls upon pictures of Southern life. In 1867-8 Macrae went south from Washington through Virginia, where he talked with many Confederate officers, to North Carolina, where he visited the Highland settlement. He inspected Charleston, and traversed part of the trail of ruin that Sherman had left from Atlanta to Savannah, proceeding to New Orleans and thence northward up the Mississippi. Among the noteworthy figures with whom he reports interviews were Ben Butler and Admiral Semmes.

The best of the Northern chapters in Americans at Home *describes a visit to Boston and Cambridge. Macrae visited Longfellow in his home and dined informally there. The poet, he says, 'looked older and more venerable than I had expected to find him—his long clustering hair and shaggy beard white as snow. I was struck, too, with a look of latent sadness in his eyes—an expression that vanishes at times when he is moved to laughter, but steals back into the thoughtful eye, and into every line of the face, as soon as the passing thought is gone.' Lowell impressed him less. He saw Lowell in his Harvard classroom, an undersized man, smartly dressed in a plain shooting coat and speckled tie, his long curly brown hair parted in the middle, lecturing to an attentive class. 'Enlivening his lecture with little sparkling bits of fun . . . he went on for nearly an hour, in quiet, easy style, rarely looking up from his manuscript; his hands looped behind his back, or fingering the edges of his desk, raising the lid half an inch and letting it softly down again. At the comical bits there was a "pawky" look in his face and comical twinkle of the eye, as if he were enjoying the fun just as much as we.'*

The traveler also attended the opening lecture of Holmes's medical course at Harvard, an occasion that drew distinguished visitors. Agassiz was there, and Macrae was delighted to meet Emerson. 'He has the queerest New England face, with thin features, prominent hatchet nose, and a smile of childish sweetness and simplicity arching the face, and drawing deep curves down the cheek. Eyes, too, full of sparkling geniality, and yet in a moment turning cold, clear, and searching like the eyes of a god.' As Emerson listened to Holmes's discourse, Macrae marked 'that queer smile of his effervescing at every joke into a silent laugh, that runs up into his eyes and quivers at the corners of his eyebrows, like sunlight in the woods.' The lecture pleased everyone. 'Holmes is a plain little dapper man, his short hair brushed down like a boy's, but turning gray now; a trifle of furzy hair under his ears; a powerful jaw, and a thick strong under lip that gives decision to his look, with a dash of pertness. In conversation, he is animated and cordial, taking the word out of one's mouth. When Mr. Fields said, "I sent the boy this—" "Yes, I got them," said Holmes.' He read his lecture with the aid of eyeglasses. 'The little man, in his dress coat, stands very straight, a little stiff about the neck, as if he feels that he cannot afford to lose anything of his stature. He reads with a sharp, percussive articulation, is very deliberate and formal at first, but becomes more animated as he goes on. He would even gesticulate if the desk were not so high, for you see the arm that lies on the desk giving nervous quivers at emphatic points. The subject of his lecture is the spirit in which medical students should go into their work—now as students, afterwards as practitioners. He warns them against looking on it as a mere lucrative employment. 'Don't be like the man who said, 'I suppose I must go earn that d—d guinea.' " He enlivens his lecture with numerous jokes and bullet sallies of wit, and at every point hitches up his head, looks through his glasses at his audience as he finishes his sentence, and then shuts his mouth pertly with his under lip, as if he said, "There, laugh at that!" '

Macrae's observations were frankly superficial, but his Scotch shrewdness, his thorough education, and his entertaining style make his book one of the best of its kind bearing on the period of Reconstruction. In these selections three useless footnotes are omitted.

ROBERT E. LEE AS COLLEGE PRESIDENT

AT the time of my visit the attendance of students had increased to four hundred. About a third of these were Virginians; but twenty other states (including Massachusetts) were represented. Many of the students lodge in the college buildings, furnishing their own rooms, and feeding in town; the rest lodge and board in private families.

General Lee's business as president is not to teach but to exercise a general supervision. He is ex-officio chairman of the faculty, presides at examinations, confers all degrees, and distributes premiums. He receives weekly reports of the standing and deportment of every student, and visits the classrooms from time to time, that he may judge for himself of their diligence and behaviour. The professors, such of them at least as I had the opportunity of conversing with, said that Lee's influence upon the whole college had been very marked. He had diffused a Christian spirit, and made discipline easy. It was one of Lee's duties, as president, to admonish defaulters; and one of the professors declared that, such was the profound veneration in which he was held throughout the South, that he believed there were students in the college who would rather shoot themselves than appear before Lee in disgrace.

My first meeting with Lee was in the room reserved for the use of the college president, where he is occupied for the greater part of the day in writing. He was dressed in one of his old military coats, stripped of all its former decorations. He is a noble-looking man, tall, straight, and soldier-like, with crisp hair turning white, short trimmed beard, pointed at the chin, and dark imperial-looking eyes, very keen and searching. His manners were quiet and dignified; and there is a good deal of the old English cavalier in his look and bearing. I was struck, sometimes painfully, with what seemed a hidden sadness in his countenance. It might have been my own thought, but it seemed to me as if the shadow of the past were over him, as if one could read behind the vigilance of his dark eyes the fate of the South, and of the myriads who lay sleeping on the silent battlefields.

I knew from report that Lee was reticent on political subjects, and wisely so, his position in the country since the war demanding the utmost prudence. I, therefore, made no attempts during the interviews I had with him to 'draw him out'; at the same time I spoke freely on all subjects that came naturally in the way. Political topics were, therefore, referred to; but Lee was on his guard, and I could not but notice the admirable delicacy and tact with which, as often as the conversation threatened to become political, he contrived to turn it into another channel.

At his home I met some of the professors, and conversation went on briskly; but I noticed that whenever they introduced political topics, Lee became silent, and allowed the conversation to go on without him.

One of his sons told me that his father's answer to direct inquiries on vexed questions was that he was a soldier, not a politician. In speaking of the war, reference was made to the odds against which the South had fought, and the want there was of accurate statistics. I told Lee it was understood he was preparing a history of the conflict himself.

'I have that in view,' he said, 'but the time is not come for impartial history. If the truth were told just now, it would not be credited.'

When I mentioned a book about the war, the proof sheets of which, it was asserted, had been submitted to General Grant and himself for revision, he said,—

'It is a mistake. I have never read a history of the war, nor the biography of any man engaged in it. My own life has been written, but I have not looked into it.' He added, after a pause, 'I do not desire to awaken memories of the past.'

Speaking of Lexington and its neighbourhood, he said,—

'You will meet with many of your countrymen here. The valley of

Virginia is peopled with Scotch-Irish—people who have come from Scotland by way of Ireland. They are a fine race. They have the courage and determination of the Scotch, with the dash and intrepidity of the Irish. They make fine soldiers.'

He said it was an old wish of his to visit this country, but it would never be realized now. Stonewall Jackson had been in Scotland before the war. He had heard him speak of it.

When he spoke of Jackson I was struck with the emphasis he placed upon his piety. One cannot indeed be long with Lee without finding his Christian character revealing itself almost unconsciously in his manners and conversation. I remember with peculiar distinctness the solemnity with which, at table, standing before his family, he asked God's blessing on the food. Also, when he referred to a gentleman whom he wished me to see at Richmond, his saying that he had rarely met 'with a nobler or more Christian man.' It was only a word, and yet it showed by what standard he gauged a man's worth.

EXHAUSTION OF THE SOUTH

I was struck with a remark made by a Southern gentleman in answer to the assertion that Jefferson Davis had culpably continued the war for six months after all hope had been abandoned.

'Sir,' he said, 'Mr. Davis knew the temper of the South as well as any man in it. He knew if there was ever to be anything worth calling peace, the South must win; or, if she couldn't win, she wanted to be whipped—well whipped—thoroughly whipped.'

I was struck with another remark made by a prominent man in the North. 'God Almighty,' he said, 'has ploughed up the South—ploughed it up with a deep plough from Mason and Dixon's line to the Gulf of Mexico. The people that were on top are now below, and the people who were below are now uppermost. And God has done it, sir, to prepare the South for a new creation.'

The further south I went, the oftener these remarks came back upon me. Evidence was everywhere that the South had maintained the desperate conflict until she was utterly exhausted. At its outbreak she had poured her best men into the field. When these began to fail she supplied their places with the next best. When she could not find men enough within the military age, she sent old men who were above and boys who were below it, till, as Grant said, she robbed the cradle and the grave to fill her depleted ranks. They told me at Petersburg that in the last year of war little boys had to be brought from the Military Academy to drill the recruits, so imperative a necessity was there for every grown soldier at the front. Almost every man I met at the South, and especially in North Carolina, Georgia, and Virginia, seemed to have been in the army; and it was painful to find how many even of those who had returned were mutilated, maimed, or broken in health by exposure. When I remarked this to a young Confederate officer in North Carolina, and said I was glad to see that *he* had escaped unhurt, he said, 'Wait till we get to the office, sir, and I will tell you more about that.' When we got there, he pulled up one leg of his trousers, and showed me that he had an iron rod there to strengthen his limb, and enable him to walk without limping, half of his foot being off. He showed me on the other leg a deep scar made by the fragment of a shell; and these were but two of seven wounds which had left their marks upon his body. When he heard me speak of relics, he said, 'Try and find a North Carolina gentleman without a Yankee mark on him.'

The South had not only wasted her population but her material resources. I visited districts where the people had not only gone on paying the ruinous war tax, but had dug up every potato in their fields, pulled every apple from their orchards, taken even the blankets from their beds to make up and send to the famishing army. In Mobile I met a brave little Southern girl who had gone barefooted the last year of the war, that the money intended for her shoes might go to the poor soldier.

When medicines could no longer be sucked into the South through the rigorous blockade, the Confederate Government called upon the women and children, who went out into the woods and swamps and gathered horehound, boneset, wild cherry bark, dogwood, and everything that could help to supply the want. When there was a danger of any place falling into the hands of the enemy, the people, with unflinching hand, dragged out their last stores of cotton, tobacco, and turpentine, and consigned them to the flames. Wade Hampton of South Carolina, when Sherman was advancing on Columbia, set fire to four thousand bales of cotton that belonged to himself. The people said, 'We did it all, thinking the South would win. . .'

Nearly three years had passed when I travelled through the country, and yet we have seen what traces the war had left in such cities as Richmond, Petersburg, and Columbia. The same spectacle met me at Charleston. Churches and houses had been battered down by heavy shot and shell hurled into the city from Federal batteries at a distance of five miles. Even the valley of desolation made by a great fire in 1861, through the very heart of the city, remained unbuilt. There, after the lapse of seven years, stood the blackened ruins of streets and houses waiting for the coming of a better day. The bank capital in the city, which stood formerly at fifteen millions of dollars, had fallen to five hundred thousand. The Battery Promenade, where two or three hundred gay equipages could have been counted before the war, was almost deserted. 'People have to content themselves now with a ten-cent ride in a streetcar,' said a friend. Over the country districts the prostration was equally marked. Along the track of Sherman's army especially, the devastation was fearful—farms laid waste, fences burned, bridges destroyed, houses left in ruins, plantations in some cases turning into wildernesses again.

The people had shared in the general wreck, and looked poverty-stricken, careworn, and dejected. Ladies who before the war had lived in affluence, with black servants round them to attend to their every wish, were boarding together now in half-furnished houses, cooking their own food and washing their own linen, some of them, I was told, so utterly destitute that they did not know when they finished one meal where they were to find the next. . .

Although three years had passed since the final crash, I found the old aristocracy still in the dust, with less and less hope of ever recovering its old position. Men who had held commanding positions during the war had fallen out of sight and were filling humble situations—struggling, many of them, to earn a bare subsistence. One of the most prominent men of the Confederacy was trying to earn a living in the peanut business; a cavalry commander was keeping a boarding-school. One of Beauregard's staff officers was teaching a small day school. Other officers were keeping stores, editing little newspapers, acting as clerks, and even as farm labourers in the pay of others. I remember dining with three cultured Southern gentlemen, one a general, the other, I think, a captain, and the third a lieutenant. They were all living together in a plain little wooden house, such as they would formerly have provided for their servants. Two of them were engaged in a railway office, the third was seeking for a situation, frequently, in his vain search, passing the large blinded house where he had lived in luxurious ease before the war.

The old planters were, many of them, going about with ruin written on their faces, some of them so poor that they were trying to sell a portion of their land in order to pay the tax upon the rest. One of them, who showed me much kindness, was living in a corner of a huge house which had once been the home of gaiety and princely hospitality. It was all dismantled now and shut up, excepting three rooms below, where its owner was living in seclusion. Others had shut up their houses altogether and gone to live in lodgings.

Estimate of American Tendencies, 1882 [1] &~

HERBERT SPENCER. *Spencer's visit to America in the autumn of 1882 was a curious episode in the life of the great thinker. He came strictly incognito to the land that had offered the first full recognition of his genius and had tendered his views their greatest measure of support. A crowd of hungry reporters was waiting for him, and their chagrin when—pleading his precarious health as a reason—he eluded them, was intense. On landing, he got out of their sight so rapidly that the newspapers simultaneously chronicled 'Mr. Spencer's arrival and disappearance.' Equally great was the chagrin of a number of people of prominence who had hoped to fête him. He registered at all hotels as 'Mr. Lott's friend.' Many amusing stories are told of the fabrications of the press concerning him. One reporter wrote that he was accustomed to carry with him a bag of hops, 'which when placed under his head has a soporific effect,' and that he had arrived at his hotel carrying the hop bag under his arm. Another declared that 'he subsists entirely on dry toast and sardines.'*

To set at rest the many misstatements of the excluded interviewers, Spencer finally allowed Professor Youmans, who had promoted the subscription sale of his works in America, and who in 1866, at a moment when the philosopher was at the end of his resources, had collected $7000 in this country and invested it in Spencer's name, to interview him. This interview, which is here reproduced entire, made a profound impression. E. L. Godkin used it in the Evening Post *as the text for one of his happiest bits of social analysis. The New York* Tribune *described it as one of the profoundest studies of American life ever made.*

The single speech delivered by Spencer in America was also a curious event. A banquet was tendered him at Delmonico's, where eulogies were delivered by H. W. Beecher and others. Spencer regarded the occasion as a terrific ordeal, which indeed it was to a man of his nervous maladies. He prepared himself with scrupulous care, waited in a quiet room till the last possible moment before the banquet, and begged his neighbor at table to refrain from talking to him. The de-

[1] From *Essays, Scientific, Political, and Speculative*, New York, 1914, volume III, pp. 471-80, 481ff. Copyright 1883 by D. Appleton and Company and reprinted by permission.

livery of his address was of course indifferent, but it was heard and read with the closest attention.

AN INTERVIEW WITH DR. YOUMANS

Has what you have seen answered your expectations?

It has far exceeded them. Such books about America as I had looked into had given me no adequate idea of the immense developments of material civilization which I have everywhere found. The extent, wealth, and magnificence of your cities, and especially the splendor of New York, have altogether astonished me. Though I have not visited the wonder of the West, Chicago, yet some of your minor modern places, such as Cleveland, have sufficiently amazed me by the results of one generation's activity. Occasionally, when I have been in places of some ten thousand inhabitants where the telephone is in general use, I have felt somewhat ashamed of our own unenterprising towns, many of which, of fifty thousand inhabitants and more, make no use of it.

I suppose you recognize in these results the great benefits of free institutions?

Ah! Now comes one of the inconveniences of interviewing. I have been in the country less than two months, have seen but a relatively small part of it, and but comparatively few people, and yet you wish from me a definite opinion on a difficult question.

Perhaps you will answer, subject to the qualification that you are but giving your first impressions?

Well, with that understanding, I may reply that though the free institutions have been partly the cause, I think they have not been the chief cause. In the first place, the American people have come into possession of an unparalleled fortune—the mineral wealth and the vast tracts of virgin soil producing abundantly with small cost of culture. Manifestly, that alone goes a long way towards producing this enormous prosperity. Then they have profited by inheriting all the arts, appliances, and methods developed by older societies, while leaving behind the obstructions existing in them. They have been able to pick and choose from the products of all past experience, appropriating the good and rejecting the bad. Then, besides these favors of fortune, there are factors proper to themselves. I perceive in American faces generally a great amount of determination—a kind of 'do or die' expression; and this trait of character, joined with a power of work exceeding that of any other people, of course produces an unparalleled rapidity of progress. Once more, there is the inventiveness which, stimulated by the need for economizing labor, has been so wisely fostered. Among us in England, there are many foolish people who, while thinking that a man who toils with his hands has an equitable claim to the product, and if he has any special skill may rightly have the advantage of it, also hold that if a man toils with his brain, perhaps for years, and, uniting genius with perseverance, evolves some valuable invention, the public may rightly claim the benefit. The Americans have been more far-seeing. The enormous museum of patents which I saw at Washington is significant of the attention paid to inventors' claims; and the nation profits immensely from having in this direction (though not in all others) recognized property in mental products. Beyond question, in respect of mechanical appliances, the Americans are ahead of all nations. If along with your material progress there went equal progress of a higher kind, there would remain nothing to be wished.

That is an ambiguous qualification. What do you mean by it?

You will understand me when I tell you what I was thinking the other day. After pondering over what I have seen of your vast manufacturing and trading establishments, the rush of traffic in your streetcars and elevated railways, your gigantic hotels and Fifth Avenue palaces, I was suddenly reminded of the Italian republics of the Middle Ages; and recalled the fact that while there was growing up in them great commercial activity, a development of the arts, which made them the envy of Europe, and a building of princely mansions, which continue to be the admiration of travelers, their people were gradually losing their freedom.

Do you mean this as a suggestion that we are doing the like?

It seems to me that you are. You retain the forms of freedom; but, so far as I can gather, there has been a considerable loss of the substance. It is true that those who rule you do not do it by means of retainers armed with swords; but they do it through regiments of men armed with voting papers who obey the word of command as loyally as did the dependents of the old feudal nobles, and who thus enable their leaders to override the general will and make the community submit to their exactions as effectually as their prototypes of old. It is doubtless true that each of your citizens votes for the candidate he chooses for this or that office, from President downwards; but his hand is guided by an agency behind which leaves him scarcely any choice. 'Use your political power as we tell you, or else throw it away,' is the alternative offered to the citizen. The political machinery as it is now worked has little resemblance to that contemplated at the outset of your political life. Manifestly, those who framed your

Constitution never dreamed that twenty thousand citizens would go
to the poll led by a 'boss.' America exemplifies at the other end of
the social scale a change analogous to that which has taken place
under sundry despotisms. You know that in Japan, before the recent
revolution, the divine ruler, the Mikado, nominally supreme, was
practically a puppet in the hands of his chief minister, the Shogun.
Here it seems to me that 'the sovereign people' is fast becoming a
puppet which moves and speaks as wire-pullers determine.

Then you think that republican institutions are a failure?

By no means: I imply no such conclusion. Thirty years ago, when
often discussing politics with an English friend and defending republican institutions, as I always have done and do still, and when
he urged against me the ill-working of such institutions over here,
I habitually replied that the Americans got their form of government
by a happy accident, not by normal progress, and that they would
have to go back before they could go forward. What has since happened seems to me to have justified that view; and what I see now
confirms me in it. America is showing, on a larger scale than ever
before, that 'paper constitutions' will not work as they are intended
to work. The truth, first recognized by Mackintosh, that constitutions
are not made but grow, which is part of the larger truth that societies,
throughout their whole organizations, are not made but grow, at
once, when accepted, disposes of the notion that you can work as you
hope any artificially devised system of government. It becomes an
inference that if your political structure has been manufactured and
not grown, it will forthwith begin to grow into something different
from that intended—something in harmony with the natures of the
citizens and the conditions under which the society exists. And it
evidently has been so with you. Within the forms of your Constitution
there has grown up this organization of professional politicians altogether uncontemplated at the outset, which has become in large
measure the ruling power.

But will not education and the diffusion of political knowledge
fit men for free institutions?

No. It is essentially a question of character, and only in a secondary
degree a question of knowledge. But for the universal delusion about
education as a panacea for political evils, this would have been made
sufficiently clear by the evidence daily disclosed in your papers. Are
not the men who officer and control your federal, your state, and your
municipal organizations—who manipulate your caucuses and conven-
tions, and run your partisan campaigns—all educated men? And has
their education prevented them from engaging in, or permitting, or
condoning the briberies, lobbyings, and other corrupt methods which

vitiate the actions of your administrations? Perhaps party newspapers exaggerate these things; but what am I to make of the testimony of your civil service reformers—men of all parties? If I understand the matter aright, they are attacking, as vicious and dangerous, a system which has grown under the natural spontaneous working of your free institutions—are exposing vices which education has proved powerless to prevent?

Of course, ambitious and unscrupulous men will secure the offices, and education will aid them in their selfish purposes. But would not those purposes be thwarted and better government secured by raising the standard of knowledge among the people at large?

Very little. The current theory is that if the young are taught what is right, and the reasons why it is right, they will do what is right when they grow up. But considering what religious teachers have been doing these two thousand years, it seems to me that all history is against the conclusion, as much as is the conduct of these well-educated citizens I have referred to; and I do not see why you expect better results among the masses. Personal interest will sway the men in the ranks, as they sway the men above them; and the education which fails to make the last consult public good rather than private good will fail to make the first do it. The benefits of political purity are so general and remote, and the profit to each individual is so inconspicuous, that the common citizen, educate him as you like, will habitually occupy himself with his personal affairs, and hold it not worth his while to fight against each abuse as soon as it appears. Not lack of information, but lack of certain moral sentiment is the root of the evil.

You mean that people have not a sufficient sense of public duty?

Well, that is one way of putting it; but there is a more specific way. Probably it will surprise you if I say the American has not, I think, a sufficiently quick sense of his own claims, and, at the same time, as a necessary consequence, not a sufficiently quick sense of the claims of others—for the two traits are organically related. I observe that they tolerate various small interferences and dictations, which Englishmen are prone to resist. I am told that the English are remarked on for their tendency to grumble in such cases; and I have no doubt it is true.

Do you think it worth while for people to make themselves disagreeable by resenting every trifling aggression? We Americans think it involves too much loss of time and temper, and doesn't pay.

Exactly; that is what I mean by character. It is this easy-going readiness to permit small trespasses, because it would be troublesome or profitless or unpopular to oppose them, which leads to the habit of acquiescence in wrong, and the decay of free institutions. Free institutions can be maintained only by citizens, each of whom is instant to oppose every illegitimate act, every assumption of supremacy, every official excess of power, however trivial it may seem. As Hamlet says, there is such a thing as 'greatly to find quarrel in a straw,' when the straw implies a principle. If, as you say of the American, he pauses to consider whether he can afford the time and trouble—whether it will pay, corruption is sure to creep in. All these lapses from higher to lower forms begin in trifling ways, and it is only by incessant watchfulness that they can be prevented. As one of your early statesmen said—'The price of liberty is eternal vigilance.' But it is far less against foreign aggressions upon national liberty that this vigilance is required than against the insidious growth of domestic interferences with personal liberty. In some private administrations which I have been concerned with, I have often insisted that instead of assuming, as people usually do, that things are going right until it is proved that they are going wrong, the proper course is to assume that they are going wrong until it is proved that they are going right. You will find continually that private corporations, such as joint-stock banking companies, come to grief from not acting on this principle; and what holds of these small and simple private administrations holds still more of the great and complex public administrations. People are taught, and, I suppose, believe, that the heart of man 'is deceitful above all things, and desperately wicked'; and yet, strangely enough, believing this, they place implicit trust in those they appoint to this or that function. I do not think so ill of human nature; but, on the other hand, I do not think so well of human nature as to believe it will go straight without being watched.

You hinted that while Americans do not assert their own individualities sufficiently in small matters, they, reciprocally, do not sufficiently respect the individualities of others.

Did I? Here, then, comes another of the inconveniences of interviewing. I should have kept this opinion to myself if you had asked me no questions; and now I must either say what I do not think, which I cannot, or I must refuse to answer, which, perhaps, will be taken to mean more than I intend, or I must specify, at the risk of giving offense. As the least evil, I suppose I must do the last. The trait I refer to comes out in various ways, small and great. It is shown by the disrespectful manner in which individuals are dealt with in your journals—the placarding of public men in sensational headings, the dragging of private people and their affairs into print. There seems to be a notion that the public have a right to intrude on private life as far as they like; and this I take to be a kind of moral trespassing.

Then, in a larger way, the trait is seen in this damaging of private property by your elevated railways without making compensation; and it is again seen in the doings of railway autocrats, not only when overriding the rights of shareholders, but in dominating over courts of justice and state governments. The fact is that free institutions can be properly worked only by men, each of whom is jealous of his own rights, and also sympathetically jealous of the rights of others—who will neither himself aggress on his neighbors in small things or great, nor tolerate aggression on them by others. The republican form of government is the highest form of government; but because of this it requires the highest type of human nature—a type nowhere at present existing. We have not grown up to it; or have you.

But we thought, Mr. Spencer, you were in favor of free government in the sense of relaxed restraints, and letting men and things very much alone, or what is called *laissez faire*.

That is a persistent misunderstanding of my opponents. Everywhere, along with the reprobation of government intrusion into various spheres where private activities should be left to themselves, I have contended that, in its special sphere, the maintenance of equitable relations among citizens, governmental action should be extended and elaborated.

To return to your various criticisms, must I then understand that you think unfavorably of our future?

No one can form anything more than vague and general conclusions respecting your future. The factors are too numerous, too vast, too far beyond measure in their quantities and intensities. The world has never before seen social phenomena at all comparable with those presented in the United States. A society spreading over enormous tracts, while still preserving its political continuity, is a new thing. This progressive incorporation of vast bodies of immigrants of various bloods has never occurred on such a scale before. Large empires, composed of different peoples, have, in previous cases, been formed by conquest and annexation. Then your immense plexus of railways and telegraphs tends to consolidate this vast aggregate of states in a way that no such aggregate has ever before been consolidated. And there are many minor co-operating causes, unlike those hitherto known. No one can say how it is all going to work out. That there will come hereafter troubles of various kinds, and very grave ones, seems highly probable; but all nations have had, and will have, their troubles. Already you have triumphed over one great trouble, and may reasonably hope to triumph over others. It may, I think, be concluded that, both because of its size and the heterogeneity of its components, the American nation will be a long time in evolving its ultimate form, but that its ultimate form will be high. One great result is, I think, tolerably clear. From biological truths it is to be inferred that the eventual mixture of the allied varieties of the Aryan race forming the population will produce a finer type of man than has hitherto existed; and a type of man more plastic, more adaptable, more capable of undergoing the modifications needful for complete social life. I think that whatever difficulties they may have to surmount, and whatever tribulations they may have to pass through, the Americans may reasonably look forward to a time when they will have produced a civilization grander than any the world has known.

FROM SPENCER'S NEW YORK SPEECH

Already, in some remarks drawn from me respecting American affairs and American character, I have passed criticisms, which have been accepted far more good-humoredly than I could have reasonably expected; and it seems strange that I should now propose again to transgress. However, the fault I have now to comment upon is one which most will scarcely regard as a fault. It seems to me that in one respect Americans have diverged too widely from savages. I do not mean to say that they are in general unduly civilized. Throughout large parts of the population, even in long-settled regions, there is no excess of those virtues needed for the maintenance of social harmony. Especially out in the West, men's dealings do not yet betray too much of the 'sweetness and light' which we are told distinguish the cultured man from the barbarian. Nevertheless, there is a sense in which my assertion is true. You know that the primitive man lacks power of application. Spurred by hunger, by danger, by revenge, he can exert himself energetically for a time; but his energy is spasmodic. Monotonous daily toil is impossible to him. It is otherwise with the more developed man. The stern discipline of social life has gradually increased the aptitude for persistent industry; until, among us, and still more among you, work has become with many a passion. This contrast of nature has another aspect. The savage thinks only of present satisfactions, and leaves future satisfactions uncared for. Contrariwise, the American, eagerly pursuing a future good, almost ignores what good the passing day offers him; and when the future good is gained, he neglects that while striving for some still remoter good.

What I have seen and heard during my stay among you has forced on me the belief that this slow change from habitual inertness to persistent activity has reached an extreme from which there must begin a counterchange—a reaction. Everywhere I have been struck with the number of faces which told in strong lines of the burdens that had to be borne. I have been struck, too, with the large proportion of gray-haired men; and inquiries have brought out the fact that with you the hair commonly begins to turn some ten years earlier than with us. Moreover, in every circle I have met men who had themselves suffered from nervous collapse due to stress of business, or named friends who had either killed themselves by overwork, or had been permanently incapacitated, or had wasted long periods in endeavors to recover health. I do but echo the opinion of all the observant persons I have spoken to, that immense injury is done by this high-pressure life—the physique is being undermined. That subtle thinker and poet whom you have lately had to mourn, Emerson, says, in his essay on the Gentleman, that the first requisite is that he shall be a good animal. The requisite is a general one—it extends to the man, to the father, to the citizen. We hear a great deal about 'the vile body'; and many are encouraged by the phrase to transgress the laws of health. But Nature quietly suppresses those who treat thus disrespectfully one of her highest products, and leaves the world to be peopled by the descendants of those who are not so foolish.

Beyond these immediate mischiefs there are remoter mischiefs. Exclusive devotion to work has the result that amusements cease to please; and, when relaxation becomes imperative, life becomes dreary from lack of its sole interest—the interest in business. The remark current in England that, when the American travels, his aim is to do the greatest amount of sight-seeing in the shortest time, I find current here also; it is recognized that the satisfaction of getting on devours nearly all other satisfactions. When recently at Niagara, which gave us a whole week's pleasure, I learned from the landlord of the hotel that most Americans come one day and go away the next. Old Froissart, who said of the English of his day that 'they take their pleasures sadly after their fashion,' would doubtless, if he lived now, say of the Americans that they take their pleasures hurriedly after their fashion. In large measure with us, and still more with you, there is not that abandonment to the moment, which is requisite for full enjoyment; and this abandonment is prevented by the ever present sense of multitudinous responsibilities. So that, beyond the serious physical mischief caused by overwork, there is the further mischief that it destroys what value there would otherwise be in the leisure part of life.

Nor do the evils end here. There is the injury to posterity. Damaged constitutions reappear in children, and entail on them far more of ill than great fortunes yield them of good. When life has been duly rationalized by science, it will be seen that among a man's duties, care of the body is imperative; not only out of regard for personal welfare, but also out of regard for descendants. His constitution will be considered as an entailed estate, which he ought to pass on uninjured, if not improved, to those who follow; and it will be held that millions bequeathed by him will not compensate for feeble health and decreased ability to enjoy life. Once more, there is the injury to fellow-citizens, taking the shape of undue disregard of competitors. I hear that a great trader among you deliberately endeavored to crush out everyone whose business competed with his own; and manifestly the man who, making himself a slave to accumulation, absorbs an inordinate share of the trade or profession he is engaged in, makes life harder for all others engaged in it, and excludes from it many who might otherwise gain competencies. Thus, besides the egoistic motive, there are two altruistic motives which should deter from this excess in work.

The truth is, there needs a revised ideal of life. Look back through the past, or look abroad through the present, and we find that the ideal of life is variable, and depends on social conditions. Everyone knows that to be a successful warrior was the highest aim among all ancient peoples of note, as it is still among many barbarous peoples. . . We have changed all that in modern civilized societies; especially in England, and still more in America. With the decline of militant activity, and the growth of industrial activity, the occupations once disgraceful have become honorable. The duty to work has taken the place of the duty to fight; and in the one case, as in the other, the ideal of life has become so well established that scarcely any dream of questioning it. Practically, business has been substituted for war as the purpose of existence.

Is this modern ideal to survive throughout the future? I think not. While all other things undergo continuous change, it is impossible that ideals should remain fixed. The ancient ideal was appropriate to the ages of conquest by man over man, and spread of the strongest races. The modern ideal is appropriate to ages in which conquest of the earth and subjection of the powers of Nature to human use is the predominant need. But hereafter, when both these ends have in the main been achieved, the ideal formed will probably differ considerably from the present one. May we not foresee the nature of the difference? I think we may. Some twenty years ago, a good friend of mine, and a good friend of yours, too, though you never saw him, John Stuart Mill, delivered at St. Andrews an inaugural address on the occasion of his appointment to the Lord Rectorship. It contained much to be admired, as did all he wrote. There ran through it, however, the tacit assumption that life is for learning and working. I felt

at the time that I should have liked to take up the opposite thesis.
I should have liked to contend that life is not for learning, nor is life
for working, but learning and working are for life. The primary use
of knowledge is for such guidance of conduct under all circumstances
as shall make living complete. All other uses of knowledge are secondary. It scarcely needs saying that the primary use of work is that of
supplying the materials and aids to living completely; and that any
other uses of work are secondary. But in men's conceptions the secondary has in great measure usurped the place of the primary. The apostle
of culture as it is commonly conceived, Mr. Matthew Arnold, makes
little or no reference to the fact that the first use of knowledge is the
right ordering of all actions; and Mr. Carlyle, who is a good exponent
of current ideas about work, insists in its virtues for quite other
reasons than that it achieves sustentation. We may trace everywhere in
human affairs a tendency to transform the means into the end. . .
Hereafter, when this age of active material progress has yielded mankind its benefits, there will, I think, come a better adjustment of labor
and enjoyment. Among reasons for thinking this, there is the reason
that the process of evolution throughout the organic world at large
brings an increasing surplus of energies that are not absorbed in ful-
filling material needs, and points to a still larger surplus for the
humanity of the future. And there are other reasons, which I must
pass over. In brief, I may say that we have had somewhat too much
of 'the gospel of work.' It is time to preach the gospel of relaxation.

American Civilization in 1883-4 [1] &

MATTHEW ARNOLD, *having formed a very positive image of
American life, decided when just past his sixtieth birthday that he
would go to the United States to verify it, to contribute his mite toward
the improvement of American culture, and to reap the harvest of dollars that lay waiting for an English lecturer. It would be a little unfair
to say that his attitude toward Americans in general was disdainful;
it was almost identical with his attitude toward Britons in general, for
he believed the countries much alike. He thought that here he would
find fewer aristocrats, social and intellectual, than in England, and
fewer barbarians, the land being wholly possessed by 'my old familiar*

[1] From *Civilization in the United States*, Boston, 1888, part IV.

friend, the middle class' or Philistines. This view, as he says, he later admitted to be inadequate.

The first American expedition of Arnold covered a half year, from October 1883, to March 1884; *we have to say first, for in 1886 he made a brief visit for the purpose of seeing his baby granddaughter, though this had no literary result save some entertaining letters. When he came he was so well known that, as one informant assured him, the very conductors and brakemen of the railway lines had read his books. He still held the post of Inspector of Schools, but Americans never thought of him in that connection. They thought of him as the son of Dr. Arnold of Rugby, as a distinguished poet and a onetime professor of poetry at Oxford (1857-67), and as the author of a long shelf of works in prose, for all his books excepting those that were to result from his tour and the second series of* Essays in Criticism *had now appeared.*

In most cities Arnold's audiences were large. In Baltimore they were *unsatisfactory, and in St. Louis he spoke to gatherings of only two hundred to three hundred and fifty people. One aspect of the impression he made is seen in the famous verdict of a Chicago newspaper:* 'He has harsh features, supercilious manners, parts his hair down the middle, wears a single eyeglass and ill-fitting clothes.' *According to Justin McCarthy, who followed him only a few years on the platform as a lecturer and was accompanied by the same American who had served Arnold as agent, the critic's lectures at first threatened to be failures. His utterance was defective, his voice lacked modulation, his accent was confusing to his audiences, and he used to read his discourses from the manuscript. Friends in Boston advised him to take lessons from an elocutionist in the art of making his voice effective throughout a large hall, and he did so, with gratifying results. The comment of Charles Eliot Norton, with whom he spent several days, was favorable, and we may be sure perfectly truthful.* 'He was most pleasant and simpler than he appears in London,' *Norton wrote Lowell.* 'Mr. Arnold quite won the hearts of my girls. Materially speaking, his lectures are a success. He will go back with some money. His delivery is not good, but is striking from its thorough Anglican seriousness and awkwardness. It does not hurt the substance of his lectures, or their effect on the audience. Indeed the common hearer seems to be impressed by the fact that it is the matter not the manner of his speech that is of primary consequence.'

On returning home, Arnold published (1885) *his* Discourses in America, *which he pronounced the ripest and most representative of all his prose writings. Three years later, in the year of his death, appeared*

Civilization in the United States, *consisting of a title essay, 'A Word about America,' 'A Word More about America,' and a paper upon General Grant, whose simple and sterling character he greatly admired.*

PERHAPS it is not likely that anyone will now remember what I said three years ago here about the success of the Americans in solving the political and social problem. I will sum it up in the briefest possible manner. I said that the United States had constituted themselves in a modern age; that their institutions conformed well with the form and pressure of those circumstances and conditions which a modern age presents. Quite apart from all question how much of the merit for this may be due to the wisdom and virtue of the American people, and how much to their good fortune, it is undeniable that their institutions do work well and happily. The play of their institutions suggests, I said, the image of a man in a suit of clothes which fits him to perfection, leaving all his movements unimpeded and easy; a suit of clothes loose where it ought to be loose, and sitting close where its sitting close is an advantage; a suit of clothes able, moreover, to adapt itself naturally to the wearer's growth, and to admit of all enlargements as they successively arise.

So much as to the solution, by the United States, of the political problem. As to the social problem, I observed that the people of the United States were a community singularly free from the distinction of classes, singularly homogeneous; that the division between rich and poor was consequently less profound there than in countries where the distinction of classes accentuates that division. I added that I believed there was exaggeration in the reports of their administrative and judicial corruption; and altogether, I concluded, the United States, politically and socially, are a country living prosperously in a natural modern condition, and conscious of living prosperously in such a condition. And being in this healthy case, and having this healthy consciousness, the community there uses its understanding with the soundness of health; it in general, as to its own political and social concerns, sees clear and thinks straight. Comparing the United States with ourselves, I said that, while they are in this natural and healthy condition, we, on the contrary are so little homogeneous, we are living with a system of classes so intense, with institutions and a society so little modern, so unnaturally complicated that the whole action of our minds is hampered and falsened by it; we are in consequence wanting in lucidity, we do not see clear or think straight, and the Americans here have much the advantage of us.

Yet we find an acute and experienced Englishman saying that there is no country, calling itself civilized, where one would not rather live than in the United States, except Russia! The civilization of the United States must somehow, if an able man can think thus, have shortcomings, in spite of the country's success and prosperity. What is civilization? It is the humanization of man in society, the satisfaction for him, in society, of the true law of human nature. Man's study, says Plato, is to discover the right answer to the question *how to live?* our aim, he says, is full and true life. We are more or less civilized as we come more or less near to this aim, in that social state which the pursuit of our aim essentially demands. But several elements or powers, as I have often insisted, go to build up a complete human life. There is the power of conduct, the power of intellect and knowledge, the the power of beauty, the power of social life and manners; we have instincts responding to them all, requiring them all. And we are perfectly civilized only when all these instincts in our nature, all these elements in our civilization have been adequately recognized and satisfied. But of course this adequate recognition and satisfaction of all the elements in question is impossible; some of them are recognized more than others, some of them more in one community, some in another; and the satisfactions found are more or less worthy.

And, meanwhile, people use the term *civilization* in the loosest possible way, for the most part attaching to it, however, in their own mind some meaning connected with their own preferences and experiences. The most common meaning thus attached to it is perhaps that of a satisfaction, not of all the main demands of human nature, but of the demand for the comforts and conveniences of life, and of this demand as made by the sort of person who uses the term.

Now we should always attend to the common and prevalent use of an important term. Probably Sir Lepel Griffin had this notion of the comforts and conveniences of life much in his thoughts when he reproached American civilization with its shortcomings. For men of his kind, and for all that large number of men, so prominent in this country and who make their voice so much heard, men who have been at the public schools and universities, men of the professional and official class, men who do the most part of our literature and our journalism, America is not a comfortable place of abode. A man of this sort has in England everything in his favor; a society appears organized expressly for his advantage. A Rothschild or a Vanderbilt can buy his way anywhere, and can have what comforts and luxuries he likes, whether in America or in England. But it is in England that an income of from three or four to fourteen or fifteen hundred pounds a year does so much for its possessor, enables him to live with so many of the conveniences of far richer people. For his benefit, his benefit above all, clubs are organized, and hansom cabs ply; service is abundant, porters stand waiting at the railway stations. In America all luxuries are dear except oysters and ice; service is in general scarce and bad; a club is a most expensive luxury; the cab rates are prohibitive—more than half of the people who in England would use cabs must in America use the horsecars, the tram. The charges of tailors and mercers are about a third higher than they are with us. I mention only a few striking points as to which there can be no dispute, and in which a man of Sir Lepel Griffin's class would feel the great difference between America and England in the conveniences at his command. There are a hundred other points one might mention, where he would feel the same thing. When a man is passing judgment on a country's civilization, points of this kind crowd to his memory, and determine his sentence.

On the other hand, for that immense class of people, the great bulk of the community, the class of people whose income is less than three or four hundred a year, things in America are favorable. It is easier for them there than in the Old World to rise and make their fortune; but I am not now speaking of that. Even without making their fortune, even with their income below three or four hundred a year, things are favorable to them in America, society seems organized there for their benefit. To begin with, the humbler kind of work is better paid in America than with us; the higher kind, worse. The official, for instance, gets less, his office-keeper gets more. The public ways are abominably cut up by rails and blocked with horsecars; but the inconvenience is for those who use private carriages and cabs, the convenience is for the bulk of the community who but for the horsecars would have to walk. The ordinary railway cars are not delightful, but they are cheap, and they are better furnished and in winter are warmer than third-class carriages in England. Luxuries are, as I have said, very dear—above all, European luxuries; but a workingman's clothing is nearly as cheap as in England, and plain food is on the whole cheaper. Even luxuries of a certain kind are within a laboring man's easy reach. I have mentioned ice; I will mention fruit also. The abundance and cheapness of fruit is a great boon to people of small incomes in America. Do not believe the Americans when they extol their peaches as equal to any in the world . . . ; they are not to be compared to peaches grown under glass. Do not believe that the American Newtown pippins appear in the New York and Boston fruit shops as they appear in those of London and Liverpool; or that the Americans have any pear to give you like the Marie Louise. But what laborer, or artisan, or small clerk ever gets hothouse peaches, or Newtown pippins, or Marie Louise pears? Not such good pears, apples, and peaches as those, but pears, apples, and peaches by no means to be despised, such people and their families do in America get in plenty.

Well, now, what would a philosopher or a philanthropist say in this case? which would he say was the more civilized condition—that of the country where the balance of advantage, as to the comforts and conveniences of life, is greatly in favor of the people with incomes below three hundred a year, or that of the country where it is greatly in favor of those with incomes above that sum?

Many people will be ready to give an answer to that question without the smallest hesitation. They will say that they are, and that all of us ought to be for the greatest happiness of the greatest number. However, the question is not one which I feel bound now to discuss and answer. Of course, if happiness and civilization consist in being plentifully supplied with the comforts and conveniences of life, the question presents little difficulty. But I believe neither that happiness consists, merely or mainly, in being plentifully supplied with the comforts and conveniences of life, nor that civilization consists in being so supplied; therefore, I leave the question unanswered. . .

But we must get nearer still to the heart of the question raised as to the character and worth of American civilization. I have said how much the word civilization really means—the humanization of man in society; his making progress there toward his true and full humanity. Partial and material achievement is always being put forward as civilization. We hear a nation called highly civilized by reason of its industry, commerce, and wealth, or by reason of its liberty or equality, or by reason of its numerous churches, schools, libraries, and newspapers. But there is something in human nature, some instinct of growth, some law of perfection, which rebels against this narrow account of the matter. And perhaps what human nature demands in civilization, over and above all those obvious things which first occur to our thoughts—what human nature, I say, demands in civilization, if it is to stand as a high and satisfying civilization, is best described by the word *interesting*. Here is the extraordinary charm of the old Greek civilization; that it is so *interesting*. Do not tell me only, says human nature, of the magnitude of your industry and commerce; of the beneficence of your institutions, your freedom, your equality; of the great and growing number of your churches and schools, libraries and newspapers; tell me also if your civilization—which is the grand name you give to all this development—tell me if your civilization is *interesting*.

An American friend of mine, Professor Norton, has lately published the early letters of Carlyle. If anyone wants a good antidote to the unpleasant effect left by Mr. Froude's *Life of Carlyle,* let him read

those letters. Not only of Carlyle will those letters make him think
kindly, but they will also fill him with admiring esteem for the qualities, character, and family life, as there delineated, of the Scottish
peasant. Well, the Carlyle family were numerous, poor, and struggling.
Thomas Carlyle, the eldest son, a young man in wretched health and
worse spirits, was fighting his way in Edinburgh. One of his younger
brothers talked of emigrating. 'The very best thing he could do!' we
should all say. Carlyle dissuades him. 'You shall never,' he writes,
'you shall never seriously mediate crossing the great Salt Pool to
plant yourself in the Yankeeland. That is a miserable fate for anyone,
at best; never dream of it. Could you banish yourself from all that is
interesting to your mind, forget the history, the glorious institutions,
the noble principles of Old Scotland—that you might eat a better
dinner, perhaps?'

There is our word launched—the word *interesting*. I am not saying
that Carlyle's advice was good, or that young men should not emigrate.
I do but take note, in the word *interesting,* of a requirement, a cry of
aspiration, a cry not sounding in the imaginative Carlyle's own breast
only, but sure of a response in his brother's breast also, and in human
nature.

Amiel, that contemplative Swiss whose journal the world has been
reading lately, tells us that 'the human heart is, as it were, haunted by
confused reminiscences of an age of gold; or, rather, by aspirations
towards a harmony of things, which every-day reality denies to us.'
He says that the splendor and refinement of high life is an attempt
by the rich and cultivated classes to realize this ideal, and is 'a form
of poetry,' And the interest which this attempt awakens in the classes
which are not rich or cultivated, their indestructible interest in the
pageant and fairy tale, as to them it appears, of the life in castles and
palaces, the life of the great, bears witness in a like imaginative strain
in them also, a strain tending after the elevated and the beautiful. In
short, what Goethe describes as 'was uns alle bändigt, das Gemeine—
that which holds us all in bondage, the common and ignoble,' is,
notwithstanding its admitted prevalence, contrary to a deep-seated
instinct in human nature, and repelled by it. Of civilization, which is
to humanize us in society, we demand, before we will consent to be
satisfied with it—we demand, however much else it may give us, that
it shall give us, too, the *interesting*.

Now, the great sources of the *interesting* are distinction and beauty;
that which is elevated, and that which is beautiful. Let us take the
beautiful first, and consider how far it is present in American civilization. Evidently, this is that civilization's weak side. There is little to
nourish and delight the sense of beauty there. In the long-settled states

east of the Alleghanies the landscape in general is not interesting, the climate harsh and in extremes. The Americans are restless, eager to better themselves and to make fortunes; the inhabitant does not strike his roots lovingly down into the soil, as in rural England. In the valley of the Connecticut you will find farm after farm which the Yankee settler has abandoned in order to go West, leaving the farm to some new Irish immigrant. The charm of beauty which comes from ancientness and permanence of rural life the country could not yet have in a high degree, but it has it in an even less degree than might be expected. Then the Americans come originally, for the most part, from that great class in English society amongst whom the sense for conduct and business is much more strongly developed than the sense for beauty. If we in England were without the cathedrals, parish churches, and castles of the catholic and feudal age, and without the houses of the Elizabethan age, but had only the towns and buildings which the rise of our middle class has created in the modern age, we should be in much the same case as the Americans. We should be living with much the same absence of training for the sense of beauty through the eye, from the aspect of outward things. The American cities have hardly anything to please a trained or a natural sense for beauty. They have buildings which cost a great deal of money and produce a certain effect—buildings, shall I say, such as our Midland Station at St. Pancras; but nothing such as Somerset House or White-hall. One architect of genius they had—Richardson. I had the pleasure to know him: he is dead, alas! Much of his work was injured by the conditions under which he was obliged to execute it; I can recall but one building, and that of no great importance, where he seems to have had his own way, to be fully himself; but that is indeed excellent. In general, where the Americans succeed best in their architecture—in that art so indicative and educative of a people's sense for beauty—is in the fashion of their villa cottages in wood. These are often original and at the same time very pleasing, but they are pretty and coquettish, not beautiful. Of the really beautiful in the other arts, and in literature, very little has been produced there as yet. I asked a German portrait painter, whom I found painting and prospering in America, how he liked the country. 'How *can* an artist like it?' was his answer. The American artists live chiefly in Europe; all Americans of cultivation and wealth visit Europe more and more constantly. The mere nomen-clature of the country acts upon a cultivated person like the incessant pricking of pins. What people in whom the sense of beauty and fit-ness was quick could have invented or could tolerate the hideous names ending in *ville,* the Briggsvilles, Higginsvilles, Jacksonvilles, rife from Maine to Florida; the jumble of unnatural and inappropriate names everywhere? On the line from Albany to Buffalo you have, in one part, half the names in the classical dictionary to designate the stations; it is said that the folly is due to a surveyor who, when the country was laid out, happened to possess a classical dictionary; but a people with any artist sense would have put down that surveyor. The Americans meekly retain his names; and, indeed, his strange Marcellus or Syracuse is perhaps not much worse than their congenital Briggsville.

So much as to beauty, and as to the provision, in the United States, for the sense of beauty. As to distinction, and the interest which human nature seeks from enjoying the effect made upon it by what is elevated, the case is much the same. There is very little to create such an effect, very much to thwart it. Goethe says somewhere that 'the thrill of awe is the best thing humanity has':

> Das Schaudern ist der Menschheit bestes Theil.

But, if there be a discipline in which the Americans are wanting, it is the discipline of awe and respect. An austere and intense religion imposed on their Puritan founders the discipline of respect, and so provided for them the thrill of awe; but this religion is dying out. The Americans have produced plenty of men strong, shrewd, upright, able, effective; very few who are highly distinguished. Alexander Hamilton is indeed a man of rare distinction; Washington, though he has not the high mental distinction of Pericles or Cæsar, has true distinction of style and character. But these men belong to the pre-American age. Lincoln's recent American biographers declare that Washington is but an Englishman, an English officer; the typical American, they say, is Abraham Lincoln. Now Lincoln is shrewd, sagacious, humorous, honest, courageous, firm; he is a man with qualities deserving the most sincere esteem and praise, but he has not distinction.

In truth, everything is against distinction in America, and against the sense of elevation to be gained through admiring and respecting it. The glorification of 'the average man,' who is quite a religion with statesmen and publicists there, is against it. The addiction to 'the funny man,' who is a national misfortune there, is against it. Above all, the newspapers are against it.

It is often said that every nation has the government it deserves. What is much more certain is that every nation has the newspapers it deserves. The newspaper is the direct product of the want felt; the supply answers closely and inevitably to the demand. I suppose no one knows what the American newspapers are who has not been obliged, for some length of time, to read either those newspapers or none at all. Powerful and valuable contributions occur scattered about in them. But on the whole, and taking the total impression and effect made by them. I should say that if one were searching for the best means to efface and kill in a whole nation the discipline of respect, the feeling for what is elevated, one could not do better than take the American newspapers. The absence of truth and soberness in them, the poverty in serious interest, the personality and sensation mongering are beyond belief. There are a few newspapers which are in whole, or in part, exceptions. The *New York Nation,* a weekly paper, may be paralleled with the *Saturday Review* as it was in its old and good days; but the *New York Nation* is conducted by a foreigner, and has an extremely small sale. In general, the daily papers are such that when one returns home one is moved to admiration and thankfulness not only at the great London papers, like the *Times* or the *Standard,* but quite as much at the great provincial papers, too—papers like the *Leeds Mercury* and the *Yorkshire Post* in the north of England, like the *Scotsman* and the *Glasgow Herald* in Scotland.

The Americans used to say to me that what they valued was news, and that this their newspapers gave them. I at last made the reply: 'Yes, news for the servants' hall!' I remember that a New York newspaper, one of the first I saw after landing in the country, had a long account, with the prominence we should give to the illness of the German Emperor, or the arrest of the Lord Mayor of Dublin, of a young woman who had married a man who was a bag of bones, as we say, and who used to exhibit himself as a skeleton; of her growing horror in living with this man, and finally of her death. All this in the most minute detail, and described with all the writer's powers of rhetoric. This has always remained by me as a specimen of what the Americans call news.

You must have lived amongst their newspapers to know what they are. If I relate some of my own experiences, it is because these will give a clear enough notion of what the newspapers over there are, and one remembers more definitely what has happened to oneself. Soon after arriving in Boston, I opened a Boston newspaper and came upon a column headed: 'Tickings.' By 'tickings' we are to understand news conveyed through the tickings of the telegraph. The first 'ticking' was: 'Matthew Arnold is sixty-two years old'—an age, I must just say in passing, which I had not then reached. The second 'ticking' was: 'Wales says, Mary is a darling'; the meaning being that the Prince of Wales expressed great admiration for Miss Mary Anderson. This was at Boston, the American Athens. I proceeded to Chicago. An evening paper was given to me soon after I arrived; I opened it, and found under a large-type heading, 'We have seen him arrive,' the following picture of myself: 'He has harsh features, supercilious manners, parts his hair down the middle, wears a single eyeglass and ill-fitting clothes.' Notwithstanding this rather unfavorable introduction, I was most kindly and hospitably received at Chicago. It happened that I had a letter for Mr. Medill, an elderly gentleman of Scotch descent, the editor of the chief newspaper in those parts, the *Chicago Tribune*. I called on him, and we conversed amicably together. Some time afterwards, when I had gone back to England, a New York paper published a criticism of Chicago and its people, purporting to have been contributed by me to the *Pall Mall Gazette* over here. It was a poor hoax, but many people were taken in and were excusably angry, Mr. Medill of the *Chicago Tribune* amongst the number. A friend telegraphed me to know if I had written the criticism. I, of course, instantly telegraphed back that I had not written a syllable of it. Then a Chicago paper is sent to me; and what I have the pleasure of reading, as the result of my contradiction, is this: 'Arnold denies; Mr. Medill (my old friend) refuses to accept Arnold's disclaimer; says Arnold is a cur.'

I once declared that in England the born lover of ideas and of light could not but feel that the sky over his head is of brass and iron. And so I say that, in America, he who craves for the *interesting* in civilization, he who requires from what surrounds him satisfaction for his sense of beauty, his sense of elevation, will feel the sky over his head to be of brass and iron. The human problem, then, is as yet solved in the United States most imperfectly; a great void exists in the civilization over there; a want of what is elevated and beautiful, of what is interesting.

The want is grave; it was probably, though he does not exactly bring it out, influencing Sir Lepel Griffin's feelings when he said that America is one of the last countries in which one would like to live. The want is such as to make any educated man feel that many countries, much less free and prosperous than the United States, are yet more truly civilized; have more which is interesting, have more to say to the soul; are countries, therefore, in which one would rather live.

The want is graver because it is so little recognized by the mass of Americans; nay, so loudly denied by them. If the community over there perceived the want and regretted it, sought for the right ways of remedying it, and resolved that remedied it should be; if they said, or even if a number of leading spirits amongst them said: 'Yes, we see what is wanting to our civilization, we see that the average man is a danger, we see that our newspapers are a scandal, that bondage to the common and ignoble is our snare; but under the circumstances our civilization could not well have been expected to begin differently.

What you see are *beginnings,* they are crude, they are too predominantly material, they omit much, leave much to be desired—but they could not have been otherwise, they have been inevitable, and we will rise above them'; if the Americans frankly said this, one would have not a word to bring against it. One would *then* insist on no shortcoming; one would accept their admission that the human problem is at present quite insufficiently solved by them, and would press the matter no further. One would congratulate them on having solved the political problem and the social problem so successfully, and only remark, as I have said already, that in seeing clear and thinking straight on *our* political and social questions, we have great need to follow the example they set us on theirs.

But now the Americans seem, in certain matters, to have agreed, as a people, to deceive themselves, to persuade themselves that they have what they have not, to cover the defects in their civilization by boasting, to fancy that they well and truly solve not only the political and social problem, but the human problem too. One would say they do really hope to find in tall talk and inflated sentiment a substitute for that real sense of elevation which human nature, as I have said, instinctively craves—and a substitute which may do as well as the genuine article. The thrill of awe, which Goethe pronounces to be the best thing humanity has, they would fain create by proclaiming themselves at the top of their voices to be 'the greatest nation upon earth,' by assuring one another, in the language of their national historian, that 'American democracy proceeds in its ascent as uniformly and majestically as the laws of being, and is as certain as the decrees of eternity.'

Or, again, far from admitting that their newspapers are a scandal, they assure one another that their newspaper press is one of their most signal distinctions. Far from admitting that in literature they have as yet produced little that is important, they play at treating American literature as if it were a great independent power; they reform the spelling of the English language by the insight of their average man. For every English writer they have an American writer to match; and him good Americans read. The Western States are at this moment being nourished and formed, we hear, on the novels of a native author called Roe, instead of those of Scott and Dickens. Far from admitting that their average man is a danger, and that his predominance has brought about a plentiful lack of refinement, distinction, and beauty, they declare in the words of my friend Colonel Higginson, a prominent critic at Boston, that 'Nature said, some years since: "Thus far the English is my best race, but we have had Englishmen enough; put in one drop more of nervous fluid and make the American."' And with that drop a new range of promise opened on the human race, and a lighter, finer, more highly organized type of mankind was born. Far from admitting that the American accent, as the pressure of their climate and of their average man has made it, is a thing to be striven against, they assure one another that it is the right accent, the standard English speech of the future. It reminds me of a thing in Smollett's dinner party of authors. Seated by 'the philosopher who is writing a most orthodox refutation of Bolingbroke, but in the meantime has just been presented to the Grand Jury as a public nuisance for having blasphemed in an alehouse on the Lord's day'—seated by this philosopher is 'the Scotchman who is giving lectures on the pronunciation of the English language.'

The worst of it is that all this talk and self-glorification meets with hardly any rebuke from sane criticism over there. I will mention, in regard to this, a thing which struck me a good deal. A Scotchman who has made a great fortune at Pittsburg, a kind friend of mine, one of the most hospitable and generous of men, Mr. Andrew Carnegie, published a year or two ago a book called *Triumphant Democracy,* a most splendid picture of American progress. The book is full of valuable information, but religious people thought that it insisted too much on mere material progress, and did not enough set forth America's deficiencies and dangers. And a friendly clergyman in Massachusetts, telling me how he regretted this, and how apt the Americans are to shut their eyes to their own dangers, put into my hands a volume written by a leading minister among the Congregationalists, a very prominent man, which he said supplied a good antidote to my friend Mr. Carnegie's book. The volume is entitled *Our Country.* I read it through. The author finds in evangelical Protestantism, as the orthodox Protestant sects present it, the grand remedy for the deficiencies and dangers of America. On this I offer no criticism; what struck me, and that on which I wish to lay stress, is the writer's entire failure to perceive that such self-glorification and self-deception as I have been mentioning is one of America's dangers, or even that it *is* self-deception at all. He himself shares in all the self-deception of the average man among his countrymen; he flatters it. In the very points where a serious critic would find the Americans most wanting he finds them superior; only they require to have a good dose of evangelical Protestantism still added. 'Ours is the elect nation,' preaches this reformer of American faults—'ours is the elect nation for the age to come. We are the chosen people.' Already, says he, we are taller and heavier than other men, longer lived than other men, richer and more energetic than other men, above all, 'of finer nervous organization' than other men. Yes, this people, who endure to have the American newspaper for their daily reading, and to have their habitation in

Briggsville, Jacksonville, and Marcellus—this people is of finer, more delicate nervous organization than other nations! It is Colonel Higginson's 'drop more of nervous fluid' over again. This 'drop' plays a stupendous part in the American rhapsody of self-praise. Undoubtedly the Americans are highly nervous, both the men and the women. A great Paris physician says that he notes a distinctive new form of nervous disease, produced in American women by worry about servants. But this nervousness, developed in the race out there by worry, overwork, want of exercise, injudicious diet, and a most trying climate—this morbid nervousness our friends ticket as the fine susceptibility of genius, and cite it as a prooof of their distinction, of their superior capacity for civilization! 'The roots of civilization are the nerves,' says our Congregationalist instructor, again; 'and, other things being equal, the finest nervous organization will produce the highest civilization. Now, the finest nervous organization is ours.'

The new West promises to beat in the game of brag even the stout champions I have been quoting. Those belong to the old Eastern States; and the other day there was sent to me a California newspaper, which calls all the Easterners the 'unhappy denizens of a forbidding clime,' and adds: 'The time will surely come when all roads will lead toward California. Here will be the home of art, science, literature, and profound knowledge.'

Common-sense criticism, I repeat, of all this hollow stuff there is in America next to none. There are plenty of cultivated, judicious, delightful individuals there. They are our hope and America's hope; it is through their means that improvement must come. They know perfectly well how false and hollow the boastful stuff talked is; but they let the storm of self-laudation rage, and say nothing. For political opponents and their doings there are in America hard words to be heard in abundance; for the real faults in American civilization, and for the foolish boasting which prolongs them there is hardly a word of regret or blame, at least in public. Even in private, many of the most cultivated Americans shrink from the subject, are irritable and thin-skinned when it is canvassed. Public treatment of it, in a cool and sane spirit of criticism, there is none. In vain I might plead that I had set a good example of frankness, in confessing over here that, so far from solving our problems successfully, we in England find ourselves with an upper class materialized, a middle class vulgarized, and a lower class brutalized. But it seems that nothing will embolden an American critic to say firmly and aloud to his countrymen and to his newspapers that in America they do not solve the human problem successfully, and that with their present methods they never can. Consequently, the masses of the American people do really come to believe all they hear about their finer nervous organization, and the rightness of the American accent, and the importance of American literature; that is to say, they see things not as they are, but as they would like them to be; they deceive themselves totally. And by such self-deception they shut against themselves the door to improvement, and do their best to make the reign of *das Gemeine* eternal. In what concerns the solving of the political and social problem they see clear and think straight; in what concerns the higher civilization they live in a fools' paradise. This it is which makes a famous French critic speak of 'the hard unintelligence of the people of the United States'—*la dure unintelligence des Américains du Nord*—of the very people who in general pass for being specially intelligent; and so, within certain limits, they are. But they have been so plied with nonsense and boasting that outside those limits, and where it is a question of things in which their civilization is weak, they seem, very many of them, as if in such things they had no power of perception whatever, no idea of a proper scale, no sense of the difference between good and bad. And at this rate they can never, after solving the political and social problem with success, go on to solve the human problem too, and thus at last to make their civilization full and interesting.

To sum up, then. What really dissatisfies in American civilization is the want of the *interesting,* a want due chiefly to the want of those two great elements of the interesting, which are elevation and beauty. And the want of these elements is increased and prolonged by the Americans being assured that they have them when they have them not. And it seems to me that what the Americans now most urgently require is not so much a vast additional development of orthodox Protestantism, but rather a steady exhibition of cool and sane criticism by their men of light and leading over there. And perhaps the very first step of such men should be to insist on having for America, and to create, if need be, better newspapers.

To us, too, the future of the United States is of incalculable importance. Already we feel their influence much, and we shall feel it more. We have a good deal to learn from them; we shall find in them, also, many things to beware of, many points in which it is to be hoped our democracy may not be like theirs. As our country becomes more democratic, the malady here may no longer be that we have an upper class materialized, a middle class vulgarized, and a lower class brutalized. But the predominance of the common and ignoble, born of the predominance of the average man, is a malady too. That the common and ignoble is human nature's enemy, that, of true human nature, distinction and beauty are needs, that a civilization is insufficient where these needs are not satisfied, faulty where they are thwarted, is an instruction of which we, as well as the Americans, may greatly require to take fast hold, and not to let go. We may greatly require to keep, as if it were our life, the doctrine that we are failures after all, if we cannot eschew vain boastings and vain imaginations—eschew what flatters in us the common and ignoble, and approve things that are truly excellent.

I have mentioned evangelical Protestantism. There is a text which evangelical Protestantism—and, for that matter, Catholicism, too—translates wrong and takes in a sense too narrow. The text is that well-known one, 'except a man be born again, he cannot see the kingdom of God.' Instead of *again,* we ought to translate *from above;* and instead of taking the kingdom of God in the sense of a life in Heaven above, we ought to take it, as the speaker meant it, in the sense of the reign of the saints, a renovated and perfected human society on earth—the ideal society of the future. In the life of such a society, in the life *from above,* the life born of inspiration or the *spirit*—in that life elevation and beauty are not everything; but they are much, and they are indispensable. Humanity cannot reach its ideal while it lacks them. 'Except a man be born *from above,* he cannot have part in the society of the future.'

America the Land of Contrasts [1] &

DR. JAMES FULLARTON MUIRHEAD, *for a quarter of a century and more, was in charge of the British editions of Baedeker's handbooks of travel. He was born in Glasgow in 1853, and educated at the Universities of Edinburgh and of Leipzig. After three years of work on* Chambers's Encyclopædia, *he became associated with Karl Baedeker at Leipzig, removing first to London and then in 1903 to the United States. As the author of* Baedeker's Handbook to the United States, *in compiling which he personally visited nearly every district of the republic, he obtained the material for* America the Land of Contrasts, *which had reached its third edition in 1902. It, like the volumes by Lord Bryce and Sir A. Maurice Low, represents not a hasty impression of the country but a study made during many years of travel and residence. The treatment is generalized and analytical, not descrip-*

[1] From *America the Land of Contrasts,* London, 1898, chapter 2; reprinted by permission of Mrs. Helen Quincy Muirhead.

tive, Dr. Muirhead dealing in successive chapters with American so-
ciety, the American woman, the American child, sports and amuse-
ments, journalism, and so on.

WHEN I first thought of writing about the United States at all, I soon
came to the conclusion that no title could better than the above express
the general impression left on my mind by my experiences in the
Great Republic. It may well be that a long list of inconsistencies
might be made out for any country, just as for any individual; but so
far as my knowledge goes the United States stands out as pre-eminently
the 'Land of Contrasts'—the land of stark, staring, and stimulating inconsistency; at once the home of enlightenment and the happy hunting
ground of the charlatan and the quack; a land in which nothing
happens but the unexpected; the home of Hyperion, but no less the
haunt of the satyr; always the land of promise, but not invariably the
land of performance; a land which may be bounded by the aurora
borealis, but which has also undeniable acquaintance with the
flames of the bottomless pit; a land which is laved at once by the rivers
of Paradise and the leaden waters of Acheron.

If I proceed to enumerate a few of the actual contrasts that struck
me, in matters both weighty and trivial, it is not merely as an exercise
in antithesis, but because I hope it will show how easy it would be to
pass an entirely and even ridiculously untrue judgment upon the
United States by having an eye only for one series of the startling
opposites. It should show in a very concrete way one of the most fertile
sources of those unfair international judgments which led the French
Academician Jouy to the statement: 'Plus on réfléchit et plus on observe, plus on se convainct de la fausseté de la plupart de ces jugements
portés sur une nation entière par quelques écrivains et adoptés sans
examen par les autres.' The Americans themselves can hardly take
umbrage at the label, if Mr. Howells truly represents them when he
makes one of the characters in *A Traveller from Altruria* assert that
they pride themselves even on the size of their inconsistencies. The
extraordinary clashes that occur in the United States are doubtless
largely due to the extraordinary mixture of youth and age in the character of the country. If ever an old head was set upon young shoulders,
it was in this case of the United States—this 'Strange New World,
thet yit was never young.' While it is easy, in a study of the United
States, to see the essential truth of the analogy between the youth of
an individual and the youth of a state, we must also remember that
America was in many respects born full grown, like Athena from
the brain of Zeus, and co-ordinates in the most extraordinary way the

shrewdness of the sage with the naïveté of the child. Thïse who criticize the United States because, with the experience of all the ages behind her, she is in some points vastly defective as compared with the
nations of Europe are as much mistaken as those who look to her for
the fresh ingenuousness of youth unmarred by any trace of age's
weakness. It is simply inevitable that she should share the vices as
well as the virtues of both. Mr. Freeman has well pointed out how
natural it is that a colony should rush ahead of the mother country in
some things and lag behind it in others; and that just as you have to
go to French Canada if you want to see Old France, so, for many
things, if you wish to see Old England you must go to New England.

Thus America may easily be abreast or ahead of us in such matters
as the latest applications of electricity, while retaining in its legal
uses certain cumbersome devices that we have long since discarded. Americans still have 'Courts of Oyer and Terminer' and
still insist on the unanimity of the jury, though their judges wear no
robes and their counsel apply to the cuspidor as often as to the code.
So, too, the extension of municipal powers accomplished in Great
Britain still seems a formidable innovation in the United States.

The general feeling of power and scope is probably another fruitful
source of the inconsistencies of American life. Emerson has well said
that consistency is the hobgoblin of little minds; and no doubt the
largeness, the illimitable outlook of the national mind of the United
States makes it disregard surface discrepancies that would grate horribly on a more conventional community. The confident belief that all
will come out right in the end, and that harmony can be attained when
time is taken to consider it carries one triumphantly over the roughest
places of inconsistency. It is easy to drink our champagne from tin
cans when we know that it is merely a sense of hurry that prevents us
fetching the chased silver goblets waiting for our use.

This, I fancy, is the explanation of one series of contrasts which
strikes an Englishman at once. America claims to be the land of
liberty *par excellence,* and in a wholesale way this may be true in
spite of the gap between the noble sentiments of the Declaration of
Independence and the actual treatment of the Negro and the China-
man. But in what may be called the retail traffic of life the American
puts up with innumerable restrictions of his personal liberty. Max
O'Rell has expatiated with scarce an exaggeration on the wondrous
sight of a powerful millionaire standing meekly at the door of a hotel
dining room until the consequential head waiter (very possibly a colored gentleman) condescends to point out to him the seat he may
occupy. So too, such petty officials as policemen and railway conductors
are generally treated rather as masters than as the servants of the public.

The ordinary American citizen accepts a long delay on the railway
or an interminable 'wait' at the theater as a direct visitation of Providence, against which it would be useless folly to direct catcalls,
grumbles, or letters to the *Times*. Americans invented the slang word
'kicker,' but so far as I could see their vocabulary is here miles ahead
of their practice; they dream noble deeds, but do not do them; Englishmen 'kick' much better, without having a name for it. The right of
the individual to do as he will is respected to such an extent that an
entire company will put up with inconvenience rather than infringe
it. A coal carter will calmly keep a tramway car waiting several minutes until he finishes his unloading. The conduct of the train boy . . .
would infallibly lead to assault and battery in England, but hardly
elicits an objurgation in America, where the right of one sinner to
bang a door outweighs the desire of twenty just persons for a quiet
nap. On the other hand, the old Puritan spirit of interference with
individual liberty sometimes crops out in America in a way that would
be impossible in this country. An inscription in one of the large mills
at Lawrence, Massachusetts, informs the employees (or did so some
years ago) that 'regular attendance at some place of worship and a
proper observance of the Sabbath will be expected of every person
employed.' So, too, the young women of certain districts impose on
their admirers such restrictions in the use of liquor and tobacco that
any less patient animal than the native American could infallibly kick
over the traces.

In spite of their acknowledged nervous energy and excitability, Americans often show a good deal of a quality that rivals the phlegm of
the Dutch. Their above-mentioned patience during railway or other
delays is an instance of this. So, in the incident related in Chapter XII,[2]
the passengers in the inside coach retained their seats throughout the
whole experiment. Their resemblance in such cases as this to placid
domestic kine is enhanced—out West—by the inevitable champing of
tobacco or chewing gum, than which nothing I know of so robs the
human countenance of the divine spark of intelligence. Boston men of
business, after being whisked by the electric car from their suburban
residences to the city at the rate of twelve miles an hour, sit stoically
still while the congested traffic makes the car take twenty minutes to
pass the most crowded section of Washington Street—a walk of barely
five minutes.[3]

Even in the matter of what Mr. Ambassador Bayard has styled 'that

[2] The author refers to the train boys' practice of dumping sample magazines and other
wares into the passengers' laps, and afterwards calling for orders.
[3] The Boston subway, opened in 1898, has impaired the truth of this sentence—
[Muirhead's note].

form of Socialism, Protection,' it seems to me that we can find traces of this contradictory tendency. Americans consider their country as emphatically the land of protection, and attribute most of their prosperity to their inhospitable customs barriers. This may be so; but where else in the world will you find such a volume and expanse of free trade as in these same United States? We find here a huge section of the world's surface, 3000 miles long and 1500 miles wide, occupied by about fifty practically independent states, containing seventy millions of inhabitants, producing a very large proportion of all the necessities and many of the luxuries of life, and all enjoying the freest of free trade with each other. Few of these states are as small as Great Britain, and many of them are immensely larger. Collectively they contain nearly half the railway mileage of the globe, besides an incomparable series of inland waterways. Over all these is continually passing an immense amount of goods. The San Francisco *News-Letter,* a well-known weekly journal, points out that of the 1,400,000,000 tons of goods carried for 100 miles or upwards on the railways of the world in 1895, no less than 800,000,000 were carried in the United States. Even if we add the 140,000,000 carried by sea-going ships, there remains a balance of 60,000,000 tons in favor of the United States as against the rest of the world. It is, perhaps, impossible to ascertain whether or not the actual value of the goods carried would be in the same proportion; but it seems probable that the value of the 800,000,000 tons of the home trade of America must considerably exceed that of the *free* portion of the trade of the British Empire, i.e. practically the whole of its import trade and that portion of its export trade carried on with free-trade countries or colonies. The internal commerce of the United States makes it the most wonderful market on the globe; and Brother Jonathan, the rampant Proctectionist, stands convicted as the greatest Cobdenite of them all!

We are all, it is said, apt to 'slip up' on our strongest points. Perhaps this is why one of the leading writers of the American democracy is able to assert that 'there is no country in the world where the separation of the classes is so absolute as ours,' and to quote a Russian revolutionist, who lived in exile all over Europe and nowhere found such want of sympathy between the rich and poor as in America. If this were true it would certainly form a startling contrast to the general kindheartedness of the American. But I fancy it rather points to the condition of greater relative equality. Our Russian friend was used to the patronizing kindness of the superior to the inferior, of the master to the servant. It is easy, on an empyrean rock, to be 'kind' to the mortals toiling helplessly down below. It costs little, to use Mr. Bellamy's parable, for those securely seated on the top of the coach to subscribe for salve to alleviate the chafed wounds of those who drag it. In American there is less need and less use of this patronizing kindness; there is less kindness from class to class simply because the conscious realization of 'class' is nonexistent in thousands of cases where it would be to the fore in Europe. As for the first statement quoted at the head of this paragraph, I find it very hard of belief. It is true that there are exclusive *circles,* to which, for instance, Buffalo Bill would not have the entrée, but the principle of exclusion is on the whole analogous to that by which we select our intimate personal friends. No man in America, who is personally fitted to adorn it, need feel that he is *automatically* shut out (as he might well be in England) from a really congenial social sphere.

Another of America's strong points is its sense of practical comfort and convenience. It is scarcely open to denial that the laying of too great stress on material comfort is one of the rocks ahead which the American vessel will need careful steering to avoid; and it is certain that Americans lead us in countless little points of household comfort and labor-saving ingenuity. But here, too, the exception that proves the rule is not too coy for our discovery. The terrible roads and the atrociously kept streets are amongst the most vociferous instances of this. It is one of the inexplicable mysteries of American civilization that a young municipality—or even, sometimes, an old one—with a million dollars to spend, will choose to spend it in erecting a most unnecessarily gorgeous town hall rather than in making the street in front of it passable for the ordinarily shod pedestrian. In New York itself the hilarious stockbroker returning at night to his palace often finds the pavement between his house and his carriage more difficult to negotiate than even the hole for his latch-key; and I have more than once been absolutely compelled to make a detour from Broadway in order to find a crossing where the icy slush would not come over the tops of my boots.[4] The American taste for luxury sometimes insists on gratification even at the expense of the ordinary decencies of life. It was an American who said, 'Give me the luxuries of life and I will not ask for the necessities'; and there is more truth in this epigram, as characteristic of the American point of view, than its author intended, or would, perhaps, allow. In private life this is seen in the preference shown for diamond earrings and Paris toilettes over neat and effective household service. The contrast between the slatternly, unkempt maid servant who opens the door to you and the general luxury of the house itself is sometimes of the most startling, not to say appalling, description. It is not a sufficient answer to say that

---

[4] It is only fair to say that this was originally written in 1893, and that matters have been greatly improved since then—[Muirhead's note].

good servants are not so easily obtained in America as in England. This is true; but a slight rearrangement of expenditure would secure much better service than is now seen. To the English eye the cart in this matter often seems put before the horse; and the combination of excellent waiting with a modest table equipage is frequent enough in the United States to prove its perfect feasibility.

In American hotels we are often overwhelmed with 'all the discomforts that money can procure,' while unable to obtain some of those things which we have been brought up to believe among the prime necessaries of existence. It is significant that in the printed directions governing the use of the electric bell in one's bedroom, I never found an instance in which the harmless necessary bath could be ordered with fewer than nine pressures of the button, while the fragrant cocktail or some other equally fascinating but dangerous luxury might often be summoned by three or four. The most elaborate dinner, served in the most gorgeous China, is sometimes spoiled by the Draconian regulation that it must be devoured between the unholy hours of twelve and two, or have all its courses brought on the table at once. Though the Americans invent the most delicate forms of machinery, their hoop-iron knives, silver-plated for facility in cleaning, are hardly calculated to tackle anything harder than butter, and compel the beef-eater to return to the tearing methods of his remotest ancestors. The waiter sometimes rivals the hotel clerk himself in the splendor of his attire, but this does not render more appetizing the spectacle of his thumb in the soup. The furniture of your bedroom would not have disgraced the Tuileries in their palmiest days, but, alas, you are parboiled by a diabolic *chevaux-de-frise* of steam pipes, which refuse to be turned off, and insist on accompanying your troubled slumbers by an intermittent series of bubbles, squeaks, and hisses. The mirror opposite which you brush your hair is enshrined in the heaviest of gilt frames, and is large enough for a Brobdingnagian, but the basin in which you wash your hands is little larger than a sugar bowl; and when you emerge from your nine-times-summoned bath you find you have to dry your sacred person with six little towels, none larger than a snuff-taker's handkerchief. There is no carafe of water in the room; and after countless experiments you are reduced to the blood-curdling belief that the American tourist brushes his teeth with ice water, the musical tinkling of which in the corridors is the most characteristic sound of the American caravanserai.

If there is anything the Americans pride themselves on—and justly— it is their handsome treatment of woman. You will not meet five Americans without hearing ten times that a lone woman can traverse the length and breadth of the United States without fear of insult;

every traveler reports that the United States is the paradise of women. Special entrances are reserved for them at hotels, so that they need not risk contamination with the tobacco-defiled floors of the public office; they are not expected to join the patient file of room seekers before the hotel clerk's desk, but wait comfortably in the reception room while an employee secures their number and key. There is no recorded instance of the justifiable homicide of an American girl in her theater hat. Man meekly submits to be the hewer of wood, the drawer of water, and the beast of burden for the superior sex. But even this gorgeous medal has its reverse side. Few things provided for a class well able to pay for comfort are more uncomfortable and indecent than the arrangements for ladies on board the sleeping cars. Their dressing accommodation is of the most limited description; their berths are not segregated at one end of the car, but are scattered above and below those of the male passengers; it is considered *tolerable* that they should lie with the legs of a strange, disrobing man dangling within a foot of their noses.

Another curious contrast to the practical, material, matter-of-fact side of the American is his intense interest in the supernatural, the spiritualistic, the superstitious. Boston, of all places in the world, is, perhaps, the happiest hunting ground for the spiritualist medium, the faith healer, and the mind curer. You will find there the most advanced emancipation from theological superstition combined in the most extraordinary way with a more than half belief in the incoherences of a spiritualistic séance. The Boston Christian Scientists have just erected a handsome stone church, with chime of bells, organ, and choir of the most approved ecclesiastical cut; and, greatest marvel of all, have actually had to return a surplus of $50,000 (£10,000) that was subscribed for its building. There are two pulpits, one occupied by a man who expounds the Bible, while in the other a woman responds with the grandiloquent platitudes of Mrs. Eddy. In other parts of the country this desire to pry into the Book of Fate assumes grosser forms. Mr. Bryce tells us that Western newspapers devote a special column to the advertisements of astrologers and soothsayers, and assures us that this profession is as much recognized in the California of today as in the Greece of Homer.

It seems to me that I have met in America the nearest approaches to my ideals of a Bayard *sans peur et sans reproche;* and it is in this same America that I have met flagrant examples of the being wittily described as *sans pere et sans proche*—utterly without the responsibility of background and entirely unacquainted with the obligations of noblesse. The superficial observer in the United States might conceivably imagine the characteristic national trait to be self-sufficiency or vanity

(this mistake *has,* I believe, been made), and his opinion might be
strengthened should he find, as I did, in an arithmetic published at
Richmond during the late Civil War, such a modest example as the
following: 'If one Confederate soldier can whip seven Yankees, how
many Confederate soldiers will it take to whip forty-nine Yankees?'
America has been likened to a self-made man, hugging her conditions
because she has made them, and considering them divine because
they have grown up with the country. Another observer might quite
as easily come to the conclusion that diffidence and self-distrust are the
true American characteristics. Certainly Americans often show a saving consciousness of their faults, and lash themselves with biting satire.
There are even Americans whose very attitude is an apology—wholly
unnecessary—for the Great Republic, and who seem to despise any
native product until it has received the hall mark of London or of
Paris. In the new world that has produced the new book, of the exquisite delicacy and insight of which Mr. Henry James and Mr.
Howells may be taken as typical exponents, it seems to me that there
are more than the usual proportion of critics who prefer to it what
Colonel Higginson has well called 'the brutalities of Haggard and the
garlic flavors of Kipling.' While, perhaps, the characteristic charm
of the American girl is her thorough-going individuality and the un-
daunted courage of her opinions, which leads her to say frankly, if
she thinks so, that Martin Tupper is a greater poet than Shakespeare, yet
I have, on the other hand, met a young American matron who confessed to me with bated breath that she and her sister, for the first time
in their lives, had gone unescorted to a concert the night before last,
and, *mirabile dictu,* no harm had come of it! It is in America that I
have over and over again heard language to which the calling a spade
a spade would seem the most delicate allusiveness; but it is also in
America that I have summoned a blush to the cheek of conscious sixty-
six by an incautious though innocent reference to the temperature of
my morning tub. In that country I have seen the devotion of Sir Walter
Raleigh to his queen rivaled again and again by the ordinary American
man to the ordinary American woman (if there be an *ordinary* American woman), and in the same country I have myself been scoffed at and
made game of because I opened the window of a railway carriage for
a girl in whose delicate veins flowed a few drops of colored blood. In
Washington I met Miss Susan B. Anthony and realized, to some extent
at least, all she stands for. In Boston and other places I find there is
actually an organized opposition on the part of the ladies themselves
to the extension of the franchise to women. I have hailed with delight
the democratic spirit displayed in the greeting of my friend and myself
by the porter of a hotel as 'You fellows,' and then had the cup of

pleasure dashed from my lips by being told by the same porter that
'the other *gentleman* would attend to my baggage'! I have been parboiled with salamanders who seemed to find no inconvenience in a
room temperature of eighty degrees, and have been nigh frozen to
death in open-air drives in which the same individuals seemed perfectly comfortable. Men appear at the theater in orthodox evening
dress, while the tall and exasperating hats of the ladies who accompany them would seem to indicate a theory of street toilette. From
New York to Buffalo I am whisked through the air at the rate of
fifty or sixty miles an hour; in California I traveled on a train on
which the engineer shot rabbits from the locomotive, and the fireman
picked them up in time to jump on the baggage car at the rear end
of the train. At Santa Barbara I visited an old mission church and
convent, which vied in quaint picturesqueness with anything in Europe; but, alas! the old monk who showed us round, though wearing
the regulation gown and knotted cord, had replaced his sandals by
elastic sided boots and covered his tonsure with a common chummy.[5]

Few things in the United States are more pleasing than the widespread habits of kindness to animals (most American whips are, as far
as punishment to the horse is concerned, a mere farce). Yet no American seems to have any scruple about adding an extra hundred weight
or two to an already villainously overloaded horsecar; and I have seen
a score of American ladies sit serenely watching the frantic straining
of two poor animals to get a derailed car on the track again, when I
know that in 'brutal' Old England every one of them would have been
out on the sidewalk to lighten the load.

In England that admirable body of men popularly known as Quakers
are indissolubly associated in the public mind with a pristine simplicity
of life and conversation. My amazement, therefore, may easily be
imagined, when I found that an entertainment given by a young member of the Society of Friends in one of the great cities of the Eastern
States turned out to be the most elaborate and beautiful private ball
I ever attended, with about eight hundred guests dressed in the height
of fashion, while the daily papers (if I remember rightly) estimated its
expense as reaching a total of some thousands of pounds. Here the
natural expansive liberality of the American man proved stronger than
the traditional limitations of a religious society. But the opposite art of
cheese-paring is by no means unknown in the United States. Perhaps
not even canny Scotland can parallel the record of certain districts in
New England, which actually elected their parish paupers to the state

---

[5] This may be paralleled in Europe: 'The Franciscan monks of Bosnia wear long black
robes, with rope, black "bowler" hats, and long and heavy military mustachios (by special
permission of the Pope)'—*Daily Chronicle*, 5 October 1895—[Muirhead's note].

legislature to keep them off the rates. Let the opponents of paid members of the House of Commons take notice!

Amid the little band of tourists in whose company I happened to enter the Yosemite Valley was a San Francisco youth with a delightful baritone voice, who entertained the guests in the hotel parlor at Wawona by a good-natured series of songs. No one in the room except myself seemed to find it in the least incongruous or funny that he sandwiched 'Nearer, My God, to Thee' between 'The Man Who Broke the Bank at Monte Carlo' and 'Her Golden Hair Was Hanging Down Her Back,' or that he jumped at once from the pathetic solemnity of 'I Know That My Redeemer Liveth' to the jingle of 'Little Annie Rooney.' The name Wawona reminds me how American weather plays its part in the game of contrasts. When we visited the Grove of Big Trees near Wawona on 21 May, it was in the midst of a driving snowstorm, with the thermometer standing at 36 degrees Fahrenheit. Next day, as we drove into Raymond, less than forty miles to the west, the sun was beating down on our backs, and the thermometer marked 80 degrees in the shade.

Thirty Years' Development in American Life, 1905 [1] ⟡

JAMES BRYCE *is universally regarded in America as the foremost expositor and critic of American institutions, manners, and traits. He was born in May 1838, in Belfast, and was educated at the University of Glasgow, Oxford, and Heidelberg. Admitted to the bar in 1867, he practiced law until 1882. However, while still in his twenties, in 1862, he had attracted the attention of Americans as well as Englishmen, and had established his position as an historian by publishing his work on* The Holy Roman Empire. *In 1870 he became regius professor of civil law at Oxford, and held the office until 1893.*

Bryce entered public life as a member of Parliament in 1880, and soon became recognized as one of the heads of the Liberal party. Between 1886 and 1894, he successively held the offices of Under-secretary of State for Foreign Affairs, Chancellor of the Duchy of Lancaster,

[1] From the essay, 'America Revisited—Changes of a Quarter Century,' in the *Outlook*, 25 March 1905. Copyright 1905 by the *Outlook*.

and President of the Board of Trade. He sat continuously for Aberdeen in Parliament from 1885 to 1906, and in 1905-6 he was Chief Secretary for Ireland, in Campbell-Bannerman's Cabinet. His career in British politics ended with his appointment as ambassador to the United States in February 1907, a post he held until 1913. It is safe to say that no envoy from Great Britain or any other nation has ever been trusted or admired so much by the American people as was Bryce. To Americans he never seemed an alien, even after he received his title.

His great work, The American Commonwealth, *was published by Bryce in 1888, and in revised form in 1910. The fruit of repeated sojourns in this country, of wide reading on American history and institutions, and of correspondence with many prominent Americans on the subjects discussed, it was at once perceived to be the most thorough study of the United States yet attempted. Its position as a classic has never been questioned. Bryce wrote many other works of note, including impressions of South America and South Africa, essays in history, jurisprudence, and contemporary biography, and a careful inquiry into the workings of democratic government in various parts of the world. His principal recreations were travel and mountain climbing, and his volume on* Transcaucasia and Ararat *records his most notable feat in the latter exercise. For several years he was president of the Alpine Club. He died in 1922.*

BUSINESS AND INDUSTRY

That which most strikes the visitor to America today is its prodigious material development. Industrial growth, swift thirty or forty years ago, advances more swiftly now. The rural districts are being studded with villages, the villages are growing into cities, the cities are stretching out long arms of suburbs, which follow the lines of road and railway in every direction. The increase of wealth, even more remarkable than the increase of population, impresses a European more deeply than ever before because the contrast with Europe is greater. In America every class seems rich compared with the corresponding class in the Old World. The huge fortunes, the fortunes of those whose income reaches or exceeds a million dollars a year, are of course far more numerous than in any other country. But the absence of pauperism is still more remarkable. In 1870 I carefully examined the poor-law system of two great Eastern cities and found that, although there were very few persons needy or receiving support at the public expense, the number was expected to grow steadily and quickly as the cities grew.

Today I am told that in these cities pauperism, though of course absolutely larger, increases more slowly than population.

Life has for a long time been more comfortable and easy for the workingman and the clerk or shopman, as compared with life for the like class in Europe. But for the classes standing next above the laborers in point of income life was in 1870 in general plain and simple, simpler than the life led by the richer class in England or France. Luxury was then confined to a very few. Simplicity is not so common today. The incomes of those who correspond to the so-called 'upper middle class' of Europe are much larger than such persons enjoy in Europe, and they live on a more lavish scale.

The 'easier life,' however, does not mean that life is taken easily. It consists in having and spending more money, not in doing less work. On the contrary, the stress and rush of life seems greater today in America than it ever was before. Everybody, from the workman to the millionaire, has a larger head of steam on than his father had. Whether it be true, as many say, that the vital powers are sooner exhausted, I do not know. It would not be strange if this were so. Time is more precious. More pains are taken to save it. More work is squeezed into the hour and the day.

In this age, more than in any preceding, wealth means power, offensive power in war as well as financial power in peace. It is an old and favorite commonplace of political moralists that the rich nations, dwelling in fertile plains and enervated by luxury, became the victims of the poor nations who, inhabiting barren mountains, were harder and fiercer in fight. It is not so now. Naval war is, above all things, an affair of scientific apparatus, of ironclads, of torpedoes, of guns with long range and quick fire. Land war depends on the best artillery, the best rifles and ammunition, the best commissariat. War is an affair of science, and science is costly. All the great nations can produce good fighting men, and all may happen to have a good general. But some have far greater pecuniary resources than others. None has resources comparable to those of the United States. The Republic is as wealthy as any two of the greatest European nations, and is capable, if she chooses, of quickly calling into being a vast fleet and a vast army. Her wealth and power has in it something almost alarming.

With this extraordinary material development it is natural that, in the United States, business, that is to say industry, commerce, and finance, should have more and more come to overshadow and dwarf all other interests, all other occupations. Every European who visited the country since the beginning of last century seems to have been struck by this fact. It is more striking now than it was thirty-five years ago. But the contrast with Europe is not greater now than it was then. Rather it is less, for in this respect England and Germany have been following in America's footsteps. In them, too, business interests hold a far more conspicuous place than formerly. The land-owners, the professional man, the man of letters are in those countries relatively less important than they were; the financier and manufac-turer more important. Business is king. In American society, as I have said, this feature is an old one. But one illustration of it struck me as new. Lawyers are now to a greater extent than formerly businessmen, a part of the great organized system of industrial and financial enter-prise. They are less than formerly the students of a particular kind of learning, the practitioners of a particular art. And they do not seem to be quite so much of a distinct professional class. Someone seventy years ago called them the aristocracy of the United States, meaning that they led public opinion in the same way as the aristocracy of England led opinion there. They still comprise a large part of the finest intellect of the nation. But one is told that they do not take so keen an interest in the purely legal and constitutional questions as they did in the days of Story and Webster, or even in those of William M. Evarts and Charles O'Conor. Business is king.

Commerce and industry themselves have developed new features. Twenty-two years ago there were no trusts; and trade unions, though they existed, were much less powerful, much less pervasive, much less thoroughly organized than they were in England. Even then, how-ever, corporations had covered a larger proportion of the whole field of industry and commerce in America than in Europe, and their structure was more flexible and more efficient. Today this is still more the case; while as for trusts, they have become one of the most salient phenomena of the country. They fix the attention, they excite the alarm of economists and politicians as well as of traders in the Old World, while they exercise and baffle the ingenuity of American legis-lators. Workingmen follow, through hitherto with unequal steps, the efforts at combination which the lords of production and distribution have been making. The consumer stands by, if not with folded hands, yet so far with no clear view of the steps which he may take for his own protection. Perhaps his prosperity—for he is prosperous—helps him to be acquiescent. The example of the United States, the land in which individualism has been most conspicuously vigorous, may seem to suggest that the world is passing out of the stage of individualism and returning to that earlier stage in which groups of men formed the units of society. The bond of association was, in those early days, kinship, real or supposed, and a servile or quasi-servile dependence of the weak upon the strong. Now it is the power of wealth which enables the few to combine so as to gain command of the sources of wealth; and the stronger the employers become and the less they have a personal tie (such as employers once had) with the workmen, so much the more do the workmen feel compelled to try how they can advance their material interests by the use of similar methods. In both cases there is a loss of that individual liberty which the last generation was taught to expect from the progress of civilization. Power becomes concentrated in a few hands, be they those of the men who control the trusts or those of the men who lead the unions. Is it a paradox to observe that it is because the Americans have been the most individualistic of peoples that they are now the people among whom the art of combination has reached its maximum? The amazing keenness and energy, which were stimulated by the commercial conditions of the country, have evoked and have ripened a brilliant talent for organization. This talent has applied new methods to production and to distribution, and has enabled wealth, gathered into a small number of hands, to dominate even the enormous market of America.

The growth of manufactures might have been predicted half a century ago, for even then it was known that there were vast deposits of coal and iron, that the American people were highly inventive, and that the increase of population would create a prodigious demand for goods. One result, however, of the extension of manufactures may not have been so fully foreseen. I mean the change in the character of the occupations and dwelling places of the people. They are ceasing to be a folk of country dwellers. It is not only that the greater cities extend themselves with amazing speed, and that many of the mineral areas are becoming so covered with villages as to differ little from cities. There is a general disposition to migrate from rural districts to centers of population, where a brisker life and more amusements can be enjoyed. The change is all the more remarkable because agriculture continues to be properous. It has been accelerated by those applications of machinery to agricultural work which enable a farm to be worked by a smaller staff than was formerly needed. Wherever one travels in the Eastern and Northern States one sees new towns rising along the lines of the railroad, and the older towns spreading out. The eye as well as the census table tells one that the people are becoming a people subject to city influences. Already, though the population which lies outside towns with less than eight thousand inhabitants is numerically larger (almost two-thirds), still it is urban ways and habits, urban opinion, urban tendencies that are beginning to prevail in the United States. This process goes on steadily. It will go on all the faster because the good land of the Northwest has now—so one is told—been practically all taken up, while even the irrigation of the

dry lands of the south central West cannot redress the balance by
providing a new rural population to set against the increase of the
cities. This is one of the new facts which strikes a visitor, and especially an Englishman. Thirty-five years ago England was already a
country of city dwellers, and the United States seemed by contrast a
country of agriculturalists. Before long the United States will be like
England, and, one may almost add, like Germany also, a land in which
the urban type of mind and life will preponderate. The change may
be regrettable. Jefferson would have regretted it. But it is unavoidable.
It will tend to increase that nervous strain, that sense of tension, which
Americans are already doomed to show as compared with the more
sluggish races of Europe. There will be less repose than ever in life.
Health may not suffer, nor the death rate increase, for cities can now
be made to show as low a mortality as most country places. In London
we have brought down the rate since 1870 from 23 to 17 per thousand.
Yet the physical strength of the average man may not be quite the
same; and his mental constitution will almost certainly be different.
It may not be inferior—indeed it may be more alert and versatile.
But it will be different.

INTELLECTUAL AND SOCIAL CHANGES

All the changes I have been enumerating tend to make men occupy
themselves more than ever with their work and with material interests
in general. It is true that they have more money, and some of them
more leisure. Hours of labor are shortening, as they have shortened,
and more generally, in Australia. But as labor is more intense while
it lasts, leisure is necessarily given chiefly to amusement. Such conditions may seem unfavorable to intellectual progress. But here comes in
another remarkable change, which casts a new light upon the landscape and fundamentally affects our estimate of the prospect that lies
before the nation.

There has been within these last thirty-five years a development of
the higher education in the United States perhaps without a parallel in
the world. Previously the Eastern States had but a very few universities whose best teachers were on a level with the teachers in the
universities of western Europe. There were a great many institutions
bearing the name of universities over the Northern and Middle States
and the West, and a smaller number in the South, but they gave an
instruction which, though in some places (and especially in New
England) it was sound and thorough as far as it went, was really
the instruction rather of a secondary school than of a university in the

proper sense. In the West and South the teaching, often ambitious when it figured in the program, was apt to be superficial and flimsy, giving the appearance without the solid reality of knowledge. The scientific side was generally even weaker than the literary. These universities and colleges had their value, for their very existence was a recognition of the need for an education above that which the school is intended to supply. I ventured even then to hazard the opinion that the reformers who wished to extinguish the bulk of them or to turn them into schools, reserving the degree-granting power to a selected few only, were mistaken, because improvemnt and development might be expected. But I did not expect that the development would come so fast and go so far. No doubt there are still a great many whose standard of teaching and examination is that of a school, not of a true university. But there are also many which have risen to the European level, and many others which are moving rapidly towards it. Roughly speaking—for it is impossible to speak with exactness—America now has not less than fifteen or perhaps even twenty seats of learning fit to be ranked beside the universities of Germany, France, and England as respects the completeness of the instruction which they provide and the thoroughness at which they aim. Only a few have a professorial staff containing names equal to those which adorn the faculties of Berlin and Leipzig and Vienna, of Oxford, Cambridge, Edinburgh, and Glasgow. Men of brilliant gifts are scarce in all countries, and in America there has hardly been time to produce a supply equal to the immense demand for the highest instruction which has lately shown itself. It is the advance in the standard aimed at, and in the efforts to attain that standard, that is so remarkable. Even more noticeable is the amplitude of the provision now made for the study of the natural sciences and of those arts in which science is applied to practical ends. In this respect the United States has gone ahead of Great Britain, aided no doubt by the greater pecuniary resources which not a few of her universities possess, and which they owe to the wise liberality of private benefactors. In England nothing is so hard as to get money from private persons for any educational purpose. Mr. Carnegie's splendid gift to the universities of Scotland stands almost alone. In America nothing is so easy. There is, indeed, no better indication of the prosperity of the country and of its intelligence than the annual record of the endowments bestowed on the universities by successful businessmen, some of whom have never themselves had more than a common school education. Only in one respect does that poverty which Europe has long associated with learning reappear in America. The salaries of presidents and professors remain low as compared with the average income of persons in the same rank, and as compared with the cost of living. That so many men of an energy and ability sufficient to win success and wealth in a business career do nevertheless devote themselves to a career of teaching and research is a remarkable evidence of the intellectual zeal which pervades the people.[2]

The improvement in the range and quality of university teaching is a change scarcely more remarkable than the increased afflux of students. It seems (for I have not worked the matter out in figures, as I am giving impressions and not statistics) to have grown much faster than population has grown, and to betoken an increased desire among parents and young men to obtain a complete intellectual equipment for life. The number of undergraduates at Harvard is much larger than is the number who resort to Oxford; the number at Yale is larger than the number at Cambridge (England). Five leading universities of the Eastern States—Harvard, Yale, Columbia, Princeton, Pennsylvania—count as many students as do all the universities of England (omitting in both cases those who attend evening classes only), although there are twice as many universities in England now as there were forty years ago, and although the English students have much more than doubled in number. And whereas in England the vast majority go to prepare themselves for some profession—law, journalism, medicine, engineering, or the ministry of the Established Church —there is in America a considerable proportion (in one institution I heard it reckoned at a third or more) who intend to choose a business career, such as manufacturing, or banking, or commerce, or railroading. In England nearly every youth belonging to the middle and upper class who takes to business goes into a commercial office or workshop not later than seventeen. In the United States, if he graduates at a university, he continues his liberal education till he is twenty-one or twenty-two. This practical people do not deem these three years lost time. They believe that the young man is all the more likely to succeed in business if he goes into it with a mind widely and thoroughly trained. To say that the proportion of college graduates to the whole population is larger in America than in any European country would not mean much, because graduation from a good many of the colleges means very little. But if we take only those colleges which approach or equal the West European standard, I think the proportion will be as high as it is in Germany or Switzerland or Scotland and higher than it is in England.

This feature of recent American development has an important bearing on the national life. It is a counterpoise to the passion, growing always more intense, for material progress, to the eagerness to seize

[2] Many subjects are taught to large classes at the best Eastern universities for the study of which hardly any students can be secured in England—[Bryce's note].

every chance, to save every moment, to get the most out of every enterprise. . . It adds to the number of those who may find some occasion
in their business life for turning a knowledge of natural science to
practical account, and so benefiting the country as well as themselves.
Nor is its social influence to be overlooked. One is frequently impressed in America by the attachment of the graduates to the place
of their education, by their interest in its fortunes, by their willingness
to respond when it asks them for money. In the great cities there are
always university clubs, and in some cities these clubs have become
centers for social and political action for good public ends. Not infre-
quently they take the lead in municipal reform movements.

When I pass from the places set apart for the cultivation of letters
and learning to the general state of letters and learning in the community, it is much more difficult to formulate any positive impressions.
One feels a change in the spirit of the books produced, and a change
in the taste of the reading public, but one cannot say exactly in what
the alteration consists, nor how it has come, nor whether it will last.
Having no sufficient materials for a theory on the subject, I can venture
only on a few scattered remarks. Literary criticism, formerly at a low
ebb, seems to have sensibly improved, whereas is England many people
doubt if it is as acute, as judicious, and as delicate as it was in the 'sixties.
The love of poetry and the love of art are more widely diffused in
America than ever before; one finds, for instance, a far greater number of good pictures in private houses than could have been seen
thirty years ago, and the building up of public art galleries has occupied much of the thought and skill of leading citizens as well as
required the expenditure of vast sums. Great ardor is shown in the
investigation of dry subjects, such as questions of local history. The
interest taken in constitutional topics and economic questions, indeed
in everything that belongs to the sphere of political science, is as great
as it is in Germany or France, and greater than in Britain. This interest is, indeed, confined to one class, which chiefly consists of university
teachers, but it is a new and noteworthy phenomenon. Few people
thought or wrote on these matters thirty years ago.

On the other hand, it is said, and that by some who have the best
special opportunities for knowing, that serious books, i.e. books other
than fiction and the lighter form of *belles lettres,* find no larger sale
now, when readers are more numerous and richer, than they did in
the 'seventies. No one can fail to observe the increasing number and
popularity of the magazines, and it seems likely that they are now
more read, in proportion to books, than they used to be. The same
thing is happening in England. It is a natural consequence of the low
prices at which, owing to the vast market, magazines containing good

matter and abundant illustrations can be sold. It may also be due to that sense of hurry, which makes the ordinary American little disposed to sit down to work his way through a book. Both these factors are more potent in the United States than they were ever before, or than they are in Europe.

If in America as well as in England the growth of population has not been accompanied by a growing demand for books (other than fiction), let us remember and allow for the results of another change which has passed upon both countries. It is a change which is all the more noticeable in America because it is there quite recent. It is the passion for looking on at and reading about athletic sports. The love of playing and watching games which require strength and skill is as old as mankind, and needs no explanation. So the desire not to play but to look on at chariot races and gladiatorial combats was a passion among the people of Rome for many centuries. The circus factions at Constantinople have their place in history, and a bad place it is. But this taste is in America a thing almost of yesterday. It has now grown to vast proportions. It occupies the minds not only of the youth at the universities, but also of their parents and of the general public. Baseball matches and football matches excite an interest greater than any other public events except the Presidential election, and that comes only once in four years. The curse of betting, which dogs football as well as horse racing in England, seems to be less prevalent in America; nor do the cities support professional football clubs like those which exist in the towns of northern England and even of Scotland. But the interest in one of the great contests, such as those which draw 40,000 spectators to the great 'Stadium' recently erected at Cambridge, Massachusetts, appears to pervade nearly all classes much more than does any 'sporting event' in Great Britain. The American love of excitement and love of competition has seized upon these games, but the fashion, like that of playing golf and that of playing bridge, seems to have come from England. It is a curious instance of the more intimate social relations between the two countries that speak the same language that fashions of this kind pass so quickly from the one to the other, and do not pass from either to Continental Europe. There has been no development of the devotion to athletic sports in Germany or in France coincident with that which is so marked a feature of modern England and so novel a feature in America.

No subject fixes the attention of social philosophers in Europe who seek for light from the New World more than does the problem of divorce. The states of the union have tried many experiments, and some rash experiments, in this field. The results, momentous for America, may be instructive for the rest of mankind, and are being watched with curiosity by European sociologists. Mr. Gladstone was so profoundly interested in the matter that whenever conversation turned upon the United States he began to inquire about the divorce laws and their working. Such information as I could gather does not enable me to say whether the position is substantially different from what it was twenty years ago, when the legislation which so many observers regret had, in most states, come into operation. There does, however, seem to be a growing reaction against the laxity of procedure in divorce suits, as well as against the freedom granted by the states which have gone farthest; and though little is heard of the proposal that Congress should receive power to pass a general divorce law for the whole country, the suggestion that efforts should be made to induce the states to introduce greater uniformity, and to make the procedure for obtaining divorce less liable to abuse finds increasing favor. It is encouraging to note a stronger sense, among thinking men, of the evils which laxity tends to produce.

Serious as these evils are, the general moral standard of the United States still appears to me, as it did twenty years ago, to be, on the whole, higher than that of western Europe. (The differences between France, Germany, and England are not so great as is commonly supposed.) Even in the wealthiest class, where luxury weakens the sense of duty, and lays men and women most open to temptation, there are apparently fewer scandals than the same class shows elsewhere. Nor is the morality of any country to be measured by the number of divorces. Its condition may be really worse if people cynically abstain from obtaining divorces where there are grounds for obtaining them. Although there is more wealth in America than in England, luxury is less diffused, and that idle and self-indulgent class which sets a bad example to other classes is relatively smaller.

Among minor changes which the traveler notes, he must not forget the growth of what may be called æsthetic sentiment. The desire to have beauty around one, to adorn the house within and the grounds without, if not new, has developed apace since 1870. In one respect it is much more active in the United States than in most parts of Europe. We have in England, so far as I know, none of those Village Improvement Societies, which have arisen in some of the Northern States, and especially in New England. Neither has any English city surrounded itself with such a superb ring of parks and open spaces, some hilly and rocky, some covered with wood, some studded with lakes, as Boston now possesses. America used to be pointed at by European censors as a country where utility was everything and beauty nothing. No one could make such a reproach now. One melancholy exception may,

however, be referred to. Niagara has lost much of the charm that surrounded it in 1870. Hideous buildings line the banks of the rivers below the falls, almost as far down as the railway bridge. The air is full
of smoke. Goat Island has, indeed, been preserved; the Canadians
have laid out a park just below the Horseshoe Fall; and the volume of
the green flood that rushes over the precipice has not been visibly
diminished by all that is now abstracted to work the great turbines.
But the wildness of nature and the clear purity of the sky have departed. It is a loss to the whole world, for the world has no other
Niagara.

The sentiment which seeks to adorn cities and improve the amenity
of villages is near of kin to the sentiment which cherishes the scenes
of historical events and the places associated with eminent men. Here,
too, one feels in the United States the breath of a new spirit. Reverence
for the past and a desire to maintain every sort of connection with it
has now become a strong and growing force among educated people.
A slight but significant illustration of the changed attitude may be
found in the disposition to expect university and (in some places)
judicial officials to wear on formal occasions an official dress. Thirty
years ago no such dress was worn by any functionary in the United
States except the judges of the Supreme Court sitting at Washington.

I must pass over many other points in which new facts, disclosing
new tendencies, present themselves to the observer's eye. One among
them is the attitude of the churches towards one another, and the wider
channels in which religious opinion now flows. Another is the position of women, with the remarkable growth of women's clubs and
societies. People who seemed to be impartial told me that this had
not brought women any more into politics, as a similar change has
done in England. They said, indeed, that the woman suffrage movement, which at one time seemed to be rapidly advancing, had of late
years experienced a check. But I am far from trying to reckon up all
or even most of the changes of thirty-five years. . .

Perhaps I have been overbold in venturing, after a brief visit, to
record so many impressions, hastily formed, upon large questions. But
I am encouraged by the kindness wherewith the comments on American affairs, which I made sixteen years ago, have been received. And
it is hard to resist the temptation to express one's admiration for the
richness and variety of the forms in which civilization has developed
itself in America, for the inexhaustible inventiveness and tireless energy
of the people, for the growing passion for knowledge, the growing
desire to diffuse happiness and enlightenment through every part of
the community.

Good-bye, America! [1] &

HENRY W. NEVINSON. *No living journalist has had a career more active and cosmopolitan than that of Henry W. Nevinson, and few newspapermen in England have contributed more towards the guidance of liberal opinion. Educated at Shrewsbury School and Oxford, Nevinson obtained his first experience as a war correspondent in the Greco-Turkish conflict of 1897, writing for the London* Daily Chronicle. *He was in Spain during the Spanish-American War; in South Africa throughout the Boer War; in Russia during the revolutionary uprising of 1905; and was in the Balkans at the time of the fighting of 1911-13. Meanwhile, he had found time to visit Central Africa in 1904-5, and to expose the Portuguese slave trade in Angola and elsewhere. When the London* Nation *was founded in 1906 by Mr. H. W. Massingham, Nevinson was placed on its staff, and remained connected with it until its change of direction in 1923. He was also at different times leader-writer for the* Daily Chronicle *(1897-1903), and for the* Daily News *(1908-9). World War I saw him active in many different fields. When it broke out he was in Berlin; later he was found in Northern France, where he helped organize the Friends' Ambulance Unit between Dunkirk and Ypres; he was a correspondent for the Manchester* Guardian *in the attack on the Dardanelles, where he was wounded; and he went as a correspondent to Salonika and Egypt as soon as he recovered. Among his books are not only volumes on his experiences in various wars and discussions of current political questions, but several essays in fiction. The following paper was contributed to the London* Nation *as the author arrived home from a visit to the Washington Peace Conference.*

IN mist and driving snow the towers of New York fade from view. The great ship slides down the river. Already the dark, broad seas gloom before her. Good-bye, most beautiful of modern cities! Good-bye to glimmering spires and lighted bastions, dreamlike as the castles and cathedrals of a romantic vision! Good-bye to thin films of white steam that issue from central furnaces and flit in dissolving wreaths around those precipitous heights! Good-bye to heaven-piled offices, so clean, so warm, where lovely stenographers, with silk stockings and powdered faces, sit leisurely at work or converse in charming ease! Good-bye, New York! I am going home. I am going to an ancient city of mean and moldering streets, of ignoble coverts for mankind, extended monotonously over many miles; of grimy smoke clinging closer than a blanket; of smudgy typists who know little of silk or powder, and less of leisure and charming ease. Good-bye, New York! I am going home.

Good-bye to beautiful 'apartments' and 'homes.' Good-bye to windows looking far over the city as from a mountain peak! Good-bye to central heating and radiators, fit symbols of the hearts they warm! Good-bye to frequent and well-appointed bathrooms, glory of the plumber's art! Good-bye to suburban gardens running into each other without hedge or fence to separate friend from friend or enemy from enemy! Good-bye to shady verandas where rocking chairs stand ranged in rows, ready for reading the voluminous Sunday papers and the *Saturday Evening Post!* Good-bye, America! I am going home. I am going to a land where every man's house is his prison—a land of open fires and chilly rooms and frozen water pipes, of washing stands and slop pails, and one bath per household at the most; a land of fences and hedges and walls, where people sit aloof and see no reason to make themselves seasick by rocking upon shore. Good-bye, America! I am going home.

Good-bye to the copious meals—early grapefruit, the 'cereals,' eggs broken in a glass! Good-bye to oysters, large and small, to celery and olives beside the soup, to 'sea food,' to sublimated viands, to bleeding duck, to the salad course, to the 'individual pie' or the thick wedge of apple pie, to the invariable slab of ice cream, to the coffee, also bland with cream; to the home-brewed alcohol! I am going to the land of joints and roots and solid pudding; the land of ham and eggs and violent tea; the land where oysters are good for suicides alone, and where mustard grows and whiskey flows. Good-bye, America! I am going home.

Good-bye to the long stream of motors—'limousines' or 'flivvers'! Good-bye to the signal lights upon Fifth Avenue, gold, crimson, and green; the sudden halt when the green light shines, as though at the magic word an enchanted princess had fallen asleep; the hurried rush for the leisurely lunch at noon; the deliberate appearance of hustle and bustle in business; the Jews, innumerable as the Red Sea sand! Good-bye to outside staircases for escape from fire. Good-bye to scrappy suburbs littered with rubbish of old boards, empty cans, and boots! Good-bye to standardized villages and small towns, alike in litter, in ropes of electric wires along the streets, in clanking 'trolleys,' in chapels, stores, railway stations, Main Streets, and isolated houses flung at random over the country! Good-bye to miles of advertisement imploring me in ten-foot letters to eat somebody's codfish ('No Bones!') or smoke somebody's cigarettes ('They Satisfy'), or sleep with innocence in the 'Faultless Nightgown'! Good-bye to long trains where one smokes in a lavatory, and sleeps at night upon a shelf screened with heavy green curtains and heated with stifling air, while over your head or under your back the baby yells, and the mother tosses moaning, until at last you reach your 'stopping-off place,' and a semi-Negro sweeps you down with a little broom, as in a supreme rite of worship! Good-bye to the house that is labeled 'One Hundred Years Old,' for the amazement of mortality! Good-bye to thin woods and fields inclosed with casual pales, old hoops and lengths of wire! I am going to the land of a policeman's finger, where the horse and the bicycle still drag out a lingering life; a land of old villages and towns as little like each other as one woman is like the next; a land where trains are short, and one seldom sleeps in them, for in any direction within a day they will reach a sea; a land of vast and ancient trees, of houses time-honored three centuries ago, of cathedrals that have been growing for a thousand years, and of village churches built while people believed in God. Good-bye, America! I am going home.

Good-bye to the land of a new language in growth, of split infinitives and cross-bred words; the land where a dinner jacket is a 'Tuxedo,' a spittoon a 'cuspidor'; where your opinion is called your 'reaction,' and where 'vamp,' instead of meaning an improvised accompaniment to song, means a dangerous female! Good-bye to the land where grotesque exaggeration is called humor, and people gape in bewilderment at irony, as a bullock gazes at a dog straying in his field! Good-bye to the land where strangers say, 'Glad to meet you, sir,' and really seem glad; where children whine their little desires, and never grow much older; where men keep their trousers up with belts that run through loops, and women have to bathe in stockings! I am going to a land of ancient speech where we still say 'record' and 'concord' for 'recud' and 'concud,' where 'necessarily' and 'extraordinarily' must be taken at one rush—a hedge-ditch-and-rail in the hunting field; where we do not 'commute' or 'check' or 'page,' but 'take a season' and 'register' and 'send a boy round'; where we never say we are glad to meet a stranger, and seldom are; where humor is understatement and irony is our habitual resource in danger or distress; where children are told they are meant to be seen and not heard; where it is 'bad form' to express emotions, and suspenders are a strictly feminine article of attire. Good-bye, America! I am going home.

Good-bye to the multitudinous papers, indefinite of opinion, crammed with insignificant news, and asking you to continue a first-page article on page 23, column 5! Good-bye to the weary platitude, accepted as wisdom's latest revelation! Good-bye to the docile audiences that lap rhetoric for substance! Good-bye to politicians contending for aims more practical than principles! Good-bye to Republicans and Democrats, distinguishable only by mutual hatred! Good-bye to the land where Liberals are thought dangerous and Radicals show red! Where Mr. Gompers is called a Socialist, and Mr. Asquith would seem advanced! A land too large for concentrated indignation; a land where wealth beyond the dreams of British profiteers dwells, dresses, gorges, and luxuriates, emulated and unashamed! I am going to a land of politics violently divergent; a land where even coalitions cannot coalesce; where meetings break up in a turbulent disorder, and no platitude avails to soothe the savage beast; a land fierce for personal freedom and indignant with rage for justice; a land where wealth is taxed out of sight, or for very shame strives to disguise its luxury; a land where an ancient order is passing away and leaders whom you call extreme are hailed by Lord Chancellors as the very fortifications of security. Good-bye, America! I am going home.

Good-bye to prose chopped up to look like verse! Good-bye to the indiscriminate appetite, which gulps lectures as opiates and 'printed matter' as literature! Good-bye to the wizards and witches who ask to psychoanalyze my complexes, inhibitions, and silly dreams! Good-bye to the exuberant religious or fantastic beliefs by which unsatisfied mankind still strives desperately to penetrate beyond the flaming bulwarks of the world! Good-bye, Americans! I am going to a land very much like yours. I am going to your spiritual home.

Part V

Travelers of the Fifth Period, 1922-46

Travelers of the Fifth Period, 1922-46

Boom, Depression, and War ஜ

A NEW America and a new Britain were brought into existence by the First World War; and these new nations, shaking off most of their old antagonisms, had formed new ties. It was impossible for intelligent citizens of the two lands to forget that they had been partners in the desperate conflict, and were still to a great extent partners in facing the problems of a stormy world. It is true that Woodrow Wilson and Lloyd George did not see eye to eye in making the Peace of Versailles. It is true that the United States, after rejecting the League, retreated for a time into its old shell of political isolation. But the numerous Britons represented by Sir Robert Cecil, and the much larger body, who were long led by Ramsay MacDonald, did think and act in general harmony with the Wilsonian liberals in America and with the American exponents of social democracy. British labor and American labor increasingly shared the same outlook. Beneath surface irritations, the nations fundamentally trusted one another as lovers of peace, of freedom, and of orderly progress.

Moreover, after the Japanese seizure of Manchuria, the rise of Adolf Hitler, and the formation of the Axis for purposes of aggression, the two Powers were gradually forced to stand shoulder to shoulder in their external relations. Despite some marked differences on the question of disarmament, a serious initial failure to work harmoniously in the Orient, and sharp divergences in attitude toward the question of debts, they took paths that soon ran parallel, and that ultimately converged. The time came when Winston Churchill, speaking of this merging of British and American interests, said that, like the Mississippi, it would roll on to its appointed conclusion—nothing could stop it; while Franklin D. Roosevelt and Wendell Willkie joined in a crusading movement to make the United States, though still nominally at peace, the arsenal and storehouse of embattled Britain. Within a short period, the two countries were again partners in war, and their leaders had united in a pledge that they would be partners in making an enduring peace.

Beyond question, the American and British peoples had far more in common by the year 1940 than at any previous time. They possessed more grounds of agreement and fewer of difference than in 1865 or 1825; many more ties of likeness than in 1765, when they had been politically united. Fundamental changes in both lands had rendered them much more homogeneous. Politically and economically, Great Britain had been democratized. The series of nineteenth-century extensions of the suffrage, the shift in taxation to bear heavily upon wealth, and the social welfare measures passed under Gladstone, Campbell-Bannerman, Lloyd George, and MacDonald had in fact made Britain a much more radical democracy than the United States. Economically, the industrialization of the United States had meanwhile given its society many of the troubles, problems, and attitudes characteristic of industrial England. America, too, had become crowded, with great slums, restless laboring masses, and heavy tasks of relief. It was no accident that the first lifelong leader of the American Federation of Labor and the first two Secretaries of Labor were British born. When the United States under Woodrow Wilson and Franklin D. Roosevelt wrote its first welfare and social-insurance legislation, it turned to Britain for models. And intellectually the bonds between the two lands had been multiplied and strengthened. The free interchange of newspapers and magazines, the binational character of most great publishing houses, the mass circulation of American books in Britain as well as British books in America, the Rhodes scholarships, the increasing exchange of teachers and lecturers, the movies, the radio, and the facilities for swift cheap travel had made the countries neighbors. Meanwhile, the liberation of Ireland and the growth of the young British democracies—Canada, Australia, New Zealand, South Africa—had deepened the American friendliness toward what was no longer an Empire but a true Commonwealth of Nations.

It was an uncertain and swift-changing world that the democracies faced after Versailles; and after 1929 it became a depressed and chaotic world, with anxiety the dominant note in both lands, and war looming directly ahead. While British travelers in America were numerous, their stays were usually short, and the times were not favorable to long and careful studies of American society. Moreover, contacts between the two nations were so easy and varied that the need for sustained analyses no doubt seemed to have disappeared. At any rate, the shelf-ful of British travel works written between 1920 and 1940 is made up almost completely of brief volumes of reportorial character. Most of the visitors were intent upon giving a sharp personal impression, and attempted nothing so ambitious as the books by the German M. J. Bonn and the Frenchman André Siegfried. If brevity and impressionism stamped the construction of these English works, their spirit was informed by a distinctly new attitude—the attitude of deference. For the first time, the great majority of British visitors showed themselves distinctly respectful of the rich, powerful, and exceedingly complex nation beyond the seas. During the period that we have described as one of Tory condescension, the travelers had tended to look down upon Americans; during the later period that we have described as one of analysis, they tended to look at the United States with level gaze; but now they frequently tended to look up at America!

This change in spirit, while pleasing to most Americans, was not altogether wise or profitable. A keener critical edge would have benefited the travel literature of the time. A few books, like C. E. M. Joad's *The Babbitt Warren* and C. H. Bretherton's *Midas: The United States of the Future,* did possess an acid quality. They represented a healthy reaction against the portly-pompous and stupidly complacent United States of Harding and Coolidge, against the Age of the Golden Calf. More such books, longer, better written, and keener, would have been distinctly valuable. The two volumes named failed to do what our own satiric writers—H. L. Mencken, Sinclair Lewis, Theodore Dreiser, John Dos Passos, Upton Sinclair, John Steinbeck, and Erskine Caldwell—were accomplishing. The heavy vein of criminality and corruption in American life, the conventional hypocrisy, the surrender to tabus, prejudices, and fetishes, the widespread intolerance, the sordid commercialism, the inequalities of opportunity, the poverty, the brutal repression of labor, the smug indifference to glaring social problems, all invited a sharp exposure. It was not to the credit of British travelers that they took so little effective part in the attack. While Bretherton, Joad, and the jaunty author of *I Lost My English Accent* did not overlook the more potent evils, they failed to put them in proper perspective, to cut into them deeply, or to draw the proper conclusions from them. These three writers said much less in their reportorial books than Mencken, Lewis, and, later on, Faulkner and Steinbeck succeeded in saying; and they said it rather feebly and blunderingly.

Changes both of subject matter and of emphasis presented themselves in these writers of the lull between two world wars. Many of the old staple topics—city life, political graft, crime, food, universities, recreation, athletics, scenery, industrialism—were treated in much the old way. But the travelers manifested an increased concern over the standardization of American life. Mass production was one of the

great facts of the Harding-Coolidge-Hoover era, believed by many
fatuous Americans to be the key to a permanent prosperity; and Englishmen were keenly curious about Henry Ford's cars, Statler's hotels,
Gillette's safety razors, and Wrigley's packages of gum. It is to the
credit of two of the shrewdest of them, L. P. Jacks and J. B. Priestley,
that they refused to be worried overmuch by the machine-made uniformity in gadgets and practical appliances, seeing in it less of an
evil than an implement to liberate the spirit for individualized and
diversified self-expression. Two transitory phases of American life,
the Prohibition experiment and the worry of parents over the post-
bellum 'wildness' of adolescents, received much attention. Again it was
to the credit of British observers that they refused to take either as
gravely as many Americans did; it was too clear that they would prove
transient. For the rest, most visitors felt it important to view (rather
disapprovingly) the tinsel glories of Hollywood. Most of them looked
about in Chicago for gangsters. Most of them paid no attention to
echoes of the Revolution; rather, it was for echoes of the First World
War, especially on the debt question, that they cocked their ears. One
and all, after 1933, struggled to learn about the New Deal, and ended
by remarking that in England most of it would be thought an Old
Deal.

Classification of these books of travel, in view of their general lack
of analytical quality, is difficult; but we can clear the board of half
a dozen by simply lumping them together as trivial or ephemeral.
No permanent value whatever attaches to the Earl of Birkenhead's
America Revisited, the outgrowth of a semipolitical tour made in
1923. The eminent and bibulous author noted some important changes
since his previous visit. Among these were the northward drift of the
Negroes, transforming large areas of Chicago and New York; the immense multiplication of automobiles; and the aggressive dominance
of business. He laid down a heartfelt opinion that the Prohibition experiment must be doomed to failure, he protested against the demand
for high tariff barriers, and he pleaded for more idealism in international affairs. But as a whole the book, pieced out with his public
addresses, was thoroughly unoriginal.

Sisley Huddleston's *What's Right with America,* brought out in the
year that nearly everything became wrong in that land—1930—was
not so much unoriginal as erroneous; in fact, dismally and fatuously
mistaken. The author, a veteran journalist who had lived chiefly in
France but had enjoyed 'the closest and happiest relations with the
United States,' visited the republic for the first time at the height of
the Coolidge-Hoover bull market. Bemused by the frenzied optimism
about him, and misled by tycoons to whom he bore letters of intro-

duction, he came near penning a celebration of the boom in the wild stage just before it burst. In fact, much of his book *is* a celebration of it. 'I did not paint America as an earthly paradise,' he writes in his closing pages. 'I merely said that there is a new attitude toward industrial problems, that some cherished European doctrines have been shattered, and that America has been comparatively prosperous.' What did he mean by the new American attitude? It was Henry Ford's golden specific. You could produce cheaply if you produced in vast quantities, you could produce in vast quantities if you had a huge purchasing public, and your purchasing public could be huge if your proletariat were paid high wages. Alas! this simple rule for an endlessly swelling prosperity suddenly ceased to work just as Mr. Huddleston's book was about to reach the counters. Men passed overnight from the dreams that they had shattered the 'cherished European doctrines' of old-school economists to the harsh question: Could the American economy be restored? Could it even survive?

It was a curious melange of reasons that Mr. Huddleston gave for liking America. He praised the country for its architecture, 'the national expression of a new form of art'; for having revolted against privilege to establish a true democracy; for being the land of opportunity; for its adventurous and optimistic spirit; and for its thirst after knowledge, its avid interest in letters, drama, and music. Our suspicion that Mr. Huddleston did not see America exactly as it was is heightened when we find him praising the United States of 1928-9 because 'growth is the law of America'; because men do not worship the dollar, although they 'rightly' consider it the barometer of success in most callings; because they 'have a strict business code'; and because business is looked upon as 'a branch of public service.' All this sounded curiously on the bleak morning after, as shabby men peddled apples for a living, as Samuel Insull fled to Greece to escape trial, as the desperate Okies and Arkies streamed toward California, and as the popular wrath against bankers and industrialists carried Roosevelt into office. Mr. Huddleston's chapter on 'The Americanism of Mr. Hoover' was a gush of compliments, like his pages on Detroit and Chicago. He entitled his description of the response to the first stock-market crash, 'Invincible Optimism.' Perhaps he was on his soundest ground when he spoke an enthusiastic word for roast loin of pork and candied sweet potatoes.

A commonplace quality pervades Sir Charles Igglesden's book, *A Mere Englishman in America,* the work of one of a party of fourteen journalists who, as guests of the Carnegie Endowment, journeyed across America and back again in 1928. His volume has a certain pleasing bluntness on some points. Sir Charles thought New York's street paving deplorable. He was disgusted by a Prohibition that did not prohibit. Twice, in Los Angeles and Chicago, his hotel was invaded by hordes of university students, boys and girls attending a football match, who kept up a mad revelry all night. They danced, sang, shouted, and drank till dawn, throwing bottles out of the window until the courtyard was full of broken glass. 'In the corridors,' writes Sir Charles, 'I had almost to fight my way past excited and intoxicated young men and women, the latter mostly pretty girls in evening dress.' He heard much about the prevalent sexual laxity. 'I was staggered by the charges made against the better-class young girls of the United States by writers in books, magazines, and newspapers.' The apparent frequency of gangsterism and drug addiction appalled him. But he was pleased by the orderliness of our elections and the vitality of our culture. And he was impressed by the larger cities; the fact that Denver and Kansas City, so recently frontier outposts, should possess so much charm, opulence, and intellectual interest, such fine galleries, libraries, and museums, so many cultivated groups, struck him as really wonderful.

Other works of but minor importance and interest include the Earl of Cottenham's *Mine Host America;* Sir Anthony Jenkisson's *America Came My Way;* and A. G. Macdonell's *A Visit to America.* The good Earl drove a car across the continent, observing and moralizing as he went, and then came back by airplane. His information upon motoring facilities, hotels, and scenery is excellent if undistinguished. A more valuable feature of his book is a shrewd comparison between the methods, finances, and general efficiency of the American and British airlines. Price lists of hotels, restaurants, and garages are included. Some good vivid passages of narrative stud the volume. But perhaps its most remarkable, and certainly its most refreshing, element is its comment upon Roosevelt and the New Deal. The Earl was shocked to find how universal was the dislike of rich Americans for the President, and how intolerant they were to his own arguments in behalf of the Roosevelt reforms. He set down a frank and sensible condemnation of the blindness of our wealthy classes in ignoring the demands of the under-privileged, and he excoriated their folly in wasting money on the Liberty League and similar reactionary organizations. It is pleasant to find a member of the British 'aristocracy' so sharply rebuking the American upper crust for its Bourbonism and selfishness.

Both Sir Anthony Jenkisson and Mr. Macdonell also plainly sympathized with the great movement for reform and social betterment under way when they visited the republic, and were perplexed by the opposition to it. Sir Anthony, indeed, gives most of his space to politics. He met President Roosevelt, who impressed him deeply, and Huey Long, who did not. He was struck by the high objects of the New Dealers, and the heavy obstacles to the proper execution of their plans—the lack of a strong professional body of civil servants, the conservatism of the courts, and the conflicts between Federal and state jurisdiction. Searching for a 'real America,' which he thought he found in a clambake, a Florida steak roast, and the day coaches of his trains, he liked the plain Americans of whom God had made so many. The citizenry struck him as on the whole kindly, orderly, law-abiding, and idealistic. As for Mr. Macdonell, he offers a series of well-organized, thorough, and shrewd pictures of travel, not neglecting some places seldom visited by Britons. He includes, for example, brief graphic sketches of Brooklyn, Peoria, and Billings, while he expatiates upon the strangely Scottish look of the Dakotas. He, too, liked the plain American. Perhaps his angriest pages deal with a defect that has been partially remedied since his visit—the national neglect of historic sites and buildings.

We rise to three more smartly written works in Philip Guedalla's *Conquistador: American Fantasia* (1927), Collinson Owen's *The American Illusion* (1929), and Morgan Philips Price's *After Sixty Years* (1936). Mr. Guedalla records a 'wildly exciting' lecture tour, which began in New York, took him from coast to coast and back again, and never really gave him sufficient time to observe and reflect. But he applies his brilliant style to some admirable snapshots of widely differing scenes—a Michigan tank town, the Grand Canyon, Gettysburg under a blanket of snow, a Western legislature pausing to receive the English guest, the Huntington Art Gallery, Hollywood, and Des Moines. Although he studied and disapproved of Prohibition, he was not greatly interested in institutions, laws, or even manners. Ironic humor is his forte, epigram his pleasure, and fantasy his greatest charm. He finds a text in the Sioux Falls *Dispatch* stating of a nineteen-year-old girl, just being let out of jail for bank robbery: 'Miss Meyers has not announced her plans after gaining her freedom.' He tells how the visiting Queen of Roumania 'relieves the tedium of court life (and her country's budget) by assisting the sale of beauty specialties.' And he thinks, as he gazes at the Romneys and Gainsboroughs in San Marino, that he ought to tell these figures all the London news —how Mr. Walpole finished Strawberry Hill, Charles Fox died a minister, and the Prince of Wales married a German princess after all.

Mr. Owen's book, written by an accomplished novelist, sparkles with *bons mots*. Its distinguishing quality is a certain melodramatic tone, which at times may be called a virtue and at others a vice. Owen's long description of Hollywood (which with tongue in cheek

he terms 'The City of Romance') is melodramatic. So is his chapter
on the trial and execution of two murderers, one a white woman of
breeding, in New Orleans. What disturbed him was not their sentence,
a just retribution for their *crime passionel,* but the eighteen months of
agonizing suspense they spent between their trial and the hanging. In
Washington the place that interested Mr. Owen most was 'Where Lincoln Died'—that is, Ford's Theatre and the red-brick house near by,
where the President had expired. In New York, he treats us to some
highly colored pages on 'The Murder in Room 349'; for, asking for a
quiet hotel, he was sent to the one in which Arnold Rothstein had
recently been shot. Chicago and its gang wars amused him, and he
quotes with relish the Chicago Chief of Police: 'Well, all I can say
is that a coffin a day keeps the New York gangsters away from Chicago.' In California he met the Master of Sensationalism, William
Randolph Hearst, and had the courage to expostulate with him over
the inaccuracy of an editorial attacking England. Hearst replied with
affable boyishness, making it plain that whenever he wanted to get
his effects, a little inaccuracy (or dishonesty) did not bother him.

Altogether, it is a vivid sketchbook that Mr. Owen offers us, with
a good many significant scenes and facts set down in swift, telling
paragraphs. Hear him on a certain well-remembered tragedy in New
York:

My friend of the moment brings up—oddly enough—the subject of Prohibition. He tells me the story of two millionaire brothers of Chicago, the Dodge
brothers, famous names in America, manufacturers of motor cars, who went to
New York on a business visit. They had nothing to drink with them, and so in
the suite of their expensive hotel sent out a bellhop to find something. He returned with an atrocious liquid masquerading as whiskey, which brought a
lingering death to both of them.

One can imagine the scene. The page boy, the tip, the arrival of the waiter
with glasses, soda water, and dice, and then . . . !

'The hard luck of it was that back in Chicago, in their homes, they had cellars
packed with the best,' says my companion.

Or hear him on the industrialism that Mr. Huddleston had so much
admired:

I met a New Yorker who told me that one of the saddest sights he had ever
seen was the faces of the myriad workmen as they left one of the greatest motor-
car factories in the world, where each man had been engaged on some small,
simple mechanical task, hour after hour, and every day, and so on forever. And
of another great and famous factory, cash registers this time, where for greater
celerity and efficiency everybody, from the highest employee to the lowest, ran
about on roller skates, with slow tracks for those who were only in a normal
hurry, and speed tracks for those in a desperate hurry. And he did not seem to

think that these things made for an ideal existence. It is my shrewd belief that
he is not the only American who thinks in the same way.

An excellent idea underlies the book of Philips Price, Gloucestershire
agriculturist and Laborite M.P., who had been a correspondent of the
Manchester *Guardian* in Russia and of the *Daily Herald* in Berlin.
He offers parallel narratives sixty years apart in date. His father had
come to America in 1868, just after being elected to Parliament, partly
for sightseeing and partly to look after timber and railroad interests.
He had been accompanied by Sir Michael Hicks-Beach. Mr. Price re-
prints some sixty pages of his father's diaries. They deal with under-
currents of Canadian politics in Sir John MacDonald's day; life in
Chicago just after the great fire; the journey to the West Coast in one
of the very first transcontinental trains, for the elder Price was one of
the earliest men to use the Union Pacific. He also made an interesting
journey to the Yosemite when it was still untouched and unspoiled,
and to Salt Lake City, which, like nearly all Britons, he admired. But
he was horrified by the misrule of Southern Reconstruction. 'The
South has been shamefully plundered,' he declared, 'and as a thor-
ough-paced republican, I am heartbroken by the gigantic system of
corruption, which prevails from high to low. Office is only a means
of making a fortune.' A few interesting pages also deal with a later
visit by the elder Price on his honeymoon (1878), when he saw much
of General Sherman. He thought the great commander fascinatingly
brilliant, and compared him with Huxley in the range of his information.

But the best parts of the book are the younger Price's 'Impressions
of America under the New Deal,' in 1934-5. This sturdy Laborite got
off the beaten track in an effort to talk with plain workers and farmers. He took pains to cover the farming areas of the Middle West,
the California valleys, and the depressed cotton-growing districts of
the South. In New York he was not beguiled by skyscrapers and art
galleries into ignoring painful social problems. Going down into the
slums, he was quick to perceive the terrible hardships of life there.
He found great areas where 'probably half of the people are now unemployed or frozen in, a derelict population.' It seemed to him enormously to the credit of President Roosevelt that he had organized
measures for the relief of this submerged element. Nor, after witnessing the Congressional campaign of 1934, did he at all like the President's opponents:

During our stay in New York I paid several visits to Wall Street. I found the
bankers and stockbrokers in an unhappy and unchastened mood. They seemed
to have learned nothing and forgotten nothing. They feel that the New Deal is

a dangerous experiment and that they will have to pay for it. They ignored the fact that the Federal Government saved them when it closed the banks for a few days in the panic of 1933, and restored the public confidence which they had destroyed. They are willing to accept that species of aid, but unwilling to give any kind of guarantee that the same sort of trouble will not occur again. They talked as if they wanted Roosevelt to abandon public relief schemes for giving aid to the unemployed, and in return they had nothing to offer save cutthroat competition and the old unplanned speculation. They are the modern American Bourbons.

At the same time, Mr. Price recognized that Wall Street was largely the product of a tradition. The atmosphere of the frontier and the aggressive role of the pioneer had encouraged speculation and discouraged the more sober, plodding types of investment. American individualism had always been antagonistic to governmental intervention; American thrift had always detested heavy government spending. He was struck by the absolutely inordinate fear among industrial leaders of any sort of public expenditure. 'I found the brokers excitedly discussing principles which all political parties had long ago accepted in England.' But if he disliked Wall Street, he was also scornful of the extreme leftist elements in New York, the pink-hued editors of the radical weeklies and the brash young pseudo-intellectuals. They had gone over altogether too wildly to Marxian principles, and many of them talked about Franklin D. Roosevelt as if he were a fascist. Price shrewdly decided that New York, like other great metropolitan cities, 'is likely to become a sounding board for extremes.'

Where was the real America? Part of it, substantial, sanely progressive, and full of integrity, he found in the plain farmers of the Middle West. Going out to a typical Iowa farm, as he ate fried chicken, waffles, and pumpkin pie, he appreciatively studied his hosts. 'One could almost see the stern lines of the Pilgrim Fathers written on their faces. Their spiritual food was Evangelical Christianity, the Bible, a healthy belief that all men are born equal, and hard work.' Very certainly, he wrote, the shades of Jefferson and Lincoln were presiding over this humble home. But these farmers, he adds, had a wider outlook than their ancestors. They wanted to know about farm prices in England, and the outlook for an improved international trade. At Ames the work of the State Agricultural College deeply impressed this Gloucestershire agriculturist: its planning of farm production, its study of taxation, its efforts to organize the tillers co-operatively. He thought poorly of the radical Farmers' Union under Miles Reno. When he interviewed the leaders, he found that they realized the Roosevelt program had taken the wind out of their sails, and that they could now justify their existence only by picking out small flaws in the government's plans and magnifying them. But in the Wisconsin-Minnesota country he discovered a healthier political atmosphere:

This region is a dairy land with surplus milk which has to be made into butter and cheese. The rugged individualism of the farmers of these parts seems to have been directed into a collectivist channel. They have realized sooner than other farmers of the Middle West that their particular problem of handling surplus milk can be solved only by co-operative effort. Leaders of strong personality have arisen among them and have given their movement a political color; indeed, many of the remedies proposed are frankly socialist in all but name. For several years the Farmers' Party has ruled Minnesota with the vigorous Governor Olsen at its head. They demand a nationalization of transportation, banking, and the packing corporations. The La Follette brothers, at the head of an independent party in the neighboring state of Wisconsin, are hardly less advanced. Still, I do not anticipate the rise of a third or agrarian party in the United States.

Everywhere Mr. Price found change under way, and most of it for the better. The hothouse atmosphere of California, with its Utopias and wild radicalism on one side, its massive purblind reactionism on the other, depressed him. But even there, he found reassuring tendencies. Mr. Hoover's state was fast awakening to some of its problems. A commission on unemployment had done excellent work. When he visited the Giannini Institute at the University of California, he found that Washington had denuded it of a large part of its staff and research workers, while Secretary of Agriculture Wallace had wanted even more. 'I think this speaks volumes. The Federal Government is gradually increasing its prestige in the land. No longer are the best brains concentrated in the local centers. The United States is forced under modern conditions to centralize its talents.' Seeing Secretaries Wallace and Ickes in Washington, and finding their departments veritable hives of activity, he was confirmed in this conclusion:

One is impressed both here and in the other Federal Departments by the existence of an efficient public service, the complete absence of which is such a feature of the public administration of the states and the municipalities. The spoils system has ruined local government, but in Washington a tradition of public service is being built up and a body of men is being created, which has all the drive and efficiency which has hitherto been the monopoly only of big business and private enterprise. The growth in public conscience of the United States will soon have an adequate body of public servants to minister to its wants.

Much alarmed by the Supreme Court decisions adverse to the New Deal, Mr. Price perceived that something would have to be done to cut through them. In his father's time, he remarked, 'the wealth of a continent could still be exploited in a wild rush of individualistic effort. Today if America is to live, her citizens must learn to co-operate in housekeeping. A beginning has been made, but the way is long and difficult.' Yet he ended on a hopeful note:

Our last wish, as we saw the floodlit Statue of Liberty disappear in the winter haze of the Hudson, was that the new phase of American liberty which is now opening shall be as rich in great men and noble achievements as the past phases have been, and that the English-speaking peoples on both sides of the Atlantic, in view of the dangers to our common liberties from the rise of militarism and fascist dictators in Europe, shall understand each other as never before.

Two rather brief books by women observers, E. M. Delafield's *The Provincial Lady in America* (1934) and Mary Agnes Hamilton's *In America Today* (1932), also deal approvingly with the new tendencies that asserted themselves after the crash of 1929. Miss Delafield's volume, however, really gives little attention to politics. The novelist, visiting America at the instance of her New York publishers, naturally called in a favorite fictitious character (the Provincial Lady) as her mouthpiece. This village gentlewoman found the Atlantic liner a palace of terrors. She thought the United States only less dismaying. Everywhere she went, the Americans said (or as she put it, screamed) the same questions; and in especial, they wanted her opinion on the romance *Anthony Adverse*—the huge bulk of which daunted her. She admired the great new undertakings in Washington, but her chief interest was in quiet memorials of the past. Thus she astonished her Boston friends by remarking that the one sight she would not miss was the home of Louisa May Alcott at Concord.

Miss Hamilton, an experienced journalist, naturally wrote a very different book—one much more direct and businesslike. But her canvas was designedly small—'not America but the America of 1932 is the object of description.' Perhaps her most striking chapter is that depicting the violent side of American life (including the kidnapping of the Lindbergh baby, and the callous indifference of most people to vice and lawlessness), under the title, 'No One Is Shocked.' In treating the psychological gloom of America after the panic, she made the acute remark that its cause lay not so much in the material losses of the crash as in the terrible shock to the American sense of self-confidence. Economic success had been the universal criterion of social value, and Americans simply could not imagine a failure of private enterprise. It had come upon a stupendous scale, and they were proportionately depressed.

The four ablest books on American life in its latest period were written by four men who had a special familiarity with American affairs, and special links with the American people. J. A. Spender's *The America of Today* (1928)—the American title being *Through English*

Eyes—was the work of a journalist who had known many leaders of public life in the United States, who had read much on our history, and who had made repeated visits to our shores. In two of these visits, paid after 1920, he stayed several months each time. The trip specially described in his book was one taken as the first Senior Walter Hines Page Fellow under a scheme organized by the English-Speaking Union. He gives a budget of general impressions; a very fair survey of American life and institutions—perhaps on the whole too favorable; and in the final section, a discussion of American policies and British-American relations. The unfavorable sides of transatlantic life he puts to one side. It is on the desirable aspects that he dwells—the general zeal for education, the spirit of social equality, the grit and initiative of the young people, the scientific organization of mass production, the idealistic interest in benevolence and good works, the readiness of rich men to endow public institutions lavishly, and the receptive quality of the American mind. All this engendered a positive enthusiasm in Mr. Spender. Ignoring our faults, he failed to give a balanced picture of the country and its pursuits.

It was this balance at which L. P. Jacks, a university teacher who had been trained in part at Harvard, who had repeatedly visited America thereafter, and who had a host of friends from New York to San Francisco, aimed. He began his book on *My American Friends* (1933) by laying down three shrewd rules for works on the United States. First, he wrote, avoid generalizations; the phenomena of American life are highly varied, discordant, and fluctuating, and what at first blush seems typical soon turns out to be quite untypical. Second, judge nothing in America by the point at which it has arrived, but rather judge all things by the direction in which they are moving. Institutions and ways that are fixed in Europe are dynamic in the New World. Third, whenever the observer is struck by a feature that seems to him peculiarly good or peculiarly evil, let him at once look about for its contrary. He is sure to find it; and he is sure to find also how definitely the good and evil tendencies in America are in conflict. 'The significant fact is not the *existence* of these opposites, but the fierce struggle for mastery in which they are everywhere engaged.' The author added that the so-called American people had not yet really come into existence, but were in a state of emergence. In 1886 young Jacks, studying with William James and Charles Eliot Norton at Harvard, had scrutinized one aspect of the United States—the New England aspect—thoroughly. On later visits he had studied other aspects. But he never forgot Lord Bryce's gentle admonition to him at lunch in 1907—not to think he knew more about the country than he did.

Acting on his three rules, Dr. Jacks struck a nice balance between defects and virtues. He thought the American intelligentsia very intelligent, especially in university and journalistic circles; but he deplored its unwillingness to play any part in governing the country. In Woodrow Wilson it had furnished the republic one true statesman, but in general it left politics entirely to the professional politicians. The Rhodes scholars, he believed, had deplorably failed to take their proper part in public affairs. He admitted that American towns and cities looked highly standardized, and that Sinclair Lewis was right when in *Main Street* he attacked the universal sameness of the lumber yards, railroad stations, garages, stores, newspapers, syndicated features, packaged goods, ready-made suits, and slangy language. But all this, he pointed out, had its healthy side. Standardization in nonessentials of culture enables men to diversify the essentials of culture. Indeed, 'standardization is a condition absolutely essential to all forms of human originality.' He looked at American children, and found them undisciplined and ill-bred. But he also found them original, independent, clean, and healthy; and he was told that in many immigrant communities the children had carried higher standards of decency and order ('American' standards) into their homes. He noted that Americans did not take enough outdoor exercise, relied too heavily on automobiles, and pampered their women too much. But they had the best systems of organized community recreation to be found on the globe.

An educator himself, Dr. Jacks was particularly interested in educational tendencies. He found America the land *par excellence* of conferences, discussion, and argument, of endless public debate about all kinds of issues. Even in proletarian circles he noted a high level of intelligence and knowledge in the disputation. In Los Angeles, for example, he went to palm-shaded Pershing Square to listen to the hundreds of men of the 'Spit and Argue Club' as they talked about every conceivable subject from free will to crop control. One tightly packed group was gathered around two keen debaters who were canvassing the respective claims of Shakespeare and of Schopenhauer to be called the greatest man the human race had produced. 'Each knew well what he was talking about and a better conducted argument I have seldom heard.' Another group was discussing relativity, and a third was waging a fierce duel over modernism and fundamentalism in religion.

In organized education, Jacks discerned four major changes in process. One was the assignment of an increasing place to physical education; another was the tendency to bring the play side of school and college life into the field of education, not as a relief from classroom activities but as a positive addition to them; a third was the increasing effort to awaken the creative energy of students instead of drilling

them in mere book knowledge; and a fourth was the growth outside
the educational system of clubs, leagues, community centers, forums,
and like activities, which were doing educational work of the utmost
value on a grand scale. In all this the dominant ideal was highly practical, even technical:

> From a certain point of view, and one I have found myself constantly taking,
> not the schools alone but the whole country might be described as one vast poly-
> technic; perhaps 'polytechnic civilization' would be a better name than 'industrial
> civilization' for the stage of evolution through which America is now passing,
> with all the Western world at her heels. Technique, always in process of further
> refinement, has imposed itself on everything, invading not only the world of
> material objects but the world of human relations, where it has become estab-
> lished under the name of 'psychology'. . . Technique confronts you everywhere;
> in the imponderables no less than the ponderables; in the churches no less than
> the factories; in the wilderness no less than the city. Indeed, there is little
> exaggeration in saying that the whole country reeks and roars with technique.

No book could be less systematic in character than J. B. Priestley's
Midnight on the Desert (1937), with its accurate subtitle, *An Excursion into Autobiography during a Winter in America,* 1935-36. It is
not a travel book, but a prolonged meditative essay. Yet no formal volume of travel in this period contains keener insights into American
life. A Yorkshireman, a frequent visitor to the United States, a natural
lover of the 'hearty, plain-spoken, democratic' American people, Priestley based his judgments on a healthy common sense, a dislike of
shams and extremes, and a novelist's perceptive eye. When the volume
appeared most critics focussed their attention upon the autobiography
(Mr. Priestley's account of the fate of his latest New York play, for
example) or on the meditation (his reflections upon the nature of
time in particular), neglecting the social criticism. But of descriptive
comment and critical verdicts on life and manners from New York
to San Diego he supplied, first and last, a generous quantity.

Priestley liked the ability of Americans to improvise, but he greatly
disliked their habit of stopping with improvisation—an old criticism
of the country. Of their capacity in this line, he found one illustration
in his Arizona hut:

> This hut was a witness to the admirable spirit of Western America, and per-
> haps of all these states. When I had first stayed on the ranch, the winter before,
> I had found it hard to work in my bedroom on the patio, where people were
> always moving about and calling to one another. What I needed was a little
> place of my own to work in, well away from the main ranch buildings. So as
> soon as I came back for a longer stay, up went this shack, and within a day or
> two it had its bookshelves, stove, and electric light. Nothing very wonderful

about all this. It was easily erected, and of course I paid for it. But I feel that in any European country there would have been endless palavers and fusses, whole crops of difficulties raised, before one would have had a brand-new place to work in; if indeed one would have persisted in the face of a mountain of objections. Here, in the Far West, it was done so casually and quickly. 'You bet!' they cried and went ahead.

Unhappily, one trouble with America was that much of it looked just as jerry-built as this Arizona cabin. Fifth Avenue and Michigan Avenue were substantial and rich enough, but the prairie hamlets between seemed sketchy and poverty-stricken. The villages of the South, the towns of the Far West likewise failed to fit the image of a wealthy land:

Where are the signs of wealth along this railroad track? What disguised riches are there in these tumble-down wooden shacks passing for houses, these unpaved roads and streets, these piles of old tin cans and rusting skeletons of automobiles? Whole villages look as if they would be dearly bought at five hundred dollars, drugstore and all. These folk who stare from their old Fords at the level crossings, a yellow melancholy in their faces, do they know that they have inherited the earth? This is, of course, pioneer country still.

To English eyes the pioneering seems to begin a mile or two outside New York. Most things you see appear to be makeshift. They will do for this year; and next year perhaps we can move to California or Florida or into the city. Money has been poured out in Niagara cataracts in the big cities to build their towers. But if there is so much money between, the fifteen hundred miles of it are inhabited by misers. I have seen ghost mining towns in the West, towns that could not have had more than ten years of life, that were better built than scores of these little rural towns and villages.

For the open country in America, and especially in the Southwest, Priestley felt an ecstatic admiration. He preferred English towns, for all their stodgy gloom, to the ugly American towns; but the American was not compelled either to stay in town or go sloshing across wet fields. He could loiter in forests, ride along high mountain trails, or picnic in enchanting canyons with sparkling air, jeweled rocks, and scarlet tanagers and blue jays flitting among the aspens. The novelist reveled in ranch life and desert scenery. Santa Barbara was so brightly colored and charming that the whole place—palms, flowers, surf, and all—seemed to have been designed out of Tennyson. Boulder, in Colorado, 'a cozy little town with a brownish wooden look about it,' appealed to him at once. He hated New York, whose feverish hurry dragged him into insomnia. He thought Hollywood unreal, unhealthy, and, under its surface gaiety, a cruel and unhappy spot. But the country of the Salton Sea, a desert lake under a sky of luminous metal, fascinated him by its utter desolation. It presented water, stone, and air—nothing else. 'Here is a glimpse at once of the beginning and end of us. This is how the world was before we began to trouble it, and this is how it may be when the last man has looked reproachfully at the fading sun, cursed the freezing universe, and died.' On the Arizona plateau, nature offered a magnificent routine. The early mornings were cold, fresh, and pure; the burning noons were full of flame; the afternoons were compact of sunlight and aromatic air. 'At sunset the land throws up pink summits and saw-toothed ridges of amethyst, and there are miracles of fire in the sky. Night uncovers two million more stars than you have ever seen before; and the planets are not points but globes.' It was outdoor America that Priestley liked best.

Just so, he liked best the outdoor American, when taken individually and not in groups. Traveling over the country, he saw at stations two contrasting types. The office man, usually pasty-faced, spectacled, and worried by competition, his mind intent on salesmanship slogans, pep talk, graphs of output, and similar greedy rubbish, was rather pathetic. The outdoor workers—truck drivers, railwaymen, roustabouts—were happier and more likeable; big fellows in blue overalls, Walt Whitman lads, doing their jobs and not caring a damn, free men altogether. The women, of course, had plenty of vitality, courage, and enterprise; everybody knew that. But to Priestley they drew more heavily on these qualities than was wise or seemly. As he looked at them in the cars, heavily painted, smartly dressed, never relaxing, always on edge, always aggressively feminine, they pained him. Like the man caught in the business net, the American woman worried too much:

When she is young, she must look prettier than the girls she is with, otherwise the young males will ignore her completely. In my forty-odd years I have never yet been at any social function where all the young men crowded around one girl and left her less dazzling sisters to droop alone, but according to the advertisers this is always likely to happen in America, where the young males have a strange uniformity of taste, and a girl must either dazzle or be ignored. She must get her man. Then, having got him, she must keep him; and if she is not very careful—in various horribly intimate matters—she will not keep him. She has only to slack off for a day or two, and he has gone. But if he does not go, and she marries him, then there may be children and with them a whole host of new and terrible dangers. Mother must know, Mother must see to it, Mother must not grow careless for a moment. Suppose the children are doing well, can she afford to take it easy? No, no. She must serve the right kind of food, surround herself with the right kind of household appointments, go to the right places, read the right books; juggle with kitchen, coquetry, and culture; cultivate her body, cultivate poise, cultivate charm, cultivate personality, cultivate her mind.

Some exaggeration appears in this, but the point is clear. Mr. Priestley, like most of our British sojourners, would have Americans live
less hectically and anxiously; treat themselves to more repose; be less
artificial, less herd-minded, less concerned with the future; and create
both a material environment of homes, gardens, and towns, and an
intellectual environment of thought and emotion, on quieter, more
substantial, more durable lines.

The last of our four most discerning observers in this era, Graham
Hutton, confined himself to what is often termed the most truly American part of the republic, the Middle West. He found it 'at noon,' or
in a moment of transition. The morning of frontier newness and early
rural development was past; industrialization had covered the land
with factories, mills, and great cities; it had grown up. The afternoon
of mature power lay before it. Because the Midwest had undergone
a rapid transformation, it seemed to him stamped by a remarkable
paradox. As was natural in view of its frontier heritage and tradition
of unfettered personal effort in subduing the Indian and wilderness,
breaking the prairie, and utilizing natural resources, it was a region
that laid great emphasis on individualism. Yet as a country that had
risen to well-diffused wealth, its adult population showed an intense
respect for the average, a lack of discriminating taste in culture and
mores, and a marked emphasis on smug conformity. In short, here
was an agricultural society three generations away from the frontier
settlements, which had bloomed into prosperity and urban comfort.
It was naturally a bourgeois society; its people, decent well-to-do
farmers, solid businessmen, well-employed artisans and clerical workers, formed as sound, massive, and repectable a backbone for the nation
as the middle class in Britain. They were just about as unimaginative,
though more adventurous. But continuing economic changes, Mr.
Graham observed, were altering the Middle-Western outlook. As industry and urbanization grew, so did wealth; as wealth increased, class
consciousness was enhanced. He hoped that the section would not
abate its common-sense respectability, but that it would do more to
recapture the individualism that had marked it in the days of Boone
and Cass and Lincoln.

On one fact, for the benefit of the British public, Mr. Hutton insisted: the Middle West was insular, but it was not isolationist. Set
in the heart of a great land-mass, with wide environing oceans, its
insularity of outlook was natural and proper. Once its place in the
world was brought home to it, however, it was less isolationist than
other parts of America—and of the world. Its deep basic idealism
responded to the challenge. By 1945 the most trustworthy polls showed
that the percentage of its citizens in favor of joining a United Nations

organization 'with teeth and claws' was greater than in the South, and as great as in the East. The trait really to cause worry, he thought, was the intense Midwestern conviction that any and every problem on earth was easily soluble by a simple application of maxims of right and wrong.

Most of the travelers of this latest period, from the humorously journalistic author of *I Lost My English Accent* to the philosophical Dr. Jacks, from the caustic Mr. Bretherton to the complimentary Mr. Huddleston, agreed upon one fact: that the United States was passing out of the old phase of individualistic pioneering into a new era of socialized mass industrialism. Most of them felt that Americans had but tardily awakened to their new problems and responsibilities; that they made an excessive pother over changes and reforms, which the crowded nations of the Old World had long since accepted as inevitable. Most of those who came during the Harding-Coolidge period felt subconsciously, if not consciously, that something was wrong with the republic, and indicated the fact in their books; while most of those who arrived after 1932 strongly approved of the new controls applied by the Federal Government under Roosevelt, the new social concern manifested by the people, and the steps taken toward a more humane and co-operative commonwealth. After all, America was simply taking a road that England had traveled a little earlier, a little more willingly. But Mr. Priestley (and to some extent Mr. Wells also in his book *The New America: The New World,* published in 1935) went further. He proclaimed that political and economic reform, though important, would not be enough for Americans or for Europeans. Beyond a pacified world, if that ever came, beyond a humanized society they would need an advance in their individual relation to the universe. Nations everywhere were suffering from a numbed sensibility, a lack of imagination, a blunted religious sentiment. 'There was no longer a widespread feeling of purpose and grandeur in life'; it should somehow be restored.

And while these words of the novelist were still fresh, the world plunged into one of the ghastliest, the most tragic, and the most unnecessary of its wars, which once again altered society in both Europe and America in incalculable ways. In that war the United States and the British Commonwealth of Nations once more joined hands, to fight through it in unity, and to take the democratic world in temporary guidance when victory was achieved.

Impressions of Post-War America, 1927-8 [1] ॐ

J. ALFRED SPENDER. *The close of World War I left the United States overwhelmingly the richest and most powerful of the nations, and while Europe was painfully laboring to re-establish its economic life and meet its most pressing difficulties, America enjoyed a golden prosperity. Naturally, different foreign commentators took different views of the now colossally wealthy republic. A considerable group of European economists and businessmen wrote books full of a frank admiration of our business methods. Among these volumes were J. E. Barker's* America's Secret, *George Peel's* The Economic Impact of America, *and G. K. Simonds' and J. G. Thompson's* The American Way to Prosperity. *Our mass production, high wages, and earnest stimulation of consumption were held up to Europe as worthy of imitation. A more intellectual group, without special interest in business, turned a decidedly critical eye upon American policies and ideals. Their objections were trenchantly stated—sometimes overstated—in such books as C. E. M. Joad's* The Babbitt Warren, *and C. H. Bretherton's* Midas: The United States of the Future. *The restless money-getting evident in America, the uniformity and conformity that stamped large parts of our society, and the subjection of the country to a machine civilization struck these critics as alarming or repellent.*

Among those whose observations avoided extremes of praise or attack, none wrote more carefully than the veteran journalist J. Alfred Spender. Born in 1862, he went into journalism shortly after his graduation at Balliol College, Oxford. In 1892 he joined the Pall Mall Gazette. *The following year he became assistant editor of the* Westminster Gazette, *a Liberal organ. By 1896 he was editor, and held that post till 1922. His personality informed the whole paper, and the editorials of the green-tinted evening sheet were known the world over for their acuteness, force, and progressive temper. The entire English-speaking world regarded it as a misfortune that the vicissitudes of journalism prevented him from continuing in his editorial chair. He had already published books, and turned to the production of more ambitious volumes, among them the* Life of Sir Henry Campbell-Bannerman *and*

---

[1] From *Through English Eyes*, New York and London, 1928, chapters 3, 7, and 22. Copyright 1928 by J. A. Spender; reprinted by permission of the executors of the late Mrs. Spender.

The Public Life. *In 1921 he had spent some months in the United States. Six years later his appointment as the first Senior Walter Hines Page Fellow under a plan organized by the English-Speaking Union, with the co-operation of leading American and British newspapers, enabled him in the fall and winter of 1927-8 to make a tour of the entire country. The resulting book,* Through English Eyes, *is divided into two parts, one called 'From a Traveller's Notebook,' and the other 'Life and Institutions.' The former contains travel impressions of New York, New England, the Middle West, and the Pacific Coast; the latter chapters on politics, law, disorder, religion, racial difficulties, journalism, and universities and colleges.*

HENRY FORD

JUST as in Rome one goes to the Vatican and endeavors to get audience of the Pope, so in Detroit one goes to the Ford works and endeavors to see Henry Ford. When I had been round the Ford works—or that part of them which is comprised in the Fordson factory—I felt like the Queen of Sheba, of whom it is recorded that when she had seen Solomon's Temple and palaces there was no more spirit left in her. To be sure these buildings are not temples and palaces, but if absolute completeness and perfect adaptation of means to end justify the word, they are in their own way works of art, and they have the artistic quality of stirring the imagination till it falls back exhausted. Beginning with coal and iron, which comes from the Ford mines, everything is here, and all is self-sufficing. The Ford ore enters at one end and comes out at the other as motors or parts of motors, which are taken away on the Ford railway or in Ford ships. There is an immense power station, great blast furnaces, the largest foundry in the world, the largest steel-rolling plant, a pressed-steel building covering nine acres, a great glass factory, and heaven knows what else. The whole covers 1100 acres, and has a frontage of a mile and a quarter. What most impresses the observer is the immense size and height of the buildings, and next their cleanliness, airiness, and perfect arrangement. There is no dust or refuse in these factories. Everything that might be waste or refuse in smaller factories is mechanically gathered up to be used again. When the factory is in full work there are 250 tons daily of steel trimmings and scrap steel, which are delivered to electrical furnaces for the manufacture of alloy steel. Gather up the fragments that nothing may be lost is the rigid rule of the industry, and incidentally the way of cleanliness and hygiene.

But the secret of these works is not the size or variety of these de-

partments, but their relation to each other. The 'conveyor' is the key
to everything. All over the ground one has only to look to see 'parts'
of motors traveling methodically on overhead rails to the point on the
assembly line where the mechanic unships them and fits them into
their place in the embryo car. The synchronization which brings each
to the exact spot at the right moment is a miracle of thought and
planning and requires a regularity of output in the various departments
which can only be achieved by the most thoroughgoing discipline of
punctuality. Many of the parts have to be separately assembled before
they are finally assembled on the car; and the assembling of the mag-
neto struck me as an especially delicate and beautiful operation.

One thing is necessary to the whole process and that is an absolute
accuracy in the machining of the parts, so that they fit instantly on
reaching the assembly line; otherwise time would be lost and the whole
process thrown out of gear. To see how this is achieved one must visit
the famous Carl Johanson in his laboratory and see him at work on
his 'precision gauge blocks,' which are so accurate that placed side by
side they actually adhere to each other. This method is, of course, not
peculiar to the Ford factory, but mass production absolutely depends
upon it, and no one has done more to bring it to perfection than Mr.
Johanson. He is dealing all the time in millionths of inches.

So much for the mechanical surroundings. What of the human
agents? Since the output of cars was suspended until the new model
was ready, I could only see them at work on the tractor assembly line,
but that, I imagine, is typical of the whole process. All along the line,
which extends down a long building, the men are at their stations,
and the embryo tractors pass in an unending procession in front of
them. The 'conveyors' cross the building at right angles to the assembly
line, and in a corresponding endless procession bring to each station
just that part—motor, wheels, steering gear, et cetera—which has to
be fitted in at that station, and at the exact moment when the embryo
arrives. At each station there is precise teamwork, different rivets being
assigned to different individuals or two men working together to lift
a part into position. Often I held my breath for fear that a team should
not complete its work before the embryo moved on, but I never saw
any fail, and the time was apparently sufficient to enable the work to
be done without hustling. Indeed, the teamwork was so perfect that
it all seemed well within capacity. At a certain point the tractor was so
far completed as to be ready for painting, and then it entered a covered space in which men in masks sprayed on the paint, completing
the work in about two minutes. I walked up and down the line for
half an hour, watching every stage of the process, from the initial block
to the completed tractor, and found it fascinating. In the last stage a

little gasolene was fed to the infant now coming to life, and someone mounted its seat and drove it gaily out of the building to the railway siding, where a freight car was waiting to take it West. The whole process, from the raw ore to the finished tractor, takes 28 hours and 20 minutes, and with the present plant 1000 can be turned out in a day. . .

My own impression is that what really redeems this method from the deadening monotony, which, in spite of all these palliatives, would sooner or later overtake it, is the pervading sense of its being team-work. The workers are not, as is sometimes alleged, confined in separate compartments, so that none sees what his fellow is doing; they are all working side by side along the whole length of the assembling line, and co-operating in a process which is visible to every one. There is a certain exhilaration in working together for an intelligent purpose, which all can realize.

POLITICS AND PARTIES

After spending three months at Washington in 1921 what chiefly struck me as a British onlooker was the extreme cautiousness of American politicians. Neither of the American parties, Republican nor Democratic, seemed ready to take any of the risks that are all in the day's work for British parties. Both, as I wrote at that time, seemed to be living in a state of doubt as to what the great masses of Americans, especially those in the West, were saying and thinking at any given moment; and to give these people a lead was declared to be too dangerous a venture for wise men. Parties, I was told, had to be absolutely sure of their ground before they committed themselves to novel opinions on any subject, and the example of Wilson, who had plunged ahead without exploring the ground, was cited as a warning to all who came after.

This sense of an unexplored world of opinion hangs heavily over American politics, and strikes one as different in kind from the doubts and perplexities of politicians in Europe. It is not merely that politicians in America, as elsewhere, are waiting for signs; it is that even serious and responsible men have a real apprehension of setting forces in motion which may have incalculable results among the millions of many races spread over the American continent. To observe neutrality on all issues which might transfer the racial quarrels of Europe to American soil or divide the Europeans in America on the same lines as their kinsmen are divided in Europe is both an instinct and a tradition with the leaders of American parties. The injunction of the fathers of the Constitution to keep clear of European entanglements seems more and not less compelling as anxieties about the racial blend increase.

But apart from this an Englishman has always to remember that the politics of a Federal country differ essentially from those of unified countries with one Parliament. Large numbers of the issues, which make politics in Great Britain, are state and not Federal matters in America; and when these are subtracted, there remains in normal times little or nothing that divides parties on the familiar British lines of radical and conservative, or that ranges individuals according to their temperament and natural bias. This vacuum has to be filled with traditions and personalities, the traditions becoming always dimmer and vaguer, and the personalities more lively in the proportion that principles are lacking. In the North and West the Republican party has got itself accepted as the party of power and prosperity—the party which, if one may believe its members, has an almost hereditary right to govern the country. Big business supports it, the 'best people' belong to it as they do to the Conservative party in Great Britain. In the South these conditions are reversed, and lingering memories of the Civil War combine with the Negro question to make the 'best people' Democratic. Either affiliation seems to be inconsistent with any principles. Conservatives and Liberals, as we understand these terms, are to be found in both parties; both have their 'drys' and 'wets' and even their Protectionists and free-traders. The Southern Democrat is often a high-tariff man and the Western Republican a low-tariff man, if he is a farmer or out for the farmers' vote, and neither will be restrained from expressing his opinions by the traditional policy of his party. But through all this confusion, as it seems to an Englishman, party allegiance remains strong and militant, and the desire to win is a passion with both parties. Winning carries with it the disposal of an enormous patronage, and this glittering prize works automatically to impose discipline, for the faithful are rewarded and the faithless receive no mercy.

The Englishman has to divest himself of most of his preconceived notions before he can begin to understand this system. He sees American parties maneuvering for position on the questions of the day, and apparently in doubt up to the last moment whether they will take one stand or the other. When he inquires about Prohibition, for example, he is told that if the Democratic party goes 'wet,' the Republican party will assuredly be 'bone dry,' but that on both sides the party managers think it an uncomfortable subject, which had better be avoided. There is no tradition such as in similar circumstances in

Great Britain would compel the radical party to be dry and the Conservative party to be wet. The same is true of foreign affairs. Accidentally and incidentally, through President Wilson, the Democratic party got entangled with the League of Nations, but there was no foundation of faith or principle which made it de fide for a Democrat to advocate the cause of the League or to go on advocating it after the first failure, as, for instance, the Liberal party in Great Britain advocated Home Rule for Ireland and continued to advocate it in the teeth of failure and discomfiture. Had Mr. Gladstone been an American President instead of a British party leader, he would almost certainly have retired from the scene and have been heard of no more when he was beaten on Home Rule. On the other hand, there is nothing in the character or composition of the Republican party which requires it to go on opposing the League policy because it did so in 1920. Support or opposition is for both parties a question of time, circumstance, and expediency.

PROHIBITION

When the Volstead Act was passed it was generally supposed that the hop-grower and the wine-grower, to say nothing of the rye- and barley-growers, would be ruined. The very opposite has proved to be the case. I was assured in California that wine grapes and hops had never fetched such prices as in the last few years, and that the growers of both might now be reckoned among the staunchest upholders of the Prohibition law. Italians will have their wine, if they have to make it themselves, and if Germans can obtain hops, they know how to make beer. Some effort was made to prevent the sale of hops and wine grapes on the ground that the intention of the buyer was to convert them into an illicit product, but the courts have so far refused to impeach the unfermented product, and enforcement is apparently powerless to trace the innocent beginnings to the guilty conclusion. Wine-making, home-brewing, and the use of the domestic still are said in large parts of the country to have passed out of the crude and poisonous stage, and to be on the way to becoming highly developed domestic arts.

Certainly by all ordinary standards the existence of these practices and the daily spectacle of a large and prosperous illicit trade carrying on its operations under the nose of the authorities and with the connivance of hundreds of thousands of otherwise law-abiding and respectable citizens must be demoralizing to the general cause of law and order. It is difficult to believe that it could go on, if opinion was as overwhelmingly on the side of the law as the Prohibitionists assert. In that case one would expect a stern demand from all over the country that the iniquitous illicit trade should be rooted out at whatever cost to the taxpayer. There is no such demand: the Federal appropriation for enforcement is admitted on all hands to be insufficient for its purpose, but said to be as much as opinion will sanction. To the onlooker the United States seems to be stuck halfway in this business. The 'dry' opinion is strong enough to maintain the Volstead Act in the statute book, but not strong enough to procure anything approaching a rigid enforcement. The great company of 'wets who vote dry,' thinking Prohibition to be a good thing for other people, have no desire to see enforcement officers prying into their own habits or coming between them and their sources of supply. To be rid of the 'saloon' and to prevent its return they will keep the Government armed with powers which may in theory be applied to themselves, but they expect tolerance and common sense and a judicious turning of the blind eye when the thing comes near home.

The United States is so different from other countries and, according to British ideas, so eccentric in its legal methods that almost any judgment which an Englishman might pass would distort the American point of view. To vast numbers of Americans it is, apart from its results, a very real satisfaction to have in their Constitution a declaration which dedicates their country to a sober life. They may not for the moment live up to it, but it is an ideal held before them, which they are bound to respect and may presently achieve. The common objection that law must not run in advance of opinion gives way, in the minds of these people, to a conviction that, if the law is boldly affirmed, opinion will rise to it. It is argued that under the discouragement of Prohibition the taste for alcohol will constantly diminish until a generation arises to which it will be as repugnant as drugs are now to normal persons. From this point of view merely to make it difficult to get intoxicating liquors is said to be an advantage which far outweighs the alleged harm in the tolerance of law-breaking. There are already so many laws on the statute books which no one thinks of observing that the partial defeat of Prohibition by passive resistance is of little consequence as a blow to legality, and may even be thought of as a common-sense method of easing the burden for frail humanity. Thousands of good citizens sip their 'Scotch' with the comfortable reflection that the saloon is a thing of the past, that the output of manufactured goods is constantly increasing, and that the United States is setting a fine example to the rest of the world.

SOME CONCLUSIONS

It is not for nothing that a large part of the territory of the United States lies in a latitude which, compared with that of the British Isles, is distinctly southern. The sky has the brightness and at morning and evening the warm glow which Englishmen call Italian. But with it, and especially as one goes away from the coast, is a keen dry atmosphere which keeps the human fit, and gives trees, plants and crops a northern vigor. One sees the Italian cypress casting its black shadow on what might be an English countryside. If the ultraviolet rays have the potency that modern medicine attributes to them, it can hardly be a fancy that the transplanting of the north European from the mists and fogs of the North Sea and the British Isles to a region where he gets an Italian sun without the relaxing qualities of the Italian climate has had some effect upon his character. In fact one seems to see this effect in the quality of collective vitality which distinguishes the people of the United States from all other peoples in the world.

The stress must be on the word collective. It runs through all parts of the country, keeping it in a state of movement and ferment which extends to the whole people. In England business is still for the most part an individual occupation in which each man does his best to win bread for his family and leisure for himself. In America it is a movement. 'The business of America is business' is a saying attributed to President Coolidge, and as an Englishman looks at it, the entire country seems to be mobilized for the winning of an industrial war in just the same way as we were a few years ago mobilized for another kind of war. All the newspapers, all the means of publicity and advertisement, even the Government itself seem to be commandeered for and concentrated on an industrial campaign which is broadly conceived as a national effort. With this go the unrest and the nervous excitement which we have noted·in Europe as wartime symptoms, and they seem to be chronic in America. Men and women live so much in the future that they seem to have little time either to savor the present or to reflect on the past; they dislike solitude and do everything in common. The Englishman sees an immense gregariousness contrasting with the scattered, individual, private life of his own country; and everybody and everything being carried along on a high tide of confident expectation, which is in still greater contrast with the ebbing spirits of some parts of Europe.

But of course this movement has its casualties, though they may be veiled in the dazzling generalized impression which the traveler

brings away with him. The pace is too quick for some and especially
for the unacclimatized newcomers. The incessant scrapping of old
things and substitution of new, the unceasing search for new labor-
saving devices involve a constant displacement which at any given
moment and even in times of prosperity mean unemployment and
poverty for large numbers. Ability which cannot conform to the dominant patterns, incompetence and physical unfitness get less mercy in
this country than in Europe. If wages are high, they must be earned
to the last cent; and the average kind of worker who looks for security
in return for a moderate effort will find life harder than in the old
countries. Here the race is to the swift, and for them the constant moving on and the sense of unlimited possibilities, with the attendant risks
and chances, are what give spice, savor and color to life. For all these
America is uniquely the country of equal opportunity. . .

It follows that the great men of the United States are the big businessmen, not the politicians. When a committee of American professors and literary men is asked to name the greatest men in the world,
it puts Mr. Henry Ford high on the list, but names not a single politician or statesman. It must be said that the businessmen take their
position seriously as leading citizens. They play a leading part in all
public enterprises of a constructional kind; they give munificently to
charity, and endow universities, museums, and art galleries on a scale
unknown in any other country. In all this they show an admirable
social instinct and make the readiest acknowledgment of the duty
which wealth owes to the community. But one thing they will not do,
or do very reluctantly, and that is to take an active part in the government and administration of the country.

The onlooker gets the impression, therefore, that far too little of the
brains and character of the country is going into its public affairs. The
greater part of state and municipal administrations is left to professional politicians, and the few businessmen who come into politics do
so comparatively late in life and with little previous experience of
affairs. Taking the country as a whole, there is no large body of men
who can be relied upon to make a career in either Federal, state or
municipal politics a steady object of ambition from their youth upwards. For lack of these the bosses and machine politicians who have
their ears to the ground (and sometimes their noses in the mud)
obtain inordinate power. . .

It needs adversity to give politics the keen edge that they have in
Europe, and the United States—or that part of it which counts—is
and has long been abundantly prosperous. Mistakes in government,
which would be ruinous in old and congested countries, seem to be
of little consequence in this enormous country with its great margin

of error and easy ways of recovery. Practical men draw the conclusion that politics do not much matter, and that they have far better ways of serving their country and occupying their time than engaging in the scramble for office and spoils, which fills so large a part of the political life in the United States. Some day when they have leisure or there is a really serious emergency, they will turn about and put the politicians in their places, but until then 'the business of America is business.' There have been signs in some parts of the country, for example in these last months in Chicago, of a change in this attitude. It is beginning to be realized that if corruption and lawlessness are allowed to go too far, the remedy may not be so easy as has been supposed. The youth of the country is beginning to think new thoughts for which political expression will some day have to be found. It is a possibility which occurs to one that when the American people do finally bring their strong wills and inventive minds to bear on their public affairs, they may devise novel and drastic expedients which will astonish the world. But in the meantime, in considering their politics and especially their dealings with other nations, it is necessary to remember that they are very imperfectly organized for any quick or strong expression of the national will. For that reason their statesmen seem to be always in doubt as to the authority behind them, and their politics tend to be of the nature of experiments to discover what their own people desire or will support.

Undoubtedly the American scene is puzzling to the stranger who tries to get a consistent picture of the whole. The national virtues are immense but they seldom run through the whole of national life. A breathless futurism in industry goes with a stubborn reluctance to change in politics; the utmost economy in production with an amazing prodigality in consumption. While the manufacturer is making a science of thrift in the workshop, the salesman is all the time discouraging thrift in the household. But the moralist who tries to draw edifying conclusions from either virtues or faults will constantly find himself baffled. He goes to a city which is a by-word for corrupt government and finds there schemes of town planning and public improvements which might be the envy of the best-governed municipality in Europe. Conditions of disorder, which would be thought intolerable in Europe, exist side by side with a prosperous and refined way of life and seem to cause it no inconvenience. The majority of Americans seem to be convinced that if only they stick to business, everything else will cure itself.

It follows that an Englishman who goes to the country with the idea of interpreting its life in terms of politics is in danger of going very much astray. Its life is first of all the life of engineering, planning, developing, producing, and only a small part of its brains and thought can be spared for the doings of politicians, whether in domestic or world affairs.

M. Siegfried said recently in a lecture in Paris that the United States is 'moving away from Europe.' He thinks it was nearer Europe thirty years ago than it is now, and that thirty years hence it will be farther away still than it now is. If this means that the United States is making a characteristically American civilization in American surroundings, it is of course true and its differentiation from Europe is likely to go on. The characteristic middle and upper-middle class life, which we are apt to think of as specially representing civilization in Europe, must in America be mechanized in a way that is not called for in European conditions. The difficulty of obtaining domestic servants alone requires a different organization of the home life; the automobile habit keeps American humanity in a perpetual state of circulation, which looks feverish and restless to the European eye. A household with three cars and one servant lives in a different way from a household with three servants and no car. The habit which Americans have of doing everything in common; their flight from the fireside to the club, the lecture hall, the pictures, the theater; their liking for publicity; their willing conformity to standards set for them and ready acceptance of things produced in bulk are a perpetual surprise to Europeans brought up to think of privacy, domesticity, and individual development as things of high value.

But it is not so much an American peculiarity as the characteristics of a still unsettled and developing country. Life is not fixed and canalized as it is in old and compact countries in which the greater part of the population expects to live and die where it was born. The sense of unbounded opportunity awaiting those who have the grit and energy to seize it, the desire for new things and the discontent with old ones, which is in the blood of pioneers, forbids what the Englishman thinks of as rest and leisure. In America there are very few 'idle rich' and hardly anyone seems to look forward to retirement and old age. The class of small rentiers so numerous in France, where the possession of a little house with a little garden and a small assured income is the dream of the middle-aged, is almost nonexistent in the United States. There the rich are not idle because it does not amuse them to be, and those who are retired from one business start another and like to think that they will continue to be wealth producers until the grave closes over them.

In recent years the native energy of the American people has been the working under the artificial stimulus of the capital poured in from Europe during the war, and great as have been the results in development and wealth production, it is improbable that this phase can continue indefinitely without a reaction. Though often scoffed at by Europeans, the idealism of the American people is a very real thing, and the signs of its unease may be seen in the stream of criticism which is being poured out by the most distinguished American writers on the American way of life. The tolerance which is accorded to these writers and the wide sales that they enjoy point to a response in the American people, which presently may make itself felt in a demand for the things that money cannot buy, and the leisure which it ought to bring. All the elements are there—the mental curiosity, the zeal of youth to be educated, and of women to be informed, the response to causes and movements, the demand for beautiful things of great price —everything but leisure. But for this too there must with so lively and ingenious a people be a demand as time goes on. One sees the American people one day turning in on themselves and being fired with an ambition to lead the world in a new civilizing movement. All things are possible in this country.

At the Height of the Boom [1] &

COLLINSON OWEN. *'America,' wrote Owen in the preface to his* The American Illusion, *'is today England's greatest subject of interest.' But England, he declared, quite misunderstood America. 'She knows everything about her façade of prosperity and magnificence. She realizes little or nothing about the astonishing background to all this, in which crime, corruption, and politics are all mixed up in a fantastic manner.' As these sentences would indicate, Mr. Owen saw the United States in the gilded and delirious period of the Coolidge-Hoover Bull Market. The American scene at that time was actually far from normal, a fact that Mr. Owen did not fully appreciate. When he crossed the ocean he was already a veteran journalist, having worked on the staff of various London newspapers since 1901 (he had been born in 1885). In the years just before the First World War he was a special correspondent on the Continent, and for a time dramatic critic of the* London Standard. *During the conflict he was editor of the* Balkan

[1] From *The American Illusion*, London, 1929, pp. 14-19, 52, 53, 79-81, 100-103, 112, 113, 256-60; by permission of Mr. Owen and Ernest Benn, Ltd.

News *for the British Salonika force, and official war correspondent in
the Near East,* 1916-19. *In addition to a number of serious books, including one called* Salonika and Afterward, *Mr. Owen had published
some novels, while he had been a prolific contributor to British and
American magazines.*

PARK AVENUE

ONE discovers Fifth Avenue and at once agrees that here is something
really worth talking about. That impression is heightened by some
of the vistas of magnificence, and groupings of audacious buildings
that tower up near Central Park: soaring masterpieces of stone and
steel, which surpass in audacity anything that the Gothic masters
dreamed of—and are hotels, not cathedrals! And the climax comes
with Park Avenue.

In the most striking section of that majestic thoroughfare the buildings are not, as New York goes, of enormous height. They are principally what are known as apartment houses, flats, of about sixteen
stories. They are built of dull red brick, with sparing ornamentations
of stone, and never since the world began has brick been better used.

These communal palaces are masterpieces of restraint and good
taste. They are only a few years old. Fifty years of life should add
greatly to their beauty, although there is plenty of that already. They
are steel inside, and they are built over concealed railway tracks that
run far beneath them. If you think how it is all done they are as material as anything can be. On the other hand, they are as magnificent
as anything that architecture has given to the modern world. And
some of the flats inside them are rented at $50,000 a year. These are
duplex and even triplex flats—that is, with whole floors removed, and
no doubt baronial halls built into them, and certainly organs.

This is the richest social colony in the world. This is where all that
the naïve and possibly envious European has ever heard of American
riches is most thickly concentrated. The sensational novelist, toying
with the popular gambit of a leading character of immense wealth,
need only walk dreaming down Park Avenue and pick one from any
window. This is where wealth is so swollen that it almost bursts. And
indeed, in describing itself it does burst. Park Avenue has an imposing
publication of its own, the *Park Avenue Social Review,* which is not to
be seen by the eye of the multitude, even if the multitude wanted to see
it. And describing its own glories, and choosing its own type, the
Park Avenue Social Review says:

THERE ARE MORE MILLIONAIRES TO THE SQUARE BLOCK ON PARK AVENUE than to the SQUARE MILE of any other residential section in the world. There is at least one building—ONE APARTMENT HOUSE—on Park Avenue which houses more millionaires than ANY CITY the size of Syracuse upon this civilized, or uncivilized, hemisphere.

And much more like it, all just as astonishing. Down the center of Park Avenue runs a long and narrow street garden. In this boulevard of millionaires one would expect it to be all that a street garden can be. But instead it is almost a disgrace: a miserable affair of sparse grass, bearing evidence of nobody's care.

Here, half a century ago, there were freight yards and factories. Now a plot a hundred feet square is worth two million dollars. On such a plot live millionaires by the dozen—more than there are in all Syracuse! And yet nobody looks after the little bit of garden in the street. That is one of the oddities about New York. However its wealth may swell and its stock market boom, there is nobody in all the great city who can be found to look after such little bits of garden as there are.

A NEW YORK SPEAKEASY

In one of the city's most expensive hotels, I watch a millionaire of large dimensions shaking up a cocktail mixture. It is his own sitting room, and we are a party of four. It is my first illicit drink, and various emotions assail me as I take it. As far as fear goes there should be very little reason for it in this case. My millionaire takes every reasonable precaution. His bootlegger is very high in his profession. What is more, my rich acquaintance, like all men of his kind, has his drink analyzed before taking. 'AI at Lloyds,' so to speak. The usual Prohibition stories go round. One has read this sort of thing a thousand times. All the same it is very interesting to meet it. My first cocktail *sub rosa* is more thrilling than desperate stories of hijackers over the cable.

A few nights later, with a friend and his wife, I enter a speakeasy. It is a building of only four stories in a quiet street—a typical New York street of thirty years ago, full of what are dearly and sentimentally known as 'brownstone fronts'—and looks like a modest Brighton boarding-house. A ring at the bell. My friend has a card. We are admitted. Inside it is more than ever like a boarding-house—a rather depressing one. The wallpaper is red and dingy. There is a bar. In a room of modest size a few people are dining. They are in these dim but expensive surroundings because Bacchus may be met there.

I am in hopes that a policeman on the beat will pop in for a friendly

drink, as so often happens in these places, but that touch is missing.
Anyhow, I claim the privilege of paying. Three sherrys at a dollar
each. Half a dollar tip. I make a remark in French. The waiter, surprisingly, takes it up. 'Ça va bien, monsieur. C'est du premier qualité.'
After that one drinks with confidence. But fourteen shillings for three
sherrys of very modest quality! And that is a very humdrum experience.

KANSAS CITY'S WAR MEMORIAL

No longer a cow town, but a very thriving, modern city, with a
population in and around it of over 600,000, Kansas City has 13,169
hotel rooms, of which 8,922 are provided with bath. This is mentioned in case you ever wish to hold a convention there, which is
something that is always happening in America. If you enter a hotel
and find it thronged with earnest men all wearing their names in
their buttonholes, then you know that up on the twelfth or the seventeenth floor a convention is being held. Fortunately, we found no
convention in Kansas City, but a hotel excellent from every point of
view. Baths and efficiency, but a pleasant family touch with it.

Kansas City not only calls itself 'The Heart of America' (it is almost
the geographical dead centre), but 'America's Most Beautiful City.'
This is a touch of hyperbole which need not be taken too seriously
in a country where civic pride can become almost a religious ecstasy.
There are men in America who would die for their cities, just as there
used to be men who would die for a faith. Kansas City presumably
bases its claim to surpassing beauty on the development of its suburbs,
and one that I explored, known as the Country Club District, is certainly an astonishing example of how a very large estate may be developed for residential purposes. Hundreds of beautiful houses—Spanish, Italian, English, and Colonial in design—and the whole an outstanding example of what real estate can do when animated by real
idealism. This idealism, by the way, has to be paid for: $50,000 would
be a modest enough price for a home in the best sections of this region.

One met very pleasant people in Kansas City, all very keen on their
city's progress. There is something that stands outside the railway
station which may be said to be the embodiment of the city's desire
to make the very best of itself. This is the Liberty Memorial, the main
feature of which is a tall column, 280 feet high, rising from the top
of a hill. If you approach Kansas City by night you see issuing from
this column a flame many feet high. So does Kansas City commemo-
rate its heroes of the Great War.

The money for this memorial, $250,000, was raised in a week. It was inaugurated by Foch, Beatty, and Pershing. I forget how many of the fallen the memorial records, but it is fair to presume that Kansas City did not lose so many of its men in the war as, say, Folkestone, England. Yet in all the British Empire there is no memorial so majestic as this—not even in London, where our modest Cenotaph stands for the British Empire's 1,070,000 dead. It was notable, by the way, that the total of British dead is recorded in one of the two halls that flank the monument.

LOS ANGELES: A FOOTBALL CELEBRATION

Out at the great stadium there is a football game between two universities. It is one of the greatest athletic events of the year and 85,000 people are present. Everything one has ever learned about American college football, from the films or elsewhere, is here to be seen; the gaudy students' brass bands of the opposing teams, the organized 'rooting' of the college cheerers, the frantic enthusiasm. Every now and again, in some climax of the game, the squeals of feminine supporters pierce the din, like the sudden uncontrollable shriek of intense physical agony. It is all very wonderful, and very well worth coming to see. To the rival supporters every moment of the hotly contested game is a crisis, and final defeat, for those who have to suffer it, is a disaster.

There is a sequel later, at one of the big and luxurious hotels downtown. Up to midnight the magnificent underground ballroom, a recently built source of pride, is packed with students, youths and girls, and their parties. There are bottles on many of the tables, which contain more than was dreamt of in the philosophy of the Eighteenth Amendment—mostly bathtub gin. The fun would be very fast and furious were it not that the dance floor is a jam.

In this gathering I notice many exceptionally pretty girls. Here and there is a real beauty. The average of mere prettiness runs very high. A film director would find something worth while once every minute. Miss America, considerably excited, is looking her very best.

At somewhere about one o'clock the fun really begins. In many hundreds of hotel rooms parties are now being held. In the corridors are many young men most patently intoxicated, and some girls not much less so. From every window overlooking the various hotel courtyards figures appear and shout college cries of defiance; the lusty voices of young men, the shriller voices of girls. The coeds are fighting the football game over once again.

I saw a similar scene at a Chicago hotel, but here the pace is much hotter. It becomes a riot. The rain of soda-water bottles begins, and for hours it goes on, down into the courtyards. All sorts of other missiles go the same way, waiters' trays being a favorite. Through this window and that one may see slight but beautiful forms in pretty frocks and in negligent attitudes, on beds, in arm chairs, smoking, laughing, quaffing; a sort of studio party in every bedroom. And such a din!

HOLLYWOOD REAL ESTATE

I follow the crowd. Outside the large booth is a small wooden platform on which a man sits in a chair. The platform bears a sign, 'Check in here for lunch.' We shuffle in. The wooden room is set with chairs and tables, clean enough, but not luxurious. I have been invited to many lunches in America, but never one like this. We settle down anywhere. To each of us is brought on the bare table a cardboard box. It is marked 'Box Lunch De Luxe.'

Mr. Thorwaldsen leaves me to see about his car, which on the way out boiled badly. I dive into the cardboard box. It is all right, no doubt, but I don't feel like a box lunch de luxe. I select, gingerly, a small cheese sandwich. There is a small bar where it says bottles of milk may be obtained for ten cents. The milk in Los Angeles is very good. I lunch on the small sandwich and a bottle of milk. A good lunch, really. I wander out to find Mr. Thorwaldsen. . .

We re-enter the booth. The tables have disappeared and the chairs are arranged for the lecture. My seat is in the back row, with my guide firmly in attendance. And the Colonel begins his lecture.

Reader, you may already have guessed what it was all about. After a time I do. It is all about real estate. We are gathered there, by siren voices on the telephone, for the purpose of being persuaded to buy lots. We are a crowd almost entirely from the Middle West, where the winters are long and bitter, and where storekeepers and farmers dream of the day when they will be able to go and live on their savings in the perpetual sunshine of Southern California.

Of such is the population of Los Angeles very largely made up—elderly people with sufficient dollars put by to go in search of everlasting sun. And we have been deftly gathered up from various hotels, not to see film stars in their native surroundings, but to hear the Colonel talk about fortunes in corner lots. And thinking again of the sweet voice of Mrs. Brown on my bedside telephone, I realize how beautifully it has all been done.

But what a discourse the Colonel gave us! Never have I heard such a perfect piece of spellbinding, never seen more perfect acting. The Colonel, no doubt, was a good soldier. But at selling real estate he is a genius. Time and again he draws applause from the audience. They are his. If all he said could have been taken down in shorthand, it would have stood for all time as a perfect essay on temptation to people who may, or may not, want to invest. That, unfortunately, was impossible. But stray gems from the Colonel's lavish and glittering display find their way to the back of an old envelope.

He tells us stories of men who have become fabulously rich from buying corner lots—'right here, almost where we are now sitting.' He tells us stories of men who have not seen Fortune beckoning until too late, and have remained forever embittered. He gives us figures. In ten years land values in Chicago have increased 76 per cent; in Detroit, 350; in Los Angeles, 906; and in Hollywood, 1,666! (Cheers.)

He pays special compliments to women—their courage and enterprise. They will do things men won't. He stresses the necessity for a wife to have a separate estate. If the husband won't part with the money, then let her take it. Let her invest in just one of the lots on the map behind him. Some day the husband may prefer a blonde. 'In that case you can tell him to take his blonde and go to it. You'll be all right.' (Cheers and laughter.)

'Real estate is the best possible investment. Why? Because nobody can invent any more earth.'

'Go and ask Gilbert E. Beesmeyer where he made his money. Where was it? Why, right here in Lemon Grove.

'Now, folks, stop and think. If you tell a Frenchman, a German, or an Italian that you live in Pasadena, he won't know what you mean. But tell him you live in Hollywood and watch his eyes light up! All the world knows Hollywood. All the world wants to come to it. You can go to the naked savage living in darkest Africa, to the untutored Aborigine, who bites raw meat with his sharpened teeth so that the blood runs down his chin, and you can say to him, "I live in Hollywood," and what will he reply? He will reply, "Yes, boss, I'se thinkin' of movin' there myself." (Much laughter.)

And so on for an hour, embellished with humor, statistics, and figures of speech. A wonderful entertainment, so that, though I begin to wonder whether I am in a tight corner, and whether my young giant of a guide is serious in his business designs upon me, I enjoy every minute of it.

The lecture over, I congratulate the Colonel and try to escape. But

my young Scandinavian protests. Now that I am on the estate I must
have a look at it. The car is his and I am more or less at his mercy.
We make a long tour. Roads made and in the making, trees planted,
here and there a house erected and occupied. We inspect several pleasant little bungalows of Spanish architecture. He advises me to take
one of their small $2750 plots. I can buy it, half down, go back to
London, and leave its value to grow and grow. Or I can erect a bunga-
low court on it—six small bungalows—and rent them out. For a moment I am almost persuaded.

MR. HEARST'S LITTLE PLACE

There are thirty miles of his own seacoast, and the domain stretches
far inland, over a succession of mountain ranges in which the coyote
and mountain lion still run wild. There is a tiny private port on the
coast, which is being developed into a sort of model village, of Spanish
architecture. Its chief imports are art treasures from Europe. A little
way back from the tiny jetty lies an English manor house—all in packing cases!

A well-made mountain road winds up to the palace on the hill. A
traffic cop on a motorcycle patrols it, to enforce the rigid rule that
nobody's automobile must exceed fifteen miles an hour, up or down.
This is because of the animals that run about, and they consist of
emus, ostriches, kangaroos, elk, bison, and deer of all descriptions.
From out a shelter of their own three giraffes poke their inquiring
heads. The giraffes do not run about.

And so the visitor arrives at the top of the Enchanted Hill and finds
himself, as he walks up one terrace after another, facing a large white
and very effective building with two tall towers, which has a good
deal of the look of a Spanish cathedral, and is an amalgam of old from
Europe and new from America. In Siena, they say, Mr. Hearst saw a
wonderful wooden ceiling in an old house, which he could not buy.
So he bought the house, took out the ceiling and sold the house.

Below the main building, at the foot of the terraces, are three exquisite separate villas, in Spanish style, each one remarkable for the
appointments, and even treasures, within, so that more than one celebrated film star has slept in Cardinal Richelieu's bed. There is a swimming pool, of course. Some two or three hundred yards from the
main building—perhaps châteaux is the best word—is a real menag-
erie, containing lions, a tiger, bears, chimpanzees, mountain lions, and
various other inhabitants. . . Real cowboys ride about.

CRIME IN THE UNITED STATES

Every country has its crime. . . But killing as a result of mere law-lessness is very rare with the English. In America it flourishes as no-where else in the world. The Balkans, the picturesque warring Bal-kans, are safer to the innocent wayfarer than the average American city at night. Americans who have grown up with these frontier con-ditions do not realise them to the extent the stranger does, but even so their eyes are fairly wide open to the situation. The more serious ones are very concerned about it. There are constant evidences of this con-cern in the newspapers and periodicals. But even they do not get that same violent 'reaction' to such conditions as does the visiting English-man, even though in this respect they are constantly and wistfully holding up England as a model of law and order, which they would be very happy to see America able to copy.

In writing about this question of crime one is conscious of the feeling that Americans would much prefer one to leave it alone. One may write, and welcome, about the spread of free education, but not about the spread of unrestricted villainy. One can sympathise up to a point with this attitude. All peoples would prefer strangers to find in them only qualities which are admirable, and there is no doubt that the visitor who is prepared to find only things that please him in the United States is bound to be very much liked in return.

But how is it possible to shut one's eyes to what is undoubtedly the outstanding phenomenon of American life today? How can one write, even sympathetically or admiringly, of the great American scene with-out not merely mentioning but stressing the universality of crimes of violence in every city?

Fortunately, since I made my own observations concerning this mat-ter, there has come striking support of such a view from the highest quarter. Mr. Hoover, in his fight for what we may well call the American Throne, did not discuss the question of crime. But Presi-dent Hoover, speaking from the Throne, has shown a very different temper. In his first public pronouncement as President, on April 22nd, 1929, and speaking to that great news organisation known as the As-sociated Press of America, he admitted that 'life and property in the United States are less safe than in any other country in the world.' This is from a President who happens to know most of the other countries of the world very well.

He made the astounding statement that there are 9000 murders an-nually in the United States—and one might mention here that some students of this matter say that the available statistics do not give the full facts [2]—and went on to say: 'I am wondering whether the time has not come to realise that we are confronted with a national necessity of the first degree; that we are not suffering from an ephemeral crime wave, but from a subsidence of our foundations.'

That is the sort of thing I was feeling throughout my observations of the United States. And that sentence of President Hoover's must surely be the gravest indictment of American crime yet made within America. Its gravity lies not merely in what is said but in who said it. It is interesting that in this same speech he made some striking comparisons between crime in his own country and in Great Britain.

And further to show that my own insistence on the subject of crime is not the mere obsession of a visitor, too keenly and too critically alive to one aspect of the American scene among so many others, and perhaps too anxious to stress the importance of what must be an unpleasant subject for Americans, especially when discussed by a visitor, I will quote the words of Chief Justice Taft, ex-President of the United States and the only ex-President who has served as Chief Justice of the Supreme Court.

He was asked by his interviewer, in the *Evening World* of January 9th, 1929:

'What relation, if any, do you see between this lust for wealth at any cost and the problem of organized crime that is challenging the government of every large city in the country?'

'There is a problem,' the Chief Justice replied, 'which unquestionably menaces our civilization. Our entire machinery of justice must be geared up to cope with it. Our police forces, our prosecuting organizations and our court system must all be improved until we are able to subdue these criminal organizations. . . The nation does not yet appear to be fully awakened to the seriousness of this problem.'

After that, perhaps, the visitor may go on without feeling that he is discussing a forbidden subject. And it reminds me that a very well-known New York magistrate, discussing these questions with me, declared that he would never dream of being mad enough to go for a stroll in Central Park at night. That is the difference between New York and London. A man who strolls in Hyde Park after nightfall

[2] Mr. Wade H. Ellis, of the Crime Commission of the American Bar, and a former Assistant Attorney-General of the United States, has since given the annual figure as 12,000, this statement being made both on the wireless and in an address delivered at Washington. He says further that crime costs the United States $2,600,000,000 a year. According to him there are 30,000 criminals at large in New York and 10,000 in Chicago. (This would hardly seem to be giving Chicago a fair allowance!) He adds that the real American stock contributes little to these figures, and that the crime statistics are chiefly provided by immigrants from Europe, or the recent descendants of emigrants.

may just possibly find himself in the police court next morning. (It would largely depend on what kind of lady he met and what sort of adventures attract him.) But the man who strolled in Central Park after nightfall would almost certainly find himself in the morgue. As a stranger he might even take a considerable risk in driving through it alone in a taxi.

The average American, discussing crime, will say in effect: 'Nearly all of these murders are gang murders, and the more enthusiastically they kill each other the better we are pleased.' There is a certain amount of both truth and wisdom in this point of view, and if such a system could end in one grand climacteric of gang murdering, in which one-half the thugs and beasts who infest American city life killed the other half, it would be perfect.

But such a consummation will never happen, and meanwhile, in making this inevitable comment on their crime problem, Americans do not realise that they are making the most damaging accusation possible against their own social achievement. If gang warfare, and the inevitable terrorism it exercises on the average citizen, coupled with the business relations it must inevitably have with the police, is accepted as a normal concomitant of American life, then America is still in essence a frontier country, and her claims to be the present leader in civilisation collapse at once.

But it is not true that the great majority of America's crimes comes from the gangs. Apart from the many murders which result from bootlegging, hijacking, racketeering, and other forms of criminal organisation, there is an immense amount of plain murdering in the United States of every possible kind, due to the actions of individuals. Some of these are domestic, more of them belong to the street. Every city has a plentiful supply of underworld rats, armed with automatic pistols as a matter of course. The hold-up is practised everywhere; kidnapping, both of children and adults, is quite common. In San Francisco and in Los Angeles I met English mothers who told me that this fear for their children, going to and from school, was never quite absent from their minds. That feeling of utter security, which is such a feature of English life that we never think of it, is utterly lacking in America.

In the Great Depression [1] ℰ⤳

MARY AGNES HAMILTON. *When Miss Hamilton arrived in New York on a misty December morning in 1931, ready to begin a lecture tour, friends who met her at the dock told her that the nation was sorely stricken. 'Things are just appalling,' said one. 'A million and a half unemployed in the city alone.' 'You won't have much of a trip,' declared another. Naturally all this simply whetted her desire to learn more of the unprecedented state of affairs. She had made three previous visits, all within a period of five years, to the United States. In these she had found the country enjoying an intoxicating if somewhat spotty boom; now she looked about for tokens of a tremendous change.*

*Not many British women have had a more active public career than Mary Agnes Hamilton. The daughter of a professor of logic in Glasgow University, she was educated at Newnham College, Cambridge. For a time, in 1929-31, she was a Labor Member of Parliament from Blackburn, while she simultaneously served on the Royal Commission of Civil Service. She was twice a member of the British delegation to the Assembly of the League of Nations. She has done much strenuous work for the Labor Party, while for four years (1933-7) she was a Governor of the British Broadcasting Corporation. In the intervals of her public activities she has found time to write biographies of Margaret Bondfield, Mary Macarthur, J. Ramsay MacDonald, Arthur Henderson, and Sidney and Beatrice Webb. Among her books is also a successful detective story—*Murder in the House of Commons.

Miss Hamilton's visit in 1931-2 took her as far west as Nebraska and Iowa, as far north as Wisconsin, and as far south as Virginia. She was particularly interested in the impact of the depression upon the poor, in its political repercussions, and in the steps being taken to alleviate unemployment. But as these pages show, she did not fail to make some broader observations.

[1] From *In America Today*, London and New York, 1932, chapters 1, 5, and 6. Copyright 1932 by Mary Agnes Hamilton; reprinted by permission of Mrs. Hamilton.

BREADLINES AND BANKERS

ONE does not need to be long in New York (or for that matter in Chicago, in Cleveland, in Detroit, in Kansas, or in Buffalo) to see that there are plenty of real tragedies, as well as plenty of not-so-real ones. If those who have turned in the second or third car talk the most, the others talk—when they get the chance. In New York, one has only to pass outside the central island bounded by Lexington and Sixth Avenues to see hardship, misery, and degradation, accentuated by the shoddy grimness of the shabby houses and broken pavements. Look down from the Elevated, and there are long queues of dreary-looking men and women standing in 'breadlines' outside the relief offices and the various church and other charitable institutions. Times Square, at any hour of the day and late into the evening, offers an exhibit for the edification of the theater-goer, for it is packed with shabby, utterly dumb and apathetic-looking men, who stand there, waiting for the advent of the coffee wagon run by Mr. W. R. Hearst of the New York American. Nowhere, in New York or any other city, can one escape from the visible presence of those who with perhaps unconscious cruelty are called 'the idle.' At every street corner, and wherever taxi or car has to pause, men try to sell one apples, oranges, or picture papers. Not matches—matches, in book form, are given away with every fifteen-cent package of cigarettes, lie on every restaurant table, litter the street, half used, and exemplify how little, as yet, the depression has done to overcome the national habit of easy-going wastefulness. On a fine day, men will press on one gardenias at fifteen cents apiece; on any day, rows of them line every relatively open space, eager to shine one's shoes. It is perhaps because so many people are doing without this 'shine,' or attempting with unfamiliar hands and a sense of deep indignity to shine their own, that the streets look shabby and the persons on them so much less well-groomed than of yore. The well-shod feet of the States struck me forcibly on my first visit; the ill-cleaned feet of New York struck me as forcibly in January and April 1932. In 1930 an English friend, long domesticated in New England, told me that she hesitated to bring her children to London, since the sight of beggars would make so painful an impression on them; in 1932 there are more beggars to be met with in New York than in London. Yes, distress is there; the idle are there. How many, no one really knows. Ten million or more in the country; a million and a half in New York are reported. They are there; as is, admittedly a dark undergrowth of horrid suffering that is certainly more de-

graded and degrading than anything Britain or Germany knows.
Their immense presence makes a grim background to the talk of
depression: there is an obscure alarm as to what they may do 'if this
goes on,' and the charitable relief funds (about which more later) dry
up, as they are in many centers already doing; their existence, in numbers that grow instead of diminishing, constitutes the fact that largely
justifies the feeling of gloom.

Yet while the fact is real enough, it is the mood bred of the fact
rather than the fact itself that both strikes the visitor and makes the
substance of conversation. And the mood is really more significant
than the fact. For the depression, whether or no it is worse than the
fact justifies, is certainly feeding creatively on itself.

The American people, unfamiliar with suffering, with none of that
long history of catastrophe and calamity behind it which makes the
experience of European nations, is outraged and baffled by misfortune.
Depression blocks its view: it cannot see round it. Misled in the onset
by leaders who assured it, in every soothing term and tone, that reverse was to last but for a little while; that it was the preliminary to
recovery; that American institutions were immune to the ills that had
laid the countries of the rest of the world upon their backs; that prosperity was native to the soil of the Union, and all that was needed was
to wait till the clouds, blown up by the wickedness of other lands,
rolled by, as they were bound to do, and that speedily; the nation now
suffers from a despair of any and every kind of leadership. Every institution is assailed; even the sacred foundations of democracy are being undermined. The defeatism that has been so lamentably evidenced
in Congress is not peculiar to Congressmen, any more than is the
crude individualism of their reactions. It lies like a pall over the spirit
of the nation. It is felt by most people to be, in fact, the greatest obstacle to recovery, to that restoration of confidence for which everybody pleads, which everybody sees as necessary. But how to break it
nobody knows.

A major sign of this unhappy frame of mind is the beating about
that goes on everywhere to find some shoulders on which to lay the
blame for an evil and unnatural condition, which, so the average
American feels, has no business to have happened to him.

For this purpose, of course, Aunt Sallies exist in abundance. At any
time the critics on the American hearth are talkative, even eloquent.
They have never been so eloquent as now. On starting forth on my
own first tour of inspction, I was advised by one who had been there
often that the question, 'What do you think of the U.S.A.?' was certain to be numerously put to me, and that I should be well advised
to proffer no generalized reply. When I got there, however, I discov-

ered that apart from the real difficulty of finding anything which did,
then, seem to characterize a continent, I was amply protected from
any need to commit myself by the fact that my questioner always had
so much to say on the topic, on his own account. There was little I
could have noted, for praise or blame, in his homeland that he was not
eager to point out to me; and as he rose in the intelligence scale, the
blame tended to outweigh the praise. The natives one meets and gets
to know, who include, needless to say, some of the most delightful
human beings the world contains, as well as the most acute in analysis,
will do all and more than all the criticizing the most astonished vis-
itant can feel inclined to indulge in. This was always a habit of theirs;
today its edge has an uncanny sharpness. Abuse, leveled with fine impartiality by skilled hands, finds almost too many targets.

Since 1930, the most despised and detested group of men in the
Union is the bankers. Wall Street has long been unpopular with the
man in the prairie and on the field, and not loved of the man in the
street. Even in 1927, one of the major reasons why the American Federation of Labor would have nothing said of recognition of Russia
was that Wall Street was supposed to be favorable to such an idea. It
is a symptom of changed mood that this possibility of Russian recognition is 'up' again. But the contempt then felt for high finance, the
money magnates, and the international bankers is mild and tolerant in
comparison with the vitriolic detestation loud and universal in 1932.
A story has been going the rounds to the effect that a certain lady, distressed to know that her daughter was about to become the mother of
a fatherless infant, was told that its parentage had been accepted by
a banker. She at once refused to admit any such acknowledgment.
'Rather a bastard than a banker,' she declared, with a spirit in which
the voice of the nation is audible. So, to various 'favorite sons' and
persons otherwise qualified as serious Presidential candidates, the fact
that they are associated in some way or other with banking interests
is held to be fatal; in the present mood of the electorate, they would,
on that ground alone, be ruled out.

If one cannot cite any banker as the most unpopular man in the
Union, and must assign that position to the President, the reason is,
in part, that there is no single individual who, in his own person, so
incorporates the idea of banker as does Herbert Hoover that of Washington. Contempt and derision of politics and politicians are, of course,
an old story in the U.S.A., but they have a new edge and a new acer-
bity at the present juncture. Few Presidents have had, during their
term of office, to endure so intense and so universal a barrage of criticism and abuse as Herbert Hoover. He incarnates not only the old
contempt for politics and the politicians, but the new disappointment

with the businessman. He is, in addition to being now not only *a* politician, but *the* politician, not only *an* executive, but *the* executive. His election was hailed as the opening of an era coincident with un-exampled prosperity, and guaranteeing its continuance and amplifica-tion, in which there was going to be that longed-for thing, a business administration in Washington. So his fall, whatever be the excuses, legitimate and illegitimate, that can be brought up to explain it, has swept down more than himself in its destructive train. Brutally at-tacked in a hostile Senate and Congress, Mr. Hoover has also suffered from the publication of biographies designed to strip him of every shred of respect even in his capacity as businessman. Perhaps in the upshot these attacks, plainly animated by a corrosive bitterness and hopelessly inept as propaganda, have helped him; but it is a distressing symptom of the general level of taste that among best sellers in a period when such have been few and far between and publishers, like newspaper proprietors, are 'on their backs,' should have been a work as vulgar as the anonymous *Washington Merry-Go-Round*. There, everyone is pilloried with waspish impartiality, and the Capitol left without a rag in which to wrap itself. And this work has been the favorite reading of Americans in Depression Year. It is certainly emi-nently calculated to deepen the general gloom.

Bankers, politics, democracy, mixed races, Prohibition—to all these, together or in a happy blend, the calamity is referred. Behind them all and coloring them all is something worse. For years it has been an article of faith with the normal American—and in this connection it makes no difference what his antecedents, or how short an American heredity he could boast—that America, somehow, was different from the rest of the world. Naturally, in view of the fact that the Ameri-cans who felt this faith came from all the corners of the earth, its basis and its assurances were expressed in terms of the only vocabulary, the only system of value common to them all, and transcending all their many differences. It expressed itself, that is to say, in money terms. What made America different was that, there, money was to be had; more and more of it. In this belief, immigrants swarmed over, from all the other countries of the habitable globe, to its happier shores, and there joined in the mighty chorus of praise and hope. Prosperity, more and more abundantly, was an American institution—*the* American in-stitution. It had an almost mystic sanctity, which was more and more reverently and devoutly felt as the post-war slump hit down first one European country and then another, and left the United States un-touched, immune. Especially among those whose ancestors had left Europe in the past, there was a sense that the sufferings and the gen-eral plight of Europe were largely its own fault. This sense, if it had at times a touch of pity, more often breathed a robust and happy contempt.

The smash of 1929 did not, of itself, shake this serene conviction of American immunity and superiority. Although it provided, and still provides, an imposing array of resounding personal crashes, and of persons, in great number, who have shot from a pinnacle of wealth into the darkest *oubliettes* of failure, it looked, at the time, just because it was so spectacular and catastrophic, like a shooting star or other natural portent, disconnected with the fundamental facts and root assumptions of American civilization. It was a mere 'phase.' So the plain citizen, no matter how hard hit, believed. His dreams were shattered; but after all they had been only dreams; he could settle back to hard work and win out by that on the soberer lines of daily fact.

Then he found his daily facts reeling and swimming about him, in a nightmare of continuous disappointment. The bottom had fallen out of the market, for good. And that market was not merely a booth for telephonic speculation; it had a horrid connection with his bread and butter, his automobile, and his installment purchases. The despicable European tragedies of shrinking exports, falling production curves, slumping prices, unsaleable stocks, unrealizeable shares crossed the Atlantic and settled down there with an awful air of perpetuity. Worst of all, unemployment became a hideous fact, and one that lacerated and tore at self-respect. Ready to work, able to work, willing and eager to work, and work with supreme efficiency—so he believed —no one wanted to give even the 100 per cent American any work to do. He was in the same case as the darkie, the wop, the hunky, the dago, and all the other 'foreigners' he had so long despised at home or abroad. . .

This is the trouble that lies, unspoken and unspeakable for the most part, at the back of the American mind. This is the real poison root in the mood of depression. All other doubts, all other questions, all other uncertainties refer back to this. If America really is not 'different,' then its troubles, the same in their outward appearances as those of Old Europe, will not be cured automatically. Something will have to be done—but what? . . .

UNEMPLOYMENT

So far as any legislative or administrative action on a national scale goes, nothing has been done, and nothing is likely to be done. During the years up to the present one, the attitude of Washington was that nothing needed to be done. The President stamped on any proposals.

good, bad, or indifferent, that came up to him from Congress or the Senate. For example, in February 1931, Congress passed a measure establishing Federal Employment centers; Mr. Hoover rejected it, out of hand. Other proposals were similarly treated, or smothered by handing them over to Commissions of Inquiry—of which a vast number were set up. True, with the opening of 1932—Presidential year—a feverish activity took possession of the White House, in marked contrast to its previous aloof assurance that everything would right itself, if only it was left alone. But the long and imposing series of measures, beginning with the Reconstruction Finance Corporation Bill, which have been accepted with the utmost docility by the House, are designed to restore 'confidence' to business. None of them has any direct bearing on the provision of work for or relief to the unemployed.

Months of steadily worsening conditions, and of grave and justified apprehension, publicly expressed by responsible directors, as to the imminent running dry of relief funds, had to pass before, in mid-May, the President ventured on a timid step forward. Even then, in extending the borrowing powers of the Reconstruction Finance Corporation by 1500 million dollars to enable government support of private enterprise, Mr. Hoover was careful to stress the fact that the 'policy that the responsibility for the relief of distress belongs to private organization, local communities, and the states will not be changed.' As it is, the utilizing of the Corporation to make relief loans to the states is disliked by all those, and they are many, who take the view expressed by one of them that 'funds administered by politicians are almost always used wastefully, and because such aid will very probably undo the economy programs that the bankers have been forcing upon local governments in an endeavor to bring taxes down to a tolerable level.'

This effort to 'bring taxes down to a tolerable level' is a story in itself, and one that reads strangely enough to those who bear the British load of rates and taxes. The tax situation in Chicago has long been notorious. When I was there, the city was by its own admission bankrupt: teachers' salaries had not been paid for months, and large numbers of schools, even in wealthy suburbs like Winettka and Evanston, were closed; the difficulty of paying police and firemen was causing acute apprehension. Respectable Philadelphia was little better off. There, too, the payment of salaries was stopped; a proposed increase of local taxation to meet them was stayed by an angry demonstration of citizens. Indeed, the cities which are not in deficit, and very serious deficit, would make but a short list—a list headed by Milwaukee, with its years of socialist administration, which is, by general admission even of its most hostile critics, the 'best governed' in the Union.

Up to the opening of 1932, the negative attitude on the part of

Washington corresponded accurately enough with the outlook of the nation as a whole. There was no general sympathy for any legislative action to deal with unemployment. The American Federation of Labor was just as keenly opposed to it as were the Chambers of Commerce and the Rotary Clubs. It was 'unAmerican.' Propaganda against the British system had been widespread and effective; the belief was quite general that it was ruining, and was bound to ruin, British trade and British morale. But by 1932 unemployment on a large scale was a three-year-old phenomenon. The belief that its results could be met by charitable campaigns, no matter how spectacular or how successful, was dying; dying with the general confidence in the 'American' way as something providentially protected from the thunderstorms of calamity. The storms were sweeping the United States as heavily as they swept less deserving lands. Among the other fears that were taking hold of the national mind, fear of what the unemployed might be driven to do began to take its place. The vast procession of jobless to Washington, the demonstration outside the Ford Plant at Baton Rouge were alarming symptoms. As a result, terrifying images of what 'may happen' unless 'something is done' obsess the mind of the least thoughtful citizen, and keep the more thoughtful lying awake into the night. But what is to be done? So far, nobody knows.

At the same time, there is a marked difference in atmosphere and in attitude, when one of the interminable discussions about unemployment insurance systems opens, as between 1932 and 1930. That such a system as the British may, *inter alia,* be a form of protection for social order is beginning to be dimly apprehended; as that it is unemployment, not the existence of organized provision for meeting its results, that is undermining to the morale of the unemployed, and dangerous to their docility. When Walter Lippmann, speaking today as the accredited spokesman of the 'best opinion,' urges that unemployment insurance is no remedy for unemployment, he is not really making a point against it, or meeting the argument of fear that is moving the minds of his fellow-countrymen to look at it (provided always it is not organized through the Federal Government) as a protection to themselves.

Most of what has, so far, been done, and most of the discussion about what could or should be done proceeds strictly within the assumption that industry should make some provision for its unemployed. What has been done is, of course, so far but a modest story; but it does mark a changing attitude that may carry far. Through the initiative of the able and active Labor Commissioner for the state of New York, a Conference of Governors of six industrial states—New York, New Jersey, Ohio, Pennsylvania, Massachusetts, and Connecticut—was held at Albany in January of last year. That conference set up an Interstate commission on Unemployment Insurance, which, in February of the current year, issued its Report, a unanimous document. The essential recommendations in the Report are: first, the compulsory establishment of state-wide systems of unemployment reserves; second, such reserves, to be built up by contributions from employers only of 2 per cent of their pay roll, to constitute the fund out of which unemployment benefit, at a maximum rate of 50 per cent of the unemployed man's wages, for a maximum period of ten weeks in any twelve months, the responsibility of the employer being strictly limited by the amount of his own reserve; third, the state to administer the fund thus created, and to extend its own public employment service, and also make every effort to extend stabilization agencies. In this, two governing points emerge. First, the responsibility is laid on the employer to meet his own unemployment (or rather, in practice, the unemployment of those men whom he treats as being 'on his establishment'). Second, not only is any kind of national scheme rejected; there is also rejected any plan based on a pooling of contributions. The scheme advocated is one of insurance by industry, on a strictly individualist basis. It is admitted that, at its best, such a plan must leave out of its scope all the workers in small, unorganized establishments.

Some of the arguments adduced against a national or even a full state scheme are illuminating. Any such scheme hinges on the possession by the worker of some sort of identity contribution card, which he can carry about with him—a point one would have thought of special value in a land when labor turnover is as high, in normal times, as 300 per cent. But covering, or claiming to cover, the craftsmen, the American Federation of Labor has always set its face against the carrying of any other than a union card; and I further was told by a most experienced administrator that even in New York State there is a proportion of employees so ignorant and helpless that they could never manage a card, and of employers so dishonest that they would evade any system which depended on their co-operation.

So far, of course, the Governors' Report has not produced more than a spate of animated discussion, although in New York State, in the city of Rochester, a plan based on the voluntary co-operation of some forty largish employers is well under way. This, however, has no legislative sanction behind it; the only state in which legislative action has been taken is Wisconsin. Wisconsin is on many counts the most interesting state in the Union. Long known as the 'State of Experiment,' it is the one state in which politics, elsewhere despised, derided, and left severely alone, enlist the active co-operation and concern of the intellectuals and excite the ardent interest of citizens of all kinds. There, the University and the State Capitol work closely hand in hand. Wisconsin is also a state of vivid and arresting personalities. Its pioneer Unemployment Compensation Act, actually signed by the Governor during the time of my visit to Madison, had the further interest of associating the Grand Old Man of social experiment and constructive economic thinking in America, Professor John R. Commons—fragile, tiny, white-haired, an elflike wisp of a man—with the youthfully vigorous governor, Phil La Follette, who is only in his thirties.

In its propaganda stages, this bill was carried through a state that is predominantly agricultural, and the farmers and industrialists there alike converted to its major principle, by the eager enthusiasm of a band of young men and women, most of whom are associated with the University, either as teachers or as students. At one of the weekly evenings at which John R. Commons assembles students and others for a 'plate supper' and subsequent talk, I was lucky enough to be allowed to meet a number of them, celebrating their success, and exchanging notes as to how it had been done. 'John R.,' as they all affectionately call him, sat in the midst of an eager and animated group: there was Elizabeth Brandeis, the darkly handsome daughter of the great judge of the U. S. Supreme Court (who, himself, now looks more like Abe Lincoln than anyone I have ever seen); Paul Rauschenbusch, her husband, as fair as she is dark, but lit with the same flame-like eagerness; Harold Groves, who will be responsible for the state's share in supervising the administration; young men who had been miners and lumber men; young women who were making their university career possible by working in beauty parlors and department stores in the vacation—and so on. It was a real human workshop, that evening's gathering, and Madison altogether seemed to me one of the most alive and hopeful centers that I struck. . . Keen realization of difficulties, but no mood of quailing or wailing before them. . .

NO ONE IS SHOCKED

The penetration of the trade unions by racketeering was perturbing the president of the American Federation of Labor two years ago; and it has gone fast since. In Chicago, several powerful unions are completely under the control of Al Capone and his gang, while others have to pay heavy monthly tribute to stave the gangsters off. It is the same in New York, where, for example, the garment manufacturers alone pay between one and two million dollars a year to protect their establishments against racketeered labor troubles; and in every great industrial center. 'Protection' is indeed, next to booze-running, gambling, and dope-peddling, the most prolific and the most profitable form of racket. The organization is often exemplary in its thoroughness: whole sections will be controlled, with a boss at the head who has 'some dirt on the big boys in city politics'; his satellites then call, in twos, on all the tradespeople in the neighborhood and 'invite' them to join the Protective Association—fee, fifty or a hundred dollars a month. Anyone who refuses may—and knows he may—next morning find his windows blown out and his stock ruined, or, as he enters, have his face smashed in. In one limited area in New York, the 'take' by way of protection is reported to be round about ten thousand dollars a month. To detail the gangs' activities would be tedious: the beauty of the system is its simplicity and general applicability. They control movie houses by ruining competitors with stink bombs, and are now well in on the food business, where the dropping of chemicals into fresh milk, causing it to curdle, alternates with the puncturing of van tires, as a relatively mild method of operation. Gangs tend to amalgamate, but also, of course, to come into mutual collision; much of the shooting up that diversifies life in the big cities is fratricidal, and between rival gangs.

Do not imagine that this is a remote affair of the slums. It penetrates into the texture of ordinary daily life. A small instance will illustrate how it works, and help to bring home the fact that it is no distant phenomenon, but something with which the plain citizen comes into constant and painful contact. I met a woman who, in a quite obscure but highly respectable part of the city of New York, well away from Broadway and the angry Forties, carries on, in a large studio apartment where she also lives, a very small business in antiques and *objets d'art*. Her stock is never large; its value derives mainly from the fact that she has knowledge and great personal taste, while a considerable connection helps her to market it in a semi-private way. The other day she was visited by two men, to her totally unknown, who demanded that she pay a heavy weekly sum as 'insurance,' in order to have her premises guarded against burglars. The neighborhood is quiet and orderly; nothing of the kind had occurred there for many years. With impressive emphasis, however, her visitors assured her that it would, unless she took on their offer; they would not answer for the consequences if she refused. She might find her premises broken into at any time; come home to discover all her stuff broken up. There had been, she knew, plenty of such cases, although not so far in her own quarter. She looked at them, attempted to beat down the price; in vain. Resistance was idle; her visitors were, she knew, amply qualified to carry out their threats. There was nothing for it but to pay. Pay she does, a heavy sum—heavy in itself, and very heavy in relation to her turnover and her resources. No watchman, such as was promised her, is visible; she did not expect one. On one occasion, however, when she was behindhand with her installment, she received a warning. She knows that whatever else she has to do without in order to keep up those payments, kept up they have got to be. And her case is common, though more blatant than some. In enhanced laundry prices and a total lack of freedom to choose between laundries, in garage charges, and in a hundred ways, direct and indirect, the market is controlled by racketeers. Gun in hand they visit the shop or the factory and demand that this or that be sold, this or that source of supply employed, this or that paid per week or per month for protection. Anyone who resists is held up and, if necessary, shot up.

During the months of my stay in New York I saw only one shooting, and of course one could live there very much longer than I did —or in Chicago, Detroit, Pittsburgh, or Philadelphia, for that matter— in the part of the city where one does live, without seeing any. I heard a shot where 43rd Street crosses 6th Avenue; I saw a mass of people running. It was all over, so far as I went, in less than a minute. I heard and read, of course, of a multitude of other cases, and the sense of their possibility is kept well before the mind by the presence of armed police and the sight and sound of the armored cars in which they dash by, with or, if it suits them, against, the traffic lights. The sole occasion on which I was in any peril of sharing the fate of Mr. Winston Churchill and being run over was when, with the lights all in my favor, my ears were suddenly assailed, as I was calmly crossing 2nd Avenue, with volleys of loud imprecations, and I only by a hairsbreadth saved myself from being run down by a police motorcycle, tearing by at sixty miles an hour, in all the freedom of an officially barred street.

There are, I am told, police regulations against the possession, by the ordinary citizen, of firearms. Their main result appears to be that he is quite helpless when two or three masked men with guns enter his shop or his dwelling house and call on him to hand over his cash box, in peril of instant death. The police claim, I know, that in 1931 an increasing proportion of murderers and other criminals have been brought to justice; they cannot claim any reduction in the appalling toll of lost life, nor any increased confidence in their own efficiency on the part of the citizen of America, in town or country.

One of the questions that arises instantly to the lips of the visitor who gets to learn something of the detailed terrorism and pervasive blackmail under which his American acquaintance live, is, 'Why don't you go to the police for protection?' A man I met, who in a speakeasy was suddenly confronted with a demand for an immense sum in ransom, and promised to pay it tomorrow in the form of a check to be called for at his office, did, in the interval, go to the police. They merely shrugged their shoulders. There was nothing they could do. He had to pay. He did pay—ten times as much as he was originally asked for, since, when he met his gentlemen, they were entirely aware of the effort he had made to escape from them, and put up the tariff accordingly. Put the query to your friends in New York or Chicago or Philadelphia, and the only reply you will get will be a stare of surprise, followed by a hoot of derision. In police protection nobody believes. That indeed is a gross understatement. They feel that, at best inoperative, such an appeal would in all probability only mean putting your head right inside the lion's jaws. This feeling is, of course, far stronger among the vast helpless mass of the population, which is poor. The insecurity and dread under which the poor of the great cities live are dreadful, and justified.

While I was in the United States, Mr. Samuel Seabury was carrying out his investigation into the administration, judicial and otherwise, of the city of New York. Reports of his inquiries and of his proceedings and ultimate recommendations appeared daily in the newspapers. They disclosed a picture of sheer injustice, of inefficiency, and of corruption that was appalling. Small sign, however, that anyone was appalled. Little in these columns that was new to the New Yorker. Little hope on the part of any of them that action would follow the recommendations. Those among them with longer memories had seen the breaking of Mayor Mitchel, who really tried, with the aid of a superb band of assistants, to clean up the city, and the city government reverting to full Tammany tradition. Tammany is in control today. The present mayor, 'Jimmy' Walker, is regarded with universal contempt, but in the very expression of that contempt one often feels a humorous, almost an affectionate, tolerance. He, of course, is not trying to do anything in the way of cleaning up; on the contrary; but nobody expects him to do so. Mr. Seabury tells people what they know, perhaps deplore, but regard as practically inevitable.

In the general picture of helpless acceptance of admitted corruption, the black chapter which describes the administration of law is perhaps the dreariest spot, since it concerns, intimately, the daily lives of millions. Mr. Seabury's Report on the administration of justice in New York was issued on March 28th. It is a truly terrifying document, and certainly explains, only too amply, why the automatic recourse of the British citizen to the police or the courts for protection never occurs to the New Yorker. Mr. Seabury states that 'bad as the conditions in the magistrates' courts of Greater New York' are shown by his Report to be, 'the actual conditions are much worse:' 'It would not,' he goes on, 'be humanly possible, no matter how long the investigation might be, or how competent the staff or counsel might be, to elicit the testimony which would be required to depict the true conditions in their entirety.' A formidable obstruction was offered by the authorities. The Mayor's assurances of co-operation were 'as sincere as they were loud'; he actually did everything in his power to thwart inquiry. Yet, as it stands, the picture is impressive enough. . .

VALUES

The standard of average possession in the U.S.A. is, of course, higher than ours, in all classes. Classes in turn are divided according to their ownership of things. The upper class, for example, is made up, to quote a recent native description, of 'those who have an income of two hundred thousand dollars or more, and the regular trimmings, such as a yacht, a showplace here or there in America and another in Europe, and so on—who do, in short, the regular things in the regular way.' The middle class imitates: they have an apartment in the city and a camp somewhere in the country, a car or two, and so on. The workman, so one is continually told, and sees for oneself, expects to have his automobile and his radio. Result—the scene is cluttered up with things to an appalling extent. On Sunday, everyone who has a car—and that is everyone—goes out in it for a ride. The roads are a mere procession of packed vehicles, and the fields that fringe them a forest of filling stations. Every house has its radio, and the noise of the loud speaker makes a standing *obbligato* to existence, from which there is no escape. Things block the mind. Motion through things takes the place of thought.

Abounding material success, the possibility for everyone of accumulating more and more things, of 'rising' and 'making good,' concealed up to now the lack of mental content to these words, over and above their sheer dollar connotation. The easy abundance of means made questions about the ends to which those means were being or might be directed appear unnecessary, even otiose. Every now and then someone rose up and put a few awkward questions; but they hung unanswered in the air. The business of accumulation, absorbing and successful, had thrills that left no energy over for inquiries of purely philosophical interest, and no apparent relevance to the great job in hand.

Now, however, the doom of this system of values—or rather of this single-value system—has descended with crashing and crushing force. The world of solid and mounting prosperity and material achievement has collapsed, and there is nothing left. Even to admit that there is or could be another scale of values, wholly different, is only to deepen depression, since there is no one to tell those to whose minds such thoughts come knocking what or where it is. There are free spirits in certain universities who feel this, acutely: an experiment like the Liberal College at Madison, Wisconsin, was directly designed to meet it, and, above all, to educate the nation's educators; but that experiment has been shelved owing to the depression; and, in general, there is little help or light coming from the universities, rich and large as they are, and objects, as they are, of so much national pride. Open to every American child, no matter where born or how conditioned financially, is an education extending from the primary through the secondary school, on to the university. This looks like being an Open Sesame for the nation to genuine civilization, and as constituting an advantage over us in Great Britain rich in unmeasured possibility. But the more one sees of the actual teaching given, whether in school or university, the cooler grows one's envy. Here, at bottom, the object pursued is the familar one of putting boys and girls, young men and women, in a position to 'make good'—the terms of this making being the standard terms of business. At the colleges, the system of 'assembling credits,' by which the courses and the studies of the average student is governed, is calculated to undermine any respect for disinterested work or thinking, and is absolutely hostile to the putting of awkward questions about 'What is it all for?' Parents expect to have their offspring equipped for 'real life'—and real life means the struggle for material success. The entire atmosphere is evasive of fundamental interrogatories. . .

America under the New Deal [1] ᘓ

M. PHILIPS PRICE. *Having seen Russia during the Revolution in 1917-18, when he was a correspondent of the Manchester* Guardian, *Morgan Philips Price wished to see how the United States, with its special traditions and history, was meeting a great economic crisis. He*

[1] From *America after Sixty Years,* by M. Philips Price, London, 1936; by permission of Mr. Price and George Allen and Unwin, Ltd.

was assisted in his observations by a remarkable fund of experience. Born in 1885, he had been educated at Harrow and at Trinity College, Cambridge. He traveled in Central Asia, Siberia, Persia, and Turkey in 1908-14, and throughout World War I he served as the Guardian's *correspondent in Russia. At the close of the conflict he joined the Labor Party, and in 1919 the Labor organ, the* Daily Herald, *sent him to Berlin, where he remained until 1923. Later he became private secretary to Sir Charles Trevelyan, and in time was elected to Parliament as a Labor member from the Forest of Dean division of Gloucestershire. All sides of the New Deal interested him, but as an agriculturist he was especially anxious to learn about the workings of the A.A.A. in the West and South. As he writes in his book on the United States— one of a number from his pen, for he has published volumes on Eastern Europe, Siberia, and Asiatic Russia in wartime—he felt strongly upon the need for a better understanding between America and Britain. Central Europe was descending into barbarism; Russia, though a great and hopeful experiment, offered the Anglo-Saxon world no model to follow. 'It remains for the British and American Commonwealths to show the world that they can carry through great and critical reforms, and at the same time retain their ancient political liberties.'*

HENRY FORD AND HIS SYSTEM

ON October 23rd [1934] we reached Detroit by the night train from Buffalo, and went straight to Dearborn, where Henry Ford has his great motor works, and where a regular satellite town has grown up round an industry—a proof of the modern tendency toward decentralization. Dearborn has its own civic life, quite separate from that of Detroit, which remains a huge industrial city, but is under the direction, as far as its local government is concerned, of its own Tammany, in which, as usual, the Irish-Catholic element is predominant. I have remarked before that the one hope of breaking the power of Tammany throughout the United States probably lies in the growth of satellite towns round decentralized industries. But here in Dearborn there is another problem. From the frying pan of Tammany one jumps into the fire of the industrial paternalism of Henry Ford. Fordism, judged by bookkeeping standards, may be more efficient than Tammany, but will it permit of the development of individual liberty and happiness, and of a civic consciousness? Dearborn is really run by an industrial oligarchy centered on the person of Henry Ford. Their will determines the lives and welfare of all the inhabitants. There can be no independent thinking under these conditions, because there is no organ of free opinion. It is an industrial Tsardom, albeit of a most efficient and benevolent kind, but a Tsardom for all that.

Dearborn is a sort of mass-production workshop, museum, and scientific laboratory combined. Every comfort is provided for the visitor, in the form of a special hotel. We spent the morning in the museum, and saw the scientific laboratory from the outside. The exhibits are all housed in magnificent buildings, some in Tudor, some in Queen Anne style. There is apparently nothing original about the architecture favored by American industrial magnates. In the main the architects follow the classical models of Europe. In the museum Ford has the beginnings of a wonderful permanent exhibition of articles designed to show how transport and industry have developed down the ages, from the caveman's tool to the aeroplane and the motor car. Outside, in the parklike grounds, there are steamers and boats from early times floating on the lakes. There are examples of houses, shops, and village industries, which show how the habits of man have changed with the growth of scientific discovery and improved methods of transport. As you move from place to place in the park, old-fashioned coaches drive up and take you where you want to go. We saw Henry Ford himself walking about with some visitors. He seemed amazingly active and well for a man of over seventy. His whole life is now devoted to perfecting this great museum, a monument to himself and to his great hero and inspirer, Thomas Edison.

The most significant thing I saw that morning was the inscription over the main entrance to the scientific laboratory. It ran: 'Man's Progress takes place over a Bridge built by the Agriculturalist, the Engineer, and the Scientist.' This is the key to Ford's philosophy, but it is, of course, nothing new. The whole of the Russian Revolution is based on this theory, and writers, from poor, dreary, old Karl Marx down to H. G. Wells, have been preaching it for the last eighty years. Ford's special contribution to this philosophy has been his sincere attempt to bring the fruits of invention down to the consuming masses, while still preserving the profit motive of industry known as capitalism. The claims of the consumer on the product of industry and production for use rather than for profit have constituted the socialist case for decades. If Ford can benefit the consumer and also produce for profit, he may save the capitalist system, which is probably why the Russian Bolsheviks respect and, to a certain extent, fear him. Cheap mass production, with the main eye on the consumer, presupposes, if a certain amount of profit is still to be allowed to the managers, a high degree of planning. Ford does not love profit seekers and investors. But his weakness is that he does not realize the social effect of his cheap mass production, which can only be remedied by social services, shorter hours, and guaranteed earnings. In other words, the state must take a hand. The benevolent industrial autocrat will not be able to put the world right without the work of the social planner. The fruits of industry cannot be brought to the masses by cheap production alone. Social services must be organized as a channel through which they must pass. Yet Mr. Ford thunders against social services, and in this respect proves himself no better than the average Wall Street obscurantist, a type which, in other respects, he dislikes heartily.

In the afternoon we visited the main workshops where the mass production of cars is effected. Rows of men stand beside the conveyors, and as the components pass each man has his particular job—to bore a hole, fit a pin, or tighten a nut. At the end of the conveyor the parts are collected and placed near the chassis of a car. One large conveyor moves the chassis along, and from the end of the long shed, in about forty minutes' time, the complete car is driven off the premises. In this way 1800 cars a day were being turned out when we were at Dearborn. In the boom years the output was 3000 cars. The unskilled men were getting five dollars a day, and the skilled workers more. We could see that the pressure of work must be very great. The conveyors were keyed up to the pace of the average man, and woe to those who could not keep up with it. I heard from many sources that some men cannot stand the strain after five years at the conveyor. Moreover, there is no guarantee of earnings, even of a low minimum. In spite of all his ideas of keeping up buying power by cheap production, Ford was obliged, in the depression, to cut production and dismiss workers. Hundreds of men earned the high wages of five dollars a day for a couple of months, and then starved for the remaining ten. Until there is a guaranteed minimum for the year, or some scheme of unemployment insurance, run either by the state or by the firm, all Ford's benevolent despotism must fail to solve the gravest of our modern social problems. In spite of the many interesting and wonderful things which we saw on our visit to Dearborn, I was not swept off my feet, nor did I fail to see that with all our slowness we in England have a sounder social basis in our systems of insurance and public service. If these could be welded to the practical idealism of Henry Ford, the world might indeed be a better place.

CHICAGO AND HER PROBLEMS

On our second day at Chicago I visited the famous stockyards. These are enormous establishments on the outskirts of the city. About five great meat trusts have their killing, dressing, and packing stations there. Roughly 700 pigs an hour are killed in one of these places alone, and 150 oxen. I saw the pigs being driven into an enclosure in which there is a great wheel. A Negro slings a cord round the hind leg of one animal, and the wheel draws it up until it is suspended on a chain and slowly conveyed down the line. 'Round goes the wheel to the music of the squeal.' A man with a knife sticks the pig as it passes, another singes its hair, a score of others dress the carcass, others cut it up, and within a quarter of an hour a live pig is converted into hams and bacon ready for curing. I saw the beeves treated in much the same manner, except that they are first stunned with the pole ax and then stuck.

We were taken through acres and acres of storehouses, stockyards, and chemical laboratories, where the enormous number of by-products coming from the animals are tested. Lard, soap, and floor polish, to say nothing of every conceivable kind of prepared foods, are handled by these firms. One could not fail to be impressed by the enormous concentrated power of the capital that controls these animal products, which has the Western farmer absolutely at its mercy. I noticed that some of the independent farmers' political organizations, now active in Wisconsin and Minnesota, were beginning to talk about the nationalization of the packing corporations. Some people, in fact, were talking Socialism without mentioning the word. Nobody bothers about political theory in America, and perhaps this is just as well. But trusts and powerful corporations were never popular with the Western farmer. These enormous private vested interests have grown up at the centre where the nerve fibres of the agricultural Middle West and the industrial East meet.

The phenomenal growth of Chicago dates from the Civil War, when the old patriarchal, self-supporting farming families, who worked their land by manual labor, were broken up by the drafts of young men to the Union armies. The Chicago manufacturer saw his chance in this crisis, and pushed his labor-saving machinery across the newly built railways to the farms, where the women and old men raised and harvested the crops with half the expenditure of time and energy. It was Chicago and the industrialized Middle West that finally crushed the South, and enabled Grant to steam-roll the Confederate armies, which not even the brilliance of Robert E. Lee could hold together. From that time dates Chicago's dominance over the Middle West, as manifested in these great packing plants, which handle almost everything that the farmer wants to buy and sell. No wonder that the Middle Western farmer is liable to bouts of rebellion against the corporations, as witness Bryan's 'Cross of Gold' speech, and Theodore Roosevelt's trust-busting, and more recently Governor Olsen's

Farmer-Labor party, to say nothing of La Follette's rule in Wisconsin.

On our third day in Chicago I presented a letter of introduction to the Chief Commissioner of Police. As I had expected, I found that he and many of his assistants were Irish, and visions of Tammany Hall floated before my eyes. I had heard a lot of unsavory stories about the connection between the gangster world and the city government of Chicago, and I knew the reputation of all the larger cities and states as regards local government. But whatever may have been going on behind the scenes, we were impressed by the efficiency with which the Police Department of Chicago is run. The Irish may have a bad record of graft and corruption in the States, but we received the impression that there has been a clean-up in Chicago since the abolition of Prohibition, and it may be hoped that the atmosphere has become permanently purer. Certainly the Irish heads of the Chicago police did not appear as though they wanted to hide anything from us. They admitted that things had been very bad, but they insisted that the city was turning over a new leaf, and that the gangsters were really on the run. Things had come to such a pass that shortly before Prohibition ended the gangsters were running the liquor and the white-slave traffic, squaring the police, terrorizing the City Council, and murdering all those who dared to raise their voices against them. Now, it seemed, the tables were being turned. There was no need for foreign police to point to Chicago as a warning. On the other hand, Scotland Yard had just sent over someone to get hints on traffic management from the Chicago police. We met in the Deputy Chief's office a Police Commissioner from Chile who had come to study American methods.

And we found that modern science was being used to defeat the gangster. We were proudly shown the room which was the nerve centre of the telephone and radio connection between the public, reporting attacks or robberies, and the police cars, fitted with radio apparatus and cruising in all sections of the city and suburbs. We were there when a message came in to the effect that a robbery had taken place in a certain street. At once an order was sent out by wireless to Car No. So-and-So, to proceed to a certain spot, investigate, and report. Generally the car is on the spot within three minutes, and is able to catch the offender. We formed the opinion that our Scotland Yard might profitably study the methods of the Chicago police. After visiting the finger-print department, which seemed very efficiently run, we were taken out in one of the cruising police cars. As we drove, we kept on hearing messages being flashed out to cars from headquarters, giving them instructions as to their movements. We passed through some of the worst slum districts, and were pleased to see that some of the streets were marked down for demolition next spring under the Public Works Administration. I never saw a worse case of dilapidation, squalor, dreariness, and general degradation. I should be a gangster myself if I had to live in such a place.

But it was encouraging to hear from all the Americans we met that they were ashamed of such places, and realized that they were the real breeding grounds of crime. The real improvement in the situation was manifested, however, firstly by the pleasure with which we were told that this and that bad street was being demolished, and secondly by the talk of the Police Commissioner who accompanied us. He showed us first this house, now that, all boarded up and deserted, where two years ago policemen were killed in fights with gangsters, and then a street, now apparently quiet and respectable, which was formerly unsafe for outsiders to enter. We felt that things were definitely on the mend in Chicago.

We saw the open space where Communist and Socialist speakers address open-air meetings—a safety valve for the submerged tenth in the Chicago back streets. One wonders why the Socialist movement has made so little headway in the United States of America. When I visited the headquarters of the American Socialist Party I found as good intellectual leaders as one could find anywhere in Europe. But the Socialist movement in America suffers from two handicaps. Firstly, America was so long a land of individuals, pioneering alone in the backwoods for their own gain, that social restrictions are unpopular. If they are admitted now as a necessity, they are accepted only as practical measures of temporary significance, as palliatives, and not as the results of clear thinking based on a political theory. Secondly, the Socialist movement of America has no foundation in the great trade-union organizations, which are such a feature of English political life. It remains an intellectual movement without a great industrial organization at its back.

We left Chicago with a feeling of wonder mingled with hopefulness. The city seemed at first sight the most imposing we had yet seen in America. But appearances were deceptive. If one got behind Michigan Avenue, one had the feeling that Chicago had been, and to some extent still was, a whited sepulchre. Insulls and Rockefellers had lived on the whited exterior. Inside were the dead men's bones of the slums, the Latin and Slav quarters from which had sprung the poisonous fungus of organized crime. Now Insull's prestige has fallen and Prohibition is ended. But until the authorities clear out the sepulchre and make it a wholesome soil where the human plant can grow to its full stature, they will not be able to congratulate themselves without reserve. No other city in the United States has such a task—to live down and repair the ravages of decades of uncontrolled nineteenth-century individualism.

CALIFORNIA: RADICAL vs. REACTIONARY

California is a land of extremes—in climate, and also, perhaps consequently, in politics. The atmosphere stimulates an explosive activity in the people. The cool breeze of the Pacific is a preventive of mental sloth. Not many weeks before we arrived the whole of the San Francisco port workers struck for better conditions. Then the seasonal workers on the fruit plantations struck, at the height of the packing season, for better pay, and got it. In response to Upton Sinclair's campaign in the fall of 1934, committees in pursuance of his 'End Poverty in California' program were formed all over the state, from San Francisco to Los Angeles. On the other hand, the solid forces of conservatism were massed behind Governor Merriam. There had never been such a lineup of Conservative Republicans and Democrats in one camp before. Does this mean that the Marxian class war, as interpreted by Lenin and Stalin, is breaking out in California? I doubt it. The population of California is too heterogeneous, as regards both race and occupation, for a common objective to be easily found. But California is the home of hothouse growths. Every kind of fruit is produced here on a commercial basis, from apples on the plains of Sacramento to figs and dates in Death Valley, which is below sea level. In the same way the country breeds extremes of politics, massed reaction on the one hand and Utopian Socialism on the other. All sorts of weird movements are going on in the towns and villages along this coast. Apart from the Sinclair movement there are the 'Utopians,' a queer mixture of religious revivalism and the charlatanism of a secret society. It seems to be the result of Anglo-Saxon evangelism from New England transplanted in the hothouse atmosphere of California.

The results of the November elections of 1934 in California were surprising, and in some respects made history. The defeat of Sinclair was a foregone conclusion. But the size of his minority was surprising, and its distribution even more so. Not only did Sinclair poll a good third of the electors of California, but these votes were not confined to San Francisco, Los Angeles, and the other large cities. They were scattered fairly evenly throughout the great fruit and farming areas of the plains. Evidently not only the white and colored unskilled and dock labor of San Francisco and the artisans of the film studios in Los Angeles supported Sinclair, but also the Spanish and Mexican seasonal workers on the farms and ranches. But it was as well that Sinclair was defeated, because he could never have put his program in operation in the teeth of the rest of the United States, and chaos would have ensued if he had tried to carry it out. But his great feat was to have given the respectable and well-to-do people of California the shock of their lives, and to have shown them that do-nothing conservatism rouses opposition in every walk of life. One thing struck us greatly during this Californian election: it was extraordinarily orderly. Nowhere did we see any manifestation of undue excitement. Life went on quite normally. There were no processions, like those we saw in the Middle West. The campaign seemed to be conducted from door to door by the distribution of leaflets and literature, and by broadcasting. Americans seem to excel in this kind of propaganda. Excitement there was, of course, but it was confined to discussions between groups of people in their homes and in public places.

THE IMPOVERISHED SOUTH

We made long stops between buses at various places on our way to Charleston, our destination. We stopped at small towns or large villages, where there was generally a post office, a police station, and a store. Wooden houses of colonial type lay on either side of a deeply rutted sandy road. Unemployed and ragged Negroes were hanging about. Some white cadets from the naval training ship at Charleston were marching along the street. Insulting remarks were hurled at the Negroes, who cowered and slunk away out of sight. A Negro girl crossed the road; I heard lewd remarks bawled across to her by some whites outside a shop. About a mile down the road was a batch of wooden huts, precariously resting on stones at the four corners. The wood was hand-sawn and there was only one room in each hut. The inmates were generally a Negro man and woman. There were children of various ages. The man was the only member of the family who had proper clothes. The rest were half naked. The food, I gathered, consisted of hand-ground maize meal, baked into flat cakes. I did not see that there was anything else, except what the local store would advance on security of the cotton crop. If it failed, there would be nothing but what could be obtained by begging from the passengers who got off the buses at the halt up the road. I looked at the fields, where the hope of future food lay. The cotton field was half covered with weeds, and there were no implements for cultivation, save such as the storekeeper would lend them, repaying himself out of the price of the food which he would sell them in the winter. This food was sold only on credit. The maize cobs had been gathered, but half the crop was weeds, as I could see from what remained on the field. I walked back up the road firm in the conviction that the conditions of the peasants in Russia under the Tsar, as I had seen them, were greatly superior to those of the Negro share-cropper and the 'poor white' in South Carolina! The Tsarist government did permit a certain amount of co-operation and self-help, which the peasants organized among themselves. There was a society and a local public opinion, which could express itself in village meetings, as long as it did not speak against the Government. But here there was nothing. Everyone was free to say anything he liked and to starve. Here an old economy, based on slavery, had collapsed, and nothing had taken its place. The human wreckage released by the collapse had been allowed to drift aimlessly about for sixty years. Society had simply decayed and died here. There was in fact no society or social consciousness whatever. I remembered that Southern whites had told me from time to time that the South really understands the Negro and loves him, and that only in the South is the Negro really at home. That may be so, but even a dog likes his kennel, because he knows nothing else. Somehow I prefer the Yankee's attitude. He says openly that he does not like the Negroes, but that they are, nevertheless, entitled to a square deal and equal rights of citizenship under the Constitution.

Arrived at Charleston, we went round the town. We were much impressed by this most perfect of all the old English colonial settlements of America. Founded in the reign of Charles II, the English colonists, mostly the sons of well-to-do families, brought English customs, and even English materials for building their houses. I saw several houses of the Queen Anne style, which one might see in any south of England village today. It was only the palms growing in the streets, the absence of the English elm and oak, which prevented one from imagining that one was in Bournemouth or some Devonshire seaside resort. From the fine sea front the Atlantic Ocean was visible through a wide channel, in which stood the famous Fort Sumter, where the first shot in the War between the States was fired.

Here in Charleston one can still see what is left of the real old Southern aristocracy, or at least those of its members who have any money left. In the main, however, the fine villas along the sea front are occupied during the winter season by Northern business people from New York and Chicago. The slump has reduced their numbers somewhat, but the process of penetrating the Old South by new blood from the North is still continuing.

The monuments of the Old South are still visible everywhere. Foremost among them is the statue and house of John C. Calhoun, that grim figure and eloquent warrior of dying causes. In the City Hall the walls were hung with portraits of Confederate leaders, whose memory still lives in Charleston. But the life of this fine old city of the South is being slowly drawn into the main stream of American life, both economic and cultural. Chain stores, Woolworths, overland bus services, and wireless are breaking down the barriers of particularism which have held South Carolina apart from the rest of the United States. Nevertheless I think this Old South will continue to contribute something to the life of the new America. I was shown with pride by a Charlestonian those words on the grave in St. Michael's Church of James Louis Petigru, jurist, statesman, and orator of South Carolina, who died in 1863: 'Unawed by Opinion, Unseduced by Flattery, Undismayed by Disaster, He confronted Life with Antique Courage and Death with Christian Hope.' These words were much appreciated by the late President Woodrow Wilson.

After our motor drive through South Carolina we caught the night express northwards and found ourselves landed next morning at a little wayside junction deep in the heart of North Carolina. We were anxious to round off our impressions of Dixieland in this the state that was supposed to be the most progressive and the most closely in touch with the North. My first impression may have been a superficial one, but I thought it important at the time. The little branch-line train that was to carry us to the town of Durham consisted of two coaches. The engine was driven and fired by two Negroes in the full cotton overall uniform of the qualified American mechanic. Even the peaked forage cap was there. Now I had not seen this anywhere in either Georgia or South Carolina. Evidently the white railway workers have not raised any objection to working in the same grades and on the same line as the Negro workers. Arrived at Durham we found the station full of Negroes who had come into town for market day. In the streets there was an atmosphere of bustle and hurry that struck us forcibly, for we had not encountered it since we had been in the South. I saw no dejected Negroes hanging about the streets. They all seemed as busy as the white Americans. There were plenty of Negro shops, and everybody was dressed reasonably well and tidily. Indeed, I soon learned that this town supports a Negro millionaire, who is the head of a prosperous insurance business. There was a good deal of industry in the town too, mostly connected with tobacco and cigarette manufacture. We saw Duke University, which was founded and financed by influential people in the tobacco industry. But of late years the tobacco interests have extended their influence into electric power, and have been behind some of the utility corporations which have come into such disfavour with the President and the public because of their high charges. These tobacco-power interests have been working very hard against the President's Tennessee Power Scheme, and their methods have not stopped short of trying to mobilize the services of the professors and college authorities, whom they can control through the power of the purse. The latter were expected to go to Washington and lobby in Congress against the President's Tennessee Power Scheme. From other sources I learnt that these interests were not averse to exploiting the Negro also, and exciting race prejudice against the employment of white labour on the Power Scheme. I confess I was not favourably impressed by the position of certain American universities. While financial influences in England are not against lobbying in their interests, and exert an appalling control over the press, they stop short of trying to control the universities and colleges. From what I could learn it seemed that public opinion in America was hardening against this sort of thing. I heard some very candid remarks during my stay here, and later in Washington.

In the next place that we visited we saw a model type of educational institution. About twenty miles to the south, after motoring through undulating woodlands and cornfields, interspersed with large built-up areas, we reached the beautiful little university town of Chapel Hill. The town seemed to have been carefully planned, with wide streets and spacious gardens and parks. It is always a pleasing feature of American towns that the gardens of one house run into the gardens of another, without a hedge or even a fence, such as one would see in England. This seems to indicate the greater sociability of the Americans. It is in keeping too with the lack of snobbishness to which I have referred elsewhere. This was particularly noticeable in Chapel Hill. The houses were mostly of the wooden colonial type, and the University of North Carolina buildings were fine brick imitations of European eighteenth-century architecture. A graceful clock tower rose above the rest, and every evening a carillon of bells, played by students, resounded over the gently undulating forests and fields, that stretched away to the horizon on every side. If the physical aspect of Chapel Hill was pleasing, the intellectual aspect of its university was equally so. Being under the state of North Carolina, its work was not hindered by the political views of trust magnates. Through Mrs. Lyman Cotton, one of the librarians of the University, to whom we had introductions, we saw something of the educational work being done here. At a dinner party at Mrs. Cotton's we met a representative group of leaders of thought at Chapel Hill, and next day (November 25th) we lunched with Dr. Frank P. Graham, the President of the University. We were immediately struck by the attitude towards the Negro, very different from that which we had noticed in Georgia and South Carolina. Here there was a feeling of anxiety about the condition of the Negro, and a desire to educate him, so that he could appreciate the full responsibilities of citizenship. There was not that patronizing declaration of love for the Negro, coupled with a supreme indifference to his economic and spiritual welfare, which we had noted further south. The Chapel Hill university was clearly creating a liberal outlook on the race question, and on all problems, social and economic, was cultivating an inquiring and sympathetic approach. I felt that while an American form of fascism or communism might develop at any time in the more southerly states, such a development would be impossible in North Carolina, if Chapel Hill was at all typical of its outlook. The general atmosphere was like that evoked by reading the Manchester *Guardian,* or talking with progressive thinkers at Oxford or Cambridge. The students were being taught by the creation of a mental state, rather than by the assertion of dogma, that sympathy with the less fortunate was necessary, and that the method of democratic and open discussion is the way to achievement.

On our first afternoon in Chapel Hill I received another striking impression. I witnessed a football match between two Negro teams, which the white students at the University attended in considerable numbers, and cheered enthusiastically. On the following day we attended a concert given by Negro singers, the proceeds of which were in aid of a Negro college in a neighbouring town. The chairman at the concert was none other than President Graham, and more than half the audience were whites.

Some Public Occasions [1] ⅋

C. V. R. THOMPSON, *in* 1933, *after eight years in newspaper harness, was assistant news editor of the London* Daily Express. *Suddenly summoned to Stornoway, the London home and office of Lord Beaverbrook, he was asked, 'How'd you like to go to America for us?' A fortnight later found him on the* Majestic; *and he was plumped down in New York some two months after Roosevelt began his first administration. Before long he was thoroughly acquainted with the country, including Chicago and Hollywood, and had married one of*

[1] From *I Lost My English Accent,* London and New York, copyright 1939 by C. V. R. Thompson, chapters III, XII, and XVIII; by permission of Mr. Thompson and G. P. Putnam's Sons.

its daughters, Miss Dixie Tighe. His book of 1939 is rather an account of how he became Americanized than an ordinary work of travel. If it seems to play up all the eccentricities and idiocies of American life, from Palm Beach and the New York night clubs to the wilder phases of the election of 1936, and if the author is pretty severe upon gangsters, Father Coughlin, American sensationalism, and the multimillionaires, the general tone of his book is sympathetic and even affectionate. He liked the country so much that he could call attention to its weaknesses in a spirit of gentle raillery or of reprimand.

A WHITE HOUSE PRESS CONFERENCE

ROOSEVELT had been President for nearly three months when I met him. He had produced the famous Bank Holiday and 3.2 per cent beer, which, by the way, was just 3.2 per cent beer. But no one was quite sure yet what the New Deal was all about. Not even Roosevelt, I suspect. Washington was still waiting for the President to put the cards of the New Deal face up on the table.

The crowd of supposedly tough Washington correspondents were, therefore, nearly as excited as I when press-conference time came near. There were about fifty of us gathered at the executive entrance to the White House in a sort of marble forum that looked more like a public lavatory. If a man with a gun had arrived, I am sure every one of us would have crouched down and got on his mark. There was more fighting to get to the front of the line than at the sewing circle's weekly bun fight. At last someone must have said, 'Go,' for I was swept forward suddenly in a hundred-yard sprint. Presently, by standing on tiptoe, I could see the President over a score of heads.

There was a round-the-campfire atmosphere about the whole conference. Roosevelt was leaning back in a swivel chair placed behind a desk littered with bric-a-brac. His smile, already famous as the Roosevelt smile, formed the circumference of a circle around a well-bitten cigarette holder. His face was slightly tanned and weather-beaten, like the complexion of the seafaring man he would have liked to have been. He already had his favorites among the correspondents, and he called those by their first names. He made some quite personal pleasantry, and they replied in similar vein, although they did not let down sufficiently to drop the 'Mr. President.' I was surprised. I expected them to call him Frank.

I didn't care for it at first. I had seen too much of Whitehall. In Whitehall a reporter is taught to look at a minister from his boots up.

Their bearing is as stiff as their wing collars. The Prime Minister himself is as untouchable as an oriental joss, and only when a Whitehall reporter feels really informal does he talk about him as the 'P.M.' When I recalled that it once took me a whole day to obtain a five-minutes' chat with not even the Minister of Health but his press officer, the informality of President Roosevelt's conference seemed almost indecent.

But the general good humor was infectious. In a few moments I was laughing with the rest of them. In a few more moments I was as much under the Roosevelt spell as they.

In a woman you would call the quality that is Roosevelt's charm. But charm is a word not masculine enough to describe his particular brand of it. I suppose the best word is—if it exists—likeability, but that again does not describe that feeling that hundreds of invisible tentacles are reaching out and drawing your warming heart toward him. It is a quality equally effective in a tête-à-tête, a conference room, or a mass meeting. It is a fortunate fact that those who see fit to attack Roosevelt can hurl their thunderbolts from a safe distance, or, I am sure, those thunderbolts would melt into silken pompons, like those with which the women of France pelt their heroes, long before they reached their mark.

I did not get to ask my question. It was about war debts. That subject seemed to be paramount in my mind at that time. But I cannot be blamed. It was drummed into me before I left England that America could never be really friendly with England until that great mysterious area, the Middle West, had forgotten about the war debts. And since my arrival in New York I had found that whenever I had the courage to utter a criticism it was answered, usually good-humoredly, with, 'Why don't you pay your debts and keep quiet?' But that was not why I did not ask my question. I did not ask it because it seemed to strike too serious a note. . .

THE HAUPTMANN TRIAL

One day, Flemington, New Jersey, was a sleepy, agricultural town; a handful of yokels strolling along its Main Street; a few butter-and-egg buyers living in its hotel; a few drunks and traffic violators in the prisoner's chair in its white steepled courthouse. And next day Flemington was a hippodrome.

There wasn't a room to be bought in the hotel. There wasn't even a room to be bought in a private house. Main Street looked more like

Broadway. Reporters, cameramen, special writers, columnists, tittle-tattlers, criminologists, broadcasters, they were all there.

In the courthouse telegraph engineers worked night and day installing wire rooms. Through their efforts there were soon facilities for handling millions of words, words for New York, words for Chicago, words for San Francisco, words for London, words for Tokyo, words for Montreal, words for Paris, words for everywhere save Germany. And near the courthouse radio engineers worked night and day putting up transmitters and microphones so that the housewife sweeping her living room, the traveling salesman driving his car, and the office worker propping up the mantelpiece with his slippered feet might listen to a running commentary on the Trial of the Century—by courtesy of Tutchurtoze Reducing Tonic.

Very different, all these preparations for the organs of public opinion, from what I was used to. Slinking to a telephone in a grocery store half a mile from the courthouse. Taking care to give the defendant just as much space as the prosecution. Not even describing the prisoner's eyes in case it should prejudice him.

Very different, too, were the hours immediately before the trial. An English reporter would have as much difficulty interviewing a barrister on the eve of a trial as the Berlin correspondent of the *Jewish Daily Forward* would have in getting a scoop from Hitler. These American lawyers not only talked to reporters beforehand. They blurted out their whole case over the radio. I was afraid that by the time the trial opened there would be nothing more to write.

Before Hauptmann was brought to court, dapper, weak-nosed David Wilentz, the Attorney General for New Jersey, was already calling him a snake-eyed monster, as guilty as hell, who might as well get ready for the hot seat right now. And his opponent, red-faced, blustery Edward Reilly, boasting that he had never lost a client to the electric chair, was barking into a microphone to the housewives, the commercial travelers, and the office workers, his promise that he would show them something, that he would prove that not Hauptmann but so-and-so and so-and-so were the kidnapers of the Lindbergh baby. It was all a dream to me. At any moment I expected to find that Hauptmann was Hitler in disguise.

I was surprised they didn't charge admission for the opening. They did issue tickets. I had one. A red ticket, which entitled me to Seat No. 7 in Row No. 2. A state trooper, in a uniform of powder blue, examined the tickets at the door, and, like an usher, showed me to my seat. If there had been a little more talking I should have thought I was at a Broadway first night. A noted actress, a playwright or two, the columnists, novelists in droves, a prize fighter and his wife, and scores of mink-coated matrons. They all had their red tickets too.

An invisible curtain went up. The principals entered, and a murmur of comment from the audience greeted each of them. Lindbergh bareheaded and frozen-faced as usual. Mrs. Lindbergh, frail, shy, and looking as if she were not sure where she was.

Mrs. Hauptmann took her seat by the defense table. A plain, ordinary woman. A cook on her day off, you would have said, had you not seen the expression in her eyes, and the determined keep-up-a-good-front look on her face. And then Hauptmann came in. I thought the audience was going to hiss, as they used to hiss the man with the drooping mustache in the old melodramas.

The attorneys could not surprise me after their eve-of-trial tactics. So I hardly noticed that they wore gray and brown suits, instead of black coats and tramline trousers, or that their heads were bare instead of wigged. Wilentz swaggered and posed as if he were making a screen test for the role of district attorney in a gang film. Reilly, more red-faced than ever, sniffed at the white carnation in his buttonhole. I asked myself what an English judge would have said to a lawyer who came into court wearing a carnation.

When Lindbergh and Mrs. Lindbergh had given their evidence, the lawyers warmed up to their job. They abused witnesses. They abused each other. They abused even the judge. English barristers have a subtle way of telling the judge he doesn't know what he's talking about. With silky smoothness they say, 'Perhaps, m'lud, I may presume to suggest,' or, 'If his ludship will graciously permit me to point out.' There was none of that in Flemington. When the attorneys disapproved of the bench's ruling, they almost said, 'You stink.'

In England, too, the lawyers have even a gracious manner of calling each other damned fools. They will say, 'I am afraid my learned friend is not fully aware of the question at issue.' If I had heard one of the Hauptmann lawyers talk of his 'learned friend' I should have thought he was trying to be funny.

There were, it seemed, two ways to confound a witness: to ask him so many questions about nothing in particular that he forgot some perfectly trivial fact, and then you could accuse him of having a bad memory or of being a downright liar; or to scream at him at the top of your lungs so that he became frightened and confused, and you could still accuse him of a bad memory, or an evasion of the truth. Both were to be recommended to discredit any witness of lowly standing. But neither method should be used with a witness of the caliber of Colonel Lindbergh. Excellent subjects for browbeating were cashiers of movie palaces, farmers' wives, bakers' assistants, plumbers, and —sometimes—country policemen.

The days flew by, and the show became, if possible, better. More actresses, more mink coats came to Flemington. It was unfashionable not to have watched, for one day at least, this hopeless struggle of a man for his life.

Then the trial became dull. Experts came to the stand. Expensive experts, but the State of New Jersey did not mind. Such expensive experts that the impoverished defense could not afford to produce any impressive enough to confound them.

The mink coats got restless. There was chatter in the courtroom. Members of the smart audience began to fix their hair and their complexions. Books and magazines were brought into the courtroom. Court officers were called with beckoning finger, and asked to 'open the window, please, officer darling.' One woman brought her knitting. Even the reporters were bored, and sent rude notes to each other, drew crude caricatures of the prisoner and his wife, and chewed sweetmeats and candy.

After weeks of testimony that did not bring out one new fact, the audiences became more commonplace. Flemington went out of fashion. But a new mob began making the ghoulish pilgrimage—the picnic mob. Guides brought them, and showed them the bars of Hauptmann's cell. They might have been pointing to Henry VII's tomb. The more morbid tourists tried to scratch their names on Hauptmann's car, parked outside the courthouse. Hawkers moved among them. They sold kidnap ladders—crude reproductions of the ladder that was propped against the courtroom wall all through the trial— and people fought to get them autographed, chasing with pens and pencils after the judge, the lawyers, the witnesses, even Mrs. Hauptmann. Book ends, wallets, handkerchiefs, all marked 'Flemington, N. J.,' were sold in thousands. Names were carved in the courtroom furniture. Something like 'Sammy loves Sarah' was etched across my desk. Chips were shaved off the chairs, the jury box, the hotel opposite. And lawyer Reilly had some new stationery printed. It had a red kidnap ladder for the letterhead.

Then the show moved toward its climax. Reilly made his final speech to the jury, a piece of oratory upon which Mr. Reilly depended.

He was brilliant. Emotional but restrained. For a few moments I felt I was back in England. And then Wilentz rose to his feet. With tears for the Lindberghs in his voice one minute and hatred for Hauptmann in his voice the next minute, he bombarded the jury for hours.

World's Public Enemy No. 1. Snake. Lowest creature on earth. He hurled the words with a tongue curved like the basket of a pelota player at the man who remained cold and passionless under nearly all his invective.

'The most venomous snake would pass that child by,' screamed Wilentz. 'An American gangster would not take it. It had to be a fellow with ice water in his veins, a fellow who thought he was bigger than Lindy. Yes. He's cold. But he'll thaw out when he hears that switch on that electric chair.'

I shuddered and felt sick. I looked round, but no one else seemed to flinch. I supposed they were more used to it than I.

Wilentz, striking a dozen poses, shook his fist at Hauptmann, and then introduced an entirely new theory of how Hauptmann had killed the Lindbergh baby, a theory for which not one morsel of evidence had been presented, a theory, in fact, which the prosecution had discarded before the trial began. I waited for a thunderbolt from the Bench, a thunderbolt which at home would have singed the wig of every barrister in town. None came.

At last Hauptmann's fate was left to the jury, a jury of men and women. Long before there was a verdict, the public had made up its mind. They were crying outside: 'He's guilty; let him burn.' The newspapers were crying for his blood. On the radio criminologists were pointing out the danger of Hauptmann's acquittal. Mob hysteria, that most dangerous of all emotions, which in the less enlightened South would, I was sure, have brought a lynching long before this, was spreading. There were crowds outside the courthouse. Crowds who wanted their blood lust satisfied.

By contrast there was a merry scene inside the courtroom. Messenger boys, relieved for a few hours from their endless errands with newspaper copy, were turned into waiters, and sent for coffee and soft drinks for the reporters. There were cigarette ends all over the floor. Reilly sat in the witness chair, trying on a telegraph boy's hat. Once more he yelled across the courtroom to Wilentz, but now it was a friendly yell. 'We'll go to Florida,' he said, 'and lay the ransom notes on a good horse.'

'Yes,' answered Wilentz, excitedly, 'and we'll try and find a horse called "Electric Chair."' Reilly, who not so long ago had been calling this man a liar, roared with jovial laughter.

Then Reilly began singing. Another defense lawyer started a dice game. Someone began throwing paper darts from the gallery. And suddenly a bell began tolling. It was the signal. The jury had reached its verdict.

There was a roar of disappointment outside when it became known that one of the press associations had sent out a verdict favorable to Hauptmann. But there was a cheer a few moments later when that verdict was denied. Then there was silence.

Hauptmann, given back his braces and his tie and his shoe laces, was led back into court. He tried to smile when he looked at his wife. The judge sat on his bench. The jury filed in. Their faces betrayed them. Two of the women were fighting back tears. The foreman need not have bothered to whisper, 'Guilty.' Slips of paper, passed by the reporters under locked doors, gave the news to the waiting mobs. Guilty. Hooray! Hooray! Hauptmann turned a pale yellow when the death sentence was announced. Hooray! Hooray! Mrs. Hauptmann collapsed. Hooray! Hooray!

That was a wild night in Flemington. There were parties all over town. People were as excited as if they had just been told their salaries had been raised. One reporter in the Union Hotel went crazy and ran around the place paging himself. At last the reporters began to move away. Suitcases and trunks were trundled down Main Street to the station. The telegraph wires were torn down.

The last to leave were the souvenir hunters. They grabbed more shavings from the courtroom, cones from a pine tree which had been an exhibit in evidence, chairs that had been occupied by famous people. They took away all the reporters' desks. Someone said he was going to varnish mine and use it as a bar. . .

Fourteen months passed. Fourteen months, during which the case of the People of the State of New Jersey *vs*. Bruno Richard Hauptmann, carpenter, broke all records for sensation.

Colonel Charles Lindbergh chose to become an exile from his own land, because he was hounded by photographers trying to obtain exclusive pictures of his second son, Jon. A midnight visit was paid to Death Row by New Jersey's governor, pudgy Harold Hoffman, so that he might convince himself of his belief that Hauptmann was not guilty. Ellis Parker, a rustic model of Sherlock Holmes, produced a disbarred barrister who perjured himself by confessing that he, and not Hauptmann, kidnaped the Lindbergh baby. Parker was arrested. Defense Counsel Edward Reilly went to a lunatic asylum. And all the time the Germans of New York paid a voluntary tax on everything they bought to finance the unearthing of new evidence to assist Hauptmann.

Faithful Mrs. Hauptmann, unrecognizable now as the plumpish, neat-looking housewife she had been at the beginning of the trial, pursued the mirage of that new evidence until late in the afternoon of April 3, 1936. Tired, but hopeful that she had obtained a clue or two which would force another stay of execution, she went to lie down in her Trenton hotel. Toward dusk a minister, who had turned detective in her behalf, came and sat with her. They waited for the messengers to come with the news that Hauptmann would not die that night.

Knitting in her hotel room, Mrs. Hauptmann realized that hope was gone as soon as the photographers burst open the door and took her picture. 'God, why did you do that to me?' she cried. They took her picture again. Hiding her eyes from the exploding flashlights, the widow of Bruno Richard Hauptmann ran into the bathroom and locked the door.

'Leave me alone!' she screamed from her sanctuary. 'We've got to get some more pictures,' cried the photographers.

Mrs. Hauptmann refused to come out, so they went downstairs to borrow the pass key. They opened the bathroom door and took pictures until Mrs. Hauptmann collapsed. They took a last picture of that and then left her to her grief.

American justice was done.

The police of America need never suspect me of murder. They need never suspect me of any crime. If what I saw in Flemington was a sample of what I might expect, I shall be a model citizen for always.

THE KING AND QUEEN VISIT AMERICA

I had looked forward to watching how the legislators who had so often attacked the royal visit would behave when they met the King and Queen face to face. They behaved just as I expected they would behave. Before the King and Queen arrived they were like the overgrown schoolboys that all legislators seem to be. Vice-President John Nance Garner was demonstrating his version of a curtsey. Representative Sol Bloom, conspicuous in spite of his size because he wore a topper, was being ragged by Congressmen while he tried to tell them what to do. 'You are not to shake their hands,' ordered Bloom, 'and you are not to talk to them.'

Well, the King and Queen arrived. There was loud applause. Senator William E. Borah walked past, aloof but polite, like a lion who had suddenly found himself in a bird cage. Then a senator broke the rules and put out his hand. They all put out their hands after that. Then someone called the Queen 'Cousin Elizabeth.' After that they all tried to say something. Even Senator Robert Reynolds, who had attacked the King, the Queen, the British Empire, the President, almost everyone save himself and God (and I don't think he saw much difference between the last two), was seen running down the corridors to get there in time. When I telephoned his office to check if he was present, his secretary said, 'Very much so.'

There were some holdouts. Congressman Martin L. Sweeney sent his regrets in a telegram, and a request that the King drop off a check at the U.S. Treasury on account of the war debt. But most of them enjoyed themselves. Their applause as the King and Queen left the Capitol rattled around the rotunda until it reached the dome, where it flattened itself against an allegorical painting of the figure of American Liberty squashing the figure of Kingly Power.

For twenty-four hours the King and Queen were allowed to discover that America was not populated entirely by Roosevelts. They were let loose on New York. The King and Queen wanted to see New York. They wanted to see Fifth Avenue and Broadway. They wanted to climb the Empire State Building. They wanted to go into a New York apartment house. They wanted to see the New York that I knew. But the police wouldn't hear of it. They had to be whisked through at high speed—until the King himself ordered them to go more slowly so that they might be seen by the crowds—and were taken straight to the World's Fair and Grover Whalen, who by now had discovered that the King would be wearing morning clothes.

The King and Queen were very impressed by the police of New York. They sent many of them pairs of cuff-links. They didn't see the police as we saw them.

We arrived too late to see the landing at the Battery. It had been carefully arranged that we who were aboard a coastguard cutter would precede the destroyer from Red Bank, New Jersey, to the Battery. But the destroyer suddenly decided to go full speed, which was seventeen knots. We went full speed, which was twelve knots. So the King and Queen had left the Battery by the time we were passing the Statue of Liberty. The police had sent our cars—empty, of course—to the World's Fair long before we landed. We had to follow democratically by subway. . .

It was a relief to reach Hyde Park, where F.D.R. becomes R.F.D. But not for long. Mrs. Roosevelt and the question of hot dogs or no hot dogs kept us too busy. There were several press conferences on the subject of hot dogs, as if they formed part of a trade pact or of an international problem. At one conference it was solemnly announced that they were going to be served. At the other it had been decided that they would not be served. But they were served.

The Pilot Train correspondents weren't invited to the picnic. I suppose Mrs. Roosevelt wanted to keep the story exclusive for her column. But we were given the bare but official announcement that the King and Queen had eaten the American delicacy that turns a snob into a damned good fellow. The members of the royal suite objected to its being put that way. 'We would prefer,' they said, 'that you write that the King and Queen attended a picnic at which hot dogs were served.'

Some correspondents reported they didn't eat them, but I had it on unimpeachable authority, as the diplomatic correspondents say, that they did. An official of the Treasury Department cooked them and brought them round. 'How do I take them?' asked the King, not sure whether to use his fork or his fingers. 'Just spear them,' said the official of the Treasury Department. The reporters attached to Buckingham Palace couldn't believe it when they were told the King drank beer. A whisky-and-soda, yes. But beer, never. They didn't send the story.

There was a last press conference. Michael MacDermott, doing his best for us, gave out two little items. There was a loud shout from the correspondents. Yelled they: 'That was in Mrs. Roosevelt's column two days ago.' MacDermott just laughed.

That evening we left Hyde Park. The King stood on the back platform watching the Roosevelts wave. He was biting his thumb, as if perplexed that a country existed where a President could be so informal. I think he was surprised that Mr. Roosevelt didn't call out, 'Don't forget to write.'

Later we crossed the border into Canada again. A great peace came over us all.

Midwest under Roosevelt [1] ح

GRAHAM HUTTON. *The importance of sections or regions in American life was little realized until Frederick J. Turner devoted a considerable part of his scholarly career to the subject. The physiographic provinces of the United States, he pointed out, are in some ways comparable to the countries of Europe, each having its own history of occupation and development. Except for the Deep South, no region is more clearly marked off or more individual in culture and spirit than the Middle West. With a history reaching back to French fur traders and British garrisons, to the campaigns of George Rogers Clark and William Henry Harrison, and the political movements led by Douglas and Lincoln, with an economic development built on*

[1] From *Midwest at Noon,* Chicago, 1946, chapters iii-v; by permission of Mr. Hutton and the University of Chicago Press.

corn, wheat, pork, and Mesabi iron, and with a special temper expressed in Grangerism and Populism, it is proudly conscious that it is the heart of the republic. In this great central valley Northerners mingled with Southerners, and Britons and Yankees with Germans (Turner thought that the culture was dominated by Puritan and German influences), Scandinavians, Irish, and newer stocks. Here the spirit of nationalism flourished as it never could in New England, or in the Cotton Kingdom. Here, too, the simplicity of the early society—every pioneer family a self-sufficing unit, each community on the flat prairies a cordial neighbor of other communities—gave birth to a hearty type of democracy. If the Middle West suffered from too much simplicity, flatness, and uniformity, it benefited from the implicit faith of its people in the common man, free opportunity, co-operation, and equality.

The versatile young Englishman Graham Hutton—businessman, editor, specialist in international affairs, teacher, writer—who gave the region its best single portrait in Midwest at Noon, had the advantage of seeing it in both peace and war. Arriving in 1937, he spent the next eight years in the Midlands. He became director of British information activities there. Duty and pleasure led him to travel more than 100,000 miles in the section. He lectured, wrote, and above all made friends, talking with men of every calling, farmers, tradesmen, newspapermen, factory hands, preachers, lawyers, policemen, automobile mechanics. Very few natives of the Middle West ever acquire half the knowledge of their country that he gained. He was a friendly observer and he met a friendly reception. 'There has not been one unpleasant experience in my journeyings,' he testifies. 'The number of hotels in which I have stayed passes account; but I have been singularly fortunate in the number of homes—homes, not houses, in which I have been lodged as a stranger, only to leave as a friend. I have never lost a dime or anything else—not even my English accent! I have never met with anything but kindness, helpfulness, and a generosity beyond the bounds of the imagination.' His book deals with the physiographic setting, with the tenacious influence of the frontier, with the conditions of agriculture, with the rise of the cities with 'the cult of the average' (which like nearly all observers he finds too strong), with politics, education, and crime, and with prospects for the future. But his warmest chapters are given to the folks, the people.

Liking the mass of Middle Westerners, he liked most of all the agricultural population in which he rightly saw not only the backbone of the area, but of the nation. The fund of honest character, the taste for slow, tenacious reflection, and the calm poise that he found among the farming folk appealed to him. In the rural area, too, democracy was *a reality. While he found many of the cities extremely attractive (and he says an emphatic word on the frequent beauty of Midwestern scenery), and appreciated their optimism and progressiveness, his appraisal of the urban population is full of reservations. He found too much hurry, as if the world might end in three months; too much noisiness, frustration, distrust of intellect, and addiction to potted culture. Class lines in many city areas seemed to him sharper than in England; racial and religious intolerance dimmed the section's trust in its own destiny. He worried over the mass production of party politics by machines, and the standardization of ideas and opinion. But if the Midwest faced the future with much perplexity and anxiety, he concluded, it did so with greater confidence than the East or Europe. The great question was whether, in politics, social affairs, and culture, it could 'develop the rich variety of the creative spirit in the individual man.'*

THE TRAITS OF THE FARMERS

I RECALL many winter evenings with Midwest farmers—in Illinois, Wisconsin, Iowa, Ohio, Minnesota—when, neighbors having been advised (or, perhaps I ought to say, warned), about twenty would foregather in one farmhouse just to talk. The visiting wives would get someone to look after their children and come over to the host's farm to help the hostess with the baking and preparations. They would bring jars of this or that, or a pie, or a cake. The men would bring bottles of this or that, too. The icicles would hang by the barn door, swordlike. The snow would crackle underfoot in the temperature of zero to 30° below. Through the double storm windows far away the little lights of nearest neighbors would twinkle like grounded stars. At six we would see the headlights of cars steadily eating up the straight, white, snow-deep roads and finally snaking along the driveway up to the farm. Muffled, their occupants would come in, greeting each other only by first names: 'Ned,' 'Matt,' 'Charlie,' 'Mis' Clarke.' There would be an intense, hushed, and entirely propitious bustling in the kitchen in the rear. The summons would come, and we would sit down, nine or ten a side, host and hostess at either end, the other ladies 'in waiting,' to a dinner which fairly sang of Midwest hospitality: fresh mushroom soup; two kinds of chicken or pork; lima and string beans, baked potatoes, corn biscuits, preserve of baby strawberries and butter with the biscuits; salad of lettuce with fresh cranberry and pomegranate jello thereon; ice cream and maple syrup or three kinds of pie; and coffee. (I know they did not eat like that ordinarily.

But I also know they could do it regularly for the enjoyment of their friends and for an evening in their own home.) In the offing, over the banisters, curious and wide-eyed youngsters, regularly shooed off to bed and as regularly returning, would give the false impression of Christmas eve. Afterward the ladies washed dishes—none would dream of leaving that pile for the hostess next morning—and then we would talk, and the ladies would join us.

Of all the talk and discussion I had in the Midwest, I think I relished that in the farmhouses most; and not only because of the preliminaries. It was direct, elemental, simple, often oversimplified, but extremely rational and open-minded. There was an evident readiness to change opinions upon fair, logical conviction. Those fundamental and remarkably searching political discussions in the stores, taverns, farms, and courthouses of Ohio and Indiana and Illinois before the Civil War do not seem so long ago when you go among Midwest farmers today. This may seem very near to romantic idealism; but it goes on. It simply is not heard of by the three-fifths of the population who are city dwellers in the Midwest. And that seems to me a pity for both of the great divisions of the Midwest people. 'There is a great gulf fixed. . . .'

One reason for this division is the greater speed with which the Midwest farming community has assimilated foreign or other American immigrants to an over-all pattern of rural life. This assimilation is almost complete and utterly unlike the state of affairs in the cities and middle-sized towns. Almost anywhere in the region today, if you take one of the county seats and look at the land titles or records, or comb the area around, you will find American farmers of Anglo-Saxon, Celtic, German, Scandinavian, Bohemian, Ukrainian, and other Slav origins. You will find Methodists, Baptists, Presbyterians, Congregationalists, Unitarians, Episcopalians, Lutherans, Roman Catholics, Greek Orthodox, Jews (only in the town), Quakers, Christian Scientists, Seventh-Day Adventists, Jehovah's Witnesses, and many you may never have heard of before. But if you leave an area with a majority of German or Scandinavian Lutheran farmers and go to one with a majority of Anglo-Saxon Methodists, or to one with a majority of Russian Orthodox (and I have been to some), or to one with a majority of Bohemian Hussites, you will note only slight and superficial differences among those communities, no different pattern of life, and only small differences in politics or outlook on national or international affairs.

In one county seat of 14,000 souls in Ohio, for instance, I found Americans of fifteen national origins with twenty-three different churches, excluding different branches of one and the same church.

Mason City in Iowa, with 27,000 inhabitants, when I was last there, had Episcopalian, Roman Catholic, Presbyterian, Baptist, Congregational, and Greek Orthodox churches and a synagogue; but it had two Methodist churches, five Lutheran—two German, a Norwegian, a Swedish, and another Eastern United Lutheran church—two Negro churches, and one remarkable evangelical, undenominational 'radio church' with a big unseen congregation of listeners. The people of the city came from forty different national origins in Europe, including Iceland, and some years ago they were from fifty-five such national origins. Mason City, apart from being the seat of an agricultural county, is partly a manufacturing town and is, in any case, not 'truly rural'; it is a middle-sized town. I mention it again in this context because I have described its near-by farmers. But these cases could be paralleled, with variations, throughout the agricultural areas of the region. Yet the social uniformity and single pattern of farm life covers them all.

The morality of the farmers in the Midwest is strict. In both their private and their community life their religions, no matter how great their differences of dogma or theology, have budded forth into an ethic of fair dealing. The sins of the rural families and communities in the region are naturally as human as those of any city dweller, but they are less varied and more elemental: mainly crimes of sex and personal violence, often ascribable to liquor. There is more looseness in sex morality than appears on the surface—or in court! The 'shotgun wedding' is still common, even if a shotgun is no longer necessary; and the two parties resume a respected position in society. There is much less theft and almost no housebreaking, robbery with violence, hold-ups, racketeering, blackmail, and so on. In the farming and rural community, the greater social uniformity is reflected in a greater uniformity of morality. Indeed, there is a more commonly recognized and observed code of behavior there than in the middle-sized manufacturing towns and cities.

I have already noted the unparalleled neighborliness and mutual help of the rural community in the Midwest; but it is worth noting that there are severe and recognized limits to this. Kindness in 'trouble' and mutual aid—'trouble' is a capacious portmanteau word in the region—are general and dependable. But the same farmer who will help out on a sick neighbor's farm will not give him an ounce of seed, or yield an inch while bargaining, if he feels that the context is one of trade or business and not of human need. They are as tender, sympathetic, kind, and hospitable as their womenfolk toward the visiting stranger or the needy; but with the non-needy they will drive the hardest and closest bargain possible. And townsmen are an object of initial distrust—with good reason, if you are to go by the history of prairie settlement or the ubiquity of smoking-room stories about the behavior of 'drummers.'

The severe self-reliance in the farmer's struggle with soil and elements, his geographical insulation from others most of the time, individual responsibility for his acts and decisions, the dependence of his kith and kin and way of life on those acts and decisions, the headship of his little family community in its isolated acres—all these things make him tend to bring up his children with a sense of the hardness and unpredictability of life. Wherever the children go in the rural community they get the same philosophy, except at school. It is part of the social uniformity. Accordingly, the rural background of the Midwest has been a forcing bed to so many promising youngsters. The better they were at school, the more, by contrary tugging and opposition and rebellion, did they strive to leave the rural life. Thus the farms and the rural community have engendered much ambition and energy—especially the energy of contrariness and 'anti' feelings—and have tended to say what the Scotch say of Scotland or the Irish of Ireland: 'A fine country to get away from!' And look what the Scotch and Irish have done in the world—or in England, for that matter—and where they now are in it! The farm boys of the Midwest have been, and still are, its 'Scotch and Irish.' Again, perhaps it is the contrariness and desire for change which drive so many farm boys away to sea, or into the air, or into the cities. Moreover, there is no room in the Midwest for every son of every farmer to become a farmer, and the room is shrinking.

Few city dwellers realize how pervasive in the Midwest is this influence from farms or rural towns. Some states in the region—Wisconsin, Minnesota, and Iowa—are more dependent on farms and farm products than on anything else. With few large cities, these states form the newest, northwest section of the region. It is predominantly agrarian in its pattern of life and therefore different in atmosphere, political outlook, and attitude from the other five Midwest states. This has significant results. For example, of the roughly two and a half million souls in Iowa, about half form the male and female electorate; and, after less than a century of settlement in the state, a surprisingly large proportion of them actually know, or know of, nearly all political candidates personally and have relatives or connections by marriage throughout the state. Such social compactness in an overwhelmingly agricultural region is rare. It is not found in Europe or in the East of America, where families have been settled far longer but have forgotten or ignore their relatives. I should like to add here, as a pointer to the impact of war on the farms, that, of Iowa's one and a half million souls of both sexes and all ages over eighteen, more than 300,000 went into the armed forces of the United States in the Second World War.

This vast reserve of farming communities throughout the Midwest, always going on with their steady life behind the cities and towns, is of enormous importance to the region as a whole—and to the people of the towns and cities, even if they only think of the farmers when they go motoring or cannot get something for their table. For, vastly different as the life of the cities is, many of the city dwellers' characteristics came, and are still being renewed, from the farming communities.

THE MENTAL CLIMATE OF THE FARMER

All these influences have combined to create a mental climate of the Midwest farmer—a climate different from that in which the city dweller grows up. This mental climate naturally declares itself in the farmer's characteristics. Perhaps only the visitor to the Midwest clearly sees that region's most striking paradox and extremes; what Karl Mannheim called in his portentous phrase the 'contemporaneity of the noncontemporaneous.' In this case it means the existence of a farming people, whose folk memories are longer, alongside one of the most highly industrialized city-dwelling people of the world whose memories, if any, scarcely go back two decades. The farming community is a more uniform society, both in national origins and in social structure. The cities and towns are melting pots, always bubbling. Here is the real division of the Midwest; the real tension; the real cleavage in attitudes. Two-fifths of the Midwesterners are still bound up with the soil, leading an agrarian way of life, serving the cities and to a less extent served by their manufactures, yet not of these cities. They were once a majority. The region once belonged to them and to their way of life. There is much influence and counterinfluence between the two divisions of the people; yet the cleavage remains, and in many ways it is greater now than it ever was.

Farmers, unlike city dwellers, have 'time on their hands'—or perhaps it would be more accurate to say they have 'time on their minds,' for their hands are always busy. As soon as the foreign visitor leaves a Midwest city or middle-sized town and spends a few days on the farms, wholly with farmers, he feels that he is on more familiar ground. More especially does he feel that he is in a familiar mental climate, even if he knows nothing of agriculture. The Midwest farmer has long and arduous tasks, but, while his limbs are coping with them, he can ruminate or contemplate or just not think at all. He cannot cart the radio about on his tractor or on his horses or cattle, though I know of one who does! The farmer cannot dash for the newspaper. The movie is a long way away. Unlike the first settlers, with their 'groceries' among every little group of cabins, the farmer today is sober. He drinks, but very little and hardly ever to excess—if he does, he fails as a farmer and very definitely loses caste among his fellows. (Here is a change in a century!) He is at the mercy of Nature and knows it. He is more profoundly religious than city dwellers; and he seems to be more philosophical, more profound, and to think more deeply about current affairs, domestic and foreign. He may not think as often or as frequently on these matters as most city dwellers think *they* are thinking on them. But he does think, and, like all real thought, it is painful. His mental climate is both more elemental and more fundamental than that of the city dweller. It is often confused and contradictory—whose isn't in our day and age?—but he gives the visitor the impression that he is not regurgitating predigested conclusions or snap judgments, that he speaks thoughts which are his own, that he has thought them out for himself, and that he has 'looked before and after.' He sees things over a longer run, and on a more general canvas, than do his contemporaries in the city. He is what Midwestern city dwellers call more unsophisticated than they. But he is also more direct, more sober in judgment and habits, more obstinate when his mind is made up, less volatile and mercurial.

For this there are many explanations. First, the competitive tempo of Midwest city life is lacking; the farmers do not so obviously have to compete with each other in trade, nor do their wives in social events. 'The Joneses' live in towns; they are not so frequent, they are not ubiquitous, in the country.

Secondly, life on the farm has a prescribed annual, seasonal, weekly, and daily routine, which dare not be flouted; and routine, contrary to popular belief among city people, does not kill; it economizes life. You can try to run your business or profession in the city on a hectic nine-hour day, then meet your wife (whose day now dawns) for cocktail parties, do a theater or party of some kind, crawl into bed in the wee sma' hours, and get up again for the new day's business when the hours are only a little bigger. You can even try to do this regularly, breaking into city 'society,' and learning to pay for it, as so many businessmen and professional men do. But if you are a farmer, want to remain a farmer, and cannot be anything else but a farmer, you cannot do that even if the opportunities are at hand—which, happily, they are not. The overwhelming majority of Midwest farmers today conform to a routine and pattern of life which is partly prescribed by

Nature, partly by tradition, partly by the compelling force of local uniformity. All other farmers are in the same boat. They save their bodies
—the Midwest rural areas produce long lives, as long as those of the
two other best regions of longevity, upper New England and the West
Coast, to which so many Americans retire to die—and it can be argued
that they save more of their souls, too.

Thirdly, they are, in fact, more interested in their souls than are the
city dwellers. As you would expect, their religions—overwhelmingly
Protestant and evangelical 'nonconformist,' with scattered pockets of
Roman Catholicism and Episcopalianism—contain stronger doses of
determinism than the same sects show in cities: doses of Calvinism,
fundamentalism, verbal inspiration, and Seventh-Day Adventism. Religion is also still more directly emotional in the farm communities, as
it was in the beginning of the Midwest. There is more dogma and
theology in the sermon and in the minds of the congregation. But, in
addition, there is an evident admixture of natural philosophy. In many
places—Ohio, downstate Illinois, Iowa, Missouri—there is at times
almost a pantheistic tinge to discussions in the narrow circle formed
by the pastor and a few others. Wordsworth would have been quite at
home on the prairie. The 'genius of the place' would have affected
him as it affects all who stay in it; who see its remorseless growth and
movement, its tough obduracy, its vast skies, its vigorous and luxuriant
life.

MIDWESTERN CITIES

The Easterner who makes fun of Kansas City, Omaha, Lincoln,
Sioux Falls, or Fargo knows little of what he is talking. Passers-by or
casual reporters from the East sent to 'write them up' do not spend
the time or have neither the inclination nor the equipment to discern
the energy, the constructiveness, the great sense of community which
have raised up these cities and thereby developed vast agricultural
regions around them. They do not see what prompted the leading
citizens who made them to pass on to their home towns such beautiful and valuable collections as that of William Rockhill Nelson at
Kansas City, and the museums and other public collections at Omaha,
Lincoln, and other such cities. Their peoples are far more interested
in music, in the other arts, in history, and in the tide of current affairs
than New Yorkers, or, for that matter, Chicagoans, imagine. British
and continental European conductors of orchestras have been surprised
by the keenness of audiences there and by the reception accorded to
them by thousands drawn from all economic ranks of their citizenry.

(That was certainly the experience of the great orchestra of the Royal Air Force, with its leading British instrumentalists, on its tour of America in 1944.) On these western confines of the Midwest, big cities and large towns are fewer and farther between. Their peoples are in touch with, and surrounded by, the atmosphere of the 'great open spaces,' like islanders. They have fewer local and social problems; and in consequence their interest in such things seems to be greater than in many bigger, more central, and more closely located cities or towns of the region.

Des Moines, capital and biggest city of Iowa, is also a city set apart in the Midwest. With about a quarter of a million people, it is still a dominant city in a big region, the region of the richest farm land in America. In the main it is also a flat city, but the state capital is perched on a dominating hill, and the expanding suburbs run along bluffs above the river valley. You see more farmers and more evidences of them in Des Moines than in any Midwest city of its size; but you also see great stores, a fine university, and big commercial and public buildings. The open country is nearer. You can see fields and water meadows from the railroad tracks. Country birds fly round the eaves and columns of the Capitol and Polk County Courthouse. Life goes forward easily, regularly, and in order in Des Moines, perhaps because it is more of an agricultural, commercial, and administrative center and has comparatively less of modern industry with its attendant social problems. Like the people of the Twin Cities, Kansas City, and a few others, those of Des Moines seem more keenly interested in the great issues of the day and display tolerance and open-mindedness to a more marked degree. I throw out this suggestion at a venture: it may be because the life of the city has remained more intimately linked to that of the farmers; but, as we shall see later, there are other reasons, too. The people of Des Moines led the American nation in their treatment of the Nisei—the American-born Japanese—displaced from the West Coast after 1941. So also in their many public forums and discussions, the earnestness and fair-mindedness of the people are striking. There is also another point worth emphasis: though Des Moines is both the capital and the metropolis of Iowa, it is relatively small; accordingly, the political, administrative, industrial, agricultural, and commercial life of the state comes closer to the average citizen of Des Moines, whatever his or her calling may be, than it does in states with far bigger metropolitan cities and far smaller state capitals.

All these big cities of the Midwest are new. None of them is older, as a city, than a hundred years, and some have only become cities within the last half century. The story is not quite the same with the smaller cities. These differ enormously one from another. The capitals of the states are generally smaller cities and often have an air of quiet distinction, beauty, and culture—for example, Madison (Wisconsin), Springfield (Illinois), Lansing (Michigan), and Jefferson City (Missouri). Of all these, Madison is the most beautiful, with an artistic capitol and a famous university poised between two big lakes. Columbus, the capital of Ohio, is really a big industrial city with more than 300,000 inhabitants; yet the city which Mr. James Thurber has immortalized seems still to be more administrative, more dependent on life in its central square, than the many smaller industrial cities of Ohio. It is somewhat like Indianapolis, the center of a region of cities and good agricultural land. Abraham Lincoln would not recognize industrial Springfield, though the old buildings and the center are still there, much as he knew them, and the trees now meet over the wide suburban avenues. The smaller industrial cities of Ohio are legion, and they are more alike than are the big cities of the region. Machinery, metal trades, fittings, devices, gadgets, accessories, household and office and farm equipment—these are the basis of their existence. These made them. You find such cities, nearly all new, throughout the region: the many cities of Michigan; Peoria, Rock Island, and Rockford in Illinois; Iowa has Clinton, Davenport, Cedar Rapids in the bend of a beautiful river among bluffs and woods, Waterloo, Sioux City, and others, all linked with both agriculture and industry; and there are many in Wisconsin—Racine, Beloit, Janesville, Kenosha, Sheboygan, Green Bay, and Manitowoc. Indiana is almost as full of them as Ohio—Gary, South Bend, Fort Wayne, Evansville, Plymouth, and Terre Haute are but a few examples. Each has a life of its own.

Yet among the smaller cities and large towns, quite different, are some of remarkable beauty. They are less industrialized; happily, modern times seem to have merely skirted them: Vincennes, 'on the banks of the Wabash' in Indiana, the capital of the Old Northwest and still as handsome as when the Lincolns came through it with young Abraham; Madison (Indiana) with its lovely old homes; Marietta in Ohio with its beautiful colonial and slightly Southern buildings, and Athens in the same state. Quite apart from the beauty of age and the elegance of the old-time architecture of the eighteenth century, which is confined to those Midwest towns in the southern part of the 'marginal belt,' there is an extraordinary profusion of quiet and well-ordered, modern, small towns in the region: towns with between 10,000 and 50,000 inhabitants, dependent on one or more big factories or industries, retaining at their center and in their everyday life much of the ordered regularity of the old rural Midwest. I think particularly of Ottawa, Kewanee, Quincy, Dixon, and Alton in Illinois; of Mexico and Columbia in Missouri; of Winona, Minnesota; of many such towns in Indiana and Ohio, which have more of them than any other state in the Union except Pennsylvania; of Battle Creek and Holland, Michigan; of Eau Claire, La Crosse, Prairie du Chien, and Fond du Lac in Wisconsin; and of Mason City, Ottumwa, and Marshalltown in Iowa. In poking fun at 'small-town life' in the Midwest, inhabitants of America's big cities have not often troubled to go and stay in them. The authors of *Middletown* did, with valuable results. The millions who talk glibly do not.

When I think of the smaller cities and towns of the region, I think first of wood-frame or brick and clapboard homes, little gardens, vines, and big trees whose leaves mingle above straight streets; of big but clean and new factories; of the workers who know each other and the inside of their fellow-workers' homes; of the garish and incongruous neon signs of Main Street at night in 'Middletown'; but also of goings and comings known to all, the great importance of the wrongly and too often derided service clubs, the birthplaces of men of genius and leaders of business, the centers of down-to-earth religion and faithful ministers of it. I think of places like Salem, Illinois, whence William Jennings Bryan—and the teacher against whom he argued in the famous 'monkey trial' at Dayton, Tennessee—both came. I think of county and other public buildings around or near the square; of people who still make time in which to meet and gossip; of old wood-frame houses near the center and new brick and clapboard homes farther out, but still within walking distance of work. I think of housewives who know tradesmen, and vice versa, and whose children know each other. I think of the longer continuity of life among these small-town families and the life of their town or city. All this needs to be remembered whenever anyone talks or writes of the standardization, boring uniformity, and constricting narrowness of small-town life.

Even the smaller cities have not yet lost all their small-town characteristics. Peoria, a city which plays the same part in American as Wigan in English vaudeville, contains three cities: the old one along the level Illinois river bank; the newer industrial one on rising ground; and, farther back, tree-lined streets of trim suburbs on the bluffs. There are the buildings and the life of the old Peoria which Lincoln knew; there is that of the huge distilleries and the caterpillar-tractor factories, and the taverns and city life which go with it; and, finally, there is the quiet home life of the suburbs. Yet Peoria has but 100,000 inhabitants. South Bend, Indiana, has Studebaker's plants, but also Notre Dame. Fort Wayne has General Electric, but also its art school, museum, civic theater, and parks. Grand Rapids has its furni-

ture factories, but also its art gallery, museums, and libraries. The
contrasts of the big cities are there, but there is also more of the small-
town sense of community, too, and more of its neighborliness.

MIDWESTERN LETTERS AND ART

There was never a Midwest leisure class, though Thorstein Veblen,
who invented a theory of it, was a son of Wisconsin. There is no leisure class today. The Old South and the East developed men of
leisure, patrons of the arts and learning. Many of them, like Henry
Adams, lived a life so remote from that of their people that they
despaired of America, or went to Europe, like Henry James; just as,
more recently, many European artists despaired of Europe and settled
in America. In Cincinnati, St. Louis, and many smaller Southern cities
of the region there are still a few traces of gentle Southern influence,
but in no other big city of the Midwest. Those who live in the region
must work as long as they can. Those who are rich enough not to
work leave the Midwest—probably for its good, and certainly for their
own. In all Midwest cities and towns there are a few well-to-do people
whose enjoyment and cultivation of the rarest and finest pleasures of
the mind are as keen as those found anywhere in the world. But they
are few.

Much of the relaxation and diversion of the region must therefore
be for the many tired or busy men. It means standardization: Mr.
Babbitt on Main Street. But it also means that, like other Midwest institutions, the art and culture of the region come from the people,
from working people, from the bottom working upward, and not
from a narrow social layer at the top. So the culture of the region
itself was bound to be rebellious and explosive, breathing frustration,
protests, sweat, and corn liquor. From about the middle of last century onward this provoked a great cultural struggle in America.

It began with the Mississippi and Ohio writers, Mark Twain, W. D.
Howells, and others, though they 'went East.' It exploded in Walt
Whitman's correspondence and arguments with Emerson; the men of
the people against the 'elect' of Boston and New York. It was carried
on by Midwestern realists against Eastern stylists and transcendental-
ists, who were often narrowly linked to European currents and modes:
by a whole band of virile, vigorous, and vulgar (in the true sense of
the word) Midwest novelists, storytellers, and poets. Writers of the
people who were the people, as well as those who described the
people's convulsive flexing of their muscles, began to thrust a new
image of America under the noses of more delicately minded Ameri-

cans and of nearly all foreigners. They did not tell of a Promised Land. They told of broken promises, tragic struggles on the land or in mean streets, of nobility amid poverty, of sordidness amid unparalleled wealth, and of the seamy side of life in all groups.

Theodore Dreiser, from Indiana, told of Chicago and many another Midwest town or city: not stylishly, not even artistically, but with the vigor of the region. Booth Tarkington, another 'Hoosier,' smoothed over the effects of Dreiser's savage work with the palette knife. Frank Norris took the lid off Chicago's 'wheat pit' and off the homes of its wealthiest citizens. Sherwood Anderson of Ohio and Hamlin Garland revealed their Midwest beginnings. So did Sinclair Lewis, who 'covered' many Midwest lives, protesting at their standardized pattern. Ring Lardner's and George Ade's sketches mixed comedy and tragedy and all the extremes of Midwesterners. Ernest Hemingway's 'toughness' took him even to European lands in search of inspiration.

James Whitcomb Riley, Eugene Field, Edgar Lee Masters, Vachel Lindsay, and Carl Sandburg beat out new measures, new verse, generally as virile as it was strange. The seething life of the region's towns and cities, the quieter struggles on the farms and in the rural towns, these were portrayed not as the public preferred to see them, or as myths embodied them, but in terms of the individual's feelings: pride, frustration, resignation, loyalty, defiance, despair, bitter resentment, and revolt. Upton Sinclair and others came into the region as reporters, fascinated by this rawer Midwest life, and told of the stockyards in 1906 and all of its rawness, aspect by aspect. Willa Cather wrote of the pioneer wives and their search for inner horizons to match the width of those on the prairie and the plains. In the period of disillusion after Prohibition, amid gangsters and corruption, James T. Farrell wrote the three volumes on young Studs Lonigan and his career in Chicago. Biographers, like Lloyd Lewis, brought out the unrealized richness of Midwest life and history.

The literary life of the Midwest, poetry as well as prose, is extraordinarily luxuriant and tenacious, like prairie vines. Fierce and uneven in quality, it has lost one stem after another. The East or California or the new Southwest plucked them away. This regional culture itself was with equal persistence spurned and rejected by the overwhelming majority of Midwest city dwellers and townsmen. It was as if the writers said to their own people, rich and not-so-rich alike: 'This is how you live: now learn of us'; and the people, almost to a man and woman, replied: 'No, thank you; we prefer our own myths, our own synthetic fairyland!' The writers and artists tended to leave the region in order to find like minds with which to consort; or, as Norman Douglas said, to 'avoid the attrition of vulgar minds.' It is a pity for the Midwest that other regions offered more material rewards to the outstanding Midwest authors. And most were human enough to take them, to go where their all-American influence would be greater. But in this way the Midwest stamped much of its life and thought upon the whole of America—more than Americans realize.

Yet many stayed; much goes quietly and steadily on; and today the Midwest has a host of young authors and poets who promise to repeat, in the next generation, what the Midwest school did between 1890 and 1930—but differently. The strange features of this regional culture are its vigor and its quiet persistence in so many different institutions and centers—in Chicago, in many places in Iowa, in the Twin Cities, in Madison, Kansas City, St. Louis, in Ohio, and many another locality. It goes on often without anyone in another city of the same state knowing it is there. Local historians and topographers, societies interested in life in the Mississippi Valley, state historical associations, collectors, bibliophiles, private printing presses, bookbinders, music societies, amateur chamber musicians, curators of museums, university students' groups, librarians, and journalists—they form an intellectual leaven which is constantly at work in the Midwest lump. The universities and colleges, which still put emphasis on the humanities, often against criticism from businessmen who think them out of date, are actually more up to date than many businessmen and are making more of a contribution to the future stability of Midwest society. The lineal descendant of a banker in Springfield in Lincoln's time, also a banker, now writes, illustrates, and prints his own books on a Washington hand press in the basement of his Springfield home and collects fine books and the productions of other private presses. Chicago's Caxton Club and its unique Lakeside Press have been continuously exchanging men, books, and ideas with Britain and other lands for nearly half a century, forming a center of fine arts in Chicago and the Midwest as a whole. Typographers and calligraphers in Chicago have been in constant touch with those of the leading European countries since the early days of Gill, Morison, and Edward Johnston in England. The fine bookstores, museums, and libraries of the region testify to the persistence and discrimination of a surprisingly broad stratum (though a minority) of people, old and young, whose interest in the erudite and one or other of the arts is not dictated by modes or critics. Special collections and libraries—for example, the Newberry Library in Chicago or the Nelson collection in Kansas City—have become influential forces in the arts and the life of the mind, the more influential, perhaps, because their work is not considered newsworthy.

Art collectors in the region are many; yet apart from a few names, known to all Americans, painting of as high an order as the region's literature is rare. But anyone who examines the paintings of the children in rural schools and in big cities must be impressed with their imagination, self-expression, and execution. These are children of many different national groups. Their work is full of promise; if they can pursue their medium, the region will be the richer. Architecture is not distinctively Midwestern—except for some functional architecture: the grain elevators, some office buildings, the barns and silos of farms, the homes and public buildings of Frank Lloyd Wright, or the libraries and other buildings designed for many towns, universities, and cities.

To a great and encouraging extent, big commercial firms have joined with artists and writers to bring elegance into everyday life: to store windows, displays, signs, exhibits, advertising, printing, paper, packaging, containers, household equipment, and railroad cars. There have been great and frequent changes in all these, and always toward higher levels of artistic form or taste.

Thomas Wolfe left the South but wrote of it and saw all humanity in terms of the folk he best knew. Ben Hecht, Archibald MacLeish, and many another left the Midwest; yet the stamp of the people, of people's hopes and fears, is clear on their work. Here, too, the genius of the place proves inescapable, even if men abandon the family altar. What regions lose, in all lands, the country and mankind gain. So it is with the culture of the Midwest. The region is a rich forcing bed. Many of its plants are bedded out, blossom, and seed in other fields; but much seed comes back on the wind.

In all this, too, the Midwest paradox is traceable. The artist is peculiarly individualistic, though he tells, sings, or portrays the life of many people. In the region of the greatest individualism and of its opposite, collective standardization, the artist, the most individualistic of rebels, is practically unhonored and unsung. He departs from the average. He won't conform. He depicts the average and the mass of conformists, often in uncomplimentary terms. He reminds comfortable Midwesterners of the unpleasantness around them. He tells Wheaton or Barrington about 'back of the yards' Chicago. He tells suburbanites outside St. Louis or Kansas City of the river-bank flophouses. He tells the comfortable about the segregated uncomfortable. Whether he is white or colored—the artists' trade union is in this respect more democratic than most—he tells white workers and employers about the Negro. He tells capital about labor. He tells labor about capital. He tells ministers of religion more about sin and human nature than they care to know. He is a confounded, confounding nuisance. But, as so often elsewhere, he is a vanguard, the herald of a movement that

much later gets things done, a voice in a wilderness. Like many a vanguard, he gets shot up.

The comfortable, tolerant, and often intolerant Midwesterners may
ignore or shoot up their own artists; but they cannot ignore the results.
Slowly more and more people are being influenced. Their thirst for
something spiritually satisfying, something more than material, is
driving them to seek new wellsprings. A growing number, even if
still a small minority, of Midwesterners in all income brackets in big
cities and small towns learn music, follow good music, discuss novels,
read criticism, and write 'appreciations' for a little group of local
friends. It does not matter if much of their curiosity and of their desire
for potted knowledge and culture enters into this. At least they want
knowledge and culture, to begin with. That is more than many seem
to want in other places; and in the Midwest their demands are
growing.

My America [1] ❧

LORD TWEEDSMUIR. *'I first discovered America through books,'*
writes Lord Tweedsmuir—the great New England writers, and Col-
onel Henderson's life of Stonewall Jackson—'chiefly because I fell in
love with the protagonist.' He developed a strong admiration for Lin-
coln, and a fervent desire to visit the United States and see Valley
Forge and the Shenandoah and the Wilderness. In due time he came,
first as a well-known author and publisher, then as historian of the
First World War, then finally as Governor-General of Canada. Gifted
with qualities that appealed irresistibly to Americans—frankness,
humor, love of adventure, versatility of interests, unquenchable energy
—John Buchan (that name fitted him better than Lord Tweedsmuir)
was always at home in the United States. Few Britons have been more
warmly loved or deeply respected in the New World. Born in 1875
at Perth, Scotland, educated at Glasgow University and Brasenose Col-
lege, Oxford, he was admitted to the bar, and went to South Africa
as private secretary to Lord Milner. But his heart was in literary pur-
suits, and he found his true vocation when he returned to Britain to
become a member of the publishing house of Thomas Nelson and
Sons. In World War I he served on the British Headquarters Staff,

[1] From *The Pilgrim's Way*, London and New York, 1940; by permission of Susan
Caroline, Lady Tweedsmuir, and Houghton Mifflin Company.

*and became director of information under Lloyd George. He was sent
to Parliament as member for the Scottish Universities in 1927, and
made his mark there. But by that time he was world-famous as a novelist and historian. Appointed Governor-General of Canada in 1935,
he wore himself out in the service of the Dominion, and died in 1940.
Though his* Pilgrim's Way *is an autobiography, not a book of travel,
a selection from it fitly closes this volume.*

THE AMERICAN CHARACTER

No country can show such a wide range of type and character, and
I am so constituted that in nearly all I find something to interest and
attract me. This is more than a temperamental bias, for I am very
ready to give reasons for my liking. I am as much alive as anyone to
the weak and ugly things in American life: areas, both urban and
rural, where the human economy has gone rotten; the melting pot
which does not always melt; the eternal colored problem; a constitutional machine which I cannot think adequately represents the efficient good sense of the American people; a brand of journalism which
fatigues with its ruthless snappiness and uses a speech so disintegrated
that it is incapable of expressing any serious thought or emotion; the
imbecile patter of high-pressure salesmanship; an academic jargon,
used chiefly by psychologists and sociologists, which is hideous and
almost meaningless. Honest Americans do not deny these blemishes;
indeed they are apt to exaggerate them, for they are by far the sternest
critics of their own country. For myself, I would make a double plea
in extenuation. These are defects from which today no nation is ex-
empt, for they are the fruits of a mechanical civilization, which perhaps are more patent in America, since everything there is on a large
scale. Again, you can set an achievement very much the same in kind
against nearly every failure. If her historic apparatus of government
is cranky, she is capable of meeting the 'instant need of things' with
brilliant improvisations. Against economic plague spots she can set
great experiments in charity; against journalistic baby talk, a standard
of popular writing in her best papers which is a model of idiom and
perspicuity; against catch-penny trade methods, many solidly founded,
perfectly organized commercial enterprises; against the jargon of the
half-educated professor, much noble English prose in the great tradition. That is why it is so foolish to generalize about America. You
no sooner construct a rule than it is shattered by the exceptions.

As I have said, I have a liking for almost every kind of American
(except the kind who decry their country). I have even a sneaking

fondness for George Babbitt, which I fancy is shared by his creator. But there are two types which I value especially, and which I have never met elsewhere in quite the same form. One is the pioneer. No doubt the physical frontier of the United States is now closed, but the pioneer still lives, though the day of the covered wagon is over. I have met him in the New England hills, where he is grave, sardonic, deliberate in speech; in the South, where he has a ready smile and a soft, caressing way of talking; in the ranges of the West, the cowpuncher with his gentle voice and his clear, friendly eyes which have not been dulled by reading print—the real thing, far removed from the vulgarities of film and fiction. At his best, I think, I have found him as a newcomer in Canada, where he is pushing north into districts like the Peace River, pioneering in the old sense. By what signs is he to be known? Principally by the fact that he is wholly secure, that he possesses his soul, that he is the true philosopher. He is one of the few aristocrats left in the world. He has a right sense of the values of life, because his cosmos embraces both nature and man. I think he is the most steadfast human being now alive.

The other type is at the opposite end of the social scale, the creature of a complex society who at the same time is not dominated by it, but, while reaping its benefits, stands a little aloof. In the older countries culture, as a rule, leaves some irregularity like an excrescence in a shapely tree-trunk, some irrational bias, some petulance or prejudice. You have to go to America, I think, for the wholly civilized man who has not lost his natural vigor or agreeable idiosyncrasies, but who sees life in its true proportions and has a fine balance of mind and spirit. It is a character hard to define, but anyone with a wide American acquaintance will know what I mean. They are people in whom education has not stunted any natural growth or fostered any abnormality. They are Greek in their justness of outlook, but Northern in their gusto. Their eyes are shrewd and candid, but always friendly. As examples I would cite, among friends who are dead, the names of Robert Bacon, Walter Page, Newton Baker, and Dwight Morrow.

But I am less concerned with special types than with the American people as a whole. Let me try to set down certain qualities which seem to me to flourish more lustily in the United States than elsewhere. Again, let me repeat, I speak of America only as I know it; an observer with a different experience might not agree with my conclusions.

First I would select what, for want of a better word, I should call homeliness. It is significant that the ordinary dwelling, though it be only a shack in the woods, is called not a house, but a home. This means that the family, the ultimate social unit, is given its proper status as the foundation of society. Even among the richer classes I seem to find a certain pleasing domesticity. English people of the same rank are separated by layers of servants from the basic work of the household, and know very little about it. In America the kitchen is not too far away from the drawing room, and it is recognized, as Heraclitus said, that the gods may dwell there. But I am thinking chiefly of the ordinary folk, especially those of narrow means. It is often said that Americans are a nomad race, and it is true that they are very ready to shift their camp; but the camp, however bare, is always a home.[2] The cohesion of the family is close, even when its members are scattered. This is due partly to the tradition of the first settlers, a handful in an unknown land; partly to the history of the frontier, where the hearth fire burned brighter when all around was cold and darkness. The later immigrants from Europe, feeling at last secure, were able for the first time to establish a family base, and they cherished it zealously. This ardent domesticity has had its bad effects on American literature, inducing a sentimentality which makes a too crude frontal attack on the emotions, and which has produced as a reaction a not less sentimental 'toughness.' But as a social cement it is beyond price. There have been many to laugh at the dullness and pettiness of the 'small town.' From what I know of small-town life elsewhere, I suspect obtuseness in the satirists.

Second, I would choose the sincere and widespread friendliness of the people. Americans are interested in the human race, and in each other. Deriving doubtless from the old frontier days, there is a general helpfulness, which I have not found in the same degree elsewhere. A homesteader in Dakota will accompany a traveler for miles to set him on the right road. The neighbors will rally round one of their number in distress with the loyalty of a Highland clan. This friendliness is not a self-conscious duty so much as an instinct. A squatter in a cabin will share his scanty provender and never dream that he is doing anything unusual.

American hospitality, long as I have enjoyed it, still leaves me breathless. The lavishness with which a busy man will give up precious time to entertain a stranger to whom he is in no way bound remains for me one of the wonders of the world. No doubt this friendliness, since it is an established custom, has its fake side. The endless brotherhoods and sodalities into which people brigade themselves encourage

[2] In the Civil War homesickness was so serious a malady that the 'printed forms for medical reports contained an entry for nostalgia precisely as for pneumonia'—Douglas Freeman, *The South in Posterity,* p. 4 [Lord Tweedsmuir's note].

a geniality which is more a mannerism than an index of character, a tiresome, noisy, back-slapping heartiness. But that is the exception, not the rule. Americans like company, but though they are gregarious they do not lose themselves in the crowd. Waves of mass emotion may sweep the country, but they are transient things and do not submerge for long the stubborn rock of individualism. That is to say, people can be led, but they will not be driven. Their love of human companionship is based not on self-distrust, but on a genuine liking for their kind. With them the sense of a common humanity is a warm and constant instinct and not a doctrine of the schools or a slogan of the hustings.

Lastly—and this may seem a paradox—I maintain that they are fundamentally modest. Their interest in others is a proof of it; the Aristotelian Magnificent Man was interested in nobody but himself. As a nation they are said to be sensitive to criticism; that surely is modesty, for the truly arrogant care nothing for the opinion of other people. Above all they can laugh at themselves, which is not possible for the immodest. They are their own shrewdest and most ribald critics. It is charged against them that they are inclined to boast unduly about those achievements and about the greatness of their country, but a smug glorying in them is found only in the American of the caricaturist. They rejoice in showing their marvels to a visitor with the gusto of children exhibiting their toys to a stranger, an innocent desire, without any unfriendly gloating, to make others partakers in their satisfaction. If now and then they are guilty of bombast, it is surely a venial fault. The excited American talks of his land very much, I suspect, as the Elizabethans in their cups talked of England. The foreigner who strayed into the Mermaid Tavern must often have listened to heroics which upset his temper.

The native genius, in humor, and in many of the public and private relations of life, is for overstatement, a high-colored, imaginative, paradoxical extravagance. The British gift is for understatement. Both are legitimate figures of speech. They serve the same purpose, for they call attention to a fact by startling the hearer, since manifestly they are not the plain truth. Personally I delight in both mannerisms and would not for the world have their possessors reject them. They serve the same purpose in another and a subtler sense, for they can be used to bring novel and terrrible things within the pale of homely experience. I remember on the Western Front in 1918 that two divisions, British and American, aligned side by side, suffered a heavy shelling. An American sergeant described it in racy and imaginative speech which would have been appropriate to the Day of Judgment. A British sergeant merely observed that 'Kaiser 'ad been a bit 'asty.' Each had a twinkle in his eye; each in his national idiom was making frightfulness endurable by domesticating it.

THE AMERICAN LESSON

The United States is the richest, and, both actually and potentially, the most powerful state on the globe. She has much, I believe, to give to the world; indeed, to her hands is chiefly entrusted the shaping of the future. If democracy in the broadest and truest sense is to survive, it will be mainly because of her guardianship. For, with all her imperfections, she has a clearer view than any other people of the democratic fundamentals.

She starts from the right basis, for she combines a firm grip on the past with a quick sense of present needs and a bold outlook on the future. This she owes to her history; the combination of the British tradition with the necessities of a new land; the New England township and the Virginian manor *plus* the frontier. Much of that tradition was relinquished as irrelevant to her needs, but much remains: a talent for law, which is not incompatible with a lawless practice; respect for a certain type of excellence in character, which has made her great men uncommonly like our own; a disposition to compromise, but only after a good deal of arguing; an intense dislike of dictation. To these instincts the long frontier struggles added courage in the face of novelties, adaptability, enterprise, a doggedness which was never lumpish, but alert and expectant.

That is the historic basis of America's democracy, and today she is the chief exponent of a creed which I believe on the whole to be the best in this imperfect world. She is the chief exponent for two reasons. The first is her size; she exhibits its technique in large type, so that he who runs may read. More important, she exhibits it in its most intelligible form, so that its constituents are obvious. Democracy has become with many an unpleasing parrot cry, and . . . it is well to be clear what it means. It is primarily a spiritual testament, from which certain political and economic orders naturally follow. But the essence is the testament; the orders may change while the testament stands. This testament, this ideal of citizenship, she owes to no one teacher. There was a time when I fervently admired Alexander Hamilton and could not away with Jefferson; the latter only began to interest me, I think, after I had seen the University of Virginia, which he created. But I deprecate partisanship in those ultimate matters. The democratic testament derives from Hamilton as well as from Jefferson.

It has two main characteristics. The first is that the ordinary man believes in himself and in his ability, along with his fellows, to govern his country. It is when a people loses its self-confidence that it surrenders its soul to a dictator or an oligarchy. In Mr. Walter Lippmann's tremendous metaphor, it welcomes manacles to prevent its hands shaking. The second is the belief, which is fundamental also in Christianity, of the worth of every human soul—the worth, not the equality. This is partly an honest emotion, and partly a reasoned principle—that something may be made out of anybody, and that there is something likeable about everybody if you look for it—or, in canonical words, that ultimately there is nothing common or unclean.

The democratic testament is one lesson that America has to teach the world. A second is a new reading of nationalism. Some day and somehow the peoples must discover a way to brigade themselves for peace. Now, there are on the globe only two proven large-scale organizations of social units, the United States and the British Empire. The latter is not for export, and could not be duplicated; its strength depends upon a thousand-year-old monarchy and a store of unformulated traditions. But the United States was the conscious work of men's hands, and a task which has once been performed can be performed again. She is the supreme example of a federation in being, a federation which recognizes the rights and individuality of the parts, but accepts the overriding interests of the whole. To achieve this compromise she fought a desperate war. If the world is ever to have prosperity and peace, there must be some kind of federation—I will not say of democracies, but of states which accept the reign of Law. In such a task she seems to me to be the predestined leader. Vigorous as her patriotism is, she has escaped the jealous, barricadoed nationalism of the Old World. Disraeli, so often a prophet in spite of himself, in 1863, at a critical moment of the Civil War, spoke memorable words:

> There is a grave misapprehension, both in the ranks of Her Majesty's Government and of Her Majesty's Opposition, as to what constitutes the true meaning of the American democracy. The American democracy is not made up of the scum of the great industrial cities of the United States, nor of an exhausted middle class that speculates in stocks and calls that progress. The American democracy is made up of something far more stable, that may ultimately decide the fate of the two Americas and of 'Europe.'

For forty years I have regarded America not only with a student's interest in a fascinating problem, but with the affection of one to whom she has become almost a second motherland. Among her citizens I count many of my closest friends; I have known all her presidents, save one, since Theodore Roosevelt, and all her ambassadors to the Court of Saint James's since John Hay; for five years I have been her neighbor in Canada. But I am not blind to the grave problems which confront her. Democracy, after all, is a negative thing. It provides a fair field for the Good Life, but it is not in itself the Good Life. In these days when lovers of freedom may have to fight for their cause, the hope is that the ideal of the Good Life, in which alone freedom has any meaning, will acquire a stronger potency. It is the task of civilization to raise every citizen above want, but in so doing to permit a free development and avoid the slavery of the beehive and the ant heap. A humane economic policy must not be allowed to diminish the stature of man's spirit. It is because I believe that in the American people the two impulses are of equal strength that I see her in the vanguard of that slow upward trend, undulant or spiral, which today is our modest definition of progress. Her major prophet is still Whitman. 'Everything comes out of the dirt—everything; everything comes out of the people, everyday people, the people as you find them and leave them; people, people, just people!'

It is only out of the dirt that things grow.

An Annotated Bibliography ❧

WHILE this bibliography does not pretend to be exhaustive—for a complete list
of books would require too much space—it is believed to contain practically all
the titles of importance to students of American history and society. Volumes
that have been treated in the body of this work are marked with an asterisk.
A brief descriptive note is appended to some of the more important of the other
titles, especially those subsequent in date to 1850. A critical and descriptive
treatment of travels written before 1850 is so easily accessible to students in
four well-known volumes, Henry T. Tuckerman's *America and Her Commentators* (1864), John Graham Brooks's *As Others See Us* (1908), Jane Louise
Mesick's *The English Traveller in America, 1785-1835* (1922), and Max Berger's
The British Traveller in America (1836-60), that annotation of them here would
usually be superfluous. Students should also consult the chapter by Professor
Lane Cooper upon 'Travellers and Observers' in the first volume of the *Cambridge History of American Literature* (1917), with a good bibliography; and
an essay, 'The Point of View of the British Traveller in America,' by Professor
Ephraim Douglas Adams, in the *Political Science Quarterly* for June 1914. Bibli-
ographical lists may be found in Solon J. Buck, 'Travels and Descriptions (Illinois), 1765-1855, in Volume IX of the *Collections of the Illinois State Historical
Society;* J. P. Ryan, 'Travel Literature as Source Material for American Catholic
History,' in the *Illinois Catholic Historical Review,* Volume X, pp. 179-238, 301-
63; Laura White, 'The United States in the 1850's as Seen by British Consuls,'
in the *Mississippi Valley Historical Review,* Volume XIX, pp. 509-36; and Richard
G. Wood, 'Bibliography of Travel in Maine, 1783-1861,' in the *New England
Quarterly,* Volume VI, pp. 426-39.

In this bibliography only the essential part of each title is given in instances
where the title or subtitle is unmanageably long.

Abdy, Edward Strutt, *Journal of a Residence and Tour in the United States,*
    London, 1835, 3 vols.
Acton, Lord, 'Lord Acton's American Diaries.' *Fortnightly Review,* London,
    1921, Vols. 110, 111.
    A most valuable travel record, from which the editor of this book regrets that he was
    denied permission to quote *in extenso;* it should be republished in some form.
    Acton's essay on the American Revolution may be found in his *Lectures on Modern
    History;* his essay on the Civil War in his *Historical Essays and Studies.*
Adams, W. E., *Our American Cousins,* London, 1883.
Alexander, Sir James Edward, *Transatlantic Sketches, Comprising Visits to the
    Most Interesting Scenes in North and South America and the West Indies,*
    London, 1883, 2 vols.
    The first volume of this plain, common-sense work is devoted to South America and
    the West Indies; the second covers New Orleans, the principal cities along the Mis-

sissippi and Ohio, Washington, and the North Atlantic States. The author gives some conclusions respecting Negro slavery and Canadian emigration.

Alsworth, H., *A Tour of the United States, Cuba, and Canada*, London, 1861.
The author spent about a half year on the western side of the Atlantic in 1859-60, and his very practical observations of the United States on the eve of the Civil War were first printed in the Bolton *Chronicle*.

Amphlett, William, *The Emigrant's Directory to the Western States of North America*, London, 1819.

Anburey, Thomas, *Travels Through the Interior Parts of America*, London, 1789, 2 vols.

Anonymous, *A True Picture of Emigration*, London, 1848.
The history of an English family, which emigrated to the United States in 1831, and remained in the country for fourteen years. Brief but graphic.

Archer, William, *America Today*, New York, 1899.
By a keen-minded critic of the drama, who took a friendly interest in many sides of American life.

Arnold, Sir Edwin, *Seas and Lands*, London, 1882.

Ashe, Thomas, *Travels in America*, London, 1808.

Asquith, Mrs. Herbert Henry, *My Impressions of America*, London, 1922.

Aubertin, J. J., *A Fight With Distances*, London, 1883.

Austin, Guy K., *Covered Wagon, 10 H.P.*, London, 1936.

Ayscough, John (The Right Reverend Count Francis Bickerstaffe-Drew), *First Impressions in America*, London, 1921.
Rather sketchy impressions of the Eastern States, of special interest to Catholic readers, for the author visited many Catholic institutions.

Baily, Francis, *Journal of a Tour in North America*, 1796-97, London, 1856.

Baird, Robert, *Impressions and Experiences of the West Indies and North America in 1849*, Edinburgh and London, 1850, 2 vols.

Barclay-Allardice, Robert (Captain Barclay of Ury), *Agricultural Tour in the United States and Upper Canada*, Edinburgh, 1842.

Barker, J. E., *America's Secret: The Causes of Her Economic Success*, London, 1927.

Barneby, W. H., *Life and Labour in the Far, Far West*, London, 1884.

Bartlett, William Henry, *American Scenery*, London, 1840, 2 vols.

Baxter, William Edward, *America and the Americans*, London, 1855.
A brief volume of lectures, delivered at Dundee, Scotland, on American institutions, treating our political system with high favor.

Bates, E. Katherine, *A Year in the Great Republic*, London, 1887, 2 vols.

Beadle, Charles, *A Trip to the United States in 1887*, London, 1887.

Beaufoy, *Tour through Parts of the United States and Canada. By a British Subject*, London, 1828.

Bell, Andrew (A. Thomason), *Men and Things in America*, London, 1838.

Belloc, Hilaire, *The Contrast*, London, 1923.

Bennett, Arnold,* *Your United States*, New York, 1912.

Benwell, J., *An Englishman's Travels in America*, London, 1857(?).

Berkeley, G. C. G. F., *English Sportsman in Western Prairies*, London, 1861.
This British M.P. spent about four months in the United States, and was chiefly interested in hunting on the Western plains.

Bernard, John,* *Retrospections of America, 1797-1811,* New York, 1887.

Beste, J. Richard, *The Wabash; or Adventures of an English Gentleman's Family in the Interior of America,* London, 1855, 2 vols.

Bird, Isabella L., *A Lady's Life in the Rocky Mountains,* New York, 1879-80.

—— *The Englishwoman in America,* London, 1856.

A volume entertaining in style, but confused in arrangement, and without much weight. The author's impressions were confined to the East and North, for she made a circuit that included Boston, New York, Cincinnati, Chicago, Buffalo, and New York again. Her impressions of New York city are the most valuable. Some account is given of political campaigning there the autumn of 1854. She went to the United States prejudiced, but 'I found much that is worthy of commendation, even of imitation.'

Birkbeck, Morris,* *Notes of a Journey in America,* London, 1818.

—— * *Letters from Illinois,* London, 1818.

Birkenhead, Earl of,* *My American Visit,* London, 1919.

—— * *America Revisited,* London, 1924.

Not so much a book of travel as a series of articles, dealing with the foreign policy of the United States, Prohibition, problems left by the war, and 'constitutionalism.'

Birmingham, George A., *From Connaught to Chicago,* London, 1914.

Blaikie, William Garden, D.D., *Summer Suns in the Far West,* London, 1890.

Brief and purely objective descriptions of Salt Lake City, the Mormons, Yosemite, Los Angeles, San Francisco, and British Columbia.

Blane, William Newnham, *An Excursion through the United States and Canada,* 1822-23, London, 1824.

Bloodgood, Simeon De Witt, *An Englishman's Sketch Book: or, Letters from New York,* London, 1828.

Blowe, Daniel, *A Geographical, Historical, Commercial, and Agricultural View of the United States of America,* London, 1820.

Boardman, James, *America and the Americans. By a Citizen of the World,* London, 1833.

Bodden-Whetham, J. W., *Western Wanderings: A Record of Travel in the Evening Land,* London, 1874.

Bradbury, John, *Travels in the Interior of America in the Years 1809, 1810, and 1811,* Liverpool, 1817.

Bretherton, C. H.,* *Midas, or the United States and the Future,* New York, 1926.

A markedly hostile analysis of American life and appraisal of American aims.

Bridge, James Howard, *Uncle Sam at Home,* New York, 1888.

Bristed, John,* *Resources of the United States,* New York, 1818.

Brogan, Denis W., *Government of the People: A Study of the American Political System,* with a Foreword by Harold J. Laski, New York, 1933.

Not a book of travel; but a treatise so penetrating and well informed that no survey of British studies of America can fail to give it an important place.

—— *U.S.A.: An Outline of the Country, Its People and Institutions,* London, 1940.

Brothers, Thomas, *The United States as They Are; Not as They Are Generally Described,* London, 1840.

Bromley, Mrs. Clara F., *A Woman's Wanderings in the Western World,* London, 1861.

Brown, Elijah (Alan Raleigh), *The Real America*, London, 1913.
Animated impressions of travel in the Eastern and Southern States, given in a series of letters by the author to her father.

Brown, William, *America*, Leeds, 1849.

Bryce, James,* *The American Commonwealth*, New York, 1888, 2 vols.

Brydges, Harold, *Uncle Sam at Home*, London, 1888.

Buchan, John (Lord Tweedsmuir), *The Pilgrim's Way*, New York, 1940.

Buckingham, James Silk,* *America, Historical, Statistic, and Descriptive*, London, 1841, 3 vols.

——* *The Eastern and Western States of America*, London, 1842, 3 vols.

——* *The Slave States of America*, London, 1842, 2 vols.

Bullock, William, *Sketch of a Journey through the Western States of North America, from New Orleans . . . to New York, in 1827*, London, 1827.

Bunn, A., *Old England and New England*, London, 1853, 2 vols.

Burn, James D.,* *Three Years among the Working Classes in the United States during the War*, London, 1865.

Burne-Jones, Philip,* *Dollars and Democracy*, New York, 1904.

Burnley, James, *Two Sides of the Atlantic*, London, 1880.
Hurried impressions of New England, New York, Chicago, and a trip across the prairies to Denver; with rather superficial chapters on journalism, Congress, life in the great cities, and travel.

Burns, Jabez, *Notes of a Tour in the United States and Canada*, London, 1848.

Burton, Richard F.,* *The City of the Saints and across the Rocky Mountains to California*, London, 1861.
Burton spent almost a month in Salt Lake City in 1860, and gives an admirably full and entertaining account of the Mormons. He also offers a good account of the journey thither, and chapters on the Sioux and the Carson Valley. The whole makes a valuable book of nearly 700 pages.

Butler, Frances Anne (Kemble), *Journal*, Philadelphia, 1835, 2 vols.

——* *Journal of a Residence on a Georgia Plantation*, New York, 1863.

Butler, Sir William Francis, *The Wild Northland: Being the Story of a Winter Journey with Dogs across Northern North America in 1872-73*, New York, 1904.

Caird, Sir James, *Prairie Farming in America*, New York, 1859.
A comprehensive treatise on farming in the Middle West, and especially Illinois, by a believer in British emigration to America. Contains a wealth of concrete information upon prices, labor, crops, farm methods, and similar topics.

Campbell, Sir George,* *White and Black*, London, 1879.

Campbell, John Francis, *A Short American Tramp in the Fall of 1864*, London, 1865.

Campbell, P., *Travels in the Interior Inhabited Parts of North America*, Edinburgh, 1793.

Candler, Isaac, *A Summary View of America*, London, 1824.

Carlisle, Lord, *Travels in America*, New York, 1851.

Casey, C., *Two Years on the Farm of Uncle Sam*, London, 1852.
Notes made in 1849-52 upon life in rural America, with a good account of travel in the West by stage and steamboat.

Caswell, Rev. H., *Western World Revisited,* Oxford, 1854.
   A brief visit to the Mormon city of Nauvoo, Ill., in 1842; a second visit to America in 1853; chief interest in religion.

Chambers, William, *Things as They Are in America,* London and Edinburgh, 1854.
   The well-known Scotch publisher devoted half his volume to Canada and the remainder to the United States, which he viewed as 'a field for the reception of immigrants.' He went no farther south than Richmond, and no farther west than Michigan and Detroit. He recommended the country heartily to would-be British emigrants, especially liked the 'spontaneity in well being' in the republic. He found American manners inferior to those of the British Isles, and condemned some actual abuses, such as Northern ill-treatment of the Negroes, but as a whole his book was very friendly. He expressed fears for the future of the Union.

Chandless, William, *Visit to Salt Lake,* London, 1857.
   Record of a trip in 1855-6, devoted almost entirely to the Mormons.

Chester, Greville John, *Transatlantic Sketches in the West Indies, South America, Canada, and the United States,* London, 1869.

Chesterton, Gilbert Keith,* *What I Saw in America,* New York, 1921.

Cobbett, William,* *A Year's Residence in the United States,* London, 1819, 3 vols.

—— * *The Emigrant's Guide,* London, 1830.

Coke, Edward Thomas, *A Subaltern's Furlough: Descriptive of Scenes in Various Parts of the United States, Upper and Lower Canada, New Brunswick, and Nova Scotia,* London, 1833.

Coke, Thomas, *A Journal of the Rev. Dr. Coke's Fourth Tour . . . of America,* London, 1792.

—— *Extracts of the Journals of the Rev. Dr. Coke's Five Visits to America,* London, 1793.

Collins, S. H., *The Emigrant's Guide to and Description of the United States,* Hull, 1830.

Collyer, Robert H., *Lights and Shadows in American Life,* Boston, 1836.

Colton, C., *Tour of the American Lakes and . . . Northwest Territory,* London, 1833, 2 vols.

Coombe, George, *Notes on the United States,* Philadelphia, 1841, 2 vols.

Cooper, Thomas,* *Some Information Respecting America,* London, 1794.

Cooper, William, *A Guide in the Wilderness,* Dublin, 1810.

Cottenham, Earl of,* *Mine Host America,* London, 1937.

Craig, Alexander, *America and the Americans,* Paisley, 1892.
   A good view of the North as far as St. Louis, with special attention to religion, and an excellent chapter on home life.

Crowe, Eyre, A.R.A., *With Thackeray in America,* London, 1893.
   An entertaining account of the novelist's lecture tour in 1852-3, by his secretary; made doubly valuable by Crowe's graphic sketches of many scenes in pen and ink.

Cunynghame, Colonel Arthur, *A Glimpse at the Great Western Republic,* London, 1851.

Cust, Mrs. Henry, *Wanderers: Episodes from the Travels of Lady Emmeline Stuart-Wortley and Her Daughter Victoria,* 1849-55, New York, 1928.

Dale, R. W., *Impressions of America*, New York, 1879.
Consists merely of four chapters on religion, politics, society, and education, all written with considerable thoroughness; education receives the most space.

Dalton, William,* *Travels in the United States and Upper Canada*, Appleby, England, 1821.

D'Arusmont, Frances Wright,* *View of Society and Manners in America*, New York, 1821.

Daubeny, Charles G. B., *Journal of a Tour through the United States and in Canada*, Oxford, 1843.

Davies, Ebenezer, *American Scenes and Christian Slavery*, London, 1849.

Davis, John,* *Travels of Four Years and a Half in the United States*, 1798-1802, London, 1803.

Day, Samuel Phillips, *Life and Society in America*, London, 1880, 2 vols.

Davis, Stephen, *Notes of a Tour in America*, 1832-33, Edinburgh, 1833.

Delafield, E. M.,* *The Provincial Lady in America*, London, 1934.

De Roos, John Frederick Fitzgerald, *Personal Narrative of Travels in the United States and Canada*, London, 1827.

Dickens, Charles,* *American Notes*, London, 1842.

Dlinot, Frank, *The New America*, London, 1919.

Dix, John Ross, *Transatlantic Tracings, or Sketches of Persons and Scenes in America*, London, 1853.

Dixon, James, D.D., *Personal Narrative of a Tour through a Part of the United States and Canada*, New York, 1849.

Dixon, William Hepworth,* *The New America*, London, 1867.

—— * *The White Conquest*, London, 1876.

Doyle, Arthur Conan, *Our American Adventure*, New York, 1923.
Principally concerned with spiritualism in the United States.

Dunraven, Earl of, *The Great Divide: Travels in the Upper Yellowstone in the Summer of 1874*, London, 1876.

Duhring, Henry, *Remarks on the United States*, London, 1833.

Duncan, John M.,* *Travels through Part of the United States and Canada*, New York, 1823, 2 vols.

Engleheart, G. D., *Journal of Progress of Prince of Wales through British North America and His Visit to the United States*, London, 1860.
By the private secretary to the Duke of Newcastle, a member of the entourage. Very amusing.

English Merchant, An, *Two Months in the Confederate States*, London, 1863.

Enock, C. Reginald, *Farthest West: Life and Travel in the United States*, London, 1910.

—— *America and England*, London, 1921.
Notable for a very full topographical account of the United States, one section being taken up after another; and for a sane discussion of Anglo-American relations.

Eyre, John, *The European Stranger in America*, London, 1839.

Faithfull, Emily, *Three Visits to the United States*, Edinburgh, 1884.
Written by a noted woman leader in Great Britain, this volume pays special attention to the place of women in American life.

Farnham, Thomas J., *Travels in the Great Western Prairies*, London, 1842, 2 vols.

Faux, William,* *Memorable Days in America,* London, 1823.

Fearon, Harry Bradshaw,* *Sketches of America: A Narrative of a Journey of Five Thousand Miles,* London, 1818.

Featherstonhaugh, George William,* *Excursion through the Slave States,* London, 1844, 2 vols.

—— *A Canoe Voyage up the Minnay Sotor,* London, 1847, 2 vols.

Felton, Mrs., *Life in America,* Hull, 1838.

Ferguson, Fergus, *From Glasgow to Missouri and Back,* London, 1878.

Ferguson, William, *America by River and Rail,* London, 1856.
> Scattered notes of travel in the North and Middle West in diary form, well written and readable, but confined to surface aspects, no generalizations being offered. An interview with President Pierce and one with Lewis Cass are reported. The tone of the book is friendly.

Ferrall, Simon A., *A Ramble of Six Thousand Miles through the United States,* London, 1832.

Fidler, Isaac,* *Observations on Professions, Literature, Manners, and Emigration in the United States and Canada,* London, 1833.

Finch, L., *Travels in the United States and Canada,* London, 1833.

Finch, Marianne, *An Englishwoman's Experience in America,* London, 1853.

Fitzgerald, William George (Ignatius Phayre), *America's Day,* London, 1918.
> A vivid piece of reporting, picturing America as she entered World War I; but frequently open to the charge of gross exaggeration. It treats of such subjects as immigration, newspaper sensationalism, violence, hectic advertising, political frenzies, inequalities of wealth, the power of money; producing on the whole a rather overdrawn portrait.

Flack, Captain, *A Hunter's Experiences in the Southern States of America,* London, 1866.

Flint, James,* *Letters from America,* Edinburgh, 1822.

Flower, Richard,* *Letters from Lexington and the Illinois,* London, 1819.

—— * *Letters from the Illinois, 1820-21,* London, 1822.

Ford, Ford Maddox, *New York Is Not America,* London, 1927.
> An eccentric study, emphasizing New York life and American literary circles.

Fordham, Elias Pym, *Personal Narrative of Travels,* edited by F. A. Ogg, Cleveland, 1906.

Fowler, John, *Journal of a Tour in the State of New York,* London, 1831.

Francis, Francis, *Saddle and Moccasin,* London, 1887.

Francis, Alexander, *Americans,* New York, 1909.
> A competent correspondent for the London *Times* discusses such topics as the assimilation of immigrants, social settlements, racial prejudice, education, colleges, socialism, social progress, and politics. He fears an elective despotism in the national government.

Freeman, Edward A.,* *Some Impressions of the United States,* New York, 1883.

Fuller, J. F. C., *Atlantis,* London, 1921.

George, W. L.,* *Hail, Columbia!,* New York, 1920.

Gibbs, Philip,* *People of Destiny,* New York, 1920.

Gladstone, T. H., *The Englishman in Kansas,* New York, 1857.

Graham, Stephen, *With Poor Immigrants to America,* New York, 1914.
> The narrative of an ocean trip from Liverpool to New York with a shipload of immigrants of all races, containing full reports of his talks with them. This is followed

by an account of the author's tramp from New York to Chicago, and of his chats with working immigrants on the way. An uneven but interesting book.

Graham, Stephen,* *The Soul of John Brown,* New York, 1920.

Grant, Hamil, *Two Sides of the Atlantic,* London, 1917.

Grattan, Thomas Colley, *Civilized America,* London, 1859, 2 vols.

Gray, Mr. and Mrs. Grattin, *With Uncle Sam and His Family,* London, 1911.

Griffin, Sir Lepel H.,* *The Great Republic,* New York, 1884.

Godley, John Robert, *Letters from America,* London, 1844, 2 vols.

Gordon, J. B., *An Historical and Geographical Memoir of the North American Continent,* Dublin, 1820.

Greene, Asa, *Travels in America,* London, 1833.

Grund, Francis Joseph, *The Americans in Their Moral, Social, and Political Relations,* London, 1837, 2 vols.

By an American author, but written largely for a British public.

—— *Aristocracy in America,* London, 1839, 2 vols.

Guedalla, Philip,* *Conquistador: American Fantasia,* London, 1927.

Gurney, Joseph John, *A Journey in North America,* Norwich, 1841.

Hadwen, Dr. Walter P., *First Impressions of America,* London, 1821.

Hadfield, Joseph, *An Englishman in America,* 1785, Toronto, 1933.

Haliburton, Thomas C., *The Americans at Home,* London, 1843.

Hall, Basil,* *Travels in North America in the Years 1827-28,* Edinburgh and London, 1829, 3 vols.

Hall, Francis,* *Travels in Canada and the United States in 1816 and 1817,* London, 1818.

Hall, Margaret, *The Aristocratic Journey: Being the Outspoken Letters of Mrs. Basil Hall,* edited by Una Pope-Hennessey, New York and London, 1931.

Hall, The Rev. Newman, *From Liverpool to St. Louis,* London, 1870.

Hamilton, Mary Agnes,* *In America Today,* London, 1932.

Hamilton, Thomas,* *Men and Manners in America,* Philadelphia, 1833, 2 vols.

Hancock, W., *An Emigrant's Five Years in the Free States of America,* London, 1860.

Hancock's experiences began about 1852; the story of an English emigrant family in the Middle West, with much valuable material on economic and social history.

Hannay, J. O. (George Birmingham), *From Connaught to Chicago,* London, 1914.

Hardman, William, *A Trip to America,* London, 1884.

A common-sense work by a close friend of George Meredith.

Hardy, I. D., *Between Two Oceans; or, Sketches of American Travel,* London, 1884.

Hardy, Lady Mary Anne, *Through Cities and Prairie Lands,* London, 1882.

Harris, W. T., *Remarks Made during a Tour through the United States,* London, 1821.

Harrison, Frederic, *Memories and Thoughts,* New York, 1906.

Contains incidental impressions of the United States, with many acute observations.

Hatton, Joseph, *Today in America,* London, 1881.

—— *Henry Irving's Impressions of America,* London, 1884, 2 vols.

Head, Sir Francis B., *A Narrative,* London, 1839.

Hodgson, Adam,* *Letters from North America,* London, 1824, 2 vols.

Hole, Dean, *A Little Tour in America,* London, 1895.

Holmes, Isaac, *An Account of the United States,* London, 1823.

Holyoake, George Jacob, *Among the Americans,* London, 1881.
  The eminent free-thinker and apostle of co-operation gives especial attention to economic affairs.

Houstoun, Mrs. C. J. F., *Hesperos,* London, 1850, 2 vols.
  One of the most vituperative accounts of America written after Mrs. Trollope.

Howison, John, *Sketches of Upper Canada . . . and Some Recollections of the United States,* Edinburgh, 1821.

Howitt, Emmanuel, *Selections from Letters Written during a Tour through the United States,* Nottingham, 1820.

Huddleston, Sisley, *What's Right with America,* Philadelphia, 1930.

Hudson, T. S., *A Scamper through America,* London, 1882.

Hughes, Thomas, *Vacation Rambles,* London and New York, 1895.
  Contains two long sections on the United States, one as seen in 1870, the other as seen in 1880-87, aggregating about 160 pages. Special attention is paid to the model English settlement at Rugby, Tennessee, to scenery, and to politics.

Hull, John Simpson, *Remarks on the United States of America,* Dublin, 1801.

Hulme, Thomas,* *A Journal Made during a Tour of the Western Countries of America,* London, 1828.

Igglesden, Sir Charles,* *A Mere Englishman in America,* Ashford, Kent, 1929.

Imlay, Gilbert, *A Topographical Description of the Western Territory of North America,* London, 1792.

Jacks, L. P., *My American Friends,* London and New York, 1933.

James, Thomas Horton, *Rambles in the United States and Canada,* London, 1846.

Janson, Charles William,* *The Stranger in America,* London, 1807.

Jenkisson, Sir Alfred, *America Comes My Way,* London, 1936.

Joad, C. E. M.,* *The Babbitt Warren,* London, 1926.
  Highly critical impressions of an English scientist, laying emphasis upon the uniformity and supposed dullness and mediocrity of American life; marked by much loose observation and thinking.

Jobson, Rev. F. J., *America and American Methodism,* London, 1857.
  Letters written while in America in 1856; largely sociological in content, but containing a good account of the Methodist Church.

Johnson, C. B., *Letters from the British Settlement in Pennsylvania,* Philadelphia, 1819.

Johnston, J. F. W., *Notes on North America,* Boston, 1851, 2 vols.
  By an English agricultural chemist, containing much on agriculture.

Juvenal (pseud.), *An Englishman in New York,* London, 1911.

Kelly, William, *Across the Rocky Mountains: From New York to California,* London, 1852.

Kemble, Fanny (Anne),* *Journal of a Residence on a Georgian Plantation,* 1838-1839, London, 1863.
  A famous but somewhat exaggerated work on slavery.

Kendall, Edward Augustus, *Travels through the Northern Parts of the United States in* 1806-8, New York, 1809, 3 vols.

Kennaway, John H., *On Sherman's Track; or, The South after the War*, London, 1867.

Kennedy, J. M., *Imperial America*, London, 1914.

Kennedy, William, *Texas: the Rise, Progress, and Prospects of the Republic of Texas*, London, 1841, 2 vols.
By the British consul in Galveston, Texas, 1841-7.

Kingdom, William, Jr., *America and the British Colonies*, London, 1820.

Kipling, Rudyard,* *American Notes*, Boston, 1899.

—— *Letters of Travel*, 1892-1913, New York, 1892 and later editions.
The chapters 'In Sight of Monadnock' and 'On One Side Only' are especially fine.

Kirkwood, The Rev. John, *A Holiday in the United States and Canada*, London, 1887.

Knight, John, *The Emigrant's Best Instructor*, Manchester, 1818.

Lambert, John,* *Travels through Lower Canada and the United States of America*, London, 1810, 3 vols.

Laski, Harold J., *Democracy in Crisis*, Chapel Hill, 1933.
Not a book of travel, but containing some valuable sidelights on American government and society.

Latham, Henry, *White and Black*, London, 1867.

Lawrence, G. A., *Silverland*, London, 1872.
By the author of *Guy Livingston*. A rather vapid book, written in flippant style, but with some facts of interest. The author describes Chicago just after the fire of 1873, reports interviews with Grant and Sumner, describes Salt Lake City and Mormon life, and gives an account of silver mining in Nevada and Utah.

Leng, John, *America in 1876*, 1877.
A volume of newspaper letters, the fruit of a hurried trip from coast to coast; it contains chapters on hotels and hotel life, the common school system, and—the most valuable part—churches and preaching.

Levinge, Richard George Augustus, *Echoes of the Backwoods; or Sketches of Transatlantic Life*, London, 1846, 2 vols.

Lewis, George, *Impression of America and the American Churches from the Journal of the Rev. G. Lewis*, Edinburgh, 1845.

Lewis, J. D., *Across the Atlantic*, London, 1850.
Excellent travel impressions by a young man just out of Cambridge, who later won some note as a novelist and scholar.

Logan, James, *Notes of a Journey through Canada, the United States of America, and the West Indies*, Edinburgh, 1838.

Long, John, *Voyages and Travels of an Indian Interpreter and Trader*, London, 1791.

Lorne, Marquis of, *A Trip to the Tropics, and Home through America*, London, 1867.
Contains vivid sketches of Washington and the upper South in the Reconstruction period.

Low, A. Maurice,* *America at Home*, London, 1905.

—— * *The American People*, Boston, 1909-11, 2 vols.

Lumsden, James, *American Memoranda, by a Mercantile Man*, Glasgow, 1844.

Lyell, Sir Charles,* *Travels in the United States*, London, 1845, 2 vols.

—— * *Travels in the United States. Second Visit*, London, 1849, 2 vols.

Macdonell, A. G.,* *A Visit to America,* London, 1935.

Macgregor, J., *Our Brothers and Cousins,* London, 1859.
A summer trip to the United States and Canada; rather light.

Mackay, Alexander,* *The Western World,* Philadelphia, 1849, 2 vols.

Mackay, Charles,* *Life and Liberty in America,* New York, 1837.

Mackenzie, Eneas, *An Historical, Topographical, and Descriptive View of the United States of America, and of Upper and Lower Canada,* Newcastle-upon-Tyne, 1819.

Mackenzie, William Lyon, *Sketches of Canada and the United States,* London, 1833.

Mackinnon, Capt. L. B., *Atlantic and Transatlantic Sketches,* London, 1852, 2 vols.
A fairly unbiased viewpoint, and much valuable material.

Macquarrie, Hector, *Over Here,* Philadelphia, 1918.

Macrae, David,* *The Americans at Home,* Edinburgh, 1870, 2 vols.

—— * *America Revisited,* Glasgow, 1908.

Majoribanks, Alexander, *Travels in South and North America,* London, 1853.

Manigault, G., *The United States Unmasked,* London, 1879.

Marryat, Captain Frederick,* *A Diary in America,* London, 1839, 3 vols.

Martineau, Harriet, *The Martyr Age of the United States,* New York, 1839.
A series of brief thumbnail sketches of the prominent people she met, with special reference to the anti-slavery movement.

—— * *Society in America,* London, 1839, 3 vols.

—— * *Retrospect of Western Travel,* London, 1838, 3 vols.

Massie, J. W., *The Origin of the Present Conflict,* London, 1864.

Matthews, W., *Historical Review of North America,* Dublin, 1789, 2 vols.

Maude, John, *Visit to the Falls of Niagara in 1800,* London, 1826.

Maury, Sarah M., *The Englishwoman in America,* London, 1848.

Maxwell, Archibald Montgomery, *A Run through the United States,* London, 1841, 2 vols.

Maycock, Sir Willoughby, *With Mr. Chamberlain in the United States and Canada, 1887-88,* London, 1914.

Mayne, J. T., *Short Notes of Tours in America and India,* Madras, 1869.
Travel letters recording a trip made in 1859.

Meade, Whitman, *Travels in North America,* London, 1820.

Meakin, Annette M. B., *What America Is Doing,* Edinburgh, 1911.

Medley, Julius George, *An Autumn Tour in the United States and Canada,* London, 1873.
The work of a military engineer, who pays special attention to public works, such as bridges, tunnels, and railways, and to technical schools.

Melish, John,* *Travels in the United States,* 1806-11, Philadelphia, 1812, 2 vols.

—— * *The Traveller's Directory through the United States,* Philadelphia, 1822.

Milne, James, *John Jonathan and Company,* New York, 1913.

Mitchell, D. W., *Ten Years in the United States,* London, 1862 (in the U.S. 1848-58).

Money, Edward, *The Truth about America,* London, 1886.

Moore, George, *Journal of a Voyage across the Atlantic; with Notes on Canada and the United States,* London, 1845.

Muir, Ramsay, *America the Golden,* London, 1927.

Muirhead, James Fullerton,* *America, the Land of Contrasts,* London, 1898.

Murphy, J. M., *Rambles in Northwestern America from the Pacific Ocean to the Rocky Mountains,* London, 1879.

Murray, The Hon. Amelia, *Letters from the United States, Cuba, and Canada,* New York, 1856.

The vivacious and readable diary, very detailed, of a tour North and South, penetrating even Texas, by an Englishwoman who had an entrée to the best society.

Murray, Charles Augustus,* *Travels in North America,* 1834-36, New York, 1839, 2 vols.

Murray, H. A., *Lands of the Slave and the Free,* London, 1855, 2 vols.

Murray, Hugh, *The United States of America,* Edinburgh, 1844, 3 vols.

American history and economics, with remarks on emigrant prospects and plans.

Neilson, Peter, *Recollections of a Six Years' Residence in the United States,* Glasgow, 1830.

Nevinson, Henry W.,* *Good-bye, America!,* New York, 1922

Newhall, J. B., *British Emigrants' Handbook and Guide,* London, 1844.

Newman, F. W., *Character of the Southern States of America,* Manchester, 1863.

Nichols, Beverley, *The Star-Spangled Manner,* London, 1928.

Nichols, T. L., *Forty Years of American Life,* London, 1864, 2 vols. Reprinted New York, 1937.

Valuable book, by an American-born 'libertarian' who left the United States in 1861 because it had become 'a military despotism,' and made England his permanent home. Discerning comments on institutions, manners, government, and political corruption.

Noel, Baptist W., *Freedom and Slavery in the United States of America,* London, 1863.

A defence of the North and a fierce attack upon slavery, with some travel elements.

O'Bryan, William, *A Narrative of Travels in the United States,* London, 1836.

O'Ferrall, Simon A., *A Ramble of Six Thousand Miles through the United States,* London, 1832.

Oldmixon, John W., *Transatlantic Wanderings,* London, 1855.

Oliphant, Laurence, *Minnesota and the Far West,* Edinburgh, 1855.

Oliver, William, *Eight Months in Illinois,* Newcastle, 1843.

Experiences and data on emigration.

Orpen, Mrs., *Memories of the Old Emigrant Days in Kansas,* 1862-65, London, 1926.

Owen, Collinson,* *The American Illusion,* London, 1929.

Ozanne, T. D., *The South As It Is,* London, 1863.

Pairpont, A., *Uncle Sam and His Country,* London, 1857.

Palliser, J., *Solitary Hunter,* London, 1857.

Sporting adventures on the prairies, circa 1857.

Palmer, John, *Journal of Travels in the United States of America,* London, 1817.

Parkinson, Richard, *A Tour in America in* 1798-1800, London, 1805, 2 vols.

Peel, George, *The Economic Impact of America,* London, 1928.

Peto, Sir S. Morton, *Resources and Prospects of America,* London, 1866
A highly statistical work on population, agriculture, minerals, manufactures, commerce, and so on, by a capitalist interested in American railways; takes an optimistic
view of the future of the South.

Peyton, J. L., *Over the Alleghanies and Across the Prairies,* London, 1869.

Phillippo, James Mursell, *The United States and Cuba,* London, 1857.
Badly arranged, dull in style, and lacking in personality; but contains much classified
information on history, government, physiography, commerce, manners, social life,
letters, religion, and so on.

Pickering, Joseph, *Enquiries of an Emigrant,* London, 1832.

Pidgeon, Daniel, *Old World Questions and New World Answers,* London, 1884.
By a civil engineer, especially interested in technology and economics.

Player-Frowd, J. G., *Six Months in California,* London, 1872.

Playfair, R., *Recollections of a Visit to the United States, 1847-1849,* Edinburgh,
1856.

Porteous, Archibald, *A Scamper through Some Cities of America,* Glasgow,
1890.

Power, Tyrone, *Impressions of America, 1833-35,* London, 1836, 2 vols.

Price, Morgan Philips,* *After Sixty Years,* London, 1936.

Price, Sir R. L., *The Two Americas . . . Sport and Travel in North and South
America,* London, 1877.

Priest, William, *Travels in the United States, 1793-97,* London, 1802.

Priestley, J. B., *Midnight on the Desert,* New York and London, 1937.

Rae, W. Fraser, *Westward by Rail,* London, 1870.

—— *Columbia and Canada,* London, 1879.
The first of these shrewd and friendly volumes deals especially with the Far Western
States and Territories just after the opening of the Union Pacific; the second with
the Eastern States in the centennial year.

Reed, Andrew, and Mathewson, James, *Narrative of a Visit to the American
Churches,* London, 1835, 2 vols.

Regan, J., *Emigrant's Guide to the Western States of America,* Edinburgh, 1852.

Rhys, Capt. H., *Theatrical Trip for a Wager through Canada and the United
States,* London, 1861.
Trip by an actor as a result of a wager, 1859; very light; data on the Americna theater.

Rich, Obadiah, *A General View of the United States,* London, 1833.

Robertson, J., *A Few Months in America,* London, 1855.
Trip in 1853-4; the book contains much commercial data.

Rose, George, *The Great Country,* London, 1868.
The title is ironical, and the book presents a harsh but at some points justified criticism of American disorder, lawlessness, corruption, and materialism. Worth notice
for its scathing view of America in a discreditable period.

Rubio, James Thomas Horton, *Rambles in the United States and Canada, 1845,*
London, 1846.

Russell, Charles, First Baron of Killowen, *Diary of a Visit to the United States
(in 1883),* London, 1910.
By an eminent British jurist, later Lord Chief Justice, who was especially interested in
law and education.

Russell, Robert, *North America, Its Agriculture and Climate,* Edinburgh, 1857.

Russell, W. H.,* *My Diary North and South*, Boston, 1863.

—— * *Pictures of Southern Life, Social, Political, and Military*, London, 1861.

—— * *Hesperothen: Notes from the West*, London, 1882, 2 vols.

Notes of a tour with the Duke of Sutherland. Reports an interview with President Garfield. The emphasis falls upon the Pacific States, and Russell condemns the prevalent violence in vigorous terms.

Ruxton, George F., *Adventures in Mexico and the Rocky Mountains*, New York, 1848.

This, like the next title, is a minor classic of life in the wild West as it was being opened up.

—— *Life in the Far West*, Edinburgh, 1849.

Sala, George Augustus, *My Diary in America in the Midst of War*, London, 1865, 2 vols.

—— *America Revisited*, London, 1883, 2 vols.

A journalist's breezy, superficial, and friendly comments on externals, with emphasis on the South and Far West. Shows strong sympathy for the Southerners. The 400 illustrations rival the text in value.

Saunders, William,* *Through the Light Continent*, London, 1879.

Senior, Nassau William,* *American Slavery*, London, 1856.

Shaw, J., *A Ramble through the United States, Canada, and the West Indies*, London, 1856.

—— *Twelve Years in America*, 1854-66, London, 1867.

Shelley, Henry C., *America of the Americans*, London, 1915.

Sheridan, Clare, *My American Diary*, New York, 1922.

Shipley, E. A., *The Voyage of a Vice-Chancellor*, London, 1919.

Scattered notes of a wartime visit by a well-known Cambridge biologist to the chief American universities.

Shirreff, Patrick, *A Tour through North America*, Edinburgh, 1835.

Short, Richard, *Travels in the United States*, London, 1825.

Simonds, G. K., and Thompson, J. G., *The American Way to Prosperity*, London, 1928.

Smart, George Thomas, *The Temper of the American People*, London, 1913.

Smith, Benjamin, *Twenty-four Letters from Labourers in America to Their Friends in England*, London, 1829.

Smith, J. C., *Emigrants' Handbook*, London, 1850.

Smyth, John Ferdinand Dalziel, *Tour in the United States of America*, London, 1784, 2 vols.

The second volume contains an account of the captivity of this Loyalist.

Somers, Robert, *The Southern States Since the War*, 1870-71, London, 1871.

The most valuable of all British books of travel dealing with the Reconstruction era. The author, a keen observer, offers elaborate data upon agricultural and social conditions following the upheaval of the war. A painstaking and impartial work, not to be neglected.

Soulsby, L. H. N., *The America I Saw in 1916-18*, London, 1920.

Spender, J. Alfred,* *Through English Eyes*, London, 1928.

Stead, William T.,* *The Americanization of the World*, New York, 1902.

Steevens, George W.,* *The Land of the Dollar*, New York, 1897.

Sterling, James, *Letters from the Slave States*, London, 1857.

Strachey, J. St. Loe, *American Soundings*, London, 1924.

Stuart, James, *Three Years in North America*, London, 1833, 2 vols.

—— *Refutation of Aspersions on 'Stuart's Two Years in North America,'* London, 1834.

Sturge, Joseph, *A Visit to the United States in 1841*, Boston, 1842.
By a Quaker philanthropist keenly interested in the emancipation of the slaves.

Sullivan, Edward, *Rambles and Scrambles in North and South America*, London, 1853.
A strongly Tory account.

Sutcliff, Robert, *Travels in Some Parts of North America in the Years 1804-6*, Philadelphia, 1812.

Talbot, Edward Allen, *Five Years' Residence in the Canadas: Including a Tour through Part of the United States*, London, 1824, 2 vols.

Tallack, William, *Friendly Sketches in America*, London, 1861.

Taylor, John Glanville, *The United States and Cuba: Eight Years of Change and Travel*, London, 1851.

Thomson, W., *A Tradesman's Travels in United States and Canada in 1840-1842*, Edinburgh, 1842.
Thomson went to the United States for health, and traveled as a working man; his emphasis is upon economics.

Thompson, C. V. R.,* *I Lost My English Accent*, London and New York, 1939.

Thornton, Major J., *Diary of a Tour through the United States and Canada*, London, 1850.
Rapid impressions of a tour made in the summer and early fall of 1849.

Thornton, Walter, *Criss-Cross Journeys*, London, 1873, 2 vols.
Graphic descriptions, reprinted from old magazine files, of the United States on the eve of the Civil War.

Times, London, special correspondence of, *A Visit to the United States*, London, 1887, two series.
Purely descriptive, not analytic, with much attention to natural scenery. In a series of newspaper letters the author covers New England, the Middle States, Virginia, and the Middle West to Chicago. Supplemented by a number of editorials from the London *Times*.

Towle, G. M., *American Society*, London, 1870, 2 vols.
An encyclopaedic and well-written book by the American consul at Bradford, England; it treats in systematic form of government, education, society, home life, hotels, the arts, amusements, literature, the professions, and almost every other topic of general interest. One of the best works on America before Bryce's. Cannot be called English, but written for an English public.

Townshend, J. K., *Sporting Excursions in the Rocky Mountains*, London, 1840, 2 vols.

Townshend, S. N., *Our Indian Summer in the Far West*, London, 1880.

Tremenheere, Hugh Seymour,* *Notes . . . Made during a Tour in the United States and Canada*, London, 1852.

Trollope, Anthony,* *North America*, London, 1862.

Trollope, Mrs. Frances M.,* *Domestic Manners of the Americans*, London, 1832, 2 vols.

Trotter, Isabella S., *First Impressions of the New World*, London, 1859.

Tudor, Henry, *Narrative of a Tour in North America,* London, 1834, 2 vols.

Vachell, Horace Annesley, *Life and Sport on the Pacific Slope,* New York, 1901.
    An excellent account of ranching, hunting, and fishing in California by an English
    novelist who married a California girl; the author is sympathetic toward the United
    States, but sees clearly the violence, crudity, and materialism that disfigured Western
    society.

Vigne, Godfrey T.,* *Six Months in America,* London, 1832, 2 vols.

Vivian, A. P., *Wanderings in the Western Land,* London, 1879.
    A member of Parliament describes big-game hunting in the Rockies, the scenery of
    the Yosemite and other regions, and mining in Utah and Nevada; a well-written
    sportsman's book.

Vivian, H. H., *Notes of a Tour in America,* London, 1877.

Vivian, R. Hussey, *Notes of a Tour in America,* London, 1878.

Wakefield, Alderman Sir Charles Cheers, *America Today and Tomorrow,* London, 1923.

Wakefield, Priscilla Bell, *Excursions in North America,* London, 1806.

Wallace, Alfred Russell, *My Life: A Record of Events and Opinions,* London, 1905, 2 vols.
    Contains about a hundred interesting pages on a tour of the United States in 1886-7,
    with the emphasis on scientific observations and scientific friends.

Wansey, Henry, *Excursion to the United States in 1794,* Salisbury, 1798.

Warburton, Eliot B. G., *Hochelaga, or England in the New World,* New York, 1846, 2 vols.
    Rapid travel observations in Canada and part of the United States, presented with
    great charm of style.

Warre, Captain H., *Sketches in North America and Oregon Territory,* London, 1849.
    The word 'sketches' is to be taken literally; a book notable for its fine lithographs,
    not its text.

Watkin, Sir E. W., *Canada and the States, 1851-1886,* London, 1897.
    The author reviews trips he made to America in 1851, 1861, and later.

Waterton, Charles, *Wanderings in South America, the Northwest of the United States, and the Antilles in the Years 1812, 1816, 1820, and 1824,* London, 1879.
    The famous naturalist devoted part of his 'fourth journey' to the United States, and
    gives precise impressions of Philadelphia, New York, the Hudson Valley, Buffalo,
    and so on. He found 'our Western brother a very pleasant fellow.'

Welby, Adlard, *A Visit to North America and the English Settlements in Illinois,* London, 1821.
    A disillusioned view of the West and its opportunities.

Weld, C. R., *A Vacation Tour in the United States and Canada,* London, 1855.
    A descendant of the Isaac Weld who had visited America a half century earlier.

Weld, Isaac, *Travels through the States of North America, and the Provinces of Upper and Lower Canada, during 1795-7,* London, 1807 and later editions.

Wells, H. G., *The Future in America, A Search After Realities,* New York, 1906.

—— *The New America, The New World,* New York, 1935.

—— *Social Forces in England and America,* New York, 1914.

Weston, Richard, *A Visit to the United States and Canada in 1833,* Glasgow, 1836.

Whibley, Charles, *American Sketches*, London, 1908.

A beautifully written series of essays on three cities (New York, Boston, Chicago), and on the press, the language, American literature, and American patriotism; some of the views are decidedly eccentric.

Wilkie, David, *Sketches of a Summer Trip to New York and the Canadas*, Edinburgh, 1837.

Wilson, Charles Henry, *The Wanderer in America*, Northallerton, 1820.

Winterbotham, William, *An Historical, Geographical, Commercial, and Philosophical View of the American United States*, London, 1795, 4 vols.

A compilation from sundry sources.

Woodley, William, *The Impressions of an Englishman in America*, London, 1910.

Woodruff, Douglas, *Plato's American Republic*, London, 1926.

A dialogue on government, education, public opinion, the Prohibition experiment, and other topics, done with cleverness but not penetration.

Woods, John,* *Two Years' Residence in the Illinois Country*, London, 1822

Wortley, Lady Emmeline, *Travels in the United States*, New York, 1851.

The author, whose full name was Lady Emmeline Stuart-Wortley, landed in New York in the spring of 1849, traveled through the Eastern States, called on President Zachary Taylor in Washington, descended the Ohio and Mississippi, and spent some time in Louisiana and Alabama. She found much to criticize in means of travel, and remarked that Washington would be a fine city if it were only built. But her general tone was cordial—'What a future! What a country! What a noble people, too, to work out its grand destiny . . . !' Americans praised her as 'a noble lady differing from a Trollope.' Her daughter Victoria accompanied her and published in 1852 *A Young Traveller's Journal of a Tour in North and South America during the Year* 1850.

Wyse, Francis, *America, Its Realities and Resources*, London, 1846.

Yelverton, Therese (Viscountess Avonmore), *Teresina in America*, London, 1875, 2 vols.

Youngman, Rev. W. E., *Gleanings from Western Prairies*, Cambridge, 1882.

Zincke, F. B., *Last Winter in the United States*, London, 1868.

Especially valuable for its picture of the South in 1867; the author reporting that he found the Cotton States in particular almost ruined by the war and the effects of Reconstruction.

Index 𝄞